COMPARATIVE JUDICIAL POLITICS

COMPARATIVE JUDICIAL POLITICS

The Political Functionings of Courts

THEODORE L. BECKER

University of Hawaii
New York University

Rand McNally & Company · Chicago

To
"Teddy Becker's Cousin"
GARY
Incomparable Friend

Preface

PREFACES CAN BE many things; this one is a channel for my thanks to the numerous friends and colleagues who have tolerated my various intrusions, seclusions, and delusions for some six years of conceptualizing, reconceptualizing, research, and writing, and an outlet for my relief that I have finally called it quits.

I think I could spend the rest of my life writing this book. It is almost impossible for me to sidle by anything that even remotely touches on the subject without plugging it in somewhere, without tailoring it to fit someplace, without reworking my concepts and categories. Like all attempts at systematic analysis, this book falls short of total enclosure—but the urge to have a try at it is unflagging. Even after I set the seventeenth final deadline, it was impossible for me to glance at a new book on law without breaking into a cold sweat. In other words, I don't think much of the theory of the leisure of the theory class. There's not much to the theory because there's not much to the leisure. But enough of the complaining; on to the plaudits.

First and foremost, I wish to express lasting indebtedness to my closest friends, past and present, long-term and ephemeral, for their general support of my intimate involvement in this project, despite the attendant dislocation, disgruntlement, distemper, and depression. Foremost among them are Kathy Wise, Mara Montelibano, Dick Pintane, Gary and Shary Skoloff, Don Dvorin, Bill and Linda Fleming, Arthur Laupus, Chris Longo, Harry and Cappy Friedman, Henry and Sheila Kariel, Ed and Jackie Heubel, Martha Carrell, and Joyce Steins. Each is hereby tendered one multicolored battle ribbon.

Two political scientists did more than the ordinary share of intelligence work by helping a capture-prone comrade out of many intellectual traps: Martin Shapiro and Robert Mendelsohn read the manuscript and did not shy away from doing their critical best. Henry Abraham, Harry Ball, David Danelski, Kenneth Dolbeare, Marshall Goldstein, Edward Greene, Joel Grossman, Michael Haas, Henry Kariel, Donald Kommers, Stuart Nagel, Fred Riggs, Robert Stauffer, and Kenneth Vines added encouragement and commentary on various chapters. Each is entitled to wear a unit citation, but all are absolved of responsibility for what is contained in this book—

except for those errors they failed to detect and the insightful critiques they failed to make. What could be fairer?

I also wish to thank several secret agents who were in the right place at the right time and who lent vital institutional support. Midnight Requisition awards go to Richard D. Schwartz of Northwestern University and its Law and Social Sciences Program; Victor G. Rosenblum, formerly of Northwestern, now president of Reed College; William Lebra of the Social Science Research Institute of the University of Hawaii; Norman Wengert, former chairman of the Department of Political Science of Wayne State University; C. Willard Heckel, dean of the Rutgers University School of Law; and Frank Jay Moreno, former chairman of the Department of Politics, Washington Square College, New York University. I would also like to express my appreciation to Professors Winston Fisk and Gerald Jordan of the Claremont Colleges and Donald Reich of Oberlin College for inviting me to bombard their students with some wild ideas.

Finally, many students have been recruited to man electric typewriters, desk calculators, computers, pencils, scissors, paste, felt-tipped pens, Xerox machines, and other instruments of modern academic warfare. I hereby present the following with the Good Humor medal for their ability to smile under barrages of bad puns and unwarranted abuse: Susan Bernard, Anthony D. Castberg, Lueva Dixon, Shirley Dow, David Engels, Victor E. Flango, Ronald Hellman, Geoffrey Pommer, Mike Scarcella, Lucille Takesue, and Arthur Webb.

THEODORE L. BECKER

New York City
Spring, 1969

Foreword

THIS STUDY might be classified as an exploratory investigation. In some respects, it is an exploration; in others it is not. The notion of exploration connotes vast *uncharted* areas; and by the time the reader finishes this book he will be well aware that he has been led to and through the mere fringes of a dense wilderness of ignorance. The number of brambles will rouse dismay, but I hope these initial probes will let in enough shafts of light to suggest that the jungle is penetrable, even to its heart. In such manner, then, this study has been an exploration.

On the other hand, I have expended a substantial amount of energy on less quixotic and exotic matters. By the time the reader navigates the course of this book, I hope he will be convinced that a reconceptualization of an academic area can help organize much ostensibly disparate literature. Also, I hope it will become clear that this type of undertaking is a powerful tool for transforming old knowledge into new. Such a reexamination of previous research is not properly called an exploration, by my definition of the term, but rather a redevelopment. Thus, this study is both an exploration and a redevelopment of an area of political science.

Now, it seems to me that researchers who engage in exploratory or redevelopment projects cannot help being painfully aware of the coarseness of their instruments and the superficiality of their first findings. Almost all apologize; many attempt justification. I have done my share on a number of occasions. Although there will be the usual amount of this patent diffidence in the following pages, I wish to assure each and every reader that there is a new pride in these initial bumbles. Perhaps it is like the English boast of "muddling through." Although I am certain that I have not scoured every possible source of data on the subject, I am confident that all materials included are well enough organized at this point to provoke further and better work in the specified areas, and that the tools are sharp enough to stimulate refinement, variation, and (heaven help us) replication.

My purpose should materialize quite rapidly: I wish to motivate and redirect thinking into an area of politics long touched upon but seldom treated. I hope to enlist the energies of people already interested in politics and the law—and to get them to move out of the law libraries. One thing is certain: they will never stumble over any politics thereabouts; that is, of course, unless they try to wheedle something out of a rule-wary librarian. If we are ever to construct an empirically based general theory of politics, I think that it is indispensable to learn about the place and role of the court system and court procedures. If we are ever to hammer out an understanding of the development of political systems, it is equally important that we learn about the development of the judiciary. Yet little or nothing has been done along these lines, mainly because of a lack of articulation of this belief. That is why I've decided to try.

In order to accomplish this, I've taken the academic liberty of stipulating some definitions and devising a conceptual scheme. From that point on the task is simply one of putting the skin on the bones. I admit there is still little flesh, but I think a physique is taking shape.

A few words are in order on two other points: on the use of court case materials in this area of the study of politics and on the importance of comparative study. Case materials—that is, reports of the opinions of the Supreme Court of the United States—are not new to books dealing with court systems. In fact, up to very recently, they were the *sine qua non* of any respectable course or textbook on public law. True to my calling, I am including several case opinions within the covers of this book. Moreover, like a good new casebook, this tome can be offered as containing "some of the most recent landmark cases decided by the Supreme Court." So far, so similar. These are the few gestures to traditionalism.

The dissimilarities seem more noteworthy. For one thing, I am including foreign cases. Though this is done in comparative *law* books, to my knowledge it has not been done before in any book stressing court procedure, politics, and processes. Furthermore, I am not the least bit concerned with the legal merits or content of any of the cases, nor with the quality of the logic or illogic, in itself, of the judges who decided them. I am content to leave that sort of thing to the law bastions and the law profession in general. Why not spare the poor unsuspecting political science major the painful unlearning he must go through in the law school con-law course? In a more positive vein, I utilize case material as illustrations of specific examples of political situations that are handled by courts in the various countries where they have occurred; in other words, they are political data and political science data. Finally, I use the case material as political theoretical statements on the interrelationship of courts and politics by some eloquent political scientists camouflaged as judges. Strangely enough, some of the most elegant are other than American.

As for comparative study, I believe I have established a way (not *the* way) to incorporate the tremendous body of so-called public law material into a scheme capable of promoting much politically oriented research pertaining to the courts. This, it seems to me, is the nucleus of a separate area of study in political science which till now has almost exclusively consisted of various modes of research into U.S. Supreme Court reports and some limited aspects of the American court system. Up to now a unified field of study has not existed; comparative politics people have been largely unapprised of the theory concerning courts that is relevant to their comprehensive understanding of politics. Up to now, men who have studied courts have been largely unapprised of the relevance of comparative study and certain concepts to their understanding of the judicial system. I don't believe in shotgun marriages—I hope only to be persuasive in my choice of words. It is my hope that the men who have studied the courts and judicial processes will see that their really important contribution must come through a move to the domicile of the comparative analysts. For a happy marriage, the major burden is upon them.

This book is part of the proposal.

CONTENTS

xiii

PART A

Introduction

THE RECONCEPTUALIZATION OF THE SEARCH: TOWARD A JUDICIAL THEORY

ONE OF THE principal objects of this book is to dramatize a past and current narrowness and shallowness in the work of many political scientists professionally committed to the study of the law and courts. By and large these scholars have been limited by the questions they have posed, the materials they have chosen to study, and the approaches to knowledge they have employed. Up to now, their orientation has been permitted to define and thus to delimit the field of public law.

A large body of subject matter of the field of public law has been, and continues to be, a presentation and analysis of appellate court decisions (principally of the Supreme Court of the United States) and some description of the judicial structure of the federal government and (occasionally) state governments. The overriding emphasis is on the American system.

By analogy, the field of public law would resemble the field of international relations if that field consisted exclusively of two courses: one on American foreign policy (using a case approach) and one called Organization and Procedures of the U.S. State Department. This is not to say that such courses do not belong in the field of international relations; but they could by no means be said to comprise a major part.

Of course, in the past fifteen years or so, political scientists such as Harold Lasswell, C. Herman Pritchett, Jack Peltason, Henry J. Abraham, Victor Rosenblum, Kenneth Vines, Walter Murphy, and Glendon Schubert have made contributions to the study of courts in politics, going far beyond legalistic case analysis and the legal structural description mentioned above. Moreover, a rapidly growing group of younger political scientists follows in their footsteps.[1] Yet it seems to me that the steadily increasing weight of the body is too heavy to permit even all these extra legs to move it very far. The trouble is that many in the first wave of innovative political scientists were actually bound more than they thought by traditional ways and by traditional fascinations. In other words, they were liberal rather than radical.[2] Had they been radical, an equivalent force of their number and of the ranks of their followers might have wrought a more significant change in direction. Nonetheless, it still seems timely to suggest a reconceptualization of the field, that is, to suggest alternatives in concept that are capable of qualitatively broadening the traditional concerns. The main point is that we *must* drop the label "public law" immediately. It isn't particularly euphonious; it hardly evokes nostalgia; it misleads the uninitiated; and it has absolutely no relationship to the development of any theory whatsoever.

A few words about the process of reconceptualizing any field or subfield of study may be appropriate: The criteria established to guide the process of formulating or reformulating concepts should be the same as those employed in the natural and social sciences. For where goals are similar (i.e., the development and redevelopment of conceptual tools to improve teaching and to further empirical research in a discipline), the sciences and their procedures are excellent models to follow. Thus, each new or redefined concept must refer to observable, distinguishable, but similar phenomena. Moreover, operations involving quantification should be devised. Third, each concept must have substantial lexical grounding.[3] To put this latter point another way, it is desirable to avoid the kind of in-group jargon that creates ill will, duplication of effort, and confusion in the literature. Coining of words ought to be kept to a minimum; traditional concepts ought to be used with as close adherence to their general usage as is consistent with maximum precision. To subscribe to these criteria is to favor the fostering of eventual understanding of the world about us

---

[1] Instead of producing a lengthy footnote containing the names of all of these people and their books, I refer the reader to C. Herman Pritchett, "Public Law and Judicial Behavior," *Journal of Politics*, 30 (May, 1968), pp. 480–509. Also, an updated résumé by Kenneth Vines can be found in Michael Haas and Henry S. Kariel, eds., *Approaches to the Study of Political Science* (San Francisco: Chandler, forthcoming).

[2] My first argument that the behavioral movement in the study of the judiciary has not been much of a revolution was set forth at length in *Political Behavioralism and Modern Jurisprudence* (Chicago: Rand McNally, 1965). See the Introduction and chap. 1.

[3] I rely heavily on Carl C. Hempel, *Fundamentals of Concept Formation in Empirical Science* (Chicago: University of Chicago Press, 1952).

through making (*a*) the relationship between the world and our vocabulary as clear as possible and (*b*) the relationship between our past and present efforts at gaining knowledge as cooperative as possible. Of course I realize that I am simply calling for the performance of a task that has been under way for some time now in other areas of political science. I am also aware that several theoretical frameworks have been advanced recently concerning the subject matter traditionally conceived of as public law.[4] Unfortunately, although all are highly sophisticated, all suffer from one basic flaw. Each of them (again being fascinated by traditional concerns) uses the United States Supreme Court as its central area of interest. Though a theory of the Supreme Court would be a step in the right direction, it is very limited. A further step is a theory about courts in general: judicial theory, as it were. Specifically, it is up to us to come up with a theory of the interrelationships of judiciaries (of all kinds and at all levels) and the entire political system.

I suggest that we redefine the field of public law, at least partially, in terms of courts, the judicial structure, or the judicial process as that phenomenon interacts with politics. Of course, I claim no originality in using and combining these words. Murphy and Pritchett have employed these concepts in the title of their reader, *Courts, Judges, and Politics,* in which they note:

> The attention of most lawyers and scholars of the law has been primarily on the law produced, not on the process by which it was produced . . . But political scientists have sought more and more to develop an approach to the judicial process which would give activities of the courts new meaning by placing them within the mainstream of political relationships.[5]

However, though Murphy and Pritchett and others utilize and interrelate these general concepts, they present this interrelation implicitly and unsystematically and, as I noted, with an acute case of American myopia. To be sure, they take the all-important first step of discussing some interaction of some of the key abstractions. What follows is a second step— an explication of each of the main concepts (as I see them) and of some of the mechanics of their interrelationship.

---

[4] Walter Murphy, *Elements of Judicial Strategy* (Chicago: University of Chicago Press, 1964), especially chap. 2; Glendon Schubert, *Judicial Policy Making* (Chicago: Scott, Foresman, 1965), especially chap. 5; Joel Grossman, "Social Backgrounds and Judicial Decisions: Notes for a Theory," *Journal of Politics,* 29 (May, 1967), pp. 334–51.

[5] Walter Murphy and C. Herman Pritchett, *Courts, Judges, and Politics* (New York: Random House, 1961), p. vii.

The Concepts of Function and Structure

To start, the concept of judicial function is frequently employed synonymously with the concept of court, but the description of that function entails so much that it turns out to describe very little. Some time ago, Frank Goodnow stated that the judicial function is really only part of the law-enforcement function. And in 1944 Charles Beard said that "from another point of view the judiciary may be regarded as an executive organ engaged in the interpretation, application and enforcement of the law."[6] More recently a book popular in political science introductory courses pointed out that the judicial function is the enforcement of law through legal or court processes.[7] But the same book also notes, as do many others, that the judiciary is a policy-maker, and policy-making is ordinarily considered to be the function of the legislature and executive. Indeed, the courts' function as policy-makers has now been widely accepted by political scientists. Therefore, we find the courts functioning in forming policy, enforcing it, and interpreting it. Apparently, courts and the judicial functions are government and all governmental functions. It should be noted that writings in political science contain many similar formulations concerning legislatures and executives. All too often we find that the executives, the legislators, and the administrative agencies are described as engaging in, or are defined by, the functions of making, interpreting, and enforcing policy. These words utterly fail as primary definitional terms in so far as they fail to discriminate between separate phenomena.

Political scientists also tend to interchange the words "branch" and "power" with "function." Accordingly, I believe them to be dealing incorrectly with a functional type of definition. Certainly if branch, power, and function are not being used synonymously, no one bothers to specify the differences. An excellent representative example of the intermingling of these particular concepts is found in a recent edition of a widely used textbook:

> Our fundamental law separates and limits power, even as it confers it. Congress is endowed with "legislative" *power:* it may not, therefore (except as a result of a specific grant or by implication), exercise executive or judicial *power.* The same restrictions apply to the other *branches* of the national government: the terms judicial *power* and executive *power,* like legislative *power,* have a technical meaning. In the exercise of their respective functions, neither Congress, President nor Judiciary may, under the principle of separation of

---

6 Charles A. Beard, *American Government and Politics* (New York: Macmillan, 1944), p. 194.

7 Austin Ranney, *The Governing of Men* (New York: Henry Holt, 1958). See chap. 20, especially pp. 49–91.

powers, encroach on fields allocated to the other *branches* of government.[8]

One is forced to conclude that there is either a great confusion in conceptualization or in reality no distinctive governmental phenomena to study. All branches have all powers and all functions. Surely, our concepts should be isomorphic with an empirical reality. There ought to be considerable correspondence between our concepts and their empirical referents. If all is indeed such confusion in reality, then confusion in our conceptualization is understandable (if not justifiable). I do not happen to think this is true. In other words, I believe that there are distinguishable governmental phenomena in the societies of the world that can be set off conceptually. For example, I think there are distinguishable phenomena that can be called courts, councils, or whatever, but that concepts like branch and function and law enforcement or policy-making are quite inadequate to set them apart. Indeed, as they are traditionally and presently employed, they have confused whatever distinctions exist in their structure. In any event, much politico-juridical theory rests upon the assumption that there are structural differences in various governmental phenomena. But the traditional-legalistic usage of such terms as structure, function, branch, power, and the like have been less than helpful in our search for knowledge on the interaction and consequences of these phenomena.

Perhaps another perspective will provide a clearer comprehension of my concern. When a committee of Congress is listening to witnesses in a hearing or an investigation, what goal is served by referring to this panel as "quasi-judicial" or as having a "quasi-judicial function"? Do the congressmen *really* constitute a court? Or are they a semicourt? Perhaps they are a pseudocourt? Were Gestapo inquests courts? Is it proper to use the word "court" at all in the term "kangaroo court"? Or are all of the above designations sloppy uses of the English language? Did the man wearing a black robe and called Judge Thayer, along with the district attorney and the jury that tried Sacco and Vanzetti, really constitute a court? Were the proletarian courts of 1919 Soviet Russia or today's People's Courts in the USSR (when they interpret the Anti-Parasite Law) really courts? Were the men who heard some of the sit-in demonstration cases against Negroes in the South really judges? Several ACLU lawyers reported a proceeding in 1963 in which a man came out of a chamber marked "Judge" wearing a pistol over a black robe and carrying a copy of the decision before the argument was made. Was the following proceeding quasi-judicial, semijudicial, or

---

[8] Alpheus T. Mason and William M. Beaney, *American Constitutional Law*, 4th ed. (Englewood Cliffs, N. J.: Prentice-Hall, 1968), p. 12 (emphasis mine). Another major offender in this category is R. M. MacIver. See his *The Modern State* (London: Oxford University Press, 1926), particularly chap. 12.

almost judicial? After all, he *was* wearing a black robe and he was inside a courtroom.

This set of questions might be construed to categorize the author as a Platonist. This would be an error, because there is no assumption made that these questions deal in what Hermann Kantorowicz has called "verbal realism"[9] (which is very similar to what usually is called real or true definition). Although the word "really" is employed, this should not be construed to mean that one can know that the "essential" court exists or what the "real" definition of the word "court" is. What is meant is that various political phenomena exist in the world which are useful to separate in the mind, with the aid of a series of verbal symbols, from similar sociopolitical phenomena. Of course, whether these phenomena are of any importance to the understanding of politics can be revealed only through study. At any rate, one such phenomenon is frequently defined as "court," and this phenomenon can be distinguished from others usually defined as "legislature," "inquisition," and the like. As I noted earlier, political science jargon has obscured differences between what is frequently termed in its lexicon "court" and the phenomena often termed "legislature" and "inquisition" under a mass of prefixes and qualifications and through a tautological usage of the concept of "function."

As a result of this confusion, the understanding and testing of politico-juridical theory have been hindered and the development of wider and more comprehensive and incisive political-juridical theory has been retarded. Sadly, we have conducted very little research into the structural nature of courts and into what results they can and do achieve. My first job, then, must be to isolate a politically relevant reality through precisely defining *judicial structure* or *judicial process* or *court*. These concepts, together with that of *function*, seem to me to have great potential in helping us understand and redevelop past and present politico-juridical theory.

At the outset, I must confess that I think it will be most parsimonious *and* fruitful (a rare combination) to adopt the *sociological* concepts of structure and function in our effort to develop judicial theory. I also think that little would be gained for the purpose of this volume by engaging either Kingsley Davis[10] or Irving Louis Horowitz[11] or Joseph La Palombara[12] in a polemic over the value of structural-functional analysis, or in

---

[9] See *Definition of Law* (Cambridge University Press, 1958), pp. 1ff.

[10] Kingsley Davis, "The Myth of Functional Analysis as a Special Method in Sociology and Anthropology," *American Sociological Review*, 24 (December, 1959), pp. 757–73.

[11] Irving Louis Horowitz, "Sociology and Politics: The Myth of Functionalism Revisited," *Journal of Politics*, 25 (May, 1963), pp. 248–64.

[12] Joseph La Palombara, "Macrotheories and Microapplications in Comparative Politics," *Comparative Politics*, 1 (October, 1968), pp. 52–78. La Palombara, however, withholds his favor from structural-functional analysis of "whole political systems,"

engaging in a more philosophical discussion on structure-function with such scholars as Carl Hempel and Ernest Nagel.[13] However, several points made in a recent essay by Walter Goldschmidt seem worth treating, for his arguments, made to persuade social scientists to abandon structural-functional analysis, help to clarify my limited goals.

[One of Goldschmidt's major points is that the attempt to compare structures and institutions cross-culturally is doomed to failure, as it is an attempt at a "comparison of incomparables."[14] According to Goldschmidt, institutions are not sufficiently similar from society to society: ["What is consistent from culture to culture is not the institution; what is consistent are the social problems.] What is recurrent from society to society is solutions to these problems."[15] He suggests that the best approach is one he calls "comparative functionalism"; that is, since all societies have the same problems to solve, these problems should be foundational units of comparative analysis, as the methods toward solution (i.e., institutions, structures) vary so greatly.

This contention packs some power. Still, I am not certain that it should sway political scientists at this stage in the development of the discipline, but particularly those who would pursue the development of judicial theory or the study of judicial politics. Sciences must grow as they can grow, given their peculiar circumstances. Sometimes it may be necessary to use a conceptual device that can guide and stimulate the collection and analysis of information in order to test some durable, though possibly confusing, theories. In the study of case law and courts, concepts akin to those of structure and function as used in sociology and anthropology have a peculiar pervasiveness in the existent theory. For this reason I believe structural-functional analysis as practiced in sociology and anthropology will help to illuminate gaps and resolve ambiguities in judicial theory as well as provide a framework by which much important information that can be relevant to subsequent testing of that theory can be gathered. The question may be asked, and correctly: Must we make the same mistakes as others before us? My answer must be yes, for in this case it is primarily important to ask questions in a way that will be understood, and to moti-

---

and thus his criticism does not apply here. He seems unaware of the possible uses of structural-functional analysis for the study of segments of political systems—and that is what this book is about; i.e., a structural-functional cross-cultural study of one segment of many political systems, the courts.

[13] Carl G. Hempel, "The Logic of Functional Analysis," in *Symposium on Sociological Theory*, ed. Llewellyn Gross (Evanston, Ill.: Row, Peterson, 1959); Ernest Nagel, *The Structure of Science: Problems in the Logic of Scientific Explanation* (New York: Harcourt, Brace & World, 1961).

[14] Walter Goldschmidt, *Comparative Functionalism* (Berkeley and Los Angeles: University of California Press, 1966), p. 28.

[15] *Ibid.*, p. 31.

vate field research where heretofore there has been very little. What may be a fatal mistake to an old man may be priceless help to an adolescent.

There is one further reservation to Goldschmidt's argument. It must be noted that Goldschmidt's solution appears to be vulnerable to the same charge he makes against structural-functional analysis. Why should one, for instance, accept the assumption that social problems (the focus of comparative functionalism) are more precisely classifiable than the attempted institutional solutions? The so-called needs of man are, at this point in time, so intricately mixed into the cultural solutions as to make them next to indistinguishable. Furthermore, as long as researchers remember that the culturally bound conceptualizations they employ in structural-functional analysis are simply verbal convention and flexible approximations, there would seem to be little damage done to the collection of data or the analysis that follows. Of course, structures vary from place to place and over time— but there may well be some core structural phenomena that are classifiable and that do exist in many cultures. Why can't we study where that core exists and where it does not? Why can't we study the variations of phenomena around that core; that is, variations in the structure where it exists? In other words, though Goldschmidt's alternative is appealing, it is not compelling.[16]

For our teaching and research purposes, then, I think it would be fruitful to use the term "structure" when there is a reasonably close correspondence between defined and expected formal and informal behavior patterns set by rule, custom, and law, on the one hand, and some actual adherence by participants within a system on the other. In other words, structure, whether systemic or procedural, is a degree of consistent behavior observed between the laws and customs (rules, statutes, consti-

---

[16] I am cognizant of the recent heavy assault on the political scientific usage of structural-functional analysis launched by A. James Gregor in his "Political Science and the Uses of Functional Analysis," *American Political Science Review*, 62 (June, 1968), pp. 425–39. Professor Gregor scores many telling points on those who employ systems and functional analytic approaches, so modish nowadays. My own use of the concepts of structure and function is not meant to bear any analogy to animal cells or galaxies; it is totally nonteleological; and it purports no positive organization of interrelated propositions. My intent is simply to bring together a widely disparate range of materials under a convenient rubric, to ask some questions systematically, and to spur research in order to obtain some answers. Although Talcott Parsons (Gregor's *bête noire*) also says he uses structural-functional analysis for these less glamorous purposes, Gregor is quick to point out that they pale in the light of Parson's use of these concepts in order to formalize a general theory. Gregor points out the differences between a theory and an analytic conceptual scheme. I think that the reader and Professor Gregor will agree that I opt for the latter in this volume. I am not trying to slip any theory over on unwary students and colleagues. In this instance, the adoption of some sociological concepts is not for "redescribing reasonably well-confirmed . . . low-order empirical generalizations," to which Gregor rightly objects (p. 438); it is to penetrate the murky depths of many "intuitively grasped" truths by turning some beliefs into questions and to generate excitement over the prospect of finding some answers.

tutions, etc.) of a group, association, or society and the human behavior within that system. If the norms of custom and law differ, there may be no structure. That would depend on behavioral patterns. If behavior were substantially consistent with either the law or the custom, the expectancy-behavioral convergence would comprise the extant social structure in that system. In light of the tendency toward merger of customary and/or expected behavior with the society's customary or legal system, there is some difference between my concept of structure and that employed by Fred Riggs. He states:

> A structure is defined as any pattern of behavior which has become a standard feature of a social system. Thus, a government bureau is a "structure," or rather a whole set of structures consisting of the many things the officials in the bureau do regularly: the decisions they make, the people they see, the papers they sign. The structure is not composed of the people and things themselves, but *of their actions.* It does not include all their actions, but only those actions which relate to the goals and work of the bureau. The bureau also includes relevant actions of "outsiders" with whom it interacts in the normal course of business, its clientele or "audience." They may be served or regulated by it; they may be the subjects as well as the objects of its activity.[17]

The difference lies simply in the fact that I choose to take behavioral expectation (particularly custom or law) into account and Riggs does not. Riggs is not at all concerned with formalized or traditional expectations. My concern with such expectations centers on the effect on the superego when they are violated, undermining (making invisible or unstable) prior or latent structural-behavioral regularities. I am also willing to take such psychological concepts as belief systems and attitude patterns into account as elements in structure or at least as strong indicators of it. The concept of structure, then, as I define it, is closely akin to Marion Levy's concept of analytic structure in contrast with concrete structure.[18]

The sociological concept of function as contrasted with the civics type discussed earlier is one that some modern political scientists ostensibly have adopted to assist them in the behavioral study of politics. In fact, one might say that the concept of function, in its new garb, is now fashionable on the political science scene. It seems to me, however, that such political scientists as David Easton[19] and Gabriel Almond[20] misunderstood the no-

---

[17] Fred R. Riggs, *Administration in Developing Countries* (Boston: Houghton Mifflin, 1964), p. 20 (emphasis mine).

[18] Marion J. Levy, *The Structure of Society* (Princeton: Princeton University Press, 1962).

[19] David Easton, *Framework for Political Analysis* (Englewood Cliffs, N.J.: Prentice-Hall, 1965).

[20] Gabriel Almond and James S. Coleman, eds., *The Politics of Developing Areas* (Princeton: Princeton University Press, 1960).

tion of function to which they seem oriented, for they appear to define it differently from the way it seems commonly accepted by sociologists. They too have equated function with what political science institutionalists call "branch." Perhaps they have refined the concept of branch a bit, and surely they have broken down what government does into myriad components. Yet modern political science's concept of function seems much the same as the traditional political science concept and resembles the sociological term only barely.

Robert Merton discusses function—and this is important to understand—in the following way:

> It is the fifth connotation which is central to functional analysis as this has been practiced in sociology and social anthropology. Stemming in part from the native mathematical sense of the term, this usage is more often explicit adapted from the biological sciences, where the term function is understood to refer to the vital or organic processes considered in the respects in which they contribute to the maintenance of the organism.[21]

Merton then goes on to say that:

> Radcliffe-Brown is the most often explicit in tracing his work conception of social function to the analogical model found in the biological sciences. After the fashion of Durkheim, he asserts that the function of a recurrent physiological process is thus a correspondence between it and the needs (i.e., the necessary condition of existence) of the "organism." And on the social sphere where human beings, "the essential units," are connected by networks of social relations witn an integrated whole, the function of any recurrent activity, such as the punishment of crime, or a funeral ceremony, is the part it plays in the social life as a whole and therefore the *contribution* it makes to the maintenance of the structural continuity.[22]

Now, Merton does not really *define* function, although some cite his statement that "social function refers to observable, *objective consequences* and *not* to subjective dispositions"[23] as a definition. It seems to me, however, that what Merton, Radcliffe-Brown, and others have said quite clearly is that structure is one thing, *effect* of structure quite another. In other words, function as a concept referring to something structural or process-like does not exist in a static state. We can speak only of nonexistence ("X is not functioning") and shades of existence of an actual functioning relationship ("X is not functioning to peak capacity and a repair in structure is needed to maximize the effect that is desired"). As Riggs would have it: "Thus a

---

21 Robert K. Merton, *Social Theory and Social Structure*, rev. ed. (Glencoe, Ill.: Free Press, 1957), p. 21.
22 *Ibid.*, p. 27 (emphasis mine).
23 *Ibid.*, p. 24.

function is a . . . *relationship between variables.*"[24] In linking this concept of function with those of structure and system, Robert Holt states:

> It is typical for those who have made important contributions to functionalism to define function more or less explicitly as an *effect*. Merton speaks of functions as "observed consequences"; Radcliffe-Brown refers to "functions of any recurrent activity"; Levy, more explicit than most, defines function as "a condition or state of affairs resultant from the operation of a structure through time." Hempel points out with devastating simplicity, however, that the term *function* cannot be used synonymously with the term *effect*. He presents the following statement for consideration: "the heartbeat has the function of producing the heart sounds; for the heartbeat has that effect." No functionalist would accept this proposition. Function is not a synonym for effect; it is a subtype of effect. Functions are system relevant effects of structures. The term has meaning, therefore, only if the terms of structure and system relevant are explicitly defined and if the system under study is explicitly identified.[25]

Thus, it seems to me that Almond and Coleman's idea that a governmental (judicial) function is to "interpret the rules" falls more comfortably within the concept of structure. After all, is this not simply a description of a pattern of behavior of certain men playing certain roles? So it would be with "apply the rules," "policy-making," and "judicial review." Categorization of such activities as functions is something that Glendon Schubert, too, seems to have misunderstood, since he declares the function of judicial review to be "to *consider* the constitutionality of acts."[26] This error finds persistent and widespread acceptance. Kenneth Dolbeare has also noticed the fact that judicial scholars use the concept of function as a synonym for decision-making, i.e., "interpret the laws."[27] Another recent illustration of this may be found in the chapter on "The Judicial Process" in John Wahlke and Alexander Dragnich's *Government and Politics.*[28]

---

[24] Riggs, *op. cit.*, p. 20 (emphasis mine).

[25] Robert T. Holt, "A Proposed Structural-Functional Framework for Political Science," in *Functionalism in the Social Sciences*, ed. Don Martindale (Philadelphia: American Academy of Political and Social Science, 1965), pp. 86–87.

[26] Glendon Schubert, *Judicial Policy Making*, p. 58.

[27] "The use of the term 'functions' with reference to courts is a frequent one in the literature, but it almost always is as a label only and not as a means of linkage to other elements in the system; it is another way of saying that courts decide cases—their 'function' is to interpret laws, for example" (Kenneth M. Dolbeare, *Trial Courts in Urban Politics* [New York: Wiley, 1967], p. 10). Dolbeare indicts Vines as well as Schubert. See Kenneth Vines, "Political Functions of a State Court," in Vines and Herbert Jacob, *Studies in Judicial Politics*, Tulane Studies in Political Science, vol. 8 (New Orleans: Tulane University Press, 1963). Cf. Donald Kommers' definition of functionalism in his "Professor Kurland, the Supreme Court, and Political Science," *Journal of Public Law*, 15 (1966), pp. 230–52.

[28] Alex N. Dragnich and John Wahlke, *Government and Politics* (New York: Random House, 1966), pp. 372ff. It might be argued that "introductory texts" are simply straw men. I would dispute that—in this case, at any rate. Indeed, the chapter on "The Judicial Process" is more sophisticated in its rhetoric and choice of materials than some of the more specialized political science monographs on the courts.

Therein one discovers the political functions of the legal system, and they, as usual, include judicial review, which is simply a type of rule interpretation, and thus a structural variation.

Definition of the Concept of Court

A good place to locate widely accepted definitions of a concept in any field is an introductory textbook. Dell Hitchner and William Harbold, for instance, describe the "essential nature" (verbal realism) of a court as follows: (1) it "administers justice" (a functional type of relationship); (2) it is "the provision by the state of an impartial judge to decide a cause" (structural factor involving normative, formal expectation); and (3) "the third characteristic of the judicial process is its conduct by determinate standards that causes disputes to be resolved according to law. It is this feature of the proceedings which gives the qualities of order and predictability to the disposition of individual interests. . ." (structural and functional).[29] Similarly, we have political scientist Herman Finer's structural notion:

> *The Courts of Justice:* . . . their whole procedure has been built up on the basis of impartial umpireship between two parties. They have had no personal interest in the result, for they are irremovable, exempted from suit for any fault; there is little question of promotion; and the acceptance of gifts is forbidden. . . . Procedure makes the discovery and presentation of all evidence fully possible, and gives all parties the opportunity of stating their case with expert help. Proceedings are public; reports are published; records are kept; and precedents have weight. Moreover, the principles of the law, as they are taught, include these things, and they are revered . . . counsel comes before a court with strict etiquette, presided over by justices who jealously guard the traditional morals of the profession. These things produce definite principles which all may know with considerable certainty, and a process and convention of impartial and impersonal attention to the claims of the parties.[30]

And, according to a prominent jurist, "The conclusive reason why judicial independence is necessary is that without it there can be, properly speaking, no judgment and no judge."[31]

---

29 D. G. Hitchner and W. J. Harbold, *Modern Government: A Survey of Political Science*, 2nd ed. (New York: Dodd, Mead, 1965).

30 Herman Finer, *The Theory and Practice of Modern Government*, rev. ed. (New York: Henry Holt, 1949), p. 114.

31 Henry T. Lummis, *The Trial Judge* (Chicago: Foundation Press, 1937), p. 10.

A fuller examination of the relevant materials would take us little further. These excerpts contain the ingredients of that mixture known as a judicial structure or a court. [A court is (1) a man or body of men (2) with power to decide a dispute, (3) before whom the parties or advocates or their surrogates present the facts of the dispute and cite existent, expressed, primary normative principles (in statutes, constitutions, rules, previous cases) that (4) are applied by that man or those men, (5) who *believe* that they should listen to the presentation of facts and apply such cited normative principles impartially, objectively, or with detachment ("judicial role," *bungangeli*),[32] and (6) that they may so decide, and (7) as an independent body.]

Two of the concepts used above will require some explication at this point because (*a*) they serve as important boundary points as to what constitutes a court (if they are not present in reality, the decision-making institution will not be classified as a court) and (*b*), once present, as they vary, they comprise a structural shading (in degree or kind) of that particular court. The concepts are those of impartiality and independence. In both cases, in order for the observer to include a particular man or decision-making body of a given society within the confines of the concept of court (contrasted with noncourt), there must be a visible manifestation that the society expects (and the relevant decision-makers themselves expect) a measure of impartiality in the decision-makers, and/or that the body has a measure of independence. The Norwegian sociologist Vilhelm Aubert had this to say in his own recent conceptualization of court: "The nature of the particular 'service' which judges contribute, its origin in a conflict between two parties, implies that the service can only be contributed when an atmosphere of objectivity prevails."[33]

A manifestation or indicator of impartiality can be simply a formalized, visual norm (e.g., a constitutional provision, a law, or a ritual), or it can be made ostensible through the existence of some trappings of political insulation. Some actual objective *behavior* must be discovered, however, before we know that impartiality exists—at least to a minimal degree; in other words, that it is possible because it has happened.

Perhaps a few words about the usage of impartiality, objectivity, and detachment might be in order. At this point, I use the terms interchangeably, though it may become necessary in the near future to make distinctions. For instance, it is risky to employ the term "impartiality" if a scholar confuses the decision-making process with its output. Another Scandi-

---

[32] Max Gluckman, *Judicial Process among the Barotse of Northern Rhodesia* (Manchester: Manchester University Press, 1954), p. 234.

[33] Vilhelm Aubert, "Courts and Conflict Resolution," *Journal of Conflict Resolution*, 11 (March, 1967), p. 42.

navian scholar, Torstein Eckhoff, asks how a judge who strictly applied Nazi laws to Jews could be considered impartial (from the pro-Jewish point of view).[34] Since the law was highly partial against this group, the resulting decisions could not be considered impartial. In the study of judicial politics from my perspective, impartiality will be conceived of as applying only to the decision-making process; it is tantamount to the concept of objectivity. It might be easier on the nerves of some to say that a judge can objectively (rather than impartially) apply a partial law—but it is no clearer once one recognizes that we are primarily concerned with structure and process when we speak of impartiality.

Independence in decision-making, it seems to me, must be manifested by some decisions that are clearly in opposition to the thinking of other politically significant decision-makers in society. Only one such instance need be found in order to classify the decision-maker as independent and the structure as a court. It would have, at that point, only the minimum degree of independence. Of course, the degree of independence of courts varies greatly from society to society. Finally, "independence" as used in relationship to the advocates is not meant to imply that the parties themselves or their relatives may not argue the case.

Of course, there are several inclusionary choices made in this definition that are arbitrary. One of those is reasonably significant, and I will discuss it briefly. Items 3 and 5 in the foregoing definition include the structural factors of the presentation and application of some normative principles—formal or informal, but extant and theoretically compelling. This inclusion is probably best explained by the fact that the author is a product of the mind-training process of the Anglo-American law school tradition. This tradition is based on the assumption that both these structural factors may be incorporated into any societal decision-making situation in the hope that they will provide for a measure of impartiality in the authoritative allocation of values for the society. It is this requirement of impartiality in judgment that is necessary to my working concept of the judiciary.[35]

Nevertheless, it is equally clear that there are ways that impartiality can be accomplished other than by the presentation and application of law and custom. Impartiality also can be achieved by reliance on chance factors just as well as on the use of reason in the application of law.[36] After all, the person desiring judicial impartiality when he is hauled before the court for judgment must be concerned that the judge's own biases *toward*

---

[34] Torstein Eckhoff, "Impartiality, Separation of Powers, and Judicial Independence," *Scandinavian Studies in Law,* 9 (1965), pp. 9–52.

[35] This theoretical requirement is frequently cited. See, for instance, David H. Bayley, *Public Liberties in the New States* (Chicago: Rand McNally, 1964), p. 129.

[36] See Vilhelm Aubert, "Chance in Social Affairs," *Inquiry,* 2 (1959), pp. 1ff.

him do not dictate his decision-making in the name of society. A judge who
is free to vent personal animosities toward a litigant is a feared instrument,
and an impartial determination of innocence or guilt is highly valued in
many societies. Obviously the application of generally applicable, rigidly
applied normative rules is only one way for this to be guaranteed. Man
has devised others, e.g., trial by ordeal and trial by combat. E. Adamson
Hoebel has described the Eskimo song duel as a juridical form in which
victory is the result of singing skill.[37] The song duel would then not be
a court within my definition, as it has a basis of impartiality other than the
application of a primary normative principle. There may be vigorous argument for the inclusion of trial by ordeal, song duels, or butting contests as
court proceedings, but they offer no data by which I would be willing to
test the hypotheses of judicial theory.

Before we proceed any further, a few words about the concept of expressed, primary normative principles are also in order, because this phrase
has a few ambiguities that are best eliminated. When Solomon, for instance,
ordered the baby cut in half, he was not acting as a judge, was not a "court"
in a legal sense, because he was not applying or interpreting any *expressed*
normative principles. Actually, what principles were involved? The whole
decision-making process in this fable was little more than a gimmick; it
was a guess; it was a clever prediction about the true response of mother
love. The only law involved was a behavioral one (instead of normative)
about the reaction of a mother under certain conditions. There was surely
no prescriptive rule applied. Another situation that would have to be classified as lacking in expressed rules is to be found in the period following
the Russian Revolution, when the early Soviet judges were empowered to
interpret "the interests of the proletariat." A similar one was the Nazi
party's removal of judges who did not decide cases in conformance with
the "tradition and instinct of the *Volk*."[38] The interpretative leeway for
each judge is so great here that only the most amorphous sort of subjec-
tively defined justice can really be applied. There is no guide for the decision-maker. There is no precedent and no tradition to apply to these
words. A judge (a judicial decision-maker) interprets reasonably definite,
expressed prescriptions, and if the words are extremely vague, one would
have to find at least some historical fact that guides the judge as to specific
applications. Alf Ross, the noted Scandinavian jurisprudent, put it this way:

> The judge shall not be like the Homeric king who received his *themistes*
> direct from Zeus, or like the Oriental cadi who makes his decision

---

[37] E. Adamson Hoebel, *The Law of Primitive Man* (Cambridge: Harvard University Press, 1954), p. 92.
[38] See Philip W. Buck and John W. Masland, *The Governments of Foreign Powers*
(New York: Henry Holt, 1947), p. 272.

out of an esoteric wisdom. The idea of the supremacy of law makes us react against the tendency in the totalitarian states to authorize the judge, disregarding all fixed rules, to decide according to the "sound legal consciousness of the people" or "the interests of the proletariat" —which we look upon as a denial of the very idea of law.[39]

The Concept of Politics

Harold D. Lasswell, in one of his enduring and celebrated works, has defined the practice of politics as "who gets what, when, how."[40] In the same work, he defines the study of politics as the "study of influence and the influential." Implicitly crucial to both of these definitions is the concept of values. Values are the "what" in the first Lasswell definition and are what one wants to wield influence for in the second. Of course, there are many values—and Lasswell has been in the process of refining his typology for many years. In the early 1960's, Lasswell's value classification scheme was as follows:

1. Wealth
2. Power (e.g., high office or a voice in party councils)
3. Respect (e.g., favorable publicity)
4. Well-being (e.g., luxurious entertainment)
5. Affection (e.g., acceptance in a family circle)
6. Enlightenment (e.g., inside dope)
7. Skill (e.g., access to advanced training)
8. Rectitude (e.g., moral support from a cynical group)[41]

This specific set of values might be helpful in our explication of the concept of politics since it is reasonably extensive and specific.

David Easton has offered what is probably America's most widely quoted and professionally accepted definition of politics, or at least of the concept of the political system. I mention it here to emphasize the place of the concept of value in a definition of politics. According to Easton, politics is "the authoritative allocation of values for a society."[42] Unfortunately,

---

[39] Alf Ross, *On Law and Justice* (London: Stevens, 1958), p. 281. See also Sir Henry Maine, *Ancient Law* (London: J. M. Dent, 1917), chap. 1.

[40] Harold D. Lasswell, *Politics: Who Gets What, When, How?* (New York: McGraw-Hill, 1936).

[41] Harold D. Lasswell and Arnold Rogow, *Power, Corruption, and Rectitude* (Englewood Cliffs, N.J.: Prentice-Hall, 1963), p. 133.

[42] David Easton, *The Political System* (New York: Knopf, 1951), p. 129. His current definition is very much the same. In *A Framework for Political Analysis* (Englewood Cliffs, N.J.: Prentice-Hall, 1965), Easton defines politics indirectly by discussing the "essential variable" in the political system: (1) "making and execution of decisions for a society" and (2) "their relative frequency of acceptance as authoritative or binding by the bulk of society" (pp. 96–97).

Easton says little here about specific values. No typology is advanced; there is no detail.

On the other hand, Dahl and Lindblom have worked out an intricate adaptation of Lasswell's taxonomy:

> The important prime goals of human beings in Western societies include existence or survival, physiological gratification (through food, sex, sleep and comfort), love and affection, respect, self-respect, power or control, skill, enlightenment, novelty and many others. These are the ultimate criteria by which we would like to test alternative politico-economic devices. But to use criteria of this kind would force one to a level of specificity that would require an encyclopedia of particular techniques.
>
> On the other hand, there are seven goals that govern both the degree to which these prime goals of individuals are attained and the manner of deciding who is to attain his goals when individuals conflict in their goal seeking. . . . These seven instrumental goals are freedom, rationality, democracy, subjective equality, security, progress, and appropriate inclusion.[43]

The specificity of the value systems offered by Dahl, Lindblom, and Lasswell helps us see certain problems more clearly. For instance, if we keep these more specific lists of values in mind when we think about what courts (for instance, in the United States) ordinarily do, the realm of courts and politics becomes wider than commonly conceived:

1. When a court grants a divorce, this is an authoritative allocation of freedom and perhaps well-being. Is this decree of divorce a *political* act by the court? Should political scientists be interested in this type of subject matter?

2. When a court acquits a defendant in a burglary case, it again is authoritatively allocating well-being and reinforcing the values of freedom and well-being to the defendant. Ought the political scientist to be interested in this type of decision *per se* (that is, without any raising of due-process issues or the like)? What about a court's decision in favor of a tenant in an eviction case? Is this political?

3. When a court awards a plaintiff money in a tort case, it is authoritatively allocating wealth. Is that politics? Political scientists almost totally ignore such subject matter—at least traditionally. Yet political scientists would be interested in a decision by a court which held a corporation merger to be the creation of a monopoly. But is not that tort case an authoritative allocation of wealth? Why does political science emphasize the values of power—economic power (different from wealth?)—in the monopoly case? Has this distinction in scrutiny any conceptual foundation? If

---

[43] Robert A. Dahl and Charles E. Lindblom, *Politics, Economics, and Welfare* (New York: Harper, 1953), p. 28.

wealth and economic power are indeed so different, would a court's decision on the validity of an election of a board of directors of a corporation then be considered to be within the bailiwick of political science? Surely that is an authoritative allocation of the value of power in the society as well as on behalf of society.

4. When the Supreme Court holds that a state statute that prohibits a Negro from going to the state law school is unconstitutional, the court is authoritatively allocating (potential) skill. Is this political?

The list of these situations is nearly inexhaustible, yet I think that these four make the point fairly clearly. The combination Dahl-Easton-Lasswell definition would allow us to treat *everything* the court finally does as a proper study for political scientists, since by its very nature the court is authoritatively allocating a value allocated by the political system. It is precisely at this point that the individual teacher-researcher must make his own definitional choices. What is his research interest? What does he wish to include in his syllabus? A scope broad enough to include all these specific situations is surely justifiable when one defines government as the monopolized force of society organized to distribute some values authoritatively and to maintain internal order. Under this definition, a divorce decree is as much a political output as a major constitutional statement. As such, it is certainly relevant to the study of political science.

But is this the best delineation of judicial politics, that is, the most fruitful way for political scientists to conceive of the interrelationship of courts and politics? If we define government in this way, the linkage between judicial and politics is through an emphasis on "authoritatively." Surely judicial decisions on torts and divorces can be deemed political in the sense that the process treating them is authoritative, but this centers on an institutional and internal process and not on a *relationship* at all. Why must we focus on the nature of the prescribing process, that is, the authoritative stating of the ought-to-be? That is a throwback to older days when the legalists held sway, and it has sapped our intellectual vigor. To my mind, at this stage of the development (or lack thereof) of this area of political science, it would be far more stimulating to orient our outlook on what is political by focusing on the actual degree of distribution and dispersal of the political and social systemic values after the decision has been made and to look to political and societal influences on such decisions. If a political scientist is interested in the actual degree of distribution of freedom and wealth in the society, the judicial settlement of divorces and wills and torts would still be within the purview of judicial politics. In short, judicial politics would be best conceived as two distinct relationships: (1) direct impact and feedback relationships between the judicial structure (and its output, a decision) and other components of the political system (govern-

ment and its appendages) as well as the society at large, and (2) the political and societal influences felt within the judicial structure as it progresses toward its decision.

At this point, then, now that we have somewhat explicated the concept that might add up to judicial politics, it is appropriate to demarcate the general boundaries of a conceptual scheme that I believe necessary to guide the teaching and research programs important for the future of this field.

The Conceptual Scheme and a Paradigm

I use the notion of conceptual scheme rather than that of theoretical framework because I define them differently and that difference matters here. In my view this distinction relates to two different degrees of closeness between words and their empirical referents. Quite simply, the former concept is just one step further removed from material reality than the latter; that is, I take the term "conceptual scheme" to imply a lesser relationship to empirical data and induction than "theoretical framework." The former is a product of a mind roaming at will within the confines of two or more high-level concepts; it is systematic interrelationship at the same level and deduction to a lower, more explicit level. Its cardinal function is to guide research in a new area. The term "theoretical framework," on the other hand, is taken to mean a scheme that is rooted in some tested and verified (or disverified) proposition. There are data and propositions, and "islands of theory"[44] that are placed in a framework primarily as inventory and then only as help to guide further, more advanced research.

Because of the dearth of data and low-level theory on judicial politics, this study must operate at a fairly high level of abstraction, and a few words on political metatheory may be helpful. It seems that almost all major theoretical constructs involved in a field of political science can be placed within one of three or so phases of theory. These phases can be theorized to interrelate, even at their highest level of abstraction.

James Robinson has worked out a splendidly simple but inclusive model of all political theories in his attempt to develop a case for a general strategy for future political science research.[45] After discussing the general

---

[44] This is a phrase often used by Harold Guetzkow. I like it because it seems more apt than "some theory," since it implies that one can have ostensibly independent but invisibly connected areas of theory. The connection is that afforded by a bedrock of data—some of which have not yet reached a general theory surface.

[45] "Problems in Political Science," in *Politics and Public Affairs*, ed. Lynton K. Caldwell (Bloomington: Indiana University Press, 1962).

set of boundary problems for political science, he discusses the intervening
and independent variables. In his words and picture:

> When we try to translate political factors or political units into more
> specific form for studying their impact on public policy, we are seek-
> ing to identify the independent and intervening variables related to
> our dependent variable. . . .

Political Units and Policy

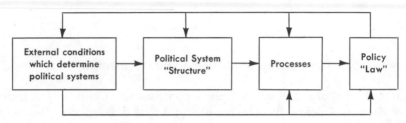

The arrows show relationships among these factors or variables. Moving from left to right, some external conditions give rise to some type
of political system which adopts some kind of processes for making
and executing policies. Hypothetically, there may be high correlations between external conditions and policy, as indicated by the
longest arrow at the bottom of the diagram. Political systems may also
be directly related to policy, or process to policy, as indicated by the
shorter arrows at the bottom. However, what one would expect to
be more likely is that conditions and systems are mediated by process.
Furthermore, policy may well have reciprocal impact on the other
variables as noted in the "feedback loops" at the top of the diagram.
Most noticeably, one would expect policy outcomes.[46]

For my purposes here, the word "structure" would replace "system." System and procedure are easily conceived as two subareas under structure.

Another recent attempt to create a research strategy includes a similar
political-metatheoretical pattern. Robert Cahill and Harry Friedman, in
arguing for the "merits of a strategy for the comparative study of local
government," discuss five questions that they deem central to almost all
(if not all) the "Western tradition of political inquiry":

1. What kinds of alternative political arrangements are *conceivable
   and/or possible?*
2. What kinds of alternative political arrangements can actually be
   discerned to exist or to have existed?
3. What are the underlying causes of alternative kinds of political
   arrangements?
4. What are the consequences of alternative kinds of political arrangements for other aspects of human life?

---

[46] *Ibid.*, pp. 172–73.

5. What are the respective *advantages and disadvantages* of alternative kinds of political arrangements?[47]

It is not too drastic a leap to liken the notion of political arrangements
to that of political structure, or causes to external conditions, or consequences to policy and/or structure and process feedback onto external
conditions. In other words, the perceived overall pattern of theory in political science by Robinson, Cahill, and Friedman is very much the same, and
I believe that this model can guide efforts to establish a general conceptual
scheme for the field of judicial politics.

Our interest centers on courts or judiciaries and their interrelationship
with politics. The key phase of any potential theory in this area is that of
structure, i.e., the judicial structure, i.e., system and procedures. This variable can well serve as the core of the field. The real observable phenomena
bounded by my conceptualization might prove to have no explanatory
value (the conceptualization may be found to relate to no phenomenon in
any orderly way). However, this is not a flaw at this point. It is the very
essence of the scientific enterprise, the key point of the exploration, to
formulate a conceptualization of reality and then go look into reality to see
if the conceptualization is at all isomorphic, if it is at all consistent with
reality. For as Easton says:

> We do not need to conclude from this generalized description of
> what is involved in the delineation of boundaries that, once estab-
> lished, they are eternally fixed. If it should turn out that owing to
> some mistaken interpretation or lack of insight, in order to improve
> our understanding of the political system we must include within it
> some element previously assigned to the environment, we are faced
> with no crisis. *We simply redefine the system to meet our analytic
> needs.* Each time that we enlarge our system we simultaneously shrink
> the environment. If this seems to introduce an element of indeter-
> minacy into our conceptualization, I can only refer to our discus-
> sion of what we mean by a system. *It is a device to help us to
> understand a defined and redefinable area of human behavior, not a
> strait jacket to imprison analysis permanently within a preconceived
> mold or model.*[48]

Within this suggested reconceptualization and metatheoretical position I submit that a new field of knowledge awaits development by and
for political science. Within this suggested reconceptualization and metatheoretical position, political scientists can stake out a relatively undisputed
virgin area that needs creative exploitation. It takes only a pinch of zest,
an ounce of playfulness, and a teaspoon of science.

---

[47] Robert S. Cahill and Harry J. Friedman, "A Strategy for the Comparative Study
of Local Governments," *Thai Journal of Public Administration*, 6 (July, 1965), pp. 1–
34; Social Science reprint no. 15 (Honolulu: University of Hawaii Press, 1966).

[48] *Framework for Political Analysis*, p. 67 (emphasis mine).

The questions that await answers (if indeed there are any answers) may be usefully placed into several major categories. First of all, there is the question of whether the phenomenon I have defined as court or judicial structure exists at all in the world. And if it does, its very dynamic needs extensive examination. It is within this context that we must pursue the inquiry into judicial role and into the mechanics of the judicial decision-making process. Actually, most of the so-called judicial behavioral work falls comfortably within this category, but by failing to conceptualize what judicial is, it fails to ask the right questions. Thus much of its output will be found to be irrelevant and immaterial despite its technical competence.

Another major question involves the societies that are without courts. We must find those societies that do not have the dispute-settling structure that I have conceptually labeled judicial structure or court. These societies must then be described. Thereafter, the task is twofold. First, it will be necessary, within the theoretical model's dictate, to determine what (if any) factors are associated with the existence of this structure. Second, we must ask what are the functions (i.e., actual effects) of the bare existence of this structure or of the nonexistence of this structure. Are courts necessarily related to order? to the maintenance of the societal status quo? to the administration of justice? to the maintenance of democracy? There is much lore and implicit theory on this topic. The time has come to be explicit in our theory and then to observe the real world systematically. Perhaps there will be corroboration; perhaps not.

The next major category posits the existence of judicial structure in society and suggests a host of questions that involve the vast array of differences in judicial structure that exist (and have existed) in the world. In slightly different terms, I suggest that many societies have judicial structure of one sort or another. Political scientists interested in the policy-science and system-science aspects of gaining knowledge must seek answers to questions that arise as to the consequences of these variations upon the social system of which the courts are but one part. How can we best explain the development of the English court system from the thirteenth to the fifteenth centuries? How can we explain the use of the particular trappings employed by the Ghanaians in the twentieth century? Why do some judiciaries have more independence than others? How can we explain the specific consequences (the function) of the use of judicial review (as a structure) in a democracy—why not employ legislative committees with no structures of political isolation? Is a nation less democratic because it has no jury system? These, too, are questions that theorists have only implicitly answered, and rarely without internal inconsistency. Again the theory must be explicit and a long, hard, systematic, and hopefully rigorous look must be taken—for the first time.

For far too long, political scientists have played alien roles concerning their interest in the court system. They have played the role of lawyer, in attempting case analysis; historian, in sketching judicial biographies and constitutional developments; philosopher, in pondering problems of jurisprudence; statistician, in describing judicial decisions with quantitative exactitude. Yet the main area of the field remains almost barren of analysis and study, and it is this field that is peculiarly their own. It is time to develop judicial theory; it is time to do the research that can lead to a large body of scientifically collected, comparatively based knowledge; it is time we pulled the field of judicial politics together.

The twentieth century may become known as that time when a large scientifically oriented group of men began to inquire openly, seriously, and objectively into their institutions and those of others, as to both cause and effect. The social sciences, as a major system of social thought underlying this inquiry, have their roots in the nineteenth century and before. But the force, size, and technological competence of this search are uniquely of the twentieth century. Its hope is in the past, its momentum is contemporary. I interpret William Golding's *Lord of the Flies* to mean that man's institutions are delicate and that the flaws in man's nature can drive him, this time, to his own destruction by fire. If this is correct, then of course there is little for us to worry about. The social sciences (as men currently practice them) involve a faith that something *can* be done by man himself. The twentieth century has become an era when man has thought much and done much about changing his institutional environment on a scale qualitatively different than ever before. One major area substantially overlooked by researchers, however, has been the political and societal significance of the judicial structure and process. I believe that it is potentially an important area, even if the ultimate conclusion may turn out to be that the existence of or variations in judicial systems and structure are of no social value or social consequence whatever. It is one primary role of the political scientist to pursue the truth of this matter.

CHAPTER 1

THE SEARCH FOR JUDICIAL ROLE AND THE COURTS: LOCATION AND MEASUREMENT

([Becket] turns to the jeweled crucifix above the bed and says simply:) I hope You haven't inspired me with all these holy resolutions in order to make me look ridiculous, Lord. It's all so new to me. I'm setting about it a little clumsily perhaps.

(He looks at the crucifix and with a swift gesture takes it off the wall.)

And you're far too sumptuous too. Precious stones around your bleeding Body . . . I shall give you to some poor village church.

(He lays the crucifix on the chest. He looks around the room happy, lighthearted, and murmurs:)

It's like leaving for a holiday. Forgive me, Lord, but I never enjoyed myself so much in my whole life. I don't believe You are a sad God. The joy I feel in shedding all my riches must be part of Your divine intentions.

(He goes behind the curtain into the antechamber, where he can be heard gaily whistling an old English marching song. He comes back a second later, his bare feet in sandals, and wearing a monk's coarse woolen robe. He draws the curtain across again and murmurs:)

There. Farewell, Becket. I wish there had been something I had regretted parting with, so I could offer it to You.

(He goes to the crucifix and says simply:)

Lord, are You sure You aren't tempting me? It all seems far too easy.[1]

—JEAN ANOUILH
Becket

IS THERE ANYTHING in reality isomorphic to that which I have conceptualized as court and judicial structure? How does it differ from other structures? If we learn that no such phenomenon really exists, or if we find good

---

[1] Reprinted by permission of Coward-McCann, Inc., from *Becket, or The Honor of God* by Jean Anouilh, translated by Lucienne Hill. Copyright © 1960 by Jean Anouilh and Lucienne Hill.

reason to doubt its existence, then all the other questions would be dross. Instead of dealing with a political institution, we would be dealing with a phenomenon more aptly conceptualized as ideology or as a political belief. It would then become senseless to discuss theories dealing with the development of court structure and its impact upon society. Rather we should be obliged to transfer the entire section of political theory treating courts to those scholars interested in epistemology, the sociology of knowledge, and the formation and consequences of political mythology.

The reader is urged to recall the definition of court stipulated in the Introduction (page 13), and to keep in mind that each item in the definition is essential. Our task is to see if any social-political phenomenon matches *all* the properties included in the definition. Other components may combine with the judicial critical mass, and as long as they are not totally contradictory or destructive of any of the key elements, the organism will remain judicial. However, if any aspect called for by the definition is missing in reality, then that particular phenomenon cannot be considered to be a court (it may have some juridical form, but it is not a court) for the purposes of this study.

There is one component of my definition that is discussed most frequently and is theorized about most intensively (at least in American circles). This is the role requirement for the judicial decision-maker to exhibit impartiality. The judicial decision-maker is expected to be at least somewhat objective in the disposition of disputes before him (item 5 in the definition). Kenneth Dolbeare goes so far as to say he believes that "the way in which the judge conceives of his judicial role is probably the most significant single factor in the whole decisional process."[2] It seems to me that this is surely *a* crucial element, though not necessarily *the* crucial one.

More specifically, I take judicial role to mean that the judicial decision-maker (1) is expected to decide concrete disputes in some accordance with the way the expressed, relevant, and specific rules of the society would have them settled, (2) believes he should decide in this manner, and (3) does indeed decide some cases in this manner, or approaches all cases in this manner. The judge, then, is supposed to perform (to some degree) as intermediary between the contestants and the rules; he is to decide a specific disposition that is found within the abstract boundaries of the rules, within the "leeway," as Karl Llewellyn puts it.[3] His own personal feelings about the individual disputants or about the wisdom of the general rules

---

[2] Kenneth M. Dolbeare, *Trial Courts in Urban Politics* (New York: Wiley, 1967), p. 69.

[3] Karl Llewellyn, *The Common Law Tradition* (Boston: Little, Brown, 1960), pp. 29ff. Cf. Richard Wasserstrom, *The Judicial Decision* (Stanford: Stanford University Press, 1961).

are to be kept as much as possible to himself and out of the decision he makes. At any rate, both the external role requirement—i.e., what *should* be done by the decision-maker (a normative prescription)—and some minimal evidence of a correspondence between this expectation and actual behavior—i.e., objectivity in the decision-making process—must be found in order for impartiality to exist in and govern society.

Widespread belief and strongly stated norms for such impartiality seem *prima facie* evidence for the existence of some such role behavior. The surprising ecstasies in actually assuming a role that is the religious equivalent of that of judge are well expressed by Anouilh's Becket on his ascendance to the archbishopric. Surely the chief cleric—like the judge at any level—is supposed to leave his personal predilections behind; he is supposed to meet various role requirements of honesty and impartiality (adherence to moral rules) by actually acting honestly and impartially. This is rewarding in and of itself.

Of course, there are other essential components to the conceptualization of court also closely associated with the ideal of impartiality in the judicial process. Two of these are the concept of independence of the decision-maker from sanction due to the content of his decision, and the impediments to access by others for the purpose of influencing the content of his decision, i.e., the laws and trappings of insulation. Although these two components are of great importance in distinguishing the court process from other official, authoritative, value-allocating decision-making processes, the *sine qua non* is the role requirement of impartiality, in at least some degree. In other words, this is what is considered the heart of the judicial process; *this is the central notion implicit in most theorizing done about the functioning of courts.* Freedom from sanction and impediments to access do reinforce or strengthen the ability of judges to internalize this role requirement, but they would scarcely be enough in themselves to ensure an orientation toward rule-deference or even to distinguish one governmental decision-making process from another. Furthermore, the objectivity requirement seems to have a centralizing, cluster-attraction force for the other two factors. For these reasons, it seems to me that search for the very existence (or nonexistence) of the judicial decision-making structure in any culture may well center around the search for the existence of this role requirement, its acceptance by those empowered to act as judges, and some evidence of their acting in accordance with it. It is important to keep in mind. however, that in those societies in which it exists, it will be found in many different degrees—as will the measure of actual independence of a judiciary. These are just some of the structural variations to be discussed subsequently.

Unfortunately, there has been very little done toward conducting the necessary pertinent research; that is, there has been little inquiry made to find patterns of judicial role belief and corresponding behavior. Moreover, the scant amount of work accomplished along these specific lines frequently has lacked system and rigor. Where the research on the judiciary has been rigorous, it has been highly tangential to research into the existence or non-existence and degree of the *judicial* structure. Although I and some others have been critical of much of this work before, it is important to couch the criticism within the conceptual framework of this book, so that the criticism may have more positive meaning. The following critical commentary is meant to serve as a backdrop for the types of research that need to be done in terms of one constructive theoretical orientation (structural-functional analysis).

Early Misdirection and Failure in the Contemporary Search

There has been a good deal written and said in American political science about the United States court system and its case output. In fact, almost all the discussion of the court system in the United States prior to the 1950s dwelled on the content of case decisions of the Supreme Court and on the formal structure of the American legal-judicial system. It is fair to say that American political science once operated upon the implicit assumption that judges simply read the law and applied it, and that the content of the law was in itself of enormous importance. This was pure and unabashed slot-machine jurisprudence. However, the fifties reflected and portended change.

At first, political scientists began to speak of the courts as policy-makers and not as law finders.[4] The Supreme Court found itself studied by far more people and in numerous different ways, and court decisions, *qua* law, were no longer the exclusive preoccupation of political scientists. Yes, the opinions were studied still, but they were being studied more and more to yield information about the judges themselves or about the court as a group of individuals, rather than about "the law." Of course, the judicial biographer and the constitutional historian have been traditional members of political science departments (and some remain so), and they have long been inter-

---

[4] Following in the steps of C. Herman Pritchett's *The Roosevelt Court* (New York: Macmillan, 1948) were such works as Victor G. Rosenblum's *Law as a Political Instrument* (New York: Doubleday, 1955) and Jack Peltason's *The Federal Courts in the Political Process* (New York: Random House, 1955). These three books are frequently cited as "founding" the "new" approaches to the study of courts by political scientists. The "founding father" of the quantitative approach to this study was Glendon Schubert. See his *Quantitative Analysis of Judicial Behavior* (New York: Free Press, Macmillan, 1959).

ested in the lives and viewpoints of judges. So some of this was not really too new, though some aspects of the study of the judge as a man came into clearer focus. The so-called modern breed of political scientists began to cull, gather, and organize different types of materials as psychological and sociological data on judges, in addition to "political" information. Far more precise techniques were employed in this endeavor. Those who used the more advanced psychometric paraphernalia were called judicial behavioralists.[5] Mainly they studied patterns of *votes* of judges; presently, more attention is being given to the content of judicial *opinions*. Whether the focus is on votes or opinions, this judicial behavioral research has failed either to establish or to disprove the existence of judicial structure. In fact, from their choice of data and their methods of analysis one can infer that the early, and largest, group of judicial behavioralists chose, a priori, to discount (not ignore) the importance, if not the very existence, of judicial role, and therefore of judicial structure. The discussion in this section focuses on the voting studies, but some attention will be paid to the opinion-content research afterward.

The pioneer and premier (and still most productive) researcher in this undertaking, Glendon Schubert, takes umbrage with my opinion on this matter. He claims that his work and that of several of his emulators did indeed investigate the concept of judicial role (in applying precedent).[6] He does manage to uncover a few studies in which the concept of *stare decisis*, precedent orientation, or judicial role was loosely employed,[7] but this does not refute the charges that these studies, as designed, were incapable of such investigation and actually betray a bias on the part of the researchers. For instance, it is true that Schubert did state in 1963 that "the major error in our prediction must be attributed to our failure to include such a traditional legal variable as *stare decisis* within the frame of reference deemed relevant."[8] Yet it is equally true that in the same year he also wrote that, added together, judicial behavioral studies substantially

---

[5] The judicial behavioral movement is just one aspect of a more general movement in modern American political science. The best discussions of this general movement can be found in Robert Dahl, "The Behavioral Approach," *American Political Science Review*, 55 (December, 1961), pp. 763–72; Heinz Eulau, *The Behavioral Persuasion in Politics* (New York: Random House, 1963); and in chap. 1 of David Easton's *Framework for Political Analysis* (Englewood Cliffs, N.J.: Prentice-Hall, 1965). Schubert reviewed the *judicial* behavioral work up to 1963 in his "Behavioral Research in Public Law," *American Political Science Review*, 57 (June, 1963), pp. 433–45.

[6] "There are, on the other hand, several reports of behavioral research in which the possible influence of stare decisis has been investigated" (Glendon Schubert, "Ideologies and Attitudes: Academic and Judicial," *Journal of Politics*, 19 [February, 1967], p. 18).

[7] Schubert lists these several reports in his footnote 22, *ibid.*

[8] Glendon Schubert, "Civilian Control and Stare Decisis in the Warren Court," in *Judicial Decision-Making*, ed. Schubert (New York: Free Press, Macmillan, 1963), p. 72.

had "*debunked* legal principles as factors controlling decisions."[9] Since the doctrine of *stare decisis* consists largely of the role expectation that legal doctrine must control decisions, one might reluctantly conclude that Schubert speaks with a forked tongue. Additionally, attention to the factor of judicial role as defined in these studies is still only an infinitesimal fraction of the work.

Though Schubert and his followers refuse to admit that they assume the controlling factor in the judicial decision-making process to be the personal bias (attitudes and values) of the judges, and have limited their search mainly to corroborating this, their assumption shines through with unmistakable clarity. The very methods with which they study this phenomenon, coupled with their interpretation, can yield no other well-rationalized explanation. Their procedures and their conclusions prove only their assumptions and "debunk" only the claim to an impartial study of impartiality. There is no way that the mere examination of judicial votes can demonstrate either the existence or the nonexistence of the factors that make up the beliefs and execution of judicial role, no more than that data can tell us about judicial attitudes, judicial personality, judicial intelligence, or judicial eating habits. Therefore, whatever the researchers label their findings, we know only what they assumed initially. Let me illustrate this in greater detail.

The information foundation of the bulk of these studies, as I have noted, are the votes of the individual members of various appellate courts in time and space. The written opinions of the judges are used mainly to classify their votes in some way. After dividing cases into legal subject-matter areas by an analysis of the opinions, the researchers tabulate the votes of individual judges as being either for or against in these areas, designating them on various types of charts with plusses and minuses respectively. Joseph Tanenhaus recently described and illustrated this procedure while discussing the cumulative scaling of judicial decisions:

> In cumulative scaling one seeks to arrange respondents (for example, judges) and stimuli (for example, cases) in a matrix in an effort to determine whether persons who respond affirmatively to a weak stimulus do in fact respond affirmatively to all stronger stimuli—and, in addition, whether persons who respond negatively to a strong stimulus will also respond negatively to all weaker ones. If a single well-structured set of attitudes is shared by all or virtually all respondents, a continuum of stimuli representing varying degrees of intensity should reveal an identifiable point at which each respondent ceases to react affirmatively and begins to react negatively. Table I illustrates such

---

[9] Glendon Schubert, "Judicial Attitudes and Voting Behavior: The 1961 Term of the U.S. Supreme Court," *Law and Contemporary Problems*, 28 (Winter, 1963), p. 104 (emphasis mine).

a matrix for six classes of respondents and five stimuli. Each class of respondents constitutes a perfect scale type. As the matrix makes clear, scale type A respondents react affirmatively to all stimuli to which type B respondents react affirmatively and to weaker stimuli as well. Type B respondents hold a similar relationship to type C respondents and so on. These relationships are clearly transitive and asymmetrical, and so the structure of the scale is unquestionably cumulative, or ordinal.

TABLE I

Model of a Perfect Cumulative Scale

Classes of Respondents (or Scale Types)	Intensity of Stimuli				
	Very Strong	Strong	Moderate	Weak	Very Weak
A	+	+	+	+	+
B	+	+	+	+	−
C	+	+	+	−	−
D	+	+	−	−	−
E	+	−	−	−	−
F	−	−	−	−	−

Should an unexpected response occur (an affirmative where a negative is expected, as in − + − − −, or a negative where an affirmative is expected, as in + − + + +), the response would be considered an inconsistency or error. Perfect consistency is not to be expected in most areas of human endeavor and especially not in adjudication, where competing interests are almost always involved. As Justice Frankfurter observed in the *Dennis* case: "Adjustment of clash of interests which are at once subtle and fundamental is not likely to reveal entire consistency in a series of instances presenting the clash." And so this thorny question necessarily arises: How much inconsistency can be tolerated without destroying the fundamentally cumulative character of a scale?[10]

Tanenhaus' criticisms, as the reader can see, are oriented toward the mechanics of scalogram analysis. For one thing, he is concerned over whether various assumptions that underlie the Guttman technique are met by the way the judicial behavioralists use vote data. Moreover, Tanenhaus is not alone in his technical suspicions, for there have been many essays voicing similar criticisms.[11] My concern, however, is more theoretical.

---

[10] Joseph Tanenhaus, "The Cumulative Scaling of Judicial Decision," *Harvard Law Review*, 79 (June, 1966), pp. 1586–87. Copyright © 1966 by The Harvard Law Review Association.

[11] See Joel Grossman, "Role Playing and the Analysis of Judicial Behavior," *Journal of Public Law*, 11 (1962), pp. 285–309; John Sprague, *Voting Patterns of the*

In the scalogram, the object is to see if a number of cases can be reduced to one unidimensional scale, such as libertarianism, on which the judges may be ranked. Errors—that is, inconsistencies between an individual judge's responses and a hypothetical unidimensional pattern—are counted and expressed statistically as the coefficient of reproducibility for each scale. The frequently high figure (usually over .90) is alleged to indicate that single psychological and sociological factors are related to judicial decisions; that is, that judicial behavior is motivated consistently by single variables. However, this consistency is an artifact of the attempt (à la Occam's razor) to find a single scale in which to collapse votes on a large set of cases. For instance, most of the judges analyzed actually appear quite inconsistent in their behavior. Judges rarely decide all cases in any category in a single direction, and they vary their decisions on cases because they are not fully doctrinaire in their views. Scalogram analyses of votes, however, deliberately bury the rationale that judges present for their votes, and individual deviations from hypothetical standards are obscured by arranging cases so as to minimize "errors." The very desire to find consistency and to overlook deviation frequently blinds the analysts to the existence of the multidimensional aspects present in judicial decision-making, one aspect of which may possibly be judicial role.

As a culmination of the practices of the scalogram researchers in judicial behavior, Harold Spaeth has presented a case for a unidimensional model to explain judicial decision-making. Not only does he remain unconvinced that scalogram analysis creates artifacts and cannot be used to disconfirm multidimensional hypotheses, but he argues that one need know only one variable to account for all judicial behavior. This long-sought variable is baptized as "attitude." Aware of the very uncomplicated notion he is advancing, but by no means deterred, Spaeth insists that justices will respond in case X to the stimulus of civil liberty, and not to the separable component aspects of search and seizure, police, right to counsel, lawyers, cruel and unusual punishment, and methods of dealing with criminals. The unidimensional model is obviously simplistic and, admittedly, loses the asserted "richness" and "variation" of judicial decision-making.[12]

The very dynamic of this approach ignores the probable influence of many factors, such as conflicting attitudes, underlying values, institutional

---

United States Supreme Court (Indianapolis: Bobbs-Merrill, 1968), especially pp. 157–60; Sidney Raymond Peck, "A Behavioral Approach to the Judicial Process," *Osgoode Hall Law Journal* (Canada), 5 (April, 1967), pp. 1–28. See also the critical portions of Daryl R. Fair, "An Experimental Application of Scalogram Analysis to State Supreme Court Decisions," *Wisconsin Law Review*, 1967 (Spring, 1967), pp. 449–67.

[12] Harold J. Spaeth, "Unidimensionality and Item Invariance in Judicial Scaling," *Behavioral Science*, 10 (July, 1965), pp. 290–304. See also his *The Warren Court* (San Francisco: Chandler, 1966), especially chap. 1.

role, the dynamics of the judicial conference, and political elements.[13] Tanenhaus, who was one of the original workers in this area of research, fled from the search for "the existence of a unidimensional continuum."[14] Even Schubert admits the possibility that the bulk of the work along these lines may have conceptualized such "efforts in terms of a search for uni-dimensionality."[15]

The main point is, though, that even if "unidimensionality" were found, there is no more reason to believe that it ought to be christened "attitude" rather than "judicial role" or "adherence to the judge's perception of the law," or "good" versus "bad" legal skills. The fact that Guttman scalograms have traditionally been attitude measurements is no reason to believe that an observable scale of case votes necessarily reflects attitudes. After all, the responses that Guttman was measuring were to questions on an attitude questionnaire. Though Schubert is more than willing to equate a judge's decision with a respondent's answer on a check-the-right-box question-naire, I am not.[16] The stimulus and the choice process of an appellate judge are infinitely more complex than those of an undergraduate respondent an-swering a questionnaire and *are thus subject to infinitely more possibilities of interpretation.*[17] To identify any factor that shows up on a scalogram as "attitude" is a misapplication of a technique that, as I have said above, be-trays only the bias of the researcher. But more important, this would be the same argument I would use if these researchers had discovered by their methodical analysis of the scalogram that indeed the voting consistency *was*

---

[13] One of the best arguments against the hypothesis that other factors "intervene" substantially between the attitudes of Supreme Court justices and their decisions is advanced by J. Woodford Howard, Jr., in "On the Fluidity of Judicial Choice," *American Political Science Review*, 62 (March, 1968), pp. 43–56. Using materials other than case opinions and votes, Howard notes the probably large influence of such factors as "bargains" and "pragmatism" (where "ideological values were tempered by strategic judgments") (see p. 49).

[14] Tanenhaus, *op. cit.,* p. 1594.

[15] Glendon Schubert, "Ideologies and Attitudes, Academic and Judicial," *Journal of Politics,* 29 (February, 1967), p. 25.

[16] "The cases which the Court has docketed for decision-making on the merits of the issues presented are conceptualized as being equivalent to the items of a question-naire. Each case asks the justices to respond to the question: Is your attitude toward value sufficiently favorable that you believe that a claim of degree Y should be upheld?" (Schubert, *The Judicial Mind* [Evanston, Ill.: Northwestern University Press, 1965], p. 75).

[17] Schubert scoffs at the "naïveté" of legal scholars who use judicial opinions to arrive at conclusions about "the law" (*ibid.,* p. 76). Similarly, Sidney Ulmer has found occasion to attack my usage of statements made by judges in private as an undue reli-ance on the veracity of these statements. But the question remains: How can Schubert and Ulmer cast the first stone when both of them use the verbiage of the case opinion as the basis of their classification of cases and thus as the basis for deciding what "atti-tudes" are responsible for the decision? See the exchange of correspondence between Ulmer and me in the *American Political Science Review*, 61 (December, 1967), pp. 1098–1101.

due to an assiduous adherence to the law as the judges perceived it. Walter Murphy makes the same point regarding Sidney Ulmer's inference from similar voting data that group interaction factors were at work. In Murphy's words: "The fact that two or more Justices vote together is rather weak evidence that their votes are the result of interaction; standing alone, voting records tell us *very little* about the force or direction of any interpersonal influence that may exist."[18] The fact is that it is utterly impossible for the researchers to know which factor or factors are responsible for a judicial decision—and in what (if any) pattern of interaction. *This is certainly as true in determining whether—and if so, to what degree—judicial role factors are operative in the decision-making process.*

It must be conceded, however, that vote classification information does yield some incidental service. For example, it serves a practical purpose for lawyers, even though it does not serve a theoretical or practical one for political scientists. Stuart Nagel (a "lawyer–political scientist hybrid")[19] has been working on quantitative *prediction* of court cases for some time now. Accordingly, he is refining a device already on the market for lawyers which allows them better (more precisely) to predict the response of judges toward particular sets of facts. But of what possible use could this be to someone not concerned with particular outcomes? Of what interest is a fair prediction potential for a *particular* decision outcome *per se* for political science? I'd say none. Ulmer, currently adapting newer statistical techniques for better prediction of judicial decision-making behavior, likens his study to the Kentucky gambler's interest in foreseeing the winner of the Derby.[20] This is close to the mark. Political science must be interested in better prediction (than proffered by traditional legal analysis) *only* as it is a manifestation of greater understanding (more powerful theory). Perfect (or near-perfect) prediction based solely on similar past performances is simply equivalent to seeing certain patterns—not explaining them. It is like observing that it rains eight out of every ten Mondays in Tahiti, and thus accurately predicting rain, even though no one knows or cares why. That is the question that these devices cannot answer. Mere precision on judicial behavior tells us nothing about whether judicial role exists, or if it does, to what extent it influences judicial behavior—and under what combination of circumstances.

---

[18] Walter Murphy, "Courts as Small Groups," *Harvard Law Review*, 79 (June, 1966), p. 1566 (emphasis mine).

[19] I am indebted to Glendon Schubert for ingeniously coining this descriptive epithet. See his *Judicial Policy Making* (Chicago: Scott, Foresman, 1965), p. 169.

[20] S. Sidney Ulmer, "The Discriminant Function and a Theoretical Context for Its Use in Estimating the Votes of Judges," in *Frontiers of Judicial Research*, ed. Joel Grossman and Joseph Tanenhaus (New York: Wiley, 1969), p. 336.

Finally I would like to turn to the possible trend in studying the content of case opinions, as several researchers foresee much promise in this approach. The general format here is to use the case-opinion material as data for factor analysis and content analysis instead of simply as a basis for categorization of votes. Through such statistical devices, these researchers believe they can isolate with some precision a number of elements and grade their importance in the judge's arrival at the decision (the vote). Schubert, for instance, believes he has detected a number of the values that influenced the decision-making pattern of Mr. Justice Jackson over the years.[21]

Some serious (if not debilitating) analytical problems inhere in using these techniques on the judicial opinion, particularly if the researcher has, or claims to have, any interest in locating a judicial role factor. Difficulties also exist, I might add, for the researcher's desire to locate attitudes or values other than those concerning judicial role. First, the statements made in American Supreme Court opinions are highly public and political statements as well as legal statements. Thus, when and if there are references to the judicial role, one must take them with the same grain of salt as political statements made for public consumption by the President or senators on the nature of their respective roles. Second, if these techniques are employed in searching for the element of judicial role and its importance, they will seriously short-change the salience and influence of this factor, for judicial statements about role in an opinion are by and large irrelevant to any decision. They are made, in the main, rarely, and when made, they are issued usually for propagandistic, educational, or highly political purposes. When picked up by a factor or content analysis technique, they represent a rarity, not the potential degree of their importance. Third, if *law* (with its force of guidance and direction) is inextricably intertwined with the values of the judge in the operation of judicial role, how can they be separated by statistical techniques? I am aware of no one who has managed to do this by any *qualitative* analysis, and I cannot see how it can be done by quantitative analyses that are completely dependent for their interpretations on equally fallible analysts. I do admit, however, that written opinions by judges constitute one place to seek an indication of the first degree of expectations of impartiality and objectivity. It is just that these statistical methods cannot get an accurate measurement.

---

[21] Glendon Schubert, "Jackson's Judicial Philosophy: An Exploration in Value Analysis," *American Political Science Review*, 59 (December, 1965), pp. 940–63. David J. Danelski has worked this area in a similar fashion. See his "Values as Variables in Judicial Decision-Making: Notes Toward a Theory," *Vanderbilt Law Review*, 19 (June, 1966), pp. 721–40. For a more literary illustration, see Schubert, ed., *Dispassionate Justice: A Synthesis of the Judicial Opinions of Robert H. Jackson* (Indianapolis: Bobbs-Merrill, 1969).

Redirection: The Search for Judicial Role Expectations and Role Behavior

The concept of role has been used in an impressionistic manner in political science for some time. Only recently, with the successful insurgence of the political behavior movement, has political science bothered to explicate this concept with some precision and with regard to its usage by the other social sciences. To date, the leading political science work based on role is *The Legislative System*, by John Wahlke and his several associates.[22] I have written at some length on that conceptualization of role and have attempted to adapt their notion in explicating the concept of judicial role.[23] My own definition of judicial role is simple, perhaps too simple. It goes like this: Judicial role is "the expected behavior of the judge characterized as being precedent-oriented, i.e., in an objective decision by referring to established legal precedent as the grounds for such a decision."[24]

Quite clearly, considering the broad conceptualization of courts and judicial structure in the Introduction to Part A of this volume, my early concept of judicial role must be expanded. This is a simple enough task. All it takes, it seems to me, is to substitute a few phrases for the limiting words "legal precedent." Thus, I propose to redefine judicial role as follows: Judicial role is the expected behavior of the judge characterized as being law-oriented, i.e., in an objective decision by referring to and abiding by existent, expressed, primary normative principles.

Even so, there is some difference of opinion about my conceptualization of judicial role—the main objection being that it is too narrow. For one thing, it is becoming clearer and clearer that modern jurisprudence and the practice of the judicial craft have altered, and that expectations concerning a strict adherence by judges to norms are no longer sure to be fulfilled. Indeed, the argument goes, the exception may be becoming the rule. Thus, as expectations change, so does the concept of judicial role (as the concept of role is ordinarily defined in social science circles). To help clarify matters, let me confess that when I speak of judicial role I am simply referring to the *judicial factor* within the broader conception of judicial role. It is this nuclear element that makes the judicial role in general conceptually different from other governmental decision-making roles, or so the theory goes.

---

[22] John Wahlke, Heinz Eulau, William Buchanan, and Leroy C. Ferguson, *The Legislative System* (New York: Wiley, 1962). But for another important step in conceptualizing a political role, see James N. Rosenau, "Private Preferences and Political Responsibilities: The Relative Potency of Individual and Role Variables in the Behavior of U.S. Senators," in *Quantitative International Politics*, ed. J. David Singer (New York: Free Press, Macmillan, 1968).

[23] Becker, *Political Behavioralism and Modern Jurisprudence* (Chicago: Rand McNally, 1965). See especially chaps. 3 and 4.

[24] *Ibid.*, p. 99.

It is the restraint on personal values in favor of original reference to and some substantial deference to precedent, the law, and the like that distinguishes the judicial role from others, at least theoretically. Do legislators have such expectations built into their roles? Do administrators? The *judicial factor* in judicial role is what is supposed to give it its own peculiar flavor, its own eccentric *Gestalt*.

Of course, there is obviously a multitude of more technical troubles inherent in my definition of judicial role. For one thing, the notion of expectation implies an obligation on the part of the incumbent. But who defines this obligation and who are the most effective role definers? This is not easily answered. Jaros and Mendelsohn articulate other perplexities in the concept of role expectations: "Though we might intuitively feel that 'society' expects judges to make decisions in accord with 'norms rooted in the law,' such an assumption is highly dangerous. 'Society' as such holds no consensual expectations about a given position. Different role definers may have quite inconsistent expectations."[25] These are but a few of the myriad wrinkles that social scientists must smooth out of the concept of role.[26] It has proved itself, however, to be of great use in explaining some, if not much, human behavior. Moreover, as defined above, I believe it will prove of great value in locating and measuring judicial structures. In fact, it seems to me that role is the middle-range concept that best connects the high-level one of structure to the regularities in behavior to which structure refers.

I submit that in order to learn whether judicial objectivity exists anywhere in this world—and if so, to what extent and under what conditions—the best tactic is to go and ask the primary role definers, e.g., the judges and legal scholars, about their personal views on this matter. In addition, we must find ways to infer judicial role from the wide variety of institutional practices and societal symbols that foster or reflect judicial role expectations. Such inferences can also be made from the writings of diverse people in other cultures, whether they be legal scholars or not. The following three

---

[25] Dean Jaros and R. I. Mendelsohn, "The Judicial Role and Sentencing Behavior," *Midwest Journal of Political Science*, 11 (November, 1967), p. 474.

[26] The most well-known sociological treatment of this concept in an empirical study is that by Neil Gross, Ward S. Mason, and Alexander McEachern, *Explorations in Role Analysis* (New York: Wiley, 1958). However, a recent anthology, edited by Bruce J. Biddle and Edwin J. Thomas, is perhaps the next best thing to the current "definitive" treatment of the topic. See *Role Theory: Concepts and Research* (New York: Wiley, 1966). Even the editors are forced to admit:

Despite the impressive growth of [role] language and the fact that it probably serves to articulate complex real-life behavior as well as or better than any other single or analogous vocabulary, the language is only partially articulate. The battery of concepts necessary to describe and study complex real-life behavior is incomplete, and too many of the existing concepts are denotatively imprecise [p. 18].

sections briefly discuss some of the work that has been done along these lines. The reader is cautioned, however, to note its highly impressionistic quality. Furthermore, it must be pointed out that all of this work has little to do with objective behavior on the part of judges; it simply gets at the expectations that are reasonably manifest. The big questions that we need to answer are when and how the expectations fit into behavior patterns. Thus, we have to go to judicial decision-making, whether genuine or artificial, and see what links we may be able to find, keeping in mind, of course, that simple inference from general behavioral regularities is insufficient unto itself. Therefore, the last section of this chapter will discuss the relative merits and demerits in observing argumentation over judicial role in actual decision, in asking judges questions about their role perceptions, and then in either posing hypothetical cases for them to decide or looking at their decisional behavior in the court reports (if any exist), and finally in observing their minority decision-making behavior.

INTERVIEWS AND SURVEYS OF ROLE DEFINERS

As to role-definers, at this point one can employ samples of the general population of a society, judges (would-be and otherwise), officials, or all of these as role-definers. Contrary to Jaros' and Mendelsohn's fears, one recent study of an American state (Kansas) has demonstrated, in fact, that there was near-unanimity in the judicial role definition among Supreme Court justices, a sample of citizens in the state, a purposive sample of lawyers, and a group of senior law students.[27] In point of fact, the item of impartiality received the highest degree of consensus among these people, some 97 percent of whom expected impartiality of judges.

One of the first social-scientifically oriented inquiries into the mysteries of a *foreign judicial role* was conducted by anthropologist Max Gluckman, of Manchester University, in the 1940s.[28] He was interested in describing the judicial structure and process of the Losi tribe of the Barotse people. Additionally, he tried to show that the same phenomena that Cardozo described in *The Nature of the Judicial Process*,[29] which was based exclusively on Cardozo's personal experience as an American jurist, also existed in a

---

[27] Gene L. Mason, "Judges and Their Publics: Role Perceptions and Role Expectations" (unpublished Ph.D. dissertation, University of Kansas, 1967). See also his "Elements of Judicial Decisions: What Is Expected?" *Journal of the Bar Association of the State of Kansas* (Spring, 1967), pp. 25–27.

[28] Max Gluckman, *Judicial Process among the Barotse of Northern Rhodesia* (Manchester: Manchester University Press, 1954). See also his *The Ideas in Barotse Jurisprudence* (New Haven: Yale University Press, 1965), especially chap. 1.

[29] Benjamin N. Cardozo, *The Nature of the Judicial Process* (New Haven: Yale University Press, 1921).

relatively isolated and independent African tribe. It is mainly for this reason that this work by Gluckman has fallen into disrepute among some social scientists.

James March, for instance, mounted a broad attack against Gluckman, complaining bitterly about several aspects of his work.[30] Chief among his complaints were that Gluckman (1) spent much time making trivial, if not faulty, comparisons between the Barotse and the Anglo-American systems, and (2) made many false inferences from his own data. I am not about to defend Gluckman against attack along these lines, for I think that both March and Victor Ayoub (in another analytically penetrating essay)[31] take him to task appropriately. However, March himself has complimented Gluckman for certain excellences in his work. For instance, March commented that Gluckman, through his usage of direct observation, summaries of cases obtained from informants, and responses to direct questions, created "a judicious portrait of the Barotse kuta (court) and its operation."[32] Later, in summarizing part of his descriptive material, March noted that:

> Time after time in the book we are given testimony in support of the fact that most people among the Losi believe that there exists a certain body of rules—"The Law"—that judges ought to, and usually do, enforce. Interestingly enough, almost all of the citations on this point are made in the context of the reports of the uncertainty of litigation. That is, the clear implication is that despite all evidence to the contrary, people believe in "The Law." Moreover, this belief extends to the judges and influences their behavior. Members of the kuta believe that they *should* and *do* pursue "The Law"—even when they change it considerably to fit a particular case—and *their behavior is different from what it would be if they did not believe this to be their function.* The general conclusion reached is that "the certainty of law in a stable society is a fact accepted by almost all members of the society."[33]

A close look at March's complaint will reveal that he is upset by certain of the conclusions drawn by Gluckman from his data, and small wonder. The major point of interest from the perspective of this volume is that there is virtually no quarrel over the fact found by Gluckman that the judges themselves (as primary role definers) believe, and there is widespread and deep belief among the members of the society, that there is law, and that the judges must adhere to it. This, of course, is quite consistent with one aspect of the definition of judicial structure and judicial role as

---

[30] James G. March, "Sociological Jurisprudence Revisited," in *Judicial Behavior*, ed. Glendon Schubert (Chicago: Rand McNally, 1964), pp. 132–52.
[31] "The Judicial Process in Two African Tribes," in *ibid.*, pp. 124–31.
[32] *Ibid.*, p. 136.
[33] *Ibid.*, p. 145 (emphasis mine).

set out above. It surely serves as strong evidence, gained from a close surveillance of a society, that a major aspect of judicial structure exists there, that is, expectations. In an equally intensive study of the Tiv, Bohannan concludes that the decision-making unit that resolves personal disputes "determines a modus vivendi" and does not "apply laws."[34] This would seem to identify the Tiv society as one devoid of judicial role and therefore without courts. On the other hand, since there is also a body of natural law reflected in a general injunction not to "spoil the Tiv," an argument could be made that this meets the minimal requirement of application. I would disagree—in interpreting my own definition—as it is far too discretionary; i.e., it is nothing but leeway; it is not a specific guideline.

Gluckman is quite graphic in his description of the judicial role expectations among the Barotse, judges and laymen alike. For instance, consider the following material:

> The judges thus exercise considerable discretion in applying the law in particular disputes, and some of them do so seemingly without appreciating that they may be changing the law and introducing considerable uncertainty. Nevertheless these judges clearly believe that they are applying the law and the ethical end—they consider they are enforcing what they ought to enforce and that they are not giving arbitrary decisions. Other Losi see that such decisions do not conform with the law, and do not consider such judges to be good judges—impartial, knowledgeable in law, courageous, and wise. *They explicitly say that a good judge is not influenced by morality to give a decision that is bad in law; he must have courage (bungangeli) to face the consequences when justice conflicts with law. A judge ought to abide by the law even if its application is inequitable. Thus though there is considerable judicial discretion, this discretion is in theory and in practice restricted by established law.*[35]

Gluckman's tragic flaw came in his unabashed and careless inferences about judicial *behavior*. The major contribution of this type of work, and of Gluckman's Barotse study in particular, is that it demonstrates how anthropologists can help us in determining where judicial role *expectations* may exist and to what degree.

INSTITUTIONS AND TRAPPINGS

Another way to determine whether there is a judicial-role belief system in a society is to see if there are any institutions and/or trappings that mani-

---

[34] Paul Bohannan, *Justice among the Tiv* (New York: Oxford University Press, 1957).

[35] Gluckman, *Judicial Process*, p. 234.

fest its existence. In other words, are there any structures (physical, symbolic, social, etc.) from which we can infer that the society values impartiality in decision-makers given authority to resolve specific disputes?

David J. Danelski went to Japan in 1965 to interview the justices of the Supreme Court of Japan. From his talks with them he was quite convinced (impressionistically) that these judges highly valued a manifest impartiality and objectivity, and considered this to be a criterion of excellence in their own decision-making process. He was further convinced of the existence of this aspect of judicial role through many other observations he made.

For instance, Japan has a professional judiciary (somewhat along the lines of the French model) and maintains an institute for the training of judges. Moreover, it requires a lengthy and rigorous apprenticeship program, through which neophytes must pass in order to achieve their career goals. The Judicial Institute and apprenticeship program, in Danelski's view, can be perceived as a socialization structure to foster the value of impartiality. Mainly, of course, the Institute and the apprenticeship set the young judge-to-be apart from the rest of society. He becomes insulated from certain social and political pressures (and perhaps from understanding them and their dynamics). Aside from this, according to Danelski, the desirability of impartiality is emphasized by the fact that it is considered an indicator of legal craft.

Another observation made by Danelski concerned the decor of the room in which the Supreme Court of Japan sits while listening to appeals. This is known as the Grand Bench Chamber and is in the Supreme Court Building in Tokyo. It is a well-appointed room with fifteen chairs arranged in a semicircle. But the interesting feature, for one trying to learn of the existence or nonexistence of the value of impartiality, is the content of three large oil paintings (approximately five by seven feet) that hang upon the walls. One hangs to the right rear of the judges, one to the left rear, and the other directly facing the judges. All the paintings concern Prince Shotoku, who in 604 A.D. gave the Japanese people their constitution. The painting to the right rear depicts a group of women holding a baby. This represents the birth of Prince Shotoku; but it also symbolizes the virtue of love—womanly, motherly love. Thus one might well infer that the Japanese include love as part of the judicial role. The Western equivalent is probably mercy. The painting to the left rear shows the Prince's delivery of the constitution to the people. It is a written constitution, and it is said to symbolize wisdom. This is probably an admonition to the judges to be bound by law. And the third painting—facing the judges most directly—portrays the Prince upon a black charger, sword in hand. This is an admonition to the judges to have courage, which could bring us right back to Gluckman's observation of the Barotse and their use of the concept of courage (*bungangeli*) in connection with those judges who would stick to the law even when it creates an obvious injustice (perhaps by not yielding to natural and societally valued cravings for mercy).

WRITINGS OF INDIGENOUS SCHOLARS AND FOREIGN EXPERTS

Another way of determining the possible existence of judicial structure and judicial role in a society, once the basic legal foundation is established, is to look at the writing of various indigenous scholars and foreign exports.

M. Hidayatullah has served in the capacity of judge of the Supreme Court of India since 1958. In a lecture entitled "Judicial Process in India" Judge Hidayatullah states:

> You will notice that what the judiciary does, it does from within the Constitution. It has no will of its own. *It can only reasonably expose the inner meaning* of the brief words, which it does, keeping in view the future evolution of society and the limits set by the Constitution.[36]

I would say that aside from the fact that Judge Hidayatullah does mention the "evolution of society," the statement about the exposure of "inner meaning" of words of the Constitution is a very clear indicator of his own very strong precedent orientation. First, it is far different to talk of inner meaning than of the outside boundaries that words might create. The latter would be far more consistent with praising the exercise of great leeway and discretion, and thus with a situation orientation consistent with the tenets of American legal realism. This squares with a previous statement of Hidayatullah's, that judges "interpret" the constitution and "do not add to it." In the context of the entire lecture, his few statements about evolution and a quotation from Frankfurter appear to be mainly lip service to modern American jurisprudence. Later in his lecture the judge explains his strong precedent orientation as a result of his having been "brought up in the conservative English tradition under which the judge must depart as little as possible from precedent."[37] Moreover, he worries about this is in the context of India's problems. All in all, then, analyses of such words can be guides to the existence and degree of judicial structure extant in the society from which they come.

---

[36] M. Hidayatullah, *Democracy in India and the Judicial Process* (New York: Asia Publishing House, 1966), p. 69.
[37] *Ibid.* p. 71.

LINKING ROLE EXPECTATIONS
AND JUDICIAL BEHAVIOR

Earlier I noted that each of these approaches—through analyses of interviews and surveys, institutions, and writings—has the same serious limitation: each fails to establish a connection between role expectations discernible in the society and any decision-making behavior that is consistent with them.[38] As is so often true in life, the most difficult task is the most critical as well; for it is role expectation plus role behavior that equal the existence of at least the first measure of judicial structure. Statements and writings of judges, interviews with scholars and laymen, observations of symbols, and analysis of institutions all are sources of data that evidence role expectations and perceptions of judges. In a sense, they are simply indicators of the reality we wish to measure. It remains to establish a direct linkage between these factors and *decision-making behavior* in order to classify it as *judicial* behavior. There are a number of ways of going about this; some have been tried, others have not. I would like to suggest one way that has not been tried, purely as an illustration of the way we might utilize foreign case materials in fields other than comparative law. Following that, I shall review a few devices that have been developed and tested in order to further this important part of our inquiry.

The Appendix to this chapter consists of the *Chancery Lane Safe Deposit* case, decided by the House of Lords in 1965. Ordinarily, as I have taken pains to argue, one must treat gingerly the statements of judges about judicial role that he chances across in case opinions. However, it seems to me that under some circumstances, case opinions might well afford insight into the links between judicial role expectations and behavior, and the *Chancery Lane* case is, to abuse an expression, a case in point. In this decision, the reader will enjoy a rather spirited debate among the judges on the proper utilization of precedent in the House of Lords. In other words, *Chancery Lane* is a formal legal argument in a judicial opinion over the principle of the application of precedent, some judges saying it should be applied and some saying it should not. This type of public polemic may well be a far more reliable indicator than a judge's informal (or even formal) musing, no matter how apparently sincere. The latter *could* be nothing more than a self-serving statement on the judge's own great rationality and impartiality. A formal argument over the application of precedent, embodied in differing decisions by the differing judges, gives us *behavioral* (decisional) data, clearly manifesting some objective decision-making.

---

[38] See Dorothy B. James, "Role Theory and the Supreme Court," *Journal of Politics*, 30 (February, 1968), p. 162.

Insofar as the decision that was reached by following precedent differs from others that might be reached through an expressed breach of precedent, we have a vivid illustration of the existence of the expectation of using precedent, with obvious effect on behavior, as opposed to contrasting views with opposite behavioral effects. The *Chancery Lane Safe Deposit* case is therefore a strong datum for the simple property description that there is some degree of behavioral impartiality in the judicial decision-making of the House of Lords in England. The arguments presented by Lords Reid and Upjohn in their dissent is strong evidence that the majority slavishly applied precedent in arriving at their decision. They also evidence some judges' desire for greater personal latitude for decision-making in that body.[39]

However, there are better ways of looking into societies to discover some relationship between judicial role expectations and decision-making behavior, and therefore whether judicial structure exists and if so to what degree. After all, we can't expect too many debates by judges in case opinions on the local or current jurisprudential contentions about judicial role. Also, relying on the same source of information to establish both parts of a relationship (expectation and behavior) is lazy—and perhaps sloppy—social science. Even when it is done rigorously, the practice leaves much to be desired. For instance, Joel Grossman recently tested the hypothesis that some Supreme Court justices formed blocs when dealing with certain types of cases (e.g., civil liberties cases, economic cases, and the like).[40] Actually, he was quarreling with the assumptions behind a large body of

---

[39] On July 26, 1966, the Lord Chancellor issued a "Practice Statement (Judicial Precedent)," which reads as follows:

> Their Lordships regard the use of precedent as an indispensable foundation upon which to decide what is the law and its application to individual cases. It provides at least some degree of certainty upon which individuals can rely in the conduct of their affairs, as well as a basis for orderly development of legal rules.
>
> Their Lordships nevertheless recognize that too rigid adherence to precedent may lead to injustice in a particular case and also unduly restrict the proper development of the law. They propose therefore to modify their present practice and, while treating former decisions of this House as normally binding, to depart from a previous decision when it appears to do so. . . .

This has caused a grand debate in English legal and political circles over whether the House of Lords can do this without sanction of legislation. Harold F. Birnbaum has presented much relevant information on this debate in his "Stare Decisis vs. Judicial Activism: Nothing Succeeds Like Success," *American Bar Association Journal*, 54 (May, 1968), pp. 482–88. He notes that to the time of his writing, no case could be found in which the House of Lords had overruled any of its prior decisions.

[40] Joel Grossman, "Dissenting Blocs on the Warren Court: A Study in Judicial Role Behavior," *Journal of Politics*, 30 (November, 1968), pp. 1068–90.

voting-bloc analyses spearheaded by Professors Schubert and Sidney Ulmer.[41] Schubert and Ulmer conclude that voting blocs exist in the U.S. Supreme Court. They infer this almost exclusively from a coincidence in voting records of Supreme Court justices. In other words, they have classified opinions as being of one genre or another and then tabulated how often certain justices have voted in agreement with certain other justices. When a high rate of agreement is found to persevere over time, they pronounce that a bloc exists. Grossman, on the other hand, feels that a bloc exists (by his definition) only when the justices explicitly join together in a dissenting opinion, i.e., hammer out an accord and sign their names together. In Grossman's view, only when justices write an opinion together can the consciousness of purpose so essential to bloc behavior be inferred. Such is Grossman's view, and his argument and data make much sense. However, my primary concern here is not with Grossman's excoriation of Schubert and Ulmer's theory of the persistence and significance of judicial voting blocs, but rather with his conclusions about judicial role. According to Grossman:

> The data presented in this paper would seem to indicate that the dissenting behavior of Supreme Court justices conforms more closely to the hypothesized role expectation that dissents are largely individual acts than to the idea that decision-making consists largely of interactions among persistent sub-groups or blocs.[42]

Simply by using judicial votes, Grossman has managed to test, albeit circuitously, the empirical attack on one aspect of the American Supreme Court's judicial subrole expectations. The reader would do well to note how Grossman phrases his findings; he is very cautious. He realizes that he has not proved any theory about this aspect of the justice's role; that is, that justices should work "largely in isolation."[43] All Grossman has done is to *disconfirm* the rival Schubert-Ulmer hypothesis, that justices in some ways feel and act together as a policy-making group. Grossman states that his data are *more* consistent with the judicial role expectation on individual dissents than with interpretations of voting data that would deny the relationship between such expectations and behavior. This is hard to accept.

---

[41] See in particular Glendon Schubert, *Quantitative Analysis of Judicial Behavior* (New York: Free Press, Macmillan, 1959), chaps. 3 and 4; S. Sidney Ulmer, "The Analysis of Behavior Patterns on the U.S. Supreme Court," *Journal of Politics*, 22 (November, 1960), pp. 629–53; Louis S. Loeb, "Judicial Blocs and Judicial Values in Civil Liberties Cases Decided by the Supreme Court and the United States Court of Appeals for the District of Columbia Circuit," *American University Law Review*, 14 (June, 1965), pp. 146–77. For the most extensive critique of other bloc analyses, see Sprague, *Voting Patterns of the United States Supreme Court*.

[42] Grossman, "Dissenting Blocs on the Warren Court," p. 1089.

[43] Robert Jackson, *The Supreme Court in the American System of Government* (Cambridge: Harvard University Press, 1955), p. 16.

Actually, Grossman's study only provides evidence that there may still be a link between this part of judicial role and judicial behavior. By disconfirming the contrary hypothesis, he only keeps the role-behavior hypothesis alive. His inference about the data's greater relative support for his hypothesis is not well founded. For instance, it could be that some justices, instead of following role expectations to write individual opinions, are simply intellectually cantankerous, and, as it were, literally disagreeable. Role conceptions may not be involved at all. Grossman's data support this contention equally well. In truth, this is a very limited study of judicial role and it shows once again the weakness inherent in work that draws upon votes alone for testing relationships between expectations and behavior. No relationship can be established; many other inferences remain possible. We still have only half of the equation.

The best method for testing this relationship is to gather fresh and independent information on judicial role expectations and to see to what extent these are adhered to in decision-making. Along this tack, I recently attempted to devise and revise a questionnaire device that could serve this purpose. Actually, the technique was a refinement of the method I described and used in *Political Behavioralism and Modern Jurisprudence* in order to see whether any objectivity (as therein and herein defined) could be discovered in judicial decision-making procedures.[44] Nonetheless, one aspect of this refinement is calculated to reveal the degree to which the role requirements of impartiality and objectivity are accepted (or at least verbally favored) by the judges.

In the American system, all judges are supposed to handle legal precedent in some way and to some extent in various types of cases and under varying circumstances and phases of litigation. There is much written literature on this point and it serves as an indicator that such a role expectation does indeed exist to some noticeable degree among the members of the American judiciary. In actuality, this expectation would probably be but one major element judges believe to comprise part of their role. Some other elements have been theorized to be: (1) what the public needs, as the times may demand; (2) what the public demands; (3) the decision-maker's view of justice in the particular case; (4) common sense; (5) a highly respected lawyer *qua* advocate; and (6) a highly respected lawyer as an esteemed and/or influential member of the community.

Since these six factors are those that many American jurisprudents, jurists, lawyers, and political scientists believe judges consider crucial in

---

[44] The original report of this method and the findings are to be found in Theodore L. Becker, "A Survey Study of Hawaiian Judges: The Effect on Decisions of Judicial Role Variation," in *American Political Science Review,* 60 (September, 1966), pp. 677–80.

their roles as judicial decision-makers, they were incorporated as question-naire items presented to a substantial portion of the Hawaiian judiciary.

The judges were first asked:

How influential do you believe the following factors to be in your deciding a case?

They were then instructed:

Please circle one number from 4 to 0 in the space on the left of each specific factor. The numbers stand for the following:

4   Extremely influential
3   Very influential
2   Influential
1   Not too influential at all
0   Uninfluential

The rating sheet read as follows:

A. Highly respected advocate (as a lawyer).   4 3 2 1 0
B. My view of justice in the case.   4 3 2 1 0
C. What the public needs, as the times may demand.   4 3 2 1 0
D. Precedent, when clear and directly relevant.   4 3 2 1 0
E. Common sense.   4 3 2 1 0
F. Highly respected advocate (as a member of the
    community).   4 3 2 1 0
G. What the public demands.   4 3 2 1 0
H. Other (please specify: place a 4, 3, 2, 1, 0 after
    each such factor).

The results were interesting enough. Of the 22 Hawaiian judges who gave codable responses, 17 rated factor D (precedent, when clear and directly relevant) as the single or modally most important factor. Only 9 of the 22 (41 percent) considered it to be *the* single most important factor. Still, this does demonstrate that the Hawaiian bench is quite precedent-oriented in its role portrait; there is a subtantial core of the judicial factor operating in the Hawaiian courts.

In criticism, many would ask: "What do you expect?" Such criticism misses the point. For it is what the *judges* expect (or even what they might think the interviewer expects them to expect) that is important. If they be-lieve it to be important to tell the interviewer that precedent adherence (objectivity) is significant, this tends to support the view that there is a judicial structure in that society. The expectation exists that judges are precedent-bound, legally constrained, objective.

My own presentation of the data in this study indicates that there is some direct linkage between a precedent-oriented judicial role and objective decision-making. However, Glendon Schubert has drawn an even clearer picture of this effect on judicial behavior (see Table 2).[45] Ironically, this is despite the fact that he has seriously misinterpreted the data of the table in the body of his essay and therefore arrived at a contrary, and erroneous, conclusion.

At any rate, it was a matter of conjecture whether judges from other cultures would respond to such a questionnaire, and if so, whether any visible differences could be observed between their responses and those of the Hawaiian judges.

Victor E. Flango, traveling through Hong Kong and the Philippines in the summer of 1965 in conjunction with an East-West Center grant, attempted to distribute a lengthy questionnaire to the judges there. This questionnaire was much like the one used in Hawaii. Three out of four Hong Kong judges and all six Philippine judges approached did respond.

Incidentally, the long-standing idea that judges are inaccessible to serious, social-scientifically oriented research is rapidly disintegrating. The facts are to the contrary. Recent research ventures into state judiciaries and the U.S. Supreme Court have managed to persuade a very large percentage

TABLE 2

Judicial Attitudes and Simulated Decisions (Hawaiian Sample)

Outcome	Dominant Role Orientation	
	Precedential (D Is Most Important)	Policy (D, C, or E Is Most Important)
"Objective" (Agrees with precedent)	4	0
"Subjective" (Disagrees with precedent)	2	5

SOURCE: Victor E. Flango and Glendon Schubert, "Two Surveys of Simulated Judicial Decision Making: Hawaii and the Philippines," in *Comparative Judicial Behavior*, ed. Schubert and David J. Danelski (New York: Oxford University Press, 1969).

---

[45] See Victor E. Flango and Glendon Schubert, "Two Surveys of Simulated Judicial Decision-Making: Hawaii and the Philippines," in *Comparative Judicial Behavior*, ed. Schubert and David J. Danelski (New York: Oxford University Press, 1969). I have laid the blame of faulty analysis upon Schubert alone since he assumes full responsibility for the analysis in n. 1 of the essay.

of high-bench incumbents to agree to questionnaire interviews.[46] Besides this great success in America, Danelski managed to get all eleven members of the Japanese high court to open themselves to an American-based social-scientific investigation, and I gained two long interviews with each of the members of the Philippine Supreme Court in less than two weeks. I don't feel overly optimistic in asserting that the future for systematic interviews of foreign judiciaries shines brightly.

The answers of the Philippine and Hong Kong judges indicated what we might expect; that is, that judicial structure appears to exist to a degree in those two political units.[47]

It is clear enough from Table 3 that judges from all three cultures *expect* that the existence of clear, directly relevant precedent *should at least be stated to be an important, influential factor in judicial decision-making*. Despite the minuscule amount of data, this is a strong indicator, I should think, that the notions of judicial role and judicial impartiality exist in these societies.

Of course, as estimated, there are noticeable variations in emphasis in the entire judicial role profile among the judges of the several cultures studied. For instance, note that *all* the Hong Kong judges saw fit to rate the precedent factor as extremely influential (factor D), while only two of six Philippine judges (33 percent) did so. Interestingly, no Hong Kong judge rated his own view of justice in the case (factor B) as either singly or

TABLE 3

Judicial Role Expectations in Three Cultures

		Factors						
Judiciary	Number	A	B	C	D	E	F	G
Hawaiian	25	1.4	2.8	1.9	**3.6**	3.1	1.0	0.6
Hong Kong	3	0.7	1.5	1.7	**4.0**	3.0	0.0	0.7
Philippine	6	1.0	3.4	1.9	**3.2**	3.4	0.8	1.0

NOTE: The score of each factor is a mean of the justices' ratings on their perception of influence of each factor.

[46] See Theodore L. Becker, "Surveys and Judiciaries, or Who's Afraid of the Purple Curtain," *Law and Society Review*, 1 (November, 1966), pp. 133–43; David L. Brey managed to persuade eight out of nine U.S. Supreme Court justices to grant interviews averaging about twenty-five minutes—to a social scientist with a questionnaire! See his "Interviewing at the Court," *Public Opinion Quarterly*, 31 (Summer, 1967), pp. 285–89. Both of these articles also discuss certain precautions that researchers who are contemplating interviews of foreign court judges should consider.

[47] A previous report of the procedures and data were included in Theodore L. Becker, "Judicial Structure and Its Political Functioning in Society: New Approaches to Teaching and Research in Public Law," *Journal of Politics*, 29 (May, 1967), pp. 302–33.

modally the most important factor in his judicial decision-making, but five out of six (83 percent) Philippine judges did. This might be an internal indicator that precedent is not *really* very important in judicial-decision behavior in the Philippines (in other words, has little constraining power upon judges).

In deciding a hypothetical case, the Hong Kong judges were 67 percent (two out of three) objective while only 40 percent of the Philippine judges (two out of five) were.[48] Of course, these are data unworthy of reportage as either raw findings or interpretation. They are presented here only to demonstrate how one might go about a cross-cultural search for judicial structure, and for variations in judicial role perceptions and behavior from culture to culture. In a continuation of this study, Flango and I obtained a much wider sample of Philippine judges. Indeed, some fifty-nine of them responded to the questionnaire, and the results confirm the fact that many of them are precedent-oriented. In comparison to Hawaiian judges, who scored 3.54, the mean response for factor D on the questionnaire for Philippine judges was 3.10. Actually, however, there were some slight differences. First of all, the item "my view of justice" was more highly thought of by Philippine judges, and no Philippine judge thought clear precedent the single most important factor in the expectations for judicial role. (See Figure 1.) There were some differences also in the decision-making behavior of these judges, but these will be discussed in the next chapter.

Kenneth Vines constructed a questionnaire to accomplish a similar task in a four-state study of judiciaries in 1966–67. His device was far less structured than the one described immediately above.[49] Such flexibility has many desirable features, particularly at this stage of development of research in the area. In order adequately to construct a forced-choice questionnaire like the one employed in the Hawaii–Philippines–Hong Kong study, one really needs some hard data from which to build categories, and these were missing. Vines elicited the type of data necessary for the job. In addition, the Vines questionnaire is far superior for cross-cultural studies. There is some irony in this, for his questionnaire was used only upon American judges, while mine was employed on foreign judges. Vines's method is superior at this point because we have such an imprecise notion about the role pictures of judges of non-Anglo-American systems. It is almost naïve to ask them to check boxes that are based on theory that in turn is based chiefly on data concerning the Anglo-American system. In a sense,

---

[48] The Hong Kong judges may be manifesting the supposedly stricter adherence to precedent that most legal scholars believe to be characteristic of English judges in general. For example, see Delmar Karlen's comparative study *Appellate Courts in the United States and England* (New York: New York University Press, 1963), pp. 86ff.

[49] Kenneth Vines, "The Judicial Role in American States: An Exploration," in *Frontiers of Judicial Research*, ed. Grossman and Tanenhaus, pp. 461–88.

Judicial Role Expectations, Philippines and Hawaii, 1966

*A. Respected advocate.
 B. My view of justice.
 C. What the public needs.
 D. Precedent, when clear and directly relevant.
 E. Common sense.
 F. Advocate as community member.
 G. What the public demands.

the forced choice required of foreign judges is even worse than the "leading question," because the concepts have cultural bias as well as the power of suggestion. Furthermore, respondents to open-ended questions can signal ambiguities, but they have no such degree of freedom in a forced-choice questionnaire. The Vines questionnaire is clearly better for use in future cross-cultural research into the judicial process because it can systematically collect more reliable data.

The relevant sections in the Vines questionnaire can be easily broken down into two levels of abstraction and tabulated according to whether the questions directly or indirectly concern the matter of impartiality-objectivity (use of precedent). For instance:

Abstract and indirect: What qualities should a judge have to attain to hold the respect of his fellow judges?

Are there any things that would cause a judge to lose the respect of his fellow judges?

Specific and indirect: The statement is sometimes made that judges should incorporate the important values of the community in their work. What do you think about this?

Abstract and direct: How would you describe the way a judge should go about reaching a decision in a case?

Specific and direct: How important should precedent be in de-
                            ciding a case?

                            What are the circumstances under which
                            a judge should depart from precedent?

                            There often appears to be a number of cases
                            that bear on a present case before the court.
                            How should a judge select the ones most
                            appropriate for use in a case?

Vines saw the replies to these questionnaires as placing the respondents in
three distinct categories of judicial role: (1) law interpreter, (2) lawmaker,
and (3) pragmatist. He tried to uncover any relationship between these role
orientations and a judge's tendency to make liberal or conservative decisions while he was on the bench. In analyzing, for the most part, one year's
complement of the nonunanimous decisions of the courts upon which these
judges sat, Vines found little such relationship; that is, there was scant
correspondence between any judicial role position and any general *political*
orientation.

It may have occurred to the reader that this study by Professor Vines,
though linking judicial role to the actual voting behavior of judges, circum-
vents the issue of whether the judicial role *constrained* the preexistent personal attitudes of the judges. In other words, this study as designed does
not advance our understanding of the links between role expectation and
role behavior; it advances our knowledge only of the relationship between
judicial role expectations and what some term "political" behavior. The
former could have been accomplished had Vines first developed some measure of the judges' personal political beliefs independent of their decision-
making behavior and then tested to see if the judicial role expectation of
objectivity ("law interpreter") was an intervening factor. Because of this
omission, Vines's study is more pertinent to the next chapter, which discusses the wide range of factors that influence the particular substantive
content of judicial decisions—once it is established that we are dealing with
a *judicial* decision-making body.

I admit that there is already ample evidence that judicial role (judicial
structure) exists in most parts of the contemporary world. All of Western
Europe, North America, Latin America, and vast portions of Africa and
Asia undeniably maintain decision-making structures that are well within
the confines of the definition of court set forth earlier in this volume. Studies
in judicial role expectations and behavior are needed not so much to establish the existence of the judicial structure as to calibrate the degrees of it.
Formerly we had some rough indexes as to how much (or how little) judges
defer to normative prescriptions and proscriptions. One of these was the

common law vs. civil law distinction, but the "free law" school of continental jurisprudence and some modern strains of American jurisprudence may well have lessened (or obscured) any real, but erstwhile, differences in actual behavior. In other words, we have been confusing potential conditions for behavioral differences (philosophy influencing actions) with the behavior itself. We need measurements of degrees of difference in judicial role behavior so that we can advance to the next two stages, that is, (1) investigating what variables influence such differences, and (2) investigating the functioning of judicial structure in society.

The next two chapters are closely related to these questions about judicial role and judicial structure. Chapter 2 is a treatment of the entire context of judicial decision-making. For example, given the fact that we have judicial role operating, how heavy a factor is it in the decision-making process in connection with all other factors, and what conditions are responsible for differences in its interactions with these factors? Within the context of the conceptual scheme presented in the Introduction, this chapter has focused on the ways we might go about finding judicial structure when there is doubt and measuring it when there is not. In gaining measures of judicial structure, we set the stage for an examination of the ways this variation operates to influence the decision, on the one hand, and society and politics, on the other. Chapter 2 will contain a discussion of the inner mechanics of the judicial decision-making structure and process. Although we are interested in the influence of external conditions (culture) on the variation in judicial decision-making structure, as well as the nature of the interactions within it, a further concern of the next chapter is the ways in which variations in decision-making structure and process affect the content of the decision. Does the judicial decision actually have a peculiar flavor as contrasted with administrative decisions? Chapter 2 consists partially, then, of my attempt to locate the relevance of the judicial decision-making research to this key question. Chapter 3 will focus on the *causes* of the very existence of the first measures of judicial role and judicial structure, i.e., those conditions that stimulate its first appearance, and will go on to include some observations on the impact that judicial structure has on the outer world, that is, the feedback effect onto the external conditions. Strictly in terms of function, Chapter 2 is centered on the potential function of judicial role in the decisional output, while Chapter 3 is centered on its potential function in society, and more specifically in the political system.

APPENDIX

Chancery Lane Safe Deposit and Offices Co., Ltd.,
v. Inland Revenue Commissioners
(England, 1965)

The taxpayer company borrowed large sums on mortgage from 1954 to 1957, reaching £650,000 in 1957. On the advice of its auditors it charged a certain proportion of the mortgage interest payments to capital in its accounts. During the years in question there were profits out of which that portion of interest might have been paid. The company was assessed to tax for the years 1954–55 to 1958–59 inclusive under section 170 of the Income Tax Act, 1952, on the ground that the portion of interest that was debited to capital account was in fact paid out of capital and not out of profits and gains brought into charge to tax. The company appealed to the special commissioners, claiming that these sums had been paid out of taxed income, although charged to capital in the accounts. The company also contended that an agreement had been made in 1957 within the terms of section 510 of the Act, which barred the assessment for the year 1955–56. The question of liability under section 170 in respect of mortgage interest charged to capital had not been raised until 1959.

Held (Lord Reid and Lord Upjohn dissenting), that the company, having of its own free choice made a deliberate attribution, having practical effects, of the sum in question to capital, was precluded from subsequently making an inconsistent attribution and could not treat a payment actually made out of capital as notionally made out of income; accordingly it was liable to tax under section 170.

Central London Railway Co. v. *Inland Revenue Commissioners* (1937) A.C. 77; 52 T.L.R. 581; (1936) 2 All E.R. 375 H.L. applied

Decision of the Court of Appeal (1965) 1 W.L.R. 239; (1965) 1 All E.R. 335, C.A. affirmed.

APPEAL from the Court of Appeal (HARMAN, DANCKWERTS and SALMON L.JJ.).

* * *

Dec. 15. LORD REID. My Lords, the appellants were assessed to income tax under section 170 of the Income Tax Act, 1952, for the five years 1954–55 to 1958–59 in respect of sums amounting in all to some £35,000. Subject to slight reduction in amount, these assessments were confirmed by the special commissioners. On appeal Plowman J. discharged the assessments but they were restored by the Court of Appeal.

The appellants have owned for many years premises in Chancery Lane consisting of a basement which they use as a safe deposit and upper storeys which they let out. During the last war the upper storeys were destroyed by enemy action and, in order to finance reconstruction, they borrowed large sums

---

2 W.L.R. (1966) 251. Footnotes have been omitted.

from time to time. In paying interest on these sums they properly deducted tax. The sums in these assessments are part of the interest so paid so that, if these assessments stand, the appellant will have to pay over to the respondents the amounts of tax which they have deducted and retained in respect of this interest. It is admitted by the respondents that the parts of the interest not included in the assessment fall within the scope of section 169 so that the appellants are entitled to retain the income tax deducted with respect to these parts.

The respondents make this difference because of the way in which the appellants treated this interest in making up their accounts. On the advice of their auditors the appellants debited to capital those parts of the interest which are now the subject of this assessment, and debited the rest to revenue account. Apart from one year about which no question now arises, the appellants had in each year ample profits to cover the whole of this interest and admittedly it would have been quite proper both from an accounting and from a legal point of view for them to have debited the whole of the interest in each year to revenue account. But the appellants chose to follow their auditors' advice and it is not disputed that in so doing they acted quite legally and followed the better accounting practice. But the respondents assert that by taking this course the appellants have increased their tax liability, though they gained no financial advantage by doing so. I find it impossible to suppose that Parliament can have intended such a strange result but I must proceed to consider whether we are compelled either by the wording of the relevant section or by weight of authority so to find.

*   *   *

There has been in the past a good deal of misunderstanding of section 169 (or of the old rule 19 which it replaced) so I think it best to begin by analysing its language. There is no doubt that in applying section 169 each year must be taken separately—there is no question of carrying forward any balance, real or notional, from a previous year. So you must first find an annual payment actually paid during the year in question, and it is not disputed that the sums now assessed are such payments. Then the annual payments must have been "payable wholly out of profits or gains." I shall have to return to this phrase later and I only note here that the word is "payable," not "paid." And finally the annual payment must have been payable out of "profits or gains brought in charge to tax." And that requires a good deal of explanation.

If these conditions are satisfied the taxpayer is entitled to deduct tax when paying the annual payment to his creditor and he is permitted to retain that tax. That produces a fair result. In making up profit and loss accounts for income tax purposes these annual payments are not permissible deductions although ordinary principles of commercial accounting would require them to be deducted before the taxpayer's real profit was determined. So in the first instance the taxpayer pays too much tax but as against that he gets the right under section 169 to retain the tax which he deducts. But the working out of this scheme is complicated by the fact that the "profits or gains brought into charge to tax" for a particular year are not the actual profits for that year. They are a notional sum computed on income tax principles from the trader's accounts for the previous year. So the apparent difficulty arises—how can a real annual payment be payable out of such a notional sum? The solution of that problem requires a close examination of the authorities. But if one carries the matter a stage further the real situation may become clearer. The profits brought into charge may be a notional sum, but the tax which the taxpayer has to pay on that notional sum is a very real sum, and there is no difficulty in comparing that sum with the amount of tax which he actually deducts in making the annual payments to his creditor. The practical result is that, if the taxpayer actually pays for a particular year a larger amount of tax than the amount of tax which he deducts in that year in making the annual payments, then he is entitled to retain the tax which he has so deducted.

If one were entitled to adopt such a straightforward approach, the point for decision in this case would become simple. In each of the years in question the appellant company did pay more tax than the amounts of tax deducted in making the annual payments. It is not disputed that, but for the way in which they chose to make up their accounts, they were entitled to retain the whole of the tax so deducted. So why should the way in which they kept their accounts produce a windfall for the Revenue and in effect produce double taxation?

The true interpretation of the old rule 19 was first explained by Lord Macmillan in his speech, unanimously adopted, in *Central London Railway Co.* v. *Inland Revenue Commissioners* and it was further developed by Lord Greene M.R. in *Allchin* v. *Coulthard* and his explanation was unanimously accepted in this House. As Lord Macmillan pointed out, the real difficulty was not discussed in the earlier cases in this House. So it can hardly be profitable to analyse the language used in these earlier cases. The decisions are easy to explain and justify but the reasoning is not. The law appears to me to be accurately stated by Lord Macmillan:

> Whenever in any year the amount of interest paid by the taxpayer does not exceed the amount of his profits or gains as assessed for income tax purposes for that year, then the interest paid in that year is, within the statutory meaning, "payable out of profits or gains brought into charge to tax" and the taxpayer is entitled to retain the tax which he deducts in paying the interest. There are qualifications of this principle but that is the general effect of the decision.

Lord Greene took up two questions propounded by Lord Atkinson in *Sugden* v. *Leeds Corporation*—(1) Has the interest been in fact paid or must it in the circumstances of the case be taken to have been paid out of profits or gains brought in to charge, i.e. out of the so-called taxed fund? (2) Was it lawful to pay them out of the fund? It is not disputed that the appellants satisfy the second question in the present case. Then Lord Greene went on to explain what is meant by the taxed fund. And then he said:

> The word can only be used in the accountancy sense of a fund of profits ascertained for the purposes of an account between the taxpayer and the revenue. As the result of taking that account the taxpayer is deemed to have in his hands a fund of taxed profits up to, but not exceeding, the amount of the assessment. Accordingly, it becomes necessary for the purpose of giving effect to rules 19 and 21 to draw up a further account as between the taxpayer and the revenue. On the one side is entered the interest paid, and on the other side the "taxed fund," which may consist of profits as assessed to tax under different schedules. The taxpayer is not entitled to bring in on this side of the account a taxed fund if the profits in respect of which the relevant assessment is made cannot lawfully be applied in payment of the interest. Subject to this, in the absence of special circumstances to which I will refer later, the taxpayer is, in my opinion, entitled to treat the interest entered on one side of the account as having been paid out of the items of taxed profit entered on the other side. In the accountancy sense, he has paid

it, since as between him and the revenue he is entitled to have the account drawn in this way and to debit his payments to the taxed fund. It follows from this that (again apart from special circumstances) the question out of what cash resources was the payment made is entirely irrelevant.

Then later he says:

To speak of this as rewriting the trader's accounts is a misdescription. His domestic accounts stand, and there is no question of rewriting them. The account which is drawn up between himself and the revenue is a totally different account drawn up for totally different purposes . . . If I have correctly grasped these principles, it follows that, in the present case, the fact that the corporation in their domestic accounts have chosen, without any legal compulsion, to show the profits of their undertakings for the year as having been wholly applied for the purposes of the undertakings does not in any way disentitle them from saying that the interest has been or must be deemed to have been paid pro tanto out of the taxed fund at which these profits are quantified by assessment.

If the authorities stopped there—and that is the latest pronouncement—I would think it clear that the appellants must succeed. And I did not understand counsel for the Revenue to deny that in order to succeed he must bring the facts of this case within the category of what Lord Greene calls special circumstances. What then is special about this case? In their domestic accounts the appellants debited part of this interest to capital with the inevitable result that the balances in their profit and loss accounts are larger than they would have been if the whole of the interest had been charged against revenue. I do not understand the respondents to rely on any other circumstance. But there is nothing special in that. It must always happen if a company debits to some other account interest which it could have debited to revenue account. So if the Revenue are right, there can be few, if any, cases in which a company can disregard their domestic accounts made up at the end of the year, although Lord Greene says that as a general rule the taxpayer is entitled to do that under section 169. The Revenue is not bound by domestic accounts in questions of income tax; admittedly a private trader would not be bound by his accounts in such circumstances. *Allchin's* case shows that a local authority is not bound, so why should a company be bound?

One can see what Lord Greene meant by special circumstances by looking at the two instances which he gives. There is no difficulty in seeing the special reason in *Birmingham Corporation* v. *Inland Revenue Commissioners*. He says with regard to that case:

The decision turned entirely on the special nature of the exchequer subsidy and the action of the corporation in basing its claim for subsidy on the assertion that it was out of pocket to the extent of the gross amount of the interest.

The corporation was, in effect, claiming the same sum from the Crown twice.

Lord Greene also dealt with the *Central London Railway* case. He said that the circumstances were very special but, before I explain why he thought that, I must go back to the *Central London Railway* case itself. In that case three similar appeals were dealt with together. It now appears on a close examination of the facts in these cases that in two of them (but probably not in the third) the facts were virtually indistinguishable from those in this present case. But as I shall try to demonstrate, the language used by Lord Macmillan in his speech shows that he must have misapprehended the facts, and his ground of judgment does not apply to the present case. Moreover, the language used by Lord Greene in the *Allchin* case shows that he must have shared Lord Macmillan's misapprehension. On appeal *Allchin's* case was argued for eight days in this House and there is no indication in the reported argument of any attempt to correct this misapprehension: it would have been most relevant to do so because, if the *Central London Railway* case really decided what the Revenue now say it decided, Lord Greene's treatment of the whole subject would require substantial modification. In this House Lord Macmillan was a party to the decision of *Allchin's* case, but he simply adopted Lord Greene's analysis. If he had realised how inappropriate his language in the *Central London Railway* case was in relation to the true facts, he could not have said what he did, and the Inland Revenue themselves only appear to have discovered in 1959 what they now say is the true effect of the *Central London Railway* case. In connection with another point in the present case with which I need not deal, it has been brought out that until that year the Revenue were content to allow the whole of the interest in the present case to be dealt with under section 169: they only discovered in 1959 the case for applying section 170.

I must now go to what Lord Macmillan said in the *Central London Railway* case. He said near the beginning of his speech that the case was solely concerned with the company's claim to retain the tax which they had deducted in paying debenture interest in so far as that interest had been debited to capital in their accounts. He then gave the novel and illuminating explanation of the operation of rule 19 to which I have already referred, and finally and comparatively briefly he gave his reasons for deciding against the company. I must quote the whole passage:

> Now it is true that the railway company could lawfully, if they chose, have paid the interest in question out of their profits, and it is also true that the interest was paid out of a general banking account which contained sufficient profits (though these profits were not their assessed profits—a difficulty which still haunts me). But the interest was actually paid out of capital, and capital was the real source of payment. If the debiting of the interest were merely a matter of domestic accounting I should not be disposed to lay much stress upon it. But in my opinion it was much more than this. There was a deliberate decision to charge the sum in question against capital and not against revenue. That being so, I do not see how the railway company can claim to retain the tax on this interest paid out of capital when the right to retain tax is conditional on the interest being payable out of profits. If the interest had been paid out of actual profits the sum so paid would have figured in the railway company's return of profits to be charged to tax in the next year; but the £2,340 1s. 11d. has never appeared and will never appear in any return by the railway company for tax purposes, for it is a payment out of capital. Consequently the Crown will never receive any tax either from the railway company or from the debenture holders in respect of the interest paid to the latter in 1930 if the railway company

are not held accountable to the Crown for the tax which they deducted. The theory of the notional taxed fund covering the amount of the interest paid does not fit such a case, for the transaction is outside the region of profits whether notional or actual. By their own deliberate act the railway company have made this sum not payable out of profits. It is nothing to the purpose that theoretically the railway company might in some future year carry this sum of £2,340 1s. 11d. back into profit and loss account as income. As to whether in the circumstances they could competently do so I express no opinion. But in the tax year in question they have chosen not to debit this sum to revenue account, and consequently have pro tanto prevented the diminution of the dividend fund in the distribution of which among their shareholders they have deducted tax and, as they were entitled to do, have retained the tax deducted.

My Lords, I do not think that the same sum can be utilized by the railway company to render them those two inconsistent services in the same year, so as to entitle them first to attribute the £2,340 1s. 11d. to the payment of interest to their creditors and claim to retain the tax deducted therefrom as if it were paid out of revenue, and then by debiting it to capital, to enhance the dividend fund and claim to retain the tax deducted from their shareholders on paying them their dividends. Whatever view be taken of the meaning of rule 19, I do not think that the railway company can bring such a case within it.

The first point which he makes is that there was a deliberate decision to charge this interest against capital and not against revenue. He cannot have meant that that in itself would be enough to oust the company's right to invoke section 169 (then rule 19). Every decision by a company as to how their annual accounts are to be framed must surely be deliberate. A company could hardly say that their accounts had been framed casually or negligently and I can think of no other alternative to deliberate. And to hold that a company must be held to every deliberate entry in their accounts would be quite inconsistent with Lord Greene's analysis in *Allchin's* case, to which I have already referred and with which Lord Macmillan expressly agreed.

Then Lord Macmillan made a statement which I am afraid is simply erroneous. He said: "If the interest had been paid out of actual profits the sum so paid would have figured in the railway company's return of profits to be charged to tax in the next year."

As counsel for the Revenue freely admitted to your Lordships, such interest could never have figured in any return of profits for income tax purposes. If it had been put in it would have been struck out by the Revenue for the reason that interest is not a permissible deduction in striking the balance of profit for income tax purposes. And that error led Lord Macmillan to a conclusion which is equally erroneous and which may have had some influence on the ultimate decision. He appears to have supposed that the effect of charging this interest against capital would be to cause the Crown to receive less tax. But again admittedly that is not so. If the company had sufficient money in hand which had borne tax they could deduct tax in paying the interest and retain the tax so deducted whatever the actual source of the money used to pay the interest or whatever entries were in their books. But I need not consider the effect on the authority of a decision of this House if one of the grounds of judgment can be shown to be based on error.

❉   ❉   ❉

Of course one tries to avoid the conclusion that this House based its decision on a mistaken view of the facts, and counsel for the Revenue strove to show that Lord Macmillan's words could be construed so as to make them fit the true facts. I do not think that he succeeded: but if he did we should have to choose between attributing to Lord Macmillan an error in appreciating the facts or attributing to him the greatest obscurity of language. Anyone may fall into error, but I refuse to contemplate the possibility that a master of the English language, as Lord Macmillan was, could have said what he did say if he had had the true facts in mind.

It is unfortunate that in such an intricate case none of the other noble and learned lords expressed his reasons in his own words. This is by no means the first time in my experience when ambiguity or possible confusion or error in a single speech or judgment has given rise to difficulties of interpretation which would probably have been avoided if we had had a second statement with which to compare the first. But we must do our best with what we have, and in the end I have no doubt that Lord Macmillan's conclusion depends on his assumption that the company were trying to make the same sum render two inconsistent services. If that is essential to the ratio decidendi, then the ratio does not apply to the present case.

I am fortified in my conclusion by the fact that Lord Macmillan appears to have been so understood in every subsequent case where *Central London Railway* was discussed. I think that that was certainly Lord Greene's view in *Allchin*. Having said that the circumstances in *Central London Railway* were *very special*, he went on to paraphrase what Lord Macmillan said in that case in this way:

> The effect of charging the interest to capital was to swell the dividend fund on the distribution of which the company *retained* a larger amount of tax than they would have retained if the interest had been charged to revenue and the dividend in consequence reduced. They could not at *one and the same time claim to enjoy this larger retention* and treat the interest as chargeable, as between themselves and the Crown, to revenue account.

Lord Greene was not unacquainted with company accounts or with the way in which tax is retained when dividends are paid, and he could not have used the words which I have italicised if he had thought otherwise—nor could he have said that the circumstances in *Central London Railway* were very special.

This House still regards itself as bound by the rule that it must not reverse or depart from a previous decision of the House. But it would, in my view, be pedantic and unreasonable to apply that rule to the present case, and to say that, because it has now been ascertained that the facts in Central London Railway *were indistinguishable from the facts of this case, therefore we must disregard the reasoning in that case but follow its result.*

In the end the case of the Revenue was based on the submission that to allow the appellants' appeal would in some way result in falsifying their published

---

❉ Editor's note: I have supplied the italics throughout this decision.

accounts. They have represented to the Revenue, the shareholders and the world at large that they were carrying forward balances in their profit and loss accounts. But I do not see how allowing this appeal would make that representation false or misleading. It is not a representation that the whole of the balance carried forward is money which has borne tax, and it is not a representation that the whole or any part of the balance will be distributed to the shareholders. If the result of operating section 169 is to prejudice the Revenue or others, that cannot be done, and it might be that it could not be done if the result would be to falsify some deliberate representation—such a case can be decided when it arises. But I can see nothing in the facts to the present case to exclude the general rule as to the application of section 169. So I am of opinion that the sums assessed in this case fall within the scope of that section and are not within the scope of section 170. I would therefore allow the appeal.

* * *

LORD UPJOHN. My Lords, when the appellants wanted to rebuild their safe deposit premises in Chancery Lane, which had been damaged in the war, they decided to do so by financing it on borrowed money. They had, of course, to pay interest on it, and they were advised by their accountants that it would be proper to treat part of that interest as attributable to capital expenditure. That was plainly right and is not in dispute; the cost of hiring money to rebuild a house is just as much a capital cost as the cost of hiring labour to do the rebuilding. So, in their company accounts issued to shareholders for the relevant years, they debited part of the interest on the borrowed money against their profit and loss account, in the usual way, and part to capital account. This meant, of course, that the profit and loss account was not as diminished as it would have been had the whole been so debited.

As I understood the Crown's argument, in the end it was that the deliberate decision of the appellant company to attribute part of that interest to capital and not to the debit of profit and loss was the sole foundation of its claim in this case.

In the relevant years the appellant paid interest on the sums it had borrowed, and it was bound to deduct tax in making those payments; the whole question is whether it is entitled to retain the tax on that part of the interest attributable to capital or is bound to account for it to the Crown. That depends upon the true construction of sections 169 and 170 of the Income Tax Act, 1952, as interpreted by a number of decisions upon that Act, or its predecessor, nearly all in this House.

My Lords, the original difficulty lay in the proper interpretation of the words of section 169 (or the previous rule 19) that the annual payments must have been "payable wholly out of profits or gains brought into charge to tax."

Obviously these words were capable of differing constructions but, as a result of many authorities, culminating in *Central London Railway Co.* v. *Inland Revenue Commissioners* and the judgment of Lord Greene in *Allchin* v. *Coulthard,* as unanimously approved in your Lordships' House, certain matters may be taken to be clearly established.

First, if in a particular year the taxpayer pays interest on a debt to a creditor and (of course) deducts tax, that tax may, under section 169, be retained, provided that the taxpayer has in hand profits assessed to tax for that particular year which exceed the interest. The profits assessed to tax are not the profits of that year but of the previous year; this has given rise to some discussion in the cases about the difficulty of equating the payment of real interest out of a notional fund.

I confess this difficulty does not worry me very much, and the decisions lead to the clear practical conclusion: look at your interest payments for the year; look at your assessed profits for the same year (the actual profits for the previous year); compare the two and, if the latter exceed the former, the interest deducted may be retained by the taxpayer in the absence of special circumstances. . . . That is the general rule or "the rule of the road."

Secondly, and this is a cardinal principle, the actual cash fund out of which any payment is made, whether it be of the interest due to the creditor or of the tax due to the Crown, is utterly immaterial; if these payments are in fact made wholly out of the proceeds of sale of some capital assets, such as a factory, it matters not.

So we must consider the tax liability solely in reference to payment out of funds used in a purely accountancy sense or category as explained by Lord Greene in *Allchin's* case. The company's banking accounts have nothing to do with it. Now, as Lord Greene pointed out, the company's accounts prepared for submission to its shareholders are quite different from the accounts which have to be prepared in accordance with the statutory requirements of the Income Tax Acts and, in conformity to income tax principles, for submission to the Inland Revenue. In particular, interest payments, which prima facie must be deducted from the profit and loss account to show the true position to the shareholders, cannot by statute be deducted from the profits for submission to the Crown for the assessment of income tax for the relevant year. But this apparent unfairness to the taxpayer is adjusted as, under the scheme of our tax laws, the recipient of interest is not assessed to tax on it, but the payer deducts it in any event and retains it if he has paid an equivalent amount of tax for that year: so fairness is obtained and, in effect, the taxpayer only pays tax on his profits and gains less the interest paid away.

In the present case, that is what has happened, for it has been conceded throughout that, in each relevant year, the taxpayer has had sufficient profits and gains brought into charge to tax (that is assessed profits) and so why does the Crown claim to recover from him the tax so deducted?

The claim, if successful, will effect double taxation of the same fund, which, as Lord Atkinson pointed out in *Sugden* v. *Leeds Corporation*, the scheme of the Acts seemed designed to avoid. As I said at the beginning of this opinion, the claim is made solely because in his own accounts the taxpayer has attributed some part of the interest paid to capital. But the Crown is not bound, or affected in any way, by the company's accounts. There can be no question of misrepresentation or of estoppel. It is conceded that, so far as an individual is concerned, the way in which he keeps his private accounts (if any) is immaterial and, as the authorities (particularly the *Allchin* case) show, it is immaterial in the case of statutory corporations: provided that the profits could lawfully be attributed to payments of interest, it matters not whether they are so attributed in the corporation's accounts. Illegality or unlawfulness is not in point here.

I fear that much of the trouble that has arisen in this case has been the unfortunate distinction drawn by Lord Macmillan in the *Central London Railway* case between "domestic accounting" and a "deliberate decision" to allocate an interest payment to capital. Of course, domestic accounting may have a different meaning from a deliberate decision when the company's accounting branch is asked to put up some figures for the consideration of the directors; but no one has suggested that such internal accounting was in any one's mind in that case or in any of the authorities which your Lordships have considered where only the formal annual accounts of the taxpayer were under review.

With all respect to Lord Macmillan, I find it quite impossible to understand what he meant or what he intended to contrast by drawing a distinction between domestic accounting and a deliberate decision. In my opinion, the distinction is meaningless and is the real source of trouble in this case. Why should the accounts prepared for its shareholders showing lawfully and truthfully a debit to capital account or, for that matter, to any other account, such as a suspense account or a reserve account or a deduction from some property account, affect the company's liability to tax?

The Crown's plea is "special circumstances," but the mere increase of the profit and loss fund by the attribution of the interest to some other account cannot be a special circumstance, for that would destroy the whole basis of the general rule; for, as the actual cash fund as the source of payment is immaterial, so must the accountancy fund to which the payment is debited be immaterial when we have got away from some meaningless idea of a "deliberate" decision to be attributed to an accountancy allocation to some account other than the profit and loss account. So special circumstances must be sought elsewhere.

No doubt if the taxed profits are sufficient to cover the interest payment but insufficient at the same time to cover a dividend payment in the same year from which tax is deducted, that might be a special circumstance, for that would be using one amount of taxed profits for two purposes, though here one must be careful to distinguish between a taxed fund for the purposes of sections 169 and 170 and a taxed fund for the purposes of section 184, which may cover earlier profits. However, for my part, I see no reason why the Crown should be enabled to rely on that, for the only sufferer is the shareholder, part of whose dividend has wrongly been withheld from him because the company has not satisfied section 184.

The shareholder may have a complaint, but not the Crown, for it is a commonplace that dividends do not suffer deduction of tax at the hands of the Crown; the company merely has the right to deduct tax if it is paying the dividend out of profits which have borne tax.

However, that is not in point here, for it is conceded that in fact in each of the relevant years the company had sufficient tax-borne profits to cover not only the interest payments but the dividends paid.

So far, I would have thought this a very plain case and appellants must succeed, but it is the circumstance mentioned in my last sentence that has given rise to all the trouble; for the recent researches of the Board of Inland Revenue have disclosed what they had never realised before 1959, that this circumstance was the same in at least two out of three of the *Central London Railway* cases. So it is said we must follow that case, admittedly utterly indistinguishable on its facts, and dismiss the appeal.

My Lords, we are not bound to follow a case merely because it is indistinguishable upon the facts. A decision even in your Lordships' House is binding on your Lordships only because it lays down some principle of law or for its reasoning on some particular facts.

It was upon the obscure opinion of Lord Macmillan in that case, contrasted with his approval of Lord Greene's judgment in the subsequent Allchin case, that much of the argument centred before your Lordships. Upon this matter I cannot usefully add anything to the penetrating analysis and ultimate criticism by Lord Reid, whose opinion I have had the privilege of reading, of Lord Macmillan's opinion in the Central London Railway *case; I agree with every word of Lord Reid. I venture to think Lord Greene expressed himself completely accurately as to the general principles to be applied in the* Allchin *case and Lord Macmillan gave his wholehearted approval thereto. The fact that in the* Central London Railway *case taxed profits were sufficient to cover both interest and dividends must per incuriam have been overlooked.*

I would allow this appeal.

❖ ❖ ❖

CHAPTER 2

CAUSES OF THE JUDICIAL DECISION

> The hungry judges soon the sentence sign . . .
>
> —ALEXANDER POPE
> *Rape of the Lock*

ONCE WE CAN characterize a process as being judicial, it is important to comprehend how extensive and compelling the judicial factor is and how it interacts with other factors to manufacture the judicial product. Certain legal realists have treated this set of questions impressionistically (Holmes, Cardozo, Pound, Frank, Llewellyn), as have some modern European jurisprudents.[1] On the other hand, American political scientists have employed a wide range of methods and approaches to study the judicial decision; indeed, many schools of thought on how to go about doing this have flourished over the years. Recently one researcher felt the need to see whether there were any rubrics under which all of these academic entrepreneurs could be placed. He became satisfied that there were three distinct groups: (1) traditional, (2) conventional, and (3) behavioral.[2]

On Causation

Much work has been done of late in attempting to apply modern social-scientific theory and methods to arrive at some explanations of the decisions of the courts, especially of American courts. This is what is usually called

---

[1] For a brief, descriptive bibliography on the nature of the continental theories, see Arthur von Mehren, "The Judicial Process: A Comparative Analysis," *American Journal of Comparative Law,* 5 (Spring, 1956), pp. 197–228.

[2] See Glendon Schubert, "Ideologies and Attitudes, Academic and Judicial," *Journal of Politics,* 29 (February, 1967), pp. 3–40, and "Academic Ideology and the Study of Adjudication," *American Political Science Review,* 61 (March, 1967), pp. 106–29.

the behavioral approach. I am going to make a semi-arbitrary dividing line that will exclude all of the traditional and most of the conventional work done in recent yers. This is due to the fact that the causes I intend to discuss are what might be called the internal or black-box factors. The degree of external (to the court system) political or social pressure, as well as the style of this pressure, though well covered in many books and articles,[3] is not the kind of influence I shall emphasize. Suffice it to say that until some-one devises a linkage between these external political, social, and economic factors and such internal ones as attitudes, roles, values, and the law, I shall consider the external factors as being converted to attitudes, values, etc. They are certainly as nebulous as the factors known as background, and therefore as difficult to link to decision. These latter factors will be dis-cussed in some detail below, though, chiefly because there has been so much effort expended in systematically trying to connect them to decisional patterns. Scant work can be found that categorizes and measures political pressures or social pressures as effective causation of judicial decisions. An-other reason for selecting the background factors for treatment here is that these factors seem far more amenable to precise description than political pressure, and therefore seem more amenable to association with patterns of judicial decision-making.

The earlier as well as the contemporary work on causation of the judi-cial decision can be divided into two distinct categories. These correspond roughly to two phases of causal theory. A conventional way to designate these two phases is to label one direct causes and the other indirect causes. This corresponds, again somewhat roughly, to the more technical termi-nology of intervening variable and independent variable. Schubert notes that there are three phases (he calls them classes) of factors that must be understood if we are ever to develop a complete theory of judicial decision-making.[4] According to him, the most immediate or direct factor (or set of factors) is "attitudinal." This, he believes, accounts for most of the variation in the judicial decision. To him, then, it is the most important cause. The

---

[3] A few books of this type are Jack Peltason, *Federal Courts in the Political Process* (New York: Random House, 1955); Clement E. Vose, *Caucasians Only* (Los Angeles and Berkeley: University of California Press, 1959); Glendon Schubert, *Constitutional Politics* (New York: Holt, Rinehart & Winston, 1960); Alan Westin, ed, *The Third Branch of Government* (New York: Harcourt, Brace & World, 1963); David J. Danel-ski, *A Supreme Court Justice Is Appointed* (New York: Random House, 1964); Martin Shapiro, *Law and Politics in the Supreme Court* (New York: Free Press, Macmillan, 1964); Joel Grossman, *Lawyers and Judges* (New York: Wiley, 1965); Samuel Krislov, *The Supreme Court in the Political Process* (New York: Macmillan, 1966).

[4] Glendon Schubert, ed., *Judicial Behavior* (Chicago: Rand McNally, 1964). See his introduction to the section entitled "Mathematical Prediction of Judicial Behavior." A more recent and more complex model devised by Schubert to guide research on adjudicatory decision-making can be found in his "Behavioral Jurisprudence," *Law and Society Review*, 2 (May, 1968), pp. 407–28.

other factors are what he terms "attributes" and "culture." In his view, predictions from the attribute data (for instance, social background information) "will be less successful than predictions based directly upon attitudinal variables and data," and "cultural-systemic macro-variables" will yield the least successful prediction of all. He illustrates this graphically by Figure 2.[5]

FIGURE 2

Prediction Between Classes of Variables

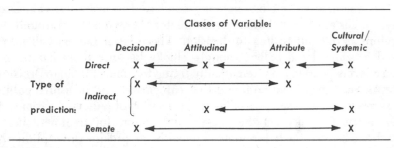

In other words, Schubert sees attitudes as the primary and most important influence (causal) factor, attributes as less important, and cultural variables as least important in determining degrees of variation in judicial behavior. In terms of the conceptual scheme of this book, the decision is seen as being influenced more by structural and process factors than by external conditions.

ON ATTITUDES, OF ALL SORTS

Almost everyone who professionally observes the courts in the United States today agrees that one major causal factor in judicial decision-making is the judges' attitudes. Whether these observers are newspapermen, presidential aspirants, political scientists, U.S. senators, law professors, or judges, this appears to be the current, if not modern, if not voguish, point of view. The legal-realism theories of the thirties (rule skepticism *and* fact skepticism)[6] have become widely shared dogma today. Most of the research has been done on the Supreme Court, and these findings should not be generalized to lower court levels. The converse holds equally true. Nevertheless, considering the heuristic emphasis of this book, I shall treat all the contemporary work as a whole.

---

[5] Schubert, *Judicial Behavior*, p. 447.
[6] Jerome Frank, *Courts on Trial* (Princeton: Princeton University Press, 1949).

It is now "known" that each member of the United States Supreme Court entertains a set of predispositions in relationship to a number of public policy areas. It is known, too, that each justice is more or less liberal or conservative toward freedom of speech, private property, procedural due process, and the like. Also, it is believed firmly that these predispositions account, at least in very substantial part, for each justice's decision in every case. In fact, it is not unlikely that some Court-watchers believe that attitudes of one kind or another (some may call them "values") are the single determinant of decisions of the Supreme Court.

Of course, there are others who would not subscribe to this theory. Other factors are seen to be probably as significant, if not more so, in determining the outcomes of any judicial process. Richard Wells and Joel Grossman have a cogent argument on this point in their claim that the Schubert type of model does not adequately explain how the judicial attitudes or values are converted into judicial decisions. They state that it is difficult to see how the attitudes or values of judges alone could possibly explain what they term the policy decisions of the court. As they put it:

> The argument is that the issue content of policy problems is a function of the conscious and rational perception of the judges. The responses of the policy-making judge depend upon his perceptions, which in turn depend upon his value system. But even assuming that this interrelationship between values and perception of issues is correct, can it be accepted as a complete and sufficient statement of process-policy conversion?
>
> We feel that it is not sufficient, fundamentally because policy outcomes cannot be considered as identical to the output of a judge's internal value system. Policy outcomes must be construed as more than the results of an accommodation between issues and values—though these are important. The conditions underlying the exercise of judicial policy functions are far too complex and diverse to be adequately contained in a simple model which purports to convert value-issue relationships into policy outcomes, and which fails to strike a balance between the personal values of the judges and the content, history, magnitude, possible solutions, and institutional route of problems which require judicial policy action.[7]

Nevertheless, whether judicial attitudes are the single most important factor or just one of several important factors, there are many specific questions that still remain about attitudinal causation of the Supreme Court decision, and the specific answers to these questions can have serious political implications. Moreover, there is a research justification in hypothesizing that these questions, as they are categorized below, may lead us to important information about other judiciaries. Exactitude in these answers

---

[7] Richard S. Wells and Joel B. Grossman, "The Concept of Judicial Policy-Making: A Critique," *Journal of Public Law*, 15 (1966), p. 308.

is a prerequisite for the development of scientific knowledge about the causes of the judicial decision. The questions about attitudes that must still be answered can be fitted into four distinct categories: (A) personal-general attitudes; (B) policy-area attitudes; (C) judicial role attitudes; and (D) highest appellate court role attitudes.

Some of these questions run roughly as follows:

A. *Personal-general attitudes*
   1. What is the relationship between the personal-general attitude universe of a justice and the more legal and political attitudes (B, C, and D)?
   2. What is the relationship between personal-general attitudes and patterns of judicial decision-making?
B. *Policy-area attitudes*
   Assuming that the policy-area orientation of justices solely determines their decisions, or is the major influence factor:
   1. What are all of these policy areas and how can we isolate and measure them precisely?
   2. How can we know which will prevail when more than one is involved in any given case (as they so frequently are, at least at the oral-argument stage)?
C. *Judicial role attitudes*
   What attitudes do justices entertain toward the use and importance of extant, relevant case law?
   1. What are the variations in these attitudes?
   2. How important are these attitudes in the making of their decisions?
   3. Under what conditions might these attitudes differ in importance? (At what stage of the litigation? Is the importance of the case a factor? Is the degree of clarity of precedent a factor?)
D. *Highest appellate court role attitudes*
   1. What are the various attitudes justices have about the place of the highest appellate court in their political system?
   2. How do these differ from those of lower court judges?

Examples of a judge's personal-general attitude would be his views on sex, religion, international affairs, and the like. Examples of his policy-area attitude would be his views on civil rights, state-federal relations, desirability of capital punishment, etc. Judicial role attitude might include the judge's views on the degree of clarity necessary to bind the judge, the importance of other high court opinions (other circuit courts, other state supreme courts, etc.). Finally, the highest appellate court role attitudes could include views on judicial activism, the importance of the Supreme Court as umpire in a federal system, etc.

I am suggesting, then, that attitude, or some other form of attitude such as value, role, philosophy, or ideology, has many dimensions as a concept. Though there is a great consensus that judicial attitudes play a leading part in the judicial decision, there is not much hard knowledge on how much importance these various types of attitude have in relationship to one another and even less knowledge on the relationship of these attitudes to various other circumstances and factors that may have some bearing on decision-making, e.g., the personal or professional relationship between various justices, the personality of the judge, strategy by the chief justice, the political atmosphere at the time (domestic and external), and the impact of debate in the conference.

There is really no way that the ordinary armchair speculator or legal scholar can answer such complicated questions with any precision, for these, by and large, are problems of measurement. The question of just how much one or another of these attitudes might weigh in the decision-making process, or in relationship to other factors, simply cannot be reasoned out. It must be found out. In fact, it is this gaping hole in our knowledge that has afforded the principal justification to the contemporary tendency in American political science circles to approach the Supreme Court decision in a social-scientific manner.

In the past decade or so, much has been researched, much has been written, and much has been published on the Court from this perspective. Sadly, though, we have not come too far beyond what was known previously, because of grievous errors made, some of which were discussed in Chapter 1. In addition to the arguments that were surveyed or made in Chapter 1 against the mainstream of the judicial behavior research, Donald Kommers has noted that the objections against using case opinions and votes to work out a theory of judicial decision-making may be even *more* valid for comparative research. According to Kommers:

> Actually, the inability to make systematic use of judicial votes may not be such a handicap after all, for the reason that it may force a search for a level of analysis that will carry one beyond the simple assumption, implicit in much of the literature on judicial behavior, that judicial policies are largely the function of personal values. Such pure behavioralism has its limits, especially in the study of *comparative judicial* politics. I should think that a politically relevant theory of the judicial process, based on comparative study, would necessitate paying greater attention to the relationship between judicial policy and adjudicatory behavior as well as the relation that these, in turn, bear to the broader aspects of the political system. It is fundamentally this kind of analysis for which Grossman and Wells are pleading when they suggest the theoretical utility of linking policy-making to judicial processes. They seriously question the validity of the "pure conversion" theory of the judicial process which holds a one-to-one relationship between policy and values.[8]

---

[8] Donald P. Kommers, "The Federal Constitutional Court of West Germany: Some Exploratory Considerations" (paper delivered at the Midwest Conference of Political Scientists, Purdue University, April, 1967). Wells and Grossman, "Concept of Judicial Policy-Making," would seem to be in accord with this view.

Nevertheless, despite the substantial misdirection of research energies, there have been some accretions to our knowledge, and the justification for a social-scientific approach remains. After all, the movement is still reasonably young; we have some new facts to show for our pains and some interesting new insights as well.

Perhaps the best work of simply testing the effect of attitudes on judicial decision-making has been done by Nagel and Danelski.[9] Their work, with that of Don R. Bowen and Joel Grossman, has furnished some strands of support to the Schubert hypotheses on the closer relationship between attitudes and decisions[10] than between attributes and decisions. In addition, the few studies done of foreign judiciaries thus far tend to confirm the hypotheses on the close and direct relationship between attitudes and judicial decision-making.

COMPARATIVE WORK ON ATTITUDES

There have been several studies of foreign judiciaries that have duplicated the approach to the U.S. courts in applying psychometric techniques to case decisions and opinions and then improperly implying attitudinal causation.[11] There is no reason to discuss them at length here. On the

---

[9] Stuart Nagel, "Off-the-Bench Judicial Attitudes," in *Judicial Decision-Making*, ed. Glendon Schubert (New York: Free Press, Macmillan, 1963); Nagel, "Judicial Attitudes and Those of Legislators and Administrators" (paper delivered at the annual meeting of the American Political Science Association, Washington, D.C., 1962); David J. Danelski, "Values as Variables in Judicial Decision-Making: Notes toward a Theory," *Vanderbilt Law Review*, 19 (June, 1966), pp. 721–40.

[10] Don R. Bowen, "The Explanation of Judicial Voting Behavior from Sociological Characteristics of Judges" (unpublished Ph.D. dissertation, Yale University, 1965); Joel Grossman, "Social Backgrounds and Judicial Decision-Making," *Harvard Law Review*, 79 (June, 1966), pp. 1551–64; Grossman, "Social Backgrounds and Judicial Decisions: Notes for a Theory," *Journal of Politics*, 29 (May, 1967), pp. 334–51. I say this with full knowledge that some scholars have found what they consider to be confounding evidence. For instance, see Werner Grunbaum, "Analytic and Simulation Models for Explaining Judicial Decision-Making," in *Frontiers of Judicial Research*, ed. Joel Grossman and Joseph Tanenhaus (New York: Wiley, 1969). However, for all the reasons argued in chap. 1, I do not feel that any design failing to provide for collection of independent attitudinal data can be taken too seriously. Cf. Sheldon Goldman, "Backgrounds, Attitudes, and the Voting Behavior of Judges: A Comment on Joel Grossman's 'Social Backgrounds and Judicial Decisions,'" *Journal of Politics*, 31 (February, 1969), pp. 214–22. Both Grunbaum and Goldman are of the opinion that a conversion process of "consensus" (small-group cohesion) or of "rationality" (*stare decisis*) alters the predispositions of judges (judicial attitudes). This fits well within a traditional vein of speculation, but their data are not pertinent support for their hunch. Their guess is still no better than that of Cardozo and Frank.

[11] Takeo Hayakawa, "Civil Liberties in the Japanese Supreme Court," in *Judicial Behavior*, ed. Schubert; Abelardo Samonte, "The Philippine and the American Supreme Courts" (paper delivered at the annual meeting of the American Political Science Association, September, 1966); Glendon Schubert, "The Dimensions of Decisional Response: Opinion and Voting Behavior of the Australian High Court," in *Frontiers of Judicial Research*, ed. Grossman and Tanenhaus.

other hand, there are some more reliable studies of this possible relationship.[12]

Danelski conducted a study of the Japanese Grand Bench in 1966.[13] Aside from background data, he arranged and analyzed a variety of cases using a variety of techniques. One he calls "linkage analysis";[14] others are cumulative scale analysis and factor analysis. He found that in Japan, as in the United States, justices tended to vote in blocs. Danelski, however, was far more prudent in his inferences than analysts of similar data on the U.S. Supreme Court. For instance, he states that: "There can be little doubt that cases from the two universes that scaled involve the same issue and measure the same dimension . . . my tentative interpretation is that they

---

[12] The most careful analysis, in terms of *justifiable inductions* drawn, of a scalogram study of a body of high court votes was done recently by a Canadian law professor, S. R. Peck. I should like to quote from his conclusion at some length, as it is a model of circumspection that future American analysis would do well to emulate. All emphasis is mine and not Professor Peck's.

> My purpose in this article is to present a report of an initial effort to apply a behavioral method to the work of the Supreme Court of Canada. I have used only one such method, scalogram analysis, and I have applied it to a relatively small number of decisions. Bearing in mind these limitations in scope, *I shall not attempt to anticipate the broad conclusions about the nature of decision-making by the court,* which may be warranted *after* further work has been done. I wish to conclude this report by drawing together some of the findings that emerge from the separate examinations of taxation, negligence and criminal law decisions.
>
> The scalogram of each group of cases indicates that some justices consistently uphold or oppose the claims of the taxpayer in taxation appeals, the plaintiffs in negligence appeals, or the accused in criminal appeals. As the appeals on each scale raise a wide variety of legal issues, it is reasonable to hypothesize that such justices (who appear near the left or right sides of the scales and have voting patterns classified as "highly pro" or "pro") base their decisions, at least in part, on the value or policy issue raised by the appeals on each scale. An examination of the three scalograms, taken together, indicates that some justices tend to have one-sided voting patterns on more than one scale. *This suggests the hypothesis that these justices pursue policy goals in more than one area of the law* ["The Supreme Court of Canada, 1958–1966: A Search for Policy through Scalogram Analysis," *Canadian Bar Review,* 45 (December, 1967), pp. 722–23].

Professor Peck is being careful to be true to his own statement that "regarded alone, the scalogram does not indicate directly the justices' attitudes to the [policy] value; nor does it establish that the justices decide cases on the basis of their attitudes, although it may suggest the possibility that they do" (p. 681). See also his "A Behavioral Approach to the Judicial Process: Scalogram Analysis," *Osgoode Hall Law Journal,* 5 (April, 1967), pp. 1ff.

[13] David J. Danelski, "The Supreme Court of Japan: An Exploratory Study" (paper delivered at the annual meeting of the American Political Science Association, September, 1966).

[14] "Linkage analysis" is defined by Danelski as intercorrelating the votes of judges, then taking the phi coefficients and arranging them in a matrix of the number of cases decided by the number of judges. Then the matrix is analyzed and judges are linked in terms of their highest and second highest positive correlation coefficients above an arbitrary cutoff point, which happened to be .28.

represent a dimension of Japanese liberalism and conservatism."[15] And later, following his factor analysis, "Whatever the factors are measuring appears to be related to the second cluster of justices in the linkage analysis. . . . I suggest very tentatively, pending information from Japanese colleagues and more precise analysis, that these justices were manifesting pragmatic behavior."[16]

Most important in his study, however, is the fact that Danelski decided to study the relationship (if any) between the decision-making behavior of Chief Justice Tanaka (who was tied for the highest positive linkage score) and his values. Tanaka's values were defined and measured in two essays he wrote before assuming the high bench. Danelski performed a content analysis on these essays and suggested that "if Tanaka is representative of the justices in the third cluster in the linkage analysis, then that cluster consists of conservatives, that is, justices who value the more traditional aspects of Japanese society."[17]

Victor Flango and I conducted a comparative study that used different techniques and gathered additional data from the study discussed in the previous chapter.[18] After discovering that the norm of impartiality existed in each society and that judges did exhibit a substantial modicum of objectivity in their decision-making, we sought a wider sample. Responses were received from fifty-nine Philippine judges on a similar questionnaire device; then it was decided to test a causal model on the expanded Philippine data and the earlier Hawaiian data in the style discussed by Charles F. Cnudde and Donald J. McCrone.[19]

Among the more interesting findings was a negative one: there were no great disparities in decision-making between the judiciaries in the United States and those in the Philippines. Differences in culture, though possibly having a marginal effect, did not seem to cause any dramatic differences in decision-making. When the relationship of such factors as the

---

[15] Danelski, "Supreme Court of Japan," pp. 13–14. Danelski is equally cautious in the revision of this paper, which appears as chap. 6 of *Comparative Judicial Behavior,* ed. Glendon Schubert and David J. Danelski (New York: Oxford University Press, 1969). Here Danelski resorts only to a *working* hypothesis that "the groupings of judges discovered by his linkage analysis and smallest space analysis are explained by differing ideologies held by the judges. He arrives at this hypothesis on the basis of converging inferences made from (1) interviews conducted with a variety of indigenous experts, (2) content analysis of some earlier written work of one of the judges, and (3) similar inferences made in earlier empirical studies of the Japanese courts.

[16] *Ibid.,* p. 15 of APSA paper.

[17] *Ibid.,* p. 12.

[18] Victor E. Flango and Theodore L. Becker, "Judicial Decision-Making in the Philippines and in Hawaii" (unpublished paper, Department of Political Science, University of Hawaii, 1967).

[19] Charles F. Cnudde and Donald J. McCrone, "The Linkage between Constituency Attitudes and Congressional Voting Behavior," *American Political Science Review,* 60 (March, 1966), pp. 66–72.

reported rank of the judges in their law school class, their orientation toward precedent (judicial role concept), their particular attitude toward the relevant policy, and their decisions were considered, no difference in decision-making could be discerned at all. Both the Hawaiian and Philippine causal models accounted for 23 percent of the total variance in decision-making, and, again, in each culture the personal attitude of the judges was most important. Figure 3 demonstrates this—although it should be reemphasized that the statistical differences are at a pretty low level.[20]

Still, these data would seem to provide basis enough to permit us to observe that:

> The most significant difference between the judiciaries of Hawaii and the Philippines is that there is a direct link between an attitude favorable to precedent and a precedent-oriented decision in Hawaii that is not present in the Philippines. Conversely, a strong policy orientation is more likely to explain more of the decision-making variance in the Philippines than it does in Hawaii.[21]

We also suggest possible reasons behind this difference:

> Perhaps Filipino judges in general possess what Agpalo considered a *pandanggo-sa-ilaw* orientation to politics, that is, legislators, administrators, and judges are moved by personalistic, concrete, material, and nonideological ends or things. In his study of the politics of the Philippine province of Occidental Mindoro, Agpalo pointed out that judges

FIGURE 3

Linkages in Judicial Decision-Making, Hawaii and Philippines

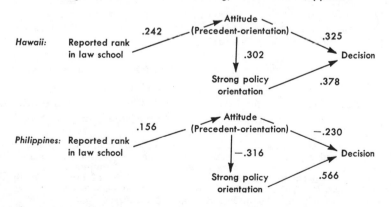

---

[20] It should also be noted that this type of extended causal analysis cannot (or should not) be carried out when there is a relationship of less than .30 between any adjacent variables. We have left in the relationship between the attribute variable and attitude variable for illustrative purposes only.

[21] Flango and Becker, *op. cit.*, p. 13.

were more interested in personal and practical matters than in ideological doctrines.[22]

Another recent probe into the attitudes and values of a foreign judiciary is one by James Allen Dator.[23] Dator managed to collect an academic
ton of material on the general-personal attitudes of a large segment of the
Japanese judiciary. The particular attitudes ranged over a wide universe.
They included the opinions of the judges on topics all the way from international relations to sexual behavior. Dator then sought to find whether or
not any of the differences in attitudes of the judges were related to any of
a wide variety of social-background factors, including their universities,
the parts of Japan from which they came, their religious backgrounds, and
the like. Unfortunately for us, despite the fact that Dator did use the Hans
Eysenck questionnaire device as adapted by Nagel for his study of the relationship between attitudes and decisions of American judges,[24] no effort
was exerted to see how these attitudes influenced the decisions of these
Japanese judges. It is to be hoped that this is on Dator's agenda.

Schubert, in the meantime, put some of Dator's data to use along these
lines. He related an analysis by John Maki[25] of seventeen Japanese Supreme
Court decisions from 1948 to 1960 to some of Dator's attitude data. The
results are supportive of the basic hypothesis:

> Only one (involving a claim of police brutality and a coerced confes-
> sion) of our seventeen civil liberties cases was decided liberally; half
> of these cases dealt with fair procedure, and the other half with political
> freedom. The responses of high court judges to Dator's survey showed
> that the item on which the Japanese most clearly prove more conserva-
> tive than American or British respondents was one which read: "Unre-
> stricted freedom of discussion on every topic is desirable in the press,
> in literature and on the stage." Eighty-five percent of the Japanese
> judges disagreed. When we recall, however, the persuasiveness of
> the consensus norm in Japan, it is easy to understand why very few
> Japanese judges could bring themselves to opt for unlimited freedom
> of speech.[26]

In summary, then, the first social-scientific research inquiries into
foreign judiciaries have produced findings consistent with the theory that

---

[22] *Ibid.* The reference is to Remigio E. Agpalo, "The Political Elite and the People" (unpublished paper, University of the Philippines). Professor Agpalo is chairman
of the Department of Political Science, University of the Philippines.

[23] James Allen Dator, "The Life History and Attitudes of Japanese High Court
Judges," *Western Political Quarterly,* 20 (June, 1967), pp. 408–39.

[24] See Stuart Nagel, "Off-the-Bench Judicial Attitudes."

[25] John Maki, *Court and Constitution in Japan* (Seattle: University of Washington Press, 1964).

[26] Glendon Schubert, "Judges and Political Leadership," in *Political Leadership in
Industrialized Societies,* ed. Lewis Edinger (New York: Wiley, 1967), p. 260. For those
readers who have observed the notion of "unlimited freedom of speech," and have
thought of the fact that only Douglas and perhaps Black on the U.S. Supreme Court

personal and policy attitudes are very important factors, and may be the most directly effective factors, in the making of the judicial decision. Thus far there is no evidence to show that cultural variation makes any significant difference in this relationship. Moreover, there has been very little scientific testing of the influence of judicial role attitudes of the judiciary.

BACKGROUND STUDY

The study of the consequences of what the judge may think and believe has taken a roundabout route as well. Various works by Danelski, Nagel, Becker, Dator, and Vines on personal values and role attitudes have been based on judges' statements of their beliefs either while they were on the bench or before they arrived at that lofty station. As far as reliability is concerned, this method has the same drawbacks as the use of questionnaires in any area of social science. Also, as has been mentioned above, various critiques warn of the inherent dangers in making inferences from the judicial decision itself about any one factor or type of factor that may be a causal agent in the decision. These limitations are great, it is true, but there are even greater dangers inherent in the attempt to infer influence of personal attitudes of judges on their decisions from the fact that there is a clear relationship between some social background characteristics of the judges and the pattern of their decisions.

---

still subscribe to it, let it be known that in contrast to the 15 percent of the Japanese judges who agreed with it, some 49 percent of the American judges agreed with the same item in Nagel's earlier use of the questionnaire (1961). Moreover, Dator himself states that

> Now it is possible, as some of the free comments indicate, that the judges were especially reacting to the notion of *unrestricted* speech, but there is nothing in the sentence as it stands in Japanese which would make this word more apparent than it is in English. It must be concluded that the judges, on the typically liberal-democratic value, are more conservative than their American and British counterparts [*op. cit.*, p. 433].

(Note also that this same item was agreed to by 75 percent of British judges. This can be found at p. 422 of Dator's study.)

One last point is worth comment. Schubert's inference about the cause of this phenomenon may be incorrect. Schubert seems to think that this indicator of conservatism is due to the widely accepted pressure toward conformity in Japan. In other words, since so many people believe that conformity is important, so do the judges. Perhaps, but Dator notes that while there are in fact many restrictions on free speech in the U.S. and the U.K., the American and British judges were willing to subscribe to the item "on principle." Could it not be, then, that Japanese judges answered the question negatively because they were simply more concerned with reconciling principle with fact? Principle is quite important to the Japanese; honor is involved in adhering to it in action. This, then, is a rival hypothesis as plausible as that posed by Schubert, and it does tend to cast some doubt on whether the Japanese response indicates the same phenomenon as the Western responses. In a sense, it depends upon the definition of the concept of value; i.e., is it a value if one considers something an *unattainable* ideal?

There has been a good deal of effort expended in the past ten years or so in studying the interrelationship of the background of the Supreme Court justice and the Supreme Court decision, and there is much evidence in the modern literature of social psychology to substantiate the view that there is frequently a high correlation between people's attitudes and aspects of their background or phases of their personal history. Therefore, the thinking goes, if one can demonstrate a close relationship (high correlation) between certain background characteristics of justices of the Supreme Court and visible patterns in their voting behavior, then it is a fair inference that it is their attitudes that are responsible for the decisions.[27] This is obviously a dangerous intellectual procedure, since the analyst relies on an inference based upon an inference. A shaky foundation and flimsy building blocks are not the best materials for a sound edifice, physical or theoretical.

Still, the proclivity of some political scientists who study the Supreme Court to give this method the old college try is understandable, since it is modish in other American political science circles today to delve into the relationships between backgrounds of political elites and certain of their attitudes.[28] A healthy proportion of the pioneering work that uses social science methods to study American politics gathers and analyzes background data. Also, to be fair, there might be some limited feasibility in studying the possible relationship between certain background factors and the direction of judicial voting so as to make slight adjustments in the structure of judicial recruitment.[29]

The first attempts to collect social background information systematically on all of the Supreme Court justices—to see if it were in any general way related to decisional tendencies—were conducted by John Schmidhauser. In his best known work, Schmidhauser accumulated all sorts of

---

[27] Sheldon Goldman, who has done some research on the relationship between social backgrounds and decisions of appeals court judges, specifically denies making such an inference. In answer to such a charge he recently stated that "certain backgrounds may provide the foundation or the setting for the development of attitudes/ values but such attitudes/values that are relevant for decision making have been tempered by a host of experiential, institutional and interpersonal variables." See his "Backgrounds, Attitudes, and the Voting Behavior of Judges." Cf. Goldman, "Voting Behavior on the United States Courts of Appeals," *American Political Science Review,* 60 (June, 1966), pp. 374–83. Actually, Goldman's disclaimer supports my view, since no one suggests, as Goldman implies, that backgrounds and attitudes are synonymous. What is being inferred is precisely that backgrounds in some ways influence attitudes (as do other collegial and procedural factors). That is the major reason for studying the background factors, i.e., to see the degree and operation of their influence on attitudes and behavior. And that is what Goldman and others are up to.

[28] See, for example, Lewis J. Edinger and Donald J. Searing, "Social Background in Elite Analysis: A Methodological Inquiry," in *American Political Science Review,* 61 (June, 1967), pp. 428–45.

[29] See David W. Adamany, "The Party Variable in Judges' Voting: Conceptual Notes and a Case Study," *American Political Science Review,* 63 (March, 1969), pp. 57–73.

facts on past and then current members of the Court, including: (1) the occupations of their fathers; (2) their places of birth; (3) their ethnic origins; (4) their religious affiliations; (5) their educational backgrounds; (6) their political party identifications; and (7) the degree of their prior judicial experience. After studying these facts, and many of the Supreme Court decisions, he alleged that:

> The social attitudes of families in the gentry class or professional upper-middle class, and particularly the traditions of the families with judicial associations, may be accounted subtle factors influencing the tone and temper of judicial decision-making. While such influence cannot ordinarily be traced in cause-and-effect formulas in specific decisions, it frequently emerges in the careers of individual justices as setting implicit limits on the scope of theoretical decision-making possibilities.[30]

This is a modest statement, as it should have been; it is so modest as to make one realize that it has simply served to verify the general assumptions made by nearly everyone conversant with the large body of judicial biographies.

On the other hand, Schmidhauser's article on *stare decisis* and dissent illustrates the fruits that can be realized by a judicious hypothesis-testing.[31] In that essay, one finds a systematic study of a large body of background and decisional information that yields data capable of refuting some conventional thinking on a quite specific relationship. Schmidhauser finds, among other things, that prior judicial experience seems to be more closely related to a tendency to overrule precedent than to honor it by rote.

Stuart Nagel, in his wide variety of studies, also has spent a good deal of time and effort trying to discover which background factors might be most important in (most closely linked with) patterns of judicial decision-making. In one of his earliest and most widely cited essays, Nagel found that one of the best predictors of how a judge will decide is his political party identification (Democrat or Republican).[32] Interestingly enough, in a very recent study of social background correlates of European elites, Edinger and Searing observed that "background factors with the widest scope . . . were again associated particularly with adult socialization experiences—especially occupation and *party affiliation*."[33]

The specific dangers and the many pitfalls in the path of those making inferences on interaction between background, attitude, and decision have

---

[30] John Schmidhauser, *The Supreme Court: Its Politics, Personalities, and Procedures* (New York: Holt, Rinehart & Winston, 1960), p. 58.

[31] John R. Schmidhauser, "*Stare Decisis*, Dissent, and the Background of the Justices of the Supreme Court of the United States," *Toronto Law Journal*, 14 (1962), pp. 194–212.

[32] Stuart Nagel, "Political Party Affiliation and Judges' Decisions," *American Political Science Review*, 55 (December, 1961), pp. 843–50.

[33] Edinger and Searing, *op. cit.*, p. 436 (emphasis mine).

been pointed up in several other recent essays. Dolbeare, for instance, in his study of the local courts in a New York county, attempted to replicate Nagel's findings of an association between the political party identifications and the ethnic backgrounds of judges with a predisposition to decide certain cases in certain ways.[34] The replication failed; Dolbeare was forced to conclude (upon admission of possible problems in his comparison) that there was "no general correlation between party identification and decision-making, except in one or two highly partisan areas. . . ."[35] The same held true for ethnic background.

Another very recent study of judicial decisions, one by Bowen, shows precious little explanatory power in a variety of background factors.[36] The Bowen study revealed that there were many low correlations between factors like party affiliation, national region, religion, and status of some 373 federal and state appellate judges and their decisions in criminal, civil liberties, and union–large-business cases. The median single correlation of all these factors in all three case areas was only .22—quite low. Upon working partial correlation and multiple regression analyses, Bowen found that no single factor in any case area explained more than 15.2 percent (status of the judge in labor–large-business cases) and that the "vast majority of the partial correlation coefficients are considerably lower than that."[37] All six factors together, Bowen notes, explain from nearly 20 percent (in criminal cases) to over 40 percent (union–large-business cases). However, he used rather conservative measures and did not include other potentially influential background characteristics in his study. Bowen is not overly pessimistic about the value of this work for the development of judicial decision-making theory. He goes on to say that "to put the situation bluntly, explaining somewhere around a quarter to better than a third of the variance is not, in current political science, to be sneezed at."[38] On the other hand, he admits that the amount of unexplained variance is "very large indeed." And indeed it is.

Grossman's assessment of Bowen's findings seems worth quoting at some length:

> Assuming that statistically significant relationships between certain background characteristics and judicial behavior have been discovered,

---

[34] The works of Nagel which Dolbeare attempted to replicate were "Political Party Affiliation and Judges' Decisions" and "Ethnic Affiliations and Judicial Propensities," *Journal of Politics*, 24 (February, 1962), pp. 92–110.

[35] Kenneth Dolbeare, *Trial Courts in Urban Politics* (New York: Wiley, 1967), p. 77.

[36] Bowen, *op. cit.*

[37] *Ibid.*, p. 18.

[38] *Ibid.*, p. 19.

to what extent can these findings be said to account for the variance in judicial vote patterns? Quantitatively, inquiry can be made through the use of partial correlations, coefficients and multiple regression analysis. Bowen's study of state and appellate judges is the only application so far of these techniques, and his findings are both encouraging and disturbing. After replicating most of Nagel and Schmidhauser's "associational" results, Bowen found that none of the variables most significantly "associated" with judicial decisions explained more than a fraction of the total variance among judges. No single variable accounted for more than 16 percent of the variance in any particular area, and most were in the 1 to 8 percent range. With one exception, the combined explanatory power of the six variables tested never exceeded 30 percent. Even allowing for errors in sampling and measurement, *Bowen's findings cast clear doubt on the explanatory power of background variables taken by themselves. Mere tests of association are inadequate, though useful,* and more powerful measures indicate the presence of other "intervening variables" between the case and the ultimate decision.[39]

Grossman goes on to make this final statement:

But [Bowen's] findings do not justify any inference that background variables are irrelevant. Rather, his results emphasize the importance of describing and analyzing the other intervening variables which interact with personal values, and of finding a way to integrate these variables in a theory which emphasizes their effect on judicial decisions.[40]

Thus, there is a visible trend in the recent work done on the social background of the judge that indicates that these factors probably have minor explanatory power as a factor in the Supreme Court decision, or any court decision. Apparently so much happens in the life of a man who ends up on the Supreme Court that what might greatly affect the behavior of lesser mortals seems all but to vanish in the behavior of the justice. This may not be too surprising, but the bulk of judicial biographical work did lend support to the contrary interpretation; that is, the justice was in many ways and to a large extent a prisoner of his background. Such may be true only in a dynamic, historical sense; it seems to be largely false in a sociological sense.[41]

---

[39] Joel Grossman, "Social Backgrounds and Judicial Decision-Making," *Harvard Law Review*, 79 (June, 1966), pp. 1561–62. Copyright © 1966 by The Harvard Law Review Association. Cf. Heinz Eulau and John Sprague, *Lawyers in Politics* (Indianapolis: Bobbs-Merrill, 1964). These men found no difference in political behavior between lawyers and nonlawyers—which contradicted the widely held belief that a lawyer's occupation would indeed affect his later political behavior.

[40] Grossman, "Social Backgrounds," p. 1562.

[41] This seems to be Jay Sigler's view, too. See his discussion in *An Introduction to the Legal System* (Homewood, Ill.: Dorsey Press, 1968), pp. 104–7.

COMPARATIVE ANALYSIS OF BACKGROUNDS

There are several comparative studies along these lines. Actually, none of these are comparative as such; that is, none systematically compares the backgrounds of the members of more than one judiciary in relationship to a set of hypotheses that are clearly and concretely explicated and advanced previously. By and large, each is simply a study of a single foreign judiciary with occasional reference to the American or other systems. I shall use the essay by Samonte as an example.[42]

One of Samonte's findings is that in a period of national development comparable to that of the Philippines, more American Supreme Court justices came from upper class families than did Philippine justices. Specifically, Professor Samonte claims that "Fewer Philippine justices (59%) came from the upper social classes than their American counterparts (90%)." Moreover,

> About 30 percent of the Philippine Colonial justices came from urban centers and 70 percent came from small towns. The Commonwealth and Republic courts (1935–66) in the Philippines were constituted almost identically in terms of their members' birthplaces: 43 percent from urban centers and 57 percent from small towns. Similarly, 44 percent of American Supreme Court justices from 1933 to 1957 had been born in urban communities, 50 percent in small towns, and 6 percent in rural areas.[43]

What is the importance of these data? Surely, these are not facts that speak for themselves. They fail to lead us to the conclusion that background factors indubitably influence judicial decisions. Can we conclude that in light of these facts, Philippine judges, in an early stage of national development, were more responsive to the claims of lower class people? Such data, in the words of Donald Kommers, would form a "slender reed" to grasp. Though Samonte and the other comparative researchers in this field engage in this type of guesstimate throughout their work, they do caution their readers to put little stock in it. Yet, in light of what we have seen of the lack of explanatory power in single (and even multiple) background factor studies, to describe these associations by using the verb "tends" is probably to overrate their importance. Yet it is done frequently. The effect of the more important intervening variables (attitudes, etc.) is either ignored or fuzzily inferred, and mention and analysis of the critical conversion process are omitted. Moreover, there is in this sort of work a good deal of precise description of comparative social background for its own sake. In fact, this

---

[42] Samonte, *op. cit.* See also the revised paper, "The Philippine Supreme Court: A Study of Judicial Background Characteristics, Attitudes, and Decision-Making," in *Comparative Judicial Behavior,* ed. Schubert and Danelski.

[43] *Ibid.,* pp. 165–66.

would appear to be true of the portion of Samonte's work that we have just quoted. Though George Gadbois affirms his trust in a significant correlation between some background factors and some judicial tendencies, he at one time forged ahead in his own background study of the Indian Supreme Court simply on the stated premise that "some background data are better than none"[44]—a highly debatable proposition.

Thus, an inventory of the several other comparative judicial politics studies that discuss social backgrounds of judiciaries does not take us very far at this stage of the development of the research. In the main, the analysts have made a few rough stabs at a variety of hypotheses as to what background factors might be related to different types of decisions. I should note that for a variety of indigenously systemic reasons, there has been little inquiry into whether political party identification is as good an indicator of patterns of judicial decison-making in other countries as it is in the United States. But one systemic variation from the American way, the existence of a professional judiciary in European and Japanese legal circles,[45] has led comparative thinkers to believe that previous judicial experience has strong influence on appellate decision-making. The reader may recall the finding of Schmidhauser that prior judicial experience seemed to correlate with a greater "liberal" tendency to repudiate past law on the part of U.S. Supreme Court justices. The comparative studies, contrarily, seem to reveal a different proclivity; that is, that prior judicial experience is related to more "conservative" decision-making in higher level cases.

Fred L. Morrison, for example, in his study of the Swiss Federal Court, has observed a rising professionalization of the highest court in Switzerland in the twentieth century.[46] That is, he notes that more and more of the professional judiciary are being recruited to the highest bench. The effect of this, to Morrison's mind, has been to make judges far more restrained, aliberal, and apolitical. According to Morrison, "this 'professionalization' has been concomitant with a change from judicial activism to one of judi-

---

[44] George Gadbois, "Indian Supreme Court Judges: Their Ascent, Attributes, and Attitudes" (paper delivered at the Shambaugh Conference, October, 1967), p. 29. In its revised form this paper appears as "Selection, Background Characteristics, and Voting Behavior of Indian Supreme Court Judges, 1950–59," in *Comparative Judicial Behavior*, ed. Schubert and Danelski. The revised version does not repeat this notion. Rather Gadbois justifies his study, as do so many others, in terms of a vague theory positing a correlation between these characteristics and the decision-making behavior. What this correlation could possibly mean is not made clear. His data leave it equally unclear.

[45] Although a professional, bureaucratic judiciary exists, some members of the highest court are not drawn from that bureaucracy, but instead come from other areas of legal or political life.

[46] Fred L. Morrison, "The Swiss Federal Court," in *Frontiers of Judicial Research*, ed. Grossman and Tanenhaus.

cial restraint," and has resulted in an abdication of any political leadership in Swiss politics.[47] Furthermore, Samonte reports a similar relationship in the Philippine system (which may be surprising, since the Philippine system is almost a duplicate of that of the United States).[48] And Kommers is in agreement with Arthur von Mehren that in view of the civil service nature of the German judiciary, there should be little wonder that it is "as staid as it is reputed to be" and fails to "attract or encourage the most forceful and energetic personality types."[49]

These findings are consistent with Ulf Torgersen's speculations on the Norwegian judiciary:

> The conservatism of civil servants is not the same as the conservatism of business and industry. It is inevitable that those who have been trained in the public bureaucracy . . . should retain a substantial part of their loyalty to the administration and its political leaders after they reach the bench. Thus, they will look with sympathy upon the government and its legislative program, and they will be extremely reluctant to propose, without the most compelling reasons, that an enacted measure is unconstitutional. As we showed in our analysis of the changes in recruitment patterns, this orientation has probably been intensified by the change in the major components of judicial experience away from the private legal practice and in the direction of the central civil service.[50]

On the other hand, the reader may be surprised to find that Danelski's study of another highly bureaucratic judicial system, that of Japan, shows no such pattern. Of five Supreme Court justices (out of nineteen) who had been judges prior to ascending the final appeal bench, two were "liberal," two were "pragmatic," and one was "conservative" along the lines Danelski defined. Furthermore, a recent six-nation comparison by Welch and Nagel revealed that an overall correlation between prior judicial experience and a liberalism-conservatism factor was "almost zero."[51]

Thus, all things considered, these studies show a good deal of conflict in their findings, and it does not seem to me to be purely a function of varying definitions. Consider, for a moment, the discrepancy between (1) Schmidhauser's findings on the American Supreme Court of a relationship between prior judicial experience and a tendency to overrule precedent and (2) the studies on Switzerland, West Germany, and the Philippines,

[47] *Ibid.*, pp. 156ff.
[48] Samonte, *op. cit.*
[49] Donald Kommers, "The Federal Constitutional Court in West Germany," in *Frontiers of Judicial Research*, ed. Grossman and Tanenhaus, p. 95. The second quotation is from von Mehren, "Judicial Process," p. 216.
[50] Ulf Torgersen, "The Role of the Supreme Court in the Norwegian Political System," in *Judicial Decision-Making*, ed. Schubert, p. 241.
[51] Susan K. Welch and Stuart S. Nagel, "Judicial Behavior on English-Speaking Supreme Courts" (unpublished paper), p. 52.

where prior judicial experience was found to be linked with conservative judicial behavior of various types. Various attempts at explanation meet a host of frustrations. For instance, later on in Chapter 4 the reader will discover a hypothesis that associates judicial independence with a common-law, nonprofessional type of judiciary. But that doesn't help at all in this case, for though the West German and Swiss systems have professional judiciaries, the Philippine system is akin to the American. Thus, the Philippine discrepancy remains unexplained unless one believes that judicial activism is not a very strong indicator of judicial independence—which it is by almost any definition of judicial independence. Moreover, Danelski's cursory look at the Japanese system, which has a professional judiciary, indicates that the Japanese judges with prior judicial experience were liberal; in fact, only one of the five Supreme Court justices studied was classed as making conservative decisions. Thus, it seems only safe to conclude that prior judicial experience, in a comparative sense, does not yet appear to be directly related to any visible pattern of judicial decision-making. Since the American studies have shown such small correlations between background factors and judicial decisional patterns, this should startle no one.

Kommers is probably quite correct, then, in shunting such background factors, *per se*, aside and pointing to another, admittedly gross, intervening factor, i.e., the political system itself as it is set within its own peculiar historical context. This theory posits that the peculiarities of the political system act as a buffer between the judicial decision and any one or more background factors, thus cushioning even moderate influence of background factors on the personal values of the judge and thence on his decisions. That prior judicial experience may indeed indicate conservative decision-making today in Switzerland, but fails to indicate similar conservatism in present-day Japan, is not too amazing when one considers the immediate past historical circumstances and the tremendously different political cultures in which these two highest courts are set. The modern Japanese Supreme Court justice may well see himself acting to integrate a whole new set of laws and political concepts, with little or no precedent, while the Swiss justice may see himself, in his professional capacity, as attempting to apply a very old and sacrosanct line of law and political concepts.

One might wonder, then, whether it is in the interest of future research efficiency to engage in any further storing of background information of foreign judiciaries. If these factors are related so indirectly, if at all, to judicial decision-making, why should we sponsor, for instance, a steady output of background materials on judges of one or another foreign culture? Should we undertake a massive cross-cultural study of *many* societies along these lines? One answer is that it is better to explain a little of something than nothing at all. This can only lead to an outbreak of shrugging among scholars. Another answer is that perhaps such studies might help us understand the degree to which these judiciaries are representative of their own cultures.

Researchers interested in the question of the representativeness of the courts are curious as to whether certain groups are over- or underrepresented. If the judiciary receives a disproportionate share of the spoils of position-holding, what groups are getting the most of what there is to get, and how does this vary, if at all, from society to society? Of course, this type of information can also be associated with the first hypothesis about social backgrounds; that is, group or class membership influences the values and attitudes of its members, and thus influences the judicial decisions of judges as well. If a group predominates, then one can expect decisional patterns favorable to that group. It seems that this set of assumptions and aims underlies the only multiculture study done along these lines—one that, I might add, seems to overlook the many reservations about attitude inference that we have noted.[52]

A glance at what the search for representativeness has uncovered is less than encouraging. All societies set certain standards for ascension to the highest court, or any court, in the land. These qualifications are remarkably similar; thus, universally there is a disproportionate number of lawyers and older people serving as judges. Moreover, the political system, as a reflection of the social system, is frequently geared to putting people of a certain social class into the judiciary. Where there is a professional judiciary, a good number of its members make the highest bench, and as they have risen to the top echelons of the hierarchy, they are always in at least the upper stratum of the middle class. Those who are chosen from outside the judicial hierarchy are also financially well off. In political appointment systems like those of the United States and the Philippines, studies show that the upper and upper middle classes contribute most of the personnel of the courts. Kommers notes, in reviewing a study of the West German lower court system, that only 3.5 percent of the lower court judges (assessors) had fathers in the laboring class.[53] Weyrauch, in another study, has noted that only 2 percent of law students in West Germany in 1962 came from working-class backgrounds.[54] Contrast this with another finding that about 45 percent of the students in a southern state university law school in the

---

[52] Glendon Schubert, "Judges and Political Leadership," in *Political Leadership in Industrialized Societies: Studies in Comparative Analysis,* ed. Lewis Edinger (New York: Wiley, 1967).

[53] Kommers, "Federal Constitutional Court in West Germany," p. 95.

[54] See Walter Weyrauch, *The Personality of Lawyers* (New Haven: Yale University Press, 1964), p. 44, n. 7.

United States came from lower class backgrounds.[55] However, the students themselves would be of far greater pecuniary means by the time they would be appointed or elected to the judiciary.

So much for all this, for the question persists: Of what use is this information? Do we need reams more to show us that certain classes or occupational groups are more highly represented than others? Of what use is the detail? Can the malapportionment of the legal profession and judiciaries (or, for that matter, legislatures) be changed? *Should* they be changed? *Should* laymen, i.e., workers, sit as judges? Aside from the question of the desirability of popular participation, these questions still imply the earlier one, i.e., that concerning the indirect causal implication. For example, Kommers goes on to say, after noting the highly middle-class, civil-service-oriented bulge in the judicial background distribution: "In any case, the available evidence suggests that West German judges are recruited from a very narrow base in the society, and largely from the most conservative . . . sector."[56] Since we are unable to demonstrate the truth of this statement universally or even for any individual society, and all we can do is find, at best, a tenuous, indirect relationship, I wouldn't be overly anxious to finance future diggings of this sort. The yield is rather sparce for the effort it necessitates. There is an awful lot of spading, much tedious sifting, and all too few chunks of gold.

FACTORS OTHER THAN ATTITUDES AND VALUES

Other pioneering studies in judicial politics have supplemented the thinking on attitudes, values, and background, although they have not yet added up to a large-scale contribution. Several factors that have captured some attention are the political considerations made by the justices, the role played by the chief justice, the influence of the personality of a justice, and the effect of judicial reasoning on the judicial decision. As usual, the emphasis has been on the American system, but there has been some significant comparative work as well.

Walter Murphy, though acknowledging the probably strong influence of attitudes upon the decisions of the American Supreme Court, goes much further in attempting to understand comprehensively how the process operates. Among his better known speculations is that the Supreme Court justice exercises a conscious political strategy in arriving at at least some of

55 Robert Agger and Marshall N. Goldstein, "Law Students and Politics: The Rising Elite" (unpublished paper, University of North Carolina Library), p. 6.
56 Donald P. Kommers, "Socialization and Recruitment of West German Constitutional Court Judges" (paper delivered at the Shambaugh Conference, October, 1967), p. 17.

his decisions.[57] In other words, Murphy has freed the Supreme Court justices from an ¡njustice, so to speak. He has helped liberate them (at least analytically) from a certain political irrationality and political impotence imposed upon them by generations of observers, from legalists to scientists. Of course, many other political analysts have been commenting for some time that the Court was playing politics; but Murphy has added a step. The justices now can be visualized as being aware of the Court as a political institution—just like everyone else. Since they are rational people, they would then be thinking in political terms as to the potential effects of their decisions. The comparative studies, up to now, have not observed the courts from this perspective, but it is to be hoped that this will be done in the near future. We have every reason to believe that foreign judges are human and political too.

A more concrete study of the possible influence of other personal factors on the American Supreme Court decision is another essay by Danelski.[58] This article delves into the potential influence of the chief justice on his colleagues. It is a study of the ways in which the Supreme Court chief justice perceives his many-sided role, and it examines the consequences of several variations in that perception. Danelski was the first to classify the various role perceptions that chief justices may entertain. According to him, the chief justice may see himself as a task leader, a social leader, a combination of both, or as neither. Danelski tries to see whether (and if so, to what degree) various chief justices who fit into one or another of these categories brought about certain results on such things as the Supreme Court's cohesion and its productivity. He found that the role of the chief justice, as it varies, has some significance in judicial behavior. On the other hand, because of the differences in systems, it seems likely, as the state of our knowledge now stands, that the American chief justice has unusually great powers. Danelski himself notes the following about the chief justice of the Supreme Court of Japan:

> In conference, attempts are made at persuasion, and at times they are successful. This may be viewed as task-leadership behavior. The concept of task leadership must, however, be understood in a Japanese context. Such leadership in the Court is far more subtle and less aggressive than it is in the Supreme Court of the United States.[59]

This leads us to another factor, the effect of the personality of the judge on the judicial process and the judicial decision. Jerome Frank's *Law and*

---

[57] See particularly his *Elements of Judicial Strategy* (Chicago: University of Chicago Press, 1964).

[58] "The Influence of the Chief Justice in the Decisional Process," in *Courts, Judges, and Politics,* ed. Walter Murphy and C. Herman Pritchett (New York: Random House, 1961), pp. 497–508.

[59] Danelski, "The Supreme Court of Japan," in *Comparative Judicial Behavior,* ed. Schubert and Danelski, p. 135.

the Modern Mind was the first serious discussion of this relationship, though Cardozo had opened the matter previously.[60] Frank was a great believer in Freudian psychology, and he applied a good deal of psychoanalytic theory to the behavior of judges. It is not surprising, then, that we find him suggesting that judges would do themselves and their society much good if they would submit themselves to psychoanalysis before assuming the bench.[61] Additionally, he felt that courts ought to have psychoanalysts on call each day should a judge feel particularly aggressive some morning and crave a bit of counseling. One of Frank's key theoretical points was that the person who strives toward success through the role of judge probably has a peculiar type of personality. Such a man yearns for the security of relying on the law and thus masks and relieves many personal problems and frustrations in acting as a sentencer of other men.

Though the notion of personality occasionally surfaces in contemporary theorizing about the causes of judicial decisions, it is still not a very popular or deeply researched theory. In the main, it is given lip service or brushed over lightly.

There have been a few recent attempts by some political scientists to think about the possible import of personality in working out a general theory of the judicial decision. Danelski is the first to try to adapt the work of another major social-psychoanalytical theorist (Karen Horney) to the study of judicial decision-making.[62] Horney identified three distinct personality types: (1) the compliant, (2) the aggressive, and (3) the detached. Each type is a syndrome of various behaviors, and of course no one person fits into any single category all of the time. Still, most people act out the behaviors included in one category far more often than any of the others. In continuing his analysis of chief justices in terms of their leadership styles, Danelski surmises that it is only the compliant personality that makes a man (a chief justice) "assert social leadership and at the same time makes it difficult for him to assert task leadership." On the other hand, the exercise of task leadership by a justice would probably be a function of his having a "mild to moderate aggressive" personality. Thus, Danelski is saying that the degree of cohesion and productivity of any court could well be a consequence of the particular personality mix of the personnel of the court at any given time.

Glendon Schubert has also tried his hand at ascertaining the possible influence of personality on attitudes and values.[63] Upon consulting his

---

[60] Jerome Frank, *Law and the Modern Mind* (New York: Coward-McCann, 1930); Benjamin N. Cardozo, *The Nature of the Judicial Process* (New Haven: Yale University Press, 1921).

[61] Jerome Frank, *Courts on Trial* (Princeton: Princeton University Press, 1949).

[62] David J. Danelski, "Conflict and Its Resolution in the Supreme Court," *Journal of Conflict Resolution*, 11 (March, 1967), pp. 71–86.

[63] Glendon Schubert, *The Judicial Mind* (Evanston, Ill.: Northwestern University Press, 1965), p. 259.

multitude of tables, figures, charts, and diagrams, Schubert concludes that in addition to the operation of the attitudes of liberalism and conservatism, he can see the influence of what he calls "pragmatism/dogmatism," a personality factor much like Milton Rokeach's "open/close mindedness"[64] and Hans Eysenck's "tender/tough mindedness."[65] As Martin Shapiro has remarked, these methods are far more "suggestive than conclusive."[66] Shapiro is kind.

Danelski continued his speculations about the effect of personality upon the role perceptions of chief justices in his study of the Japanese Supreme Court. Particularly important is the Japanese desire to resolve ostensible disharmony as quickly and informally as possible.[67] Thus, Danelski is thinking along the lines of the Schubertian hypothesis that establishes linkages among culture, attitude, and behavior, except that here the attitudinal variable is of a personality type.

Kommers ponders the same relationship in his study of the West German courts. In concordance with E. J. Cohn[68] and Arthur von Mehren,[69] Kommers believes that the German national character has established a legal-judicial system that attracts and reinforces a certain personality set, and that such a personality is, to say the most for it, not overly open-minded. "It is not difficult to see how stifling this system of advancement can be to motivation and imagination, and how it may lead to a deadening conservatism. And the norms of the civil service appear to predominate."[70] Or in Cohn's words:

> The judiciary forms in effect a civil-service-type career holding out security of tenure, statutory independence (which in practice is

---

[64] Milton Rokeach, *The Open and Closed Mind* (New York: Basic Books, 1960).
[65] Hans J. Eysenck, *The Psychology of Politics* (London: Routledge & Kegan Paul, 1954).
[66] Martin Shapiro, "Political Jurisprudence," *Kentucky Law Journal*, 52 (Winter, 1964), p. 329.
[67] Danelski cites Nabutaka Ike, *Japanese Politics* (New York: Knopf, 1957), on this point. Ike states:

Many people are prevented by training and social custom from saying what they think and of revealing their real and innermost feelings and thoughts. The pressure for social harmony and for outward unanimity is too strong. Individuals who grow to maturity in such an environment must learn to fathom another's thoughts, feelings, and intentions by reading between the lines, by observing indirect signs, and by resorting to a kind of intuitive process [p. 267].

For a similar view, see Takeyoshi Kawashima's unpublished paper, "The Notion of Law, Right, and Social Order in Japan." Professor Kawashima is a leading Japanese sociologist.
[68] E. J. Cohn, "The German Attorney—Experiences with a Unified Profession," *International and Comparative Law Quarterly*, 9 (October, 1960), pp. 580–99. See especially p. 590.
[69] Arthur von Mehren, "The Judicial Process," p. 216.
[70] Kommers, "Socialization and Recruitment," p. 16.

somewhat less imposing than in theory, owing to numerous rules of detail and traditional habits and arrangements), a reasonable, though not outstanding, social rank and the power to adjudicate upon the failings and disputes of one's fellow men. It is obvious that the type of young men who feel allured by prospects such as these will as a rule not belong to either the most brilliant or to the most strong-willed type.[71]

Kommers also seems to believe that the German legal education system both supports and is in turn reinforced by this bureaucratic-personality interaction. In contrast to the American system of exchanges of questions and answers ("bullfight between student and teacher"), the German student sits and listens "to an omniscient professor reading from his notes." In other words, the generally authoritative characteristics of the culture are seen to saturate the legal-judicial system as well.

On the other hand, Kommers' views seem to be disputed by another American observer who did a good deal of interviewing of German lawyers, jurists, and scholars. According to Walter Weyrauch:

> The first group of lawyers, expressing firm belief in the rules of logic and abstract principles, appeared to consist of power-centered and conservative individuals, aggressively and successfully pursuing their careers with conventional means. . . . *Only a few judges fitted into this category*. The second group of lawyers, stressing the function of intuition, were probably power-oriented too, though in a less dynamic fashion. . . . There was a preponderance of judges, irrespective of age, whereas practicing attorneys presumably felt that they were in no position to rely on hunches.[72]

With both Kommers and Weyrauch using open-ended interview schedules, their disagreement might lie only in their definition of conservativeness. Nevertheless, an area of possible disagreement remains. This underlines the need for much more research in this entire area, and adds great weight to the argument that the research methods need far more standardization— or at least far more rigor.

The judge's reasoning also has its effect on the judicial decision. The notion of judicial role, of course, posits that the judge will do his best to apply and reason from existent and clearly relevant law in the resolution of the dispute before him. American political science has done very little to pinpoint just how large a factor this is in judicial decision-making. The American political scientist is really no more knowledgeable about this today than he was many years ago. For instance, in meticulously documenting the fact that judges change their minds over time ("fluidity of choice")

---

[71] Cohn, "The German Attorney," p. 590.
[72] Weyrauch, *op. cit.*, pp. 184–85 (emphasis mine).

for apparently a whole host of reasons, J. Woodford Howard points out that an explanation totally in terms of attitudes or ideology is hopelessly inept. On the other hand, Howard also notes that "the evidence of the 1940's lends greater support to the lawyer's ideal of the judicial process as a system of reasoning than many legal realists would accept."[73] But just how much do personal factors, group factors, or legal reasoning factors account for judicial decisions and in what types of cases and at what levels of litigation? Just how rational is the judicial process?[74] When is the judicial process more rational than not? Nowadays, just about everyone is joining the Golden Mean Club, whose motto is that personal factors, particularly personal attitudes, have some effect; but so does precedent, so does legal reasoning. Yet, aside from the few first faltering attempts to measure judicial role mentioned in the previous chapter, one man's guess as to how much and when is as good as another's.

As poorly as we have fared in answering such questions and thus building theory about the factoral interactions, we have even less to show on more important questions. What relevance, for instance, has this knowledge—such theory—for political science? Are there any broader questions that the discovery of the precise nature of the judicial decision-making process might help to answer? Does the current research help us phrase these larger questions more explicitly? Can and has it provided any answers?

Relevance to Political Science:
Toward a General Theory of Decision-Making

Shall we continue the kind of work discussed in the first part of this chapter solely in deference to the principle of knowledge for the sake of knowledge? If so, there is nothing further to discuss. This work, if left to its own momentum, probably will increase our knowledge of the factors that, to varying degrees, under a variety of conditions, produce different types of judicial decisions. Even if this new information helps no one else and answers no questions in a broader empirical context or within any normative context, researchers can rest easy in the assurance that they are in-

---

[73] J. Woodford Howard, "On the Fluidity of Judicial Choice," *American Political Science Review,* 62 (March, 1968), p. 55.

[74] For a recent philosophical explication of this point, see selections 5, 8, 9, 10, and 11 in *Rational Decision,* ed. Carl Friedrich, Nomos VII (New York: Atherton Press, 1965). Another way in which this same basic argument is presented is in terms of judicial activism v. judicial restraint. See Wallace Mendelson, *The Supreme Court: Law and Discretion* (Indianapolis: Bobbs-Merrill, 1967). See also Martin Shapiro, *Law and Politics in the Supreme Court* (New York: Free Press, Macmillan, 1964).

creasing knowledge for its own sake. However, some may object that this is not in itself worthwhile. Hackles have been known to rise at such a bare-faced empiricism. Perhaps, then, it will help to muse aloud over other potential values of this work.

Herbert Simon, in introducing his widely respected book *Administrative Behavior,* discussed the justification for the development of administrative science.[75] By and large, those who would scientifically study the administrative decision-making process are interested in how "rationally" the decisions are made. This concept dovetails neatly with that of efficiency, which is central to evaluating administrative behavior for itself. Men wish to learn whether agencies are distributing the values they are supposed to in the most effective and economical fashion—most rationally—and frequently this is assayable in quantitative terms: cost efficiency. Are the administrators getting the most, in terms of time and money, out of their employees and their budget allotments? Are they processing data in the shortest time? Are they using the most parsimonious and accurate methods of data interpretation? Do their routines expedite the distribution of their services or goods most quickly and with least waste?

Naturally there are far more difficult problems when one begins to grade efficiency beyond the confines of the specific bureaucratic boundary and starts to think within a broader framework. For instance, though highly efficient in internal terms—or even in terms of the distribution of these values allotted to them to allocate—an organization's very efficiency may cause resentments among its clientele. Its by-product may be a large dose of dysfunction. Might there not be a strong relationship between high bureaucratic efficiency and low public morale? Businesses may have been extremely efficient in their indifference to their surrounding areas while maximizing their profits, but they may thereby have sown the seeds for the incapacitation or destruction of American cities by urban guerrillas. How efficient were they, then, in this grander context? But this need not concern us here and now. What does concern us is the more limited concept of organizational efficiency, for this concept happens to be a highly explicable criterion and is of greatest importance to the organization itself. Thus, what ought to be researched from the point of view of organizations is clear and its practicality is immediately established. It is the attempt to discover how efficient organizations are that keeps the administrative science labs humming with activity. Is the same true for the study of the judicial decision-making process? The answer must be both yes and no. Yes, the judicial decision-making process can be studied for much the same reasons, but no, it is not being studied in this way today.

---

[75] Herbert Simon, *Administrative Behavior* (Glencoe, Ill.: Free Press, 1957).

It is often stated that what the judiciary administers is justice. Whether or not the courts do this efficiently within the context of the administrative process of the judicial system would not seem to be easily measurable. After all, the ordinary governmental agencies administer programs—there is identifiable and quantifiable output that is expected and the results can be measured against the expectations. Similarly, businesses work for profit. This, too, is readily ascertainable and readily auditable. Such is hardly the case with the output of courts. How could we look to see if justice was administered efficiently? True, one might measure justice by defining it in a highly specific and measurable way. For example, one could define it as being closely related to the degree of delay a person encounters in getting to and through trial.[76] The longer it takes and the more it costs, the less likely it is that the poorer among us have an equal chance at the "artichoke of justice."[77] However, it seems clear that such data have little or nothing to do with the "black box" research that modern political science has carried out on the courts. How can such psychological and sociological approaches toward understanding the influences of judicial decisions be related to the more significant question of whether justice is administered efficiently, as we have been using the term? On its face, such research would seem to be related to efficiency very tenuously, if at all. Scratching that surface, though, one can find substantial relationship—and it is this very connection that is the basis for an original dialogue between the study of judicial decision-making and all other areas of governmental decision-making.

What if the research on judicial decision-making reveals that, despite all the institutional safeguards, plus all the legal research, plus all the courtroom polemics, judges do to a very large extent decide on the basis of their personal general attitudes and policy attitudes? What if we find out unmistakably that despite the theory and the paraphernalia of impartiality, there is precious little objectivity in fact? What justification would there be in all the cumbersomeness inherent in these procedures, and in all the concomitant delay? Why bear the burden of expense and the injustice of delay if there is little constraint of personal attitudes in the judicial role—in the judicial structure? Wouldn't it be far simpler to develop much less formal administrative hearings? Of course this begs the vital question: How much attitude constraint is there in various administrative roles? Therefore,

---

[76] Hans Zeisel, Harry Kalven, Jr., and Bernard Buchholz, *Delay in the Court* (Boston: Little, Brown, 1959). See Preface: "We became increasingly aware of the critical importance of the delay problem to the integrity of the administration of justice" (p. vii).

[77] James Davies coined this delicious metaphor, which just goes to show that justice appears differently to each beholder. To me it is an onion (having no heart and compelling him who would strip it to cry). To Martin Diamond it is a prickly pear (succulent once you get beneath the surface).

judicial decision-making specialists ought to conceive of research along such comparative lines. Their own research, as it now stands, can answer no such question by itself. We are capable of designing relevant research; that is the yes. We have not done so; that is the no.

Those who study other areas of governmental decision-making (or any organizational decision-making) almost completely ignore the study of judicial decision-making.[78] This is despite the fact that the court is an administrative agency by dint of the fact that it interprets and applies laws. Courts administer laws for and to the people; for and to the rulers as well. Whether and the degree to which the judicial factor has *any* operating effect in the process is the province of the judicial behaviorialists to answer in the context of several questions that have been and will be discussed throughout this book. Whether the judicial factor is different in kind from other attitude-constraining factors in decision-making bodies, or whether, if it is the same in kind, it is more or less effective, is the province of all those who are interested in developing a theory of decision-making.[79]

No matter what decision-making process is under scrutiny, researchers are vitally interested in understanding the effectiveness of personal attitudes and personality-constraining role factors. Certainly the judges are worried about being impartial and objective and adhering to *stare decisis.* Is this any less a constraint (in principle or in reality) than the foreign-policy-maker's concern with satisfying the "validators"[80] or with "honoring our commitments"? Is it any less than the administrator's concern with remaining detached and following the past policies of the agency? How does it differ, for instance, from Lindblom's concept of "successive limited com-

---

[78] Simon, for one, never mentions the judicial decision-making process in *Administrative Behavior,* and in the leading omnibus survey of research on organizations we find chapters on the military, political parties, unions, prisons, hospitals, and public bureaucracy, but none on the judiciary. See James March, ed., *Handbook of Organizations* (Chicago: Rand McNally, 1965).

[79] William Gore's highly abstract categories, which are not at all concerned with or based on any data related to judiciaries, seem to me to be quite pertinent to the study of judicial decision-making. They are (1) perception, (2) evaluative set, (3) estimation of consequences, and (4) manuever for position. See his *Administrative Decision-Making* (New York: Wiley, 1964).

[80] See Robert C. Noel, "Internation Simulation Participants' Manual," in Harold Guetzkow, *et al., Simulation in International Relations* (Englewood Cliffs, N.J.: Prentice-Hall, 1963). The definition of validators is as follows:

The validators are conceived as those individuals in the political system who occupy positions of power outside the immediate purview of top level governmental decision-making power. The validators have wants and goals which are more or less satisfied by the outcomes of governmental decisions. Because they occupy positions of power in the system they are able to make their satisfactions and/or dissatisfactions felt by the central decision-maker (CDM). If they are satisfied, they will support his tenure in office. If they are not satisfied, on the other hand, they will support the efforts of an aspiring decision maker (CDM$_a$) to acquire office [p. 47].

parisons" in describing administrative decision-making, or from the concept of incrementalism?[81] Is it any different in quality or quantity than state legislators' deference to their constituencies' expressed desires when these are contrary to their own preferences (Wahlke and Eulau's concept of legislative "delegate"), or James Barber's finding that some legislators see themselves as arbitrators?[82] Are these various role conceptions different, and if so, how? Is the behavior different, and if so, how? Are the behaviors more or less consistent with the role? Let me offer another example. The judge frequently resorts to the concept of justice in his role conception. How similar or dissimilar is this to the foreign-policy-maker's conception of the national interest or the administrator's concept of either the public interest or our old friend efficiency? In other words, to what extent are these equally rationalizations of the decision, rather than reasons for it? These are questions of essential concern across the decision-making board, and research in all these areas must begin to account for its failure to answer them.

I know of no study that scientifically compares the personal attitudes, role expectations, and substantive content of decisions of legislators, administrators, and judges. This is a field of exploration as yet unentered by students of either American politics or comparative politics. Stuart Nagel, in one part of an intricate study of comparative attitudes and decisions of a large grab bag of American and English officials, did make this remark:

> The personal attitudes of administrators and legislators also undoubtedly influence their decisions, but how much in comparison with that of judges? No attitude-decision study seems to have been made with administrators, but Warren Miller and Donald Stokes have made such a study with Congressmen. They found that there was a + .57 correlation between the diverse attitudes of Congressmen and their roll call voting behavior in social welfare controversies. This correlation is substantially higher than the correlations found between the attitudes of judges and their decisional voting behavior. The difference probably results from the greater restraints which law and tradition place on the personalized voting of judges as contrasted to legislators, although

---

[81] Charles E. Lindblom, "The Science of Muddling Through," in *The Making of Decisions*, ed. William J. Gore and J. W. Dyson (New York: Free Press, Macmillan, 1964), p. 155. Lindblom, though never mentioning the judiciary, does discuss the "incremental" nature of administrative decision-making. Martin Shapiro, however, has seen the relationship between this concept in administrative processes and the judicial processes. See his "Stability and Change in Judicial Decision-Making: Incrementalism or *Stare Decisis*," *Law in Transition Quarterly* (Winter, 1965), pp. 134–57. Also see his *The Supreme Court and Administrative Agencies* (New York: Free Press, Macmillan, 1968), pp. 54–55. Shapiro, however, takes much of the apparent similarity at face value. Cf. Richard Cyert and James March, *A Behavioral Theory of the Firm* (Englewood Cliffs, N.J.: Prentice-Hall, 1963); Aaron Wildavsky, *Politics of the Budgetary Process* (Boston: Little, Brown, 1964).

[82] John C. Wahlke *et al.*, *The Legislative System* (New York: Wiley, 1962); James Barber, *The Law Makers* (New Haven: Yale University Press, 1965).

legislators are restrained by party and constituency pressures which sometimes conflict with their personal attitudes.[83]

However, Nagel was comparing data from two different studies (his and the one by Miller and Stokes), and he made no attempt to get at the role conceptions held by the individual respondents. Unfortunately, his guesses are not data. This is more of a stumble than a start along the lines I have outlined.

The tone of this chapter has been less than enthusiastic about the accomplishments of the men who are moving ahead in developing judicial theory and science. I hope, though, that this does not diminish their value in the eyes of other political scientists because, in all candor, I do not feel that their achievements are much the theoretical less than the accomplishments of those working in other areas of governmental decision-making. For instance, those who would develop a rigorous theory of foreign-policy decision-making have not moved too far ahead in either operationalizing their concepts or building solid empirical and validated bases for sound inductions to even a middle level of abstraction. William Coplin, for one, believes that though there have been several conceptual schemes with the capacity to guide case studies or rigorous experimental work on comparative foreign-policy-making, they have not generated enough research to advance actual knowledge very far on the ways in which foreign-policy decisions are made. The schemes he specifically includes are the theoretical works of such as Richard Snyder, James Rosenau, Feliks Gross, and George Modelski.[84] With some dismay, Coplin sees the empirical development of his field as "rudimentary" and research attempts at understanding the psychological and sociological factors effecting foreign-policy-making as "rare."[85] Similarly, Lester Grinspoon, in one of the Craigville Papers, was uncomplimentary to the general development of theory of governmental decision-making. According to him, "Although improvements have been made in all these theories and techniques, even the optimistic decision

---

[83] Stuart S. Nagel, "Judicial Attitudes and Those of Legislators and Administrators" (paper delivered at the annual meeting of the American Political Science Association, Washington, D.C., 1962). Nagel is referring to Stokes and Miller's "Constituency Influence in Congress," *American Political Science Review*, 57 (March, 1963), pp. 45–56.

[84] Richard C. Snyder, N. W. Bruck, and Burton Sapin, *Foreign Policy Decision Making* (New York: Free Press, Macmillan, 1962); James Rosenau, "Pre-Theories and Theories of Foreign Policy," in *Approaches to Comparative and International Politics*, ed. R. Barry Farrell (Evanston, Ill.: Northwestern University Press, 1966); George Modelski, *A Theory of Foreign Policy* (New York: Praeger, 1962); Feliks Gross, *Foreign Policy Analysis* (New York: Philosophical Library, 1954).

[85] William D. Coplin, "Bibliographical Essay on Foreign Policy Decision-Making," in his *Introduction to International Politics* (Boston: Little, Brown, forthcoming). Coplin's résumé of the work in this area makes it clear that the judicial decision-making scholars are not too far behind.

theorist recognizes that exact understanding of how decisions are made remains obscure."[86]

It seems to me that those who are interested in understanding decision-making are too preoccupied with their own self-restricted bailiwicks. In and of itself, the research on one or another of the decision-making bodies is extraordinarily parochial. For political science, the significance of this approach is not in understanding the intricate working of every conceivable factor within the tight boundaries of one type of organ; the significance for political science is in understanding the variation in output as a function of structural variations (if any) in the decision-making processes. This can best be done by research that builds elements of this variation into the design *explicitly*. Survey methods and experimental methodology in particular are well up to the task.[87] What has been done thus far in judicial decision-making research has at best been a tiny step in helping develop a theory of judicial decision-making, which is, I am sorry to say, pretty uninteresting in and of itself. Until wider latitudes, briefly touched upon here, are explored, judicial science and administrative science can have only very limited practical and theoretical significance.

In summary, my argument has been that the previous studies of judicial behavior have missed the mark by failing to focus attention on the importance of judicial structure and function. While attitudinal and background studies have been helpful in breaking new ground in judicial research, they have only limited value in the development of systematic political theory. Work along judicial behavioral lines has yet to highlight its relation to general decision-making theory, and it is too broad for testing all but a smattering of low-level hypotheses that might be useful in judging the efficacy of courts in political systems. I have suggested that this theoretical weakness can be relieved by centering attention on the judicial role of the court.

---

[86] Lester Grinspoon, "Interpersonal Constraints and the Decision-Maker," in *International Conflict and Behavioral Science,* ed. Roger Fisher (New York: Basic Books, 1964), p. 238.

[87] For an excellent survey of experimental research done on the effect of variation of decision-making structure on outputs, see Charles G. Moore, "Simulation of Organizational Decision-Making," in *Simulation in the Study of Politics,* ed. William D. Coplin (Chicago: Markham, 1968). Unfortunately, the only study on a governmental decision included was of preparation and approval of budgets in city governments. There are no simulations of which I am aware that handle decision-making in reference to norms as a distinct variable. The only controlled experiment where norms were a key variable (though there was no separate third-party deciding in relationship to the norms) was the Penthouse work at Berkeley. Two lengthy monographs are relevant: Thomas A. Cowan, Donald A. Strickland, *et al., The Legal Structure of a Confined Microsociety* (*A Report on the Cases of Penthouse II and III*), Internal Working Paper No. 34 (Berkeley: Space Sciences Laboratory, University of California, August, 1965); Walter Weyrauch, *The Law of a Small Group,* Internal Working Paper No. 54 (Berkeley: Space Sciences Laboratory, University of California, 1967).

The court, when studied from the perspective of role, becomes an important structure or subsystem within the political system. As such it can be subjected to systems analysis in terms of its inputs and outputs and in terms of its impact on the environment. By using role theory I have demarcated what is functionally unique about courts and have helped to fill out the skeleton systems of Easton, Almond, and others. Thus judicial role is important for theory building because it fits so well into general systems theory and provides a useful comparative tool for generating testable propositions.

CHAPTER 3

WHETHER THERE ARE COURTS OR NOT: CAUSES AND CONSEQUENCES

> Indeed, I need not hesitate to declare that only the act of judgment which transforms the defendant into a condemned man truly confers the accolade of justice. There can be nothing nobler, nothing greater, nothing more sublime than the condemnation of a man to death. Therefore I now pronounce this sentence.
>
> —FRIEDRICH DUERRENMATT
> *Traps*

THE MAJOR DIFFERENCE between discussing the causes of the judicial decision and the causes of courts is that the former connote degrees of "judicialness" and the latter the very first appearance of it. This chapter will deal with the second area, at least as far as causes are concerned. Thus, our present focus will be on the conditions for the court/no-court variation. There is now sufficient literature on this topic to treat at some length and substantial practical justification as well.

The second part of this chapter will take up a macro-analysis of several political functions of the court/no-court variation. I shall look to see whether courts are necessary in ways they are said to be. As courts are conceptualized in this chapter, there is no room left for degrees of judicial structure as related to degrees of functioning. As we go along I shall discuss whether courts are necessary for (1) the preservation of order, (2) the maintenance of democracy, and (3) the administration of justice. I shall not, however, discuss whether more or less emphasis on courts in a society brings about more or less democracy. In self-defense let me point out that the literature on this topic rarely speaks in relative terms along these lines, and I am addressing myself to that body of work.

Court as a Dependent Variable:
The Preconditions of Courts

The fact that there is so very little thought and less research along these lines could be considered somewhat surprising. After all, as the reader will see, there has been a good deal of thought about the necessity of courts in society; that is, their necessary impact, their function. When something is so universally considered essential, one might reasonably expect that there must also be a good deal of thought given to what brings this phenomenon about in the first place; but this is not the case.

Yet the paucity of such thinking is quite understandable. It is clear that the sum of thinking about the importance of courts in society has been done by scholars who live in societies with developed legal systems. They see their own systems at work. A few might think about comparing their systems with others, but for the most part they are simply concerned with the operations of their own. It is quite understandable (though not necessarily pardonable) that these scholars are prone to overgeneralize about the impact of courts in general from observation of their own and a few similar court systems. It is even more easily understandable that these scholars would ignore systems that have no courts. Since they ignore them, as well as even the *possibility* of a society without courts, it is altogether comprehensible that so little theory has been forthcoming about the preconditions for courts. This is not so much lofty contempt as it is sheer egocentrism.

There may even be some reluctance on the part of scholars to classify certain societies as courtless. There is a tendency, in fact, to lean toward notions of "quasi courts" and the like, or to call certain administrative structures that have *some* judicial elements "courts," even though they lack other features also commonly associated with that distinctive type of decision-making body. For instance, if Jerome Alan Cohen is correct in his description of the current criminal processes in the People's Republic of China and the Soviet Union, then it would seem best to classify the former as courtless and the latter as having at least the legal prerequisites of a judicial structure.[1] Communist China, by Cohen's own description, fails to maintain even the basic legal requirement that there be a reasonably specific code to guide the decisions of the judges. Moreover, if Cohen is correct, there would appear to be much dictation of decision from the party and administrative hierarchy. Lastly, the trial is almost nonexistent; that is, there is no public airing of evidence through an adversary system. Though

---

[1] Jerome Alan Cohen, "The Criminal Process in China," in *Soviet and Chinese Communism*, ed. Donald W. Treadwell (Seattle: University of Washington Press, 1967). See also his *Criminal Process in the People's Republic of China, 1949–63* (Cambridge: Harvard University Press, 1968).

this situation also seems to characterize accurately the Soviet system of earlier years as seen by Western observers, Cohen notes that:

> When the Soviet Union undertakes to rationalize its criminal law and to clarify some of its prescriptions, abolishes the doctrine of analogy, and requires publication of all national laws and decrees of general consequence, it is beginning to move its criminal law in a direction that is significantly different from that of a China that declines to take such actions. Similarly, when the Soviet regime establishes the procurator's supervision of investigation by the state security agencies, expands the scope of the pre-trial activities of defense counsel, enhances the role of public trial, and inveighs against party interference with the adjudication of individual cases, it is moving its criminal procedure in a direction that is significantly different from that of a China that shrivels the powers of the procurator, generally dispenses with both public trials and defense counsel, and preaches and practices party control over individual cases.[2]

If Cohen's description is accurate, one should have no difficulty in classifying mainland China today as courtless. This is not shocking if one takes Chinese history into account. Apparently there was no court system under the Manchu dynasty either, and justice was administered, as today, by an administrative process that had only a few of the characteristics by which I have defined court.[3] Although Sybille van der Sprenkel does speak of a "judicial process" existing in China during the Manchu dynasty, her description more befits an administrative hearing; the major purpose was not so much to find guilt or innocence as it was to keep the peace. For instance, she informs us that there were several factors that militated against judicial impartiality:

1. The administrative magistrates were not lawyers.
2. It was in their interest to resolve the issue at any cost, as failure to do so would be construed by administrative superiors as a failure to keep order in the area.
3. Magistrates' fees came from the fines they imposed. (See *Tumey* v. *Ohio* in the Appendix to Chapter 4.)
4. "Another reason for reluctance within the *yamen* to pursuing crimes impartially was fear of personal reprisals by influential local families, some of whose members, if they held official office,

---

[2] *Ibid.*, pp. 140–41. I wish to caution the reader that I quote this material as an example of an American scholar's view of the criminal process in mainland China. This sort of evidence must be used currently only because it is the only evidence to which we have access. However, I think it fair to remind the reader that Cohen has not himself observed the phenomena he describes. The descriptive material is a synthesis of numerous interviews conducted with Chinese people who, I would suspect, have defected from their country. Such informants are not the most reliable that a social scientist can hope to interview.

[3] Sybille van der Sprenkel, *Legal Institutions in Manchu China* (London: Athlone Press, University of London, 1962).

would almost certainly out-rank the local magistrate"[4] (lack of independence).

Although van der Sprenkel does observe that there was an occasional magistrate who was more interested in working justice than in prosecuting offenders and lining his own pockets, there is still no evidence that any notions of impartiality were cherished; there was no judicial role. Indeed, it is her contention that the underlying assumption was that courts should be extremely harsh and the legal process basically unfair, since that would discourage the use of them.

This was equally so in the Ch'ing dynasty.[5] In any event, one of the principal reasons for finding those societies in which no courts exist is that we must do so if we are ever to understand what factors and conditions are prerequisite to the establishment and maintenance of courts.

It might be claimed by some of the more erudite among us that some of the greatest political thinkers of all times have made speculations very much along these lines. In a way, this claim has a kernel of truth to it. However, drastically varying philosophical viewpoints and teleologies of these Grand Observers have made their perspectives extremely disparate and the objects of their attentions greatly divergent. Their contribution, then, is vague wisdom; it is very difficult to apply in our attempt to comprehend how courts have developed, when they have developed at all.

Consider Aristotle on this topic. In *Politics,* he discusses causes of the development of courts only by implication.[6] When he discusses conditions that underlie political structures, he treats only whole political systems; only by deduction or inference is it possible to reach the conclusion that this is meant to include the judicature as well. By way of example, when Aristotle states that the size of a society is at least partially responsible for the division of governmental functions, can one assume that he means to say that the size of the society is responsible for that structural offshoot labeled judicial?[7] One can so assume, but one needn't. One can take his

---

[4] *Ibid.,* p. 73.

[5] "The magistrate heard all cases in his area. . . . But he was more than a judge. He not only conducted hearings and made decisions; he also conducted investigations and inquests, and detected criminals. In terms of modern concepts his duties combined those of judge, prosecutor, police chief and coroner" (T'ung-tsu Ch'ü, *Local Government in China under the Ch'ing* [Cambridge: Harvard University Press, 1962], p. 116). This held true in traditional China as well. See T'ung-tsu Ch'ü, *Law and Society in Traditional China* (Paris: Mouton, 1965), pp. 275–76.

[6] Aristotle, *Politics and Athenian Constitution,* ed. and trans. John Warrington (London: Dent, 1959).

[7] In discussing any constitution, particularly those of small states, it is more important to ask what kind and number of magistracies are necessary to a state's existence, and what kind (even though not necessary) help to make a good constitution. In large states it is possible for each individual function to be in the hands of a separate magistracy; the size of the population insures a plentiful supply of eligible candidates for office, and thereby

statement as a major premise, supply the obvious minor one, and conclude the inevitable; or one can simply take it as an abstraction that contains what one wishes to find.

Much the same holds true for John Locke. Locke, in his second "Treatise of Government," spends next to no time on the causes of anything other than the revolutionary movement from tacit, filial acquiescence to a conscious choice of government in general, or at least some particular form of government.[8] Truly, one might say that Locke's philosophy includes some theorizing about the impact of growing wealth and/or complexity of society on evolving government. According to him, a great increase in "ambition" and "luxury" can allow the people to see when government functions for its own sake and not for the people. At that point, a conscious change could be sought, and the legislature, executive, and other administrative units could be constructed.[9] Once again, these other units *could* be courts, but this is not spelled out. I think it fair to say that this is representative of the entire fare on courts among the more widely respected political philosophers of the days of yore.

A few more modern writers, however, have been specifically interested in preconditions of the judicial structure. One in particular, William Seagle, has speculated at great length on this subject.[10] Perhaps his most sophisticated theoretical contribution stipulates the factors of "societal complexity" and the populousness of the society as being independent variables preconditioning the existence of courts. According to Seagle, "Men put the accent on procedure when they go to law against strangers."[11] This occurs, in his view, when the society loses its foundation of kinship bonds and gravitates toward more impersonal relations as the size and complexity of the social milieu increases.

Glendon Schubert has forged a similar theory about the emergence of the judicial structure. He concludes, upon scanning some relevant literature in this area, that "the need for courts is a direct function of the concentra-

---

enables some offices to be held by the same person at very long intervals or only once in his lifetime. Besides being possible, it is *desirable* that this should be so; for a task is always carried out more efficiently when the man responsible can give it his undivided attention. A different situation arises in small states, where numerous functions must be concentrated in the hands of a few individuals. . . . I grant that small states do sometimes need the same magistracies as large ones, and the same laws governing their tenure and administration. But the point is that large states need those magistracies most of the time" [*ibid.*, p. 127].

[8] John Locke, *Two Treatises of Government,* ed. Peter Laslett (Cambridge: At the University Press, 1963).

[9] *Ibid.*, p. 361 (section III of the second treatise).

[10] William Seagle, *The Quest for Law* (New York: Knopf, 1941); see especially chap. 8.

[11] *Ibid.*, p. 92.

tion of people and wealth,"[12] and he points to the fact that the Cheyenne Indians, a nomadic tribe, had no need for courts, but that the Barotse, as subsistence farmers, did.[13] Once people stop wandering about the landscape, up go the courts. Factors such as industrialization and urbanization, he believes, are responsible only for *variations* in judicial structure, not for the very *existence* of a court system itself.[14]

Seagle and Schubert seem to be in substantial agreement about what factors are necessary to the establishment of a court system, but they do not appear to be completely in accord about the dynamics concomitant to these factors. Their theories raise a question as to whether (1) ecological relationships that are dependent on economics, or (2) social systemic disruptions, as dependent on economics, are proximate causal factors behind the development of a court structure. Whatever the case, both Seagle and Schubert isolate much the same factors as do those scholars interested primarily in the development of a certain formalization and/or rationalization of legal codes, e.g., Sir Henry Maine, Emile Durkheim, Henry Wigmore.[15]

Interest in courtless societies and the birth of courts is not simply the manifestation of a desire to satisfy idle curiosity about smaller, less developed or ancient societies. Some of the contemporary work is motivated by the gravity of our present world condition. Some academicians are seriously worried over the persistently chaotic state of the international system. They are concerned over the fact that individual nations act like individual men in Hobbes's "state of nature." They fear, at this stage of nuclear technology, that a war of all men against all men might be totally disastrous to Western civilization as we know it, if not to all mankind. *Dr. Strangelove* comes too close for comfort. Thus, some of the current appeal of this topic is related to the long-standing hope of many men to see some kind of international court (would the Court of International Justice fit within my definition of court, set out in the Introduction to Part A?) which would be capable of maximizing peaceful and final resolutions of conflict, thus helping to preserve humanity. They have decided to look into any courtless societies that might exist—or that have existed in the past—because they wish to limit the danger they perceive in courtlessness. It is for this reason that they are

---

[12] Glendon Schubert, *Judicial Policy Making* (Chicago: Scott, Foresman, 1965), p. 12.
[13] Schubert cites E. Adamson Hoebel and Karl Llewellyn's *The Cheyenne Way* (Norman: University of Oklahoma Press, 1941).
[14] Schubert, *Judicial Policy Making*, p. 12.
[15] Sir Henry Maine, *Ancient Law* (London: J. M. Dent, 1917); Emile Durkheim, *The Division of Labor in Society* (New York: Macmillan, 1933). This type of study is what Wigmore termed "comparative nomogenetics" in his monument of comparative law, *Panorama of the World's Legal Systems* (Washington, D.C.: Washington Law Book Co., 1928).

interested in finding out whether there are any factors directly related to the evolution of courts. In other words, there are a few scholars who are trying to develop some theory on the causes of judicial structure with a view to applying it to the international system.

Perhaps the earliest social-scientifically constructed, empirically based work along this line is a study by Richard Schwartz.[16] Again, much was written in the parallel field of sociology of *law* long before Schwartz went to work on the structure of *courts*. He duly notes this by prefacing his study with the following quote from Ehrlich, which sets the tone for the theory he subsequently proposes: "The substance of every attempt to state the fundamental principles of the sociology of law [is that] the center of gravity of legal development lies not in legislation, nor in juristic science, nor in judicial decision, but in society itself."[17] Of course, this is extremely broad; it tells us very little.

Schwartz, on the other hand, is quite specific. The phenomena he studied were two Israeli kibbutzim. He observed that they had much in common. Both had been founded about the same time (1921) by two groups of "young settlers who had come from Eastern Europe 'to build a new life.'" They were about the same size (2,000 acres). Their geographic settings were very similar (they were close to each other). Each had a mixed farming economy and both populations had approximately the same religious outlook. In other words, many variables that could have served as the bases for confounding rival hypotheses were controlled. Yet, according to Schwartz, "Despite these similarities, the two communities have differed from the outset in their members' ideas about economic organization."[18] One was the usual type of kibbutz, known also as a *kvutza*, a word meaning literally "group" but with the connotation of "collective"; the other was a *moshav*, a cooperative rather than a collective.

> In the *kvutza*, members felt they could implement the program, "from each according to his abilities, to each according to his need," as the way to create a "just society." *Moshav* members, many of whom had spent a few years in collectives, decided that the family should be the unit of production and distribution, and that thus a class of small, independent farmers could be developed in the *moshav* which would provide a strong agricultural base for the country.[19]

In the *moshav* there was a structure called the Judicial Committee. (Schwartz's description of it places it squarely within this book's definition

---

[16] Richard D. Schwartz, "Social Factors in the Development of Legal Control: A Case Study of Two Israeli Settlements," *Yale Law Journal*, 63 (February, 1954), pp. 471–91.

[17] Eugen Ehrlich, *Fundamental Principles of the Sociology of Law* (Cambridge: Harvard University Press, 1936), quoted in Schwartz, *op. cit.*, p. 471.

[18] Schwartz, *op. cit.*, p. 474.

[19] *Ibid.*

of court.) The *kvutza* developed no such structure. Instead, it had an elaborate system of informal social controls that operated mainly through sanction by public opinion. It was public opinion that kept internal order and settled personal disputes in the *kvutza* whenever they arose. Thus Schwartz hints at a relationship between the social theory (ideology) and consequent social organization of the community and the existence or non-existence of legal organization. Clearly the situations in these kibbutzim do not support the usual hypothesis that complexity of social grouping is related to complexity of organization, since one was as complex as the other. Rather, a confounding variable is introduced: the *type of complexity* of social interrelationships.

It seems of crucial importance to the development of a formal legal system that there be a lack of certain primary social interactions among people living within a reasonably complex society. Where these interactions do not exist, the necessary communication of information about a sanctionable action by a community member and the rapid implementation of sanctions will not occur automatically or informally. Instead a formal mechanism will be established to transmit the information accurately and deftly to sanctioners and to enforce any deprivations deemed deserved. Thus, in a more impersonal, segmented, and complex social organization, social control will be carried out within the context of identifiable, regular procedures by people to whom such authority has been specially delegated.

Schwartz presents a graphic description of the informal sanctioning process operating within the *kvutza*:

> Public opinion can be manifested often, swiftly, subtly and with varying degrees of intensity in the *kvutza*. In the course of a day's continual interaction, positive or negative opinion may be communicated by the ways in which members glance at an individual, speak to him, pass him a requested work implement or dish of food, assign him work, give him instructions, sit next to him and listen to his comments. To an experienced member, these small signs serve to predict more intense reactions of public acclaim or social isolation. They therefore acquire sanctioning power in and of themselves and become able to control the behavior in question before extremes are reached. In the *moshav*, by contrast, there are fewer opportunities to convey public opinion quickly and accurately because there is so much less contact between members in the course of the daily regime.[20]

This study, then, can be cited as further empirical evidence for the view that complexity of social system is a necessary condition of a legal system. However, complexity alone would not seem to be a sufficient condition, as the *kvutza* has prerequisite complexity—but no court system! Surprisingly, perhaps, the Schwartz study indicates that a greater amount of social interaction of a primary sort might stunt the growth of legal organization or

---

[20] *Ibid.*, p. 479.

judicial structure. A close communal interaction, though highly complex in the number and intensity of interrelationships, might be seen to eliminate the need for formal, specialized judicial agencies.

Yet, several years later, Schwartz teamed with James Miller in another study of some fifty societies which expressly states support for the simpler hypothesis that societal complexity leads to judicial structure.[21]

Schwartz and Miller were interested in the *evolution* of what they defined as "legal organization" and the relationship of its emergence to specified variations in societal complexity. To their way of thinking, legal organization develops in three major stages. According to Schwartz and Miller, the three steps are as follows:

1. Mediation—regular use of non-kin third-party intervention in dispute settlement.
2. Police—specialized armed force used partially or wholly for norm enforcement.
3. Counsel—regular use of specialized non-kin advocates in the settlement of disputes.

What is most incredible is that the two researchers discovered an almost perfect scale, i.e., that when the police factor was found to exist, there was *always* mediation extant in the society (except among the Lapps), and when there was counsel there was *always* mediation and policy.[22] In fourteen of the societies, none of the factors appeared. Thus, there are at least this number of societies that, by my definition, are courtless.

Having scaled the evolution of a legal (judicial/court) structure (organization), Schwartz and Miller then found some extremely high correlations with societal complexity factors. In their words (while explaining the development of counsel):

> It is a striking feature of the data that damages and mediation are characteristic of the simplest (as well as the most complex) societies, while legal counsel are found only in the most complex. The societies with counsel also have, without exception, not only damages, mediation and police, but, in addition, all of the complexity characteristics identified by Freeman and Winch. These are: (1) a symbolic means of

---

[21] Richard D. Schwartz and James C. Miller, "Legal Evolution and Societal Complexity," *American Journal of Sociology*, 70 (September, 1964), pp. 159–69. For an elaboration of this point, see Michael Barkun, *Law Without Sanctions* (New Haven: Yale University Press, 1968), chap. 7, especially pp. 146–48.

[22] But see Vilhelm Aubert, "Courts and Conflict Resolution," *Journal of Conflict Resolution,* 11 (March, 1967). Aubert's thesis seems to be that counsel could come first or second in the international system and help develop the legal system at an earlier stage. Perhaps, given the large number of lawyers in the world, this is a feasible suggestion. John Wigmore also felt that counsel is a critical factor in the development and maintenance of a legal system even after the death of the political system. "The rise and perpetuation of a legal system is dependent on the development and survival of a highly trained professional class [of legal thinkers]" (Wigmore, *op. cit.*, p. 1129).

exchange; (2) punishment for wrongs against the society; (3, 4, and 5) religious, educational, and governmental specialization; and (6) writing.[23]

I think it appropriate to note that this study is correlational and should not be taken to establish any general cause-and-effect relationships. Aside from the logical flaws in assuming cause and effect from such data, one must take into account the fact that in the Schwartz study of the two kibbutzim, all the prerequisites for classifying the *kvutza* as a complex society were present, yet the style of social interrelationship that characterized the life in the commune seemed to *retard* the development of a legal organization.

Nagel also probed the interrelationship between several societal factors and the existence of judicial structure.[24] Actually, his study is broader in its scope of inquiry regarding both the independent and the dependent variables handled in the research done by Schwartz. As independent variables, Nagel was interested in such societal dichotomies as "manufacturing/nonmanufacturing," "mainly dictatorial/mainly democratic," and "collectivistic property system/individualistic property system." As the dependent variable, he was concerned with "adjudicative characteristics," but his concept includes many more aspects of legal order than I include in mine. Suffice it to say that he specifically isolates several factors that basically add up to my notion of judicial structure: "presence of professional judges or dispute settlers," "frequent presence of lawyers or professional pleaders," and "mainly rigid precedent following or norm following resulting in considerable judicial restraint versus mainly case individualization resulting in considerable judicial discretion."[25] Nagel used ten societies as his source of data: the five in Hoebel's *The Law of Primitive Man* (Cheyenne, Ifuago, Trobriand, Eskimo, and Ashanti), the United States, precommunist China, pre-Nasser Egypt, the Fourth French Republic, and the Soviet Union.

Among his findings is a relationship between manufacturing and elements of judicial structure. He cautiously advances a theory to account for this—and some of it should have a familiar ring by now:

> The disproportionate presence of professional judges, jurors, lawyers, promulgating bodies, and appellate courts among manufacturing societies can probably be partially explained by the fact that increased industrialization brings increased specialization within the economic

---

[23] Schwartz and Miller, *op. cit.*, p. 167. Copyright © 1964 by the University of Chicago. See Linton C. Freeman and Robert F. Winch, "Societal Complexity: An Empirical Test of a Typology of Societies," *American Journal of Sociology*, 62 (March, 1957), pp. 461–66.
[24] Stuart Nagel, "Culture Patterns and Judicial Systems," *Vanderbilt Law Review*, 16 (December, 1962), pp. 147–57.
[25] *Ibid.*, pp. 147–48.

system of a society which carries over into the political and adjudication systems. The relationships can also be partially explained by the fact that increased industrialization better enables a society to have enough of an economic surplus to be better able to support political and judicial officials who are not directly producing food, shelter, or clothing for the society.[26]

Nagel goes on to say that:

> The disproportionate presence in non-manufacturing societies of divination, trial by ordeal, and judicially supervised duels . . . can possibly be explained by the fact that with increased industrialization there comes a greater emphasis on materialistic explanation of phenomena rather than on supernaturalistic explanation.[27]

It is important to observe that Nagel's discussion of the relationship between the individualistic vs. collectivistic property orientation of the societies is directly in line with the first Schwartz study. There is at least the appearance of some confirmation of what Schwartz observed. From Nagel's tables, it seems that only one out of three (33 percent) of the collective-oriented societies have judges, while four out of six (67 percent) of private-property–oriented societies have them. Similarly, Nagel found lawyers in only one out of three (33 percent) societies that were collective-oriented, but in five private-property societies, there were lawyers in three (60 percent).

The Nagel study, then, serves to reinforce both sets of hypotheses generated by the two Schwartz studies, i.e., the complexity-judicial structure relationship and the intervening-variable relationship, which postulates a collectivistic orientation acting as an obstruction to the development of judicial mechanism despite prerequisite complexity.

An immediate American reaction to this intervening-variable hypothesis might be that it is patently absurd in light of what we know (or think we know) about the USSR and the other Communist-bloc countries. However, the current state of development of judicial systems in the so-called Iron and Bamboo Curtain countries (we know that they have complex machinery) does not necessarily refute the above set of interrelated hypotheses. For these systems may well be dynamic and changing (there is some reason to believe so in light of occurrences in Czechoslovakia before August, 1968, and in Rumania) and their operating theory predicts a future state of affairs somewhat along the lines of what Schwartz observed in the *kvutza*. Furthermore, a recent book by George Feifer on the lower court system of Greater Moscow makes many observations that should give pause to any cavalier

---

[26] *Ibid.*, pp. 151–52.
[27] *Ibid.*, p. 153.

discounting of the Schwartz-Miller-Nagel findings.[28] After all, much of what is popularly believed about the Russian judicial system is based on numerous American newspaper and magazine descriptions of the political-inquisition type of procedure associated with the purge trials of the middle and late 1930s and reinforced by more recent (but infrequent) trials like that of Daniel and Sinyavsky. This type of trial and the type of trial portrayed by a set of political novels are by no means the whole of what the Russian judicial system is, was, and is capable of becoming.

At this point only the vague outline of a theory concerning causative agents of courts has been formulated.[29]

The three studies cited above are explorations into a new area and they tell just enough to be considered heuristic—which is not a negligible function or achievement. Nevertheless, there must be substantial improvement in the future studies conducted in this area, particularly in the methodology employed. For instance, there are serious coding problems in any cross-cultural type of study. Neither Nagel, Schwartz, nor Miller has been precise enough in conceptualization to allow for even the most rudimentary replication. Still, the way is becoming clearer as to what needs to be done. As far as this area is concerned, the first steps toward a scientifically based understanding have been taken.

Court as an Independent or Intervening Variable: The Effects of Courts

INTERNAL ORDER; STATUS QUO

As I noted in the first part of this chapter, one major motivation behind the study of the preconditions of courts is the desire to bring about a more stable or placid society (more orderly system). Schwartz and Miller stated at the conclusion of their essay:

> The study also raises but does not answer questions concerning the evolution of an international legal order. It would be foolhardy to generalize from the primitive world directly to the international scene

---

[28] George Feifer, *Justice in Moscow* (New York: Simon & Schuster, 1964).

[29] Of course, courts may exist in a society in juxtaposition to other available means of resolving conflicts, e.g., family or associational group mediation. For an interesting theoretical probe into the factors that may lead to greater or less usage of courts, namely, other modes of dispute settlement, see Laura Nader and Duane Metzger, "The Distribution of Conflict Resolution in Two Mexican Communities" (unpublished paper). Professor Nader is with the Department of Anthropology, University of California at Berkeley.

and to assume that the same sequence must occur here as there. There is no certainty that sub-trial units can be analogized to nations. . . .

Nonetheless, it is worth speculating that some of the same forces may operate in both situations. We have seen that damages and mediation almost always precede police in the primitive world. This sequence could result from the need to build certain cultural foundations in the community before a central regime of control, as reflected in a police force, can develop. Hypothetically, this cultural foundation might include a determination to avoid disputes, an appreciation of the value of third-party intervention, and the development of a set of norms both for preventive purposes and as a basis for allocating blame and punishment when disputes arise. Compensation by damages and the use of mediators might well contribute to the development of such a cultural foundation, as well as reflecting its growth. . . . This raises the question as to whether the same kind of cultural foundation is not a necessary condition for the establishment of an effective world police force and whether, in the interest of that objective, it might not be appropriate to stress the principles of compensatory damages and mediation as preconditions for the growth of a world rule of law.[30]

Now no one could deny that all of this implies a factual assumption; namely, that the courts are in some way related to social order. Also, no one (including Schwartz and Miller) could say that such an assumption is an original theoretical stance. In fact, it would probably not be too bizarre to say that the development and maintenance of social order are probably the most frequently cited functions of all court systems. Specifically, it is repeated time and time again that courts are related to social order in the international political arena as well. The entire set of beliefs involving world order through *law* implies a similar association, but there is a distinction between the traditionally perceived relationship between *law* and order and the concern of this part of this book. The major difference, it seems to me, is that the focus of international juristic attention has been placed upon the *output* (that is, the law) rather than upon the *structure* and *process* themselves. This is not meant to say that scholars of international law have completely overlooked the role of the court or the existence of arbitration and mediation procedures as potentially (or presently) powerful factors in the bringing about of at least a semblance of world order. They have not. The judicial structure is *mentioned* in many different but vague ways, e.g., as a "source" of law. Still, the focus of the discourse and the research has been and strongly continues to be on papers, documents, and principles as the influential agents for world pacification.

Only in recent times has anyone begun to make *explicit* references and systematic analyses of the role of the various institutional factors in world

---

order. Hopefully, this might mean that we are at least escaping from indirect observation of and thinking about human behavior (inferences from documents) to direct observation and thinking about human behavior (studying *people in action*).

Morton Kaplan and Nicholas de B. Katzenbach co-authored a highly imaginative book several years ago in which they attempted to separate those diverse factors that were more or less and directly or indirectly related to international stability.[31] One factor they treated at some length was judicial structure, or (in their words) the "legal process."[32] According to them: "It is a commonplace that law is a process, not a body of self-executing rules, and that the institutional framework in which doctrine is created, invoked and applied is of decisive importance in understanding the decision-making process."[33] I might note also in passing (1) that this has only recently become a "commonplace," and (2) that even so, it has rarely been thought through thoroughly so as to afford any specific meaning or to give any practical understanding. For instance, the following Kaplan-Katzenbach statement is precisely the kind of hypothesizing that should saturate our literature and spur our research, but it is actually quite novel:

> The extent to which one can persuasively relate a decision to past decisions of others is a technique of disarming opposition and gaining acceptance on grounds of reasonableness and moderation. Consistency is a political as well as a legal virtue, for the expectations of others are conditioned by past experience and by past statements and acts. For the judge, cast in an impartial role, consistency helps to establish his lack of bias or favoritism among litigants as well as assisting future claimants to predict future judicial responses to various facts and arguments. For the political decision-maker impartiality is not a formal requirement of the role, but consistency is no less important if conflict and collision are to be held to a minimum.[34]

This is an engagingly complex hypothesis. It stipulates the existence of a social pacification program through the medium of a particular structure of decision-making behavior. What the decision-maker does, in this view, is to bestow an opportunity upon disputants for rationalization *if* that is an acceptable course for them at the time. The individual or social rationale is grounded on the belief (or the hope, or the tactic of saying that one believes) that there is moderation, consistency, or impartiality inherent in the decision-making behavior of the judge. Of course, Kaplan and Katzen-

---

[31] *The Political Foundations of International Law* (New York: Wiley, 1961).

[32] By their definition, "The essence of legal process lies in the fact that the authority of public officials is limited by formal norms and processes, and is thus imbued with a degree of objectivity" (*ibid.*, p. 232). This is reasonably close to my definition; at least, close enough for my purposes here.

[33] *Ibid.*, p. 231.

[34] *Ibid.*, p. 233.

bach aren't the first political theorists to muse over the placation function. In a slightly more general sense, an earlier political scientist of some renown had this to say about it:

> As for the paternal rule, it possesses neither strength nor compulsory power, nor in fact does the rule of any one man, unless he is a king or someone in like case, but the law has power to compel, since it is a declaration emanating from practical wisdom and intellect. And people feel enmity towards their fellow men who oppose their impulses. However rightly they may do so: the law, on the contrary, is not the object of hatred, though enforcing right rules.[35]

Confronted by such supposed excellence in procedure, how could combatants be anything but serene? Indeed, not only is it a structure to resolve conflict and restore order and placate the irate, but, according to Almond and Powell, it also simultaneously manages to keep from "expanding the pressure on the rule makers to make new laws or to become intimately engaged in the administration of old ones."[36] Professors Almond and Powell, being true to science, cite a dialogue between Moses and Jethro as empirical evidence of this function. So go aspects of the dynamics of this theory, as applied to the international scene as well as to any social grouping, from families to tribes to cities and states to complex national systems.

On the other hand, Kaplan and Katzenbach are equally quick to show that the theory does not work so neatly in practice, at least not at the international level.

> Courts must make new rules slowly, conservatively and, of necessity, interstitially; a court is ill equipped to rewrite a whole area of law within the limits of a single, narrow controversy. For these reasons the ICJ cannot really contribute greatly to relieving international tensions even should its jurisdiction be expanded; it can seldom get at the basic causes of which the particular dispute is merely symptomatic.[37]

Furthermore,

> . . . the clarification of important rules in the context of particular disputes is a questionable device. It has the difficulties of an interstitial approach, and *lacks the moderating influence* that can come from more flexible institutions capable of broadening the area of negotiation and compromise, and of recommending more comprehensive solutions.[38]

---

[35] Aristotle, *Nichomachean Ethics*, tr. D. P. Chase (New York: Dutton, 1950), p. 275.
[36] Gabriel A. Almond and G. Bingham Powell, Jr., *Comparative Politics: A Developmental Approach* (Boston: Little, Brown, 1966), p. 160. Characteristic of the handling of courts by comparative analysts, their treatment of the functions is at best conservative and at worst naïve.
[37] Kaplan and Katzenbach, *op. cit.*, p. 280.
[38] *Ibid.*, p. 281 (emphasis mine).

Thus, by sabotaging their first point in good dialectical fashion, they convincingly make the point that this procedure (the judicial structure) has paradoxical tendencies within it which may equally mollify and antagonize participants in a quarrel. Though objectivity and impartiality might well be seen (as they are so often theorized to be) as order-inducing agents of a decision-making process, the very same structural elements (decision-maker being bound by law in the invoking of it) might serve to fan the sparks of basic discontent in the social system and induce later disorder (if not overt violence).

It should be conceded that Kaplan and Katzenbach are dealing with a reasonably strange phenomenon (international relations)—one that might be an inappropriate source of empirical information upon which to base theories applicable to sociopolitical units of lesser magnitude and far greater cohesion and homogeneity. After all, it is as appropriate to warn against generalizing from greater to lesser social units as to issue the more frequently heard warning about generalizing from lesser to greater units. The international society, it is true, is difficult even to contemplate as a society, as that word is ordinarily used in the social sciences. How many other social units, for instance, would tolerate such frequent outbursts of violent self-help to achieve individual goals? I doubt that any exist or could exist. Nonetheless, Kaplan and Katzenbach's countertheory of the disordering effects that may possibly flow from the very nature of judicial structure do merit serious reflection.

On the other hand, their theory diverts us from another important question about the relationship between the existence of a court in a social system and the maintenance and preservation of order within it. Although it may well be true that the seeds of future conflict might inhere in the judicial structure (just as well as the basis of conflict resolution), the critical causative factor might be psychological rather than sociological. In other words, the key determinant of the effect the court structure has in society may well be a *widely believed myth* that the court is an instrument for social order. The fact that most people in a social group believe that order is forthcoming because of the courts may be the sufficient condition to the maintenance of that very order. That this is held as likely (both consciously and subconsciously) by certain elites probably accounts for the vast amount of literature that supports this belief and helps to reinforce it over time.[39]

---

[39] Walter Weyrauch, on the other hand, believes that this is a subjective belief held by the legal elite that inheres both in their personality and in the very existence of the legal system, which is, like all systems, proficient in trying to reproduce itself.

Assuming a society that places emphasis on class stratification in whatever form, it may be one of the functions of lawyers, and perhaps of law, to counteract social change, thus protecting the prevailing distribution of enlightenment, skills, respect, affection, rectitude, wealth, power, and well-

Plato, the master mentor of all who would manipulate a society, once upon a time offered the advice that "rulers will find considerable doses of falsehood and deceit necessary for the good of their subjects." It is hardly beyond the realm of possibility that the frequently cited relationship between the continued existence of a judicial structure and a well-ordered community might just be a myth we have accepted without much skepticism for too long. It may be good ideology, but is it good political theory and sound political science?

Perhaps this point might become clearer when looked at from the perspective of another widely held belief, that courts support the status quo. For instance, Kaplan and Katzenbach say that "judicial institutions must essentially preserve the status quo. Neither the methodology nor the function really permits otherwise."[40]

The status quo and *slow, orderly change* are quite similar phenomena in a social context. The interstitial nature of the process occurring within the structural confines of the court makes this inevitable. Dean Levi's excellent little book, *Introduction to Legal Reasoning*,[41] furnishes a vivid illustration of the way the legal (judicial) process changes its concepts (and thus the law). It is assumed that this subsequently has an effect upon the germane social, economic, and political relationships in the society. However, actually this is an illustration of the way the judiciary has *reacted*, belatedly, to catch up with basic economic and technological advances. Economic pressures build up, and eventually the governmental structure may acknowledge them; or it may *not* expressly acknowledge them. Frankly, it is easy to imagine that excessive reliance upon court decisions to react eventually to changes might have the effect of allowing pressures to build until they maximize *disorderly* change. This may help to explain the inner-city riots that rocked America in the summers of the middle and late 1960s. When large segments of our city population came to disbelieve in the ability of the legislatures to bring about orderly change, it is more than likely that they also came to disbelieve in the efficacy of the courts. Authoritative sensitivity to actual pressures for change is probably located in more direct and open political structures like councils and chiefs and legislatures and executives. The very trappings of judicial isolation might impede responsiveness to necessary modifications, the lack of which might again stimulate violent efforts for change. This might hold particularly

---

being among the privileged strata of society. The lawyers' personality characteristics, with allowances for deviant cases, may conform to this social function of maintaining the status quo in the distribution of social values [*The Personality of Lawyers* (New Haven: Yale University Press, 1964), p. 46].

[40] Kaplan and Katzenbach, *op. cit.*, p. 280.
[41] Chicago: University of Chicago Press, 1949.

true in a society that puts excessive faith in such procedures—as could be said about the United States.

In fact, the relationship between judicial structure and status quo and/or the maintenance of order and/or the slow, orderly change of things was not demonstrated in Schwartz's study of the *kvutza*. Was there less social order in the *kvutza* than in the *moshav?* Was the status quo maintained more readily in the *kvutza* than in the *moshav?* The Schwartz data afford us no foundation for belief in either hypothesis.

No less a social theorist than Talcott Parsons stated that:

> It may become evident that the prominence of and the integrity of a legal system as a mechanism of social control is partly a function of a certain type of social equilibrium. *Law flourishes particularly in a society in which the most fundamental questions of social values are not currently at issue or under agitation.*[42]

If we substituted "order" or "status quo" for "law" in the above quotation, we would have an explanation of the phenomenon of the *kvutza*. Heavy reliance on legal procedure to foster the status quo or order in a time of potential value reorientation in a society might be a good formula for violent disorder.

In a similar vein, but more directly contrary than the Parsons statement to the hypothesis that courts foster order, is a study by Michael Barkun.[43] In this essay, Barkun makes the point that societies of a "segmentary" social pattern maintain substantial order and enjoy reasonably peaceable conflict resolution through a device he calls "implicit mediation." There is no war of all men against all, and no unlimited, ever spiraling blood feuding, despite the absence of a formal, explicit mediation device that would structurally approach what I have defined as a court. This, then, is a finding similar to Schwartz's in his essay on the kibbutzim.

Barkun believes that the social condition that supports this state of affairs is what he terms a "legal consensus," and this in turn results in what he calls a "jural community." A strong legal consensus itself supposes peace. Legal organizations and judicial edifices are not necessary to this state of affairs in this simple community. Barkun goes even further: "In fact, municipal legal systems—despite codes, judges, courts and police—ultimately rest on consensus. Its operation is subsurface, while institutions with coercive powers achieve high visibility."[44] The reader should be alerted to the fact that all the segmentary societies of which Barkun speaks are what

---

[42] Talcott Parsons, "The Law and Social Control," in *Law and Society*, ed. William M. Evans (New York: Free Press, Macmillan, 1961), p. 71 (emphasis mine).

[43] Michael Barkun, "Conflict Resolution through Implicit Mediation," *Journal of Conflict Resolution*, 8 (June, 1964), pp. 121–30.

[44] *Ibid.*, p. 124.

social scientists call primitive, preliterate, or underdeveloped. Some social scientists would argue that the necessary amount of value consensus that Barkun discusses is possible only in simple societies that are segmented, but quite impossible in a highly industrial society. They would argue that a modern society, though resting on some consensus, cannot attain the type or degree of societal homogeneity necessary to support implicit mediation. This is particularly true, they would contend, in the face of the division of labor and function so characteristic of the complex technological and technocratic society of the modern world. Still, we have seen that the *kvutza,* which was reasonably complex, did pretty well without courts. But there are even better examples than this to support the contention that a complex society can have a highly homogeneous value system and do well with a minimal reliance on courts. Consider Japanese society, particularly up to very recent (post–World War II) times.

The Japanese mode of doing things casts doubt on the generally accepted court–internal-order hypothesis and adds much to the value-consensus–internal-order hypothesis. This is not to imply that there were no courts in Japan up to the middle of the twentieth century. As must be obvious by now, courts are only one means by which a social system can restore itself to a serene equilibrium. A society can use them more or less or not at all. Although the Japanese system traditionally has included courts, it used them very infrequently up to present times. Thus, the Japanese legal system, even today, raises the question about *differences of degree in the use of formal courts in order to resolve internal conflicts.* According to Kenzo Takayanagi:

> It has often been pointed out that the elaborate, imported Western apparatus for administering justice and settling disputes has not been utilized in Japan to the same extent as in Western countries. The Japanese people prefer the mediation method to the black-and-white judicial method in the resolution of disputes.[45]

Takayanagi goes on to offer a few possible explanations:

> Some account for this attitude by the deep influence of the Confucian teaching that "harmony is to be valued," that is to say, by the general feeling that the judicial method is not conducive to abiding harmony between the parties concerned. Others attribute the attitude to the feudal sentiment that it is morally wrong to trouble the mind of the lord about private matters. Still others say it is due to the Japanese national character. . . .[46]

---

[45] Kenzo Takayanagi (assisted by Thomas L. Blakemore), "A Century of Innovation: The Development of Japanese Law, 1868–1961," in *Law in Japan,* ed. Arthur von Mehren (Cambridge: Harvard University Press, 1963), p. 39. See also, in the same volume, Takoyoshi Kawashima, "Dispute Resolution in Contemporary Japan."

[46] Takayanagi, *op. cit.,* p. 39.

Although there may be dispute as to all the precise factors involved in the reluctance of the Japanese to make use of courts, most observers agree in general that the principal one is some convergence of elements in the social value system. For instance, there is great social consensus in Japan to the effect that one's honor must be protected and that family honor is a cardinal virtue. Losing in litigation could be nothing less than a scar upon honor. Thus, for fear of suffering such a catastrophe, or for fear that one might create a greater enemy by defeating him publicly, Japanese avoid the court despite the availability of its procedures.[47]

Glendon Schubert, in his comparative study of foreign cultures, also has observed that the Japanese culture has been peculiarly low in litigational tendencies:

> There has been no Japanese tradition—as there have been in the Philippine and American political cultures—that lawyers have a special set of roles to play in negotiating nonlitigational settlements of most economic and political disputes. Neither has it been true in Japan, as it has in all three of the other countries in our sample, that litigation itself is a specialized structure for the functioning of mediation and negotiation as primary decision-making processes, since only a small proportion of either civil or criminal cases that are docketed with courts ever persist to the stage where they are resolved by a formal decision of a trial judge. Instead of being the quasi-monopoly of the bar, conciliatory roles in Japan are the very warp and woof of the social structure.[48]

Japan, then, furnishes an excellent illustration of a highly complex society —even a highly industrialized society—minimizing the usage of courts as a device to maintain order.

The fact that order is actually maintainable by other decision-making bodies within a system where the legal device would fail is the subject of an interesting study by Richard Walton.[49] Walton develops a scheme that posits the existence of three types of conflict-resolution decision-making processes within a system: (1) "legal-justice," (2) "power-bargaining," and (3) "social-science intervention." His description of several types of labor disputes indicates that bargaining, by relating to current power distribution, can keep a system from being disrupted better than resort to legal machinery (which reflects past power settlements). Legal victories, indeed,

---

47 For instance, as Kawashima notes, in 1958 there were 6,044 victims of physical injury (including death) involving the Japanese National Railways, yet only 18 lawsuits were brought (*op. cit.*, p. 63).

48 Glendon Schubert, "Judges and Political Leadership," in *Political Leadership in Industrialized Societies,* ed. Lewis Edinger (New York: Wiley, 1967), p. 236.

49 Richard E. Walton, *Legal-Justice, Power Bargaining, and Social Science Intervention: Mechanisms for Settling Disputes,* paper no. 194 (Lafayette, Ind.: Institute for Research in the Behavioral, Economic, and Management Sciences, Purdue University, March, 1968).

might maintain a superficial order (no strike) but promote dysfunction in terms of systemic efficiency.[50] This again raises the serious question as to how overuse of the legal mechanism to resolve disputes may sow the seeds for greater dispute and thus for greater disorder.

Finally, the current Soviet practice of using the *obshchestvennost* in the Comradely Courts of Moscow also warrants some attention, as a way of maximizing order while simultaneously lessening other serious societal stresses and strains.

According to George Feifer, the Comradely Court is the next best thing to no judicial procedure at all—and indeed it seems to be quite an informal and almost anarchistic get-together. Yet it convenes (if that is the proper word) on occasion to resolve local disputes. From the way Feifer describes the institution, it would seem closely to resemble a Quaker meeting: some people sit up front, but most of the talking emanates from the assembly. The assembly itself is made up of people from the particular community in which the contending parties reside. Soviet theory has it that

> The drawing of *obshchestvennost* into battle with crime . . . is one of the most important and topical questions in the theory and practice of Soviet criminal procedure, because in the conditions of full-scale building of Communism there is taking place a transformation of socialist *étatism* into Communist *obshchestvennoye* self-administration.[51]

Feifer duly notes that Westerners (and particularly Americans) are inclined to view this in a different way. The Westerner will construe it as opening the door for mass Big Brotherism and for a grass-roots authoritarianism. Theoretically, it is equally plausible to construe this system as very basic grass-roots democracy. Theory aside, Feifer did some direct observing and described his own reaction to what seemed to be really occurring.

> The Young Communist group of the Juridical Faculty provided a vivid example of this democracy while I was there. At one of its general meetings, the committee—that is, the activist, official leadership— recommended the expulsion of a nonconformist student for poor studies and wild behavior, and in the course of an hour's discussion it furiously assailed him. Yet the rank and file voted almost unanimously not to expel him.[52]

---

[50] Walton recognizes the fact that these various conflict-resolution devices exist to differing degrees in different systems. Much of his paper discusses the process element of each device and the conditions prerequisite to the use of one or another of these three ways to resolve disputes. Cf. Richard E. Walton and Robert B. McKersie, *A Behavioral Theory of Labor Negotiations* (New York: McGraw-Hill, 1965).

[51] Feifer, *op. cit.*, p. 106. Copyright © 1964 by George Feifer. Reprinted by permission of Simon & Schuster and Harold Matson Co., Inc.

[52] *Ibid.*, pp. 125–26.

Thus, we have one heavily industrial society serving as an example of how a noncourt societal system might be workable to reestablish peace and harmony upon the occurrence of a disturbing disequilibrium.

Theoretically, the innovation of *obshchestvennost* at the lower, trial-court level is a practical start toward the achievement of what Erich Fromm has long stated to be the most workable type of societal arrangement: the decentralization and deformalization of procedures to a local, smaller-unit basis. This, Fromm believes, would help to eliminate the major dysfunctional by-product of modern, industrialized society, alienation. It would help, from Fromm's point of view, to eliminate what many modern American political scientists have begun to observe with some dismay: political apathy due to feelings of political ineffectiveness.[53]

At least since the time Socrates was condemned by a mob acting under some sort of judicial procedure, powerful men have feared to allow the people to be the judge; that is, a court. It seems to me that many men believe that the more formal and remote the court system is, the better for the stability of the society. I would guess that these are the same people who push the complexity-friction-court hypothesis; it makes a neat tautology. That none of this is necessarily true at all should be clear by now. This is not to say that the converse is true; the information discussed in this section simply casts doubt on this stanza in our political-judicial folklore.

DEMOCRACY; INDIVIDUAL AND MINORITY RIGHTS (LIBERTY)

One of the major difficulties in analyzing statements of this type is deciding whether any given writer is really discussing a *relationship* between courts and democracy or *defining* democracy by insisting that it has a court system. All too often, I fear, authors define democracy by linking it inextricably with the concept of court. They are so impressed by data that manifest a *compatibility* between democracies and court systems and procedures that they tend to define one in terms of the other. For instance, Piero Calamandrei, the famous Italian jurisprudent, once observed that "in the judicial process the lawyers represent freedom; they are the living symbol of what is perhaps the vital principle of modern democracy."[54] It is difficult to see why this must be so. One wonders how he can speak so

---

[53] See Erich Fromm, *The Sane Society* (New York: Holt, Rinehart & Winston, 1955), especially chap. 8. For a good survey discussion on political inefficacy, see Lester Milbrath, *Political Participation* (Chicago: Rand McNally, 1965).

[54] Piero Calamandrei, *Procedure and Democracy* (New York: New York University Press, 1956), pp. 80–81.

assuredly of lawyers as symbols of democracy when in Italy during the reign of Il Duce they surely served fascism. Much was also heard at Nuremberg on the role of lawyers in Nazi Germany; they served the cause of a legitimized Hitler as well as the Weimar Republic. On the other hand, the *kvutza* in Israel had many democratic procedures and no lawyers.

Aside from the inconsistency of his theory with his own nation's experience, Calamandrei's concept falters definitionally. If a freely elected and representative legislature established a subcommittee to hear and decide statutory and constitutional disputes, this would be a democratic-republican system within the usual meaning of those terms. It would remain so even if the body of the legislature reserved the power to alter decisions of this committee, and to replace the members for committing too many "errors." Why is representative democracy, the government of and by the people, dependent upon an independent council of interpreters of its laws?

However, a more clearly relational type of statement is one by Arthur T. Vanderbilt, the late chief justice of the Supreme Court of New Jersey and dean of New York University Law School:

> It must be apparent to all who consider the matter that the local courts of first instance are the very foundation of the enforcement of the criminal law. On them rests the primary responsibility for the maintenance of peace in the various communities of the state . . . and . . . for development of respect for law on the part of our citizenry, on which, in the last analysis, all of our democratic institutions depend.[55]

Now this, I believe, is representative of a type of causal statement that is often accepted *in toto*. I suspect that statements of this sort from this high a source are rarely pondered and even more rarely challenged. This type of rhetoric has become so deeply entrenched in American legal-political mythology that people rarely dispute it.[56] In essence, Vanderbilt's statement posits an indirect relationship between the courts (or one level of them) and the entire democratic structure. True, in his proposition the intervening and direct variable is a popular attitude (respect for the law), but Vanderbilt is propounding a theory that insists that the trial courts are the necessary if not sufficient conditional force for the maintenance of democracy. Even if he meant his statement to apply only to the American system of democracy, it is hard to see why this one factor is so important,

---

[55] Arthur T. Vanderbilt, "The Municipal Court," *Rutgers Law Review*, 10 (Summer, 1956), p. 650.

[56] The same sort of thing may well be happening in modern Japan. Chief Justice Tanaka (perhaps the most prestigeous jurist to hold that position) said that the people "often fail to perceive that the maintenance of the social order by means of the justice administered by the courts is the cornerstone of a democratic community". (Kotaro Tanaka, "Democracy and Judicial Administration in Japan," *Journal of the International Commission of Jurists*, II [1959], p. 15).

and why our system hasn't already collapsed, considering the current sorry state of the American civil and criminal courts.[57]

But perhaps the clearest, most explicit, and most developed argument along these lines is David Bayley's. He states:

> Democratic government is based upon the concept of the rule of law, meaning that community power shall impinge upon individuals according to written prescriptions publicly implemented and publicly adjudicated. Democratic theory further stipulates that rules and procedures affecting the lives of individuals must be established by men representing the community, not a small coterie or cabal. The working of the rule of law founded on community consensus is dependent on two institutional mechanisms, an independent court system and free elections.[58]

Upon closer analysis, though, this appears more glib than enlightening. All we really need do is substitute the word "any" for "democratic" at the beginning of the above excerpt. The Western form of democracy is hardly unusual or unique in resting upon a legal basis. In fact, all modern governments do. Also, Western democracies are not unique in having (not necessitating) formal, independent adjudication of the laws. The current Soviet political system might not fit Bayley's concept of democracy (no "free" elections), yet there is substantial independence of the judiciary at the trial levels, and this despite the existence of the Procuracy. Feifer reminds us that "The question of whether the procurator exercises any kind of control over the court is a hot one in legal circles."[59] He goes on to note that procurators take both sides of a case—indeed, the procurator is known to argue the case for the defendant. No less a Soviet expert than Harold Berman also notes that the procurator "cannot annul [a doubtful judicial decision] but can only protest it to a higher administrative or judicial body."[60] It would seem that a politically independent judiciary can exist in a political system not usually labeled "democracy" by Americans.

Specifically, Bayley tries to demonstrate that the existence of a court, particularly in its role of an independent, power-checking, decision-making body, is an indispensable condition to the maintenance and support of individual liberties in a society. He seems to believe quite firmly that without such a structure, the individual is all but lost. In Bayley's view, without the court, without the independence of the judges, the solitary person stands helpless before the whim and caprice of the police, the executive branch in general, and the legislature; against the mighty array of power they

---

[57] See Harry W. Jones, ed., *The Courts, the Public, and the Law Explosion* (Englewood Cliffs, N.J.: Prentice-Hall, 1965).

[58] David H. Bayley, *Public Liberties in the New States* (Chicago: Rand McNally, 1964), p. 127.

[59] Feifer, *op. cit.*, p. 132.

[60] Harold J. Berman, *Justice in the U.S.S.R.* (Cambridge: Harvard University Press, 1963), pp. 239–40.

wield. He goes on to show how the ruling elites of many underdeveloped countries have gone to great pains to establish the shell of a judicial system —many fine trappings—but have insidiously deprived it of efficaceousness by retaining power to remove recalcitrant or contrary-minded judges at their will or by preestablished limitations of term. It is this type of proposition he has in mind when he and others state that "the tenure of judges should certainly not be at the discretion of government." When that occurs, it is reasoned, individual liberties are imperiled to the point of non-existence.

Yet other conditions must also be met for the court structure to perform the function Bayley believes it does. "The effectiveness of courts in defending human rights will then depend upon the discretion allowed to them and the personality and character of the individual judges."[61] He also observes that "a judiciary which assumed the power to judge the propriety of all laws whatsoever might fail to defend liberty due to aristocratic bias or laziness. If a legislature infringes rights, what certain guarantee is there that a second legislature will not likewise allow the infringement of rights?"[62]

One is tempted to inquire: What guarantee is there that a court would not allow the infringement of individual rights as well? What did the Supreme Court of the United States do during the increasing dangers to individual liberties inherent in the congressional investigations of McCarthy days? What sort of sentinel of liberty is the state court system in the southern parts of the United States today when a Negro or civil rights worker's rights or life is at stake? Yes, and one need not cite only such highly unusual instances to recognize that the judicial structure has a rapidly dissolvent membrane when placed next to social, economic, and political heat. Moreover, it can become part of an oppressive machinery when its own values so suit it—even in America—as Klonoski and Mendelsohn have observed so well:

> One function clearly demonstrated today in the South and only yesterday in the American labor movement is the use of the local legal subsystem to suppress and frustrate political, economic and social demands. Leaders of the movements—and their followers—are arrested, cited with numerous charges and convicted. Workers attempting to alter the economic status quo are stopped for various "violations" and charges pressed, all within the bounds of legality and the law. In more subtle fashion, in "better" communities, "trouble-makers" are singled out and treated with less sympathy.[63]

---

[61] Bayley, *op. cit.*, p. 132.
[62] *Ibid.*, p. 129.
[63] James R. Klonoski and R. I. Mendelsohn, "The Allocation of Justice: A Political Approach," *Journal of Public Law*, 14 (1965), p. 334.

Many a young peace demonstrator has found the American courts somewhat less than the bastion of free speech he supposed it to be.

Professor Bayley seems to be a bit at odds with himself. He seems inclined to believe that the structure of the judiciary is quite necessary to the guarantee of individual rights, but recognizes that it is far from a sufficient condition. He seems to believe that what is sufficient is the actual quality and understanding of the importance of freedom and liberty of the individual judges themselves. But if that is true, it is equally reasonable to argue that presidents, prime ministers, council members, various administrators, legislators, and even policemen can be so enlightened. What is there inherent in the *judicial* structure that is so important for the guarding of minority rights? I fail to see anything in it at all. I see no more reason for looking to structures in this regard than I do to looking at the words of a constitution. This type of theory (or area of theory) seems, instead, to be explained more in terms of a manipulation of symbols by one part of the elite. It may well be the last resort of a conservative institution *against* democratic procedures. In a very recent and excellent analysis of the English legal system, the authors have this to say about English judges:

> By convincing influential opinion of each generation that they were the champions of English liberties, they have been able to ward off attempts to dilute their quality, reorganize their deployment, or alter their responsibilities as dangerous challenges to the liberties of individual Englishmen. The judges have long had a vested interest in the *status quo*, as well as possessing more than one forum for expressing their opposition to change [64]

Finally, the judicial structure, purely in terms of its personnel, is not necessarily supportive of democracy. In the first place, there are tremendous variations in how and to what degree the lay populace can participate in the judicial process. Certainly, whether or to what degree the court, as a decision-making process, involves laymen relates to whether or not the judicial structure sustains or encourages the growth of democratic values. Frequently courts are quite unrelated to democracy in this respect. In fact, to Western eyes and within the definitions of this book, the more a judicial structure involves the layman, the less it appears to be a court. Happily, there are some exceptions that allow for the probabilistic nature of this statement, but this will be discussed in full in Chapter 6.

The question also arises as to whether judicial structure can function to bring about or support democracy *unless* the judges are elected (or chosen by lot). After all, appointing judges for life does not seem the best

---

[64] Brian Abel Smith and Robert Stevens, *Lawyers and the Courts* (Cambridge: Harvard University Press, 1967), p. 460.

way to keep them responsive to the wishes of the majority, and this is the method employed at the national level of the American political system. It is a fact that causes some discomfort to democratic purists. Additionally, there is weight to the argument that even the election of judges does not put them into close proximity to the will of the people. Dolbeare's study of some local courts in the United States revealed that "even though judges were technically elected, nominations were usually bipartisan and therefore choiceless, and in any event the public knew little about the candidates."[65] Considering the evidence gathered on American voters' knowledge of issues and candidates, even for what they believe to be important and partisan offices, this should take few people aback.

Moreover, Dolbeare's study is unique in trying to evaluate the relative worth of the functional propositions concerning status quo and democracy on the basis of some systematically conceived and rigorously executed research. The courts' role in protecting individual liberties, as contrasted to their delight in protecting the status quo, was not a spectacular success.

> The enforcement of private property rights by the courts means that the status quo has a potent final line of defense—a line which can be held by a few individuals after popular inattentiveness and governmental inertia have been overcome. . . . Nor are private rights the only basis on which the status quo may be defended, for this emphasis extends to a general resistance to any new or unfamiliar practices.
>
> ✿   ✿   ✿
>
> What values were upheld in these courts? Our data indicate that they were property rights, the status quo, and the openness and regularity of the political process, in that order. In order to supplement this catalogue if possible, an atypical incursion into the criminal law field was made in search of decisions dealing with such civil rights issues as free speech, free assembly, segregation, etc.—all Bill of Rights liberties except those involving criminal due process. Very few cases were found. . . . In most cases, civil rights claims were unsuccessful. With as well rounded a view of the activity of these courts as was practical, then, we can hardly conclude that the courts make a major substantive contribution to the democratic qualities of the urban political process.[66]

If this holds true generally in the United States, it is a fact well worth knowing, even if it must give rise to dismay. Dolbeare's finding calls for replication before political theorists, philosophers, and ideologues need go to work explaining, justifying, or obscuring it.

I am inclined to agree most heartily with those who have warned that the guarantees of freedom and liberty found in the United States Consti-

---

[65] Kenneth M. Dolbeare, *Trial Courts in Urban Politics* (New York: Wiley, 1967), p. 130.

[66] *Ibid.*, pp. 127 and 130.

tution are just so much ink on so much yellowed parchment. Among others, Learned Hand has noted that courts cannot save democracy—particularly in times of crisis, when democracies most need saving.[67] There is no guarantee of liberty and freedom other than the understanding and practice of maintaining and supporting it on the part of *all* the individual role-players in government and on the part of the effective, validating portion of the populace. If freedom and liberty are truly values in a society, and if police and administrators, legislators and executives are properly trained, they will be an absolute guarantee. For this function, institutions and structures seem irrelevant in themselves.[68] Thus, as far as democracy or freedom of individuals is concerned, the existence of courts would seem to be neither a necessary nor a sufficient condition.

JUSTICE; FAIRNESS; EQUITY

Perhaps the most frequently cited manifest consequence of judicial structure is its rendering of justice in society. Where does one find the heraldry of justice? It is in front of the courthouse. One would search in vain to find such symbolism flanking the portals of the legislature, a palace, or any governmental office building. The very essence of man-made, governmentally dispensed justice resides within the power of the judge and the entire courtroom procedure. It resides nowhere else. At least, that is the position that so many jurisprudents and political theorists seem to hold. In fact, this notion is so deeply imbedded in political lore that I feel no need to string together a line of quotations to convince the reader of the wide acceptance of the proposition. I would like to inquire, without pretending to have developed *the* definition of justice, how true this is. At least from the following perspective of justice, in terms of the relationship of procedure to result, this proposition, too, is highly questionable.

Suppose, if you will, that four men have been working at planting a row of trees. At the lunch break, the foreman comes along and tells the men that he has three apples. Upon being asked, each worker says he would like one. Then the foreman asks them how he should decide who

---

[67] See Irving Dilliard, ed., *The Spirit of Liberty: Papers and Addresses of Learned Hand,* 2nd ed. (New York: Knopf, 1953), p. 164. One of the "others" is Robert Dahl. He has observed that "so far as there is a general protection in human society against the deprivation by one group of the freedom desired by another, it is probably not to be found in constitutional forms" (*Preface to Democratic Theory* [Chicago: University of Chicago Press, 1963], p. 134).

[68] "To assume that this country has remained 'democratic' because of its Constitution seems to me to reverse the relation; it is much more plausible to suppose that the Constitution has remained because our society is essentially 'democratic'" (Dahl, *op. cit.,* p. 143).

gets what. One of the workers suggests that the foreman simply choose the worker or workers he likes best and distribute the fruit according to whim. The foreman quickly rejects this suggestion. A second worker recommends an election. He believes that the men themselves should vote on who the three best workers are. A third worker suggests that the foreman himself decide who the three best workers are and reward them accordingly. The foreman listens to all these suggestions but is displeased with each. He is still undecided as to how to divide the apples in the fairest, most "just" way. Then the last worker says to him: "Well, in order to be most fair, I guess we ought to draw straws. The one who pulls the short straw is the loser." "Aha!" says the foreman. "That's more like it." He immediately senses that this is the "only" way to share the spoils *fairly* so as to eliminate any feelings of hostility on the part of the man left out of the unanimously desired dessert. He agrees. So do all the men. One man loses. He neither resists nor resents the fact that three men are eating apples and he is not. "That's the breaks of the game," says he ungrammatically and foolishly.

It is true that the procedure was one of pure chance. Each did have an equal chance to lose. One lost. The distribution *thereafter* was fair. But was justice done? Not necessarily. For one thing, justice and equality and fairness could have been construed to mean that, in this case, each man should receive three-quarters of an apple. In other words, there was a certain amount of valued goods to be distributed. There were no preset standards of distribution. From a positivistic point of view, there is no universally correct standard, e.g., greater need, greater ability. One's particular preference probably is dependent on various background factors ranging from the personal (intelligence) through the psychological (personality type) through the sociological (social status) through the anthropological (culture). However, men seem almost universally to have some misconceived notion about some natural or mysterious interrelationship between procedures and fairness. In the case of the workmen and the apples, the men could not see that in the absence of any previous agreement on appropriate standards for distributing the values, they were allowing a random procedure to be substituted. These men were simply surrendering their fortunes to caprice. There was an unperceived alternative that many would consider just. All it would have taken would have been for one to take out a penknife and cut the apples into quarters and then to distribute three to each worker. We tend to think so much in terms of procedures that we fail to perceive that they may conceal fundamental unfairnesses occurring under our very eyes.

Political scientists, jurisprudents, philosophers, historians, and lawyers speak at great length about justice. But their descriptions, analyses, and discussions are quite frequently couched in rather high-level abstractions that carry rather eccentric or specialized meanings. Frankly, many of these tracts seem more perplexing than enlightening. There seems to be an undue and entirely unhelpful sophistication of terminology in academic discussions of justice. The professional student of the topic, whether legalist or *philosophe*, whether anthropologist or political scientist, tends to discourse with a precious few beyond himself and has failed to help the rest of us much in understanding the relationships between court processes and justice.

Some of the clearest insights into this phenomenon that have come to my attention are from the pens of playwrights and novelists. This may be so because their data are not a series of definitions of theories, but instead are specific, factual situations. They may also have less interest in justifying the system than most legal academicians and jurists who write on this subject. Thus, I am suggesting that men such as Bertolt Brecht, Ugo Betti, and Friedrich Duerrenmatt may offer more help to political behavioralists in search of hypotheses about the interrelationship among courts, justice, and politics than most jurisprudents.

Probably the single common denominator in three literary works I have selected for analysis (Betti's *Landslide*, Brecht's *The Caucasian Chalk Circle*, and Duerrenmatt's *Traps*) is the viewpoint that the judicial process, as a set of procedures in human motion, and as practiced in society, is a great hoax. It is a fraud on the society and on all individuals living within it, and almost without exception upon the practicing judge himself.[69]

Brecht, the brilliant sociologist playwright-poet, heaped his scorn on common conceptions of the relationship between courts and justice by

---

[69] Ugo Betti, *Landslide*, Act III, in *Three Plays on Justice* (San Francisco: Chandler, 1964), pp. 55–56. As Parsc, the judge in *Landslide*, says to Goetz (a man who seems to represent the state):

PARSC (*picking up some papers from his desk, and getting ready to read the judgment*) Now then, let's see . . . "In the name of God, in accordance with the law . . . the law of the State, it is our free and impartial conviction . . ." (*hesitates, drops the papers onto the table, takes off his gown; to Goetz, calmly*) Sir, I would rather be struck dead than pronounce this judgment.

GOETZ (*gravely*) Judge Parsc, what is the matter with you?

PARSC I have something rather curious to tell you, Mr. Goetz. Perhaps, in all these years, I've never really believed in all this. (*He pushes aside the papers and lawbooks bound in red that lie on the table in front of him.*)

GOETZ Do you realize what you're saying?

PARSC (*with growing exasperation*) Of course I realize! And I'll tell you something else; for most of my life I've been a pleasure-seeking pig and an egoist. . . . And yet I've always been unhappy, sir. I used to lie in bed every night listening to the tap dripping in the yard or the ticking of the clock in my room. I wanted to kill myself. I would lie awake thinking about the cord at the side of the curtains! It was being alone that made me so unhappy! I kept myself

placing a vulgar rogue on the bench immediately following a successful (though temporary, as it turned out) revolution. This man, named Azdak, knew nothing of "the law" and cared even less about it. Its role, in his administration of the settling of disputes, was to serve only a physical function in the judicial procedure. Azdak sat upon the thick tomes of the legal code. Brecht believed that the law elevated justice in only the basest sense.

Azdak's actions upon the bench would be considered boorish and erratic by anyone with an eye and taste for the more sophisticated Western judicial procedures. He was arbitrary and his decisions were fashioned frequently upon whimsy rather than any more objectively based or visible system of values. Yet, by and large, if any pattern emerges, it is one in which the peasant folk received a far better deal (won many more cases) than under the former order of things. In fact, one might venture the thought that Brecht believed that the less judiciously Azdak acted (the less he comported himself as a proper judge in the courtroom), the more he would distribute victory to the people. But all good (just?) things come eventually to an end, and we learn that:

> . . . Azdak disappeared and was not seen again.
> The people of Grusinia did not forget him but long remembered
> The period of his judging as a brief golden age
> Almost an age of justice.[70]

Yet, to believe that Brecht made such a simple point would do injustice to his artistic and intellectual genius. Brecht had more in mind than the idea that feudalistic or capitalistic control was an instrument of oppression that could be converted into an instrument of justice by simply ignoring procedure and the very law it is set up to interpret. Otherwise, why would Brecht tell us of Azdak's lust (in seducing a farmer's daughter who had piously complained of rape) and of the fact that though he "granted their shrill demands, [he] took bribes from the empty hands of the simple and the poor"?

I think that Brecht is saying that judicial procedure has an importance for man beyond that which is usually stated (particularly by academicians

---

going by pretending to believe . . . to believe in so many fine things. (*frenziedly*) Nothing of the sort, my friend, I didn't really believe in anything at all! If you were to ask me now, I couldn't tell you why it is that I'm sitting here with these baubles in front of me. Justice, the law . . . ha! I'm sick to death of sitting up here playing the fool. Here, take your stupid papers. (*He picks up the papers and documents from his table, and scatters them about the floor.*) You can write out the judgment yourself. Do you want to know what I think? Well, I'll tell you. I think there's too much confusion, too much filth, too much cowardice. . . .

[70] *Seven Plays by Bertolt Brecht*, ed. Sir Eric Bentley (New York: Grove Press, 1961), pp. 586–87.

and jurists of all sorts). In the *Caucasian Chalk Circle,* the caprice involved in Azdak's administration comes very close to approximating the random natural injustices in the world that man tries so hard to avoid. In contrast to the plight of the poor peasants under the law before his ascendance, Azdak's personal justice was more desirable. After all, under the prior administration of the law they *always* were deprived. True, there was a consistency and a certainty, but this only assured them of misery. Who wouldn't be happier in a state of inconsistently administered pain and pleasure than in one of consistent and certain pain? Brecht is one person who does not equate procedures, order, certainty, and justice. He is surely not an advocate of the position that judicial procedure and just distributions of values go hand in hand.

So both Brecht and Betti have endowed their judges with an objectivity about what they do on the bench, and through these judges we are told that judicial structure has many functions other than that of functioning in the realm of justice. Indeed, it may do precisely the opposite. That is also a point made by Friedrich Duerrenmatt in his novel *Traps.*

Traps is a strange tale of a man who finds himself forced to stay overnight at an inn. He is the guest, after a time, of three men who persuade him to play at being a defendant in a trial for his own life while the trio acts as a court to prosecute and judge him. The four agree and have a go at it. Shortly, the man finds himself admitting that he has been guilty of murder. In the real world, he would not have been indicted or convicted of any crime at all. The murder was not a murder in the sense accepted by Western criminal codes, although it was in any human ethical sense. The defendant (Traps) had wished that a certain man would die, and had assisted nature to take its course more rapidly than it might otherwise have done.

Upon the recognition that he is actually guilty of this murder, Traps becomes elated and eventually takes his own life, dying with a smile upon his face. Why the smile? That's the point of it all. Duerrenmatt, like Betti and Brecht, is hardly convinced that the adjudication process in society does much to bring about justice. In *Traps,* Duerrenmatt is arguing that the law and the legal organization of a business society are not geared to prosecute people who take the market ethic to heart. Only an isolated, remote, unofficial, and informal juridical form is able to ferret out the truth and bring about proper punishment; the court system of the society is unable to do this.

Duerrenmatt is also telling us something more about why men need the adjudication structures that I have called courts. Very much like Betti, Duerrenmatt seems to believe that man needs a process that can affix guilt —rightly or wrongly, justly or unjustly. It is simply the statement of right or wrong that is important for most men; *it is the certainty of decision* (no matter what the content of the decision may be).

> The fatality that comes to the average man, to the man in the street, as chance will have it, in the form of an automobile accident, or as a mere imposition of nature, disease, the obstruction of a blood vessel by an embolism, a malignant growth, here emerges as the moral and indispensable outcome; in our sentence, life is perfected with logical consistency, like a work of art, and the human tragedy is revealed in all its beauty, shines radiantly, is welded into flawless form. . . .[71]

Poor man, facing so many dreadful possibilities and with no eternal father to tell him the truth, to tell him the good from the bad, to tell him the right from the wrong, craves answers, any answer. Is it irrational for man to establish such an elaborate set of procedures in order to accomplish this for himself? What nature has neglected, man has erected. Vilhelm Aubert, a contemporary Norwegian sociologist, sees very much the same function being performed by the court:

> Getting an unpredictable answer from the law may, to the legally naïve individual, mean a verification or falsification of important assumptions about his moral worth and standing in the social realm. It may even take on religious overtones, law being in some measure perceived as a manifestation of divine justice.[72]

This is also very much Betti's view, although Betti sees the certainty for which man hungers related to a direct, internal force rather than an indirect, external one.[73]

---

[71] Friedrich Duerrenmatt, *Traps* (New York: Ballantine Books, 1960), p. 115.

[72] Aubert, *op. cit.*, p. 47. Durkheim was perhaps the first to make this point explicit. He saw the punishment of crime as a great societal morale booster. See his *Division of Labor*, p. 277. This is discussed also by Christian Bay in his *The Structure of Freedom* (Stanford: Stanford University Press, 1958), p. 277. Sybille Bedford seems to have much the same impression about the function of English courts:

> The emotional climate of a trial is strange; it breeds a compound of scepticism and faith, an alert weighing of the facts and the sound of the facts, and an ultimate turning to the man in the chair, the more than arbiter, the oracle, the last word. And afterwards, it is a shock to find that one had looked to him to provide the miracle. The third shock is that of course he must be right [*The Faces of Justice* (New York: Simon & Schuster, 1961), p. 48].

[73] Betti, *Landslide*, pp. 57–58:

PARSC	Considering . . . that all those who stand before us, in this tribunal and elsewhere, have struggled hard to produce the dark, uneven bread whereby they exist . . . and that the good ingredients and the bad which this bread contains are not easily distinguishable because perhaps these men, while they breathed and walked upon the earth, were unable to be any different . . . Considering . . .
GOETZ	Go on!
PARSC	. . . that they have suffered greatly, dragging with them a most heavy burden . . .
GOETZ	Go on!
PARSC	. . . but that nothing is more dear to them than their own suffering . . . They are afraid that they will lose it . . . they feel it, like a whip

Betti sees the judge doing more than simply passing a judgment, any judgment. He sees him as a *potential* dispenser (whether he actually dispenses it or not) of compassion. For man at least has at times, in certain places (no matter how rarely), been known to parcel out compassion and mercy (even though with great parsimony). Nature, on the other hand, is universally and relentlessly cruel, indiscriminate, and without an atom of leniency.

The fact that academicians are so preoccupied with the idea that courts are the dispensers of justice seems to me somewhat ridiculous. The fairness of the procedure can do little but reflect the distribution of values inherent in the laws that the courts administer. Under the laws of Nazi Germany, the most impartial judge, using the most sophisticated rules of evidence, would have had to sentence Jews to concentration camps, and by no standard can that be considered a just act.

Of course, there may well be injustices—grossly unfair discriminations built into some juridical form—but the court itself does not discriminate. This many believe—and would have us believe—is essential to justice. That is precious little upon which to spend so much time and so many words. It is true, as some contend, that the judiciary is occasionally the avenue of access to the powers-that-be, through which more equitable distributions of the values of the society are authoritatively allocated. Thus, Victor G. Rosenblum can say:

> The judiciary is a primary and coordinate, though not plenary or exclusive, channel for the communication and critical appraisal of men's attitudes, latitudes, lassitudes, and achievements. It functions, of course, within a disciplined and stylized framework of preconditions and procedures, and sometimes serves constituencies different from those of legislature and executive. But communication and confrontation are preconditions of justice; and, to the extent the judiciary provides access to our central decision-making mechanisms for individuals

---

>   cracking over their heads, striking them and yet befriending them; it wounds them, but it also reassures them; and it forces them to walk on, and on, towards further wretchedness, further suffering . . .
>
> GOETZ   Go on, Parsc!
>
> PARSC   Considering, therefore, that they suffer because they want to suffer; that they suffer both when they possess the land and when they work it for others; both when they are called good and when they are called evil, when they oppressed, when they allowed themselves to be oppressed, when they deceived and when they were deceived . . .
> For these reasons. In the name of God; in the name of the law; we declare that these men . . . have pronounced their just and proper sentence. They pronounce it every day, in the lives that they lead and the torments that they suffer. We declare that by themselves they have found their certainty. And from the hands of the judge they will need to have something else, something higher; compassion. Compassion.

or groups otherwise excluded from effective participation, it enlarges the practicability of justice as well as the commitment of the otherwise alienated populations to justice as ideal and ideology.[74]

It must be noted, though, that the justice Rosenblum sees served here is not a function of the judicial structure, *per se*, but only of the existence of another route to equality of distribution regardless of the way that route is run. The fact that it is one structure of access among others will be handled in a later chapter. On the other hand, the fact that it *apparently* dispenses justice, just by its peculiar decision-making process, may have substantial political effect.

The most enduring function of the court—indeed of judicial structure —seems best described as the appeasement of the outrage felt in the soul and mind of man at the instability, tedium, amorphousness, and basic arbitrariness of our natural environment and our mortality. Whether man's mind should be eased of worry over these aspects of the human condition is a question that both social and political philosophers should discuss, at least as to whether such pacification should be a political function.

It has been my intent in this chapter to look at the phenomenon of courts somewhat more systematically than political scientists have done in the past. Many writers have taken an interest in courts because they believe them to be deeply involved in various phases of politics. However, their concern about courts has been uneven, for some aspects essential to a deeper understanding have been largely ignored.

Though much has been written on the origins and development of law, very little has been accomplished toward understanding the origins and development of courts. In this chapter I have tried to marshal those few works that have treated factors hypothesized to be associated with the rise of judicial structure in society. At this point in the development of a general theory of the evolution of courts, we must still consider the concept of societal complexity to be of some importance. However, it must be considered only *one* necessary condition. The sufficient conditions are yet far from clear. As we have seen, there are a few studies that, taken together, suggest that society must be segmented by some social philosophy or system before judicial structure can appear. When the social philosophy or social system is what we might call "communitarian," there seem to be fewer support factors for courts.

On the other hand, much has been written about the political functions of court systems and procedures. Unfortunately, this work is char-

---

[74] Victor G. Rosenblum, "Justiciability and Justice: Elements of Restraint and Indifference," *Catholic University Law Review*, 15 (1966), p. 152.

acterized more by the flowery quality of its rhetoric than by its clarity of thought. The lack of thoroughness in this vast literature is probably due to two tendencies: the tendency of scholars to overemphasize the importance and significance of their own personal interests and involvements, and the inclination of these scholars to disseminate knowledge rather than to put it to question or to scientifically oriented test. A close analysis raises many doubts about that literature which has blithely assumed that courts have been quite essential to public order, democracy, individual liberty, and justice. I don't believe that either the lexical definitions of these terms or reality itself justify much faith in these long-established propositions. This is not to say that judicial structure is functionless for society as a whole or for the individuals within it. The thinking of those who see courts as a social structure that helps procreate existing social values and which serves some very deep psychic need of individuals within society seems sound. It is also probably safe to say that courts *can* serve the functions for which they are said to be necessary. But they are neither the necessary nor the sufficient conditions for the performance of these functions. They are accidents coupled with vested interests.

PART B

Introduction

ON STRUCTURAL VARIATIONS OF COURTS

POLITICAL SCIENCE has long counted among its ranks a large number of men eager to describe political systems and processes, comprehensively and in part. Their descriptions have been, by and large, extensive and adroit. Surely Aristotle's study of 158 constitutional governments demonstrates the historical aspect of this proposition; and a simple browsing in the government section of any library will corroborate the scope, thoroughness, and excellence of these studies. But alas for him who would study the cause-effect relations between various conditions and structural variations in the *judicial* subsystem, for there are almost no data, no extensive descriptions.

Aside from the long manifested lack of interest by American political scientists in court systems of other societies, one necessary approach to gathering data on this phenomenon has fallen into disrepute: the notion of merely describing the legal/structural/historical/institutional aspects of some political structure is frowned on today as being a "traditional" activity. In some political science circles traditionalism is denounced in tones reminiscent of true Marxists drumming revisionists out of their ranks or of true Christians condemning heretics. It is true that political scientists did, as a matter of past practice, mainly describe general political structure and certain subsystems, including the judicial, in a legalistic and simple chronological fashion. Is it not the case, though, that such badly cropped pictures still have significant, though limited, value to those who wish to develop theories of political processes? I can see nothing wrong with such description as long as it is part of a more comprehensive description. One cannot understand such contemporary fashionable notions as role or attitude or process without initially knowing about the germane legal and historical facts that constrain human behavior.

Traditional concerns are indispensable as a context of more modern research foci, as well as a context of normative political theoretical enterprises. Furthermore, accumulating and presenting quantified data in charts, graphs, or statistical forms are entirely within the competence of the well-trained, legally and historically oriented researcher. Of course, traditional researchers would be of even further assistance to the behavioral types of researchers and theorists if they would also busy themselves with data related to social-scientific concepts and methods. It is not too difficult, and, after all, we are all engaged in a common endeavor.

Yet the general research picture is not so gloomy as I may have led the reader to believe, for some political scientists have managed to reconcile and employ diverse research approaches. A type of research that integrates traditional and behavioral research approaches is being carried out today by some American political scientists in what has been called the field of developmental politics. Yet these scholars display next to no enthusiasm for casting more than a passing glance at the prominent and important relationship between courts and politics. Even in descriptions of the development of a single nation, very little is written about the courts. It is as though they didn't exist, didn't perform important political functions in the society. There is little descriptive matter and less hypothesizing about any cause-effect relationships involving courts. Comparative-minded political scientists of such prominence as Gabriel Almond, David Apter, Leonard Binder, Lucian Pye, and Fred Riggs have almost totally ignored the court system and its political functions in their all but exhaustive studies of diverse underdeveloped lands. It seems somewhat shortsighted of them to exclude this aspect of political reality from their theoretical musings on the development of particular structural typologies. So it is not possible to be very happy with the state of the political science discipline in its treatment of an important aspect of politics—the interrelationship of the judicial structure and system with other components of the political system. The traditional comparative people present only barren legal and historical data, and the more modern comparative people rarely grant that courts exist.

THE PAUCITY AND VAGUENESS OF THE DATA AND THE THEORY

One way to demonstrate the near vacuum of work on the courts by the comparative development movement is to scan the index portions of its books. Next to nothing is to be found under the rubric of court, judiciary, legal system, justice, rule adjudication, or any other closely related concept. Incidentally, this is equally true of the more statistical mode of contemporary comparative work, such as *A Cross-Polity Survey*[1] and *Comparing Nations*.[2]

Let me use some of David Apter's work as a first example, mainly in deference to the aesthetics of alphabetical order. It amazes me how a theorist as important as Apter can manifest such total disinterest in and/or unawareness of the theoretical position of the relationship between courts and politics. If he has reason to believe that his studies disprove or disverify these theories, a few pages of his observations—systematic or otherwise— would be invaluable to us laboring under the attractions of such theory. But we are not treated to this at all. We are left frustrated by both his specific, one-nation studies and his more abstract, general theoretical creations.

In *Ghana in Transition* there is no mention of the courts' role either in the text or in the new Preface (1963).[3] This is particularly distressing in a study of a country like Ghana, where the Anglo-American legal system has been so closely (in a formal, structural sense) emulated. For instance, the constitution of the Republic of Ghana contains a very lengthy part concerned with "Law and Justice." In it we find some provision for judicial review. Furthermore, there have been some extremely important and highly publicized political trials in Ghana. Perhaps the most visible and significant one occurred in the latter days of 1963—though the courts did make some highly important decisions before then. The case against *Adamafio et al.* ended in an acquittal of several defendants brought to trial by Nkrumah himself for an assassination attempt on his life. This judicial action (the acquittal) led to the dismissal of the chief justice, a changing of the judiciary laws, and ultimately to a constitutional amendment![4] That's quite an impact for a court decision—and since it did happen in Ghana, one can surely

---

[1] Arthur S. Banks and Robert B. Textor, *A Cross-Polity Survey* (Cambridge: M.I.T. Press, 1963). Although this is a broad-gauge attempt to compare political systems on many dimensions, there is almost a total lack of reference to the judiciary. True, there is an attempted modification of Wigmore's typology of some forty years ago—but this is of the law (the legal system), not a classification of judicial systems. The only mention of judicial structure that I found in this book comes in section 43: "Horizontal Power Distribution" (or separation of powers)—and this could be of only limited value in a comparative study of the role of judiciaries. The reason is that only one unit of the typology ([A] Effective allocation of power to functionally autonomous legislative, executive, and judicial branches) contains a clear statement on the judiciaries. In B and C there is a lumping of branches without ever indicating wherein the courts are classified. Wesley Gould and Michael Barkun, in their forthcoming *The Science of Order*, find the same fault in this lack of finesse in classifying types of law.

[2] Richard L. Merritt and Stein Rokkan, *Comparing Nations* (New Haven: Yale University Press, 1966).

[3] David Apter, *Ghana in Transition*, rev. ed. (New York: Anthenium, 1963).

[4] For a detailed treatment of this case, see William Harvey, "The Ghana Treason Trials: A Study in Political Irrationality," in *Political Trials*, ed. Theodore L. Becker (Indianapolis: Bobbs-Merrill, forthcoming).

question the thoroughness of a political analysis of that country which failed to provide even a simple structural description of the court system. Apparently some very important people in Ghana—ex-Chief Justice Korsah, for one—took the structural requisites and expectations of the Ghanaian constitution and the history of the country quite seriously—much to their political and personal disadvantage.

A similar question can be posed about a similar omission in Apter's study of Uganda.[5] In another recent work, *The Politics of Modernization,*[6] he discourses at a high enough theoretical level to avoid discussion of the courts; the closest he gets to discussing the courts is through such phrases as "the mechanics of government."[7] He does, however, mention political parties, the bureaucracy, and the military, which seem to me to be at about the same level of abstraction as the concept of courts. Since Apter has theoretical interest in "legitimation" and the formation of political values, both of which are theoretically related to traditional concerns of courts, the omission is all the more glaring.

Lucian Pye and Fred Riggs have done work equally pertinent to this discussion. Again we have men who have published well-received single-nation studies that fit within more comprehensive nation-system political theories developed elsewhere, and again, both in Riggs's *Thailand: The Modernizing of a Bureaucratic Polity*[8] and *Administration in Developing Countries: The Prismatic Society*[9] and in Pye's *Politics, Personality, and Nation Building*[10] and *Communication and Political Development,*[11] there is nearly complete silence on the courts' relationship to the polity. One may argue, of course, that Riggs can limit his studies to administration and avoid discussing courts without fearing criticism. This argument misses the mark; I am not criticizing Riggs, I am exhorting a group of scholars. My point is simply that there is a developing body of theory, built upon the American experience, which covers a broad range of propositions on the interrelationship between courts, politics, and bureaucracies. If it does not apply in Thailand or the rest of the developing countries, it would be of no small importance for us to know it. Political science can surely benefit from Riggs's speculations on this subject matter relevant to his descriptions and theorizing. The same may be said about Pye and his theoretical orientations of personality, nation-building, communication, and politics. Do the courts have *no* bearing on these phenomena?

5 *The Political Kingdom in Uganda* (Princeton: Princeton University Press, 1961).
6 Chicago: University of Chicago Press, 1965.
7 *Ibid.,* p. 34.
8 Honolulu: East-West Center Press, 1966.
9 Boston: Houghton Mifflin, 1964.
10 New Haven: Yale University Press, 1962.
11 Princeton: Princeton University Press, 1963.

Moreover, I think it would be extremely worthwhile if political scientists dealing in comparative data in general (whether of developing or industrialized societies, or of Occidental or Oriental cultures) concentrated a reasonable span of attention on the courts, as this would help in the construction of that area of empirical political theory related to courts. That is, as societies develop *in toto* or vary systemically, whither the structure or function of courts?

I have noted that there are some materials on the judiciary in the body of research on general comparative government and politics. My point has been that they are of lesser quality than those dealing with other political subsystems. Aside from the shallowness and narrowness of the theory handled, it frequently smacks of the worst of the traditional ideologizing. Where it makes an attempt to say something more than this, it becomes either naïve, trivial, vague, impressionistic, or opaque.[12] Of course, there are occasional exceptions. I will say for it that the areas of judicial structural variation that are treated, when they are treated at all, seem to me to include the most important ones. These are: the degree, if any, of judicial independence; the existence of the power of judicial review or some power akin to that; and the formal interrelationships and real power distribution between the courts and the other governmental subsystems. One major structural variable that the comparative government and politics and judicial behavior researchers completely ignore (or forget about) is the degree of lay participation in the judicial system.

The following chapters are divided along lines of structural variation. The common lesson will become painfully clear: a strong tinge of Western or conservative bias is easily discernible in what has been said about judicial structure. It is therefore not extraordinary that the evidence proffered to support these statements is scarcely adequate or reliable. In sum: we have almost nowhere to go but up.

---

[12] I should like to mention, once again, Gabriel A. Almond and G. Bingham Powell, Jr., *Comparative Politics: A Developmental Approach* (Boston: Little, Brown, 1966), as a glaring illustration of this. In a few short pages they intermingle poor theory, flimsy evidence, and thoroughly confused concepts of judicial impartiality and independence.

CHAPTER 4

THE MEASURE, CONDITIONS, AND FUNCTIONS OF JUDICIAL INDEPENDENCE

> Neither slave nor master. I *am* my
> freedom. No sooner had you created
> me than I ceased to be yours.
> —JEAN-PAUL SARTRE
> *The Flies*

THE BEST STARTING POINT for a discussion of judicial independence is an explication of the concept. Once again, there has been all too little definitional exactitude. What is accepted as a definition of judicial independence is an occasional passing remark, a shrugging of the shoulders, a "You know what I mean," or an *obiter dictum*. This will be demonstrated in the following pages as the reader becomes aware of some political scientists' penchant for talking around this topic, and their proclivity to discuss conditions that must precede something they have not bothered to describe adequately. After working out a comprehensive conceptual definition, since I intend to do social science in lieu of metaphysics, I shall stipulate (at first arbitrarily) the phenomena deemed to be indicators of independence. The second step will be to develop an operationalizable definition.

An implicit assumption at the operationalization stage will be that the concept of independence is not a dichotomous variable; it refers to a potentially continuous phenomenon. We shall tackle the problem of assigning relative weights to the various indicators.

Once we find that independence exists (to some minimal degree), the differences in degree of that quality (from small to large) become structural variations, and at that point we would do well to see what theories have been advanced to account for judicial independence. Until the functional importance of various degrees of judicial independence is disconfirmed, ample justification exists (given the tremendous amount of theory that supports these hypotheses) to ponder and inquire into the causes of the varying degrees of judicial independence.

Lastly, much of the literature that speaks of the importance of independence of the judiciary implicitly presents some functional hypotheses. The final section of this chapter will be devoted to these, so as to state them as clearly as possible and to suggest pertinent research ventures.

The Concept Defined

The most appropriate starting point for a definition, I think, is the distinction between the sister concepts of judicial independence and judicial impartiality, particularly as I have defined the latter in Chapter 1.[1] Within my definitional scheme (and I think within a reasonably close reference to reality as well) one may exist without very much correspondence with the other.[2] That is, much independence may exist without much impartiality and much impartiality may exist without much independence. A decision-maker may be (1) very impartial and objective and (2) appear to be a judge; that is, he may have a structurally defined position clearly distinct from the executive, replete with trappings, yet he may still enjoy little independence. Such a decision-maker may slavishly apply law in the same way as the promulgating legislative committee or the decreeing king; that is, he may be 100 percent in accord with the viewpoints of the legislature and the executive. It is probably true that he is not very independent of them, if at all. The big question, however, is how could we tell? In this case we couldn't, because there was nothing but agreement. We can find independence only if we define it in terms of overt, observable behavior that manifests a respect for opposition or opposition itself.

This, I suspect, is the only meaningful (in a research and analytic sense) way to define it. I tend to think that we can get a fair idea of whether or not there is any independence at all, and attain some crude measurement

---

[1] As evidence of the fact that these concepts are very close to one another, it can be shown that they are frequently interchanged by scholars in the field, and that little distinction is made in their use. For instance:

> These two aspects of relationship between judiciary and bureaucracy have not appeared in any way detrimental to the impartiality and independence of the courts or the judges. As in the *Conseil d'État* of France, the fact that some judges belong to the same [civil service] cadre as administrators has not resulted in impartiality for or against administration [Ralph Braibanti, "Public Bureaucracy and Judiciary in Pakistan," in *Bureaucracy and Political Development*, ed. Joseph La Palombara (Princeton: Princeton University Press, 1963), p. 416].

[2] The best explication of the difference and relationship between these two concepts is Torstein Eckhoff's "Impartiality, Separation of Powers, and Judicial Independence," *Scandinavian Studies in Law*, 9 (1965), pp. 9–52. One of the most intriguing parts of Professor Eckhoff's examination of these concepts is his perception of their interaction.

of the degree to which it exists, when indeed it does exist. Of course, beliefs about judicial independence have some importance, for if no one (judges, officials, citizenry) believed the judiciary independent, it would be highly unlikely that we would find judges acting independently. I also believe that these are far better indicators than legalistic ones—though this remains to be seen.

A common approach to the concept of judicial independence is to skirt the problem of defining it by assuming that everyone knows what is meant, and then to describe its *legal* guarantees. This, of course, confuses statute books with the living law. For instance, Henry Abraham has, on occasion, dealt with the notion of judicial independence. Once upon a time, he presented a rather legalistic representation of what one usually finds in the judicial politics work on this topic.

> Essential to an independent judiciary is security of tenure, and it is particularly so in the case of appointed judges. . . . Without a lengthy term of office, preferably life tenure, decent remuneration, and stringent safeguards against removal for other than statutorily or constitutionally carefully circumscribed serious breaches of official trust, the concept of judicial independence becomes a mockery.[3]

Of course, this is not a definition, and I doubt that Abraham meant it as such. Frequently, though, when the concept is dealt with in such a way as this, the statement is easily confounded with a definition. Not only is the concept of judicial independence subject to confusion bred of the vagueness of terminology used, but further confusion results from the usual absence of any explicit definition elsewhere in the book or article employing the concept. Actually, Abraham's statement is a set of hypotheses in the form of a widely held theory; of several interrelated and tested propositions. Still no explication of the dependent variable (judicial independence) is anywhere to be found in the book in which these propositions are stated. This is common practice.

In constructing a modal (or lexical) conceptualization of judicial independence, one might include concepts of honesty and integrity as primitive terms, but they have a high emotional charge and tell us little. Moreover, reference to some doctrine of separation of powers and to freedom from various types of external political pressure would have to be made. Finally, the conception of self-containment in decision-making would have to be included. The following three illustrations are specific examples of the ways in which these components get mixed in much of the traditional literature.

---

[3] Henry J. Abraham, *The Judicial Process: An Introductory Analysis of the Courts of the United States, England, and France,* 2nd ed. (New York: Oxford University Press, 1968), p. 39.

Justice Bernard Botein, in his treatise on the trial judge, approaches the concept of judicial independence in the following way:

> When a lawyer looks up at a judge, that judge wants to read in his eyes the unspoken expression: "You may rule for me or against me, you may get the point of my argument or miss it: I know my client's cause will receive earnest and *honest* consideration in your hands."[4]

This, however, could well be referring to impartiality, and thus does not help us distinguish between impartiality and independence.

The concepts of dispassionate decision, separation from politics, and independence are frequently linked in the literature,[5] but on occasion someone singles out the concept of independence for special treatment. For instance, according to Ranney: "If the judicial process is to be well performed, it must operate in an atmosphere of calmness, deliberation, *and above all, freedom from pressures by parties and pressure groups with axes to grind.*"[6]

Similar to this view is that of another jurist, Henry Lummis, who quite explicitly defines the boundary between judicial independence and nonindependence as follows:

> The moment a decision is controlled or affected by the opinion of others or by any form of external influence or pressure, that moment the judge ceases to exist. One who pronounces a decision arrived at even in part by other minds is not a judge . . . the courts must be above intimidation, *control* or influence, or they cease to be courts.[7]

I think that the discussion by Lummis and the following one by Glendon Schubert come close to a sound behavioral (substantive attitudes, values, or actions relative to judicial decisions and strategies) type of definition of judicial independence, and at the same time distinguish the phenomenon from its legal prerequisites, which is what Abraham failed to do. Schubert states that:

> To say that the justices enjoy job security and legal independence from the power of direction and policy *control* of the President and the Congress is only the beginning rather than the end of significant inquiry into the meaning of judicial independence, however. The justices clearly are not independent from the legal profession; and guild restraints and distraints are a major channel of judicial responsibility. By this we mean that the justices normally retain active affiliation with bar associations; they find that *noblesse oblige* requires,

---

[4] Bernard Botein, *The Trial Judge* (New York: Cornerstone Library, 1963), p. 292 (emphasis mine).

[5] See in particular Gray Thoron, "A Report on Judicial Ethics," *Annals of the American Academy of Political and Social Science* (January, 1966), pp. 36–43.

[6] Austin Ranney, *The Governing of Men*, rev. ed. (New York: Holt, Rinehart & Winston, 1966), p. 497 (emphasis mine).

[7] Henry T. Lummis, *The Trial Judge* (Chicago: Foundation Press, 1937), p. 10 (emphasis mine).

pretty much, that they make recurring guest appearances at the better-known law schools; they write for and read the major law journals. Neither are the justices independent of the past, which surely includes, for each, the sociopsychological factors which have helped to shape his character and personality to say nothing of friendships which, not infrequently, survive a man's accession to the Court. With the possible exception of occasional Olympians who eschew the reading of daily newspapers, the justices are aware of what is going on in the world; and with different degrees of zest, they participate in the social life of official Washington. Moreover, the justices are not independent of each other, or of their clerks or other elements of the organization of which they are the formal leaders. They are dependent, necessarily, upon many other human beings in order to do their work; and, being men with substantial experience in political affairs, they need not ask for whom the bell tolls—they know that it tolls for them together with the rest of humanity.[8]

The only difficulty with Schubert's conceptualization is that much about judicial independence still remains implicit, and Lummis' idea of control is too stringent to aid us in discovering *degrees* of independence. A key may lie in some definitional distinction between control and influence. The way in which control is used by Lummis and Schubert seems to present an either-or proposition: There is or there is not control. Influence usually implies a matter of degree; control does not refer to degree unless it is explicitly so qualified: e.g., partial control of behavior. Influence, I believe, is in itself only a question of degree of effect on behavior. At any rate, Lummis seems to be a product of an age of mechanical jurisprudence; Schubert probably would agree with my point, though perhaps not with my choice of words. Elsewhere his use of the word "extent" in prefacing "control" strongly implies he considers judicial independence capable of measurement, not just dichotomization.[9]

I propose that a definition of judicial independence that would go a long way in helping in the study of comparative judicial politics might read something like this:

Judicial independence is (a) the degree to which judges believe they can decide and do decide consistent with their own personal attitudes, values, and conceptions of judicial role (in their interpretation of the law), (b) in opposition to what others, who have or are believed to have political or judicial power, think about or desire in like matters, and (c) particularly when a decision adverse to the beliefs or desires of those with political or judicial power may bring some retribution on the judges personally or on the power of the court.

---

[8] Glendon Schubert, *Constitutional Politics* (New York: Holt, Rinehart & Winston, 1960), pp. 67–68 (emphasis mine).
[9] *Ibid.*, p. 67.

Those with retaliatory powers against judges would include hereditary officials, appointed officials, elected officials, lobbyists, or an electorate. This definition would exclude much of the influence on judges coming from the sources Schubert believes to be so important, e.g., past friendships and their clerks. By now, few believe judges can be totally independent of their society and their own values; judicial independence, if taken to mean this, could not exist, and thus there would be no courts. If judicial independence is indeed a variable (as it differs in degree), then it can only refer to the degrees of freedom the judge has from *official* and *political* sources of influence. Finally, as the judge is dependent upon the law (bound to interpret and apply it), he is impartial; as he would resist those in other positions (or those who support them) who would have him violate this dependency, he is independent. To insist that "influence" or "control" of judicial decision-making by the content of laws is a constraint on judicial independence is to insist on obscuring any differences between the concepts of independence and impartiality.

I am including an edited version of the American case of *Tumey* v. *Ohio* (1927) in the Appendix to this chapter for two reasons. First, it is illustrative of the distinction between impartiality and independence. Second, it is an unusual judicial discussion of the concept of independence. In my view, the fact that the judge's salary was based on the fines he levied discounts his impartiality. His own personal interests could easily hinder his objective reading of the law. The fact that, as mayor, the judge was interested in drumming up revenue discounts his independence. His role and outside support in another governmental structure prejudices the possibility that as a judge he could arrive at a conclusion opposite to the interests of the mayoralty.

I elected to use the word "decide" instead of "act" since I am not referring to the possible dependence that judges may have on a prosecutor, in an inquisitorial system, for information and evidence. The emphasis here is on *independence to decide*, given the judges' own perception of the law and facts.

Indicators and Measures

Although I have gone to some lengths to delineate the boundaries of this concept, the real trouble comes in trying to evaluate which data best indicate judicial independence, directly and indirectly, and which data are essential to measure its variations cross-culturally. Clouds may indicate rainfall, but measuring their density is no valid calibration of the inches of rain that will fall. As far as judicial independence is concerned, all kinds of data are available; the problem has long been to separate the indicators from the reality. For instance, what are we to do with the legal guarantees for judges (tenure, etc.)? Obviously, they are not, in and of themselves, true measures of judicial independence. Probably they do have a significant relationship to the extent to which it exists in any given society. Other problems confront us: If judicial independence is a relationship between sets of attitudes and actions on the parts of various political actors and judges, what methods are feasible for measurement? What data are reliable? Dr. Hans Frank, the Nazi commissioner of justice, once told a group of German judges that "There is no independence of the law against National Socialism. Say to yourselves at every decision which you make: 'How would the Fuehrer decide in my place?' "[10] This, of course, suggests that the court should have no independence whatever. If this were believed by all judges who were appointed, or who remained, and if they so stated and really tried to think like Hitler, it could be all but definitive proof of a complete lack of independence. Though the German judges could still decide with great impartiality (adhering to the Nazi laws and codes despite strong *personal* views to the contrary), there would be no court in operation.

Some may argue that the extent of belief in independence cannot be an indicator of the actual degree of independence. I tend to think otherwise, though I do not feel there is anywhere near a perfect fit. It seems to me that if judges do believe they have independence, then that attitude, and the degree of its pervasiveness, to some extent will indicate the degree (or lack) of judicial independence in the society. It may not be an *accurate* indicator of degree—but that is open to question. In like manner, the amount of freedom actually present in a society in general is partly commensurate with how much freedom the people believe they have. If they fear they have little, then there will be little actual freedom, for few would be willing to risk imminent sanctions. If they believe they have great liberty to speak, assemble, and act, then that society is likely to demonstrate more liberty than another where people do not believe they have much liberty. When the U.S. Supreme Court states that certain governmental actions tend to "chill" liberty, it means that people become afraid, and hence are far less likely to act. So once again, some distribution of an attitude must exist in order to justify any attempts to measure the phenomenon that is the object of the belief. Such attitudes can be inferred, it should be noted, from the existence of the legal safeguards of political insulation for judges. In other words, with such laws on the books, it can be assumed that judges and

---

10 See William Ebenstein, *The Nazi State* (New York: Farrar & Rinehart, 1943).

others believe that the judges themselves can make at least some decisions with relative impunity. Thus, our attention must then focus on the occasions when these decisions are made. Once again we are faced with the problem of getting at some vital attitudes: those of judges and those of some warring politicos. If there is no substantial degree of difference between them, i.e., if the elite is not visibly fragmented in its deeper values, the structure of judicial independence must be extremely fragile and permeable.

The Soviet system (at a local level) as described by Feifer is a good one to compare with the American local court system.[11] The data suggest that Moscow judges are more in accord with their superiors or other political or party officials on questions of system, policy goals, guilt, and/or proper sentence than are their American counterparts. More specifically, it appears that Soviet judges and prosecutors agree more—and thus judicial decisions are more in line with executive policy—than American judges and district attorneys. This may be due more to a pervasive ideology in the USSR (with widespread sharing of values among all members of the elite) than to any structural-systemic variations. All that is important at this point is to find the best ways to determine the relative degrees of judicial independence from society to society or within any given society from time to time. Surely, information along these lines will be hard to come by. Political actors are infrequently anxious to put many of their beliefs on record. Judges, too, are cautious in this regard. Still, ways must be found to get at these data. The attitudes of the populace, on a variety of issues, must also be gauged occasionally, in order to determine whether judicial independence was exercised.

There also may be some "unobtrusive measures" for judicial independence.[12] For instance, Braibanti observed what he believed to be a reliable indicator for a high degree of independence of the Pakistan Supreme and High Courts. This was, in his words, the fact that decisions "are read avidly and discussed with fervor in the coffee houses and other gathering places."[13] Another one could be the fact that the speeches of certain justices are reprinted at great length in the newspapers. Still another indicator could be that, as Braibanti notes, the courts constitutionally or statutorily have the power to issue one or several of the prerogative writs—*mandamus, habeas corpus*, etc. What should be checked here are the records of the raw number of applications for any of these writs. If records are not available, an observer could watch the courts for the percentage of actions therein that consist of pleadings commensurate with the nature of these writs. Braibanti

---

[11] George Feifer, *Justice in Moscow* (New York: Simon & Schuster, 1964).
[12] Eugene J. Webb, Donald Campbell, Richard D. Schwartz, and Lee Sechrest, *Unobtrusive Measures* (Chicago: Rand McNally & Co., 1966).
[13] Braibanti, *op. cit.*, p. 412.

has attempted to corroborate his view that Pakistan's courts have a great degree of independence by noting the great number of such writ applications *and* the notable degree to which this number increased over time.[14]

On the other hand, it is possible that the impressionistic wisdom of the ages is true. It is possible that if the statute books of a culture reveal all the structural guarantees ordinarily considered to promote judicial independence, judges there are far more likely to think and act independently than are judges in states and cultures where the statute books are devoid of such guarantees. If we do not need to test out traditional beliefs, then— *and only then*—can we accept these statutory provisions as indicators of independence by simply summing the quantity of indicators that are present.

As indicators and degrees of indicators, one might propose the following scheme, purely for illustrative purposes:

Salary	Cannot be lowered while in office.	1	Can be lowered.	0
	Is sufficient to live on in culture in comfort without resort to other occupations.	1	Not sufficient.	0
Tenure	Lifetime (with checks by other branches on each other for removal).	3	May be removed at pleasure of other (executive).	0
	Period of years, then lifetime (with checks).	2		
	Period of years only (with checks).	1		
Recruitment	Election by people. Appointment (with checks).	2 1	Appointment by executive alone (no checks).	0

It would be of interest to determine, through questionnaires and interviews, the degree of correlation between the degree of independence to be inferred from these guarantees and the independence judges (or those who study politics in general or courts specifically) believe they have. All of these legal factors are discussed frequently in the literature on the judicial process, particularly that body of work concerned with the political rele-

---

[14] "After the 1956 Constitution went into effect, the number of writs sought in the courts increased markedly. The total number sought through July 31, 1962, approximates 14,000. Of these, approximately 3,000 . . . were writs sought by government employees seeking redress of grievance relating to employment matters. This does not mean that these actions resulted in granting of writs or even of admitting them for consideration. The number of writs sought is symptomatic of its wide use as a means of redress" (*ibid.*, p. 421).

vance of courts. In fact, according to Vines: "Questions about the selection of judicial personnel and their conditions of tenure dominate discussion of the politics of judicial institutions."[15] Yet I am unaware of any discussion that relates these statutory requirements to *any variation in degree of judicial independence* that may or may not exist in the judiciaries under study. Isn't this the critical question? Is this not the significance of such data? Vines, for instance, in his comparative study of the American state judicial systems, equated the whole factor of "court personnel" (selection, tenure, etc.) to the factor "taking the judiciary out of politics."[16] As I noted above, "taking the judiciary out of politics" is at least a substantial part of the concept of judicial independence. Thus Vines is attempting to relate some variations in judicial selection structure to judicial independence; yet he never mentions this latter concept (by that label) or even defines concretely what "taking the judiciary out of politics" means. Although the background data that Vines analyzes in relationship to the variations in selection procedures can be taken as indicative of an indirect relationship to judicial independence, Vines is probably implying a relationship between the background information and the closeness with which a judge's vote coincides with his own personal values (as indicated by socioeconomic status characteristics). Therefore, he is studying the lack of objectivity of the judge rather than the degree of his independence.[17]

A quote from Harold Berman may be helpful in illuminating the problems of relying on legal sources to indicate the degree of independence. The major drawback is the inclination to confuse legal prerequisites with reality.

> The Soviet judge is an important means of reconciliation of the abstract "will of the state" with the personal actions of individual citizens. He is a figure in whom the state seeks to have public confidence reposed. He identifies himself with the parties who come before him. He does equity. He has not merely the interests of the state but also the interests of the litigant at heart. Indeed the People's Courts *sometimes* show a remarkable leniency, a *tendency* to acquit, a *tendency* to mitigate the harshness of the law; *on appeal, they are sometimes rebuked for their soft-heartedness.* But even here, the conscientious attitudes of the Soviet judges are subject to *far greater pressure* from outside political authorities. They owe their election to the Communist Party . . . Their tenure is relatively short (five years) and they *may* be

---

15 Kenneth Vines, "Courts as Political and Governmental Agencies," in *Politics in the American States*, ed. Herbert Jacob and Kenneth Vines (Boston: Little, Brown and Company [Inc.], 1965), p. 257.

16 *Ibid.*, p. 259.

17 *Ibid.*, pp. 261–62, 279–83.

recalled in the interim by their constituents for misconduct. Their conscience is *subject to the demands* of Party campaigns to stamp out this or that type of activity among the population.[18]

Even as excellent a scholar as Berman fails to avoid the trap. He has emphasized that the legal prerequisites are more indicative of the degree of judicial independence than the actual *behavior* of the judges ("remarkable leniency," "tendency to acquit," "sometimes rebuked"). How great a tendency? How frequently rebuked? Are they threatened generally with removal? How often have the lenient ones been recalled, or *not* recalled? Berman downgrades the degree of independence only because of certain of the Soviet *laws* on the makeup of the judiciary. The mere fact that judges are nominated by the party, have short terms, and are subject to policy-motivated programs by a political party does not seem to me to make them *qualitatively* different from the judiciaries of many American states. Many American judges are party choices, must run for reelection, and are quite aware of the same pressing needs in a community as party or governmental officials (a stamp-out-crime-by-being-hard-on-criminals campaign). It is what is in the judge's mind and how he and the government act—not the statute books—that will tell us what we wish to know about judicial independence. For instance, Frank Lacy's statement on judicial independence in modern Yugoslavia seems to illustrate a more objective study of the phenomenon, and possibly a more accurate appraisal of its nature:

> On the score of independence, one man told me: "They [the judges] aren't really so secure as the permanent-tenure law would suggest. They can always get rid of them if they want to." Another: "It all depends on the man. Certainly we have some who are too responsive to the party's wishes, but we have strong judges too," and he went on to describe a one-time zealous police officer who upon election to the bench became a zealous civil rightist and a great thorn in the flesh of the prosecuting authorities.[19]

The Communists, it seems, may have their Musmannos, Coxes, and Warrens as well. This raises a very important point regarding the American study of a variety of aspects of Communist systems. For instance, this statement by Lacy hardly squares with one made some fifteen years previously by a Yugoslav Communist party dignitary, Aleksander Rankovic, that "there exists no abstract independence of the court."[20] Indeed, there can

---

[18] Harold J. Berman, *Justice in the U.S.S.R.*, rev. ed. (Cambridge: Harvard University Press, 1963), pp. 270–71 (emphasis mine).

[19] Frank R. Lacy, "Yugoslavia: Practice and Procedure in a Communist Country," *Oregon Law Review*, 43 (December, 1963), p. 15.

[20] Vladimir Gsovski and Kazimierz Grzybowski, eds., *Government, Law and Courts in the Soviet Union and Eastern Europe* (New York: Praeger, 1959), p. 803.

be little doubt that many changes and practices forced upon the court systems of Eastern Europe by the newly ruling Communist parties dominated (if not obliterated) the judicial independence in those countries in the late 1940s.[21]

Is it possible to equate legal restrictions and administrative sanctions on judicial independence during a revolutionary era with those of the same legal system now? Once a regime feels securely entrenched, may it not tolerate abundant amounts of judicial discretion? How also can one explain the establishment, zealousness, and great impact of the Yugoslavian Constitutional Court since 1964?[22] We know that structural and administrative factors that theoretically bind *our* lower court judges do not yield anything close to perfect compliance; lower court judges defy higher judicial authority in the United States as well.[23] What we must find out is the degree of difference in this level of actual judicial independence. What the law says, and how the system is set up, and what was the case in revolutionary circumstances—these things tell us far too little about judicial behavioral realities.

Relying exclusively on attitudes about judicial independence, or on unobtrusive measures of it, or doting upon laws that guarantee it, is a risky business. All should be used to the exclusion of none; even when they are taken together, however, the analyst must realize that he has, at best, only approximated the reality of this aspect of judicial behavior. To obtain a reasonably precise measuring stick, we must get at the actual decision-making patterns of the judges as well. For example, to go Braibanti one further, it is not merely the number of prerogative writs applied for that measures independence directly—it is the ratio of favorable to unfavorable dispositions. This does illustrate, however, one way we can approach the measurement of judicial independence without being compelled to tap the attitudes of the other governmental officials. We can readily infer their policy preferences from the action or inaction on their part that triggered the trial proceedings. Still, on other occasions we shall find it necessary to sample the views of officialdom in order to evaluate the degree of discrepancy between

---

[21] This is extensively documented in Gsovski and Grzybowski, *Government, Law and Courts.*

[22] See Winston M. Fisk and Alvin Z. Rubenstein, "Yugoslavia's Constitutional Court," *East Europe,* 15 (July, 1966), pp. 24–28. It is an excellent survey, with illustrations, of the seriousness with which the court exercises its power. It also discusses the impact of this innovation on Yugoslavian officials. For a general handling of this topic, see chap. 6 of this volume.

[23] Walter Murphy, "Lower Court Checks on Supreme Court Power," *American Political Science Review,* 52 (December, 1959), pp. 1017–31; Kenneth N. Vines, "Federal District Judges and Race Relations Cases in the South," *Journal of Politics,* 26 (May, 1964), pp. 337–57. Cf. Richard J. Richardson, "Review, Dissent and the Appellate Process: A Political Interpretation," *Journal of Politics,* 29 (August, 1967), pp. 597–616.

them and corresponding judicial activity. All of this leads us to another difficulty: even when we know (1) the governmental official attitudes, (2) the judicial attitudes, and (3) the exact configuration of the judicial behavior, we are still not ready to measure judicial independence with any degree of accuracy until we have gauged it (remember section *c* of the definition on page 144) not only against governmental or political powers, *per se,* but also against those who possess the *power to injure* the judges or the court (as an institution) in response to their decision or decisions. This power varies from one society to another. We cannot rely on structural similarity.

To American eyes, the claims made by Braibanti about the great independence exercised by the Supreme Court of Pakistan might appear unjustified in light of this latter definitional component. This would be due to Braibanti's nearly exclusive focus on cases wherein the Supreme Court of Pakistan held only against the civil service bureaucracy. This is, of course, not a negligible exercise of judicial power. The bureaucracy is an arm of the executive. If the court also handed down many decisions against, say, the legislature, then all these decisions taken together would add up to an exceedingly high measure of judicial independence. But it appears to be an excessively high evaluation of the degree of judicial independence to state that it reached "climactic heights" when the Supreme Court upheld a contempt citation against the Secretary of the Law Ministry for public statements attacking the writ jurisdiction of the judiciary (*The State* v. *Sir Edward Snelson*).[24] In the main, the "high degree of courage and independence of the judiciary," for all we can see, is to be found only in the Pakistani judiciary's dictations to various levels of the bureaucracy. On the other hand, convicting and affirming the conviction of an important governmental official, in the face of manifest executive displeasure, is a measure of a healthy degree of judicial freedom. Furthermore, Braibanti is probably justified in his extremely high rating of Pakistani judicial independence, for in Pakistan, power is held in the bureaucracy, military and civil, not in the legislature.[25]

Of course, what this points up is that in attempting to measure judicial independence itself (instead of only its indicators), one must locate and evaluate the strength of diverse sources of power potentially toxic to the courts. Then one must observe the extent to which the courts actually flaunt these opposing power centers. There may be a rough scale of independence. Cases in which courts invalidate police actions as being inept or foolish

---

[24] See Appendix to this chapter.
[25] I am indebted to Fred Riggs for this observation (in a personal communication).

administrations of law, though important acts of independence *per se,* are not necessarily indicative of the higher echelons of independence. Contrariwise, the existence of higher strata of independence, as we shall see in the following chapter on judicial review, almost inevitably indicates that the court system at least will run the gauntlet of police displeasures.

In many countries, however, the most lethal danger lurks in the courts' willingness to tussle with the legislature. Courts have their ways, though. The main one is statutory construction. Moreover, it can go either way; that is, the court can either shrink or inflate policies promulgated by the legislature. Even when the highest court has the power of judicial review, it may forgo the exercise of it and more subtly subvert specific value allocations determined by the legislature. I have appended two American cases as examples of this. The first, *Kent* v. *Dulles* (1958), exemplifies a contraction of the legislative intent. In the second, *Cleveland* v. *United States* (1946), the Court feels that the legislature has not gone far enough down a path the Court believes desirable. As an example of where and how a high court can indirectly tangle with a strong president, I am appending the recent Philippine case of *Gonzales* v. *Hechanova* (1963). This is a fine cameo of a supreme court's preventing a powerful chief executive from producing a timely political *tour de force.* The President was attempting to get extra rice distributed to poor people prior to an election, but the court became an insurmountable obstacle, even without resorting to judicial review.

An interesting example of lower reaches of judicial independence may be found where a court system is just beginning to stir in a new legal setting. Danelski has described the post–World War II Japanese judiciary's initial high-level skirmishes with other sources of political power in a modernizing Japan.[26]

Considering the variations in the loci of anticourt power and the variety of methods open to courts, the rating of the degree of judicial independence will not be easy. This is particularly true if one intends to rely solely on actions of *supreme* courts. I have not appended these several graphic examples (case opinions) because they are the best behavioral instances of the degree of judicial independence in the societies from which they come. They are simply the most visible examples, the most accessible, and fascinating. The real work will have to come in field research, and chiefly by fieldwork will we be able to measure the relationship between the legal indicators (guarantees), the attitudinal indicators, and the actual exercise of the means of judicial independence.

---

[26] David J. Danelski, "The People and the Court in Japan," in *Frontiers of Judicial Research,* ed. Joel Grossman and Joseph Tanenhaus (New York: Wiley, 1969), pp. 49–52.

The Conditions for the Existence and/or Degrees
of Judicial Independence

The fact that no one has operationalized the concept of judicial independence has not prevented some theorizing on what does or does not relate to the existence of either some or a lot of it. This is not to derogate the discrete insights of the comparative people who are occasionally concerned about judicial independence. Their theories are intriguing, to say the least. However, the trouble comes when one tries to glue these together into a consistent set of propositions: they refuse to stick together. That is one of the setbacks one should expect when cross-cultural researchers work in their separate fields with quite dissimilar conceptual tools. Still, there is something to be gained by sifting through them.

Let's start with Fred Riggs. According to him:

> The autonomy of judges in diffracted politics reflects the relative separation of values, which also differentiates learning, wealth and prestige from political power. The traditions of an independent legal profession, with many opportunities for lawyers to make a living outside the bureaucracy, in private practice and working for free enterprise, have laid the basis for an independent judiciary in democratic Western countries. But in the prismatic system legal careers are either directly bureaucratic, or parasitic to the bureaucracy. An effective basis for an independent judiciary is lacking.[27]

Riggs might be saying that the prismatic/nonprismatic variable determines whether there is independence or not. If prismatic, then there will not be any independence, and thus, by my definition of court (page 13), there would be no court at all. On the other hand, the Riggs statement is subject to other interpretations. For instance, it could be construed to mean that there may be several effective bases for independence of the judiciary, independent-of-the-bureaucracy-legal-profession being just one. We do not know. It is unclear.

Support for the theoretical link between judicial independence and the independence of the legal profession comes from Lewis Mayers, a long-time student of the American judiciary and the American legal system.[28]

> The career judge, until he reaches such an age and position that the desire for promotion is no longer a major motive, is dependent for his professional future wholly upon the approval of his superiors (even if

---

[27] Fred R. Riggs, *Administration in Developing Countries* (Boston: Houghton Mifflin, 1964), p. 235.

[28] Lewis Mayers, *The American Legal System*, rev. ed. (New York: Harper & Row, 1964). For a discussion of the relationship between the judicial personality ("independence" of mind) and the career system, see Arthur von Mehren, *The Civil Law System* (Englewood Cliffs, N.J.: Prentice-Hall, 1957), p. 843.

they be judicial superiors, and not, as in the Continental countries, bureaucratic superiors, in the ministry of justice). He is thus in reality *less* independent, it is argued, than is the judge who has come from the bar and can return to it if need be, who does not, characteristically, expect or hope for higher judicial office, and who can discharge his duties without fear of reprisal or hope of reward.[29]

The reader would do well to notice that judicial independence in this proposition is not simply a dichotomous concept, it is a matter of degree, though Fred Riggs's characterization of it as a "polar" concept may be the most apt. Mayers is saying definitely that there can be independence in a judiciary that is part of the bureaucracy, but, all other factors being held constant, the judge who rose from the bar will be more independent. This, by the way, may be testable, since some national supreme courts derive their personnel from both the professional bureaucratic judiciary and the practicing bar (this is true in West Germany and in Japan).

A good example of the struggles of a student of comparative politics with the concept of judicial independence and its causes is Leonard Binder's study of Iran. Binder appears to believe that there is only a small measure of judicial independence in Iran, but his statements are confusing. We can make out this much, though: Binder believes there is less judicial independence in Iran than in the West. According to him: "Neither civil rights nor the independence of the judiciary have become great issues, nor have they been realized in any approximation of the manner developed in Western constitutional countries."[30] He attributes the minuscule amount of judicial independence to the pervasive Islamic religion. He notes, furthermore, that what little independence Iranian courts did enjoy is fading with time.

A fourth characteristic has been the subordination of the judiciary to the executive. This last has always been partly true, even when the traditional Islamic courts applied Islamic law, but during the present century, when even the restricted sphere of Islamic personal status law has come to be applied by secular courts, this is even more the case.[31]

Note the use of words like "partly" and "more." He is, in a sense, measuring. But how? Upon what information does he base his calibration? We do know that there is at the very least a structurally established system of courts. That is an important basis for assuming that there is a measure of independence; still that is not enough. Binder says subsequently:

The discrepancy between the asserted character of the courts and their actual subordination to the executive branch is analogous to the

---

[29] Mayers, *op. cit.*, p. 380.
[30] Leonard Binder, *Iran: Political Development in a Changing Society* (Berkeley and Los Angeles: University of California Press, 1962), p. 83.
[31] *Ibid.*, p. 99.

situation of the majlis [parliament] and cabinet. The press, the radio, and official public persons high and low, including some judges, readily declare the whole system corrupt . . . several members of the judiciary go to great lengths to insist upon their own honesty and to show with what courage they have withstood pressures from the police, the ministry of the interior or the minister of justice. Few will admit to what extent such defiance represents or is protected by a bargain made outside of the ministry of justice.[32]

These self-styled independent judges insist they have defied hierarchical controls. Aren't they Moslems? Then why would they so insist? Why would they defy and make bargains to assure their independent judgment? Why does secularization *lessen* the degree of independence? Though Binder estimates the amount of independence to be low, his description makes it sound substantial enough to measure. There are manifest judicial attitudes supporting independent behavior.

Similar to Binder, two professors of law, one an American (Samuel Shuman), the other a Norwegian (Torstein Eckhoff), believe a philosophical variable is influential on the degree of judicial independence in a society.[33] According to Eckhoff, "We expect to find connections between the prevailing *legal philosophy* of a society on the one hand and the conditions of judicial independence on the other."[34] Eckhoff is in substantial agreement with Shuman, who explains it in terms of the acceptance or nonacceptance of a legal theory such as that of the eminent jurisprudent Hans Kelsen.[35]

Many of my jurist friends in Italy have told me that Kelsenite positivism continues to be influential in Italy because it does offer some assistance to the judiciary in resisting church as well as state pressures. Also in Argentina and some other South American countries, Kelsen has been and continues to be popular because it is believed that his theory does offer assistance in assuring judicial independence. What is thought to be useful in Kelsen is his absolute insistence that law and morals are wholly separate and that what is law is decided without an appeal to moral criteria.[36]

One big question is why such positivism can be accepted in juxtaposition to Roman Catholicism but not in relation to Islam. Another is to what extent this is true and accounts for any actual degree of difference in the amount of judicial independence in Argentina and Iran.

At this rather high level of abstraction (philosophical variables), other comparatively oriented observers have noted a similar lack of much judicial

---

[32] *Ibid.*, p. 277.

[33] Samuel Shuman, "Philosophy and the Concept of Judicial Independence," *Wayne Law Review*, 8 (Spring, 1962), pp. 363–78; Eckhoff, *op. cit.*

[34] Eckhoff, *op. cit.*, p. 44 (emphasis mine).

[35] See Hans Kelsen, *The Pure Theory of Law*, trans. Max Knight (Berkeley: University of California Press, 1967).

[36] *Shuman, op. cit.*, p. 368.

independence in a certain grouping of countries they were studying. For instance, George Blanksten, in his contribution to *The Politics of Developing Nations*, lavishes little praise on the judiciary of Latin America. In noting a strong tendency toward centralized, monolithic power in those nations, Blanksten writes:

> The final arbiters of the area are the executive, the Church, and the military. Everywhere in Latin America, the presidents are regarded, with considerable accuracy, as government personified. Frequently, Hispanic Americans do not think of the work of legislative bodies and courts as government, too. The president is the government, and he is a major adjudicator. As for the Church, Mexico is the only country in the region where the clergy has been ousted from its powerful position. Elsewhere, the Church is unrivaled in its ability to endow one side or another in a controversy with legitimacy, and the adjudicating force of the clergy is in most cases irresistible. The same is in general true of the army. *Historically, arms have been the court of last resort in Latin America.* This pattern has become so firmly embedded in the political culture of the area that appeal to arms to decide fundamental questions is generally an accepted procedure. Indeed, the armies in many of the countries regard rule adjudication as an official function of the military in cases where division on an issue is deep and strong. There have been instances of attempts to indoctrinate Latin American armies with the proposition that they should be apolitical, but these have not been effective. At any given moment, anywhere from ten to fifteen army officers may be counted among the nineteen incumbent Latin American presidents. "Oh, people of Paraguay, how long will you remain idiots?" a president once asked his people. "Bullets are the only saints you have."[37]

Perhaps Blanksten is correct in his generalization, though it does seem a bit gross and a trifle overbearing. There are numerous vignettes that can be told to contradict it. For example, in late 1967, during the throes of a very rigid dictatorship in Argentina, the government of President Juan Carlos Onganía banned the printing of a weekly magazine called *Prensa Confidencial*. A presidential decree had banned all publications of its editor, Jorge Vago. Vago's recourse was to the courts—which is strange if Blanksten's view is true. After all, why? True enough, the lower court upheld the decree, but the intermediary appellate did not. In point of fact, the Argentine Federal Court of Appeal reversed the lower court decision and upheld Vago's right to publish. This, I might add, was in the face of a presidential (if not dictatorial) edict. In this case the court's word was reversed, but by an arbitrary and extralegal raid by a political police unit that not only confiscated the copy, but melted down the print.[38] Still, this

---

[37] George Blanksten, "Latin America," in *The Politics of Developing Nations*, ed. Gabriel Almond and James S. Coleman (Princeton: Princeton University Press, 1960), pp. 528–29 (emphasis mine).

[38] "Argentine Police Block Magazine," *New York Times*, November 29, 1967, p. 15.

action by certain Argentine government officials indicates at least enough independence to establish a distinguishable judicial structure in that country. On the other hand, Argentina is highly industrialized. Thus, this evidence does not contradict a theoretical proposition based on much of the reading in this field, that there is a close relationship between underdevelopment and low degree of judicial independence.

Yet underdevelopment cannot be a condition that precludes judicial independence (or, I should say, a substantial measure of judicial independence), Iran and Blanksten's Latin America notwithstanding. Other facts just will not support it. For instance, Ghanaian courts did stand up quite dramatically to the very strong political leader Kwame Nkrumah. The Philippines and India also furnish many inconsistent data.

One is led to recognize, from the Ghanaian experience, that perhaps, as William Harvey has speculated, many elements of judicial independence might be manifest, and there might be actual belief in and past action consistent with such independence—until strong *"internal political pressures"* arise.[39] In Ghana in the mid-1960s there were very considerable internal political pressures:

> There is no doubt that the Nkrumah Government has been confronted with the problem of dealing with dissident groups that have not limited themselves to political activity of a constitutional and democratic kind. The nature of the forces opposing Nkrumah and the CPP explains in some measure the resort to such methods. These forces have been largely composed of persons oriented toward the traditional order where authority was status-determined and to whom mass political organization and methods were alien. That they should be such organizations and employ such methods, and that this frustration should lead to violence would not be surprising.[40]

This violence-prone condition, plus Nkrumah's own brand of charisma, may well (with 20-20 hindsight) be seen as the proximate cause of the downfall of a serious exercise in expansion of judicial independence in a developing nation.[41] Why then does this demonstrate judicial *independence?* Those who sought to exercise it were fired and their jurisdiction was curtailed. How now judicial independence? The critical point is that the belief in freedom was there, and action was taken by the court in the face of expressed, strong-armed disapproval. The fact that sanctions were imposed against the court does not show a lack of independence. It merely shows an *upper limit* on that independence. Should

---

[39] William B. Harvey, *Law and Social Change in Ghana* (Princeton: Princeton University Press, 1966).

[40] *Ibid.*, pp. 341ff.

[41] See Aristide R. Zolberg, *Creating Political Order: The Party-States of West Africa* (Chicago: Rand McNally, 1966), pp. 82–83.

this have been the *only* instance of behavior necessary to establish the existence of a measure of independence, then it would not be sufficient. However, there were other instances of judicial independence in Ghana previously, and this incident simply established the ceiling on it under Nkrumah.[42] Still, the conditions that underlay the original establishment of such a degree of independence could again prevail in Ghana.

At any rate, even the scarceness of literature in this field does not allow us to rest with the hypothesis that strong internal political pressures cause judicial independence to collapse in underdeveloped countries. Other evidence is once again available to serve as disconfirmation for this too. Observations by American scholars on various situations in Burma and the Philippines are cases in point. For instance, Josef Silverstein, in his essay in *Government and Politics of Southeast Asia,* notes that even in times of great danger, the independence of the Burmese upper courts were not apparently threatened: "Despite the grave conditions prevailing at the time, the court worked to protect the individual against the arbitrary actions of the government."[43] Even when the government of Burma decided that risks to the very survival of Burma were present in the early sixties, and a preventive-detention act existed and was being implemented by a very strong executive, the Burmese courts were releasing detained people because "grounds must be sufficient to support" detention, but were not.

In a similar vein, the Philippine judiciary seems to have a good deal of independence from the policy-making and enforcement branches. In fact, according to Wurfel: "The Philippine Supreme Court has usually been willing to decide on political questions framed in legal terms to a much greater extent than its American prototype."[44]

Since almost all American political scientists think of the American federal system as displaying the maximum of judicial independence, this is really saying something.

In the heated Philippine presidential campaign of 1965, the challenger (now president), Ferdinand Marcos, was affected adversely by an execu-

---

[42] Fred Riggs notes (in a personal communication), quite correctly, that American comparativists tend to forget that many institutions in newly independent states existed in fact—or were more strongly entrenched—under colonial auspices.

Under British rule separate tribunals were established in the dependencies and many of them achieved a high degree of detachment and discretion. I would guess that in most of the ex-British dependencies the degree of detachment and discretion of these tribunals has declined, not risen, since independence. The critical points arise when a judge tries to make a decision which he could have made with impunity under British rule. He later discovers, to his discomfiture, that such decisions are unsafe to make under new rulers.

[43] Josef Silverstein, "Burma," in *Government and Politics in Southeast Asia,* 2nd ed., ed. George McT. Kahin (Ithaca: Cornell University Press, 1964), p. 120.
[44] David Wurfel, "The Philippines," *ibid.*, p. 737.

tive branch decision. A friend of Marcos' produced a motion picture (entitled *Written by Fate*) which tried to portray Marcos as a man of destiny. Apparently the film was quite dramatic and very effective. On the day of its official opening in Manila, the national board of censors decided to ban it on the official grounds that it offended Philippine morality. The political overtones were clear; the government did not want what promised to be a very successful image-builder for Marcos circulating around the countryside at election time.

The Marcos forces, however, were not cowed. Of the alternatives available, they chose public trial. After they had won an injunction from the court of first instance and appealed from a reversal by the intermediate court of appeals, the case finally reached the Supreme Court. Now the political pressures were really on, and it so happened that several of the justices were appointees of the incumbent president, Macapagal. The court not only took the case, it set aside all delaying procedures in order to decide it well before election. It is not insignificant to note that the court *unanimously* (including the three Macapagal judges) upheld the lower court's grant of injunction, which restrained the government from interfering with the exhibition of the picture. Certainly the internal political pressure from Macapagal forces and the effective political majority was great upon the Philippine court. Yet the justices exercised their independence in taking the case for decision and deciding it as they did.[45] Moreover, they had decided against Macapagal on several other occasions during his tenure of office.

Thus, neither underdevelopment nor the strain of great political pressure necessarily forebodes the collapse of a good measure of judicial independence. It is even possible that extra pressure may stimulate the motivation and genius to expand it, as was the case in another underdeveloped country, the United States, in 1803.

At this point we are left in a state of wonderment. What, if anything, does the political science literature—particularly that on developing nations—offer us in the way of theory on the development of judicial independence? David Wilson has observed that "Modern Thai jurisprudence is an uneasy amalgamation of Napoleonic, Anglo-Saxon, and traditional Thai notions. From such a background and in the atmosphere of unstable constitutional forms, the bulwarks of the courts against political pressures are not impenetrable."[46] Can we say then that judicial independence is de-

---

[45] See Theodore L. Becker, "*Iginuhit ñg Tadhana:* The Written-by-Fate Case," in *Political Trials,* ed. Becker (Indianapolis: Bobbs-Merrill, forthcoming). The court, it should be noted, did not decide that the action was "unconstitutional"; it simply handed down a "Minute Resolution" affirming the trial court's disposition by saying that there was no question of fact. It was purely a judicial side-step.

[46] David Wilson, "Thailand," in *Government and Politics in Southeast Asia,* p. 51.

pendent upon a homogeneous code? Hardly. The Philippines are disproof enough of that simple hypothesis. The Philippines have an amalgam of Spanish and American law, and British as well. Silverstein's proposition may help some: "Venerating a legacy of the British period—the rule of law—the justices of the Supreme and High Courts [of Burma] established an enviable record for independence of action and for creating a respect for courts. . . ."[47]

There may be some relationship between the existence of an Anglo-American judicial pattern and a measure of judicial independence. Though other European judicial structures have substantial judicial independence, it is particularly emphasized in legal systems in the English and American traditions. Actually, the reason for this is probably the fact that there is a relationship between impartiality and independence. As Professor Eckhoff has noted, "It should be borne in mind that dependence on one source of influence often provides for independence of others."[48] Thus, where judges can rely, in a common-law system, on norms that *they* produce, they need to rely less on the other norm-producing structures, i.e., the legislature, the administrative agencies, etc. This is not a transaction in tautology. If such a relationship can be empirically established, then certain words have been accepted, internalized, and acted upon. Of course, research may yet demonstrate no association between the Anglo-American pattern and degree of judicial independence, though this seems extremely doubtful. It appears much more likely that a readily visible degree of this association will be discovered, though many European judiciaries, some Asian, and perhaps a few others may well be found to be more independent than some systems patterned on the Anglo-American model. Indigenous cultures have many ways of rejecting grafts, modifying them, or enhancing them. The independent variable, the Anglo-American judicial system, is a virile transplant. Its growth in alien cultures may take many forms, but it will still exhibit manifestations of its main characteristics. In any event, factors that scholars seem to think are relatable to degree of judicial independence are the type of legal system in general, religious philosophy, legal philosophy, and level of social development. How important one or the other is and how they interact is something political science has yet to find out.

The Political Functions of Judicial Independence

But judicial independence, as a structural variable, engages our interest only insofar as it has a function or functions in society. Quite frequently the theoretical functioning of judicial independence is couched in more con-

---

[47] Silverstein, *op. cit.*, p. 119.
[48] Eckhoff, *op. cit.*, p. 44.

ventional and vague terms, like "rule of law"—though that slogan probably includes the concepts of judicial objectivity or impartiality as well. In other words, the slogan "America is ruled by law, not men," includes the concept of the independence of judges.[49] "Rule of law" is just one of those conceptual potpourris comprising the popular writing that needs dissection and analysis.

It is often said (explicitly enough) that judicial independence is necessary in order for the judge to be able to determine the truth in a dispute. A judge subject to outside meddling because he is dependent upon others for his livelihood (i.e., the legislature at its whim) may easily become the finder of falsehoods in order to protect his privileges. The proposition "The more judicial independence extant in a court system, the more reliably the courts will operate as a fact-finding mechanism" is a functional one— but it is of little concern here. Though accuracy of fact-finding might have some political significance in a societal system, it seems to me to be a bit too far removed to capture the contemporary concern of political science. Lines must be drawn somewhere, and I think there are far more directly political propositions to treat.

One last note: The functions of judicial independence are the same as those of courts in general. For judicial independence is an indispensable component of courtness. Thus, the following discussion on functions simply will elaborate on the discussion of functions of courts in general, by approaching it from a slightly different angle, and by discussing some issues implicit in relating the varying degrees of independence (as a structural variation) to varying degrees of consequences (functions).

MAINTENANCE OF THE STATUS QUO

Thinkers in the area of judicial politics have made much of the alleged importance of judicial independence, as well as judicial impartiality, for the maintenance or orderly change of the status quo in society. Judicial independence is seen as helping in the preservation of law; that is, in the continuation, over a period of time, of the established formalized rules in the society. By virtue of being a separate decision-making institution, insulated from normal pressures for change, the court can be and is employed as a slowing-down process in society. It is another channel into which currents of dissent can be diverted. It is another impediment to leaders' attempts to alter processes in order to produce reforms. This role of the court

---

[49] See A. V. Dicey, *The Law of the Constitution*, 8th ed. (London: Macmillan, 1915), pp. 183–84. Cf. J. Roland Pennock, *Administration and the Rule of Law* (New York: Rinehart, 1941), p. 9.

is couched, by those who have had their preferences previously institution-
alized and formalized as "laws," in terms akin to "preserving law and
order."

In one objective sense, it does do this, and it is peculiarly suited to this
task. Many eloquent scholars have lent their talents to articulating this fact
in its most favorable symbolic form. Charles McIlwain, the noted constitutional historian and analyst, puts it as follows: "If jurisdiction is essential to liberty, and jurisdiction is a thing of the law, it is the law that must be
maintained against arbitrary will. *And the one institution above all others
essential to the preservation of law has always been the judiciary.*"[50] And as
one famous jurist states: "Our way of life can only be preserved by a calm
and dignified running of our judicial system by men of loyalty and sincerity
who call them as they see them coming over the plate."[51]

Modern political scientists like Glendon Schubert, however, have seen
the court's role as a preserver in a less favorable legalistic light (to elites
and conservatives) and in a more objective political light. Schubert knows,
as we saw in Chapter 2, that judges are strongly bound by their social and
professional heritage and will decide from such a perspective; the past can
thus be served by their very independence from the political waves that
beat more heavily and with more telling effect on other branches.

Yet it seems important to observe that the courts can also be viewed
as innovators in social and political change—ironically enough, by virtue of
the same independence.[52] This is very true in the American system. To
avoid noting this would be tantamount to ignoring the entire run of cases
that have legally spared and spread various rights "guaranteed" in the federal constitution. On the other hand, these cases can also be viewed as conservative. As I suggested in the previous chapter, the more representative
decision-making agencies may be so unresponsive to pressures that serious
societal upheavals may be impending. If a sufficient legal basis is available,
the courts can act to preserve the comprehensive systemic status quo
through limited systemic adjustments or major policy changes. This is
probably a very rare occurrence. But it happens.

What is implicit in much of the foregoing discussion is that the more
independence there is in a judiciary, the more likely it is that a status quo

---

[50] Charles McIlwain, *Constitutionalism: Ancient and Modern*, rev. ed. (Ithaca:
Cornell University Press, 1947), p. 140 (emphasis mine).

[51] Harold Medina, "Some Reflections on the Judiciary: A Personal Viewpoint,"
American Bar Association Journal, 38 (February, 1952), p. 110.

[52] The ostensible reversal of the *London Tramways case* (1898) by the House
of Lords' 1966 statement (see chap. 2, n. 37) has thus opened the door to admitting
the personal biases and values of the judges into the decision-making process, making
judges more subjective. Yet, in so doing, the House of Lords, as a court, has gained
an independence from Parliament, thereby lessening one conservative proclivity in
its structure.

will be maintained, or the longer it will be maintained intact. A court system that has a significant degree of independence, i.e., power in its own right, gives an added avenue of access to decision-makers. This can be the method by which counter power elites are co-opted into a system. They have a place in which to operate and there is less demand for change of the system. The Federalists' refuge in the American court system after Jefferson's victory in 1800 is an excellent example of this. That they took this route, and paved it, may have preserved the institution of American government in its present form for so long. Then again, it may have had no long-range structural effect at all.

PROTECTION OF INDIVIDUAL RIGHTS AGAINST GOVERNMENT

Much has been written to the effect that independent judiciaries are essential to, prerequisite for, and a necessary condition of the maintenance of individual liberty and freedom. Thus, courts can act to *conserve* a classic *liberal* doctrine embedded in the comprehensive formal structure of a political system, e.g., a written constitution. When they do that, they may indeed become the conservative mainstay against pressure for diminishing individual freedom, and are thus simultaneously liberal: an apparent but not real paradox.

I would like to demonstrate briefly how the individual-freedom–judicial-independence proposition is treated in the literature. For instance, Herbert Jacob, a political scientist, states: "Judicial independence has long been thought *necessary* to prevent tyrannical government. To an unusual extent, Americans have viewed the courts as a bastion *against* governmental intrusion rather than as an instrument of government itself."[53]

Lummis is, I believe, more representative of the elaborateness and forcefulness with which the subject is usually discussed in American political-legal academic circles:

> The independence of the judiciary is *imperatively necessary* for the liberty of every citizen. When judges are not free [i.e., dependent], no man can be said to have rights, for the forms of justice can be twisted to serve the tyranny of the numerous, the wealthy, the powerful, or the demogogues and schemers who are enabled to govern in their names. . . . It is the weak and the poor who need most the safeguard of a strong and independent judiciary. One cannot be sure of always running with the pack; he may find himself the pursued rabbit. A man cannot tell when in a civil or criminal case he may be unjustly accused; the object of widespread calumny and popular

---

[53] Herbert Jacob, *Justice in America* (Boston: Little, Brown and Company [Inc.], 1965), p. 147.

hatred, with the result that his property, his liberty, or even his life, is in danger. In that day his only refuge is a firm and independent judiciary, governed by conscience and not by glamor, and free to do justice even to a hated individual in the face of an angry crowd.[54]

And so it goes. There is little doubt that I could stock well over a hundred pages with a harvest of similar pieties, but that would avail us little. Statements about an empirical relationship are not proof of the relationship; they are only proof of agreement among scholars. The obvious disproof of this proposition is in the very progenitor of the American system, the English system. In England the courts would be helpless if Parliament decided to do in various English civil liberties. In short, can the relative civil-liberties situations in England and the United States support the hypothesis that the greater the independence of the judiciary, the greater the liberty?

It is the shortsightedness of many American scholars, once again, that makes them overgeneralize from the American system to more universal reality. Though American courts do indeed protect the liberties of individuals from encroachment by various governmental agencies (Congress included), this is a rather unusual role for courts. Besides, there is a less sanguine way of looking at this. Indeed, the extent to which individual rights are protected against a superambitious or overly authoritative officialdom can be seen equally in terms of the preservation of the status quo of the general political system (as the real, though latent, function). "Protection of personal liberties" may be scarcely more than a euphemism. After all, no matter where the system—America, England, the British Commonwealth, Africa, or Asia—freedoms are *always* severely menaced by nervous power elites in unstable periods that they are quick to interpret as "clear and present danger," "state of siege," and the like. At such times the courts become next to powerless, and these times seem to have great frequency and amazing durability. In short, when a system is perceived by its elite or elites to be threatened, there is little leeway for judicial protection of individual rights—*particularly against strong antisystem counterelites (or those perceived as strong)*. More often than not, I fear, what "protection of individual rights" means is that the elite is or has become variegated enough to see benefit in providing breathing space for discussion of minor systemic adjustments or substantial policy change. Recognizing that different factions will be in power at different times, the elite sees that it is beneficial to keep any faction (intellectual, financial, commercial, military) from imposing silence on any other. Having an organ that guarantees a forum is simply a device to maintain the structure

---

[54] Lummis, *op. cit.*, pp. 11–12 (emphasis mine).

of the system that is beneficial to the entire elite. All segments of this elite desire the silence, if not the elimination, of implacable opponents of the system (though they insist on it only under certain conditions).

From this perspective, "protecting the little man" and the "guarantee of liberty to all" can be seen as symbols that make the system appear far more open that it is, and which stimulate a maximum amount of popular support by keeping the mass base from believing that it is limited in its options for changing the system. This view holds that the mass is manipulated into thinking it can exchange opinions and ideas on the systemic superstructure when in reality it cannot even have them presented—particularly if the going gets tough and the mass support seems to the elite to be susceptible to any restlessness or recalcitrance. Some regimes (elites) are edgier than others; all are touchy about criticism of the system; all manifest extreme anxiety at the first sign of any overt action to make changes in it, even if only in key parts of the subsystem. Even in America.

Thus, when a formerly very closed system begins to move toward a much greater flexibility, newly enfranchised factions of the elite may call for sweeping reforms in the courts to provide for more "individual liberty." One way this will be phrased will be as a demand for an independent (or more independent) judiciary. This was the case in Czechoslovakia under Dubček.[55] The best interpretation of this phenomenon would seem to be that the elite (the new faction of it that had taken over power) had come to feel secure enough to provide a governmental structure that could simultaneously generate policy (not system) debate and engender a wider base of legitimacy for the system among the people. An independent judiciary is a wide boulevard to both objectives.

Once we recognize that in no system will courts protect freedom of speech, assembly, and the like geared to doing away with the system when there is the slightest chance that this speech might actually generate the action it calls for, we can begin to talk about the degrees to which courts protect individual policy and subsystem disagreement within the system. Courts frequently are employed for this purpose—and the more independent the judiciary, the more likely that they will be employed in this way. This does not necessarily mean that the courts actually function in this way. Judicial protection of individual liberty may indeed be nothing more than a co-variation, and thus the independence of the judiciary is simply an *indicator* of personal freedom.

The one prerequisite to this maintenance of individual liberties against governmental oppression is a low threshold of popular outrage toward such actions developed among the citizenry as a whole or among the society's

---

[55] *New York Times*, Saturday, March 9, 1968, p. 4.

influentials. (Among the influentials such outrage is likely to be a concomitant of an ideology or a sense of *noblesse oblige.*) John Roche is probably correct in tracing the great role the American courts have played in the maintenance of individual freedom at least partially to the peculiar nature of the whole complex structure of the American political system, including the very strong role the courts have played within it generally.[56] For instance, he asks, would Roosevelt have failed to pack the court in 1937 if there had been strong party discipline (as in England)? Probably not. Roche also notes the rather undemocratic overtones to this theory, i.e., that highly independent courts are essential to liberty in a democratic republic. This is especially true when the judge is not elected, but appointed.

> Essentially it is a Platonic graft on the democratic process—a group of wise men insulated from the people have the task of injecting truth serum into the body politic, of acting as an institutional chaperon to ensure that the sovereign population and its elected representatives do not act unwisely.[57]

Particularly under the system of the appointment of judges, the more independence of the court, the less democratically republican is that form of government.[58]

Be this as it may, I think it should be clear enough that degrees of independence of the courts, as a structural variable, neither logically nor empirically appear to be a necessary condition to any significantly changing degree of political liberty in a society. It just happens that an independent judiciary is seen as the guarantor of personal liberty in the United States of America because it is so written in its basic law, the Constitution. This is another paradox running through our system: an undemocratic institution (the appointed permanent court) maintains democratic values against the representatives of the people clamoring to impair them. Other systems may put greater responsibility upon the masses to protect their own individual liberties, which may be better for the maintenance of such liberties in the long run. Others may mimic the American system on paper but permit no exercise of the measure of judicial independence in this substantive area whatsoever. To date, this too is an area of comparative study that is still empirically unexplored.[59] We speak, but we do not find. We mutter something about science, but write only a stilted and turgid philosophy.

[56] John Roche, *Courts and Rights,* 2nd ed. (New York: Random House, 1966).

[57] *Ibid.,* pp. 121–22.

[58] As Brian Abel-Smith and Robert Stevens put the question: "What was the justification of judicial independence in a democracy with responsible government?" See their *Lawyers and the Courts* (Cambridge: Harvard University Press, 1967), p. 313.

[59] Christian Bay discusses the cross-cultural study of relative degrees of freedom, and suggests the desirability of much case study. Trends might then become discernible. See his *Structure of Freedom* (Stanford: Stanford University Press, 1958), p. 375.

There is nothing wrong with philosophy, of course, but philosophy by another name is not science. It would be very nice indeed if we could devise some instrument that would measure degrees of judicial independence and degrees of liberty, so that we could compare data on a wide range of societies and discover the association, if any, that might exist between liberty and judicial independence.

Finally, the measurement of judicial independence is also, in some regard, an indicator of the degree of influence the court system has on the political and social system, and vice versa. (This will be discussed in Chapter 7.) Dolbeare developed a very rough index of the independence of the local courts in a New York county when he noted that "claims brought to court have about a 50-50 chance of succeeding in over-ruling governmental action or forcing government to act in ways which they were disinclined to do."[60] Certainly, this hints at a good measure of judicial independence from the people in power and suggests a great degree of impact on the local system of government and politics. But let us not forget Dolbeare's findings as presented in the preceding chapter (p. 124). Despite this high degree of independence by the court, little protection of individual civil liberty was found. Even in this relative sense, the first indications are that the data will not support a hypothesis that there is a close relationship between increasing degrees of judicial independence and corresponding increases in the protection of individual freedom. Indeed, we have much serious thinking to do about the heretofore blindly and blithely accepted functions of increased judicial independence, and much serious research to do as well.

---

[60] Kenneth Dolbeare, *Trial Courts in Urban Politics* (New York: Wiley, 1967), p. 36.

APPENDIX

Tumey v. Ohio
(U.S.A., 1927)

Tumey, the plaintiff in error hereafter to be called the defendant, was arrested and brought before Mayor Pugh, of the village of North College Hill, charged with unlawfully possessing intoxicating liquor. He moved for his dismissal because of the disqualification of the mayor to try him under the Fourteenth Amendment. The mayor denied the motion, proceeded to the trial, convicted the defendant of unlawfully possessing intoxicating liquor within Hamilton county as charged, fined him $100, and ordered that he be imprisoned until the fine and costs were paid. He obtained a bill of exceptions and carried the case on error to the court of common pleas of Hamilton county. That court heard the case and reversed the judgment, on the ground that the mayor was disqualified as claimed. . . .

The defendant was arrested and charged with the unlawful possession of intoxicating liquor at White Oak, another village in Hamilton county, Ohio, on a warrant issued by the mayor of North College Hill. The mayor acted under the sections of the state Prohibition Act and Ordinance No. 125 of the village of North College Hill adopted in pursuance thereof.

Section 6212—15, General Code, Ohio, provides that.

"No person shall, after the passage of this act . . . manufacture . . . possess . . . any intoxicating liquors. . . ."

* * *

The mayor has authority, which he exercised in this case, to order that the person sentenced to pay a fine shall remain in prison until the fine and costs are paid. At the time of this sentence, the prisoner received a credit of 60 cents a day for each day's imprisonment. By a recent amendment, that credit has been increased to $1.50 a day.

* * *

Under the authority of the last section, the village council of North College Hill passed Ordinance No. 125, as follows:

* * *

Section V. That the mayor of the village of North College Hill, Ohio, shall receive or retain the amount of his costs in each case, in addition to his regular salary, as compensation for hearing such cases.

* * *

The fees which the mayor and marshal received in this case came to them by virtue of the general statutes of the state applying to all state cases, liquor and otherwise. The mayor was entitled to hold the legal fees taxed in his favor. General Code Ohio, § 4270; State v. Nolte, 111 Ohio St. 486, 146 N. E. 51, 37

---

47 S. Ct. 437 (1927).

A. L. R. 1426. Moreover, the North College Hill village council sought to remove all doubt on this point by providing (section 5, Ordinance 125, supra), that he should receive or retain the amount of his costs in each case in addition to his regular salary, as compensation for hearing such cases. But no fees or costs in such cases are paid him, except by the defendant, if convicted. There is, therefore, no way by which the mayor may be paid for his service as judge, if he does not convict those who are brought before him; nor is there any fund from which marshals, inspectors and detectives can be paid for their services in arresting and bringing to trial and furnishing the evidence to convict in such cases, except it be from the initial $500 which the village may vote from its treasury to set the court going or from a fund created by the fines thereafter collected from convicted defendants.

* * *

Between May 11, 1923, and December 31, 1923, the total amount of fines for violation of the prohibition law collected by this village court was upwards of $20,000, from which the state received $8,992.50, North College Hill received $4,471.25 for its general uses, $2,697.25 was placed to the credit of the village safety fund, and the balance was put in the secret service fund. Out of this, the person acting as prosecutor in the liquor court received in that period $1,796.50; the deputy marshals, inspectors and other employees, including the detectives, received $2,697.75; and $438.50 was paid for costs in transporting prisoners, serving writs and other services in connection with the trial of these cases. Mayor Pugh received $696.35 from these liquor cases during that period as his fees and costs, in addition to his regular salary.

[2] That officers acting in a judicial or quasi judicial capacity are disqualified by their interest in the controversy to be decided is of course the general rule. . . . Nice questions, however, often arise as to what the degree or nature of the interest must be. One is in respect to the effect of the membership of a judge in a class of taxpayers or others to be affected by a principle of law, statutory or constitutional, to be applied in a case between other parties and in which the judge has no other interest. Then the circumstance that there is no judge not equally disqualified to act in such a case has been held to affect the question. . . . We are not embarrassed by such considerations here, for there were available in this case other judicial officers who had no disqualification, either by reason of the character of their compensation or their relation to the village government.

[3] All questions of judicial qualification may not involve constitutional validity. Thus matters of kinship, personal bias, state policy, remoteness of interest would seem generally to be matters merely of legislative discretion. Wheeling v. Black, 25 W. Va. 266, 270. But it certainly violates the Fourteenth Amendment and deprives a defendant in a criminal case of due process of law to subject his liberty or property to the judgment of a court, the judge of which has a direct, personal, substantial pecuniary interest in reaching a conclusion against him in his case.

[4] The mayor of the village of North College Hill, Ohio, had a direct personal pecuniary interest in convicting the defendant who came before him for trial, in the $12 of costs imposed in his behalf, which he would not have received if the defendant had been acquitted. This was not exceptional, but was the result of the normal operation of the law and the ordinance. Counsel for the state do not deny this, but assert the validity of the practice as an exception to

the general rule. They rely upon the cases of Ownbey v. Morgan, 256 U.S. 94, 41 S. Ct. 433, 65 L. Ed. 837, 17 A. L. R. 873; Murray's Lessee v. Hoboken Land & Improvement Co., 18 How. 272, 276–280, 15 L. Ed. 372.

[5] These cases show that in determining what due process of law is, under the Fifth or Fourteenth Amendment, the court must look to those settled usages and modes of proceeding existing in the common and statute law of England before the emigration of our ancestors, which were shown not to have been unsuited to their civil and political condition by having been acted on by them after the settlement of this country. Counsel contend that in Ohio and in other states, in the economy which it is found necessary to maintain in the administration of justice in the inferior courts by justices of the peace and by judicial officers of like jurisdiction, the only compensation which the state and county and township can afford is the fees and costs earned by them, and that such compensation is so small that it is not to be regarded as likely to influence improperly a judicial officer in the discharge of his duty, or as prejudicing the defendant in securing justice, even though the magistrate will receive nothing if the defendant is not convicted.

We have been referred to no cases at common law in England, prior to the separation of colonies from the mother country, showing a practice that inferior judicial officers were dependent upon the conviction of the defendant for receiving their compensation. Indeed, in analogous cases it is very clear that the slightest pecuniary interest of any officer, judicial or quasi judicial, in the resolving of the subject-matter which he was to decide, rendered the decision voidable. Bonham's Case, 8 Coke, 118a. . . .

*   *   *

We conclude that a system by which an inferior judge is paid for his service only when he convicts the defendant has not become so embedded by custom in the general practice, either at common law or in this country, that it can be regarded as due process of law, unless the costs usually imposed are so small that they may be properly ignored as within the maxim "de minimis non curat lex."

The mayor received for his fees and costs in the present case $12, and from such costs under the Prohibition Act for seven months he made about $100 a month, in addition to his salary. We cannot regard the prospect of receipt or loss of such an emolument in each case as a minute, remote, trifling, or insignificant interest. It is certainly not fair to each defendant brought before the mayor for the careful and judicial consideration of his guilt or innocence that the prospect of such a prospective loss by the mayor should weigh against his acquittal.

[6] But the pecuniary interest of the mayor in the result of his judgment is not the only reason for holding that due process of law is denied to the defendant here. The statutes were drawn to stimulate small municipalities, in the country part of counties in which there are large cities, to organize and maintain courts to try persons accused of violations of the Prohibition Act everywhere in the county. The inducement is offered of dividing between the state and the village the large fines provided by the law for its violations. The trial is to be had before a mayor without a jury, without opportunity for retrial, and with a review confined to questions of law presented by a bill of exceptions, with no opportunity by the reviewing court to set aside the judgment on the weighing of evidence, unless it should appear to be so manifestly against the evidence as to indicate mistake, bias, or willful disregard of duty by the trial court. It

specifically authorizes the village to employ detectives, deputy marshals, and other assistants to detect crime of this kind all over the county, and to bring offenders before the mayor's court, and it offers to the village council and its officers a means of substantially adding to the income of the village to relieve it from further taxation. The mayor is the chief executive of the village. He supervises all the other executive officers. He is charged with the business of looking after the finances of the village. It appears from the evidence in this case, and would be plain if the evidence did not show it, that the law is calculated to awaken the interest of all those in the village charged with the responsibility of raising the public money and expending it, in the pecuniarily successful conduct of such a court. The mayor represents the village and cannot escape his representative capacity. On the other hand, he is given the judicial duty, first, of determining whether the defendant is guilty at all; and, second, having found his guilt, to measure his punishment between $100 as a minimum and $1,000 as a maximum for first offenses, and $300 as a minimum and $2,000 as a maximum for second offenses. With his interest as mayor in the financial condition of the village and his responsibility therefor, might not a defendant with reason say that he feared he could not get a fair trial or a fair sentence from one who would have so strong a motive to help his village by conviction and a heavy fine? The old English cases . . . in the days of Coke and Holt and Mansfield are not nearly so strong. A situation in which an official perforce occupies two practically and seriously inconsistent positions, one partisan and the other judicial, necessarily involves a lack of due process of law in the trial of defendants charged with crimes before him. . . . It is, of course, so common to vest the mayor of villages with inferior judicial functions that the mere union of the executive power and the judicial power in him cannot be said to violate due process of law. The minor penalties usually attaching to the ordinances of a village council, or to the misdemeanors in which the mayor may pronounce final judgment without a jury, do not involve any such addition to the revenue of the village as to justify the fear that the mayor would be influenced in his judicial judgment by that fact. The difference between such a case and the plan and operation of the statutes before us is so plain as not to call for further elaboration.

The State v. Sir Edward Snelson
(Pakistan, 1961)

✿ ✿ ✿

JUDGMENT

SHABIR AHMAD, J.—This case, the proceedings of which were marked by some unexpected events, each of the most outstanding of which will be dealt with in its proper place, arises out of a notice issued to Sir Edward Snelson, K.B.E., Secretary to the Government of Pakistan, Ministry of Law (who will hereinafter be referred to as "the respondent"), to show cause why he should not be punished under the Contempt of Courts Act, 1926.

2. The material facts briefly stated are these. On the 15th of February 1960,

---

P. L. D. 1961 (W.P.) Lahore 78. Citations have been omitted.

the respondent gave a Talk at Rawalpindi to the Section Officers of the Government of Pakistan with regard to the Transitional Constitution of 1958. On the 17th of September 1960, two thousand pamphlets containing this Talk and some other matter were printed by the Manager, Government Pakistan Press, Karachi, as is clear from certain entries in the pamphlets themselves. Twenty-five of these pamphlets were sent by the Director of Training and *Ex-officio* Deputy Secretary to the Government of Pakistan, President's Secretariat, Secretariat Training Institute, Rawalpindi, to the West Pakistan Government and with his letter No. S. VIII-3-116/60, dated Lahore, the 10th of October 1960, Section Officer VIII, acting for the Additional Chief Secretary to the Government of West Pakistan, sent a copy of the pamphlet to the Registrar of this Court for information. As is usual when pamphlets are sent to the Registrar of this Court by Government, Central or Provincial, this pamphlet was circulated amongst the Judges of this Court stationed at Lahore and would have been sent to the Benches of the Court at Karachi and Peshawar in due course. Some of the Judges at Lahore read the pamphlet and as they were of the view that it contained matters open to grave exception, all the Judges were asked to read it before consideration of the question whether any, and if so, what action should be taken in the matter. When the matter came up for consideration on the 25th of October 1960, the Judges of this Court present at Lahore were of the view that as parts of the Talk of the respondent which occurred in the printed pamphlet, in paragraphs numbered by the Judges as 9 and 10, contained matter which, in addition to being entirely irrelevant to the subject-matter of the Talk, was calculated to lower this Court in the eyes of those who heard the Talk as well as of those who read the pamphlet and to undermine the authority of this Court, notice should issue to the respondent to show cause why he should not be dealt with under the Contempt of Courts Act, 1926, whereupon a formal order was passed by me which directed the respondent to appear in this Court on the 14th of November 1960. The last sentence of this order was to the effect that as usual in cases of this kind intimation should be sent to the Advocate-General, West Pakistan. No notice was issued to those who have been, to some extent, responsible for publication of the Talk given by the respondent because the Talk having been given by a person who must have been presumed not to have broken the law, the others responsible for publication could, at worst, be held to have been guilty of a venial lapse. A day or two later his Lordship the Chief Justice passed an order that as the respondent was an important law officer of the Central Government, the case against him should be heard by a Bench of the three senior most Judges present at Lahore. On the 29th of October 1960, the order dated the 25th of October 1960 as well as paragraphs Nos. 9 and 10 of the Talk, a copy of which paragraphs had been sent to the respondent along with the notice, appeared in some newspapers. The notice, which conformed to the order, directed the respondent to be present at the hearing as it was probable that it would be necessary to ask him some questions. On the 31st of October 1960, Chaudhri Nazir Ahmad Khan, the Attorney-General of Pakistan, presented before me an application on behalf of the Pakistan Government praying that it should be made a party to the case and notice should be issued to the Attorney-General. This application was granted on the same day.

3. On the service on him of the notice to appear in this Court on the 14th of November 1960 to show cause why action should not be taken against him under the Contempt of Courts Act, the respondent presented a petition in the

Supreme Court of Pakistan for obtaining special leave to appeal against the order. This petition, if the press reports regarding the proceedings in the Supreme Court were correct, had the support of the Attorney-General of Pakistan who appeared for the Central Government. The petition was, however, rejected by the Supreme Court of Pakistan on the 10th of November 1960. A copy of the order of the Supreme Court of Pakistan rejecting the petition has not been received in this Court so far, but if the reports in the press were correct, the petition was rejected on the ground that as this Court, as a Court of Record, had exclusive jurisdiction to deal with a contempt of itself, the Supreme Court was not prepared to interfere at the stage at which the case taken was.

4. The case came up for hearing before the Bench nominated by his Lordship the Chief Justice on the 14th of November 1960 and the respondent appeared along with Mr. A. Haque, Advocate, to show cause against the notice issued to him, while the Pakistan Government, which had become a party at its own request, was represented by Chaudhri Nazir Ahmad Khan, Attorney-General of Pakistan. And now occurred the second of the unexpected events to which I have alluded in the first paragraph of this order. The first of these unexpected events was the application by the Attorney-General of Pakistan to the effect that the Central Government should be made a party to the proceedings. This was an unusual application because as far as my knowledge based on some experience with regard to these matters goes the practice, which is probably based on some rules, is that whenever action is taken in a Court or by a Court against a public servant, Government leaves him to fight out his own battle and decides only after the determination of the proceedings by the Court whether the public servant is to be paid the expenses by the Court whether the public servant is to be paid the expenses incurred by him to defend himself. I have no doubt in my mind that the application of the Pakistan Government to be impleaded as a party in a case arising out of a notice to a public servant under the Contempt of Courts Act can claim to be entirely unique.

5. As I have already indicated, the second of the unusual events occurred in these proceedings on the 14th of November 1960. This was that instead of appearing in support of the notice issued to the respondent by this Court and thereby acting according to the decision of the Provincial Government with regard to cases of Contempt of Court communicated to the Registrar of this Court by the Law Department, Government of West Pakistan, letter No. Genl. (91)/57/1828, dated the 21st of March 1958, which was to the effect that the Advocate-General, the Additional Advocate-General and Assistant Advocate-General will appear in contempt cases before the High Court on behalf of the Court and not on behalf of the respondent, Mr. M. Anwar, Advocate-General, stated that he had been instructed by the Provincial Government to pray. because the issue involved was delicate, for the adjournment of the case for one week to permit the Provincial Government to decide whether or not the Advocate-General for the Province should appear in the case. I have already indicated that intimation regarding the issue of notice to the respondent had been sent to the Advocate-General, West Pakistan, on the 25th of October 1960, and as the time at the disposal of the Provincial Government to decide the question mentioned by the learned Advocate-General had been long enough, his request was not acceded to. The press reports had made it clear that the Central Government had aligned itself with the respondent and it was considered necessary by the Bench to request Mr. Mahmood Ali Qasuri, an Advocate of this Court, to give

his views in the matter to this Court, and it was heartening to note that Mr. Mahmood Ali Qasuri undertook without hesitation this duty which had been thrust unexpectedly on him. It is, however, somewhat gratifying that the Provincial Government agreed to pay to Mr. Mahmood Ali Qasuri such fees as the Bench may consider proper for rendering to the Court the assistance that should have been rendered by the Advocate-General, West Pakistan. At the hearing arguments were addressed by Mr. A. Haque on behalf of the respondent, by Chaudhri Nazir Ahmad Khan, Attorney-General of Pakistan, on behalf of the Pakistan Government as well as by Mr. Ghias Muhammad, Standing Counsel of the Pakistan Government on behalf of that Government, on the last two days of hearing, as the Attorney-General had to leave for Karachi to appear in the Supreme Court which was in session there, and by Mr. Mahmood Ali Qasuri, who appeared as *amicus curiae* at the request of the Court.

6. The respondent and the Central Government put in separate written statements and the contents of the written statement of the latter were the third unexpected event of these proceedings. This written statement reads as follows:

Written statement on behalf of the Central Government

Respectfully showeth:

(1) The speech including the two paragraphs in question was delivered by Sir Edward Snelson, K.B.E., Secretary to the Government of Pakistan, Ministry of Law, Karachi (respondent), in his official capacity, to the Section Officers of the Central Government stationed at Rawalpindi. It was exclusively meant for officials and no part of it could in view of the provisions of the Official Secrets Act, 1923, be disclosed to the public. The speech was later on printed and copies thereof were supplied in normal routine to certain offices of the Government.

(2) No official to whom the speech or copies thereof were addressed could under the law communicate the same to the public. So far as is known to the Central Government, the public at large did not come to know of this speech till it appeared in the press as an enclosure to the notice for contempt issued to Sir Edward Snelson.

> (Sd.)   Nazir Ahmad Khan,
> Attorney-General of Pakistan

It cannot escape the notice of anyone that this written statement had not said even a single word about the matter that was before the Court and merely hinted that by making paragraphs Nos. 9 and 10 of the Talk of the respondent as printed in the form of a pamphlet a part of the judicial record of this Court and thereby making it a public document which could be published in the newspapers, the Judges of this Court had contravened the provisions of the Official Secrets Act of 1923. That the written statement did not bear any meaning other than that which its plain words conveyed is clear from the fact that even the learned Attorney-General who had signed it for the Pakistan Government did not claim that it had any other meaning as well as from the fact that the notice that issued from the Court had said clearly that the offence was committed because this Court was sought to be lowered in the eyes of those who had heard the Talk and of those who had read the pamphlet and no reference had been made to the public learning about it. This plea was raised before the Court dealing with the culpability or otherwise of the paragraphs in question and could be nothing but a hint that the sword of Damocles in the shape of appropriate action for contravention of the Official Secrets Act, 1923, hung over the heads of the Judges of this Court and therefore the Judges hearing the case should watch their steps lest they themselves and their colleagues come to grief. If anyone were to describe the written statement put in on behalf of the Pakistan Government as the least law respecting document ever presented by a responsible party before a Court of Law of any civilised country, he would not be held by an impartial critic to have indulged in misdescription. By the laws of no civilised country is it open to any person, howsoever highly placed, and whether that person be a natural person or a juristic person, to say or do anything which may even hint at a threat to the Court, however humble that Court may be, and this applies with greater force to persons who are parties to the proceedings in which the threat is held out or is hinted at. This sort of conduct would amount to Contempt of Court by the laws of all civilised countries, including America, where the law relating to Contempt of Court is less stringent than in Great Britain and the Commonwealth countries. The written statement put in on behalf of the Central Government makes it clear that its author was either entirely ignorant of the law relating to Contempt of Court or else had scant regard for it. It is a matter of no small regret that a written statement which clearly held out a threat to the Court to which it was presented should have been presented in a case in which the original respondent was the Secretary of the Law Department of the Government of Pakistan, of which department the Minister, Mr. Muhammad Ibrahim, had for some years been a Judge of a High Court in Pakistan and as such had dealt with law judicially and has for a couple of years been dealing with law in an executive capacity as the Minister for Law. The objectionable nature of the written statement is no whit reduced by reason of the fact that the members of the Bench hearing the case had not allowed the insidious exhibition of the iron hand through extremely sizable holes in the velvet glove—the only vestige left of the velvet glove being the words "respectfully sheweth" with which the written statement opens—to deter them from the performance of their delicate duty.

7. It is true that though final orders in that regard are passed by the President of Pakistan, the Pakistan Government, and especially the Law Ministry of that Government, has a say in the matter of appointment and advancement of Judges of the High Courts. However, no law in force in Pakistan permits anyone how-high-so-ever to try to affect the decision of a Judge with regard to a judicial matter before him. . . . As far as my knowledge goes, the only other person of eminence who held out a threat to a Court in the course of judicial proceedings was the son of a king of England who walked into a Court and tried to interfere with the course of justice. The result was that the monarch's eldest son, who was to ascend the throne after his father, was sentenced by Lord Chief Justice Cascoigne to a term of imprisonment for Contempt of Court. This case finds mention in Chapter III of Oswald's book on Contempt of Courts. The authority for what is written therein is the book "Governour, ed. Croft," Volume 2, by Sir Thomas Elyot. The passage from Sir Thomas Elyot's book has been reproduced in Oswald's book in the English language used near about the time when the incident occurred and in the English language in use at the present time reads as under:

> The most renowned prince King Henry the fifth, late King of England, during the life of his father was noted to be fierce and of wanton courage. It happened that one of his servants, whom he favoured very

much, was arraigned before the King's Bench for felony committed by him and the prince learning of this in furious rage came hastily to the bar where his servant stood as a prisoner and commanded that he be set at liberty, whereat all men were abashed, except the Chief Justice, who humbly exhorted the prince to be contented that his servant might be ordered according to the ancient laws of the realm, or if he would have him saved from the rigor of the laws, that he should, if he liked, appeal to the King, his father, to grant him his gracious pardon. By this answer the prince was not appeased, but rather more inflamed, and made an attempt to take away his servant. The Judge considering the perilous example and inconvenience that might thereby ensue with a valiant spirit and courage commanded the prince upon his allegiance to leave the prisoner and depart his way. As the prince was still in fury, he in a terrible manner, came up to the place of judgment and the men present in Court thought that he would slay the Judge or cause him some injury. The Judge, however, sitting still, without moving, declaring the Majesty of the King's place of judgment, and with an assured and bold countenance, addressed the prince with these words:

"Sir, remember yourself: I keep here the place of the King, Your sovereign lord and father, to whom you owe double obedience. In his name, I charge you desist from your wilfulness and unlawful enterprise and thereby give good example to those who hereafter shall be your subjects. And now for your contempt and disobedience I send you to the prison of the King's Bench where I commit you and direct that you shall remain there until the pleasure of your father, the King, be further known."

Upon these words the prince was abashed and laying his weapon apart and doing reverence, departed and went to the King's Bench as he was commanded. His servants felt disdainful at this and came and told the King of what had happened, whereupon, in all gladness, the king holding his hand upward said in a loud voice: "O merciful God, how much am I above all other men bound to Your infinite goodness, especially because You have given me a Judge who fears not to administer justice and also a son who can suffer and obey justice.

I make no secret of this that if the learned Attorney-General had disclosed—which in spite of repeated questions by me he did not do—the name of the person who had directed him to put in on behalf of the Central Government the written statement which was not only irrevelant but threatening also, I would have unhesitatingly dealt with the person in the same manner in which Lord Chief Justice Cascoigne had dealt with the Prince of Wales. This action of mine would have been in accord with the law of the land and I have no doubt in my mind that even if the erring party were a Minister in the Cabinet, my action would have been accorded the same approval by the Head of the State as the action Lord Chief Justice Cascoigne was accorded by the Sovereign of England whose son and heir had been sent to jail by that Judge.

8. I would have been a happier man if an occasion to find fault with the written statement put in on behalf of the Central Government had not arisen, but the occasion having arisen I would have failed in my duty if I had omitted to point out in what respects the document was open to exception. In view of the fact that the written statement in question purports to have the blessings of the Central Government of Pakistan, overlooking its defects would perhaps have

been the safer course for me and I would have followed that course had it not been for the certain knowledge that if, for fear that what I say may at some future time be sought to be used by interested persons as the documentary proof of my incompetence, I omitted to deal with this written statement in precisely the same manner in which I would have dealt with it if it were that of a private party, the oath of office as a Judge of the High Court of West Pakistan, whereby I solemnly affirmed to do justice between the parties before me without fear or favour, affection or ill-will, would for a very long time, mockingly ring in my ears. Moreover, I believe that there is a good deal of truth in the following lines:

> He either fears his fate too much or his deserts are small
> Who does not put it to the touch to gain or lose it all.

Extremely irregular in the circumstances of the present case though it would have been on the part of the respondent to have done so, I would have preferred that the learned Attorney-General reply to my questions on the point that the written statement was based on the instructions given by the respondent, purporting to act for the Central Government as he is perhaps competent to do under the Rules of Business. If the written statement was based on the instructions given by the respondent, it would, to a slight extent, lose its objectionable character because it could then be construed as an attempt of a man finding himself in a tight corner to extricate himself by every possible means, but the learned Attorney-General did not state that the respondent had given him the instructions. I might mention that even if some unbiased person were to say that I have erred in dilating on the objectionable nature of the written statement of the Central Government, I would have no regrets because if I have erred [I have done so] in a good cause, that cause being an attempt at keeping scrupulously pure and entirely unadulterated the stream of justice not in theory only but in practice also, not merely in the speeches of those in power from the public platform but also in their actions at the bar of the Courts as well.

9. But the unexpected events which I have hinted at in the first paragraph of this judgment have not ended and another yet remains. This was that whenever it was pointed out to Chaudhri Nazir Ahmad Khan, the learned Attorney-General of Pakistan, or Mr. Ghias Muhammad, the learned Standing Counsel of the Central Government, that the thing said or done by him was not allowed by law, the reply was that the thing had been done or said, as the case might be, under the orders of the Central Government. I confess that this answer amused me not a little and in fact reminded me of the early days of my practice in the Courts of Magistrates where it was not unusual to hear the police officer conducting the prosecution telling a Magistrate in plain words that the Superintendent of Police was opposed to the grant of bail to an accused person or that that exhalted personage would not like the acquittal of an accused person. The name of the Central Government was mentioned by both its counsel in precisely the same manner as I had heard the name of the Superintendent of Police mentioned in Courts of Magistrates about a quarter of a century earlier. I, however, hope that the learned counsel who appeared for the Central Government did not believe that the words "Central Government" were an "open Sesame" which would help them in demolishing all barriers set up by the law of the land. The written statement of the Central Government was presented by the learned Attorney-General and when after going through it I pointed out to him that it offended against the law of the land, I was surprised to hear him reply that he was per-

forming his duty as he was putting it in under the orders of the Central Government. Again, when Mr. Ghias Muhammad wanted to refer to a speech made by an *ex*-Chief Justice of Pakistan and to two made by the present Chief Justice of West Pakistan, I pointed out to him that as those speeches had not been the subject of decision by any Court, a reference to them was entirely irrelevant for the present proceedings, and he came out with the reply that he had been instructed by the Central Government to refer to those speeches during the course of his arguments. In what respect the person who issued these instructions on behalf of the Pakistan Government thought that the case of the respondent would be improved by a reference to these speeches passes my comprehension. It may be that the object of the person who instructed that a reference to the speeches of the Chief Justice of this Court, published in the press very long ago, be made was to point out as politely as he could that an application will be made to take proceedings against his Lordship the Chief Justice on the basis of these speeches; but if that was the object it is hardly open to question that it was reprehensible for more reasons than one.

*   *   *

11. I will now take up the question whether or not the respondent had been proved guilty of contempt of Court and will in this connection, first of all, deal with some contentions of a general nature that were raised. I have indicated in paragraph 2 of this judgment that the decision to issue notice was taken in a meeting of the Judges which was held to determine whether any, and if so what, action should be taken with regard to the Talk of the respondent given on the 15th of February 1960. Two courses were open to the Judges, one being to send a complaint to the Central Government and the second to take action under the Contempt of Courts Act, and the latter course was followed. The position which was taken on behalf of the Pakistan Government during the proceedings of this case has proved that in deciding to take action under the law of the land rather than by a complaint to the Central Government the Judges had adopted the better course. The main reason why this course was adopted at that time was that the pamphlet, of which, as I have said already, two thousand copies were prepared, was printed at public expense and would on the face of it appear to have the support of the Pakistan Government. It was deemed inconceivable that a pamphlet which dealt with so important a subject as the Transitional Constitution of Pakistan which had been printed at public expense had not been read by any one of those in Government who would notice that paragraphs No. 9 and 10 of the Talk were irrelevant to the subject on which the respondent had been asked to give the Talk and yet the distribution of the pamphlet to Government servants was not stopped. The Judges expect the same protection by Government as any of its servants, and the Talk having been printed at the public expense without any objection from Government, the Judges had no course open to them but to take action under the Contempt of Courts Act. A contention was half-heartedly raised in this Court that the respondent was, to some extent, prejudiced by reason of the fact that all the Judges present at Lahore on the 25th of October 1960 had decided upon the issuance of the notice and the three hearing the case had attended the meeting in which this decision was taken. No decision on the question had been arrived at in the meeting of the Judges and all that was said in the meeting was that *prima facie* paragraphs No. 9 and 10 of the Talk contravened the provisions of the Contempt of Courts Act under which action should be taken. The law is clear on the point that a Judge who had, at the preliminary

stage, considered the question whether or not proceedings under the Contempt of Courts Act should be taken is not precluded from hearing the case. There are a large number of cases on record in which a Judge who had been maligned, and maligning whom was considered to be contempt of Court, had sat on the Bench which heard the case.

* * *

14. Coming now to the passages about which notice was issued to the respondent, it should be borne in mind that the Talk which the respondent gave related to the Transitional Constitution of Pakistan as contained in the President's Order (Post-Proclamation) No. 1 of 1958, known as Laws (Continuance in Force) Order, 1958. After dealing with some other matters the respondent said in his Talk that the stand of the Law Ministry of Pakistan to the effect that the sovereign power lay in the Governor-General and not in the Constituent Assembly had been proved to be correct as the decision of the Federal Court of Pakistan in *Maulvi Tamizuddin's case* would show. He explained some provisions of the President's Order (Post-Proclamation) No. 1 of 1958, and then came to the discussion with regard to writs. This is what he said on this subject:

> 9. I think everybody has heard about the writs or, as the Law Ministry prefers to call them—to indicate the source of the power—the prerogative writs. Between 1956 and 1958, the High Courts had used the language of the 1956 Constitution—with its reference to orders and directions in the nature of writs—to claim a jurisdiction to interfere with the Government itself without reference to the strictly defined frontiers of the prerogative writs. A Court can issue a writ only because the sovereign function is to that extent delegated to it by the Sovereign, that is to say, by the State. Clearly the delegate cannot exercise the power against the Sovereign itself, and that has been made clear over centuries of decisions by the Courts in England, where the writs first originated by delegation from the King, and this has been followed in the United States, where the sovereign power descended to the people and is exercised in their name by the President. As an American Judge recently said:
>
> "There cannot be two sovereigns, and the sovereign will not issue a prerogative writ against itself." The Law Ministry has had to appeal a large number of times to the Supreme Court to have the position properly established, and has succeeded in every appeal but one. All this has cost a very great deal of money, and to try and put the situation right without having to spend more money on more appeals a clause was inserted in the Order we are discussing giving the High Courts the power to issue the named "writs" (not "orders or directions" and so on, but writs) of *mandamus* and the rest. This was to indicate as politely as possible, that a writ was a writ, confined to known limits, and the limits could not be exceeded. I have to confess that, even with this civility, we have not entirely succeeded even yet, but this clause on the one side, and some very severe observations by the Supreme Court on the other, have at least had the effect of indicating that after all there are limits and that the limits must be observed. The great thing, in any orderly system of Government (and without orderliness there is chaos), is that every organ of the Government should be best adapted to the work it has to do and should know what that work is

and what its own frontiers are. This avoids duplication. It avoids fraction. It prevents usurpation of function and consequent uncertainty, with all the public confusion and private misery that it can lead to.

10. I apologize for taking up so much time over this Order, but on it the whole fabric of the constitutional Government of the country rests until we have the new Constitution. Perhaps you would have wished me to say something about the services, seeing that what was originally a single paragraph, Article 6, has now been increased to a further six paragraphs, some modifying the terms and conditions of service already guaranteed—but not all: one of the additions establishes the power to grant extensions of service, a power which was denied by the High Court. We have never been able to understand the judgment: We would, of course, have appealed against it, and I have no doubt we should have succeeded, but there was no time—a certain loan from abroad was made conditional upon the continued retention of certain people, and since the High Court had denied the power to retain, and we could not wait for the months an appeal would take, the existence of the power was formally asserted in an explanation. We chose this particular way of doing things, if you are interested to know, so as not to concede that the power had to be created: We took it for granted that, notwithstanding the judgment, and in order not to prejudice our appeal if we ultimately did appeal in any other case, the power does exist.

15. It will be noticed that this part of the Talk is entirely incongruous with other parts of it and, at any rate, no one who reads the Talk from the beginning can easily understand how the question of the decisions of the Judges of the High Courts in writ petitions presented against Government had cropped up. The purpose for which the Government had desired the respondent to give the Talk was to explain the Transitional Constitution of 1958, and one fails to see how, even if the views of the respondent be assumed to be correct, the question arose that the High Courts in Pakistan had completely failed to understand in what cases the powers to grant writs could be exercised. The manner in which the High Courts have been brought into the discussion makes it clear that the respondent wanted to tell his audience that the High Courts in Pakistan were manned by incompetent people who did not understand a branch of law which they had been administering for about five years. In the tenth paragraph of the Talk the respondent made a reference to a judgment of this Court, the correctness of which he incorrectly asserted had not been tested by an appeal to the Supreme Court. With regard to this judgment the respondent said in unequivocal terms that it was incomprehensible and added that if an appeal had been taken against it, there was no doubt that the appeal would have been accepted. How any person can say what the decision of a Court would have been in any particular case is beyond my comprehension, and if the respondent had prophesied what the decision of this Court in any particular case would be, as he has done with regard to the Supreme Court, it is by no means unlikely that action under the Contempt of Courts Act would have been taken against him. It will also have been noticed that the respondent had told his audience that though the Law Ministry, of which Ministry, I might mention, the respondent has been the Secretary for about ten years, had been trying to impress upon the Judges of the High Courts that a writ was a writ and nothing more than a writ, it had taken

some very severe remarks of the Supreme Court to make the Judges of the High Courts understand that obvious thing and that even the severe remarks of the Supreme Court had not succeeded entirely. The burden of paragraph No. 9 is that in spite of the fact that no writ could issue against Government and the fact that all appeals in which the Law Ministry had raised this point before the Supreme Court had succeeded, the High Courts had not been able to fully grasp the implications of the words used by the Legislature. It says that the Judges of the High Courts had been issuing writs to Government though no writ could issue to Government and the Judges had been pressing into service the words "directions and orders" which occurred in the Constitution of the Islamic Republic of Pakistan, which came into force on the 23rd of March 1956, and was abrogated on the 7th of October 1958, for issuing writs to Government which they could not do. Anyone reading the pamphlet would think that the meaning of the Talk, patent at some places and latent at some, was that the Judges of the High Courts in Pakistan were either half-witted persons who did not understand the law or persons who deliberately misinterpreted it.

* * *

18. . . . I have given my views on the plain meaning of the two paragraphs of the Talk of the respondent which are under consideration in this case, and will now consider whether the respondent had any basis for making the assertions he made about the High Courts. The purport of the first few lines of paragraph 9 is that between 1956 and 1958 the High Courts in Pakistan had been issuing writs to Government, which they could not have done. The reasoning adopted was that the power to issue writs was delegated to Courts by Government and consequently no writ could have been issued to Government. I might point out that in Pakistan the power to issue writs was given by the Legislature and not the Government, but that point need not be emphasised. The respondent was clearly talking of the period between 1956 and 1958, the period during which the abrogated Constitution was in force. Article 170 of that law was in the following terms:

> 170. Notwithstanding anything in Article 22, each High Court shall have power, throughout the territories in relation to which it exercises jurisdiction, to issue to any person or authority, including in appropriate cases any Government, directions, orders or writs, including writs in the nature of *habeas corpus, mandamus,* prohibition, *quo warranto* and *certiorari,* for the enforcement of any of the rights conferred by Part II and for any other purpose.

Can anyone who has read Article 170 even once—and I can safely presume that the respondent had read this Article a number of times—justifiably say that between 1956 and 1958, the High Courts in Pakistan did not possess the power to issue writs against the Central or a Provincial Government in Pakistan? In his statement before the Court the respondent tried to indicate that his impression all along had been that even under the abrogated Constitution a writ could not be issued to Government. I would have believed that assertion of the respondent if he were not an educated man who has held the post of the Law Secretary to the Government of Pakistan for about ten years.

* * *

19. But the impeachment of the highest Courts in the Provinces of Pakistan, namely the High Courts, does not finish there. The respondent went on to say in

paragraph 9 of the pamphlet that in spite of the fact that the Law Ministry had tried to point out to the High Courts the limits of their jurisdiction and in spite of some very severe remarks of the Supreme Court, they had not been able to fully grasp the law about writs and the High Courts had been encroaching on the preserves of the Government. The paragraph ends by saying that if the frontiers between the functions of the different organs of the Government are not kept in view, the result is chaos, but if the frontiers are observed, then no usurpation of functions results and uncertainty with all the public confusion and private misery that usurpation of functions can lead to is avoided. When making his statement before the Court the respondent did not say that in this part of the Talk his reference was to any other organ of the Government than the High Courts in Pakistan, but in his affidavit he has asserted that his intention was to tell his audience that if the frontiers of functions are not kept in view, chaos and disarray results. I am prepared to accept the assertion of the respondent in the affidavit that he did not intend to say that it was only the usurpation of powers by the High Courts that will lead to chaos and other things mentioned by him, but the question is whether his audience and those who read the pamphlet will think of any other organ of the Government than the High Courts which had led to chaos and disarray with all its public confusion and private misery, when no other organ of Government has been mentioned even once in the paragraph in question. The answer to this question has to be in the negative.

✿   ✿   ✿

27. What I have said [before] about the Talk and its meaning will have made it clear that the respondent had indulged in what is called scandalizing the High Courts in Pakistan, and there will be no escape from the finding that he had been guilty of contempt of Court unless it be proved that he was protected. The learned counsel for the respondent argued that the respondent having given the Talk in question at the instance of the Government and the Talk having been given to the Section Officers of the Pakistan Government only, he was protected. I cannot accept either of these contentions. Assuming that the person at whose request the respondent gave the Talk in question was above the law, I do not see how the respondent can escape liability if he has contravened the law. There is no evidence on the record that the person who asked the respondent to give the Talk had told him to give the Talk that he actually gave. But assuming that he had and that he was superior in rank to the respondent, the law is clear on the point that the orders of a superior can be of no avail if the person who obeys those orders contravenes the law of the land. This proposition of law can be aptly brought out by taking the example of a soldier who has been ordered by his officer to kill a man without any legal justification. If the soldier does not obey the officer he thereby makes himself liable under the military law for disobedience of the orders of an officer, but if he obeys them he is guilty under the law of the land and may suffer the extreme penalty for the murder that he has committed under orders of his officer. The fact, therefore, that the respondent had no intention of giving the Talk and gave it only because he had been requested to do so would not make any difference to his liability if the Talk has contravened the law of the land. Nor does the second part of the argument of the learned counsel for the respondent have any force. The mere fact that the respondent was addressing only a gathering of eighty or a hundred Section Officers of the Pakistan Government and not a large gathering would not make any difference

to his culpability, though the fact that the Judges were scandalized before a small number of people may be taken into consideration when considering the question of the sentence.

✿   ✿   ✿

30. It was next contended by learned counsel for the respondent that as the respondent in his capacity of Secretary of the Law Ministry of the Pakistan Government had to deal with legislation and the appeal work of the Government and in the performance of that duty had to comment upon judgments of the High Courts in Pakistan, the Talk could not be held to have been made with the object of scandalizing this Court or the other High Court in Pakistan. It is undeniable that in his capacity of Secretary of the Ministry of Law, the respondent has the right to express his own views about judgments of the High Courts, but those views can be expressed by him on confidential official files, the contents of which are not broadcast to the world at large or to public servants other than those having official concern in the matter. If the intention of the respondent was that because of what he considered to be the incompetence of their Judges the High Courts in Pakistan should be deprived of the power to issue writs, it was open to him to address a secret and confidential communication through the Law Minister to the President of Pakistan, but as he was not discussing the matter with an authority competent to take away the powers of the High Courts to issue writs but was addressing people who would scarcely know the difference between a writ and any other process issued by a Court, he cannot claim the protection which would attach to his secret communications in the discharge of his official duties. No one should have the mistaken impression that the fact that he can in certain circumstances do a thing gives him the right to do that under all circumstances. This may be explained by giving an example. A Judge can punish a man after trial and can send him to prison, but the same Judge cannot, sitting at home without holding a trial, send anyone to prison, and if he were to do that he would certainly be guilty of the offence of wrongful confinement. A case similar to that of the respondent arose when a litigant wrote disparaging things about a Judge of this Court in an application presented to a Court subordinate to this Court. His case, which is *The State* v. *Abdur Rahman*, was dealt with by me and he was sentenced. I held in that case that though it may be permissible to say certain things about a Judge in the Court which is hearing an appeal against the judgment of that Judge, the same thing, if it is derogatory in nature, cannot be said in a Court from whose judgments the Judge hears appeals. While, therefore, it may have been open to him to scathingly criticise the Judges of the High Courts before the President of Pakistan, the respondent could not do that before anyone else except the Supreme Court of Pakistan when that Court was engaged in hearing an appeal against a judgment of the Judges in question, and even then, as is clear from the decision of the Federal Court of Pakistan in *S. M. Haq* v. *The Honourable Judges of the High Court of Judicature at Lahore*, the privilege would not be unlimited.

31. Learned counsel for the respondent also urged that what was contained in paragraphs 9 and 10 of the pamphlet was to a great extent correct and, therefore, contempt of Court could not be said to have been committed. He contended that the respondent believed that even under the abrogated Constitution no writ could be issued to Government, but as the words of Article 170 of that Constitution were clear, I am not prepared to accept the contention that the respondent believed what his counsel said he did. And if the respondent did

have that belief, he should not have had it. His learned counsel added that this at least was correct, that no writ could be issued to Government even under Article 170 of the abrogated Constitution in service matters. This contention too is devoid of force because when it was raised on behalf of the Government before the Supreme Court in Civil Appeals No. 95, 96 and 97 of 1956, decided on the 10th of November 1958, which were appeals against a decision of this Court in *Mahmood Ali Khan etc.* v. *The Islamic Republic of Pakistan* the contention was repelled by their Lordships of the Supreme Court. Mr. A. Haque, learned counsel for the respondent, further contended that the respondent had not been far wrong when he said in his Talk that some severe remarks were made by the Supreme Court with regard to the mode of exercise of writ jurisdiction by the High Courts, and in this connection referred to *Tariq Transport Company, Lahore* v. *The Sargodha-Bhera Bus Service etc., The State of Pakistan* v. *Mehraj-ud-Din* and *Pakistan through The Secretary, National Assembly* v. *Khandker Ali.* It may be that some remarks in these judgments of the Supreme Court are severe, but I do not see why it should have been necessary to mention to the Section Officers of the Pakistan Government that severe remarks were made by the Supreme Court against the High Courts in Pakistan, if the only object of the respondent was to apprise them of the purport of the Transitional Constitution of Pakistan.

*   *   *

34. I will now take up the most difficult of the questions that arose in the case, namely, what punishment should be awarded. In this connection Mr. Mahmood Ali said that the Court should pass no sentence and should content itself with recording a conviction. Though he did not say so, one could see that Mr. Mahmood Ali had adopted that attitude because the fact that the Government of Pakistan having supported the respondent so completely would make it appear that if a sentence is passed it would be commuted by Government. That, however, is a matter which cannot weigh with the Court. The circumstances that are to be kept in view by the Court are:

(1) That an institution in which all and sundry should have implicit confidence so that there should not be chaos has been maligned and its authority has been attempted to be undermined by an individual, and an institution cannot be sacrificed for an individual;

(2) that the person who has indulged in the reprehensible act is a high official and as he is the Secretary to the Law Ministry of the Government of Pakistan, what he said about legal matters must have been considered to be true by all those who did not know the correct position;

(3) that the respondent is a foreigner in Pakistan; and

(4) that the respondent has been in the service of Pakistan for about twelve years.

The first two of these four circumstances call for the imposition of the maximum sentence prescribed by law for the offence, namely, simple imprisonment for six months and a fine of Rs. 2,000, while the last two call for exercise of leniency. Weighing all the circumstances together, I would sentence the respondent to pay a fine Rs. 2,000, default of payment of which will entail simple imprisonment for one month. I would further direct that the respondent pay as costs of these proceedings the sum of Rs. 2,000 which is to be paid by the Provincial

Government as fee to Mr. Mahmood Ali, Advocate, out of public money. The respondent is granted time till the 9th of February 1961 to pay the amounts mentioned above.

* * *

Kent v. Dulles
(U.S.A., 1958)

MR. JUSTICE DOUGLAS delivered the opinion of the Court.

This case concerns two applications for passports, denied by the Secretary of State. One was by Rockwell Kent, who desired to visit England and attend a meeting of an organization known as the "World Council of Peace" in Helsinki, Finland. The Director of the Passport Office informed Kent that issuance of a passport was precluded by § 51.135 of the Regulations promulgated by the Secretary of State on two grounds: (1) that he was a Communist and (2) that he had had "a consistent and prolonged adherence to the Communist Party line." The letter of denial specified in some detail the facts on which those conclusions were based. Kent was also advised of his right to an informal hearing under § 51.137 of the Regulations. But he was also told that whether or not a hearing was requested it would be necessary, before a passport would be issued, to submit an affidavit as to whether he was then or ever had been a Communist. Kent did not ask for a hearing but filed a new passport application listing several European countries he desired to visit. When advised that a hearing was still available to him, his attorney replied that Kent took the position that the requirement of an affidavit concerning Communist Party membership "is unlawful and that for that reason and as a matter of conscience," he would not supply one. He did, however, have a hearing at which the principal evidence against him was from his book *It's Me, O Lord*, which Kent agreed was accurate. He again refused to submit the affidavit, maintaining that any matters unrelated to the question of his citizenship were irrelevant to the Department's consideration of his application. The Department advised him that no further consideration if his application would be given until he satisfied the requirements of the Regulations.

Thereupon Kent sued in the District Court for declaratory relief. The District Court granted summary judgment for respondent. On appeal the case of Kent was heard with that of Dr. Walter Briehl, a psychiatrist. When Briehl applied for a passport, the Director of the Passport Office asked him to supply the affidavit covering membership in the Communist Party. Briehl, like Kent, refused. The Director then tentatively disapproved the application on the following grounds:

> In your case it has been alleged that you were a Communist. Specifically it is alleged that you were a member of the Los Angeles County Communist Party; that you were a member of the Bookshop Association, St. Louis, Missouri; that you held Communist Party meetings; that in 1936 and 1941 you contributed articles to the Communist Pub-

---

78 S. Ct. 1113 (1958). Footnotes and interlinear citations have been omitted.

lication "Social Work Today"; that in 1939, 1940 and 1941 you were a sponsor to raise funds for veterans of the Abraham Lincoln Brigade in calling on the President of the United States by a petition to defend the rights of the Communist Party and its members; that you contributed to the Civil Rights Congress bail fund to be used in raising bail on behalf of convicted Communist leaders in New York City; that you were a member of the Hollywood Arts, Sciences and Professions Council and a contact of the Los Angeles Committee for Protection of Foreign Born and a contact of the Freedom Stage, Incorporated.

The Director advised Briehl of his right to a hearing but stated that whether or not a hearing was held, an affidavit concerning membership in the Communist Party would be necessary. Briehl asked for a hearing and one was held. At that hearing he raised three objections: (1) that his "political affiliations" were irrelevant to his right to a passport; (2) that "every American citizen has the right to travel regardless of politics"; and (3) that the burden was on the Department to prove illegal activities by Briehl. Briehl persisted in his refusal to supply the affidavit. Because of that refusal Briehl was advised that the Board of Passport Appeals could not under the Regulations entertain an appeal.

Briehl filed his complaint in the District Court, which held that his case was indistinguishable from Kent's and dismissed the complaint.

The Court of Appeals heard the two cases en banc and affirmed the District Court by a divided vote. . . . The cases are here on writ of certiorari. . . .

The Court first noted the function that the passport performed in American law in the case of Urtetiqui v. D'Arcy (US) 9 Pet 692, 699, 9 L ed 276, 279, decided in 1835:

> There is no law of the United States, in any manner regulating the issuing of passports, or directing upon what evidence it may be done, or declaring their legal effect. It is understood, as matter of practice, that some evidence of citizenship is required, by the secretary of state, before issuing a passport. This, however, is entirely discretionary with him. No inquiry is instituted by him to ascertain the fact of citizenship, or any proceedings had, that will in any manner bear the character of a judicial inquiry. It is a document, which, from its nature and object, is addressed to foreign powers; purporting only to be a request, that the bearer of it may pass safely and freely; and is to be considered rather in the character of a political document, by which the bearer is recognized, in foreign countries, as an American citizen; and which, by usage and the law of nations, is received as evidence of the fact.

A passport not only is of great value—indeed necessary—abroad; it is also an aid in establishing citizenship for purposes of re-entry into the United States. . . . But throughout most of our history—until indeed quite recently —a passport, though a great convenience in foreign travel, was not a legal requirement for leaving or entering the United States. See Jaffe, "The Right to Travel: The Passport Problem," 35 *Foreign Affairs* 17. Apart from minor exceptions to be noted, it was first made a requirement by § 215 of the Act of June 27, 1952, 66 Stat 190, 8 USC § 1185, which states that, after a prescribed proclamation by the President, it is "unlawful for any citizen of the United States to depart from or enter, or attempt to depart from or enter, the United States unless he bears a valid passport." And the Proclamation necessary to make the restrictions of this Act applicable and in force has been made.

Prior to 1952 there were numerous laws enacted by Congress regulating passports and many decisions, rulings, and regulations by the Executive Department concerning them. Thus in 1803 Congress made it unlawful for an official knowingly to issue a passport to an alien certifying that he is a citizen. 2 Stat 205. In 1815, just prior to the termination of the War of 1812, it made it illegal for a citizen to "cross the frontier" into enemy territory, to board vessels of the enemy on waters of the United States or to visit any of his camps within the limits of the United States, "without a passport first obtained" from the Secretary of State or other designated official. 3 Stat 199–200. The Secretary of State took similar steps during the Civil War. See Dept. of State, *The American Passport* (1898), 50. In 1850 Congress ratified a treaty with Switzerland requiring passports from citizens of the two nations. 11 Stat 587, 589–590. Finally in 1856 Congress enacted what remains today as our basic passport statute. Prior to that time various federal officials, state and local officials, and notaries public had undertaken to issue either certificates of citizenship or other documents in the nature of letters of introduction to foreign officials requesting treatment according to the usages of international law. By the Act of August 18, 1856, 11 Stat 52, 60–61, 22 USC § 211a, Congress put an end to those practices. This provision, as codified by the Act of July 3, 1926, 44 Stat, Part 2, 887, reads, "The Secretary of State may grant and issue passports . . . under such rules as the President shall designate and prescribe for and on behalf of the United States, and no other person shall grant, issue, or verify such passports."

Thus for most of our history a passport was not a condition to entry or exit.

It is true that, at intervals, a passport has been required for travel. Mention has already been made of the restrictions imposed during the War of 1812 and during the Civil War. A like restriction, which was the forerunner of that contained in the 1952 Act, was imposed by Congress in 1918.

The Act of May 22, 1918, 40 Stat 559, made it unlawful, while a Presidential Proclamation was in force, for a citizen to leave or enter the United States "unless he bears a valid passport." See HR Rep No. 485, 65th Cong, 2d Sess. That statute was invoked by Presidential Proclamation No. 1473 on August 8, 1918, 40 Stat 1829, which continued in effect until March 3, 1921. 41 Stat 1359.

The 1918 Act was effective only in wartime. It was amended in 1941 so that it could be invoked in the then-existing emergency. 55 Stat 252. See S Rep No. 444, 77th Cong, 1st Sess. It was invoked by Presidential Proclamation No. 2523, November 14, 1941, 55 Stat 1696. That emergency continued until April 28, 1952. Proc No. 2974, 66 Stat C31. Congress extended the statutory provisions until April 1, 1953. 66 Stat 54, 57, 96, 137, 330, 333. It was during this extension period that the Secretary of State issued the Regulations here complained of.

Under the 1926 Act and its predecessor a large body of precedents grew up which repeat over and again that the issuance of passports is "a discretionary act" on the part of the Secretary of State. The scholars, the courts, the Chief Executive, and the Attorneys General all so said. This long-continued executive construction should be enough, it is said, to warrant the inference that Congress had adopted it. See Allen v. Grand Cent. Aircraft Co. 347 US 535, 544, 545, 98 L ed 933, 941, 942, 74 S Ct 745; United States v. Allen-Bradley Co. 352 US 306, 310, 1 L ed 2d 347, 350, 77 S Ct 343. But the key to that problem, as we shall see, is in the manner in which the Secretary's discretion was exercised, not in the bare fact that he had discretion.

The right to travel is a part of the "liberty" of which the citizen cannot be deprived without due process of law under the Fifth Amendment. So much is conceded by the Solicitor General. In Anglo-Saxon law that right was emerging at least as early as the Magna Carta. Chafee, *Three Human Rights in the Constitution of 1787* (1956), 171–181, 187 et seq., shows how deeply engrained in our history this freedom of movement is. Freedom of movement across frontiers in either direction, and inside frontiers as well, was a part of our heritage. Travel abroad, like travel within the country, may be necessary for a livelihood. It may be as close to the heart of the individual as the choice of what he eats, or wears, or reads. Freedom of movement is basic in our scheme of values. See Crandall v. Nevada (US) 6 Wall 35, 44, 18 L ed 745, 747; Williams v. Fears, 179 US 270, 274, 45 L ed 186, 188, 21 S Ct 128; Edwards v. California, 314 US 160, 86 L ed 119, 62 S Ct 164. "Our nation," wrote Chafee, "has thrived on the principle that, outside areas of plainly harmful conduct, every American is left to shape his own life as he thinks best, do what he pleases, go where he pleases." Id., at 197.

Freedom of movement also has large social values. As Chafee put it:

> Foreign correspondents and lecturers on public affairs need firsthand information. Scientists and scholars gain greatly from consultations with colleagues in other countries. Students equip themselves for more fruitful careers in the United States by instruction in foreign universities. Then there are reasons close to the core of personal life— marriage, reuniting families, spending hours with old friends. Finally, travel abroad enables American citizens to understand that people like themselves live in Europe and helps them to be well-informed on public issues. An American who has crossed the ocean is not obliged to form his opinions about our foreign policy merely from what he is told by officials of our government or by a few correspondents of American newspapers. Moreover, his views on domestic questions are enriched by seeing how foreigners are trying to solve similar problems. In many different ways direct contact with other countries contributes to sounder decisions at home. [Id., at 195–196. And see Vestal, "Freedom of Movement," 41 *Iowa L Rev* 6, 13–14.]

Freedom to travel is, indeed, an important aspect of the citizen's "liberty." We need not decide the extent to which it can be curtailed. We are first concerned with the extent, if any, to which Congress has authorized its curtailment.

The difficulty is that while the power of the Secretary of State over the issuance of passports is expressed in broad terms, it was apparently long exercised quite narrowly. So far as material here, the cases of refusal of passports generally fell into two categories. First, questions pertinent to the citizenship of the applicant and his allegiance to the United States had to be resolved by the Secretary, for the command of Congress was that "No passport shall be granted or issued to or verified for any other persons than those owing allegiance, whether citizens or not, to the United States." 32 Stat 386, 22 USC § 212. Second, was the question whether the applicant was participating in illegal conduct, trying to escape the toils of the law, promoting passport frauds, or otherwise engaging in conduct which would violate the laws of the United States. See 3 Moore, Digest of International Law (1906), § 512; 3 Hackworth, Digest of International Law (1942), § 268; 2 Hyde, International Law (2d rev ed), § 401.

The grounds for refusal asserted here do not relate to citizenship or allegiance on the one hand or to criminal or unlawful conduct on the other. Yet, so far as relevant here, those two are the only ones which it could fairly be argued were adopted by Congress in light of prior administrative practice. One can find in the records of the State Department rulings of subordinates covering a wider range of activities than the two indicated. But as respects Communists these are scattered rulings and not consistently of one pattern. We can say with assurance that whatever may have been the practice after 1926, at the time the Act of July 3, 1926, was adopted, the administrative practice, so far as relevant here, had jelled only around the two categories mentioned. We, therefore, hesitate to impute to Congress, when in 1952 it made a passport necessary for foreign travel and left its issuance to the discretion of the Secretary of State, a purpose to give him unbridled discretion to grant or withhold a passport from a citizen for any substantive reason he may choose.

More restrictive regulations were applied in 1918 and in 1941 as war measures. We are not compelled to equate this present problem of statutory construction with problems that may arise under the war power. Cf. Youngstown Sheet & Tube Co. v. Sawyer, 343 US 579, 96 L ed 1153, 72 S Ct 863, 26 ALR2d 1378.

In a case of comparable magnitude, Korematsu v. United States, 323 US 214; 218, 89 L ed 194, 199, 65 S Ct 193, we allowed the Government in time of war to exclude citizens from their homes and restrict their freedom of movement only on a showing of "the gravest imminent danger to the public safety." There the Congress and the Chief Executive moved in coordinated action; and, as we said, the Nation was then at war. No such condition presently exists. No such showing of extremity, no such showing of joint action by the Chief Executive and the Congress to curtail a constitutional right of the citizen has been made here.

Since we start with an exercise by an American citizen of an activity included in constitutional protection, we will not readily infer that Congress gave the Secretary of State unbridled discretion to grant or withhold it. If we were dealing with political questions entrusted to the Chief Executive by the Constitution we would have a different case. But there is more involved here. In part, of course, the issuance of the passport carries some implication of intention to extend the bearer diplomatic protection, though it does no more than "request all whom it may concern to permit safely and freely to pass, and in case of need to give all lawful aid and protection" to this citizen of the United States. But that function of the passport is subordinate. Its crucial function today is control over exit. And, as we have seen, the right of exit is a personal right included within the word "liberty" as used in the Fifth Amendment. If that "liberty" is to be regulated, it must be pursuant to the law-making functions of the Congress. Youngstown Sheet & Tube Co. v. Sawyer (US) supra. And if that power is delegated, the standards must be adequate to pass scrutiny by

the accepted tests. . . . Where activities or enjoyment, natural and often necessary to the well-being of an American citizen, such as travel, are involved, we
will construe narrowly all delegated powers that curtail or dilute them. See
Ex parte Endo, 323 US 283, 301, 302, 89 L ed 243, 255, 256, 65 S Ct 208.
Cf. Hannegan v. Esquire, Inc. 327 US 146, 156, 90 L ed 586, 592, 66 S Ct 456;
United States v. Rumely, 345 US 41, 46, 97 L ed 770, 775, 73 S Ct 543. We
hesitate to find in this broad generalized power an authority to trench so heavily
on the rights of the citizen.

Thus we do not reach the question of constitutionality. We only conclude
that § 1185 and § 211a do not delegate to the Secretary the kind of authority
exercised here. We deal with beliefs, with associations, with ideological matters.
We must remember that we are dealing here with citizens who have neither
been accused of crimes nor found guilty. They are being denied their freedom
of movement solely because of their refusal to be subjected to inquiry into their
beliefs and associations. They do not seek to escape the law nor to violate it. They
may or may not be Communists. But assuming they are, the only law which
Congress has passed expressly curtailing the movement of Communists across
our borders has not yet become effective. It would therefore be strange to infer
that pending the effectiveness of that law, the Secretary has been silently granted
by Congress the larger, the more pervasive power to curtail in his discretion the
free movement of citizens in order to satisfy himself about their beliefs or associations.

To repeat, we deal here with a constitutional right of the citizen, a right
which we must assume Congress will be faithful to respect. We would be
faced with important constitutional questions were we to hold that Congress by
§ 1185 and § 211a had given the Secretary authority to withhold passports to
citizens because of their beliefs or associations. Congress has made no such
provision in explicit terms; and absent one, the Secretary may not employ that
standard to restrict the citizens' right of free movement.

Reversed.

SEPARATE OPINION

MR. JUSTICE CLARK, with whom MR. JUSTICE BURTON, MR. JUSTICE HARLAN,
and MR. JUSTICE WHITTAKER concur, dissenting.

❈   ❈   ❈

The Court purports today to preclude the existence of such a ground by
holding that the Secretary has not been authorized to deny a passport to a Communist whose travel abroad would be inimical to our national security.

In thus construing the authority of the Secretary, the Court recognizes that
all during our history he has had discretion to grant or withhold passports. That
power, first exercised without benefit of statute, was made the subject of specific
legislative authority in 1856 when the Congress consolidated all power over
passports in the hands of the Secretary. 11 Stat 60–61. In 1874 the statutory
language, "shall be authorized to grant and issue," was changed to "may grant
and issue." 1874 RS § 4075. In slightly modified form, the Secretary's power
has come through several re-enactments, e.g., 44 Stat, Part 1, p. 657 in 1926,
to its present-day embodiment in 44 Stat, Part 2, p. 887, 22 USC § 211a.

This discretionary authority, which we previously acknowledged in Perkins
v. Elg, 307 US 325, 349, 350, 83 L ed 1320, 1333, 1334, 59 S Ct 884 (1939),

was exercised both in times of peace and in periods of war. During war and other periods of national emergency, however, the importance of the Secretary's passport power was tremendously magnified by a succession of "travel-control statutes" making possession of a passport a legal necessity to leaving or entering this country.

*   *   *

The legislative history of the 1918 Act sharply indicates that Congress meant the Secretary to deny passports to those whose travel abroad would be contrary to our national security. The Act came to the floor of the House of Representatives accompanied by the following explanation in the Report of the House Committee on Foreign Affairs, HR Rep No. 485, 65th Cong, 2d Sess 2–3:

*   *   *

It is essential to meet the situation that the Executive should have wide discretion and wide authority of action. No one can foresee the different means which may be adopted by hostile nations to secure military information or spread propaganda and discontent. It is obviously impracticable to appeal to Congress for further legislation in each new emergency. Swift Executive action is the only effective counterstroke.

*   *   *

During debate of the bill on the floor of the House, its House spokesman stated:

"The Government is now very much hampered by lack of authority to control the travel to and from this country, even of people suspected of not being loyal, and even of those whom they suspect of being in the employ of enemy governments." 56 Cong Rec 6029.

*   *   *

"Our ports are open, so far as the law is concerned, to alien friends, citizens, and neutrals, to come and go at will and pleasure, and that notwithstanding the Government may suspect the conduct and the intention of the individuals who come and go." Id. at 6065.

His counterpart in the Senate stated in debate:

The chief object of the bill is to correct a very serious trouble which the Department of State, the Department of Justice, and the Department of Labor are having with aliens and alien enemies and renegade American citizens, I am sorry to say, entering the United States from nests they have in Cuba and over the Mexican border. They can now enter and depart without any power of the departments or of the Government to intercept or delay them. There is no law that covers this case. It is believed that all the information which goes to Germany of the war preparations of the United States and of the transportation of troops to France passes through Mexico. The Government is having a great deal of trouble along that border. It is an everyday occurrence, and the emergency of this measure is very great. The bill is supplementary to the espionage laws and necessary for their efficient execution in detecting and punishing German spies. [56 Cong Rec 6192.]

The implication is unmistakable that the Secretary was intended to exercise his traditional passport function in such a manner as would effectively add to the protection of this country's internal security.

That the Secretary so understood and so exercised his passport power in this period is evident from two State Department documents in 1920. A memorandum of the Under Secretary of State, dated November 30, 1920, declared, "Any assistance in the way of passport facilities which this Government may render to a person who is working either directly or indirectly in behalf of the Soviet Government is a help to the Soviet Government. . . ."

* * *

By its terms a war statute, the 1918 Act expired in March 1921, see 41 Stat 1359, after which no more travel controls existed until 1941. In that year, Congress amended the 1918 Act so as to provide the same controls during the national emergency proclaimed by the President on May 27, 1941, should the President find and publicly proclaim that the interest of the United States required that such restrictions be reimposed. . . . The legislative history of the 1941 amendment is as clear as that of the 1918 Act: the purpose of the legislation was to so use the passport power of the Secretary as to block travel to and from the country by those persons whose passage would not be in the best interests and security of the United States.

* * *

While the national emergency to which the 1941 amendment related was officially declared at an end on April 28, 1952, Proc No 2974, 66 Stat C31, Congress continued the provisions of the Act in effect until April 1, 1953. 66 Stat 54. In that interim period, Congress passed the Immigration and Nationality Act of 1952, which both repealed the 1918 Act as amended in 1941, 66 Stat 279, and re-enacted it as § 215 of the 1952 Act, amending it only to the extent that its provisions would be subject to invocation "during the existence of any national emergency proclaimed by the President." . . .

At the time of the 1952 Act, a national emergency proclaimed by President Truman on December 16, 1950, in response to the Korean conflict, was—and still is today—in existence. Proc No. 2914, 64 Stat A454. In reliance on that, the President invoked the travel restrictions of § 215 on January 17, 1953. Proc No. 3004, 67 Stat C31. The proclamation by which this was done carefully pointed out that none of its provisions should be interpreted as revoking any regulation "heretofore issued relating to the departure of persons from, or their entry into, the United States." Id. Among the regulations theretofore issued were those now attacked relating to the issuance of passports to Communists, for they had been promulgated to be effective on August 28, 1952, shortly after passage of the 1952 Act. 17 Fed Reg 8013.

Congress, by virtue of § 215 of the 1952 Act, has approved whatever use of his discretion the Secretary had made prior to the June 1952 date of that legislation. That conclusion necessarily follows from the fact that § 215 continued to make legal exit or entry turn on possession of a passport, without in any way limiting the discretionary passport power theretofore exercised by the Secretary. . . . But the Court then determines (1) that the Secretary's denial of passports in peacetime extended to only two categories of cases, those involving allegiance and those involving criminal activity, and (2) that the Secretary's wartime exercise of his discretion, while admittedly more restrictive, has no relevance to the practice which Congress can be said to have approved in 1952. Since the present denials do not involve grounds either of allegiance or criminal activity, the Court concludes that they were beyond the pale of congressional authorization. Both of the propositions set out above are vital to the Court's final conclusion. Neither of them has any validity: the first is contrary to fact, and the second to common sense.

*   *   *

In a wholly realistic sense there is no peace today, and there was no peace in 1952. At both times the state of national emergency declared by the President in 1950, wherein he stated that "world conquest by communist imperialism is the goal of the forces of aggression that have been loosed upon the world" and that "the increasing menace of the forces of communist aggression requires that the national defense of the United States be strengthened as speedily as possible," was in full effect. Proc No. 2914, 64 Stat A454. It is not a case, then, of judging what may be done in peace by what has been done in war. Professor Jaffe has aptly exposed the fallacy upon which the majority proceeds:

> The criterion here is the defense of the country from external enemies. It is asserted that the precedents of "war" have no relevance to "peace." But the critical consideration is defense against an external enemy; and communication abroad between our citizens and the enemy cannot by its nature be controlled by the usual criminal process. The facts in a particular case as to the citizen's intention are inevitably speculative: all is to be done after the bird has flown. Now our Congress and the Administration have concluded that the Communist International is a foreign and domestic enemy. We deal with its domestic aspect by criminal process; we would seem justified in dealing with its external aspect by exit control. If an avowed Communist is going abroad, it may be assumed that he will take counsel there with his fellows, will arrange for the steady and dependable flow of cash and information, and do his bit to promote the purposes of the "conspiracy." [Jaffe, "The Right to Travel: The Passport Problem," 35 *Foreign Affairs* 17, 26.]

Were this a time of peace, there might very well be no problem for us to decide, since petitioners then would not need a passport to leave the country. The very structure of § 215 is such that either war or national emergency is prerequisite to imposition of its restrictions.

Indeed, rather than being irrelevant, the wartime practice may be the only relevant one, for the discretion with which we are concerned is a discretionary control over international travel. Yet only in times of war and national emergency has a passport been required to leave or enter this country, and hence only in such times has passport power necessarily meant power to control travel.

Finally, while distinguishing away the Secretary's passport denials in wartime, the majority makes no attempt to distinguish the Secretary's practice during periods when there has been no official state of war but when nevertheless a presidential proclamation of national emergency has been in effect, the very situation which has prevailed since the end of World War II. Throughout that time, as I have pointed out, the Secretary refused passports to those "whose purpose in traveling abroad was believed to be to subvert the interest of the United States." Report of the Commission on Government Security, supra.

Numerous specific instances of passport denials on security grounds during the years 1947–1951 were reported in a February 1952 law review article, nearly half a year prior to passage of § 215. Note, "Passport Refusals for Political Reasons," 61 *Yale LJ* 171.

On this multiple basis, then, I am constrained to disagree with the majority as to the authority of the Secretary to deny petitioners' applications for passports. The majority's resolution of the authority question prevents it from reaching the constitutional issues raised by petitioners, relating to claimed unlawful delegation of legislative power, violation of free speech and association under the First Amendment, and violation of international travel under the Fifth Amendment. In view of that, it would be inappropriate for me, as a dissenter, to consider those questions at this time. . . . Accordingly, I would affirm on the issue of the Secretary's authority to require the affidavits involved in this case, without reaching any constitutional questions.

Cleveland v. United States
(U.S.A., 1946)

MR. JUSTICE DOUGLAS delivered the opinion of the Court.

Petitioners are members of a Mormon sect, known as Fundamentalists. They not only believe in polygamy; unlike other Mormons, they practice it. Each of petitioners, except Stubbs, has, in addition to his lawful wife, one or more plural wives. Each transported at least one plural wife across state lines, either for the purpose of cohabiting with her, or for the purpose of aiding another member of the cult in such a project. They were convicted of violating the Mann Act (36 Stat. 825, 18 U. S. C. § 398) on a trial to the court, a jury having been waived. . . . The judgments of conviction were affirmed on appeal. . . . The cases are here on petitions for certiorari which we granted. . . .

The Act makes an offense the transportation in interstate commerce of "any woman or girl for the purpose of prostitution or debauchery, or for any other immoral purpose." The decision turns on the meaning of the latter phrase, "for any other immoral purpose."

United States v. *Bitty*, 208 U. S. 393, involved a prosecution under a federal statute making it a crime to import an alien woman "for the purpose of prostitution or for any other immoral purpose." The act was construed to cover a case where a man imported an alien woman so that she should live with him as his concubine. Two years later the Mann Act was passed. Because of the similarity of the language used in the two acts, the *Bitty* case became a forceful precedent for the construction of the Mann Act. Thus one who transported a woman in interstate commerce so that she should become his mistress or concubine was held to have transported her for an "immoral purpose" within the meaning of the Mann Act. *Caminetti* v. *United States*, 242 U. S. 470.

It is argued that the *Caminetti* decision gave too wide a sweep to the Act; that the Act was designed to cover only the white slave business and related vices; that it was not designed to cover voluntary actions bereft of sex commercialism; and that in any event it should not be construed to embrace poly-

---

67 S. Ct. 13 (1946). Footnotes have been omitted.

gamy, which is a form of marriage and, unlike prostitution or debauchery or the concubinage involved in the *Caminetti* case, has as its object parenthood and the creation and maintenance of family life. In support of that interpretation an exhaustive legislative history is submitted which, it is said, gives no indication that the Act was aimed at polygamous practices.

While *Mortensen* v. *United States, supra,* p. 377, rightly indicated that the Act was aimed "primarily" at the use of interstate commerce for the conduct of the white slave business, we find no indication that a profit motive is a *sine qua non* to its application. Prostitution, to be sure, normally suggests sexual relations for hire. But debauchery has no such implied limitation. In common understanding the indulgence which that term suggests may be motivated solely by lust. And so we start with words which by their natural import embrace more than commercialized sex. What follows is "any other immoral purpose." Under the *ejusdem generis* rule of construction the general words are confined to the class and may not be used to enlarge it. But we could not give the words a faithful interpretation if we confined them more narrowly than the class of which they are a part.

That was the view taken by the Court in the *Bitty* and *Caminetti* cases. We do not stop to reexamine the *Caminetti* case to determine whether the Act was properly applied to the facts there presented. But we adhere to its holding, which has been in force for almost thirty years, that the Act, while primarily aimed at the use of interstate commerce for the purposes of commercialized sex, is not restricted to that end.

We conclude, moreover, that polygamous practices are not excluded from the Act. They have long been outlawed in our society. As stated in *Reynolds* v. *United States,* 98 U. S. 145, 164:

> Polygamy has always been odious among the northern and western nations of Europe, and, until the establishment of the Mormon Church, was almost exclusively a feature of the life of Asiatic and of African people. At common law, the second marriage was always void (2 Kent, Com. 79), and from the earliest history of England polygamy has been treated as an offence against society.

As subsequently stated in *Mormon Church* v. *United States,* 136 U. S. 1, 49, "The organization of a community for the spread and practice of polygamy is, in a measure, a return to barbarism. It is contrary to the spirit of Christianity and of the civilization which Christianity has produced in the Western world." And see *Davis* v. *Beason,* 133 U. S. 333. Polygamy is a practice with far more pervasive influences in society than the casual, isolated transgressions involved in the *Caminetti* case. The establishment or maintenance of polygamous households is a notorious example of promiscuity. The permanent advertisement of their existence is an example of the sharp repercussions which they have in the community. We could conclude that Congress excluded these practices from the Act only if it were clear that the Act is confined to commercialized sexual vice. Since we cannot say it is, we see no way by which the present transgressions can be excluded. These polygamous practices have long been branded as immoral in the law. Though they have different ramifications, they are in the same genus as the other immoral practices covered by the Act.

The fact that the regulation of marriage is a state matter does not, of course, make the Mann Act an unconstitutional interference by Congress with the police powers of the States. The power of Congress over the instrumentalities of inter-state commerce is plenary; it may be used to defeat what are deemed to be im-moral practices; and the fact that the means used may have "the quality of police regulations" is not consequential. *Hoke* v. *United States,* 227 U. S. 308, 323; see *Athanasaw* v. *United States,* 227 U. S. 326; *Wilson* v. *United States,* 232 U. S. 563.

Petitioners' second line of defense is that the requisite purpose was lack-ing. It is said that those petitioners who already had plural wives did not trans-port them in interstate commerce for an immoral purpose. The test laid down in the *Mortensen* case was whether the transportation was in fact "the use of interstate commerce as a calculated means for effectuating sexual immorality." 322 U. S. p. 375. There was evidence that this group of petitioners in order to cohabit with their plural wives found it necessary or convenient to transport them in interstate commerce and that the unlawful purpose was the dominant motive. In one case the woman was transported for the purpose of entering into a plural marriage. After a night with this petitioner she refused to continue the plural marriage relationship. But guilt under the Mann Act turns on the pur-pose which motivates the transportation, not on its accomplishment. *Wilson* v. *United States, supra,* pp. 570–71.

It is also urged that the requisite criminal intent was lacking since pe-titioners were motivated by a religious belief. That defense claims too much. If upheld, it would place beyond the law any act done under claim of religious sanction. But it has long been held that the fact that polygamy is supported by a religious creed affords no defense in a prosecution for bigamy. *Reynolds* v. *United States, supra.* Whether an act is immoral within the meaning of the statute is not to be determined by the accused's concepts of morality. Congress has provided the standard. The offense is complete if the accused intended to perform, and did in fact perform, the act which the statute condemns, viz., the transportation of a woman for the purpose of making her his plural wife or cohabiting with her as such.

We have considered the remaining objections raised and find them without merit.

Affirmed.

Mr. Justice Black and Mr. Justice Jackson think that the cases should be reversed. They are of opinion that affirmance requires extension of the rule announced in the *Caminetti* case and that the correctness of that rule is so dubious that it should at least be restricted to its particular facts.

Mr. Justice Rutledge, concurring.

I concur in the result. Differences have been urged in petitioners' behalf between these cases and *Caminetti* v. *United States,* 242 U. S. 470. Notwith-standing them, in my opinion it would be impossible rationally to reverse the convictions, at the same time adhering to *Caminetti* and later decisions per-petuating its ruling.

It is also suggested, though not strongly urged, that *Caminetti* was wrongly decided and should be overruled. Much may be said for this view. In my opinion that case and subsequent ones following it extended the Mann Act's coverage beyond the congressional intent and purpose, as the dissenting opinion of Mr. Justice McKenna convincingly demonstrated. 242 U. S. at 496. Moreover, as I also think, this legislation and the problems presented by the cases arising under it are of such a character as does not allow this Court properly to shift to Congress the responsibility for perpetuating the Court's error.

Notwithstanding recent tendency, the idea cannot always be accepted that Congress, by remaining silent and taking no affirmative action in repudiation, gives approval to judicial misconstruction of its enactments. See *Girouard* v. *United States*, 328 U. S. 61, 69. It is perhaps too late now to deny that, legislatively speaking as in ordinary life, silence in some instances may give consent. But it would be going even farther beyond reason and common experience to maintain, as there are signs we may be by way of doing, that in legislation any more than in other affairs silence or nonaction always is acquiescence equivalent to action.

* * *

I doubt very much that the silence of Congress in respect to these cases, notwithstanding their multiplication and the length of time during which the silence has endured, can be taken to be the equivalent of bills approving them introduced in both houses, referred to and considered by committees, discussed in debates, enacted by majorities in both places, and approved by the executive. I doubt, in other words, that, in view of all the relevant circumstances including the unanticipated consequences of the legislation, such majorities could have been mustered in approval of the *Caminetti* decision at any time since it was rendered. Nor is the contrary conclusion demonstrated by Congress' refusal to take corrective action.

The *Caminetti* case, however, has not been overruled and has the force of law until a majority of this Court may concur in the view that this should be done and take action to that effect. This not having been done, I acquiesce in the Court's decision.

Mr. Justice Murphy, dissenting.

Today another unfortunate chapter is added to the troubled history of the White Slave Traffic Act. It is a chapter written in terms that misapply the statutory language and that disregard the intention of the legislative framers. It results in the imprisonment of individuals whose actions have none of the earmarks of white slavery, whatever else may be said of their conduct. I am accordingly forced to dissent.

The statute in so many words refers to transportation of women and girls across state lines "for the purpose of prostitution or debauchery, or for any other immoral purpose." The issue here is whether the act of taking polygamous or plural wives across state lines, or taking girls across state borders for the purpose of entering into plural marriage, constitutes transportation "for any other immoral purpose" so as to come within the interdict of the statute.

The Court holds, and I agree, that under the *ejusdem generis* rule of statutory construction the phrase "any other immoral purpose" must be confined to the same class of unlawful sexual immoralities as that to which prostitution and debauchery belong. But I disagree with the conclusion that polygamy is "in the same genus" as prostitution and debauchery and hence within the phrase "any other immoral purpose" simply because it has sexual connotations and has "long been branded as immoral in the law" of this nation. Such reasoning ignores reality and results in an unfair application of the statutory words.

It is not my purpose to defend the practice of polygamy or to claim that it is morally the equivalent of monogamy. But it is essential to understand what it is, as well as what it is not. Only in that way can we intelligently decide whether it falls within the same genus as prostitution or debauchery.

There are four fundamental forms of marriage: (1) monogamy; (2) polygyny, or one man with several wives; (3) polyandry, or one woman with several husbands; and (4) group marriage. The term "polygamy" covers both polygyny and polyandry. Thus we are dealing here with polygyny, one of the basic forms of marriage. Historically, its use has far exceeded that of any other form. It was quite common among ancient civilizations and was referred to many times by the writers of the Old Testament; even today it is to be found frequently among certain pagan and non-Christian peoples of the world. We must recognize, then, that polygyny, like other forms of marriage, is basically a cultural institution rooted deeply in the religious beliefs and social mores of those societies in which it appears. It is equally true that the beliefs and mores of the dominant culture of the contemporary world condemn the practice as immoral and substitute monogamy in its place. To those beliefs and mores I subscribe, but that does not alter the fact that polygyny is a form of marriage built upon a set of social and moral principles. It must be recognized and treated as such.

The Court states that polygamy is "a notorious example of promiscuity." The important fact, however, is that, despite the differences that may exist between polygamy and monogamy, such differences do not place polygamy in the same category as prostitution or debauchery. When we use those terms we are speaking of acts of an entirely different nature, having no relation whatever to the various forms of marriage. It takes no elaboration here to point out that marriage, even when it occurs in a form of which we disapprove, is not to be compared with prostitution or debauchery or other immoralities of that character.

The Court's failure to recognize this vital distinction and its insistence that polygyny is "in the same genus" as prostitution and debauchery do violence to the anthropological factors involved. Even etymologically, the words "polygyny" and "polygamy" are quite distinct from "prostitution," "debauchery" and words of that ilk. . . . The result here reached is but another consequence of this Court's long-continued failure to recognize that the White Slave Traffic Act, as its title indicates, is aimed solely at the diabolical interstate and international trade in white slaves, "the business of securing white women and girls and of selling them outright, or of exploiting them for immoral purposes." . . . The Act was suggested and proposed to meet conditions which had arisen in the years preceding 1910 and which had revealed themselves in their ugly details through extensive investigations. The framers of the Act specifically stated that it is not directed at immorality in general; it does not even attempt to regulate the practice of voluntary prostitution, leaving that problem to the various states. Its exclusive concern is with those girls and women who are "unwillingly forced to practice prostitution" and to engage in other similar immoralities and "whose lives are lives of involuntary servitude." *Ibid.* A reading of the legislative reports and debates makes this narrow purpose so clear as to remove all doubts on the matter. And it is a purpose that has absolutely no relation to the practice of polygamy, however much that practice may have been considered immoral in 1910.

Yet this Court in *Caminetti* v. *United States*, 242 U.S. 470, over the vigorous dissent of Justice McKenna in which Chief Justice White and Justice Clarke joined, closed its eyes to the obvious and interpreted the broad words of the statute without regard to the express wishes of Congress. I think the *Caminetti* case can be factually distinguished from the situation at hand since it did not deal with polygamy. But the principle of the *Caminetti* case is still with us today, the principle of interpreting and applying the White Slave Traffic Act in disregard of the specific problem with which Congress was concerned. I believe the issue should be met squarely and the *Caminetti* case overruled. It has been on the books for nearly 30 years and its age does not justify its continued existence. *Stare decisis* certainly does not require a court to perpetuate a wrong for which it was responsible, especially when no rights have accrued in reliance on the error. . . .

Gonzales v. Hechanova
(Philippines, 1963)

❊   ❊   ❊

JUSTICE CONCEPCION delivered the decision of the Court.

This is an original action for prohibition with preliminary injunction.

It is not disputed that on September 22, 1963, respondent Executive Secretary [Hechanova] authorized the importation of 67,000 tons of foreign rice to be purchased from private sources, and created a rice procurement committee composed of the other respondents herein for the implementation of said proposed importation. Thereupon, or on September 25, 1963, herein petitioner, Ramon A. Gonzales—a rice planter, and president of the Hoilo Palay and Corn Planters Association, whose members are, likewise, engaged in the production of rice and corn—filed the petition herein, averring that, in making or attempting to make said importation of foreign rice, the aforementioned respondents "are acting without jurisdiction or in excess of jurisdiction," because Republic Act No. 3452—which allegedly repeals or amends Republic Act No. 2207—explicitly prohibits the importation of rice and corn by "the Rice and Corn Administration or *any other government agency*"; that petitioner has no other plain, speedy and adequate remedy in the ordinary course of law; and that a preliminary injunction is necessary for the preservation of the rights of the parties during the pendency of this case and to prevent the judgment therein from becoming ineffectual. Petitioner prayed, therefore, that said petition be given due course; that a writ of preliminary injunction be forthwith issued restraining respondents, their agents or representatives from implementing the decision of the Executive Secretary to import the aforementioned foreign rice; and that, after due hearing, judgment be rendered making said injunction permanent.

❊   ❊   ❊

Respondents question the sufficiency of petitioner's cause of action upon the theory that the proposed importation in question is not governed by Republic Act Nos. 2207 and 3452, but was authorized by the President as commander-in-chief "for military stock pile purposes" in the exercise of his alleged authority under Section 2 of Commonwealth Act No. 1; that in cases of necessity, the President "or his subordinates may take such preventive measure for the restoration of good order and maintenance of peace"; and that, as Commander-in-

---

Decision Law Journal 842 (1963). Footnotes have been omitted.

Chief of our armed forces, "the President . . . is duty-bound to prepare for the challenge of threats of war or emergency *without waiting for any special authority.*"

Regardless of whether Republic Act No. 3452 repeals Republic Act No. 2207, as contended by petitioner herein—on which our view need not be expressed—we are unanimously of the opinion—assuming that said Republic Act No. 2207 is still in force—that the two Acts are applicable to the proposed importation in question because the language of said laws is such as to include within the purview thereof *all* importations of rice and corn into the Philippines. Pursuant to Republic Act No. 2207, "it shall be unlawful for *any* person, association, corporation or *government agency* to import rice and corn into any point in the Philippines," although, by way of exception, it adds that "*the President of the Philippines* may authorize the importation of these commodities through any government agency that he may designate," if the conditions prescribed in Section 2 of said Act are present. Similarly, Republic Act No. 3452 explicitly enjoins "the Rice and Corn Administration or *any government agency*" from importing rice and corn.

Respondents allege, however, that said provisions of Republic Acts Nos. 2207 and 3452, prohibiting the importation of rice and corn by any "government agency," do not apply to importations "made by the Government itself," because the latter is not a "government agency." This theory is devoid of merit. The Department of National Defense and the Armed Forces of the Philippines, as well as respondents herein, and each and every officer and employee of our Government, are government agencies and/or agents. The applicability of said laws even to importations by the Government, as such, becomes more apparent when we consider that:

1. The importation permitted in Republic Act No. 2207 is to be authorized by "*the President of the Philippines,*" and, hence, by or on behalf of the Government of the Philippines;

2. Immediately after enjoining the Rice and Corn Administration and any other government agency from importing rice and corn, Section 10 of Republic Act No. 3452 adds "that *the importation of rice and corn is left to private parties* upon payment of the corresponding taxes," thus indicating that *only* "private parties" may import rice under its provisions. . . .

* * *

The attempt to justify the proposed importation by invoking reasons of national security—predicated upon the "worsening situation in Laos and Vietnam," and "the recent tension created by the Malaysia problem"—and the alleged powers of the President as commander-in-chief of all armed forces in the Philippines, under Section 2 of the National Defense Act (Commonwealth Act No. 1), overlooks the fact that the protection of local planters of rice and corn in a manner that would foster and accelerate self-sufficiency in the local production of said commodities constitutes a factor that is vital to our ability to meet a possible national emergency. Even if the intent in importing goods in anticipation of such emergency were to bolster up that ability, the latter would, instead, be impaired if the importation were so made as to discourage our farmers from engaging in the production of rice.

Besides, the stockpiling of rice and corn for purposes of national security and/or national emergency is within the purview of Republic Act No. 3452.

Section 3 thereof expressly authorizes the Rice and Corn Administration "to *accumulate* stocks as a *national reserve* in such quantities as it may deem proper and necessary to meet *any contingencies.*" Moreover, it ordains that *"the buffer stocks held as a national reserve . . . be deposited by the Administration throughout the country under proper dispersal plans . . .* and may be released only upon the occurrence of calamities *or emergencies. . . ."* (Underscoring supplied.)

Again, the provisions of Section 2 of Commonwealth Act No. 1, upon which respondents rely so much, are not self-executory. They merely outline the general objectives of said legislation. The means for the attainment of those objectives are subject to congressional legislation. Thus, the conditions under which the services of citizens, as indicated in said Section 2, may be availed of, are provided for in Sections 3, 4 and 51 to 88 of said Commonwealth Act No. 1. Similarly, Section 5 thereof specifies the manner in which resources necessary for our national defense may be secured by the Government of the Philippines, but only *"during a national mobilization,"* which does not exist. Inferentially, therefore, in the absence of a national mobilization, said resources shall be produced in such manner as Congress may by *other* laws provide from time to time. Insofar as rice and corn are concerned, Republic Acts Nos. 2207 and 3452, and Commonwealth Act No. 138 are such laws.

Respondents cite Corwin in support of their pretense, but in vain. An examination of the work cited shows that Corwin referred to the powers of the President during "war time" or when he has placed the country or a part thereof under "martial law." Since neither condition obtains in the case at bar, said work merely proves that respondents' theory, if accepted, would, in effect, place the Philippines under martial law, *without* a declaration of the Executive to that effect. What is worse, it would keep us *perpetually* under martial law.

It has been suggested that even if the proposed importation violated Republic Acts Nos. 2207 and 3452, it should, nevertheless, be permitted because "it redounds to the benefit of the people." *Salus populi est suprema lex*, it is said.

If there were a local shortage of rice, the argument *might have* some value. But the respondents, as officials of this Government, have expressly affirmed again and again that there is no rice shortage. And the importation is avowedly for stockpile *of the Army—not* the civilian population.

But let us follow the respondents' trend of thought. It has a more serious implication than appears on the surface. It implies that if an executive officer believes that compliance with a certain statute will not benefit the people, he is at liberty to disregard it. That idea must be rejected—we still live under a rule of law.

* * *

It is lastly contended that the Government of the Philippines has already entered into two (2) contracts for the purchase of rice, one with the Republic of Viet Nam, and another with the Government of Burma; that these contracts constitute valid executive agreements under international law; that such agreements became binding and effective upon the signing thereof by representatives of the parties thereto; that in case of conflict between Republic Acts Nos. 2207 and 3452 on the one hand, and the aforementioned contracts, on the other, the latter should prevail, because, if a treaty and a statute are inconsistent with each other, the conflict must be resolved—under the American jurisprudence—in favor of the one which is latest in point of time; that petitioner herein assails the validity of acts of the Executive relative to foreign relations in the conduct of which the Supreme Court cannot interfere; and the aforementioned contracts have already been consummated, the Government of the Philippines having already paid the price of the rice involved therein through irrevocable letters of credit in favor of the sellers of said commodity. We find no merit in this pretense.

The Court is not satisfied that the status of said contracts as alleged executive agreements has been sufficiently established. The parties to said contracts do not appear to have regarded the same as executive agreements.

* * *

The alleged consummation of the aforementioned contracts with Vietnam and Burma does not render this case academic. Republic Act No. 2207 enjoins our Government *not* from *entering into contracts* for the purchase of rice, but from *importing* rice, except under the conditions prescribed in said Act. Upon the other hand, Republic Act No. 3452 has two (2) main features, namely: (a) it requires the Government to purchase rice and corn *directly* from our local planters, growers or landowners; and (b) it prohibits *importations* of rice by the Government, and leaves such importations to private parties. The pivotal issue in this case is whether the proposed *importation*—which has *not* been consummated as yet—is legally feasible.

Lastly, a judicial declaration of illegality of the proposed importation would not compel our Government to default in the performance of such obligation as it may have contracted with the sellers of the rice in question, because, aside from the fact that said obligations may be complied with *without importing* the commodity into the Philippines, the proposed importation may still be legalized by complying with the provisions of the aforementioned laws.

The members of the Court have divergent opinions on the question whether or not respondents herein should be enjoined from implementing the aforementioned proposed importation. However, the majority favors the negative view, for which reason the injunction prayed for cannot be granted.

WHEREFORE, judgment is hereby rendered declaring that respondent Executive Secretary had and has no power to authorize the importation in question; that he exceeded his jurisdiction in granting said authority; that said importation is not sanctioned by law and is contrary to its provisions; and that, for lack of the requisite majority, the injunction prayed for must be and is, accordingly, denied.

IT IS SO ORDERED.

(Chief Justice Bengzon and Justices Padilla, Labrador, J. B. L. Reyes, Dizon and Makalintal concurred; Justices Bautista and Barrera each concurred separately. Justices Paredes and Regala concurred in the result.)

CHAPTER 5

VARIATIONS IN COURT STRUCTURE: JUDICIAL REVIEW

> What we call necessary institutions
> are often no more than institutions
> to which we have become accus-
> tomed.
>
> —ALEXIS DE TOCQUEVILLE
> *Democracy in America*

BY NO MEANS unwittingly, I omitted from the previous chapter all discussion of the indicators and measurement of the highest possible degree of judicial independence. The formal prerequisites, existence, and function of this phenomenon are so widely heralded and frequently discussed that they deserve separate treatment. I am referring, of course, to the formal legal power, actual usage, and measurable consequences of *judicial review*.

Definitions of judicial review float about like so much flotsam. As is par for any course in academe, each definition is fitted to the eccentric purposes of the individual definer. So it is here. There is no need to rekindle controversy over what judicial review *really* means. I do not know and it is more than likely that no one else does either. Here there is need only to make it consistent with the other concepts constituting the framework of this book. Indeed, because of my prior conceptualizations and reconceptualizations, my definition of judicial review is nearly predetermined. Still, it is well within the mainstream of the opinion of my fellows. I opt to define it as does Henry Abraham: "the power of any court to hold unconstitutional and hence unenforceable any law, any official action based upon a law, and any other action by a public official that it deems . . . to be in conflict with the Basic Law."[1] Perhaps the major peculiarity of my

---

[1] Henry J. Abraham, *The Judicial Process: An Introductory Analysis of the Courts of the United States, England, and France,* 2nd ed. (New York: Oxford, 1968), p. 283. McWhinney also defines judicial review in this way. However, he considers this to be "direct" judicial review. We shall not be concerned with his concept of "indirect" judicial review here. (See Edward McWhinney, *Judicial Review,* 4th ed. [Toronto:

definition was suggested as early as the Introduction to Part A; that is, that judicial review is a structural variation. To call it a "function" is only to perpetuate confusion.

In this chapter I intend first to spend some time describing the *types* of judicial review to be found around the globe through time, and the *degrees* of it as (or as a degree of) judicial independence. After that we shall examine the theoretical functions of judicial review and expose them to some searching questions.

The Wide, Wide World of Judicial Review

Like any other nation, America has had its fair share of misinformed scholars. So it is not too astonishing to find a famous American historian saying most authoritatively:

> Just as a written Constitution amendable only by the people was wholly an American idea, so the proposal of a court with authority to determine when Congress had overstepped the bounds set by the Constitution and to curb attempts by Congress to amend or alter the Constitution was purely American.[2]

Wouldn't it be just as true to say the same thing about pizza pie and chicken chow mein? In each instance, the basic idea was spawned elsewhere well before America became a gleam in Vespucci's eye. And in each instance a new and improved product, distinctively American, has evolved. That is the truth of the matter, and so it is with judicial review.

Plato probably first discussed a form of judicial review when he prescribed the establishment of a "nocturnal council of magistrates" to be the "guardians of our god-given constitution."[3] One must admit that this has a familiar ring to it. Max Radin also notes Cicero's contention that certain legislation was void as having gone beyond the competence of the Roman Senate.[4] Thus the idea that a representative body's laws might be void

---

University of Toronto Press, 1969], p. 13.) Nor shall I be concerned with some of the more peculiar usages of this concept. As an example of one of these, see the pre-scientific Glendon A. Schubert, Jr., in his article "Judicial Review of Royal Proclamations and Orders-in-Council," *University of Toronto Law Journal*, 9 (1951), pp. 69–106. The more technical Schubert is closer to my definition. See his *Constitutional Politics* (New York: Holt, Rinehart & Winston, 1960), p. 188.

2 Charles Warren, *Congress, the Constitution and the Court* (Boston: Little, Brown, 1928), p. vi. Reprinted by permission from the President and Fellows of Harvard College, Cambridge, Mass., 1969.

3 *The Laws of Plato*, trans. A. E. Taylor (London: J. M. Dent, 1934), p. 357. The council of magistrates was considered, strangely enough, "the State's custodian and preserver" (p. 364).

4 Max Radin, "The Judicial Review of Statutes in Continental Europe," *West Virginia Law Quarterly*, 41 (December, 1934), p. 114.

from the beginning has walked a long mile. The theory of judicial review started a long time ago. As to practice, there were shades of what might be called judicial review way back in ancient Greece, too. In Athens it was an indictable offense to cause a bill to be passed that ran "counter to the basic principles of the state."[5] The body that passed on this was called the Helliaea. But enough of this; it is but a trifle to haggle about who was first—or to brag of it. All agree that the American version became *the* model after which many cultures have fashioned a structure akin to judicial review. In fact, statistically speaking, this variant in court systems has sprouted in about 40 percent of the existing independent states and abounds in every geopolitical area except mainland China and the Soviet Union.[6]

There are many ways one can classify types of judicial review. I shall attempt a trichotomy. First, the power of judicial review is exercised by one of two different judicial reviewing organs. Second, there are a few crucial differences in accessibility to the body reviewing the constitutionality of acts in question. Third, there are important distinctions regarding the type of proceedings and jurisdiction of the reviewing body. I shall survey them briefly for illustrative, rather than taxonomic, purposes, though they may have some research value as well.

THE NATURE OF REVIEWING ORGANS

There are two major variations in the type of judicial organ possessing the power of statutory or rule review. Probably the most familiar is the regular general-jurisdiction court within the formal judicial structure. Regular courts possessing judicial review are found in the United States, Australia, Brazil, Burma, Canada, India, Pakistan, Colombia, and Japan. Continental Europe has given us the other type of reviewing court. Italy, West Germany, and Austria have designated special constitutional courts to exercise judicial review. In other words, these courts are "usually found *outside* or astride the ordinary court structure."[7] They supplement the regular system, and the regular system is not troubled by the problem of tangling with legislatures and a variety of executives over whether they have usurped power.

Incidentally, the Fourth French Republic established a Constitutional Committee to determine whether laws "implied amendment of the constitution." The Fifth French Republic also withheld the power of review from any type of court by establishing a Constitutional Council

---

[5] *Ibid.*, p. 112.

[6] David Deener, "Judicial Review in Modern Constitutional Systems," *American Political Science Review*, 46 (December, 1952), p. 1098.

[7] Abraham, *op. cit.*, p. 299.

composed of thirteen political officials, including the president of the republic and the president of the National Assembly. Thus, although a review procedure (of a sort) exists in modern-day France, it is not *judicial* review. This might better be called statutory review, or perhaps constitutional review.

ACCESSIBILITY TO THE STRUCTURE

Many systems limit accessibility to persons injured by the alleged unconstitutional act. This is true in the United States and Mexico. In the United States the "case or controversy" rule means that only those with a direct, personal interest in the case—e.g., those who are injured physically or fiscally by an alleged unconstitutional act—can institute suit. Even then a litigant can obtain a ruling on the constitutionality of an act only incidentally, i.e., when a party maintains that the application of a statute in a concrete case is an illegal violation of its interests because the statute is unconstitutional. In Mexico, however, the use of the writ of *amparo* is the established procedure for deciding when a law, either state or federal, violates any one of the rights or privileges secured by the Constitution. The use of this writ is open to anyone whose private rights are violated.[8]

On the other hand, many countries don't allow those injured by an alleged unconstitutional act to bring a case to the reviewing body. In these countries accessibility to the reviewing organ is the exclusive prerogative of certain designated officials. This is true of the Constitutional Courts of Italy, West Germany, and Austria. For instance, in Austria a case can come to the Constitutional Court only at the request of certain official bodies: on application of the federal ministry, on application of a state government, or if the judges on either the Supreme Judicial Court or Supreme Administrative Court request it. Private parties can only "call the attention of the courts to the question of the constitutionality of statutes and ordinances. They [have] no right to put such procedure in motion." The reason for this restricted accessibility is simple: "It [is] exclusively the public interest protected by the courts and not the private interest of the parties which [is] decisive from the point of view of the procedure."[9]

Other countries have seen fit to adopt still another variation in the judicial review structure. Here all restrictions to the reviewing body are

---

8 Benito Flores, "The Writ of Amparo under Mexican Law," *American Bar Association Journal,* 7 (August, 1921), pp. 388–92. James L. Busey has stated that this guarantee is resorted to frequently by Mexicans, and that the dockets are clogged because of its exercise. See James L. Busey, *Latin America: Political Institutions and Processes* (New York: Random House, 1964), pp. 38–39.

9 Hans Kelsen, "Judicial Review of Legislation: A Comparative Study of the Austrian and the American Constitution," *Journal of Politics,* 4 (May, 1942), pp. 195–96.

removed so that anyone can bring a case to the reviewing organ. In Latin America, *recurso de inconstitucionalidad* is the general term used to describe the power of judicial review. One author calls the Colombian system of accessibility (in 1910) "the most dramatic manifestation of the *recurso*."[10] *Anyone* could introduce a petition of unconstitutionality directly to the Supreme Court, without even having to prove a case or controversy existed, or that he had any real or personal interest in the constitutionality of the law in question.[11] The reason for this open accessibility to the court of last resort was simple: it was believed that everyone, not just an injured party, had an interest in ensuring that the constitution not be violated.[12]

SCOPE OF THE REVIEW

Another variation in type of judicial review is the latitude of power that the court may have. Americans are familiar with a very broad range of situations into which the Supreme Court can intrude. Cultures entertain widely divergent ideas about which official acts courts should or should not be allowed to invalidate. Compare the Norwegian and American versions of judicial review. The Norwegian is the lesser insofar as, at least theoretically, Norway's Supreme Court can knock a statute down as unconstitutional only when the legislature has failed to follow certain procedural guidelines laid down by the constitution. Indeed, as one justice of the Supreme Court of Norway said at the turn of the century: "It is presumably considered as one of the best features of the Norwegian Supreme Court that only reluctantly has it been willing to take stands on the basis of principles."[13] Torgersen seems to think that this hesitance to overrule the legis-

---

[10] William S. Stokes, *Latin American Politics* (New York: Crowell, 1959), p. 475.
[11] *Ibid.*

A novel contribution to constitutional machinery was made by Colombia in allowing any citizen to challenge the constitutionality of any law by means of the so-called "public action" *(acción pública)* or "popular action" *(acción popular)*. For the first time in the New World the Citizen became Champion of the Constitution. This remarkable device is directly parallel to the Athenian *graphe paranomon*, which could be brought by any citizen to question the constitutionality of a law. Under the Athenian conception of democracy every citizen had a direct interest in the commonwealth; as the State was a partnership of citizens under a constitution, any member of the partnership could take action to conserve the charter . . . the Supreme Courts of the United States and of Canada have consistently and definitely refused to allow a citizen as such to challenge the constitutionality of a law" [George Jaffin, "New World Constitutional Harmony: A Pan-Americanadian Panorama," *Columbia Law Review*, 42 (April, 1942), p. 566].

[12] J. A. C. Grant, "Judicial Control of Legislation: A Comparative Study," *American Journal of Comparative Law*, 3 (Spring, 1954), p. 195.
[13] Ulf Torgersen, "The Role of the Supreme Court in the Norwegian Political System," in *Judicial Decision-Making*, ed. Glendon Schubert (New York: Free Press, 1963), p. 222.

lature lies more in the philosophy of the justices than in the words of the constitution, but it is the actuality rather than the legality that counts.[14]

Hitchner and Levine note another variation in the scope of judicial review in their discussion of the Israeli Supreme Court.[15] According to them, the high court has competence to overturn all local laws and even actions on the part of ministers of the cabinet. It may not, however, lay a hand in anger on any acts emanating from the Knesset, the national legislature. Thus judicial review would seem to have a narrower latitude in Israel than in the United States, though it would appear to have broader latitude there than in Norway. The Swiss system offers us an illustration of a further difference in scope. In Switzerland the highest tribunal can set aside any act of any official at the cantonal, or provincial, level, but it has absolutely no judicial review power over acts at the national level—of cabinet ministers or otherwise.

Sometimes constitutions speak with directness and explicitness as to what kinds of acts the courts may and may not review. For instance, the Thai constitution of 1949 puts social and economic objectives in a separate section and declares them to be unenforceable by the courts.[16] Meanwhile, other countries bestow directly political jurisdiction on the scope of judicial review. Perhaps the best example of this is the power of the Constitutional Court of West Germany to decide whether a political party is unconstitutional if it endangers the democratic-political order. I am appending a translation of the *Party Finance Case* (1966), which exemplifies this power of that court.[17] It is an example *par excellence* of the scope and style of the exercise of this power. It shows the tremendous power exercisable by that court and raises some intriguing questions on what value, if any, this typology of the power of judicial review has for us. Keep in mind, too, that any variation within a structural variation also concerns us only in terms of its potential political function.

TYPICAL FUNCTIONING

The reader may wonder what earthly purpose some of these variations in judicial review types could have. I do not intend to exhaust all the possibilities, but a few of them may help, once again, to illustrate what I have

---

[14] *Ibid.*, pp. 222–23.

[15] Dell G. Hitchner and Carol Levine, *Comparative Government and Politics* (New York: Dodd, Mead, 1967), p. 174.

[16] Deener, *op. cit.*, p. 1097.

[17] I am deeply indebted to Donald Kommers for his cooperation on this project. It was given freely, efficiently, and in the spirit of collegial rapport essential to the advancement of our science.

in mind. For example, the reader might ask (quite understandably) what political function could be served through the differing natures of the reviewing organs. What political consequences might ensue from removing judicial review from the regular system and entrusting it to a special high court, such as the Constitutional Court of West Germany (*Bundesverfassungsgericht*)? One possibility comes to mind. When heavy emphasis is placed on the fact that such a power as judicial review exists, as will be discussed shortly, the visibility of the reviewing court could increase and the light in which it is seen could change. Both visibility and affect are theoretically important factors in the degree of employment and effectiveness of judicial review. This could be either an expressed or a latent reason for putting it into effect where the prior history and culture of the country by and large were devoid of such an institution. A super-court reflects itself. On the other hand, some experts believe that in West Germany the establishment of a separate court for judicial review simply reflects a cultural trait: the Germans frequently create special courts and otherwise compartmentalize when they wish to emphasize expertise. Other observers consider that the establishment of the special Constitutional Court is a necessary adjustment of a Roman law system to a predominantly common-law type of practice (i.e., judicial review).[18] Nonetheless, the "spotlight" function may still attend this structural variation regardless of the reasons behind its establishment, and actual functioning may vary from the projected functional effects that brought about the adaptation of a structure.

The reader may wonder as well what political function or functions could inhere in a variation in the range of accessibility to judicial review proceedings. It seems to me that the performance of the function of this variation depends entirely on the legal impact that the judicial review can have. For example, in Mexico, as noted, the writ of *amparo* extends to all aggrieved people. On its face, this would appear to be a strong popular check on the executive and legislative branches, but it is not. The reason for this is that a court decision holding that an act is unconstitutional is not generalizable; it covers only the case in front of the court. Thus, while a case may reach the highest court and be decided in favor of the individual bringing suit, the highest court does not come into direct confrontation with its peers: the President and the Congress. The *law* or *decree* is not unconstitutional, only its enforcement on the claimant is—and there is no

---

[18] Mauro Cappelletti and John Clarke Adams, "Judicial Review of Legislation: European Antecedents and Adaptations," *Harvard Law Review,* 79 (March, 1966), pp. 1207–24. See also Mauro Cappelletti, John Henry Merryman, and Joseph Perillo, *The Italian Legal System* (Stanford: Stanford University Press, 1967), especially p. 76.

doctrine of precedent, either.[19] The court is simply directing its power against the lower bureaucracy. Thus there is no "check," as we might think of it in terms of "checks and balances," though there is strong force available against unlimited power in the lower echelons of government. This kind of judicial review reflects a comparatively low level of independence and therefore its functions are not very imposing, though they are none the less real. Though it does not curb the executive, it does curb administrators, and thus is an operating organ that protects individuals in the society against a limitless degree of governmental arbitrariness. This kind of judicial review may then function toward increasing feelings of loyalty toward the party, the regime, and the like. After all, the courts *are* part of the regime.

Unfortunately for us, no systematic categorization of the many variations in judicial review has been undertaken with a view to empirically testing any hypotheses, functional or otherwise. Similarly, no one has tried to assess weights (greater and lesser power) to these legal variables, even as possible indicators of more or less judicial independence. Yet they seem susceptible enough to a degree-of-power-potential indexing (as in the writ of *amparo*). In short, some formal judicial review provisions bestow more power (in terms of potential visibility, access, and functional impact) than others. This brings us to the important relationship between judicial independence and judicial review.

The Relationship between Judicial Independence and Judicial Review

I stated at the outset of this chapter that the presence of judicial review in a society is best understood as some supplementary degree of judicial independence in that society. In short, judicial review is analogous to the highest summit of a range of mountains. The average altitude of the range might be thought of as the measure of judicial independence. I think this is a far more realistic appraisal of the relationship than some that have been offered. According to one American legal scholar, "The judiciary, minus the power of review, is, simply enough, a shriveled appendage, rather than a third arm, of the government."[20] He goes on to say that judicial review is "the alternative to an insipidly weak judiciary."[21] This view completely fails

---

[19] In Mexico, however, once five separate cases converge on a single point of law, the point generalizes and becomes part of "the jurisprudence," which thereafter has precedential influence on the judiciary.

[20] Alan Kent Shearer, "The Political Utility of Judicial Review," *University of Kansas Law Review,* 2 (May, 1954), p. 380.

[21] *Ibid.*

to consider important aspects of less glamorous but still highly significant demonstrations of judicial muscle vis-à-vis the executive and the legislature, as noted in the previous chapter. Moreover, it utterly bypasses the daily, low-level, eyeball-to-eyeball confrontation of government and the governed at the local level through judicial administration of the law.

In other words, the corpus of judicial independence—an essential ingredient in the study of comparative judicial politics—is downgraded, if not ignored. Scholars dizzy themselves at the apex and impair their vision of the base. This is not to say that the panorama at the top is unimportant or dull. Still its proper value materializes only if appropriate surveying is done on the climb.

This relation between judicial independence and judicial review is not well understood. If it were, there would be less confusion in the literature, particularly in the comparative or foreign descriptive materials on this topic written by Americans. In a traditionalist vein, they are awed by the power and glory of judicial review. Also, there is some penchant to see the legal and judicial system from a purely American perspective. Thus, they tend to get discouraged when judicial review is present legally but is largely a farce in reality. Overgeneralizing, they throw up their hands in disgust. This is peculiarly apparent in some work done by comparative researchers on Latin America. It seems that Latin Americanists spend relatively more time on the judiciary than do Middle East or Asian experts. This is probably due to the fact that Latin American governments emphasize the tripartite separation of powers (constitutionally, at least), and almost without exception, Latin American countries provide the judiciary with some formal type of judicial review. Indeed, in 1965 Alexander Edelmann could write that "every one of the [Latin American] nations today has some form of review by the courts."[22]

An example of the overgeneralizing that manifests a misunderstanding of the relationship between judicial independence and judicial review is an essay by J. Lloyd Mechem in which he discusses the fablistic qualities of constitutionalism in the countries of Latin America. At one point Professor Mechem notes:

> Freedom and equality of the courts is also a fiction, for the judiciary, like the legislature, is subordinate to the executive. . . . Rare, indeed, are the judges who will tempt fate by invalidating acts of congress or presidential decree laws.[23]

---

[22] Alexander T. Edelmann, *Latin American Government and Politics* (Homewood, Ill.: Dorsey Press, 1965), p. 466. For a legalistic detailing of this up to 1952, see Helen L. Clagett, *Administration of Justice in Latin America* (New York: Oceana Publications, 1952).

[23] J. Lloyd Mechem, "Latin American Constitutions: Nominal and Real," *Journal of Politics*, 21 (May, 1959), reprinted in *The Dynamics of Change in Latin American Politics*, ed. John D. Martz (Englewood Cliffs, N.J.: Prentice-Hall, 1965), p. 42.

However, not much later Professor Mechem observes that in "routine matters" and situations where there are no strong executive interests, the courts "are usually free of political interference."[24] My point is simply that *the presence or absence of judicial review, whether legally or in practice, is only one* (and perhaps not the most convincing) *indicator of the degree of judicial independence extant in a culture.* Professor Mechem sees the courts of Latin America as having no freedom (freedom of the courts is a "fiction") because of rare exercise of judicial review. Yet in the next breath he confesses there is much freedom from political interference at the grass-roots level. This judicial flexibility is nothing to dismiss so cavalierly. The degree of this freedom is the foundation that may well support the carrying out of important functions. Norway and Denmark are two countries where *reputedly* very independent judiciaries rarely invoke their legal power of judicial review, yet no one says that the freedom of their courts is a "fiction."[25]

Another Latin American specialist, Martin Needler, denigrates the degree of actual independence in Latin America because of the existence of several vague legal indicators: first, the different legal limitations on the exercise of judicial review (e.g., it is applicable only to the official action and not to the law itself); second, the rigidity inherent in civil law jurisprudence (codes); and third, the gigantic amount of strength given to the executive constitutionally throughout Latin America (which gives courts scant leeway to oppose the executive). Needler concludes his terse discourse on the judiciary with this cynical statement: "The fact that the milder dictators permit the courts to continue functioning normally (Getulio Vargas, for example) should not be regarded as evidence of the strength of the courts, as it has been by some commentators, but as an indication of their ultimate political weakness."[26]

In my view, however, downgrading judicial independence because of such high-level legal indicators is as much in error as downgrading it because of the rare exercise of direct, high-level judicial review. It misconceives the relationship, which in fact is a more complex phenomenon than my mountain metaphor would suggest. Judicial review is not simply the most visible and dramatic example of judicial independence; it is related to (a function of) the force of judicial independence. If the judicial independence is a paper independence, then the judicial review, if provided for at all, can be only a sham review (and I would guess that it would be de-

---

[24] *Ibid.*

[25] Cappelletti and Adams, *op. cit.*, p. 1217.

[26] Martin Needler, *Latin American Politics in Perspective* (Princeton: Van Nostrand, 1963), p. 155; see pp. 152–55. There is some evidence, though, that the Supreme Court gave Vargas more than a little trouble in his day. See John W. F. Dulles, *Vargas of Brazil* (Austin: University of Texas Press, 1967), pp. 79, 262–63, 266.

signed only to perform some latent function). Thus, the former is an indispensable, though not a significant, precondition for any existence of the latter. This is very much the position of M. J. C. Vile in his penetrating study of the doctrine of the separation of powers. According to Professor Vile:

> Clearly some form of separation of powers is a necessary prerequisite of judicial review. The long evolution of judicial independence in England, the development of Montesquieu's theory through the medium of Blackstone's interpretation, and the importance attached to judicial independence in the colonial period in America, are all essential steps in the development of the power of the American courts. However, the separation of powers, in itself, is not a sufficient basis for the establishment of a doctrine of judicial review: indeed, taken to its logical extreme, as in France after 1789, or by the Jeffersonian Republicans in the United States, the separation of powers is incompatible with the idea that one branch can interfere with the functions of another to the extent of invalidating its acts. Like the veto power, the establishment of judicial review depended upon the acceptance of the idea of checks and balances as essential barriers to the improper exercise of power.[27]

Just because a society promulgates a constitution that expressly gives its court system a power of judicial review (Japan, Brazil) does not mean that the judiciary in that country is more independent than that of a country that makes no provision for judicial review (England, France). I feel that the judiciary's independence is relative to the degree to which the power of judicial review is exercised—and that the power of judicial review is relative to the actual degree of independence (potential and actual) extant in that society. If judicial review is exercised frequently, and if it is of a wide latitude and is available at the national level as well as at the local (state, province, canton), then it is highly probable that such a judiciary possesses a higher level of independence than a system wherein courts can only flaunt executive and legislative desires in the construction of statutes but cannot overrule those statutes by declaring them invalid. This is why everyone agrees that the American courts are more independent than the English. Thus, all other things being equal, a *substantial exercise* of judicial review means that the highest level of judicial independence exists and that we can expect that judges in such a system are not easily cowed by cross glowers from police officials, bureaucrats, legislators, premiers, presidents, or potentates.

The existence of the legal power of judicial review is thus a rough indicator (at best) of a high level of judicial independence, but by no means a measure of it. The degree of actual exercise of judicial review is a far

---

[27] M. J. C. Vile, *Constitutionalism and the Separation of Powers* (New York: Oxford University Press, 1967), pp. 157–58.

better measurement. And there may be a high level of judicial independence despite a lack of exercise of judicial review (where legally available) or despite the absence of the power of judicial review. However, it is senseless now to speak of high or low degrees for any one society or for any society in one area of the world. It is even more senseless—and downright parochial—to speak of anything as "low" because it is less than the American practice. Indeed, all sorts of problems of coding and measurement must be faced before we can get a meaningful comparison.

I have included three American cases in the Appendix to this chapter to show how the American Supreme Court fears not to tread anywhere political angels play. In *Baker* v. *Carr* (1962) the Court takes on the state legislatures, if not the entire structure of state politics and state power interests. In *Youngstown Sheet and Tube Company* v. *Sawyer* (1952) the Court does violence to a President's definition of his own power during a time of national emergency. In *Watkins* v. *United States* (1957) the Congress of the United States is victimized by the Court's interpretation of the allowable limits of congressional action.

Obviously, these few selected cases are simply three stakes at the outer reaches of the Court's independence. They manifest an awesome display of judicial brawn. What is interesting is to compare them with the foreign cases I have included as well. Can the reader notice any difference, for instance, between the degree of strength that the Indian Supreme Court manifests in its combat with a state legislature in *Keshav Singh* v. *Uttar Pradesh* (1964) and that detectable in *Baker*? As an initial exercise in the flexing of judicial biceps, is *Nakamura et al.* v. *Japan* (1963) more or less promising than *Marbury* v. *Madison* was in 1803? Considering the institutionalization of the German parties in the federal constitution of West Germany, does the *Party Finance Case* (1966) show more or less courage, independence, or power than *Watkins* or *Youngstown Sheet and Tube*? Keep in mind, though, that many saw the U.S. Supreme Court's decision in *Barenblatt* v. *United States* (1959) as a retreat in the face of stormy congressional reaction to the *Watkins* case.[28]

A cross-cultural index and measurement must be developed in relationship to many factors, including history, stage of economic development, and the like, before quantitative adjectives reflect anything more than the bias of American researchers. What must be measured is the relationship between comparable actions of judicial independence and judicial review

---

[28] "It may be suggested that the Court itself contributed to the defeat of the anti-Court legislation by subsequent moderation. . . . The primary example concerns *Watkins* and *Barenblatt*" (C. Herman Pritchett, *Congress versus the Supreme Court* [Minneapolis: University of Minnesota Press, 1961], p. 121). *Barenblatt* can be found at 360 U.S. 109. See also Stuart Nagel, "Court-Curbing Periods in American History," *Vanderbilt Law Review*, 18 (June, 1965), pp. 925–44.

over time and across cultures. There are many questions the researcher must pose and answer. How often is judicial review exercised—how often do acts of judicial independence occur? In what kinds of cases? Against whom (keeping in mind the varying power positions from culture to culture)? Are the decisions generalizable and/or do they become precedent? Are there adverse reactions? What form do these take? Are there judicial reversals (explicit overrulings or subtle backpedaling)? Are reprisals taken against the judiciary?[29] If so, what are the long-range effects? How often do reprisals occur? The list of questions is long and involved. These are just a few.

Clearly, case law is only *one* source for the data that would be necessary to answer the questions, but it is a primary one. The comparative literature on Latin America does yield a few tidbits of relevant knowledge along these lines. Furthermore, there are definite signs that there is greater exercise of judicial review in some of those countries than the more pessimistic might lead us to believe. William Stokes, for example, tells us that since 1910, "well over fifty national statutes and a far larger number of executive decrees" have been declared unconstitutional in Colombia, and many of them were "important."[30] Similarly, James Busey offers several quantitative judgments about the actual degree of usage of judicial review in Latin America. He has already processed his data and leaves us with only impressionistic judgments rather than specific facts, like Stokes. This is far better than nothing, however. For instance, James L. Busey notes the following about the writ of *amparo* in Mexico: "Applications for *amparo* are numerous, and Mexican court dockets are burdened with many cases that are related to it. It is quite clear that *amparo* is no hollow formality. . . . Numerous judgments do in fact serve to defend humble citizens against abusive acts by minor officials. . . ."[31] Edelmann is far more specific. The Mexican Supreme Court in 1950 "handled 33,957 matters of judicial business [and] still had a backlog of 27,026 cases, *almost all concerning writs of amparo.*"[32] Busey also observed (again impressionistically) that judicial review in Brazil has been "no empty gesture" and has served to "moderate the impact of arbitrary legislative or executive behavior."[33]

---

[29] In dealing with reprisals, the researcher must use some care. After all, there may just be a period of repression against the courts following a period of judicial independence. Instances of repression are not in themselves reason to downgrade the independence of the courts as a whole—even if the period of repression is in existence at the time the research is conducted. See George Blanksten, *Peron's Argentina* (Chicago: University of Chicago Press, 1953), pp. 125–29. Remember Franklin D. Roosevelt's "court-packing" scheme and the "switch in time that saved nine."

[30] Stokes, *op. cit.*, p. 475.

[31] Busey, *op. cit.*, p. 39.

[32] Edelmann, *op. cit.*, p. 468 (emphasis mine).

[33] Busey, *op. cit.*, p. 114.

All of this serious utilization of judicial review in some Latin American systems, plus an apparently healthy flexing of judicial independence in others (where there is rare or no exercise of judicial review), probably accounts for occasional statements that the judiciary is more independent of the executive in Latin America than is the legislature. This would seem to dispute conclusions reached by others; for instance, Blanksten's statement discussed in the previous chapter.[34]

All in all, this promises to become a fruitful area for comparative judicial politics empirical research. There are great variations from country to country legally and in the actual operations of the judiciary. A rigorous descriptive study could furnish the basis for answers to many cause-and-effect questions.

The Conditions for Judicial Review

Whereas only a few people have taken the trouble to figure out what pre-conditions support judicial independence, many have thought about the factors that influence the instituting of judicial review. It is such an obvious appurtenance! But all of this speculation comes off the top of the head. As far as I can see, there has been no systematic study of this topic. After flipping through reams of reflections upon it, however, one begins to sense a consensus among the speculators on what brings judicial review about in any given culture.

Most scholars, as well as laymen intrigued by this topic, seem to agree that the American experiment with judicial review was the critical starting point. I don't think it necessary to belabor the wealth of material available that discusses the development of judicial review in this country, but I would like to touch on it lightly.

One of the leading theories concerns the existence of the Privy Council in England during colonial days. This august body could review and over-rule any act of any colonial legislature. In point of fact, "of 8,563 acts submitted by the colonies, 469 or 5.5 percent were disallowed by order in council."[35] According to no less a solon than Charles Grove Haines: "In this

---

[34] However, even Blanksten stated a few years earlier that in Ecuador, "of the three national functions [*sic*], the judiciary has operated most effectively" (George Blanksten, *Ecuador: Constitutions and Caudillos* [Berkeley: University of California Press, 1951], p. 172). Even Needler has stated that though the court's sphere is limited, it "play[s] a more independent role than does the legislature" (*op cit.*, p. 154).

[35] Charles Grove Haines, *The American Doctrine of Judicial Supremacy*, rev. ed. (New York: Russell & Russell, 1959), p. 49.

respect the practice of English colonial administration agencies and of the assertion of authority by the Privy Council influenced the colonists in that they realized the possibility of having their judgments reviewed and in certain instances their statutes invalidated by a superior tribunal."[36]

The point is that the colonial Americans became accustomed to a form of judicial review. After their successful revolution, under the Articles of Confederation, several of the states granted their own highest courts the very same power. It is reasonable to suggest that once they became accustomed to such a practice as colonies, it was a short step toward adaptation at the state level, and many of them took it. Moreover, not only was adoption of judicial review a deference to local custom, but it had the added prestige of being in direct disagreement with contemporary English practice. Indeed, it was early in the seventeenth century that Lord Coke's contention that the English courts could overrule any act of Parliament (*Bonham's Case,* 1610) went down to dismal defeat. Thus we have another instance of those deep-seated American quirks: (*a*) love of one's own traditions and (*b*) rejection of European governmental institutions.[37]

McWhinney believes that the same traditionalism, custom, and/or inadvertence is directly responsible for the establishment of judicial review in several of the Commonwealth governments:

> Since none of the constitutions of the Commonwealth contains express provision for direct judicial review, the carry-over of the practice by both the Privy Council and local appellate tribunals, long after these parliaments have ceased to be subordinate legislative bodies vis-à-vis the United Kingdom Parliament, would seem primarily due to the fact that the practice has become ingrained over the years and its historical roots and justification have been forgotten, an example perhaps of long-time use and practice ripening into a binding "convention" of constitutional law.[38]

At any rate, there is still a wide chasm between explaining the adoption of judicial review in several of the states under the Articles and its adoption at the national level. Haines and many others document the tremendous amount of argumentation over judicial review before, during, and after the Constitutional Convention in Philadelphia. As we all know, this power was not explicitly granted the Supreme Court, though there was argument aplenty that it should be. These two facts help to explain why many think that it was John Marshall's ingenuity and nerve in the *Marbury* case that was proximately responsible for the injection of judicial

---

[36] *Ibid.,* p. 44.

[37] For a greater detailing of factors that may have contributed to a preconditioning of American judicial review, see Deener, *op. cit.,* pp. 1081–82.

[38] McWhinney, *op. cit.,* p. 14.

review into the operating American system, and nothing else. Certainly its nourishment and growth on American soil in several of the states helped, but judicial review at the national level in no way flowed directly from the local way of doing things. It did not *have* to happen the way it did. It came to pass purely from the machinations of a highly political man who engineered something extraordinarily clever at precisely the opportune moment—and then let it weather a tempest. It is probably not by accident that no other act of Congress was declared unconstitutional for over fifty-four years—which by any standard is a long, long time. The power, though once exercised, was far from invulnerable to attack, if not to obliteration. Thus, I believe that peculiarly American historical and cultural patterns and traits harbored essential support for this near-novel institution designed to govern the internal affairs of a society. Because of its unique history, American society nurtured the foundation for *any* free option of judicial review: an accepted (or acceptable) belief system to the effect that there can be a law higher than that of any given legislature or administration.[39] Still, all these historical and institutional factors together cannot be said necessarily to have generated judicial review in the United States at the national level. The brazenness, sharp-wittedness, and good luck of John Marshall are necessary (and probably sufficient) elements in any explanation of its specific implementation at that time.

Having considered what factors in concert might have artificially inseminated judicial review in the American womb, we must consider whether this helps us explain its proliferation elsewhere. McWhinney has observed, as we noted earlier, that much these same general factors explain the adoption of judicial review in a good portion of the British Commonwealth. Of course, try as we may, we will not find indigenous versions of John Marshall in each country at just the propitious moment in history. On the other hand, a different factor was present to combine with the essentially similar cultural-historical ones: the perceived "success" of the American variant. So McWhinney can say that India, for instance, has "a Supreme Court exercising judicial review on the model of the Supreme Court of the United States."[40] He also is convinced that Pakistan's constitutional proviso for judicial review was drawn from the American example.[41] In like fashion, Haines, in surveying the existence and extent

---

39 Kommers puts it this way: "A political system which regards its constitution as ordinary law, as was the case in Weimar, is not the kind of legal environment in which judicial review is likely to flourish, or even survive" (Donald P. Kommers, "The Federal Constitutional Court of West Germany: Some Exploratory Considerations" [paper delivered at the Midwest Conference of Political Scientists, Purdue University, April, 1967], p. 7).

40 McWhinney, *op. cit.*, p. 129.

41 *Ibid.*, p. 148.

of judicial review in Australia, sensed an "evident intention to adopt American principles of judicial review of legislative acts and judicial interpretation of the constitution itself."[42] This might also explain Nigeria's adoption (before the Biafran secession) of a form of judicial review;[43] but it can only raise the next obvious question: Why, then, is there no, or extremely limited, judicial review in such Commonwealth countries as New Zealand and Ghana?[44] They shared varying degrees of similar colonial experiences with Pakistan, India, and Nigeria. Thus the answer cannot lie in the Commonwealth factor alone, or even in the appearance of a Marshall-like judicial knight. One answer that comes to mind is that judicial review is frequently found in federated societies. Founding fathers in such cultures seem to be, by and large, impressed by the American experience along these lines—at least verbally.

Henry Abraham put it this way: "The practice of judicial review is not likely to be found in nonfederal states."[45] What this means is that there is a very high correlation between the explicit grant of judicial review to the courts in a society and the fact that the government has powers divided among levels. This does not mean that (*a*) once federalism exists, judicial review is sure to follow (e.g., the USSR), or that if it follows it will be granted at the national level (e.g., Nigeria; and the Swiss rejected this idea explicitly by citing the *failure* of the American experience);[46] or (*b*) judicial review will not be found in a unitary state (e.g., it exists in Italy,

---

[42] Charles Grove Haines, "Judicial Interpretation of the Constitutional Act of the Commonwealth of Australia," *Harvard Law Review*, 30 (April, 1916), p. 616.

[43] The Nigerian Constitution gives the Supreme Court a power similar to the Mexican writ of *amparo*. Persons believing their human rights have been trod upon by the executive are "given direct access to the High Court of the territory concerned. [That] court may refer any point of law to the Supreme Court and has to do so if one party to the proceedings so requests . . . no public official . . . stands between the individual and the court as far as the enforcement of his civil rights is concerned" (Oluwole Idowu Odumosu, *The Nigerian Constitution: History and Development* [London: Sweet & Maxwell, 1963], pp. 250–51). Also: "The Constitution has entrusted the Federal Supreme Court with the function [*sic*] of deciding questions about the division of legislative powers between the Federal and Regional Governments" (B. O. Nwabueze, *The Machinery of Justice in Nigeria* [London: Butterworth, 1963], pp. 285–86).

[44] C. F. Strong, *A History of Modern Political Constitutions* (New York: Capricorn Books, 1963), p. 281. Ghana's judicial review is extremely limited, as it can invalidate legislation only on three very narrow grounds. See William B. Harvey, *Law and Social Change in Ghana* (Princeton: Princeton University Press, 1967), pp. 221–22. It should also be noted that New Zealand did toy with judicial review for a while before dropping it in 1947 as a function of the choice to allow the New Zealand Parliament to amend the constitution by simple majority vote.

[45] Abraham, *op. cit.*, p. 294.

[46] "Indeed, the small American influence on the Federal Court has been largely negative in character. Whenever judicial review of national legislation has been proposed, opponents have used the example of the United States Supreme Court in successfully defeating such suggestions" (Fred L. Morrison, "The Swiss Federal Court," in *Frontiers of Judicial Research*, ed. Joel Grossman and Joseph Tanenhaus [New York: Wiley, 1969], p. 134).

Japan, and the Philippines).[47] Also, I should like to note that the reader should be wary of dismissing the USSR's failure to adopt judicial review as a necessary consequence of its being a Communist state. After all, Yugoslavia is a federal and a Communist state, and it has adopted judicial review.[48]

The fact that Italy, Japan, and the Philippines have judicial review provisions in their constitutions and are neither former colonies of Great Britain nor federal systems suggests another potentially important element to be taken into account in grasping the development of judicial review in a society. These three countries have only one historical link in common. Each of them was dominated, if not occupied, by American power in this century following a war. The Philippines was, in all but name, a colony of the United States for nearly half a century. Italy and Japan were vanquished and occupied countries after World War II. Americans have an almost religious affinity for their governmental institutions and consider them highly functional for goals that Americans hold dear. It is therefore understandable that Americans exert their influence in order to graft this revered American "innovation" onto subject (formerly "misgoverned") countries. For instance, according to one scholar, American authorities feared the possible "return to power of reactionaries" in Japan.[49] As we shall see, in American lore judicial review is considered a highly impenetrable barrier against such people; *ergo*, the American "recommendation" that this structure be imported by its client states. Such an argument was also made to West Germany, and then taken up by German legal elites. Finally, the overwhelming dominance of the Colossus of the North may also help to explain why various species of judicial review have sprouted up throughout Latin America. North Americans seem pleased by such legal deference and "good sense"; it can be a pittance to pay for the substantial material consequences of North American pleasure.

---

[47] Some who are familiar with the provision for "Regions" in the post–World War II Italian constitution may consider Italy to be a federation. That is not the view of the experts. William H. Riker, *Federalism* (Boston: Little, Brown, 1964), doesn't discuss Italy at all. Also see Norman Kogan, *The Government of Italy* (New York: Crowell, 1962), pp. 160–63; Margaret Carlyle, *Modern Italy*, rev. ed. (New York: Praeger, 1965), p. 42.

[48] Judicial review became incorporated into the Yugoslavian system in 1963 (Constitution of the Socialist Federal Republic of Yugoslavia, Article 241). See Frank R. Lacy, "Yugoslavia: Practice and Procedure in a Communist Country," *Oregon Law Review*, 43 (December, 1963), pp. 1–46.

[49] Allan P. Dionisopoulos, "Judicial Review and Civil Rights in Japan: The First Decade with an Alien Doctrine," *Western Political Quarterly*, 3 (June, 1960), p. 269. McWhinney is one of the few who has acknowledged the strong role of American pressure for the upsurge of judicial review since World War II. See his "Federal Supreme Courts and Constitutional Review," *Canadian Bar Review*, 45 (September, 1967), p. 578.

Thus we are left with a short theory of the factors that seem to be highly associated with the legal existence of judicial review in various forms. First, it occurs in erstwhile British possessions. Second, there is a very high correlation with federalism. Third, there is the strong influence (direct and indirect) on the part of American power interests.

There are a few other conditions frequently believed to have at least some influence on the institution and maintenance of judicial review. In fact, some of these theories have far more advocates than those mentioned above. I happen to think, though, that they deserve but short shrift. They are either legalistic, and thus tautological, or pseudo-psychological, and thus propagandistic.

Some scholars seem to get trapped into a legalistic explanation of cause. However, when one is dealing with the origin of a *legal* phenomenon, as we are here, then it becomes rather likely that one is explaining something by another aspect of itself. Judicial review, as we are using it here, is simply the existence of the legal power of review (though it is an indicator of a high degree of independence). When someone says, then, that judicial review arises from the fact that a constitution provides for a separation of powers and also guarantees civil liberties, this is not a scientific explanation of judicial review's appearance, though it is frequently stated as though it were. It is merely a statement of the legal prerequisites or concomitants of any judiciary's ability to invalidate acts of the other branches at its own level. *By definition*, in order for the legal power of judicial review to exist there must be in the constitution (*a*) an article that distributes and limits powers and (*b*) another or others that separate or divide powers.

Other scholars are inclined to accept the rhetoric of constitutional framers and their academic supporters (domestic and foreign) as the real reasons underlying a decision to opt for judicial review in a written constitution. For instance, it has frequently been said that judicial review has come to life on the Continent because of a growing distrust of legislative power in the twentieth century. Tyrants have run amok and popularly elected legislatures have failed miserably to block excesses loosed by dictatorship. These regrets, fears, and good intentions are thought to explain the motivations of the modern European sponsors of judicial review.[50] Taylor Cole puts it this way: "The constitutions of West Germany and Italy were the product of negative revolutions, reflecting a deep distaste for the

---

[50] Many look at the entire constitution-building of Germany and Italy along these lines—particularly those provisions that are designed to be (in a functional sense) guardians of an open, democratic system (judicial review is seen as one of these). See, for example, Herbert J. Spiro, "The German Political System," in *Patterns of Government*, ed. Samuel H. Beer and Adam B. Ulam, 2nd ed. (New York: Random House, 1962).

'dismal past.' "[51] To shore up this view, Professor Cole dusts off a few obscure and ancient principles to demonstrate that there was a background for judicial review on the Continent much akin to America's colonial heritage.[52] That, however, stretches even the most elastic credulity to the breaking point. To bolster this theory of the conditions that led to the Constitutional Court of Italy, among others, Professor Cole also tells us of an insignificant practice that "pointed to judicial review" in Sicily and quickly dismisses the monstrous suggestion that the original Allied demands for judicial review were a "direct" pressure. He admits that they might have been "indirect," and concludes again that it was a "reaction to excess" that was the principal factor.[53]

Professor Cole's staunch belief that a few vaguely related practices and doctrines preconditioned the existence of judicial review in these countries is disturbing. The arguments are too pat, the analogies are too thin, and a confounding coincidence is too great: all *four* of the nations that the United States defeated or had a hand in defeating in this century have opted for judicial review, while other independent states in their area of the globe have spurned it. That there is an undeniable consistency between Cole's kind of theoretical explanation and the rhetoric of the Cold War should give us pause to wonder: To what extent are our politico-judicial theories a function of that conflict? I am equally leery, by the way, of theories that stress the influence of an economic factor, over all others, in explaining why a particular form of judicial structure comes to pass.[54]

In summary, it must be kept in mind that by and large our focus must center on the conditions for different measures of judicial *independence*. The legal presence of some judicial review, in itself, is of little importance. We are interested, though, in the scope and depth to which it is formally exercisable and the degree to which it is really put to use without severe setbacks due to reprisal, for this represents a high (or higher) degree of independence. As I stated above, the factor of English legal heritage prob-

---

[51] Taylor Cole, "Three Constitutional Courts: A Comparison," *American Political Science Review*, 53 (December, 1959), p. 965.

[52] So does Gottfried Dietze, "Judicial Review in Europe," *Michigan Law Review*, 55 (February, 1957), pp. 539–66. Dietze's line of argument throughout is substantially similar to Cole's.

[53] Taylor Cole, "The West German Federal Constitutional Court: An Evaluation after Six Years," *Journal of Politics*, 20 (May, 1958), pp. 283–84; Giuseppino Treves, "Judicial Review of Legislation in Italy," *Journal of Public Law*, 7 (Fall, 1958), pp. 345–61.

[54] Max Radin, for example, once observed that "the question of unconstitutionality is conceived of as a struggle between an economic group in control of the courts and another group in control of the legislature" (*op. cit.*, p. 122). Thus one can infer that it behooves one economic group to have judicial review and another to be free of it. Whether or not it exists, in a Charles Beardsian sense, can then be seen as the particular outcome of a struggle between two or more economic classes. This, too, is a theoretical relic of another day.

ably has some impact on the degree of judicial independence. Still, to my mind, the influence of the United States is probably the single most important factor in bringing about the currently widespread existence of judicial review. Sometimes the pressure is quite indirect, sometimes it is directly applied. America's missionary heritage dies hard. If the reader is still skeptical about this point, I would like him to ask himself why South Vietnam joined the ranks of countries with judicial review, on April 1, 1967. The exact date of its adoption may only be ironic.[55]

The Functions of Judicial Review

The final part of this chapter will be devoted to a discussion of the consequences of a society's having (or not having) judicial review. One might wonder whether there is much to say. After all, I have repeated time and again in this chapter that the relationship of judicial review to judicial independence is a series of points at the top of a cumulative scale of the relative strength of judicial independence. For the sake of consistency, then, it would appear necessary only to refer the reader back to the corresponding section of the preceding chapter. Whatever functions judicial independence was seen to serve, judicial review can just be said to serve them better. It seems logical. Unfortunately, real life is not such a simple engine; nor is political science.

There are several ways in which a phenomenon may be simply an increase in another phenomenon ("more of the same"), yet vary in kind as well. On the one hand, it may be so much of an increase as to be like a quantum jump; that is, there may be a difference in a qualitative sense *precisely because of the effect* (function) *it will have*. By way of example, water is water, and a working water tap yields more of it than a partially filled canteen. Each has the same basic purpose: to slake thirst. But look at the difference to a man wandering, near death, in the desert. He stumbles across a canteen that is nearly empty. Functionally it may have little or reverse effect: (*a*) it carries him a trifle farther, (*b*) he despairs upon finding so little in it and loses his will to continue. Though it is simply a difference of degree, suppose this same man stumbles into a cabin where there is a faucet in good running order. The function is quite clearly of a different

---

[55] Article V of the South Vietnamese constitution provides that the Supreme Court will "decide on the constitutionality of all laws and decree laws"; see *Keesing's Contemporary Archives,* 16 (November, 1967), p. 22350. For a slightly more extended set of remarks, see Robert Devereux, "Judicial Provisions of South Vietnam's New Constitution," *Judicature,* 51 (February, 1968), pp. 262–65.

order—only because of the difference in degree. Similarly, a rainstorm may alleviate a drought while three straight weeks of downpour may well wash out the crop.

Furthermore, the extreme of a phenomenon may also contain other features (elements), concomitant with it, which in interaction have a different effect as well. In other words, there is more than the simple effect of the greater quantity. Other intrinsic properties, inseparable from the extreme quantity of the phenomenon, act with it and are potentially responsible for certain other impacts. When the extreme degree of this phenomenon exists, then, it is possible that a unique reaction ensues. An example might be the differences between waging a conventional war and resorting to the use of tactical nuclear weapons. In one sense it is just more of the same (a bigger bang and blast); in others it is not (radiation). To the extent that it is not, the consequences wrought (militarily and politically) may be quite different. In a military sense, the functions of the atomic device are far more varied than just having the bigger explosion; for instance, terrain can be denied to the enemy for a long period because of the persistence of the radiation. The political consequences that are likely to come in the wake of such a tactic are the subject of heavy controversy.

In any event, it should now be clear why the fact that judical review is an extension of judicial independence does not in any way cut off a discussion of (*a*) the extra effect it may have and (*b*) the other effects it may have.

PROTECTION OF INDIVIDUAL RIGHTS AND/OR OF DEMOCRACY

As in the thinking about judicial independence, there is much expressed belief that the structural provision for judicial review in a constitution is a safeguard against governmental infringement of individual rights.[56] Where judicial review exists, the courts are pictured as buffer and redeemer for the citizen in his eternal battle against the state. Moreover, in a slightly less direct fashion, judicial review is seen as promoting democracy. It does this, so the argument goes, by protecting the individual—by insulating him and his rights against official caprice. It is portrayed as an impermeable coating on the pillars of democracy. One contemporary scholar has gone so far as to say that democracy without judicial review is "unthinkable," and that without judicial review "free government in the

---

[56] For instance, see C. Perry Patterson, "Judicial Review as a Safeguard to Democracy," *Georgetown Law Journal*, 29 (April, 1941), pp. 829–85 (particularly "Judicial review protects personal rights," pp. 846–47).

United States is likely to come to an end."[57] Of course, this thinking is flagrantly specious.[58]

For one thing, it is perfectly clear that judicial review could be employed in a federal system that divided powers between levels but that had no explicit guarantee (or any tradition) of individual liberty. How could judicial review then function as a buffer or shield? Without a law or a tradition to uphold on this point, the court would not function in such a way, judicial review or not. For another, the judicial review might be of a very limited variety. Indeed, according to Stokes, "In most of the other [Latin American] nations, judicial review does not afford an effective protection as in Mexico to private rights. . . ."[59] He notes, for instance, that in Ecuador the high court can declare a law unconstitutional only when the legislature has failed to adhere to some proper *procedure* in promulgating that law. This is judicial review, all right, but it has no relationship to the substance of the law, and can therefore provide scant protection to individual private rights. Also, a high court with the power of judicial review might well be operating in a society (and some so operate today) to construe constitutional provisions that separate the executive, legislature, and judiciary, while at the same time the guarantees of individual liberties and the existence of competing political parties and elections have all been suspended by the executive in accordance with his clear constitutional power to proclaim a national emergency.

The courts cannot do what the society itself must do. England is the most obvious example to Americans that a culture can do without judicial review and still support a good deal of individual liberty. There are others, and this same point has been made for some time by American scholars. For instance, Charles Grove Haines said in 1930:

> The constitutions of Belgium and Switzerland, though subject to final interpretation by the legislative assemblies, have seldom been changed merely by legislative interpretation or by a refusal to obey a constitu-

----

[57] Gottfried Dietze, "America and Europe—Decline and Emergence of Judicial Review," *Virginia Law Review,* 44 (December, 1958), p. 1235. Dietze also believes judicial review is *"vital* for the protection of the individual's liberty" (*ibid.*; emphasis mine).

[58] This is so even when the thinker is of the status and quality of Mr. Justice Cardozo:

> The utility of an external power restraining the legislative judgment is not to be measured by counting the occasions of its exercise. The great ideals of liberty and equality are preserved against the assaults of opportunism, the expediency of the passing hour, the erosion of small encroachments, the scorn and derision of those who have no patience with general principles, by enshrining them in constitutions, and consecrating to the task of their protection a body of defenders [*The Nature of the Judicial Process* (New Haven: Yale University Press, 1921), pp. 92–93].

Among other greats, see James Bryce, *The American Commonwealth,* rev. ed. (New York: Macmillan, 1922), pp. 256–57, 273.

[59] William S. Stokes, *Latin American Politics* (New York: Crowell, 1959), p. 496.

tional requirement. The experience of these countries indicates that legitimate private rights and privileges are likely to receive adequate protection without a judicial guardianship of the written constitution.[60]

A more recent authority echoes this sentiment in his analysis of the functions of the Constitutional Court in West Germany. He concludes, as does Haines, that where the court has the power, as it does in Germany today, even to outlaw political parties threatening the democratic order or individual rights, "important though the judicious attitude of the courts . . . may be, what will count in the end will be the prevailing political climate in the nation."[61] Only legalists in blinders could gainsay this argument. But there are more serious charges against judicial review than these.

Perhaps the gravest indictment brought against judicial review is that it is undemocratic.[62] This is the other face of the contention that judicial review has sprung up in modern Europe as a reaction to the oppression effectuated by popularly based dictatorships. No matter how it is stated, though, the point is crystal clear. Legislatures shouldn't be authorized to defend the individual and his access to democratic processes, nor should

---

[60] Charles Grove Haines, "Some Phases of the Theory and Practice of Judicial Review of Legislation in Foreign Countries," *American Political Science Review*, 24 (August, 1930), pp. 592–93.

[61] Sigmund Neumann, "Germany," in *European Political Systems*, ed. Taylor Cole, 2nd ed. (New York: Knopf, 1959), p. 431.

[62] I prefer to avoid a long argument over the meaning of the term "democratic" in the text, although I do agree with Howard Dean that too many people engaging in the debate over the compatibility of judicial review and democracy fail to explicate what they mean by "democracy" (if not "judicial review" too). See Howard E. Dean, *Judicial Review and Democracy* (New York: Random House, 1966), especially chap. 3. I do not propose to offer "the" definition of it in either a real or a lexical sense. In fact, with so much dispute over its meaning, I doubt that there *is* a lexical definition. Before·I get to my own position on this, I would like to point out that the pretense has long been that since some 60 percent of qualified American citizens vote in presidential elections, it follows that America has a democratic setup. However, modern political science studies have shown that indifference toward politics (if not pure distrust) is rampant, even among those who bother to vote. To soothe the fears of some that this flies in the face of classic democratic theoretical assumptions, various revisions of classic democratic theories have sprung up, among them the pluralist and the elitist brands. For instance, see Lester Milbrath, *Political Participation* (Chicago: Rand McNally, 1964); Robert Dahl, *Who Governs?* (New Haven: Yale University Press, 1961); Edward Banfield, *Political Influence* (New York: Free Press, 1961). Some of the revisionists even revise the concept purely for the sake of showing the compatibility of "democracy" (as so revised) with American judicial review. See Walter Murphy and Joseph Tanenhaus, "Constitutional Courts, Public Opinion and Political Representation" (report from the Laboratory for Political Research, Department of Political Science, University of Iowa, 1967). However, the pluralist theory has recently come under heavy attack as being near-mythology. See Henry S. Kariel, *The Promise of Politics* (Englewood Cliffs, N.J.: Prentice-Hall, 1966) and Grant McConnell, *Private Power and American Democracy* (New York: Knopf, 1966). And those who argue for their own revised versions of democracy are truly setting up ideal types in very much the same fashion as the "purists" they villify. I shall simply state that one element of the possible degrees of democracy is the ratio between the amount of public interest and extent of engagement in politics to the number and importance of issues that are governmentally resolvable. There can be little doubt that judicial review, in this sense, greatly diminishes the democratic element in our governmental system.

the executive. Only the reserved, calm, and erudite judiciary is reliable in this regard. That judges are almost always appointed or rise through the bureaucracy and are difficult to remove are facts that lend a distinctly undemocratic bias to judicial review. The people cannot be burdened with their own good any more. Let the blackrobes do it. This argument has wide support, but there are those who show us that it is limited. For example, Stanley A. de Smith tells us how it is viewed in the new states of Africa:

> *In the first place,* there is a genuine and widespread feeling that judicial review is anti-democratic. Those who have long been denied the right to express their will on political questions resent an implication that they cannot be trusted to express it wisely through their chosen representatives. No doubt lawyers are experts on the construction of legal documents, but the constitution is no ordinary legal document; its spirit can be apprehended by the politicians and the people, who have no need to depute the judges to act as communal mentors. Everyone is for the rule of law . . . but why must this entail submission to the rule of lawyers?[63]

This is a good argument for democracy and for the abolition of judicial review, but it is rather defensive; that is, it makes a weak suggestion that the layman is as good at reading legal documents as the professional. But this helps the legal position, I fear, for it puts the emphasis where the layman is weakest: on his skill (or lack of it) with the law. The best argument that can be made against judicial review as being undemocratic is one that is rarely used: the existence of judicial review stunts the political growth of the individuals within the society. Among other things, judicial review relieves the people of responsibility for their own well-being. If they are to grow as political beings, if a society is to gain its own maturity, the public cannot be treated as immature and in need of some remote paternal overseers. Moreover, the existence of judicial review promotes a tendency to look at grave political issues only as sterile legal ones. By constantly jamming political stress into legal boxes, the system superimposes an artificiality on the political system, thereby hiding the true nature and dilemmas of the system from the public. Can this be functional for the development of a democratic system? Not by a long shot.[64] Herman Finer has presented both of these arguments elegantly, and I shall quote him at some length:

> A great deal of substance and dramatic effect, as distinct from transient and superficial sensationalism, are extracted from American politics by judicial review, for no politician can make a promise of major importance with the ring of truth in his declaration. Short of promising the

---

[63] In *Federalism and the New Nations of Africa,* ed. David P. Currie (Chicago: University of Chicago Press, 1964), p. 295.

[64] For an argument that judicial review provides a certain amount of "discipline" to a "constitutional" democracy, see Patterson, *op. cit.,* pp. 852–54.

almost unattainable—a constitutional amendment—he has very little
to offer. . . . When vital questions are taken from the hands of the party
organizations, these are themselves devitalized. But in England and on
the Continent, the plentitude of powers is in the hands of the legislature,
the parties, and the people. Obtain a majority in the legislature and you
may, legally, change the political and social fabric of the state. . . .
That is a spur to the people to attack or defend; and both receive an
education in political thinking and self-control. In the United States,
Congress is in a perpetual state of non-age, and the people likewise
are bound by a testament made by their forefathers. . . . In the same
line of criticism lies the fact that in the United States, political questions are discussed by Congress, the parties, and the electorate not
merely on their merits, not as to their social advantages and disadvantages, but as to their constitutionality. . . . The discussions of constitutionality are, in the United States, always an interference with the
direct consideration of political issues, and not seldom they establish
a screen around the real questions. We might, indeed, add another
phrase to the catalogue of logical fallacies: the *argumentum ad con-
stitutionem.*[65]

John Schmidhauser, after canvassing Supreme Court decisions in the
United States on federal-state relations from 1789 to 1957, put this matter
in much the same way and with much the same feeling of consternation:

A second major consequence of judicial arbitership of American federalism is the probable weakening of democratic participation in meeting major social, economic and political problems. This was especially
marked in the discouragement of social experiments by the states during the period from 1890 through 1937. Further, it is especially
marked in the contemporary period with respect to the maintenance
of fundamental freedoms and civil rights.[66]

To the further discredit of the system of judicial review, the high court
is not likely to protect individual liberty—*when it really counts*—against
the politically irresponsible mass that becomes aroused every so often.
Where final disposition of questions of constitutionality are in the traditional and legal bailiwick of a high court, the public is hardly in a position
to grasp the delicate nuances in many of the more important systemic issues. Therefore, out of a collage of frustrations, strong public aggressions
occasionally erupt. When this happens, and the clamor is great, instead of
being the towering protector of the individual victims in these cases, courts
have been known to buckle under instead of buckling down. It is a grim
circle, for the various elite factions manage to see this as further proof of

[65] Herman Finer, *Theory and Practice of Modern Government*, rev. ed. (New
York: Holt, Rinehart & Winston, 1949), p. 151. This is close to the argument made
some time ago by J. B. Thayer that judicial review may "dwarf the political capacity
of the people."

[66] John Schmidhauser, *The Supreme Court as Final Arbiter in Federal-State
Relations* (Chapel Hill: University of North Carolina Press, 1958), p. 212.

the need to maintain rather than eliminate judicial review; this despite the fact that it is they who usually support the prosecution of the more radical political dissenters.

Charles Sheldon conducted an interesting survey of public opinion polls in Australia, Germany, Canada, and the United States near the time when the supreme court in each country made a major decision about the constitutionality of a statute that outlawed or banned the local Communist party.[67] In all four nations there was strong and widespread sentiment among the populace for ridding society of Communists. (See Table 4.)

Three of the courts upheld the statutes, and Sheldon notes that this was consistent with well over 50 percent of the prevailing opinion in each nation at the time and of ancillary political pressure. Only in Australia did the court buck public opinion. Professor Sheldon believes that this was due to the fact that the Australian High Court is extraordinarily legalistic. Since the Australian people can reverse the court's rulings by referendum, a suggested hypothesis is that only the court that was most impartial and least independent of pressure managed to protect speech threatening the system. On the other hand, another authority points out that the Australian population almost always turns down the national government's request against the court's interpretations as well as for anything that can be construed as governmental aggrandizement.[68]

In any event, Sheldon's finding that three-quarters of the courts in his study retreated in the face of adversity does not do much to increase confidence in the hypothesis that judicial review protects individual liberty

TABLE 4

Public Tolerance toward Communists
(In Percentages)

	U.S. 1954	Germany 1954	Canada 1951	Australia* 1951
Favor outlawing party or jailing Communists	51	55	58	80
Not for outlawing or jailing	34	30	30	12
Undecided	15	15	12	8

*Shortly after the High Court decision.
SOURCE: Charles H. Sheldon, "Public Opinion and High Courts: Communist Party Cases in Four Constitutional Systems," *Western Political Quarterly*, 20 (June, 1967), p. 344.

---

[67] Charles H. Sheldon, "Public Opinion and High Courts: Communist Party Cases in Four Constitutional Systems," *Western Political Quarterly*, 20 (June, 1967), pp. 341–60.
[68] M. J. C. Vile, "Judicial Review and Politics in Australia," *American Political Science Review*, 51 (June, 1957), pp. 386–91.

(or democracy).[69] Thus, even at this highest degree of judicial independence, the functional hypotheses on the relationship of courts, individual rights, and democracy do not appear to be borne out by either analysis or empirical evidence.[70] Of course, some among us might argue that the Supreme Court has only recently flexed its muscles in the area of civil liberties here in the United States. Milton Konvitz, in perceiving and evaluating this recent trend, entitled a recent book *Expanding Liberties*,[71] and Henry Abraham has told us in his most recent effort:

> Since 1937 the overwhelming majority of judicial vetoes imposed upon the several states and *all* of those against the national government have been invoked because they infringed personal liberties, other than "property," safeguarded under the Constitution. This preoccupation with the "basic human freedoms" is amply illustrated by the statistics of the docket of the Supreme Court and the application of its power of judicial review. Upwards of 45 percent of all cases decided by the Court now fall into this category of "basic human freedoms"; whereas in the 1935–36 term only two of 160 written decisions had done so, in the 1965–66 term the ratio had increased to 54 out of 120.[72]

If we grant Konvitz' and Abraham's arguments about the Court's output, two questions go begging. First, in areas of liberty where the Court

---

[69] Nor does a short study by Stuart Nagel. According to Nagel, whether or not a justice upholds civil liberties seems to relate to his party affiliation. Such a factor does not appear to be the impenetrable bulwark one might hope for. See "Political Parties and Judicial Review in American History," *Journal of Public Law*, 11 (Spring, 1962), pp. 334–39. After an exhaustive survey of Court decisions on civil liberties, John Frank stated that "the actual overt exercise of judicial review of acts of Congress has been of almost negligible good to civil liberties, and has probably harmed those liberties more than it has helped them. The great inescapable fact is that in a century and a half no substantial restriction on liberty has yet been invalidated" ("Review and Basic Liberties," in *Supreme Court and Supreme Law*, ed. Edmond Cahn [Bloomington: Indiana University Press, 1954], p. 129). Shortly thereafter he noted that judicial review fosters a buck-passing tendency: Congress puts off political issues to the Court and debates these issues in constitutional terms instead of "in terms of their merits" (p. 130). Cf. S. Sidney Ulmer, "Judicial Review as Political Behavior: A Temporary Check on Congress," *Administrative Science Quarterly*, 4 (March, 1960), pp. 426–45. According to Ulmer, after an exhaustive survey of the Court's overruling or weakening of Congressional statutes, "As an administrative means of preventing legislative tyranny, judicial review of national policy appears to have marginal value" (p. 445).

[70] Perhaps it would be salutary to recall Justice Robert Jackson's statement:

> It is not idle speculation to inquire which comes first, either in time or importance, an independent and enlightened judiciary or a free and tolerant society. . . . It is my belief that the attitude of a society and of its organized political forces, rather than its legal machinery, is the controlling force in the character of free institutions [*The Supreme Court in the American System of Government* (Cambridge: Harvard University Press, 1955), p. 81].

[71] Milton Konvitz, *Expanding Liberties: The Emergence of New Civil Liberties and Civil Rights in Postwar America* (New York: Viking Press, 1966).

[72] Henry J. Abraham, *Freedom and the Court: Civil Rights and Liberties in the United States* (New York: Oxford University Press, 1967), p. 6.

has spoken out most nobly to our society—in racial integration, in separation of church and state, in protecting detainees in police custody—there has been a flood of lip service but a drought of heed. High hopes and judicial eloquence have not been converted into practical realities by any stretch of the imagination.[73] The first question is: How can we speak of expanding freedoms when so few people are willing to put them into practice? Words do not freedom make. Next, there is good reason to believe that, owing to the unprecedented technological nature of our society, our traditional liberties are being eroded at a far faster rate than even a far more sagacious and zealous court can handle. If we grant the remote possibility that as things now stand, more and more people might obey the Court over some extended period of time, a second question must still be raised: Is the Court an adequate protector against the rapidly accelerating threats of the mechanical society? I think it noteworthy that Alan Westin, in describing the frightening increase in spying and prying and the danger this augurs for the future existence of individual privacy, is not enchanted by the Court either. He places the onus squarely on society itself. When he turns to the role of government, it is primarily legislative action that he seeks. According to Westin: "A judicial opinion drawing a line between constitutional and unconstitutional conduct and relying on exclusion of illegally obtained evidence to compel obedience is not the most promising way of properly balancing the interests of privacy, disclosure, and surveillance."[74] Nor is it the most promising way of balancing *any* of the more serious conflicts between authority and individual freedom.

It is high time we began seriously to study, discuss, and reevaluate in earnest the possible *dysfunction* of judicial review for the maintenance of individual rights and for the support of democratic ideals and politics. Its functioning in this field is dubious enough to warrant it.

MAINTENANCE AND STRENGTHENING OF FEDERAL SYSTEMS

There is a sizable segment of literature on the great functional importance of judicial review for a federal system of government. This is perhaps the major functional hypothesis involving what might be called a subsidi-

---

[73] I shall deal with the specific findings on Supreme Court impact in the section on legitimization.

[74] Alan F. Westin, *Privacy and Freedom* (New York: Atheneum, 1967), p. 384. I must note that later in the book, in fact at the very end, Westin does state that a decision by the Court setting forth a "new constitutional right to privacy from unreasonable surveillance" would be desirable—but only as a "catalyst for elective-branch responsibility" (p. 398). This is a far cry from saying that the Court is a necessary protector; it is simply a statement that under our present setup the Court *can assist* the representative branches in protecting democracy and freedom.

ary property to the *cumulative* nature of judicial review (as an extension of judicial independence). What I mean by this is that if one analyzes this supposed relationship, it becomes clear that what is believed to flow from the existence of judicial review is only partially based on the fact that judicial review indicates (or demonstrates) a substantial amount of judicial *independence*. Other aspects of the judicial review structure that are felt to be of peculiar functional importance for federalism are *impartiality* and *legal expertise*. Those who believe that *judicial* review is the best structure to harmonize a federal system are highly voluble on this point.

It should be perfectly obvious that there can be no absolute, one-to-one structural-functional relationship between judicial review and the *maintenance* of a federal system (the strict perpetuation of the system intact). There are enduring and probably viable federal systems without effective judicial review (Mexico, the USSR). Thus, it is rare that one finds someone insisting that a federal system will totally collapse without a constitutional provision for judicial review.[75] One does detect a feeling, though, that most scholars interested in this topic feel that judicial review is indeed a very important factor in any federal system, though the precise effect of it is either in dispute or very poorly explicated. The area of agreement between them is based on legal and logical analysis and is reasonably easy to describe. I think it is fair to say that the following paragraph is representative of this type of thinking.

Federalism implies a constitution; that is, the spelling out of the distribution and division of powers. Frequently this is written down. Words in such documents are bound to be ambiguous and vague, as the level of abstraction in most constitutions is extremely high. Meanwhile, preexistent and ever developing tensions in the society between forces pushing for centralism and others pulling for localism will need easing. Specific conflicts will need resolution. However, the general words of the constitution fail to afford much help in and of themselves. Since the constitution is a *law*, what more reasonable solution than to let the courts interpret its provisions? After all, the courts are, by their very nature, interpreters of law. Therefore, they should construe the constitution, resolve the conflict, and thus alleviate the pressures that might eventuate in a rupture. If the independent, professional, and impartial judiciary cannot do it, there is little hope that a biased and involved party (e.g., the national legislature) can. So goes the general drift of the argument, and it makes sense. Oliver Wendell Holmes once said that the United States would not "come to an end" if the power of judicial review over congressional statutes were withdrawn

---

[75] Howard O. Eaton, *Federation: The Coming Structure of World Government* (Norman: University of Oklahoma Press, 1944). Eaton feels that it is "essential" if a *world* federation is to endure.

from the Court, but that "the Union would be imperiled" if the power over state actions were.[76] Note that he said "imperiled," not "destroyed." Carl Friedrich once put it this way:

> In the discussion of federalism it has been shown that a constitutional judiciary is an *integral part* of any federal structure. If there is to be a division of powers between the central and local authorities, conflicts over the respective spheres of authority are bound to arise, and a procedure for their settlement is obviously needed. Generally speaking, this need is analogous to the need for an arbiter between authorities dividing powers functionally under some kind of separation of powers. Therefore, it is not surprising that federalism should reinforce the idea of judicial review, along with the idea of a constitution which embodies "higher" law than ordinary legislation.[77]

Note that Professor Friedrich used the word "reinforce," rather than "require" or a stronger term. Note also that each of these two statements emphasizes the great significance of judicial review for federalism, but that neither claims indispensability for it. And yet the general tenor of these statements is that judicial review is indeed essential and logical. But even if we accept the qualified nature of these statements, they still totally fail to come to analytical grips with the probabilistic realities of federalism. *All* of the work that centers on the relationship of judicial review to federalism—from the perspective of judicial review—is utterly insensitive to shadings in or types of federalism. That there may be types or degrees of federalism and that judicial review may be more or less important (in different ways) has never occurred to any of the legal writers or traditional political scientists who have been interested in this area of judicial politics. Indeed, their naïve, black-and-white view of federalism and nonfederalism has led them into rather serious intellectual traps.

Some of the more modern analysts of federal systems have made observations that call the supposedly great importance of judicial review into serious question. For example, William H. Riker has developed a quasi scale of federal systems. It reads as follows:

A. The central government can completely overawe the constituent governments.

B. The central government cannot completely overawe the constituents, but it can keep them from overruling its own decisions [centralized].

---

[76] Oliver Wendell Holmes, Jr., "Law and the Court," in *Collected Papers* (New York: Harcourt, Brace, 1920), p. 295.

[77] Carl J. Friedrich, *Constitutional Government and Democracy: Theory and Practice in Europe and America,* 4th ed. (Waltham, Mass.: Blaisdell, 1968), pp. 222–23 (emphasis mine).

C. The constituent governments cannot completely overawe the rules of the center, but they can significantly vary the behavior of officials of the center, though central officials cannot overawe them [peripheralized].

D. The constituent governments can unilaterally completely overawe the rulers of the center.[78]

As Riker himself notes, if situation A or D exists, the federal bargain is not long for this world. Situation C, according to Riker, also courts a self-breaching of the federal contract. Only B, in Riker's view, represents a healthy and fertile situation, as far as continuing federalism is concerned. Therefore the question we have to answer is whether the structure of judicial review helps a system advance toward situation B or assists it in hovering at or near that point. Is there something inherent in the structure of judicial review *per se* that operates to the advantage of the federal bargain (the value of that bargain being quite irrelevant to our discussion)?

Most traditional analysts believe that a supreme court holding the power of judicial review is a force toward centralization. For instance, Robert K. Carr speaks of the "loyalty" of the United States Supreme Court to the national government.[79] Also, according to Gottfried Dietze, "The courts do not play the role of an umpire between national and state interests, but rather protect national law against infringements by state authorities."[80] Paul Kauper puts it this way:

> Judicial review has functioned most effectively in respect to the operation of the federal aspects of the constitutional system. The Supreme Court's most telling work is seen in its success in keeping the states within constitutional limits and subordinating their laws and policies to the national interests as reflected in Congressional policy and legislation. . . . The Court has functioned less effectively as a tribunal for restraining the federal government, particularly the Congress, from enlarging its power at the expense of the states.[81]

Now, if we could be assured that this functioning was inherent in the very structure of judicial review itself, its potential role would be clearer, though we could still not be certain that judicial review, all by itself, would operate in such a fashion. For one thing, it would become relevant to determine the tendency of the system before adopting judicial review. If there is a strong tendency in the system at its inception to move toward

---

[78] William H. Riker, *Federalism: Origin, Operation, Significance* (Boston: Little, Brown and Company [Inc.], 1964), p. 86.

[79] Robert K. Carr, *Supreme Court and Judicial Review* (New York: Holt, Rinehart & Winston, 1942), p. 87.

[80] Dietze, *op. cit.*, p. 540.

[81] Paul Kauper, "Judicial Review of Constitutional Issues in the United States," in the Max Planck Institute's *Constitutional Review in the World Today* (Köln-Berlin: Carl Tleymanns Verlag KG, 1962), p. 638.

centralism, then adopting judicial review might push the system into situation A. Thus, the federation would be *kaputt* at its commencement because it opted for judicial review; yet this possibility is *never* mentioned in the literature. Also, at some point, if judicial review has slowly moved a system that started at C to B, it could be the better part of wisdom to remove judicial review, *as an adjustment in the system,* to keep it at B and prevent it from moving on to A. That is, of course, if one wants to keep it at B. Quite logically, then, judicial review can be *dysfunctional* for federalism at various stages, depending on other factors. The time may be coming (or it may be now) to put judicial review out to pasture if we want to keep any semblance of a federal system in the United States. In making this, the best case for judicial review, apparent—i.e., granting that it has a distinguishable and predictable quality—we still find that it may backfire and that there is no way to know whether or when it will. In any case, this argument is moot, as there happens to be good reason to believe that (1) such a centralizing force is probably not inherent in the *structure* of judicial review anyway, and (2) even where the judicial review *process* manifests this centralizing tendency, it operates effectively only in conjunction with more powerful institutional and/or political and social and economic forces.

As for the first point, we find that the process of judicial review can have a peripheralizing effect on a federation—in other words, it can be centrifugal. According to Kenneth Wheare:

> In Canada . . . the net result of judicial interpretation has been to *restrict* the sphere of action of the general government. Here again it is important to emphasize that there are exceptions to the general statement. *But the trend of judicial review has been towards limiting the powers of the general government.*[82]

In view of what we know about the nature of the judicial process, this should not be too surprising. Some judges may have value positions favorable to greater centralization and others may be more favorably disposed to peripheralization. Thus, there is no particular direction inherent in the structure of judicial review itself; it all depends on the culture and the peculiar value mix of the judges through time and the precedents they have developed. If they are strongly oriented toward centralization and are heavily precedent-oriented, the reviewing body may present a rigidity that could endanger a federal system moving rapidly from situation B to situation A. If the judges are very situation-oriented in federal questions (high flexibility), the question arises why nonelected, politically remote judges should decide or are competent to resolve the value disputes inherent in (*a*) more or less centralization or (*b*) federation or no federation.

---

[82] Kenneth Wheare, *Federal Government,* 3rd ed. (London: Oxford University Press, 1953), p. 229 (emphasis mine).

As I have also suggested, another serious question can be raised as to the relative importance of any high court in the centralizing or peripheralizing processes in a political system. Other factors may well be far more potent. It probably depends on the composition of the whole system—structurally, politically, historically, and the like. Even in the American system, however, where so many of the experts believe the Court to play such a strong role in centralization, some grave reservations have been noted of late.[83] Riker's argument along these lines merits close attention.

> And in this century the *administrative centralization*, though partially occasioned by economic necessity, has usually been preceded and accompanied by exploitation of the President's military and diplomatic authority. Theodore Roosevelt, Wilson, Franklin Roosevelt, and Truman all used their military powers creatively and aggressively, often to accomplish what they could not accomplish by other means. All this is a story often told, however, so I see no need to repeat it here. Aside from the Presidency, *the other main centralizing institution is the Supreme Court. Many writers on federalism, especially those with a background in law, interpret the Court as the "arbiter of federalism"; i.e., the agency that decides on the pace and extent of centralization, and assert that the Court, by its gradual changing of the boundaries between the work of the states and the work of the nation, has been a major force for centralization.* This interpretation is on its face fallacious and could only come from an *overspecialized* view of the political process. The Court is an organization without much political or military force and therefore cannot be *expected to occasion or even to pace constitutional change. A more accurate way to interpret the role of the Court, which is by construction and its framers' probable intent admittedly a wholly centralized institution, is to say that the Court hastens the process of centralization when it is in phase with the ideology of the Presidency and cannot impede centralization when it is not.*[84]

Riker goes on to say:

> The Court is dependent on the Presidency for its renewal, but since the judges have life tenure, it is quite possible that at any particular time the ideological tone of the two institutions may be quite different. Four cases can be distinguished:
>
> 1. The President and the Court are striving for greater centralization.
> 2. The President and the Court are content to maintain the status quo.

---

[83] Francis H. Heller states that "Institutional arrangements cannot guard the balance of locality versus nation unless the political and electoral machinery function on a federal basis. . . . Therein lies more assurance for the continuance of federalism than in the attempts the Court might make to adjust and manipulate the delicate balance" ("The Supreme Court: Its Role in the Balance of the Federal System," *Journal of Public Law*, 6 [Spring, 1957], p. 330).

[84] Riker, *op. cit.*, p. 102 (emphasis mine).

3. The President is striving to centralize and the Court to maintain the status quo.
4. The President is content to maintain the status quo and the Court to centralize.

Examples of case 1 are the periods 1938–53 (Roosevelt and Truman); and 1790–95 (Washington); examples of case 2 are 1835–60 (the Taney Court) and 1869–1933 (the Republican dominance); examples of case 3 are 1861–65 (Civil War), 1933–37 (New Deal); and the only clear example of case 4 is to be found sporadically during the period 1801–34 (the Marshall Court).

The crucial question is about cases 3 and 4. *Can the Court resist the President's attempts to centralize and can the Court centralize when Presidents are not eager to do so?* A brief look at the examples demonstrates that the answer to both questions is negative. The Taney Court was powerless to inhibit Lincoln's military centralization and the Hughes Court was able to resist Roosevelt's centralization only for about two years. On the other hand, though Marshall made many bold pronouncements, the centralization that occurred in his era was mostly military, with which he had nothing to do. Economic centralization, in which he was interested, actually *declined during his period on the bench. It seems clear, therefore, that the Court has significance for federalism only when it is the handmaiden of the political branches, especially the Presidential branch.* And as a handmaiden, it is of only secondary importance for our analysis.[85]

In conclusion, then, though judicial review may have served some function for American federalism, it may well be overrated, it may well have passed its prime, and its functions may well have been performed by other institutions. It seems hard to justify its maintenance in our system on the basis of its alleged functioning for federalism. It seems harder to justify it for any other federal system because we have not begun to comprehend its functioning in past, present, and future America.

LEGITIMIZATION

One hypothesized function of judicial review receiving its share of political science attention of late is that of legitimization. As usual, an early and certainly the most celestial theoretical statement on this function flowed from the flowery pen of Cardozo. He put it this way:

By conscious or subconscious influence, the presence of this restraining power aloof in the background, but nonetheless always in reserve, tends to *stabilize* and *rationalize* the legislative judgment, to infuse

---

[85] *Ibid.*, pp. 102–3 (emphasis mine).

it with the glow of principle, to hold the standard aloft and visible for those who must run the race and keep the faith.[86]

By forsaking the heavenly in favor of the mundane, Shearer is clearer:

> The power of review, through its intrinsic dependence upon mandate, real or imagined, of the Constitution, serves to create an awareness amongst the populace of the paramount position of that charter within the political complex of the nation. The reinforced *reliance* upon an apparently stable law, in turn, has motivated within a vast body of our populace an abiding *faith* in the corresponding permanency of our government.[87]

One member of the current complement of Yale's law faculty is the main source of contemporary intrigue over this hypothesis. Allow me, then, to quote at some length from Professor Charles Black's view on this subject:

> Judicial review has two prime functions—that of imprinting governmental action with the stamp of legitimacy, and that of checking the political branches of government when these encroach on ground forbidden to them by the Constitution, as interpreted by the Court. These two functions are not independent of each other; on the contrary, they may be looked on as different aspects of the same function. The investment of a tribunal with the checking function almost necessarily makes it a legitimating organ as to those governmental actions (the great majority, in our history) to which it finds a convincing constitutional objection.[88]

In applying this to the American system he says:

> The American Government always has been and still is a government of limited power; it is idle speculation to guess whether our people would ever have accepted it on any other basis.
> . . . A government of limited powers faces a special problem in the legitimating of its actions; for a number of reasons, the task is of immense intricacy, theoretically almost insuperable. . . . The only humanly possible way to go about solving this problem (and it may or may not work) is to build a governing mechanism into the body of government itself, in the form of an institution charged with deciding on the legitimacy of actions. There are special requirements for such an agency.[89]

Black argues, it appears to me, that the Supreme Court of the United States, given its power of judicial review, by its very nature adds an air of legitimacy to the entire American system. When the Congress (or a state legislature) passes a law, the mere fact that it *could* be declared

---

[86] Cardozo, *op. cit.*, pp. 93–94 (emphasis mine).
[87] Alan Kent Shearer, "The Political Utility of Judicial Review," *University of Kansas Law Review*, 2 (1953–54), p. 589 (emphasis mine).
[88] Charles Black, *The People and the Court* (New York: Macmillan, 1960), p. 223.
[89] *Ibid.*, pp. 54–55.

unconstitutional is all that is necessary to inject legitimacy into that law. Black has powerful supporters for this argument, among them his colleague Alexander Bickel. In Bickel's view, "The truth is that the legitimating function is an inescapable, even if unintended, by-product of the checking function."[90] I think it should be clear by now that the "checking function" is simply a tautology with reference to the lexical definition of judicial review. They are one and the same thing; the "checking *function*" is the definition of the *structure* of judicial review. As a structural variable, it (judicial review or judicial checking) is supposed to legitimize. *Legitimization* is its function, but such a high-level abstraction leads to low levels of understanding. Fortunately, Cardozo and Shearer have developed some more concrete and therefore testable hypotheses. Black and Bickel remain mysterious. Cardozo and Shearer seem to be saying that judicial review lends (1) rationality in and (2) stability to the legislating process and are responsible for (3) public alertness to the meaning of constitutionality as well as some measure of (4) public faith in governmental permanence. These hypotheses are readily convertible into research designs.

At the legislative level, one could try to expose the way and degree to which a high court's power of judicial review is used by legislators. It may be employed symbolically in floor debate (the Court's expertise, etc.); it may be utilized as data in committee hearings (constitutional history); it may appear in the role expectations of legislators ("The Court should [or should not] oversee the legislature"). At the grass roots, one could inspect attitude and knowledge systems over entire spectrums of national communities. For want of more precise prose on their part, we can assume that this is what Black and Bickel think of the "air of legitimacy"; i.e., it is positively responsive attitudes, actions, and acknowledgments by officials and the people toward the role of government, judicial review, and specific Supreme Court decisions. Meanwhile, some of the modern breed of political scientists have instigated reasonably rigorous inquiries that have turned up data directly and indirectly pertinent to the above hypotheses.

The initial sally into legislative hypotheses was engineered by Harry Stumpf. Professor Stumpf was curious to learn whether the use of the Supreme Court as "our most important symbol of government" is indeed the font of legitimacy it is purported to be.[91] Once upon a time, Glendon Schubert pondered the difficulty Congress had in quashing Supreme Court

---

[90] Alexander Bickel, *The Least Dangerous Branch* (Indianapolis: Bobbs-Merrill, 1962), p. 29. It should be noted that Bickel, however, has also stated that the legitimating function "cannot be accepted as an independent justification for" judicial review. Still, he thinks legitimization "exists" (p. 30).

[91] Harry P. Stumpf, "The Political Efficacy of Judicial Symbolism," *Western Political Quarterly*, 19 (June, 1966), p. 294.

decisions; he observed that "many Congressmen are lawyers; and the argument that proponents of the amendatory bill are showing disrespect for the highest court in the land is an *effective* one."[92] The Supreme Court, then, with its power of judicial review, is believed to be the premier sign of legitimacy, and some Congressmen appeal to this legitimacy to ward off the evil designs of those who would reverse a Court decision. Professor Stumpf proceeded to look at reversal bills that were either passed or defeated, and he also looked to see if any of a variety of Court symbols were employed *effectively* in House and Senate floor debates between 1957 and 1961. His results on the use of the Supreme Court as a symbol in debate are shown in Table 5.

TABLE 5

Effectiveness of Use of Supreme Court as Symbol
in Congressional Debate, 1957–61

Disposition of Bills Debated	Use of Symbol	
	Absent or Very Low Frequency	Medium to High Frequency
Passed	35	5
Not passed	4	0

SOURCE: Harry P. Stumpf, "The Political Efficacy of Judicial Symbolism," *Western Political Quarterly,* 19 (June, 1966), pp. 67–68.

After applying the Fisher Exact Probability Test to this information, Stumpf states that "certainly there is no evidence in the present data that use of this symbol in debate on bills anti-Court in flavor or content in and of itself inhibits their passage."[93] Though this is not quite so, the evidence strongly favors this interpretation.[94] Thus, our first excursion into testing the legitimacy hypothesis leaves us feeling something less than euphoric.

If the Stumpf data create something of a credibility gap for the legislative aspect of the legitimacy-function hypothesis, the relevant data on the public aspect of it are enough to create an incredibility gap. At the outset, though, it may be helpful to go over the range of phenomena that must be observed to test fully the legitimacy function as it defines the consequences of judicial review on the public. It seems to me that legiti-

---

92 Glendon Schubert, *Constitutional Politics* (New York: Holt, Rinehart & Winston, 1960), pp. 257–58 (emphasis mine).

93 Stumpf, *op. cit.,* p. 303.

94 Glendon Schubert launched an attack on Professor Stumpf's methodology, to which Stumpf has issued a rejoinder. The details of this debate can be found in *Western Political Quarterly*, 20 (September, 1967), pp. 792–97.

mization must involve a connection between, on the one hand, a pre-conditioning set of attitudes and knowledge (potential legitimization) and, on the other, a different set of attitudes and knowledge in connection with certain behavior.

Legitimization requires that specific past Court decisions of constitutionality or unconstitutionality be known to the public, or at least to effective portions of it. And the public, or substantial or effective portions of it, must feel favorable toward these decisions. This implies, it seems to me, that the public is aware of the role of judicial review, which is to say that there must be some understanding of the traditional political operation of the Supreme Court in American politics. Further, this implies that among those who comprehend this Court role (judicial review), there is substantial positive feeling toward this role. We are dealing, in other words, with the existence and distribution of a certain unspecifiable level of knowledge and many attitudes relevant to this knowledge. In the words of Walter Murphy and Joseph Tanenhaus, this conception of legitimacy, in relation to the public, means that it must "quiet doubts and . . . promote acceptance."[95] Of course, even if studies were to demonstrate that all these elements appeared to an extremely high degree in the United States, this would still demonstrate only that the psychological *preconditions* for legitimacy existed; it would be demonstrative of only a potential legitimacy. For legitimization to occur, we would then have to find out that there was actual acceptance in the form of certain public attitudes and behavior toward then-current specific decisions of the Court, toward the specific composition of the Court (e.g., the Warren Court) and, most importantly, *toward government as a whole because of the existence of judicial review.*

Anyone familiar with studies of the American electorate is aware that the average American knows very little about specific past Supreme Court decisions, about the composition of the Court, or about the role of the Court. If "Most Americans are almost totally uninformed about legislative issues in Washington,"[96] it would be foolish to expect them to know very much detail on Supreme Court decisions or about the structure of judicial review. The data bear this out, at least tentatively.

Kenneth Dolbeare reanalyzed Gallup polls spanning approximately a twenty-year period, scrutinized the post-1964 election study of the Survey Research Center, and employed data from a 1966 survey of the adult population of the state of Wisconsin in order to examine, among other things,

---

95 Walter Murphy and Joseph Tanenhaus, "Constitutional Courts, Public Opinion and Political Representation" (report from the Laboratory for Political Research, Department of Political Science, University of Iowa, November, 1967), p. 17.

96 Angus Campbell, Philip E. Converse, Warren E. Miller, and Donald Stokes, *Elections and the Political Order* (New York: Wiley, 1966), p. 355. Cf. Angus Campbell *et al., The American Voter* (New York: Wiley, 1960), pp. 194–209.

the extent of public information on the Supreme Court.[97] Among his findings were the following: (*a*) In 1949, 14 percent of a sample of the American population didn't even know the name of the high court; (*b*) in 1945, 60 percent didn't know how many justices were supposed to be on the Court; (*c*) in 1945, upon Justice Roberts' retirement, a fabulous 4 percent of the population knew the number of Republican judges on the Court; (*d*) in the middle sixties, some 25 percent of the Wisconsinites surveyed knew that the Court had made decisions concerning the rights of defendants and 35 percent knew that the Court had made decisions concerning the redistricting of state legislatures. John Kessel, in his survey of attitudes toward the Court in the Seattle area, also found "a fairly low level of informational support for these (generalized, supportive) attitudes."[98] Of course, when the decisions are highly controversial and directly affect the personal interests of the average citizen, the public is more aware of the fact that judicial review is exercised, and more alert to what the Court has actually said. However, those who disapprove of the Court's actions and role are far more likely to know about specific Court decisions than are those who support the Court.

Walter Murphy and Joseph Tanenhaus, in a recent study that attempted to link information with attitudes relevant to the legitimacy function, noted that some 12.8 percent of the population knew a few names of Supreme Court justices, could give some vague articulation of the Court's judicial review role, and furnished a "diffuse" support as well. Fancy that. They do note, though, that this rather small group happens to be "politically attentive."[99] It would be unwise, I think, to suppose that attentiveness is linked with influence, and thence, under canons of elitist theory, to legitimizing the Court as an institution, much less the system as a whole. I fear that the Tanenhaus-Murphy finding does little to support the hypothesis of potential legitimization.

All of the studies of attitudes toward the Supreme Court itself (as an institution) interpret their data as demonstrating reasonably widespread general support for the Court, despite the fact that many who support the Court know little about its role, its decisions, or government in general. This, however, should not cause unbounded joy in the camp of the Cardozoans. Couldn't this vague, subliminal popular approval of the Supreme Court be due to the fact that people tend to support any

---

[97] Kenneth Dolbeare, "The Public Views the Supreme Court," in *Law, Politics, and the Federal Courts*, ed. Herbert Jacob (Boston: Little, Brown, 1967).

[98] John H. Kessel, "Public Perceptions of the Supreme Court," *Midwest Journal of Political Science*, 10 (May, 1966), p. 171.

[99] Walter Murphy and Joseph Tanenhaus, "Public Opinion and the United States Supreme Court," in *Frontiers of Judicial Research*, ed. Joel Grossman and Joseph Tanenhaus (New York: Wiley, 1969), p. 295.

established institution, particularly when it is as majestic and esoteric as the Court? This limp affection in no way means that the people who cherish it will back the Court specifically when it crosses swords with any other institution (federal, state, or local) or when it opposes their own personal interests. Along these lines, Murphy, Tanenhaus, and Dolbeare all note that more people repose trust in Congress than in the Court. Doesn't this seem to lend credence to the proposition that Congress is a greater legitimizing agency than the Court? In fact, Dolbeare notes that the Court even trails the President in public trust. According to Dolbeare: "The Court appears to be the only institution whose actions respondents, without further information, were prepared to question."[100]

The work that has focused on political attitudes and behavior as consequences of specific Supreme Court decisions yields even more grist for the mills of the doubters. Though there are not enough data yet reported to supply eager theorists with the raw material for a theory of judicial impact, there is fact aplenty to riddle any remaining faith in the validity of the legitimacy hypothesis. After all, if the Supreme Court cannot gain a legitimacy for its own decisions—and widespread defiance, evasion, and indifference indicate that it cannot—there is little hope that it can generate the spillover in general attitudes on government and behavior toward government implicit in the legitimization-function hypothesis. Why should people feel that a legislative act is legitimate because it can be reviewed by a high court when they don't even seem to feel that the Court's own decisions are legitimate, particularly as they conflict with their personal or organizational conceptions of right and wrong? That is what the impact studies are revealing, almost without exception. Whether we are dealing with the average restaurant owner in the South, or a local political official in his town, or a school superintendent in Tennessee, or any municipal policeman, or a neighborhood bookseller, the results form a regular pattern.

Jerome Skolnik notes the following about policemen's response to the exclusionary rule endorsed by the Supreme Court:

> The policeman perceives his job not simply as requiring that he arrest where he finds probable cause. In addition, he sees the need to be able to reconstruct a set of complex happenings in such a way that, subsequent to arrest, probable cause can be found according to appellate court standards. . . . Thus, the policeman respects the necessity for "complying" with the arrest laws. His "compliance," however, may take the form of *post hoc* manipulation of the facts rather than before-the-fact behavior.[101]

---

[100] Dolbeare, *op. cit.*, p. 197.
[101] Jerome Skolnik, *Justice without Trial* (New York: Wiley, 1966), pp. 214–15.

Based on an exhaustive inquiry into the impact of the *Miranda* decision on the New Haven police, a *Yale Law Journal* article noted the following:

> Despite increasing adherence to the letter of *Miranda,* however, both groups of detectives complied less readily with its spirit. By and large the detectives regarded giving the suspect this advice an artificial imposition on the natural flow of interrogation—an imposition for which they could see little reason. Most incorporated into their tactical repertoire some sort of hedging on the warnings, when they were given. Some changed the warning slightly. . . .[102]

Thus, the Court has enormous difficulty in appearing legitimate even to law-enforcement officers.

Its troubles with southern school administrators are well documented,[103] as is its ineptness even with federal district court judges in the South concerning the problem of racial integration.[104] Its record with school administrators on the question of religion in the public schools is not an enviable one, either. Frank Sorauf, for instance, noted widespread knowing evasion of the *McCollum* decision by Pennsylvania school superintendents.[105] Another, more recent research effort, this one into the patterns of noncompliance with the *School District* v. *Schempp* decision, showed that "of the 121 districts, 70 were reported to be still following the requirements of state law. The other 51 districts were reported to have made some changes in their policy but only one of these completely eliminated all Bible reading and devotional exercises."[106] Needless to say, the state law was in contradiction to the policy enunciated by the Court. The situation among nonofficials is equally bad. An interesting twelve-state study of booksellers by James Levine demonstrated that the content of the *Roth* case, as well as many state supreme court decisions that interpreted *Roth,* had little to do with the stocking of "obscene" literature in

---

[102] Michael Wald, Richard Ayres, David W. Hess, Mark Schantz, and Charles Whitebread II, "Interrogations in New Haven: The Impact of Miranda," *Yale Law Journal,* 76 (July, 1967), pp. 1551–52.

[103] Two of the best résumés of southern methods of avoiding the will of the Court are Robert B. McKay, " 'With All Deliberate Speed': A Study of School Desegregation," *New York University Law Review,* 31 (June, 1956), pp. 991–1090, and Albert Blaustein and Clarence Ferguson, *Desegregation and the Law* (New Brunswick: Rutgers University Press, 1957), chap. 15.

[104] See Jack Peltason, *Fifty-eight Lonely Men* (New York: Harcourt, Brace & World, 1961), and Kenneth N. Vines, "Federal District Judges and Race Relations Cases in the South," *Journal of Politics,* 26 (May, 1964), pp. 337–57.

[105] Frank J. Sorauf, "Zorach v. Clauson: The Impact of a Supreme Court Decision," *American Political Science Review,* 53 (September, 1959), pp. 777–91.

[106] Reprinted from "The Supreme Court and the Bible Belt: Tennessee Reaction to the 'Schempp' Decision," *Midwest Journal of Political Science,* 10 (August, 1966), p. 308, by Robert H. Birkby, by permission of the Wayne State University Press. Copyright © 1966 by the Wayne State University Press. The official citation for the case is 374 U.S. 203 (1963).

bookstores.[107] The cardinal factor was, quite clearly, the personal pre-disposition of the bookseller toward such literature, the Supreme Court and its decisions notwithstanding. According to Levine:

> Neither legal nor social forces can easily pierce the inner shell of personal prejudices, preferences, and inhibitions which seem to mo-tivate those who function as "gatekeepers" of public speech. The courts may command and the public may opine, but the bookseller is, by and large, the master of his own fate.[108]

And so it goes. Up to now, with one lone exception,[109] the impact studies indicate that the Supreme Court is too feeble to legitimate much of its own important action; one would suspect that it could not effectively legitimate actions of other governmental agencies by its own nonaction.

To date, only one study has attempted to test any aspect of the legiti-mization hypothesis as it might apply in another country. As we might have expected, David J. Danelski's investigation into the exercise of ju-dicial review by the Japanese Supreme Court does little to help revive the hypothesis.[110] Indeed, there is almost no legitimizing that this court could possibly accomplish, as the Japanese Supreme Court itself has extremely low visibility and, owing to the nature of Japanese legal culture, extra-ordinarily little prestige. Furthermore, there has as yet been no study done to determine whether the various preconditioning attitudes and post-decisional attitudes and behavior exist cross-culturally, to what extent, and in relationship to what conditions.

Conclusion

We have seen, then, that the most hypothesized preconditions for and functions of judicial review are subject to grave question. Indeed, there is much reason to doubt that judicial review necessarily arises or functions in the ways we have been led to believe. Yet the reader need not conclude

---

[107] James P. Levine, "Constitutional Law and Obscene Literature: An Investiga-tion of Bookseller Censorship Practices," in *The Impact of Supreme Court Decisions: Empirical Studies,* ed. Theodore L. Becker (New York: Oxford University Press, 1969), pp. 129–48.

[108] *Ibid.,* p. 148.

[109] Richard Johnson conducted an intensive study of "Eastville," a small mid-western town that, though religiously homogeneous and opposed to the Bible-reading prohibition, acceded to the Court's wishes. See his "Compliance and Supreme Court Decision-Making," *Wisconsin Law Review* (1967), pp. 170–85, and *The Dynamics of Compliance* (Evanston, Ill.: Northwestern University Press, 1967).

[110] David J. Danelski, "The People and the Court in Japan," in *Frontiers of Judi-cial Research,* ed. Tanenhaus and Grossman.

that the only functions judicial review can effectuate are illusory or negative, e.g., antidemocratic. For one thing, judicial review can keep voting
lines open (see the *Party Finance Case* in the Appendix to this chapter).
For another, it can protect individual rights, as it does structurally in Mexico and Colombia to a far greater degree than it seems to do in reality
in the United States. What I mean by this is that the wider accessibility in
these countries allows for potentially greater protection of individual rights
by the courts than seems actually to exist in America today. This is not to
deny that American courts probably rank among the leaders in supporting
liberty, though this support is more probably due to other structures in our
society (e.g., higher education) than to judicial review. Also, depending on
systemic and personnel circumstances, we have seen that a high court with
judicial review in a federal system can act as an arbiter or as a centralizing
instrument. What must be borne in mind is that judicial review does not
function *necessarily* in any specific way. I submit that its functioning depends not on its ideological place in the system, and not on its peculiar
structural characteristics; the functioning of judicial review depends on its
relationship to various social and political aspects (structures and goals) of
the entire societal system.

APPENDIX

Baker v. Carr
(U.S.A., 1961)

MR. JUSTICE BRENNAN delivered the opinion of the Court.

This civil action was brought under 42 U.S.C. § § 1983 and 1988 to redress the alleged deprivation of federal constitutional rights. The complaint, alleging that by means of a 1901 statute of Tennessee apportioning the members of the General Assembly among the State's 95 counties, "these plaintiffs and others similarly situated are denied the equal protection of the laws accorded them by the Fourteenth Amendment to the Constitution of the United States by virtue of the debasement of their votes," was dismissed by a three-judge court convened under 28 U.S.C. § 2281 in the Middle District of Tennessee. The court held that it lacked jurisdiction of the subject matter and also that no claim was stated upon which relief could be granted. . . . We noted probable jurisdiction of the appeal. . . . We hold that the dismissal was error, and remand the cause to the District Court for trial and further proceedings consistent with this opinion.

The General Assembly of Tennessee consists of the Senate with 33 members and the House of Representatives with 99 members. . . .

※　※　※

Tennessee's standard for allocating legislative representation among her counties is the total number of qualified voters resident in the respective counties, subject only to minor qualifications. Decennial reapportionment in compliance with the constitutional scheme was effected by the General Assembly each decade from 1871 to 1901. . . .

※　※　※

Between 1901 and 1961, Tennessee has experienced substantial growth and redistribution of her population. In 1901 the population was 2,020,616, of whom 487,380 were eligible to vote. The 1960 Federal Census reports the State's population at 3,567,089, of whom 2,092,891 are eligible to vote. The relative standings of the counties in terms of qualified voters have changed significantly. It is primarily the continued application of the 1901 Apportionment Act to this shifted and enlarged voting population which gives rise to the present controversy.

Indeed, the complaint alleges that the 1901 statute, even as of the time of its passage, "made no apportionment of Representatives and Senators in accordance with the constitutional formula . . . but instead arbitrarily and capriciously apportioned representatives in the Senate and House without reference . . . to any logical or reasonable formula whatever." It is further alleged that "because of the population changes since 1900, and the failure of the Legislature to reapportion itself since 1901," the 1901 statute became "unconstitutional and obsolete." . . . The complaint concludes that "these plaintiffs and others similarly

---

369 U.S. 186 (1961). Footnotes have been omitted.

situated are denied the equal protection of the laws accorded them by the Fourteenth Amendment to the Constitution of the United States by virtue of the debasement of their votes." They seek a declaration that the 1901 statute is unconstitutional and an injunction restraining the appellees from acting to conduct any further elections under it. They also pray that unless and until the General Assembly enacts a valid reapportionment, the District Court should either decree a reapportionment by mathematical application of the Tennessee constitutional formulae to the most recent Federal Census figures, or direct the appellees to conduct legislative elections, primary and general, at large. . . .

✿ ✿ ✿

The District Court was uncertain whether our cases withholding federal judicial relief rested upon a lack of federal jurisdiction or upon the inappropriateness of the subject matter for judicial consideration—what we have designated "nonjusticiability." The distinction between the two grounds is significant. In the instance of nonjusticiability, consideration of the cause is not wholly and immediately foreclosed; rather, the Court's inquiry necessarily proceeds to the point of deciding whether the duty asserted can be judicially identified and its breach judicially determined, and whether protection for the right asserted can be judicially molded. In the instance of lack of jurisdiction the cause either does not "arise under" the Federal Constitution, laws or treaties (or fall within one of the other enumerated categories of Art. III, § 2), or is not a "case or controversy" within the meaning of that section; or the cause is not one described by any jurisdictional statute. Our conclusion, see pp. 208–237, *infra,* that this cause presents no nonjusticiable "political question" settles the only possible doubt that it is a case or controversy. Under the present heading of "Jurisdiction of the Subject Matter" we hold only that the matter set forth in the complaint does arise under the Constitution and is within 28 U.S.C. § 1343.

Article III, § 2, of the Federal Constitution provides that "The judicial Power shall extend to all Cases, in Law and Equity, arising under this Constitution, the Laws of the United States, and Treaties made, or which shall be made, under their Authority. . . ." It is clear that the cause of action is one which "arises under" the Federal Constitution. The complaint alleges that the 1901 statute effects an apportionment that deprives the appellants of the equal protection of the laws in violation of the Fourteenth Amendment. Dismissal of the complaint upon the ground of lack of jurisdiction of the subject matter would, therefore, be justified only if that claim were "so attenuated and unsubstantial as to be absolutely devoid of merit." . . .

✿ ✿ ✿

Since the complaint plainly sets forth a case arising under the Constitution the subject matter is within the federal judicial power defined in Art. III, § 2 and so within the power of Congress to assign to the jurisdiction of the District Courts. Congress has exercised that power in 28 U.S.C. § 1343 (3):

> The district courts shall have original jurisdiction of any civil action authorized by law to be commenced by any person . . . [t]o redress the deprivation, under color of any State law, statute, ordinance, regulation, custom or usage, of any right, privilege or immunity secured by the Constitution of the United States. . . .

✿ ✿ ✿

In holding that the subject matter of this suit was not justiciable, the District Court relied on *Colegrove* v. *Green, supra,* and subsequent *per curiam* cases. The court stated: "From a review of these decisions there can be no doubt that the federal rule . . . is that the federal courts . . . will not intervene in cases of this type to compel legislative reapportionment." 179 F. Supp., at 826. We understand the District Court to have read the cited cases as compelling the conclusion that since the appellants sought to have a legislative apportionment held unconstitutional, their suit presented a "political question" and was therefore nonjusticiable. We hold that this challenge to an apportionment presents no nonjusticiable "political question." The cited cases do not hold the contrary.

Of course the mere fact that the suit seeks protection of a political right does not mean it presents a political question. Such an objection "is little more than a play upon words." *Nixon* v. *Herndon,* 273 U.S. 536, 540. Rather, it is argued that apportionment cases, whatever the actual wording of the complaint, can involve no federal constitutional right except one resting on the guaranty of a republican form of government, and that complaints based on that clause have been held to present political questions which are nonjusticiable.

We hold that the claim pleaded here neither rests upon nor implicates the Guaranty Clause and that its justiciability is therefore not foreclosed by our decisions of cases involving that clause. The District Court misinterpreted *Colegrove* v. *Green* and other decisions of this Court on which it relied. Appellants' claim that they are being denied equal protection is justiciable, and if "discrimination is sufficiently shown, the right to relief under the equal protection clause is not diminished by the fact that the discrimination relates to political rights." *Snowden* v. *Hughes,* 321 U.S. 1, 11. To show why we reject the argument based on the Guaranty Clause, we must examine the authorities under it. But because there appears to be some uncertainty as to why those cases did present political questions, and specifically as to whether this apportionment case is like those cases, we deem it necessary first to consider the contours of the "political question" doctrine.

Our discussion, even at the price of extending this opinion, requires review of a number of political question cases, in order to expose the attributes of the doctrine—attributes which, in various settings, diverge, combine, appear, and disappear in seeming disorderliness. Since that review is undertaken solely to demonstrate that neither singly nor collectively do these cases support a conclusion that this apportionment case is nonjusticiable, we of course do not explore their implications in other contexts. That review reveals that in the Guaranty Clause cases and in the other "political question" cases, it is the relationship between the judiciary and the coordinate branches of the Federal Government, and not the federal judiciary's relationship to the States, which gives rise to the "political question."

We have said that "In determining whether a question falls within [the political question] category, the appropriateness under our system of government of attributing finality to the action of the political departments and also the lack of satisfactory criteria for a judicial determination are dominant considerations." *Coleman* v. *Miller,* 307 U.S. 433, 454–455. The nonjusticiability of a political question is primarily a function of the separation of powers. Much confusion results from the capacity of the "political question" label to obscure the need for case-by-case inquiry. Deciding whether a matter has in any measure been committed by the Constitution to another branch of government, or whether the action of that branch exceeds whatever authority has been committed, is itself a delicate exercise in constitutional interpretation, and is a responsibility of this Court as ultimate interpreter of the Constitution. To demonstrate this requires no less than to analyze representative cases and to infer from them the analytical threads that make up the political question doctrine. We shall then show that none of those threads catches this case.

* * *

We come, finally, to the ultimate inquiry whether our precedents as to what constitutes a nonjusticiable "political question" bring the case before us under the umbrella of that doctrine. A natural beginning is to note whether any of the common characteristics which we have been able to identify and label descriptively are present. We find none: The question here is the consistency of state action with the Federal Constitution. We have no question decided, or to be decided, by a political branch of government coequal with this Court. Nor do we risk embarrassment of our government abroad or grave disturbance at home if we take issue with Tennessee as to the constitutionality of her action here challenged. Nor need the appellants, in order to succeed in this action, ask the Court to enter upon policy determinations for which judicially manageable standards are lacking. Judicial standards under the Equal Protection Clause are well developed and familiar, and it has been open to courts since the enactment of the Fourteenth Amendment to determine, if on the particular facts they must, that a discrimination reflects *no* policy, but simply arbitrary and capricious action.

This case does, in one sense, involve the allocation of political power within a State, and the appellants might conceivably have added a claim under the Guaranty Clause. Of course, as we have seen, any reliance on that clause would be futile. But because any reliance on the Guaranty Clause could not have succeeded it does not follow that appellants may not be heard on the equal protection claim which in fact they tender. True, it must be clear that the Fourteenth Amendment claim is not so enmeshed with those political question elements which render Guaranty Clause claims nonjusticiable as actually to present a political question itself. But we have found that not to be the case here.

* * *

We conclude then that the nonjusticiability of claims resting on the Guaranty Clause which arises from their embodiment of questions that were thought "political" can have no bearing upon the justiciability of the equal protection claim presented in this case. Finally, we emphasize that it is the involvement in Guaranty Clause claims of the elements thought to define "political questions," and no other feature, which could render them nonjusticiable. Specifically, we have said that such claims are not held nonjusticiable because they touch matters of state governmental organization.

* * *

We conclude that the complaint's allegations of a denial of equal protection present a justiciable constitutional cause of action upon which appellants are entitled to a trial and a decision. The right asserted is within the reach of judicial protection under the Fourteenth Amendment.

The judgment of the District Court is reversed and the cause is remanded for further proceedings consistent with this opinion.

Reversed and remanded.

Keshav Singh v. Uttar Pradesh
(India, 1964)

The Legislative Assembly of the State of Uttar Pradesh committed one Keshav Singh, who was not one of its members, to prison for its contempt. The warrant of committal did not contain the facts constituting the alleged contempt. While undergoing imprisonment for the committal, Keshav Singh through his Advocate moved a petition under Art. 226 of the Constitution and s. 491 of the Code of Criminal Procedure, challenging his committal as being in breach of his fundamental rights; he also prayed for interim bail. The High Court (Lucknow Bench) gave notice to the Government Counsel who accepted it on behalf of all the respondents including the Legislative Assembly. At the time fixed for the hearing of the bail application the Government Counsel did not appear. Beg and Saghal JJ. who heard the application ordered that Keshav Singh be released on bail pending the decision of his petition under Art. 226. The Legislative Assembly found that Keshav Singh and his Advocate in moving the High Court, and the two Judges of the High Court in entertaining the petition and granting bail, had committed contempt of the Assembly, and passed a resolution that all of them be produced before it in custody. The Judges and the Advocate thereupon filed writ petitions before the High Court at Allahabad and a Full Bench of the High Court admitted their petitions and ordered the stay of the execution of the Assembly's resolution against them. The Assembly then passed a clarificatory resolution which modified its earlier stand. Instead of being produced in custody, the Judges and the Advocate were asked to appear before the House and offer their explanation.

At this stage the President of India made a Reference under Art. 143(1) of the Constitution in which the whole dispute as to the constitutional relationship between the High Court and the State Legislature, including the question whether on the facts of the case Keshav Singh, his Advocate, and the two Judges, by their respective acts, were guilty of contempt of the State Legislature, was referred to the Supreme Court for its opinion and report.

At the hearing of the Reference a preliminary objection as to the competency of the Reference was raised on behalf of the Advocate-General of Bihar, on the ground that it did not relate to any of the matters covered by the President's powers and duties under the Constitution. It was also urged that even if the Reference was competent, the Court should not answer it as it was not obliged to do so, and the answers given by it would not help the President in solving any of the difficulties with which he might be faced in discharging his duties. The Court did not accept these contentions and proceeded to hear the parties which fell, broadly, into two groups—those supporting the Assembly and those supporting the High Court.

On behalf of the Assembly it was urged that by virtue of Art. 194(3) of the Constitution all the powers, privileges, and immunities of the House of Commons of the United Kingdom had been conferred on it. It was the sole judge of its privileges and the Courts had no jurisdiction to interfere with their exercise. In the alternative, it was contended that Courts in England never interfered with a committal by the House of Commons for contempt when the committal was by a general warrant, *i.e.*, a warrant which did not state the facts constituting the con-

---

1 S.C.R. 413 (1964). Footnotes have been omitted.

tempt, and, therefore, Courts in India were also precluded from examining the legality of the general warrants of the State Legislatures. The proceedings in the High Court in the present case were, therefore, in contempt of the legislature.

Those supporting the stand taken by the High Court urged that the Legislatures received the powers of the House of Commons subject to provisions of the Constitution and to the fundamental rights, that the power to commit by general warrant was not one of the privileges of the House of Commons, that by virtue of Articles 226 and 32, the citizen had the right to move the Courts when his fundamental rights were contravened, and that because of the provisions in Art. 211, the Legislature was precluded from taking any action against the Judges.

* * *

GAJENDRAGADKAR C. J. This is Special Reference No. 1 of 1964 by which the President has formulated five questions for the opinion of this Court under Article 143(1) of the Constitution. The Article authorises the President to refer to this Court questions of law or fact which appear to him to have arisen or are likely to arise and which are of such a nature and of such public importance that it is expedient to obtain the opinion of the Supreme Court upon them. Article 143(1) provides that when such questions are referred to this Court by the President, the Court may, after such hearing as it thinks fit, report to the President its opinion thereon. In his Order of Reference made on March 26, 1964, the President has expressed his conclusion that the questions of law set out in the Order of Reference are of such a nature and of such public importance that it is expedient that the opinion of the Supreme Court of India should be obtained thereon.

* * *

The questions referred to this Court under this Reference read as follows:

(1) Whether, on the facts and circumstances of the case, it was competent for the Lucknow Bench of the High Court of Uttar Pradesh, consisting of the Hon'ble Mr. Justice N. U. Beg and the Hon'ble Mr. Justice G. D. Sahgal, to entertain and deal with the petition of Mr. Keshav Singh challenging the legality of the sentence of imprisonment imposed upon him by the Legislative Assembly of Uttar Pradesh for its contempt and for infringement of its privileges and to pass orders releasing Mr. Keshav Singh on bail pending the disposal of his said petition;

(2) Whether, on the facts and circumstances of the case, Mr. Keshav Singh, by causing the petition to be presented on his behalf to the High Court of Uttar Pradesh as aforesaid, Mr. B. Solomon, Advocate, by presenting the said petition, and the said two Hon'ble Judges, by entertaining and dealing with the said petition and ordering the release of Shri Keshav Singh on bail pending disposal of the said petition, committed contempt of the Legislative Assembly of Uttar Pradesh;

(3) Whether, on the facts and circumstances of the case, it was competent for the Legislative Assembly of Uttar Pradesh to direct the production of the said two Hon'ble Judges and Mr. B. Solomon, Advocate, before it in custody or to call for their explanation for its contempt;

(4) Whether, on the facts and circumstances of the case, it was competent for the Full Bench of the High Court of Uttar Pradesh to entertain and deal with the petitions of the said two Hon'ble Judges and Mr. B. Solomon, Advocate, and to pass interim orders restraining

the Speaker of the Legislative Assembly of Uttar Pradesh and other respondents to the said petitions from implementing the aforesaid direction of the said Legislative Assembly; and

(5) Whether a Judge of a High Court who entertains or deals with a petition challenging any order or decision of a Legislature imposing any penalty on the petitioner or issuing any process against the petitioner for its contempt or for infringement of its privileges and immunities or who passes any order on such petition commits contempt of the said Legislature and whether the said Legislature is competent to take proceedings against such a Judge in the exercise and enforcement of its powers, privileges and immunities.

At the hearing of this Reference, Mr. Varma has raised a preliminary objection on behalf of the Advocate-General of Bihar. He contends that the present Reference is invalid under Art. 143(1) because the questions referred to this Court are not related to any of the entries in Lists I and III and as such, they cannot be said to be concerned with any of the powers, duties, or functions conferred on the President by the relevant articles of the Constitution. The argument appears to be that it is only in respect of matters falling within the powers, functions and duties of the President that it would be competent to him to frame questions for the advisory opinion of this Court under Art. 143(1). In our opinion, this contention is wholly misconceived. The words of Art. 143(1) are wide enough to empower the President to forward to this Court for its advisory opinion any question of law or fact which has arisen or which is likely to arise, provided it appears to the President that such a question is of such a nature or of such public importance that it is expedient to obtain the opinion of this Court upon it. It is quite true that under Art. 143(1) even if questions are referred to this Court for its advisory opinion, this Court is not bound to give such advisory opinion in every case.

* * *

It is hardly necessary to emphasise that the questions of law which have been forwarded to this Court on the present occasion are of very great constitutional importance. The incidents which have given rise to this Reference posed a very difficult problem and unless further developments in pursuance of the orders passed by the two august bodies were arrested, they were likely to lead to a very serious and difficult situation. That is why the President took the view that a case for reference for the advisory opinion of this Court had been established and he accordingly formulated five questions and has forwarded the same to us for our advisory opinion. . . .

* * *

That takes us to the merits of the controversy disclosed by the questions formulated by the President for our advisory opinion. . . .

Though the ultimate solution of the problem posed by the questions before us would . . . lie within a very narrow compass, it is necessary to deal with some wider aspects of the problem which incidentally arise and the decision of which will assist us in rendering our answers to the questions framed in the present Reference. The whole of the problem thus presented before us has to be decided in the light of the provisions contained in Art. 194(3) of the Constitution, and in that sense, the interpretation of Art. 194(3) is really the crux of the matter. At this stage, it is necessary to read Article 194:

194. (1) Subject to the provisions of this Constitution and to the rules and standing orders regulating the procedure of the Legislature, there shall be freedom of speech in the Legislature of every State.

(2) No member of the Legislature of a State shall be liable to any proceedings in any court in respect of anything said or any vote given by him in the Legislature or any committee thereof, and no person shall be so liable in respect of the publication by or under the authority of a House of such a Legislature of any report, paper, votes, or proceedings.

(3) In other respects, the powers, privileges and immunities of a House of the Legislature of a State, and of the members and the committees of a House of such Legislature, shall be such as may from time to time be defined by the Legislature by law, and, until so defined, shall be those of the House of Commons of Parliament of the United Kingdom, and of its members and committees, at the commencement of this Constitution.

(4) The provisions of clauses (1), (2) and (3) shall apply in relation to persons who by virtue of this Constitution have the right to speak in, and otherwise to take part in the proceedings of, a House of the Legislature of a State or any committee thereof as they apply in relation to members of that Legislature.

* * *

Our Legislatures have undoubtedly plenary powers, but these powers are controlled by the basic concepts of the written Constitution itself and can be exercised within the legislative fields allotted to their jurisdiction by the three Lists under the Seventh Schedule; but beyond the Lists, the Legislatures cannot travel. They can no doubt exercise their plenary legislative authority and discharge their legislative functions by virtue of the powers conferred on them by the relevant provisions of the Constitution; but the basis of the power is the Constitution itself. Besides, the legislative supremacy of our Legislatures including the Parliament is normally controlled by the provisions contained in Part III of the Constitution. If the Legislatures step beyond the legislative fields assigned to them, or acting within their respective fields, they trespass on the fundamental rights of the citizens in a manner not justified by the relevant articles dealing with the said fundamental rights, their legislative actions are liable to be struck down by courts in India. Therefore, it is necessary to remember that though our Legislatures have plenary powers, they function within the limits prescribed by the material and relevant provisions of the Constitution.

In a democratic country governed by a written Constitution, it is the Constitution which is supreme and sovereign. It is no doubt true that the Constitution itself can be amended by the Parliament, but that is possible because Art. 368 of the Constitution itself makes a provision in that behalf, and the amendment of the Constitution can be validly made only by following the procedure prescribed by the said article. That shows that even when the Parliament purports to amend the Constitution, it has to comply with the relevant mandate of the Constitution itself. Legislators, Ministers, and Judges all take oath of allegiance to the Constitution, for it is by the relevant provisions of the Constitution that they derive their authority and jurisdiction and it is to the provisions of the Constitution that they owe allegiance. Therefore, there can be no doubt that the sovereignty which can be claimed by the Parliament in England cannot be claimed by any Legislature in India in the literal absolute sense.

There is another aspect of this matter which must also be mentioned; whether or not there is distinct and rigid separation of powers under the Indian Constitution, there is no doubt that the Constitution has entrusted to the Judicature in this country the task of construing the provisions of the Constitution and of safeguarding the fundamental rights of the citizens. When a statute is challenged on the ground that it has been passed by a Legislature without authority, or has otherwise unconstitutionally trespassed on fundamental rights, it is for the courts to determine the dispute and decide whether the law passed by the legislature is valid or not. Just as the legislatures are conferred legislative authority and their functions are normally confined to legislative functions, and the functions and authority of the executive lie within the domain of executive authority, so the jurisdiction and authority of the Judicature in this country lie within the domain of adjudication. If the validity of any law is challenged before the courts, it is never suggested that the material question as to whether legislative authority has been exceeded or fundamental rights have been contravened can be decided by the legislatures themselves. Adjudication of such a dispute is entrusted solely and exclusively to the Judicature of this country; and so, we feel no difficulty in holding that the decision about the construction of Art. 194(3) must ultimately rest exclusively with the Judicature of this country. That is why we must overrule Mr. Seervai's argument that the question of determining the nature, scope and effect of the powers of the House cannot be said to lie exclusively within the jurisdiction of this Court. This conclusion, however, would not impair the validity of Mr. Seervai's contention that the advisory opinion rendered by us in the present Reference proceedings is not adjudication properly so-called and would bind no parties as such.

In coming to the conclusion that the content of Art. 194(3) must ultimately be determined by courts and not by the legislatures, we are not unmindful of the grandeur and majesty of the task which has been assigned to the Legislatures under the Constitution. Speaking broadly, all the legislative chambers in our country today are playing a significant role in the pursuit of the ideal of a Welfare State which has been placed by the Constitution before our country, and that naturally gives the legislative chambers a high place in the making of history today. The High Courts also have to play an equally significant role in the development of the rule of law and there can be little doubt that the successful working of the rule of law is the basic foundation of the democratic way of life. In this connection it is necessary to remember that the status, dignity and importance of these two respective institutions, the Legislatures and the Judicature, are derived primarily from the status, dignity and importance of the respective causes that are assigned to their charge by the Constitution. These two august bodies, as well as the Executive, which is another important constituent of a democratic State, must function not in antinomy nor in a spirit of hostility, but rationally, harmoniously and in a spirit of understanding within their respective spheres, for such harmonious working of the three constituents of the democratic State alone will help the peaceful development, growth and stabilisation of the democratic way of life in this country.

❖   ❖   ❖

As we have indicated at the outset of this opinion, the crux of the matter is the construction of the latter part of Art. 194(3), and in the light of the assistance which we must derive from the other relevant and material provisions of the Constitution, it is necessary to hold that the particular power claimed by the House, that its general warrants must be held to be conclusive, cannot be deemed to be the subject-matter of the latter part of Art. 194(3). In this connection, we may incidentally observe that it is somewhat doubtful whether the power to issue a general unspeaking warrant claimed by the House is consistent with s. 554(2)(b) and s. 555 of the Code of Criminal Procedure. . . .

Before we part with this topic, there are two general considerations to which we ought to advert. It has been urged before us by Mr. Seervai that the right claimed by the House to issue a conclusive general warrant in respect of contempt is an essential right for the effective functioning of the House itself, and he has asked us to deal with this matter from this point of view. It is true that this right appears to have been recognised by courts in England by agreement or convention or by considerations of comity; but we think it is strictly not accurate to say that every democratic legislature is armed with such a power. Take the case of the American Legislatures. Article 1, section 5 of the American Constitution does not confer on the American Legislature such a power at all. It provides that each House shall be the judge of the Elections, Returns and Qualifications of its own Members, and a majority of each shall constitute a quorum to do business; but a small number may adjourn from day to day, and may be authorised to compel the attendance of absent Members, in such manner, and under such penalties as each House may provide. Each House may determine the Rules of its proceedings, punish its Members for disorderly behaviour, and, with the concurrence of two-thirds, expel a Member. Contempt committed outside the four walls of the legislative chamber by a citizen who is not a Member of the House seems to be outside the jurisdiction of the American Legislature. As Willis has observed, punishment for contempt is clearly a judicial function; yet in the United States, Congress may exercise the power to punish for contempt as it relates to keeping order among its own members, to compelling their attendance, to protecting from assaults or disturbances by others (except by slander and libel), to determining election cases and impeachment charges, and to exacting information about other departments in aid of the legislative function. Nobody has ever suggested that the American Congress has not been functioning effectively because it has not been armed with the particular power claimed by the House before us.

In India, there are several State Legislatures in addition to the Houses of Parliament. If the power claimed by the House before us is conceded, it is not difficult to imagine that its exercise may lead to anomalous situations. If by virtue of the absolute freedom of speech conferred on the Members of the Legislatures, a Member of one Legislature makes a speech in his legislative chamber which another legislative chamber regards as amounting to its contempt, what would be the position? The latter legislative chamber can issue a general warrant and punish the Member alleged to be in contempt, and a free exercise of such power may lead to very embarrassing situations. That is one reason why the Constitution-makers thought it necessary that the Legislatures should in due course enact laws in respect of their powers, privileges and immunities, because they knew that when such laws are made, they would be subject to the fundamental rights and would be open to examination by the courts in India. Pending the making of such laws, powers, privileges and immunities were conferred by the latter part of Art. 194(3). As we have already emphasised, the construction of this part of the article is within the jurisdiction of this Court, and in construing this part, we have to bear in mind the other relevant and material provisions of the Constitution. . . .

Before we part with this topic, we would like to refer to one aspect of the question relating to the exercise of power to punish for contempt. So far as the courts are concerned, Judges always keep in mind the warning addressed to them by Lord Atkin in *Andre Paul* v. *Attorney-General of Trinidad*. Said Lord Atkin, "Justice is not a cloistered virtue; she must be allowed to suffer the scrutiny and respectful even though out-spoken comments of ordinary men." We ought never to forget that the power to punish for contempt, large as it is, must always be exercised cautiously, wisely and with circumspection. Frequent or indiscriminate use of this power in anger or irritation would not help to sustain the dignity or status of the court, but may sometimes affect it adversely. Wise Judges never forget that the best way to sustain the dignity and status of their office is to deserve respect from the public at large by the quality of their judgments, the fearlessness, fairness and objectivity of their approach, and by the restraint, dignity and decorum which they observe in their judicial conduct. We venture to think that what is true of the Judicature is equally true of the Legislatures.

Having thus discussed all the relevant points argued before us and recorded our conclusions on them, we are now in a position to render our answers to the five questions referred to us by the President. Our answers are:

> (1) On the facts and circumstances of the case, it was competent for the Lucknow Bench of the High Court of Uttar Pradesh, consisting of N. U. Beg and G. D. Sahgal JJ., to entertain and deal with the petition of Keshav Singh challenging the legality of the sentence of imprisonment imposed upon him by the Legislative Assembly of Uttar Pradesh for its contempt and for infringement of its privileges and to pass orders releasing Keshav Singh on bail pending the disposal of his said petition.

> (2) On the facts and circumstances of the case, Keshav Singh, by causing the petition to be presented on his behalf to the High Court of Uttar Pradesh as aforesaid, Mr. B. Solomon, Advocate, by presenting the said petition, and the said two Hon'ble Judges, by entertaining and dealing with the said petition and ordering the release of Keshav Singh on bail pending disposal of the said petition, did not commit contempt of the Legislative Assembly of Uttar Pradesh.

> (3) On the facts and circumstances of the case, it was not competent for the Legislative Assembly of Uttar Pradesh to direct the production of the said two Hon'ble Judges and Mr. B. Solomon, Advocate, before it in custody or to call for their explanation for its contempt.

> (4) On the facts and circumstances of the case, it was competent for the Full Bench of the High Court of Uttar Pradesh to entertain and deal with the petitions of the said two Hon'ble Judges and Mr. B. Solomon, Advocate, and to pass interim orders restraining the Speaker of the Legislative Assembly of Uttar Pradesh and other respondents to the said petitions from implementing the aforesaid direction of the said Legislative Assembly; and

> (5) In rendering our answer to this question, which is very broadly worded, we ought to preface our answer with the observation

that the answer is confined to cases in relation to contempt alleged to have been committed by a citizen who is not a member of the House outside the four walls of the legislative chamber. A Judge of a High Court who entertains or deals with a petition challenging any order or decision of a Legislature imposing any penalty on the petitioner or issuing any process against the petitioner for its contempt, or for infringement of its privileges and immunities, or who passes any order on such petition, does not commit contempt of the said Legislature; and the said Legislature is not competent to take proceedings against such a Judge in the exercise and enforcement of its powers, privileges and immunities. In this answer, we have deliberately omitted reference to infringement of privileges and immunities of the House which may include privileges and immunities other than those with which we are concerned in the present Reference.

Youngstown Sheet and Tube Co. v. *Sawyer*
(U.S.A., 1952)

MR. JUSTICE BLACK delivered the opinion of the Court.

We are asked to decide whether the President was acting within his constitutional power when he issued an order directing the Secretary of Commerce to take possession of and operate most of the Nation's steel mills. The mill owners argue that the President's order amounts to lawmaking, a legislative function which the Constitution has expressly confided to the Congress and not to the President. The Government's position is that the order was made on findings of the President that his action was necessary to avert a national catastrophe which would inevitably result from a stoppage of steel production, and that in meeting this grave emergency the President was acting within the aggregate of his constitutional powers as the Nation's Chief Executive and the Commander in Chief of the Armed Forces of the United States. The issue emerges here from the following series of events:

In the latter part of 1951, a dispute arose between the steel companies and their employees over terms and conditions that should be included in new collective bargaining agreements. Long-continued conferences failed to resolve the dispute. On December 18, 1951, the employees' representative, United Steelworkers of America, C.I.O., gave notice of an intention to strike when the existing bargaining agreements expired on December 31. The Federal Mediation and Conciliation Service then intervened in an effort to get labor and management to agree. This failing, the President on December 22, 1951, referred the dispute to the Federal Wage Stabilization Board to investigate and make recommendations for fair and equitable terms of settlement. This Board's report resulted in no settlement. On April 4, 1952, the Union gave notice of a nation-wide strike called to begin at 12:01 A.M. April 9. The indispensability of steel as a component of substantially all weapons and other war materials led the President to believe that the proposed work stoppage would immediately jeopardize

---

343 U.S. 579 (1952). Edited with the assistance of David Engels. Footnotes have been omitted.

our national defense and that governmental seizure of the steel mills was necessary in order to assure the continued availability of steel. Reciting these considerations for his action, the President, a few hours before the strike was to begin, issued Executive Order 10340. . . . The order directed the Secretary of Commerce to take possession of most of the steel mills and keep them running. The Secretary immediately issued his own possessory orders, calling upon the presidents of the various seized companies to serve as operating managers for the United States. They were directed to carry on their activities in accordance with regulations and directions of the Secretary. The next morning the President sent a message to Congress reporting his action. Cong. Rec., April 9, 1952, p. 3962. Twelve days later he sent a second message. Cong. Rec., April 21, 1952, p. 4192. Congress has taken no action.

Obeying the Secretary's orders under protest, the companies brought proceedings against him in the District Court. Their complaints charged that the seizure was not authorized by an act of Congress or by any constitutional provisions. The District Court was asked to declare the orders of the President and the Secretary invalid and to issue preliminary and permanent injunctions restraining their enforcement. Opposing the motion for preliminary injunction, the United States asserted that a strike disrupting steel production for even a brief period would so endanger the well-being and safety of the Nation that the President had "inherent power" to do what he had done—power "supported by the Constitution, by historical precedent, and by court decisions." . . .

❈   ❈   ❈

The President's power, if any, to issue the order must stem either from an act of Congress or from the Constitution itself. There is no statute that expressly authorizes the President to take possession of property as he did here. Nor is there any act of Congress to which our attention has been directed from which such a power can fairly be implied. Indeed, we do not understand the Government to rely on statutory authorization for this seizure. There are two statutes which do authorize the President to take both personal and real property under certain conditions. However, the Government admits that these conditions were not met and that the President's order was not rooted in either of the statutes. The Government refers to the seizure provisions of one of these statutes (§ 201 [b] of the Defense Production Act) as "much too cumbersome, involved, and time-consuming for the crisis which was at hand."

Moreover, the use of the seizure technique to solve labor disputes in order to prevent work stoppages was not only unauthorized by any congressional enactment; prior to this controversy, Congress had refused to adopt that method of settling labor disputes. When the Taft-Hartley Act was under consideration in 1947, Congress rejected an amendment which would have authorized such governmental seizures in cases of emergency. Apparently it was thought that the technique of seizure, like that of compulsory arbitration, would interfere with the process of collective bargaining. Consequently, the plan Congress adopted in that Act did not provide for seizure under any circumstances. Instead, the plan sought to bring about settlements by use of the customary devices of mediation, conciliation, investigation by boards of inquiry, and public reports. In some instances temporary injunctions were authorized to provide cooling-off periods. All this failing, unions were left free to strike after a secret vote by employees as to whether they wished to accept their employers' final settlement offer.

It is clear that if the President had authority to issue the order he did, it must be found in some provision of the Constitution. And it is not claimed that express constitutional language grants this power to the President. The contention is that presidential power should be implied from the aggregate of his powers under the Constitution. Particular reliance is placed on provisions in Article II which say that "The executive Power shall be vested in a President . . ."; that "he shall take Care that the Laws be faithfully executed"; and that he "shall be Commander in Chief of the Army and Navy of the United States."

The order cannot properly be sustained as an exercise of the President's military power as Commander in Chief of the Armed Forces. The Government attempts to do so by citing a number of cases upholding broad powers in military commanders engaged in day-to-day fighting in a theater of war. Such cases need not conern us here. Even though "theater of war" be an expanding concept, we cannot with faithfulness to our constitutional system hold that the Commander in Chief of the Armed Forces has the ultimate power as such to take possession of private property in order to keep labor disputes from stopping production. This is a job for the Nation's lawmakers, not for its military authorities.

Nor can the seizure order be sustained because of the several constitutional provisions that grant executive power to the President. In the framework of our Constitution, the President's power to see that the laws are faithfully executed refutes the idea that he is to be a lawmaker. The Constitution limits his functions in the lawmaking process to the recommending of law he thinks wise and the vetoing of laws he thinks bad. And the Constitution is neither silent nor equivocal about who shall make laws which the President is to execute. The first section of the first article says that "All legislative Powers herein granted shall be vested in a Congress of the United States. . . ." After granting many powers to the Congress, Article I goes on to provide that Congress may "make all Laws which shall be necessary and proper for carrying into Execution the foregoing Powers, and all other Powers vested by this Constitution in the Government of the United States, or in any Department or Officer thereof."

The President's order does not direct that a congressional policy be executed in a manner prescribed by Congress—it directs that a presidential policy be executed in a manner prescribed by the President. The preamble of the order itself, like that of many statutes, sets out reasons why the President believes certain policies should be adopted, proclaims these policies as rules of conduct to be followed, and again, like a statute, authorizes a government official to promulgate additional rules and regulations consistent with the policy proclaimed and needed to carry that policy into execution. The power of Congress to adopt such public policies as those proclaimed by the order is beyond question. It can authorize the taking of private property for public use. It can make laws regulating the relationships between employers and employees, prescribing rules designed to settle labor disputes, and fixing wages and working conditions in certain fields of our economy. The Constitution does not subject this lawmaking power of Congress to presidential or military supervision or control.

It is said that other Presidents without congressional authority have taken possession of private business enterprises in order to settle labor disputes. But even if this be true, Congress has not thereby lost its exclusive constitutional authority to make laws necessary and proper to carry out the powers vested by the Constitution "in the Government of the United States, or any Department or Officer thereof."

The Founders of this Nation entrusted the lawmaking power to the Congress alone in both good and bad times. It would do no good to recall the historical events, the fears of power and the hopes for freedom that lay behind their choice. Such a review would but confirm our holding that this seizure order cannot stand.

The judgment of the District Court is

Affirmed.

MR. JUSTICE FRANKFURTER, concurring.

Although the considerations relevant to the legal enforcement of the principle of separation of powers seem to me more complicated and flexible than may appear from what Mr. Justice Black has written, I join his opinion because I thoroughly agree with the application of the principle to the circumstances of this case. Even though such differences in attitude toward this principle may be merely differences in emphasis and nuance, they can hardly be reflected by a single opinion for the Court. Individual expression of views in reaching a common result is therefore important.

＊　　＊　　＊

It is not a pleasant judicial duty to find that the President has exceeded his powers and still less so when his purposes were dictated by concern for the Nation's well-being, in the assured conviction that he acted to avert danger. But it would stultify one's faith in our people to entertain even a momentary fear that the patriotism and the wisdom of the President and the Congress, as well as the long view of the immediate parties in interest, will not find ready accommodation for differences on matters which, however close to their concern and however intrinsically important, are overshadowed by the awesome issues which confront the world. When at a moment of utmost anxiety President Washington turned to this Court for advice, and he had to be denied it as beyond the Court's competence to give, Chief Justice Jay, on behalf of the Court, wrote thus to the Father of his Country:

> We exceedingly regret every event that may cause embarrassment to your administration, but we derive consolation from the reflection that your judgment will discern what is right, and that your usual prudence, decision, and firmness will surmount every obstacle to the preservation of the rights, peace, and dignity of the United States. [Letter of August 8, 1793, 3 Johnston, Correspondence and Public Papers of John Jay (1891), 489].

In reaching the conclusion that conscience compels, I too derive consolation from the reflection that the President and the Congress between them will continue to safeguard the heritage which comes to them straight from George Washington.

MR. JUSTICE DOUGLAS, concurring.

＊　　＊　　＊

If we sanctioned the present exercise of power by the President, we would be expanding Article II of the Constitution and rewriting it to suit the political conveniences of the present emergency. Article II which vests the "executive Power" in the President defines that power with particularity. Article II, Section 2 makes the Chief Executive the Commander in Chief of the Army and Navy.

But our history and tradition rebel at the thought that the grant of military power carries with it authority over civilian affairs. Article II, Section 3 provides that the President shall "from time to time give to the Congress Information of the State of the Union, and recommend to their Consideration such Measures as he shall judge necessary and expedient." The power to recommend legislation, granted to the President, serves only to emphasize that it is his function to recommend and that it is the function of the Congress to legislate. Article II, Section 3 also provides that the President "shall take Care that the Laws be faithfully executed." But, as Mr. Justice Black and Mr. Justice Frankfurter point out, the power to execute the laws starts and ends with the laws Congress has enacted.

* * *

We pay a price for our system of checks and balances, for the distribution of power among the three branches of government. It is a price that today may seem exorbitant to many. Today a kindly President uses the seizure power to effect a wage increase and to keep the steel furnaces in production. Yet tomorrow another President might use the same power to prevent a wage increase, to curb trade-unionists, to regiment labor as oppressively as industry thinks it has been regimented by this seizure.

MR. JUSTICE JACKSON, concurring.

That comprehensive and undefined presidential powers hold both practical advantages and grave dangers for the country will impress anyone who has served as legal adviser to a President in time of transition and public anxiety. While an interval of detached reflection may temper teachings of that experience, they probably are a more realistic influence on my views than the conventional materials of judicial decision which seem unduly to accentuate doctrine and legal fiction. But as we approach the question of presidential power, we half overcome mental hazards by recognizing them. The opinions of judges, no less than executives and publicists, often suffer the infirmity of confusing the issue of a power's validity with the cause it is invoked to promote, of confounding the permanent executive office with its temporary occupant. The tendency is strong to emphasize transient results upon policies—such as wages or stabilization—and lose sight of enduring consequences upon the balanced power structure of our Republic.

* * *

I have no illusion that any decision by this Court can keep power in the hands of Congress if it is not wise and timely in meeting its problems. A crisis that challenges the President equally, or perhaps primarily, challenges Congress. If not good law, there was worldly wisdom in the maxim attributed to Napoleon that "The tools belong to the man who can use them." We may say that power to legislate for emergencies belongs in the hands of Congress, but only Congress itself can prevent power from slipping through its fingers.

The essence of our free Government is "leave to live by no man's leave, underneath the law"—to be governed by those impersonal forces which we call law. Our Government is fashioned to fulfill this concept so far as humanly possible. The Executive, except for recommendation and veto, has no legislative power. The executive action we have here originates in the individual will of the President and represents an exercise of authority without law. No one, perhaps not even the President, knows the limits of the power he may seek to exert in this instance and the parties affected cannot learn the limit of their rights. We do not know today what powers over labor or property would be claimed to flow from Government possession if we should legalize it, what rights to compensation would be claimed or recognized, or on what contingency it would end. With all its defects, delays and inconveniences, men have discovered no technique for long preserving free government except that the Executive be under the law, and that the law be made by parliamentary deliberations.

Such institutions may be destined to pass away. But it is the duty of the Court to be last, not first, to give them up.

✿   ✿   ✿

MR. JUSTICE CLARK, concurring.

✿   ✿   ✿

The limits of presidential power are obscure. However, Article II, no less than Article I, is part of "a constitution intended to endure for ages to come, and, consequently, to be adapted to the various *crises* of human affairs." Some of our Presidents, such as Lincoln, "felt that measures otherwise unconstitutional might become lawful by becoming indispensable to the preservation of the Constitution through the preservation of the nation." Others, such as Theodore Roosevelt, thought the President to be capable, as a "steward" of the people, of exerting all power save that which is specifically prohibited by the Constitution or the Congress. In my view—taught me not only by the decision of Mr. Chief Justice Marshall in *Little* v. *Barreme*, but also by a score of other pronouncements of distinguished members of this bench—the Constitution does grant to the President extensive authority in times of grave and imperative national emergency. In fact, to my thinking, such a grant may well be necessary to the very existence of the Constitution itself. As Lincoln aptly said, "[Is] it possible to lose the nation and yet preserve the Constitution?" In describing this authority I care not whether one calls it "residual," "inherent," "moral," "implied," "aggregate," "emergency," or otherwise. I am of the conviction that those who have had the gratifying experience of being the President's lawyer have used one or more of these adjectives only with the utmost of sincerity and the highest of purpose.

I conclude that where Congress has laid down specific procedures to deal with the type of crisis confronting the President, he must follow those procedures in meeting the crisis; but that in the absence of such action by Congress, the President's independent power to act depends upon the gravity of the situation confronting the nation. I cannot sustain the seizure in question because here, as in *Little* v. *Barreme*, Congress had prescribed methods to be followed by the President in meeting the emergency at hand.

Watkins v. United States
(U.S.A., 1957)

MR. CHIEF JUSTICE WARREN delivered the opinion of the Court.

This is a review by certiorari of a conviction under 2 U.S.C. § 192 for "contempt of Congress." The misdemeanor is alleged to have been committed during a hearing before a congressional investigating committee. It is not the case of a truculent or contumacious witness who refuses to answer all questions or who, by boisterous or discourteous conduct, disturbs the decorum of the committee room. Petitioner was prosecuted for refusing to make certain disclosures which he asserted to be beyond the authority of the committee to demand. The controversy thus rests upon fundamental principles of the power of the Congress and the limitations upon that power. We approach the questions presented with conscious awareness of the far-reaching ramifications that can follow from a decision of this nature.

*   *   *

Petitioner's name had been mentioned by two witnesses who testified before the Committee at prior hearings. In September 1952, one Donald O. Spencer admitted having been a Communist from 1943 to 1946. He declared that he had been recruited into the Party with the endorsement and prior approval of petitioner, whom he identified as the then District Vice-President of the Farm Equipment Workers. Spencer also mentioned that petitioner had attended meetings at which only card-carrying Communists were admitted. A month before petitioner testified, one Walter Rumsey stated that he had been recruited into the Party by petitioner. Rumsey added that he had paid Party dues to, and later collected dues from, petitioner, who had assumed the name Sam Brown. Rumsey told the Committee that he left the Party in 1944.

Petitioner answered these allegations freely and without reservation. . . .

*   *   *

Rumsey had identified a group of persons whom he had known as members of the Communist Party, and counsel began to read this list of names to petitioner. Petitioner stated that he did not know several of the persons. Of those whom he did know, he refused to tell whether he knew them to have been members of the Communist Party. He explained to the Subcommittee why he took such a position:

> I am not going to plead the fifth amendment, but I refuse to answer certain questions that I believe are outside the proper scope of your committee's activities. I will answer any questions which this committee puts to me about myself. I will also answer questions about those persons whom I knew to be members of the Communist Party and whom I believe still are. I will not, however, answer any questions with respect to others with whom I associated in the past. I do not believe that any law in this country requires me to testify about persons who may in the past have been Communist Party members or otherwise engaged in Communist Party activity but who to my best knowledge and belief have long since removed themselves from the Communist movement.
>
> I do not believe that such questions are relevant to the work of this committee nor do I believe that this committee has the right to undertake the public exposure of persons because of their past activities. I may be wrong, and the committee may have this power, but until and unless a court of law so holds and directs me to answer, I most firmly refuse to discuss the political activities of my past associates.

---

354 U.S. 178 (1957). Edited with the assistance of David Engels. All footnotes have been omitted save one, which has been renumbered.

The Chairman of the Committee submitted a report of petitioner's refusal to answer questions to the House of Representatives. . . . The House directed the Speaker to certify the Committee's report to the United States Attorney for initiation of criminal prosecution. . . . A seven-count indictment was returned. Petitioner waived his right to jury trial and was found guilty on all counts by the court. . . .

We start with several basic premises on which there is general agreement. The power of the Congress to conduct investigations is inherent in the legislative process. That power is broad. It encompasses inquiries concerning the administration of existing laws as well as proposed or possibly needed statutes. It includes surveys of defects in our social, economic or political system for the purpose of enabling the Congress to remedy them. It comprehends probes into departments of the Federal Government to expose corruption, inefficiency or waste. But, broad as is this power of inquiry, it is not unlimited. There is no general authority to expose the private affairs of individuals without justification in terms of the functions of the Congress. This was freely conceded by the Solicitor General in his argument of this case. Nor is the Congress a law enforcement or trial agency. These are functions of the executive and judicial departments of government. No inquiry is an end in itself; it must be related to, and in furtherance of, a legitimate task of the Congress. Investigations conducted solely for the personal aggrandizement of the investigators or to "punish" those investigated are indefensible.

It is unquestionably the duty of all citizens to cooperate with the Congress in its efforts to obtain the facts needed for intelligent legislative action. It is their unremitting obligation to respond to subpoenas, to respect the dignity of the Congress and its committees and to testify fully with respect to matters within the province of proper investigation. This, of course, assumes that the constitutional rights of witnesses will be respected by the Congress as they are in a court of justice. The Bill of Rights is applicable to investigations as to all forms of governmental action. Witnesses cannot be compelled to give evidence against themselves. They cannot be subjected to unreasonable search and seizure. Nor can the First Amendment freedoms of speech, press, religion, or political belief and association be abridged.

❋   ❋   ❋

Clearly, an investigation is subject to the command that the Congress shall make no law abridging freedom of speech or press or assembly. While it is true that there is no statute to be reviewed, and that an investigation is not a law, nevertheless an investigation is part of lawmaking. It is justified solely as an adjunct to the legislative process. The First Amendment may be invoked against infringement of the protected freedoms by law or by lawmaking.

Abuses of the investigative process may imperceptibly lead to abridgment of protected freedoms. The mere summoning of a witness and compelling him to testify, against his will, about his beliefs, expressions or associations is a measure of governmental interference. And when those forced revelations concern matters that are unorthodox, unpopular, or even hateful to the general public, the reaction in the life of the witness may be disastrous. This effect is even more harsh when it is past beliefs, expréssions or associations that are disclosed and judged by current standards rather than those contemporary with the matters exposed. Nor does the witness alone suffer the consequences.

Those who are identified by witnesses and thereby placed in the same glare of publicity are equally subject to public stigma, scorn and obloquy. Beyond that, there is the more subtle and immeasurable effect upon those who tend to adhere to the most orthodox and uncontroversial views and associations in order to avoid a similar fate at some future time. That this impact is partly the result of non-governmental activity by private persons cannot relieve the investigators of their responsibility for initiating the reaction.

The Court recognized the restraints of the Bill of Rights upon congressional investigations in *United States* v. *Rumely*, 345 U.S. 41. The magnitude and complexity of the problem of applying the First Amendment to that case led the Court to construe narrowly the resolution describing the committee's authority. It was concluded that, when First Amendment rights are threatened, the delegation of power to the committee must be clearly revealed in its charter.

Accommodation of the congressional need for particular information with the individual and personal interest in privacy is an arduous and delicate task for any court. We do not underestimate the difficulties that would attend such an undertaking. It is manifest that despite the adverse effects which follow upon compelled disclosure of private matters, not all such inquiries are barred. *Kilbourn* v. *Thompson* teaches that such an investigation into individual affairs is invalid if unrelated to any legislative purpose. That is beyond the powers conferred upon the Congress in the Constitution. . . .

Petitioner has earnestly suggested that the difficult questions of protecting these rights from infringement by legislative inquiries can be surmounted in this case because there was no public purpose served in his interrogation. His conclusion is based upon the thesis that the Subcommittee was engaged in a program of exposure for the sake of exposure. The sole purpose of the inquiry, he contends, was to bring down upon himself and others the violence of public reaction because of their past beliefs, expressions and associations. In support of this argument, petitioner has marshalled an impressive array of evidence that some Congressmen have believed that such was their duty, or part of it.[1]

We have no doubt that there is no congressional power to expose for the sake of exposure. The public is, of course, entitled to be informed concerning

---

[1] In a report to the House, the Committee declared:

"While Congress does not have the power to deny to citizens the right to believe in, teach, or advocate communism, fascism, and naziism, it does have the right to focus the spotlight of publicity upon their activities. . . . " H. R. Rep. No. 2, 76th Cong., 1st Sess. 13.

A year later, the Committee reported that ". . . investigation to inform the American people . . . is the real purpose of the House Committee." H. R. Rep. No. 1476, 76th Cong., 3d Sess. 1–2.

A pamphlet issued by the Committee in 1951 stated that: "Exposure in a systematic way began with the formation of the House Committee on Un-American Activities, May 26, 1938." The Committee believed itself commanded ". . . to expose people and organizations attempting to destroy this country. That is still its job and to that job it sticks." 100 Things You Should Know About Communism, H. R. Doc. No. 136, 82d Cong., 1st Sess. 19, 67.

In its annual reports, the Committee has devoted a large part of its information to a public listing of names along with a summary of their activities. ". . . [T]he committee feels that the Congress and the American people will have a much clearer and fuller picture of the success and scope of communism in the United States by having set forth the names and, where possible, the positions occupied by individuals who have been identified as Communists, or former Communists, during the past year." H. R. Rep. No. 2516, 82d Cong., 2d Sess. 6–7.

the workings of its government. That cannot be inflated into a general power to expose where the predominant result can only be an invasion of the private rights of individuals. But a solution to our problem is not to be found in testing the motives of committee members for this purpose. Such is not our function. Their motives alone would not vitiate an investigation which had been instituted by a House of Congress if that assembly's legislative purpose is being served.

Petitioner's contentions do point to a situation of particular significance from the standpoint of the constitutional limitations upon congressional investigations. The theory of a committee inquiry is that the committee members are serving as the representatives of the parent assembly in collecting information for a legislative purpose. Their function is to act as the eyes and ears of the Congress in obtaining facts upon which the full legislature can act. To carry out this mission, committees and subcommittees, sometimes one Congressman, are endowed with the full power of the Congress to compel testimony. In this case, only two men exercised that authority in demanding information over petitioner's protest.

An essential premise in this situation is that the House or Senate shall have instructed the committee members on what they are to do with the power delegated to them. It is the responsibility of the Congress, in the first instance, to insure that compulsory process is used only in furtherance of a legislative purpose. That requires that the instructions to an investigating committee spell out that group's jurisdiction and purpose with sufficient particularity. Those instructions are embodied in the authorizing resolution. That document is the committee's charter. Broadly drafted and loosely worded, however, such resolutions can leave tremendous latitude to the discretion of the investigators. The more vague the committee's charter is, the greater becomes the possibility that the committee's specific actions are not in conformity with the will of the parent House of Congress.

*   *   *

It is, of course, not the function of this Court to prescribe rigid rules for the Congress to follow in drafting resolutions establishing investigating committees. That is a matter peculiarly within the realm of the legislature, and its decisions will be accepted by the courts up to the point where their own duty to enforce the constitutionally protected rights of individuals is affected. An excessively broad charter, like that of the House Un-American Activities Committee, places the courts in an untenable position if they are to strike a balance between the public need for a particular interrogation and the right of citizens to carry on their affairs free from unnecessary governmental interference. It is impossible in such a situation to ascertain whether any legislative purpose justifies the disclosures sought and, if so, the importance of that information to the Congress in furtherance of its legislative function. The reason no court can make this critical judgment is that the House of Representatives itself has never made it. Only the legislative assembly initiating an investigation can assay the relative necessity of specific disclosures.

Absence of the qualitative consideration of petitioner's questioning by the House of Representatives aggravates a serious problem, revealed in this case, in the relationship of congressional investigating committees and the witnesses who appear before them. Plainly these committees are restricted to the missions delegated to them, *i.e.*, to acquire certain data to be used by the House or the Senate in coping with a problem that falls within its legislative sphere. No witness can be compelled to make disclosures on matters outside that area. This is a jurisdictional concept of pertinency drawn from the nature of a congressional committee's source of authority. It is not wholly different from nor unrelated to the element of pertinency embodied in the criminal statute under which petitioner was prosecuted. When the definition of jurisdictional pertinency is as uncertain and wavering as in the case of the Un-American Activities Committee, it becomes extremely difficult for the Committee to limit its inquiries to statutory pertinency.

o o o

Unless the subject matter has been made to appear with undisputable clarity, it is the duty of the investigative body, upon objection of the witness on grounds of pertinency, to state for the record the subject under inquiry at that time and the manner in which the propounded questions are pertinent thereto. To be meaningful, the explanation must describe what the topic under inquiry is and the connective reasoning whereby the precise questions asked relate to it.

The statement of the Committee Chairman in this case, in response to petitioner's protest, was woefully inadequate to convey sufficient information as to the pertinency of the questions to the subject under inquiry. Petitioner was thus not accorded a fair opportunity to determine whether he was within his rights in refusing to answer, and his conviction is necessarily invalid under the Due Process Clause of the Fifth Amendment.

We are mindful of the complexities of modern government and the ample scope that must be left to the Congress as the sole constitutional depository of legislative power. Equally mindful are we of the indispensable function, in the exercise of that power, of congressional investigations. The conclusions we have reached in this case will not prevent the Congress, through its committees, from obtaining any information it needs for the proper fulfillment of its role in our scheme of government. The legislature is free to determine the kinds of data that should be collected. It is only those investigations that are conducted by use of compulsory process that give rise to a need to protect the rights of individuals against illegal encroachment. That protection can be readily achieved through procedures which prevent the separation of power from responsibility and which provide the constitutional requisites of fairness for witnesses. A measure of added care on the part of the House and the Senate in authorizing the use of compulsory process and by their committees in exercising that power would suffice.

The Party Finance Case
(West Germany, 1966)

Judgment of the Second Senate of July 19, 1966, following oral argument held on April 19–21, 1966, in the proceeding concerning the constitutionality of Paragraph 1 of the Federal Budget Law of March 18, 1965, which appropriates for fiscal year 1965, pursuant to Section 06, Chapter 02, Title 612, the sum of 38 million DM [$9.5 million] to political parties for the execution of their tasks under Article 21 of the Basic Law. *Petitioner*: The Government of the State of Hesse, represented by its Minister-President.

Decision of July 19, 1966, West German Federal Constitutional Court (Second Senate). From the official reports: *Entscheidungen des Bundesverfassungsgerichts*

HOLDING OF THE COURT

Paragraph 1 of the Budget Law of March 18, 1965, is void in so far as Section 06, Chapter 02, Title 612 authorizes the Federal Minister of Interior to disburse 38 million DM [$9.5 million] to the parties for the purpose of fulfilling their tasks under Article 21 of the Basic Law.

The motion of the Hesse State Government is accepted.

I. In its decision of June 24, 1958, the Federal Constitutional Court declared that political parties are basically election organizations and that their financial resources are to be used mainly for the support of election campaigns. Because an election is a public function and, moreover, since political parties are expressly commissioned by the Basic Law to carry out this function, it is constitutionally permissible to use public [state] funds not only for the actual conduct of elections, but also for the support of those political parties involved in the electoral process. These declarations of the Court might well be interpreted, as they have been, by federal and state governments, as rendering it constitutionally permissible to appropriate state funds for the general support of the political parties. The proceedings in this case, however, have convinced the Court that the allocation of state subsidies to the parties for their *general* activity in the area of forming both public opinion and the political will of the people is incompatible with Article 21 and Article 20, paragraph 2, of the Basic Law. Such subsidies are in fact allocated under Section 06, Chapter 02, Title 612, of the Federal Budget Law for 1965. The specific text of this title says: "Special funds for party functions under Article 21 of the Basic Law." Thus, the parties are to obtain subsidies for their general political activity. This violates the Basic Law. Paragraph 1 of the 1965 Budget Law, is therefore, invalid since it empowers the Federal Minister of Interior to disburse 38 million DM [$9.5 million] to the political parties. It is, however, compatible with the Basic Law to finance political parties for the purpose of assisting them in forming the political will of the people through parliamentary elections; but such support may only embrace necessary campaign costs.

II. 1. When the authors of the Basic Law created the liberal democratic basic order, they opted for a free and open process of forming the opinion and the will of the people. State financing of general party activity is incompatible with this decision.

a) The right of free expression guaranteed by Article 5 of the Basic Law—freedom of press, radio, television, and motion pictures—is a necessary element of a liberal democratic state order. Article 5 ·also guarantees the free formation of public opinion. The fundamental right to engage in the political process is derived from the basic right of free expression. Freedom of opinion, freedom to form associations, freedom of assembly and the right to petition are intended to secure the freedom to form the opinion and the will of the people. Articles 21, 38, and 28 of the Basic Law constitute additional safeguards of

(Tübingen: J. C. B. Mohr [Paul Siebeck], 1967), vol. 20, pp. 56–119. The decision in this case has been translated by Donald P. Kommers, University of Notre Dame, and is reproduced here with his permission. Citations have been omitted. Italics throughout are the translator's.

the right freely to form the will of the people. The attitudes, political ideas, and views embodied in public opinion have been described as the "raw materials" [*Vorformung*] out of which the political will of the people is formed. In a democratic commonwealth, especially, the forming of the political will of the people must be free, open, and unregimented. . . . This process finds its most definitive expression in parliamentary elections. The forming of the will of the people and forming of the will of the state through its constitutional organs must be distinguished. This distinction is actually grounded in the Basic Law. Article 21, paragraph 1, of the Basic Law speaks of the forming of the will of the *people;* Article 20, paragraph 2, of the Basic Law concerns the forming of the will of the *state.* Only when the people exercise state authority as an organ of the Constitution or as a *Kreationsorgan* by means of elections and voting does the concept of forming the people's will merge with the forming of the will of the state.

The expression of the people's will, however, is not solely confined to elections and voting. The citizen's right to participate in forming the political will also takes the form of influencing public opinion. First of all, public opinion, whose origin is not to be explained here, influences the decisions made by the organs of the state. Furthermore, groups and associations of various kinds seek to influence governmental decisions in the interest of their members. Above all, however, are the political parties which influence the decisions of the constitutional organs between elections, particularly those of Parliament; in so doing, not only do parties shape the opinion of the people, but they also influence the forming of the will of the state. Through the parties, whose internal organization must conform to democratic principles, the people also influence, between elections, the decisions of the constitutional organs. Indeed, numerous relationships, contingencies, and interests are involved in the complex process of forming public opinion and the people's will.

But these processes interlock in several ways. In a democracy the formation of the public will must flow from the people to the organs of the state, and not the other way around; that is, from the organs of the state to the people. The organs of the state derive their authority from the will of the people as expressed in elections. This means that the organs of the state must not themselves form the opinion and will of the people; indeed, this is a process that must remain free of state influence. The influence of governmental organs and legislative bodies upon the process of opinion formation is consistent with the democratic principle of a free political process—meaning that authority-influence must flow from the people to the state—only in very special or constitutionally justified instances.

Thus, for example, an electoral law may be devised to organize the political will of the people in a given way. The public relations work of government agencies is also unobjectionable so long as it seeks objectively to explain and present to the public the policies and purposes of government programs, or to describe the problems to be resolved by them in the future.

b) The relations between the organs of the state and political parties are particularly bound by the constitutional requirement of a free and open political process in which authority flows from the people to the organs of the state.

aa) The state is not obliged to concern itself with the financial relations between the constitutional organs and political parties, nor to see that the financial needs of the parties are satisfied, nor to employ financial means to balance the competitive situation among those parties seeking to influence the forming of the opinion and will of the people.

A state obligation to support the parties financially cannot be derived from the fact that the parties actually cooperate in the process of forming the people's political will and, therefore, assume the function of a constitutional organ, or from the fact that they have been described as an organ of the state, namely as a *Kreationsorgan* in the sense that George Jellinek uses the term.

Article 21 recognizes political parties as indispensable instruments for the construction of the political will of the people and treats them as constitutional organs. . . . Political parties, however, are not included among the *highest* organs of the state. Rather, they are voluntary organizations firmly rooted in the socio-political structure; they do, however, cooperate in forming the people's political will and, of course, function within the organized state. But parties are not integral parts of the organized state; therefore, the state is not obliged to finance them.

bb) Political parties *cooperate* in forming the political will of the people mainly through their participation in elections, which could not be carried on without them. Beyond this, of course, they constitute a link between the individual and the state, and therefore serve as instruments through which the will of citizens can be realized between elections. . . . To the extent that they support the government, they constitute a link between the people and the political leadership. When they are in the minority they constitute the political opposition, and make it effective. As intermediaries the parties assist in forming public opinion. They represent the attitudes, opinions, and interests of men oriented to political power and its exercise; moreover, parties tend to offset one another as they seek to form the public will. In modern mass democracies political parties exercise decisive influence upon those occupying the highest offices of the state. Thus, they influence the forming of the will of the state as they operate within the state's far-flung institutional apparatus, particularly where the committees and proceedings of Parliament are concerned.

The constitutional requirement that the opinions and will of the people be formed openly and freely, so that the will of the state is derived from the will of the people, imposes limits upon the role of parties, forbidding them to function as institutions of the organized state.

The entire, or even partial, subsidization of political parties out of state funds cannot be squared with the Basic Law. Partial funding of parties through yearly or monthly allocations for their general political activity would not actually transform the parties into state institutions, but would force them across the boundary that separates state from nonstate institutions. Such financing would enable the state to influence the parties and thus to influence the forming of the political will of the people. No constitutional argument can be advanced to support this development. The party finance law of 1965 is therefore unconstitutional. In so ruling, the Court is not obliged here to determine whether the law actually encroaches upon the freedom of parties which is guaranteed by Article 21, or whether it contravenes the basic principle of the equal opportunity of political parties.

(1) The use of state funds for the general support of the parties cannot be justified because Article 21 recognizes them as constitutionally essential instruments for forming the people's political will, or because it treats political

parties as constitutional organs. In other words, constitutional recognition of the parties' role in the democratic process of forming public opinion and the political will of the people does not mean that the state may finance parties for the purpose of performing this role.

(2) Nor is it possible to justify such financing on the ground that without state support the parties would be unable to fulfill their functions. This argument implies doubts about the capacity and readiness of the ordinary citizen voluntarily to support party organizations and to render them effective instruments of political expression. The argument also questions the democratic state order [regarding the role of parties] assumed by the Constitution; today, as in times past, such doubt stems from a historically conditioned or deep-seated aversion to parties in contemporary society, or from an indifference toward parties on the part of many citizens. Moreover, it cannot be shown that the parties would have been unable to fulfill their tasks had they not begun to receive state subsidies in 1959. In any case, the Constitution has not relieved the parties of the risks involved in their own self-financing. Liberal democracy, on principle, assigns the task of forming the political will to the judgment and activity of individual citizens.

(3) It does not follow, moreover, that because members of Parliament receive daily allowances and party factions in the Parliament receive state stipends [to perform their legislative functions], political parties are entitled to state funds for the purpose of carrying on their political activity.

The legislator occupies a state office. Daily allowances are intended to secure his freedom of decision—even against his parliamentary faction and extraparliamentary party organization—so that he can freely exercise the rights and duties required of him by his constitutional status [as a representative of the whole people]. The right to daily allowances is a material parliamentary right. Daily allowances are supported and justified by the principle of "liberal representative democracy." Such allowances for parliamentary representatives were in fact already sanctioned by Article 85 of the Prussian Constitution of January 31, 1850, just as they were in other state constitutions of this period, as well as by Article 95 of the Frankfurt Republican Constitution of 1849. The prohibition of such allowances under Article 32 of the Imperial Constitution of 1871 actually constituted a step backward in [the development of] representative parliamentarianism in the second half of the nineteenth century; from the struggle to nullify this prohibition, which did not succeed until 1906, no parallelism can be drawn to support the validity of party financing, which was actually foreign to [the concept of] a developing representative parliamentary government.

No more convincing is the argument that state funds for general party support are nothing more than expenditures to be used by parliamentary factions for the purpose of carrying out their legislative responsibilities. Parliamentary factions are constituent and permanent members of the Bundestag, are acknowledged in the order of the day, and are vested with their own [parliamentary] rights. They are necessary institutions of our "constitutional life," since their activity takes place in the Bundestag, while their proceedings are regulated by the Constitution and order of the day. The factions, to a certain degree, must take charge of and, accordingly, lighten the technical burdens in Parliament. It is only because party factions are permanent members of the Bundestag, not because they are parts of political parties, that they are justified, for example, in bringing suits to this court under its *Organstreit* jurisdiction. As members of the Bundestag they are part of the organized state. Therefore, subsidies may be granted to them.

It is true that party factions are closely bound to the political parties, and that the latter, especially those represented in Parliament, influence their members in Parliament as well as the policies of the state. But the fact remains that party factions in Parliament enjoy a different status than the political parties which function *within* the organized state.

It would indeed be an alarming abuse of the Constitution if Parliament were to allocate funds to the factions which are not justified by their actual parliamentary needs; this would, in effect, constitute a concealed party finance law.

(4) The financing of parties out of public funds for their ordinary political activity—as this inquiry has shown—cannot, moreover, be justified by the argument that it would render the parties less dependent than before on private sources of income and the decision of a committee of the Second Senate, June 22, 1960.

Article 21 of the Basic Law secures the freedom of the parties from the state, and does not protect them from the influence of financially powerful individuals, employers, or associations. Article 21, paragraph 1, clause 4, of the Basic Law, which commands the political parties to give a public accounting of the origin of their funds, is evidence of the fact that the Basic Law neither approves nor forbids influence that is frequently sought by means of large private contributions to the parties; instead, it accepts this rather common form of interest-group support of the parties on condition that the sources of these contributions are made public. The Constitution does not distinguish between proper and improper financing. The line between proper and improper influences upon a free political process is elusive. It is chiefly the responsibility of the parties to distinguish between legitimate and harmful financial influence, and to resist the improper pressures of special interests. Freedom from such pressure is not secured in the Basic Law. At the same time, we should recognize that not all large contributions to the parties are linked with an attempt to influence party decisions.

In requiring the parties to give a public accounting of their funds the authors of the Basic Law intended "to prevent abuses in party financing by seeing to it that the public receives proper information concerning the origin of party funds, so that it is clear who stands behind a political group." The framers sought to prevent anonymous interests from using their financial power "to control public opinion in devious ways and thus indirectly to acquire substantial political power" and secure influence over the forming of the public will. The constitutional requirement concerning this matter seeks to render the process of forming the political will of the people entirely visible to the voter and to disclose the identity of those groups, organizations, or private persons seeking political influence over the parties by means of their financial contributions. This provision [of the Basic Law] seeks to place these contributions—by means of which financial contributors enlarge the recruiting possibilities of a party and, accordingly, enable a party to increase its own influence —under the control of publicity. At the same time the equal opportunity of political parties should be secured. It is true that the legislature has not yet implemented this mandate of the Basic Law.

(5) The duty publicly to account for the source of their funds guarantees that the parties will carry out their constitutionally sanctioned role of cooperating in freely forming the political will of the people. The Constitution does not require the corresponding disclosure of funds received by various groups and associations. The Basic Law says nothing about this. Public financing of parties cannot, therefore, be justified on the ground that state subsidies are available to certain social groups, organizations, and societies. Organizations of this sort do indeed influence public opinion and the decisions of governmental agencies. The free play of organized interests vis-à-vis the state as well as the parties is an element of a free political process, guaranteed by Article 9 of the Basic Law. These groups, however, are not like political parties; they cannot be considered as *Kreationsorgane*. The former, therefore, may receive state subsidies for economic, social, and cultural purposes that the state recognizes as worthy of support. Such assistance, however, has little to do with the principle of a free *political* process. On the other hand, state subsidies to political parties, as provided in the 1965 budget law, do disturb this principle. It cannot, therefore, be concluded that state support of these various social groups and organizations is justification for state financial support of political parties.

2. To finance out of state funds all the political activity of the parties does not correspond to the intent of the framers of Article 21 of the Basic Law. This provision should in fact obviate the inconsistencies that existed under the Weimar Constitution between political reality and written constitutional law. Article 21 of the Basic Law has, however, changed nothing concerning the prevailing structure of the parties except for the fact that they must be freely competitive and independent of the state; the financial security of the parties is not a matter that concerns the state.

a) The Weimar Republic has been described as a party state. Though the Weimar Constitution did not expressly recognize political parties, it was assumed, by the decision to adopt proportional representation (Art. 17, 22), that parties would organize the will of the voters. "For the entire system recognizes the fact that organized parties strive for election victory" (Triepel, *Die Staatsverfassung und die politische Parteien*). Accordingly, the High State Court (*Staatsgerichtshof*) acknowledged that in the German Reich political parties had the capacity to bring suits involving constitutional controversies since the parliamentary systems of modern constitutions assumed the existence of parties; to carry on elections without them would have been unthinkable. The recognition of the right to form political parties has been described as "a consequence of the constitutional establishment of the party state." But the parties remained "in essence voluntary organizations which compete, openly and continuously, for their members" (Max Weber, *Staatssoziologie*). Public financial support was not considered important to the parties. Since the freedom of the parties was legally and in fact equivalent to the freedom of ordinary associations, it was regarded as a matter of course that parties would look out for themselves.

b) Under the National Socialist regime parties were either broken up or dissolved. The formation of new parties was of course forbidden. The National Socialist German Workers Party was in fact identified with the nation; it demanded the total unity of law and the will of the nation, and that there be only a "single representative of the people's will" (E. R. Huber, *Verfassungsrecht des Grossdeutschen Reiches*). The [Nazi] Party was described as the legal incorporation of the constitutional life of the nation; it was bound institutionally to the state, forced all organs of the state to do its bidding, and gave orders to the state.

c) The authors of the Basic Law, emphatically rejecting the ruling system of the National Socialists, anchored the legitimacy of parties in the newly created parliamentary democracy. At the same time, mindful of developments under National Socialism, the support it received from wealthy industrialists, and the destruction of all party competition in 1933, the authors of the Basic Law sought to adopt measures which would guarantee the security of liberal democracy. This purpose is served not only by Article 21, paragraph 2, of the Basic Law, concerning the unconstitutionality of certain parties, but also by the provision that the internal organization of parties correspond to democratic principles and that the parties should give a public accounting of the origin of their finances. Only in the interest of securing the liberal democratic basic order did the framers impose these limitations upon the freedom of parties. Finally, the framers looked decisively toward a model of parties openly competitive and independent of the state in every regard, much as had been the case under the Weimar Constitution.

The history of the Basic Law does not suggest that the framers wanted to depart from the [Weimar] model of free political parties operating on their own, and independent of state financial control.

According to the Report of Subcommittee 1 of the Constitutional Assembly held at Herrenchiemsee on August 20, 1948, there was agreement over the fact that the Basic Law should not overlook the reality of political parties. If they could not be conceived as state organs in the strict sense, they were nevertheless to be regarded as crucial elements in the life of the state. The Parliamentary Council accepted these views. The Council, by means of a *"Parteien-Artikel,"* intended to legitimize the party state [*Parteistaat*] in the text of the written constitution, and also to provide the necessary security against dangers to democracy, but at the same time intended to disassociate the parties, as far as possible, from the organs of the state. The delegate Dr. Schmid declared: "Indeed, it is certain that political parties are not organs of the state, although they are crucial factors in our public life. . . ." The delegate Brockman declared that "parties are political organizations characterized by their universality." In the third reading, without contradicting these statements, the delegate Dr. Menzel said: "We welcome the fact that for the first time political parties have been specifically mentioned in the Constitution, that we have had the courage to recognize the effective role of parties in the political life of the nation, and therefore constitutionally to legitimate them, but also to police [in certain respects] the parties without at the same time affecting the vitality of our political life. Thus, in the Second Reading before the Plenum we supported the motion that parties should be obliged to disclose their finances so that every German might be informed as to the sources of their support."

d) In the minds of the framers, therefore, political parties were to be freely formed, controlled democratically by their members, and bound to the obligations of Article 21, paragraph 1, clauses 3 and 4 of the Basic Law, and accordingly to cooperate in forming the political will of the people within the framework of the liberal democratic order. The framers' notion of parties as free and independent organizations is specifically expressed in Article 21 of the Basic Law, particularly in paragraph 1, clauses 2 through 4. The intent of the framers, in so far as Article 21 is concerned, is of even greater weight since it shows that, in addition to the objective content of the constitutional norm, the framers had taken the necessary precautions, under the influence of their historical experience, to avoid any repetition of the ominous developments under National Socialism. Article 21 of the Basic Law must be understood in terms of its historical origin; for it is a reaction to the situation of the parties toward the end of the Weimar Republic and under the National Socialist regime. This provision [Article 21] safeguards the liberal democratic order in that it forbids antidemocratic tendencies within the parties. At the same time it is intended to avoid any entanglement of the parties with constitutional organs; the state is, accordingly, forbidden, in the interest of a free party system, to finance political parties. State subsidies to the parties are therefore out of line with the language of Article 21 and the intent of the framers. Legislation which provides such subsidies for the ordinary political activity of the parties is therefore unconstitutional.

3. The appropriation of public funds provided in the 1965 budget is neither compatible with the constitutional command that political opinion and the will of the people be formed freely nor with Article 21, paragraph 1, which prescribes party structures to be formed by the parties themselves, as is the case with other groups independent of the state. It remains to be seen whether this legislation is unconstitutional on the further ground that it offends the principle of inner-party democracy.

III. State funds may not be allocated to the parties for their activity in the field of political education [*politische Bildungsarbeit*]. The proceedings before the Court have shown that no satisfactory line can be drawn between a party's general political activity [*allgemeine Parteiarbeit*] and its political propaganda.

The treasurer of the Social Democratic Party has indeed made reference to a norm by which the educational activity of parties might actually be separated from their general political activity. However, he has conceded that in the last analysis the separation of these functions would depend on the good will of the parties themselves. The treasurers of the Christian Democratic Union, the Christian-Social Union, and the Free Democratic Party, on the other hand, are of the opinion that no satisfactory line can be drawn between these functions. The representatives of the remaining parties before the Court, with the exception of the Social Democratic Party, agree.

Actually, the political propaganda and general political activity of the parties overlap. No party today can avoid discussing political issues or announcing suggestions for their solution to the electorate. Therefore, money that is provided for the educational work of the parties also assists the parties in carrying on their other political activities. It follows that state funds placed at the disposal of the parties for their educational activities are likewise contrary to the Constitution.

IV. 1. According to Article 21 and Article 20, paragraph 2, of the Basic Law, political parties may not receive state funds for their general political activity. But the state constitutionally may appropriate to the parties funds which reimburse them for reasonable campaign expenditures, to the extent permitted by the decision of June 24, 1958.

Parliamentary elections are decisive in forming the will of the people in a democratic state. In representative democracies, as the framers themselves resolved, they must take place at regular intervals in order to give the people, from whom all state power is derived, an opportunity to announce their will. The holding of an election is a public task which the constituent organs of the state are duty-bound to carry out. It is their responsibility to provide the conditions, institutions, and means necessary for the execution of this task.

Without political parties, however, elections in modern mass democracies could not take place. It is mainly through elections that voters judge the worth of party programs and thus the extent to which they influence the forming of the political will of the state. Voters cannot effectively carry out this function without being represented in the programs and aims of the various parties. It is only through campaigns that voters are motivated to participate in elections, and to make their decision. The Court has frequently emphasized that political parties are mainly election organizations, and that their principal purpose is to cooperate in forming the political will of the people, above all through participation in the electoral process. It is this conception of a political party that justifies the Court's policy of permitting parties to invoke this court's *Organstreit* jurisdiction; parties [*qua* parties] may bring cases to this court only if they are active in the field of elections and seek to defend their constitutional right against encroachment by other organs of the state.

The parties cooperate in forming the political will. But they have no monopoly over this process. Individual citizens and, above all, various groups and associations also influence the making of public opinion and the forming of the political will of the people. A consideration of Article 21, in connection with Article 38, of the Basic Law, together with the federal election law that forms part of our material constitutional law, leads to the conclusion, however, that political parties, because of their participation in parliamentary elections, are agencies superior to other groups in the society. Even if the activity of political parties is not exclusively limited to participation in parliamentary elections, still Article 21, paragraph 1, of the Basic Law emphasizes this role in particular, which is indispensable to the orderly functioning of a democratic community.

The process of making public opinion and forming the people's will reaches its climax in election campaigns. An election campaign can be distinguished from the continual [year-round] forming of the people's will. The activity of the parties in an election campaign can be distinguished from its other activity. For one thing, an election campaign assumes that an election is imminent. It is limited by time. Accordingly, the costs of an election campaign are to be measured by a party's activity during this limited period of time. Expenditures of money by the parties during election campaigns can therefore be separated from their normal expenditures. In oral argument before the Court, it was pointed out that the treasurers of the four parties represented in the Bundestag had actually received supplementary income for the election years of 1957, 1961, and 1965, thereby confirming that it is possible in practice to separate these expenditures.

The special importance that the parties have for voters constitutionally justifies, therefore, state financing of those costs which are essential for the conduct of a reasonable election campaign. It is, however, a political question as to whether the legislature should make such funds available to the parties, and hence is not a question which can be resolved by this court.

2. The competence of the Federal Government to pass such a statute is derived from Article 21, paragraph 3, of the Basic Law.

But it does not have to be decided here how far legislative power, under Article 21, paragraph 3, reaches. It is sufficient to begin with the fact that Article 21, paragraph 1, directly through clause 4 and indirectly through clauses 1 and 3, permits the close regulation of a party's finances. One cannot conclude, in considering Article 21, paragraph 1, clause 4 in relation to paragraph 3, that the legislature's right to pass legislation in regard to party financing is limited to laws which require the parties to account for the sources of their funds.

3. Only those expenditures *directly* related to an election campaign can be reimbursed by the government. The ordinary expenditures of parties for the support of their permanent organizations and their general activity are not direct election expenditures and therefore cannot be allowed. For purposes of determining such costs, parties must keep their campaign budgets separate from their regular budgets, so that the parties are not financed for activities that should be supported from contributions by party representatives, members, and followers; this is necessary to maintain the freedom and independence of parties.

Only those specific costs which enable the parties to present their programs, aims, and purposes in the course of an election campaign may form the basis of computing total election expenditures. This computation is, moreover, not to be based on the estimates of the parties themselves. The legislature must instead formulate an objective measurement of determining what are *appropriate* election expenditures.

It would be constitutionally permissible for the legislature to limit appropriations for party campaign costs to a certain percentage of their total costs, leaving it up to the parties themselves to raise the rest of the money.

4. If the legislature chooses to finance party campaigns, it must, however, ensure the freedom of the parties under Article 21 of the Basic Law. The legislature must further ensure that any formula for the distribution of such funds does not offend the principle of equal opportunity of political parties. This is a principle the validity of which extends not only to electoral rights in the stricter sense—that is, of equality among the parties in their right to carry on a preelection campaign, to solicit party funds, and to present their propaganda on radio— but also to all other campaign activities in connection with which reimbursement by the state is permissible. In all these areas the principle of equal opportunity is to be strictly followed. The authority of the legislature is narrowly limited by this principle. Every discriminatory treatment of the parties which cannot be justified by specially compelling reasons will be denied constitutional validity.

It is not this court's task to say how a constitutionally legitimate rule [for the disbursement of funds] can or must be laid down. The Court, therefore, limits itself here to asserting, as earlier decisions of this court have suggested, that the principle of equal opportunity delimits the discretion of the legislature.

a) With the ruling that parties may be reimbursed out of public funds for their necessary and rising campaign costs, the Court rules also that *only* those parties which have taken part in an election campaign are entitled to state reimbursement. Moreover, the principle of equal opportunity, strictly construed, commands that *all* parties which take part in the campaign are entitled to share in the distribution of such funds. The principle of equal opportunity is violated if these funds are allocated only to the parties which have been represented in Parliament, or which attain seats in Parliament because of a current election. But this principle does not forbid every differentiation between parties; it permits distinctions to be drawn for particularly compelling reasons. It would, for example, be legitimate for the legislature to consider the danger of an excessive splintering of votes and parties in the enactment of such a law.

The legislature actually anticipated that public financing of political parties might stimulate the formation of new parties. This development was held at bay by the 5 percent clause [forbidding representation in the Bundestag under

PR to those parties failing to get 5 percent of the national vote] which has been upheld by the Federal Constitutional Court. Thus, the legislature has already taken precautions to prevent the fragmentation of the vote and the formation of splinter parties; the same formula, in effect, has been used for purposes of allocating money to the parties. But it is not permissible to base the allocation of campaign funds on whether a party has received 5 percent of all valid votes. This measure would in fact double the effect of the 5 percent clause, and make virtually impossible the entrance of a new party into the Parliament. On the other hand, the provisions of the federal election law which limit the creation of new parties are not sufficient to prevent their formation *as a result of the availability of state financing*. Hence, the legislature may base the allocation of such funds on a party's having attained a limited number of votes. But this must indeed lie considerably below the 5 percent level, the attainment of which is necessary for parliamentary representation.

b) Some differentiation in the treatment of the various parties, in so far as disbursement of election expenses are concerned, is also compatible with the principle of equal opportunity. The Court's decision concerning the allocation of radio time to political parties for campaign propaganda would seem relevant here. The parties are distinguished by their size, their political weight, and their leadership capabilities, and thus vary—though this is undergoing change—in terms of their importance to the political system. The form of electoral participation, particularly in choice of advertising means and methods of political recruitment, is to a certain extent related to the size and political importance of the various parties. The principle of equal opportunity does not require that these differences between the parties be equalized by means of state support. It would contradict the intent behind such allocations of state funds if all parties participating in the electoral process were to receive equal amounts of money, without reference to their real or potential capabilities. In this case the actual competitive situation between the parties would be distorted. On the other hand, the legislature is obliged not to intensify existing inequalities regarding the competitive chances of the parties. Should the legislature provide for the disbursement of campaign funds, it must see to it that the quotas allocated correlate with previous disbursements to the parties. Up to now, however, parties not represented in the Bundestag have not received any public funds. This method of distribution, which merely defines the basis of the legislation, is henceforth to be extended to newly emerging parties as well as those currently involved in the electoral process. Whether other points of view concerning differentiations between the parties are compatible with the principle of equal opportunity, and would therefore permit modification of the broad formula announced in this case, will have to be considered by the legislature.

Nakamura et al. v. Japan
(Japan, 1962)

TITLE

Case Concerning Charge of Attempted Violation of the Customs Law [*Kanzeiho*]

TOPICS [*Hangi Jiko*]

1. Is it contrary to the Constitution, Articles 31 and 29, to confiscate [*bosshu*] a third party's property under the Customs Law, Article 118(1)?

2. May a *jokoku* appeal be made on the grounds of the unconstitutionality of confiscation of a third party's property?

SUMMARY [*Hanketsu Yoshi*]

1. It is contrary to the Constitution, Articles 31 and 29, to confiscate a third party's property under the Customs Law, Article 118(1).

2. In such case [of the preceding paragraph], the accused ordered to forfeit property may file a *jokoku* appeal based on its unconstitutionality even in cases concerning a third person's property.

(There are concurring opinions [*hosoku iken*] and minority opinions[*shosu iken*].)

REFERENCES [*Sansho*]

Customs Law, Article 118:

Cargo related to the crimes provided in Articles 109 through 111 (crime of importing prohibited cargo, crime of avoiding customs, etc., and crime of exporting or importing without permit), ships or airplanes used in the commission of such crimes, or cargo related to the crime provided in Article 112 (crime of transport, etc., of smuggled cargo) (hereafter referred to as "Criminal Cargo" [*hanzai kamotsu to*] in this article) shall be confiscated. However, this shall not apply to criminal cargo owned by a party other than the criminal and when such party comes under any one of the following items [*go*]:

1. When it is found that he has continuously maintained the criminal cargo as owner without knowing in advance that one or more of the crimes provided in Articles 109 through 112 were to be committed.

2. When it is found that he took possession of the criminal cargo without knowing of the circumstances after one or more of the crimes provided in the preceding subparagraph were committed.

When the criminal cargo that should be confiscated under the provision of the preceding paragraph cannot be confiscated or when the criminal cargo is not confiscated according to the provisions of item 2 of that paragraph, an amount equivalent to the value [*kakaku*] at the time when the crime was committed of such criminal cargo that cannot be confiscated or is not confiscated shall be collected as an additional penalty [*tsuicho*] from the criminal.

When tariffs [*kanzei*] should be collected in cases in which criminal cargo is not confiscated according to the provisions of Article 1(1), such tariffs shall be collected immediately from the owner. However, when criminal cargo is brought into the bonded area as foreign cargo within a period designated by the chief of customs [*zeikancho*], they shall be deemed as having not been imported.

Constitution, Article 29:

The right to own or to hold property is inviolable.

Property rights [*zaisanken*] shall be defined by law, in conformity with the public welfare.

---

16 Keishu 1593 (Sup. Ct., G. B., November 28, 1962). This case was translated by Dan F. Henderson, University of Washington School of Law, and is reproduced here with his permission.

Private property may be taken for public use upon just compensation therefor.

Constitution, Article 31:

No person shall be deprived of life or liberty, nor shall any other criminal penalty be imposed, except according to procedure established by law.

Criminal Procedure Code, Article 405(1):

A *jokoku* appeal may be lodged against a judgement in first or second instance rendered by a high court in the following cases:

(1) On the ground that there is a violation of the Constitution or an error in construction, interpretation or application [*kaishaku*] of the Constitution.

DECREE (*Shubun*)

The decision below [*genhanketsu*] and decision on first instance are quashed [*haki*].

Accused [*hikokunin*] Kazuichi Nakamura is sentenced to six months of imprisonment at forced labor [*choeki*] and accused Toshihiro Nakamura is sentenced to four months of imprisonment at forced labor, except that execution [*shikko*] of each of these sentences is to be suspended [*yuyo*] for three years from the date this judgment [*saiban*] becomes final [*kakutei*].

The *Taiei-maru*, a steam- and sail-driven ship (valued at 431,000 yen [$1,197]), which is in the custody of the Kokura branch of the Fukuoka District Procurator's Office [*kensatsucho*], shall be confiscated.

All costs on first instance shall be borne jointly by the two accused.

REASONS [*Riyu*]

Regarding the reasons for the respective *jokoku* appeals [*jokoku shui*] presented by counsel [*bengonin*] Eizaburo Ogata and Shi'itsu Matsunaga:

It is reasonable to say that confiscation as provided in the Customs Law, Article 118(1), is a disposition forfeiting and appropriating by the national treasury the ownership [*shoyuken*] of ships and cargo (etc.) that are related to the crimes as provided in the same paragraph and that do not come under the proviso clause [*tadashigaki*] of the same paragraph, whether they belong to the accused or not; and that even though the owner is a third party, not an accused, the declaration of confiscation as an additional penalty [*fukakei*] against the accused does give rise to the effect of forfeiture of such third party's ownership.

(1) However, when the property of a third party is confiscated, we must say that to deprive the owner of his ownership without giving him notice [*kokuchi*] or an opportunity for explanation [*benkai*] or defense [*bogyo*] in connection with such confiscation is extremely unreasonable and cannot be tolerated by the Constitution. For the Constitution, Article 29(1), provides that property rights are inviolable, and Article 31 provides that no person shall be deprived of life or liberty, nor shall any other criminal penalty be imposed, except according to procedure established by law; the above confiscation of a third party's property is ordered as an additional penalty against the accused, and the effect of the disposition of the criminal case extends to the third party;

thus, it is necessary to give notice and opportunity of explanation and defense to the third party who has his property thus confiscated. To confiscate the property of a third party otherwise is to impose a penalty that would result in violation of property rights without resort to procedure established by law.

Accordingly, this is a problem separate from what kind of remedy for such third party is recognized afterward. Nevertheless, the Customs Law, Article 118(1), although providing for the confiscation of ships and cargo (etc.) related to the crimes as provided in the same paragraph, even when they are owned by a third party not an accused, does not provide for giving notice or opportunity for explanation or defense to such third-party owners, nor does the Criminal Code nor any other law or order [*horei*] establish provisions concerning such procedure. Consequently, we cannot but judge that to confiscate a third party's persuant to the Customs Law, Article 118(1), violates the Constitution, Articles 31 and 29.

(2) An accused who has suffered such a declaration of confiscation may, as a matter of course, make a *jokoku* appeal on the grounds of the unconstitutionality of the judgment of confiscation, since it is an additional penalty against him, even in cases concerning a third party's property. Furthermore, since an accused obviously has an interest in the outcome because he is deprived of his possession of the property so confiscated, or is put in a situation in which he cannot use or take advantage of it, or because he is exposed to a possible claim for damages by the third party who had his ownership confiscated, we must hold that he may seek his remedy by *jokoku* appeal.

We regard it as reasonable to modify the Grand Bench precedents [*hanrei*], *Omachi et al.* v. *Japan*, 14 Keishu 1574 (Sup. Ct., October 19, 1960), and *Kiyonaga* v. *Japan*, 14 Keishu 1611 (Sup. Ct., October 19, 1960), which are contradictory to the above.

Regarding the present case, because the court below confirmed the fact that the confiscated cargo was owned by a third party not an accused, the judgment of confiscation is unconstitutional for the above reasons, and appellants' points of argument are, in this regard, well taken.

The decision below and decision on first instance must be reversed in this regard.

Therefore, we quash the decision below in accordance with the Criminal Procedure Code, Article 410(1), main clause [*honbun*]; Article 405(1); Article 413, provisio clause, and enter new judgment in the present case.

We decide as in the decree above; that is: When the law is applied to the facts found in the decision on first instance and confirmed by the court below, the acts of the accused found as above come under the Customs Law, Article 111(1) and (2) [*sic;* 118(1) and (2)], and the Criminal Code, Article 60; thus, we choose imprisonment at forced labor out of the penalties provided by law, and within the terms of penalties so provided, we sentence accused Kazuichi Nakamura to imprisonment at forced labor for six months and accused Toshihiro Nakamura to imprisonment at forced labor for four months, suspending the execution of each sentence for three years from the date this judgment becomes final by application of the Criminal Code, Article 25(1), in accordance with the circumstances. The value, 431,000 yen, of the *Taieimaru*, the steam- and sail-driven ship mentioned in the decree, is to be confiscated pursuant to the Customs Law, Article 118(1), main clause, since it is a ship used in the commission of the crime in this case and is owned by the accused Toshihiro

Nakamura. Costs are to be found applying the Criminal Procedure Code, Article 181(1), main clause, and 182.

This decision is made by the unanimous opinion of all justices except for the concurring opinions of Justices Toshio Irie, Katsumi Tarumi, and Ken'ichi Okuno, and the minority or dissenting opinions of Justices Hachiro Fujita, Masuo Shimoiizaka, Tsuneshichi Takagi, Shuichi Ishizaka, and Sakunosuke Yamada.

The concurring opinion of Justice Toshio Irie is as follows:

1. I agree with the majority opinion in this decision, holding that (1) confiscation as provided under the Customs Law, Article 118(1), is a disposition purporting to transfer ownership of ships and cargo (etc.) that are related to the crimes as provided under the same paragraph but do not come under the proviso clause of the same paragraph, to the national treasury whether they are owned by the accused or not; (2) if a third party, not an accused, is the owner, the declaration of confiscation as an additional penalty against the accused would give rise to the effect of forfeiture of the ownership of such third party; and (3) an accused who suffers such declaration of confiscation may make a *jokoku* appeal on the grounds of unconstitutionality of the judgment of confiscation, even though the object confiscated is a third party's property.

Concerning the reasons therefor, I wish to supplement the above by incorporating by reference [*enyo*] my dissenting opinion [*hantai iken*] on these points in the Grand Bench decision, *Omachi et al.* v. *Japan*, 14 Keishu 1574 (Sup. Ct., October 19, 1960).

2. The majority opinion in this judgment states that the confiscation in this case violates the Constitution, Article 31 and 29, and in this regard, I have decided to amend what I stated in my dissenting opinion concerning the above points in the decision cited above and to agree with the above majority opinion. Although I think that what the majority opinion explains suffices as reasoning, I would supplement it somewhat by additional points just for emphasis.

(1) I consider that the guarantee of procedure established by law found in the Constitution, Article 31, should be interpreted as meaning not that merely nominal establishment of procedure by law satisfies the requirements of this article, but that even though established by some law, that law does not avoid violating this article, if its content contravenes the fundamental principles of constitutions in modern democratic states; the guarantee of this article covers not only procedural provisions but substantive provisions establishing the content of rights; and it should be interpreted to mean not only that this article provides for criminal penalties, but that "No person shall be deprived of . . . liberty" covers, in addition to criminal penalties, also cases in which individual rights or property are infringed by the power of the state. (We should consider this article is also a successor to the intent of the Meiji Constitution, Article 23, which was generally interpreted as providing guarantees concerning not only criminal, but administrative arrest, detention, interrogation, and punishment.)

(2) I do not consider, however, that the Constitution, Article 31, requires, in all cases in which the power of the state infringes on the right or interest of an individual, that he be given notice and opportunity to be heard so that he may state his opinion, explain, and defend himself. For punishment, of course, we should find that such requirements are expressly provided by the other articles of the Constitution, such as Articles 32, 37, and 82, and such guarantees are given by these articles as well as Article 31; however, I should say that for mat-

ters other than criminal punishment, this should not be interpreted to mean that the lack of notice or opportunity to be heard, explain, and defend is, aside from the viewpoint of legislative policy, contrary to the Constitution, Article 31, unless, judging from the nature of the problem, such notice or opportunity is indispensable to the guarantee of fundamental human rights, as viewed from the premises of the Constitution as a whole.

(3) Since the procedure for declaration of confiscation against a third party and the procedure for the main penalty declared are inseparable and must be considered as a whole, we must say that it is necessary under the Constitution, Article 31, to join such third party in the trial procedure and to give him, in some way, advance notice and opportunity to be heard so that he may explain and defend himself. My way of thinking concerning the Constitution, Article 31, as stated above in (1) through (3), is in no way different from what I stated in my dissenting opinion in the previous case.

(4) In the previous dissenting opinion, however, I insisted on an interpretation of the Constitution, Article 31, as applied to confiscation of a third party's property, to the effect that the minimum requirement to satisfy this article would be to summon such third party as a witness to the Court and to give him notice of the proposed third-party confiscation, and thus give him an opportunity to state his opinion, explain, and defend himself; but I have this time decided to amend my view and to agree with the majority opinion in this judgment. For, because there are certain limitations on procedure for examination of witnesses under the present Criminal Procedure Code, we may hardly say that to question a witness in and of itself amounts to giving him an opportunity to defend, and there is no evidentiary requirement, under present trial procedure, that a third-party owner be questioned as a witness in order to find him in bad faith.

However, although when an accused is punished by confiscation of his property, he is naturally given, as an accused, notice, hearing, and opportunity for defense, there is no institutional guarantee of such opportunity when a third party has his property confiscated, and we must say that there is an unfavorable discrimination in treatment between an accused and a third party. Taking such circumstances into consideration (these points were raised in the minority opinions of Justices Daisuke Kawamura and Ken'ichi Okuno in the previous precedent), I have come to think it appropriate to hold that confiscation of a third party's property should be treated as a penal disposition in relation to such third party as well, because it is pronounced as an additional penalty against the accused, yet its effect extends to the third party; and I think that, analogous to the case of an accused, the third party should be joined in the trial procedure and be given notice and opportunity to explain and defend, and that it does not satisfy due process under the Constitution, Article 31, merely to examine the third party as a witness, thereby giving him notice and an opportunity of sorts to explain and defend.

The concurring opinion of Justice Katsumi Tarumi is as follows:

1. Confiscation is a deprivation of ownership on the grounds of a crime. (It was with this idea that the provisions concerning execution of confiscation were established.) Therefore, persons who are to suffer this disadvantageous disposition regarding the things used in a crime or made a constituent element in a crime must, first of all, speaking from the standpoint of substantive law [*jit-taiho*], be limited to offenders themselves, persons with bad faith (accomplices,

[*kyohansha*]), or persons with such intentions or attitudes, are strongly blame-worthy by society (a kind of negligent person [*kashitsusha*]). Secondly, speak-ing from the standpoint of procedural law [*tetsuzukiho*], to determine the fact that the owner stands in the position of an offender, accomplice, or negligent person, as noted above, such third party must be made a kind of party to the lawsuit when he is not already a party to the suit, unless there are proper reasons to the contrary, and he must be duly given notice of the factual and legal grounds for the threatened confiscation, an opportunity for his case to be heard, and the opportunity by himself or his representative [*dairinin*] to prove as a means of defense the factual or legal reasons why confiscation should not be imposed. Only when this has been done may confiscation of the property of a third party be said to follow due process as provided in the Constitution, Article 31. (This is the same as my concurring opinion in *Omachi et al.* v. *Japan*, Sup. Ct. G.B., 14 Keishu 1574, October 19, 1960, Case Concerning Charge of Violation of the Customs Law.)

But the present Criminal Procedure Code has no such special procedural provisions for protection of the interests of third parties when their property is to be confiscated. Until such special provisions are created by legislation, judg-ments confiscating a third party's property are contrary to the Constitution, Article 31, and hence Article 29(1), even though the provisions of substantive criminal law recognizing third-party confiscations are constitutional.

2. The majority opinion, which rejects indiscriminate confiscation [*musa-betsu bosshu*] and holds that if indiscriminate, there may be no confiscation, does not indicate which article of the present Criminal Procedural Code violates the Constitution, Article 31. We must interpret this to mean that if a decision confiscates a third party's property, although the Criminal Procedure Code lacks provision for due process, it violates the Constitution, Articles 31 and 29(1). (Such a decision declaring a law or order unconstitutional without clearly indi-cating any particular provision of the law or order concerned must surely be contrary to law.) The value of the property to be confiscated does not matter to the majority opinion. The confiscation of a third party's property is thus uncon-stitutional, except for certain prohibited objects which no one may legally own, objects that have lost their value, or objects the ownership of which may be regarded as abandoned by their owners (objects that an ordinary person may be regarded as having abandoned, such as a fish knife used in a murder or a blood-stained towel). Of course, even when the third-party confiscation should be allowed by the evidence presented in a criminal case, it would still violate the Constitution, Article 31, so to declare without giving him opportunity for defense (that is, without so much as hearing the third person's opinion and proof on admissibility [*shoko noryoku*] and credibility [*shin'yosei*] of the evidence).

Perhaps we may ordinarily make a confiscation judgment if the third party has failed to appear without due cause though he has received proper summons [*yobidashi*] to the confiscation proceedings. However, in Japan today, it is gen-erally difficult successfully to serve notice of confiscation by international judicial cooperation to a third party residing abroad for a long time, and even though the third party is in this country, it takes much energy, money, and time, and hence slows down the trial, to give service by public notice [*koji sotatsu*] on particular property to be confiscated from him when his residence is unknown or unsettled, with the result that it often happens that, even though fair procedural rules are established, they may not be actually operable. Since we can hardly wait a long time for the decision on the principal issue [*hon'an hanketsu*] of guilty or not guilty [against the accused] in such a case, we must declare nonconfiscation, unless appropriate legislation for such cases is enacted. In addition, would it not be possible to enact legislation providing remedies by which, after the judgment of confiscation of the third party's property becomes final, its execution might be stayed, if the Court regards grounds alleged by the third-party owner sufficient?

3. The majority opinion says that "... an accused who has suffered a declaration of confiscation against a third party's property may, as a matter of course, make a *jokoku* appeal on the grounds of the unconstitutionality of the judgment of confiscation, since it is an additional penalty against him, even in cases concerning a third party's property. Furthermore, since an accused obviously has an interest in the outcome because he is deprived of his possession of the property so confiscated, or is put in a situation in which he cannot use or take advantage of it, or because he is exposed to a possible claim for damages by the third party who had his ownership confiscated, we must interpret that he can seek his remedy by *jokoku* appeal."*

Yet there is a problem in this. It is said that the Supreme Court of the United States as a general rule has come to hold that:

> Appeals which allege the unconstitutionality of a law merely by invoking the constitutional rights of another are unlawful. For one whose constitutional rights are damaged is most qualified to present the constitutional issue before the Court, and the Court also can appropriately render judgment on constitutionality only when that person himself makes such an allegation. When the possessor of constitutional rights endures the infringement on his rights, and perhaps has abandoned or ignores his constitutional rights, it is not appropriate to decide those rights where another (going ahead of their possessor) invokes his rights. It is not desirable to render a constitutional judgment based upon a hypothetical fact situation as yet not arisen in which, although the law has not been applied to a certain other person, when the law is applied to him, his constitutional rights will probably be injured.

It is a general rule, in *koso* appeals and *jokoku* appeals, as in suits in the first instance [*uttae*], that it does not constitute proper grounds for appeal to allege infringement of another's interests without alleging concrete facts that involve possible damage to the interests of the accused himself, because otherwise the appellant is not seeking a decision beneficial to himself; that is, a decision modifying the decision below to benefit the appellant himself. The grounds for *jokoku* appeal in this case say that to confiscate the third party's property as an additional penalty against the accused is unconstitutional. As the grounds for this, the allegation is that the accused have concrete and natural interests since they will avoid the additional penalty by quashment of the confiscation decision. Assuming this, we may for the moment render a substantive judgment on the reasons for the *jokoku* appeal in this case as follows: Due process was satisfied for the accused themselves since the accused in this case received confiscation decision as provided by law after they were notified in the first instance of the facts in the information [*koso jijitsu*], gave opposing pleadings in open court, made allegations in their own behalf, were given opportunity to examine the witnesses in court through their counsel, and were defended by their counsel.

---

*Note that this, though in quotation marks, is *not* a verbatim quote.

From the standpoint of substantive law, we may answer the arguments for *jokoku* appeal as follows: (1) Even assuming the owner of the confiscated property was responsible for the crime, which as a matter of substantive law justified the confiscation because he was an accomplice or the like, the decision below is proper as a penalty against the accused, since the confiscation was imposed as an additional penalty against the accused themselves on the grounds of their criminal acts. (2) Even assuming the owner of the confiscated property had no bad faith nor any kind of negligence which would justify the confiscation, even though the accused were deprived only of their possession as an additional penalty for their own crime, the innocent owner may suffer imposition of penalty more severe than the criminal—confiscation of ownership. Therefore, it is natural that the accused have a duty to compensate him. In any event, the accused cannot be exempted from confiscation for their crime. So far as the accused themselves are concerned, there are no grounds for their arguments for *jokoku* appeal. This may well be a judgment in accordance with procedure provided by law.

However, were we to dismiss the *jokoku* appeal and regard the confiscation decision below as proper, the result would be that the third-party owner, without being found to be a person to be held liable [*yusekisha*] by lawful procedure, would be deprived of his right of ownership by the unconstitutional confiscation decision. Therefore, in this case, it is a matter requiring immediate attention and meeting the demands for justice and equity to resist deprivation of a third party's ownership by an unconstitutional procedure like this, even though it involves escape of the accused, who are criminals.

Thus, in one decision we are in the dilemma that while the confiscation against the accused found to be criminals must be allowed, the same confiscation must be denied because it deprives a third party of his right of ownership. Why this dilemma? While from the standpoint of procedure law [*soshoho*] we render a decision to deprive a third party of his right based on arguments between the litigants alone, and from the standpoint of substantive criminal law confiscation merely deprives the criminal of the right of possession [*sen'yuken*], such deprivation of a third party's right of ownership would mean neither punishment nor education to the criminal, yet we deprive the third party of his right of ownership. Perhaps the dilemma is derived from such absurdity as this. This is particularly clear in the case of indiscriminate confiscation in which it does not matter whether the owner is responsible or not. (Legislation may be justified, if confiscation of a third party's property is not allowed, but additional collection may be imposed on the criminal accused instead.) Be that as it may, even when the third-party owner has some blameworthy intent or negligence, so long as there is no law providing due process giving the right to such owner to be joined in a lawsuit to secure self-protection and to be able to receive a decision beneficial to himself and in order to find whether such fault existed, it is unconstitutional to treat the third party unfavorably by confiscating his property. Therefore, it cannot be helped that, as said in the majority opinion, such injustice may actually occur in which, for example, the third party has had bad intentions or was negligent, or the accused is unjustly exempted from a confiscation decision, until appropriate procedure is legislated.

For the above reasons, I have decided to amend my opinion regarding lawful grounds for *jokoku* appeal [*jokoku tekiho no riyu*] in the Grand Bench decision on the Case of Accused Charged with Violation of the Customs Law involving Tatsuhei Omachi *et al.*, which was cited at the beginning of my opinion, and to agree with the majority opinion regarding the substantive question of constitutionality.

The concurring opinion of Justice Ken'ichi Okuno is as follows:

What is termed "confiscation" in the Criminal Code and other laws is an additional penalty declared against articles related to a crime, and is conceived as something which, when a declaration of confiscation becomes final, has the effect that the articles confiscated go to the national treasury. The effect of such deprivation of ownership does not depend on whether the owner is an accused or a third party.

There is no statutory authority from which we may consider that confiscation of a thing owned by an accused deprives his ownership, but confiscation of a thing owned by a third party not an accused only deprives the right of possession of the accused. For, if there is, I cannot understand, regarding the confiscation of an article owned by a third party, why the law is concerned with good faith or bad faith of the owner and justifies confiscation only when the owner has bad faith knowledge. (See Criminal Code, Article 19(2); Customs Law, Article 118(1), proviso clause; and the Grand Bench decision, *Kamashiro v. Japan*, 11 Keishu 3132, Sup. Ct., November 27, 1957.)

The declaration of confiscation as part of the state's right to prosecute [*keibatsuken*] is a pronouncement of appropriation to the national treasury of an article that is closely related to a crime in the interest of public welfare, as a function of state power, and it does not merely have an effect in relation to the accused, but has the effect of appropriation to the national treasury in relation to all persons.

However, in actuality it is extremely irrational and impermissible under the Constitution, Article 31, to confiscate a third party's property, thus depriving him of ownership, without an opportunity of notice and hearing and without allowing him to explain and defend himself; therefore, I interpret such confiscation to be unconstitutional and contrary to law.

Although some may argue that, even in such a case, a third-party owner can seek relief by a civil lawsuit, we cannot possibly acknowledge such a contradiction in the state's policy; while the state adopts a system for appropriating confiscated articles to the national treasury regardless of whether the article is owned by the accused or a third party, at the same time the state allows such third-party owner to make a claim against the state by a civil lawsuit for return of the article confiscated or payment of damages for unjust enrichment [*futo ritoku*] even after the confiscation decision becomes final. That is, the argument that a third-party owner can seek relief in court by a civil lawsuit even after the declaration of confiscation becomes final can only be premised on the assumption that ownership is not taken away in spite of the confiscation judgment; in other words, that such confiscation is unconstitutional and illegal, and therefore, does not have the effect of confiscation.

Furthermore, although some may say that a third party who has suffered confiscation of an article owned by himself may claim its return under the Criminal Procedure Code, Article 497, I interpret this article to cover cases in which it becomes clear that someone else had owned the property after a confiscation decision that was made against property thought not to belong to any third party other than a criminal has become final; thus this article is not applicable when the court, upon finding a thing to be owned by a third party, has judged it to be a thing which should be confiscated, and has made a declaration of confiscation.

The minority opinion of Justice Hachiro Fujita is as follows:

Concerning the reasons for *jokoku* appeal presented by Counsel Shi'itsu Matsunaga and reasons for *jokoku* appeal presented by Counsel Eizaburo Ogata:

Their arguments come to this, in short: The cargo in this case is owned by a third party not an accused, and the decision below, which confiscated it, is unconstitutional because it infringes the rights of the third party; however, since we should hold that the accused are not allowed to file a *jokoku* appeal with a third party's right of ownership as its subject on the grounds that rights of a third party are infringed (see the Grand Bench decisions *Omachi et al* v. *Japan,* 14 Keishu 1574, October 19, 1960, and *Kiyonaga* v. *Japan,* 14 Keishu 1611, Sup. Ct., October 19, 1960), their arguments should not be accepted.

The dissenting opinion of Justice Masuo Shimoiizaka is as follows:

It is not at all necessary to pass on the question of unconstitutionality in a case like this in which the accused, who are not the owners of the confiscated article, dispute the constitutional effect of a decision that, as an additional penalty, declared confiscation of a third party's property. Consequently, this decision makes, in spite of this, an unnecessary constitutional judgment, which is against the purport of the Grand Bench decisions of this court, *Omachi et al* v. *Japan,* 14 Keishu 1574, October 19, 1960, and *Kiyonaga* v. *Japan,* 14 Keishu 1611, Sup. Ct., October 19, 1960. I, as a person who firmly insisted on the opinion included in the above-cited Grand Bench decisions, still strongly oppose the present decision and wish to point out the errors expressed in the majority opinion of this case and to add the following opinion, as well as to maintain and incorporate by reference [*in'yo*] those Grand Bench decisions.

The right to review for unconstitutionality given to the Court under the Constitution, Article 81, must be exercised within the scope of judicial power; and for the judicial power to be invoked it is necessary that a contentious case [*sosho jiken*] has been instituted concretely. The Court, when there is no concrete contentious case before it, is not empowered to give abstract judgments concerning the dubious arguments existing concerning construction [*kaishaku*] of the Constitution and other laws and orders in anticipation of the future, as has been established by the Grand Bench of this court. (See the Grand Bench decision *Suzuki* v. *Japan,* 6 Minshu 783, Sup. Ct., October 8, 1952). In concrete contentious cases when laws and orders that do not apply to oneself or that do apply constitutionally to oneself are unconstitutional if applied to another person, should we allow their attack on the grounds of unconstitutionality and hasten invocation of the right to review for unconstitutionality? In such an event, it is necessary to consider separately two kinds of cases: (1) cases in which the party concerned does not actually suffer concrete detriment under the laws and orders that are being reviewed for unconstitutionality, and (2) cases in which the party concerned does actually suffer concrete detriment under the laws and orders that are being reviewed for unconstitutionality. In the former case (when the party concerned does not actually suffer concrete detriment under the laws and orders that are being reviewed for unconstitutionality), to give a judgment on the issue of unconstitutionality is nothing but to give an abstract judgment on dubious arguments in anticipation of the future, which is to go outside the scope of the judiciary power. To do so is not permissible as an exercise of the right to review for unconstitutionality given to the Court under the Constitution, Article 81. For the latter case (when the party concerned does actually suffer concrete detriment under the laws and orders that are being reviewed for unconstitutionality), I will later touch upon the propriety of giving a judgment on the issue of unconstitutionality.

Turning to the present case, it was confirmed by the court below that the confiscated cargo was criminal cargo that the accused attempted to smuggle abroad and that was owned by a third party not an accused. The majority opinion holds that the accused may dispute the constitutionality of the confiscation judgment on the grounds that the accused obviously have an interest in the judgment for confiscation of the criminal cargo, which became final, because they are deprived of the right of possession of the confiscated article, or are put in a position in which they are unable to use or take profit from it, and further, are exposed to the risk that the third party, deprived of his right of ownership, may exercise his right to claim damages. The majority opinion points out, as one of the reasons why the accused may contest the confiscation judgment in this case as unconstitutional, the fact that the accused is exposed to the risk that the third party, deprived of the right of ownership, may exercise his right to claim damages; yet whether the third-party owner will exercise his right to claim damages is a pending question and such a risk is but indefinite and abstract. The accused have thus not actually suffered any concrete detriment from the confiscation judgment in this case. A Grand Bench decision of this court (*Kamashiro* v. *Japan*, 11 Keishu 3132, Sup. Ct., November 27, 1957) has held that the confiscation of the property of a third party who was in bad faith is not contrary to the Constitution, Article 29. Admitting that the accused are deprived of the right of possession of the confiscated cargo by the final confiscation judgment in this case and are in a position in which they are unable to use or take profit from it, as pointed out by the majority opinion, since the accused, criminals who attempted to smuggle the confiscated cargo abroad, did act in bad faith, we cannot conclude that even if the accused are deprived of the right of possession of the article by the final confiscation judgment in this case or are put in a position in which they are unable to use or take profit from it, they have as a result been illegally deprived of a property right under the Constitution, Article 29, or that they actually suffered infringement of their constitutional rights from the confiscation judgment, since the accused were given notice and an opportunity for explanation and defense. Consequently, since the accused have not suffered any actual concrete detriment, from any point of view, from the confiscation judgment in this case, I must conclude that the majority opinion, which on the issue of unconstitutionality of the confiscation judgment bases its decision on the petition of these accused who in fact have not suffered actual concrete detriment, is nothing but an abstract judgment on dubious arguments in anticipation of the future, transcending the scope of the right to review for unconstitutionality given to the courts under the Constitution, Article 81. Since the accused lack any actual concrete interest to argue the unconstitutionality of the confiscation judgment in this case, the grounds for *jokoku* appeal alleging the confiscation to be unconstitutional are legally insufficient, and the appeal in this case should be dismissed for this reason. Accordingly, I must say a word on the fact that the majority opinion has modified the Grand Bench decisions of October 19, 1960, cited above. Those decisions hold it reasonable to regard that it is impermissible in a lawsuit to interfere with rights of another and seek relief for him; therefore, it should also be regarded that it is impermissible to argue, as in this case, that confiscation is constitutionally invalid as an infringement of fundamental human rights against the property of another. The previous decisions declare, in short, that it is not permissible under any circumstances to argue that laws and orders are unconstitutional in a concrete contentious case, when they are constitutional as applied to oneself, simply because they would be unconstitutional if applied to another. Presumably, it is sound to say that when a party has not suffered any concrete detriment under the laws and orders that are being reviewed for unconstitutionality, it would result in interfering with the constitutional rights of another person to base one's case on the grounds that such laws and orders, when applied to another, would infringe the constitutional rights of that other person, and such asking for relief for others should not be allowed. In contrast to this, if the party concerned does actually suffer concrete detriment under the laws and orders that are being reviewed for unconstitutionality, I think we must consider, from another angle, whether it should be absolutely forbidden to attack such laws and orders by invoking the constitutional rights of another person on the ground that the laws and orders infringe the constitutional rights of such other person. On this point the expressions in the Grand Bench decision cited above, it seems to me, lacked clarity and breadth. I thus wish to interpret the content of the above Grand Bench decision as having wider meaning and to explain and amplify this point as follows. That is, I think that when a party does actually suffer concrete detriment under the laws and orders that are being reviewed for unconstitutionality, it is proper to say that the law does not prohibit an attack on such laws and orders by invoking the constitutional rights of another person, nor does it transcend the scope of the judicial power, even if we adjudicate constitutional issues thus raised. (However, in the present case, the accused have neither alleged nor proved that they suffered any concrete detriment from the confiscation judgment.)

Next, I would like to introduce the thinking of the Supreme Court of the United States of America on this point, which court is based on a system of review for unconstitutionality that is the same as ours.

On the attitude of the U.S. Supreme Court, which has long adhered to the principle that it does not have the power to declare laws unconstitutional except when the question is raised for judgments regarding the legal rights of litigants in actual disputes, the Court has said as follows:

> We start with the fundamental purpose of avoiding unnecessary constitutional judgments. This originates from considerations (1) of the delicate function of what is termed review for unconstitutionality, which becomes clear when the Court makes a judgment of unconstitutionality and when its effects extend to other organs established under the Constitution, the same as the Court (*i.e.,* the legislative body and executive body); (2) of the relative conclusiveness of the Court's judgment of unconstitutionality, which does not absolutely bind other organizations; (3) of the scrupulous care that should properly be given to judgments concerning the powers of the organs holding legislative power and administrative power under the Constitution along with the Court; (4) of the necessity of the holders of state power to

stay within the scope of authority given to each such holder, including the Court, in order to act in accordance with Constitutional provisions; (5) of the limitations inhering in the judicial process arising from the negative nature of the judicature, as well as the limited means by which judgments are enforced; and (6) of the important position occupied by the Court's constitutional judgments in the political structure of the United States. . . .

Declared as one of the manifestations of the above fundamental attitude is the principle that "it is impermissible to attack a law that is constitutionally applied to oneself, on the grounds that the law becomes unconstitutional when it is applied to another person or to other facts," and it is declared as an expression incidental to this principle that "the litigant may only argue his own constitutional rights and is not allowed to invoke constitutional rights of another person." This principle may be interpreted to flow from the following reasons: (1) It is the person who has his own constitutional rights infringed that is best able to raise constitutional issues before the Court, and a proper decision can only be made by a constitutional judgment when there is an attack by one whose constitutional rights are damaged. (2) Although the possessor of constitutional rights being invoked may tolerate infringement on his rights and may abandon his constitutional rights, it is undesirable to make a constitutional judgment when, in anticipation, such rights are invoked by another person. (3) It is not desirable to render a constitutional judgment based on hypothetical facts, yet to occur, that when and if the law in question is applied to another person in the future, his constitutional rights would be infringed. The attitude of the U.S. Supreme Court has consistently been as stated above, which is said to have proven most wise through time and experience.

Because I think that in Japan, as well, the above principle would be wise and a way of thinking endorsed by reason, it seems to me that the above points might well be considered fully in connection with review for unconstitutionality handled by the Courts in our country. However, since the above principle should be interpreted not as a principle ordered by the Constitution to the Court, but rather as a frame of mind for the Court, or a standard with which to form a fundamental attitude in the exercise of the right to review unconstitutionality, we probably cannot avoid violating the principle in exceptional instances when the third party's constitutional rights invoked by another are infringed, yet the third party has no means effectively to preserve his rights by himself.

The majority opinion says that an accused who has suffered a declaration of confiscation may, as a matter of course, make a *jokoku* appeal on the grounds of the unconstitutionality of the confiscation judgment since it is an additional penalty against the accused, even in cases concerning a third party's property. In the final analysis it only says something or other about the additional penalty and is completely a formalism. Does such a basis of argument have reasonable grounds as constitutional theory? The accused neither do nor attempt to allege or prove that they have suffered actual concrete detriment from the declaration of confiscation in this case. Even going so far as to concede that the *jokoku* appeal is lawful on the grounds that the confiscation judgment in this case is unconstitutional as said in the majority opinion, I do not consider it necessary to make a constitutional judgment in this case in which constitutionality of the judgment of confiscation is disputed by invoking only the constitutional rights of a third party who is an outsider to the lawsuit. My understanding is that a third party whose property is confiscated without being given notice or an opportunity of explanation and defense may be categorized as a person having rights under the Criminal Procedure Code, Article 497 (1), and so long as the owner of the thing confiscated alleges that the confiscation violates the Constitution, Article 31, he may institute an administrative lawsuit [*gyosei sosho*] against the state claiming return of the confiscated thing. Consequently, since a third-party owner may later assert his constitutional rights and validly argue the unconstitutionality of the confiscation, it is unnecessary to make a constitutional judgment in anticipation during the criminal proceedings at the stage in which it is not determined yet whether the third party will tolerate the infringement on his constitutional rights. Thus, I firmly believe that the decision in this case should embody the following judgment:

Although the accused allege the unconstitutionality of the declaration of confiscation as their grounds for *jokoku* appeal, the accused, merely invoking the constitutional rights of a third-party owner of the thing confiscated, do not argue that their own constitutional rights were infringed. We should hold then that an attack on constitutionality by invoking only constitutional rights of another is allowed only in exceptional cases when it is impossible for the possessor of constitutional rights to allege existence of his rights himself later, or when there is no practical benefit if such allegation is made at a later date; in the ordinary case, an attack on constitutionality is not permissible when invoking only the constitutional rights of another. Since the present case falls under the category of a case in which it is possible and valid for the owner of the confiscated thing to dispute the matter of constitutionality himself later, we need not give a judgment on the unconstitutionality alleged by the accused in the present case. Consequently, the argument alleging unconstitutionality of the confiscation in this case is thus groundless, and cannot be accepted.

The minority opinion of Justice Tsuneshichi Takagi is as follows:

Since my opinion on the reasons for *jokoku* appeal presented by Counsel Eizaburo Ogata and Shi'itsu Matsunaga is the same as my concurring opinion in the Grand Bench decision, *Omachi et al* v. *Japan*, 14 Keishu 1574, Sup. Ct., October 19, 1960, I refer to that opinion as my opinion here.

The dissenting opinion of Justice Shuichi Ishizaka is as follows:

I oppose the majority opinion expressed in this case. I adopt the dissenting opinion of Justice Masuo Shimoiizaka since I am in agreement with it.

The minority opinion of Justice Sakunosuke Yamada concerning the reasons for *jokoku* appeal of Counsel Eizaburo Ogata and Shi'itsu Matsunaga is as follows:

1. The majority opinion says that "It is reasonable to say that confiscation as provided in the Customs Law, Article 118(1), is a disposition depriving, and appropriating by the national treasury, ownership of ships and cargo (etc.), owned or possessed by criminals that are related to the crimes as provided in the same paragraph and that do not come under the proviso of the same paragraph, and even when a third party (not an accused) is the owner, the declaration of confiscation as an additional penalty against the accused does give rise to the effect of depriving the ownership of such third party";* the majority

---

*Note that this too is not a verbatim quote though in quotation marks.

opinion also recognizes that the effect of the decision extends to persons who are not even parties to the action, and then develops its position based on this premise; however, on this point I cannot agree.

2. Concerning things covered by the Customs Law, Article 118 (1) (etc.), such as smuggled jewelry, I consider it neither unjust nor unconstitutional to provide that these things may be confiscated under substantive law (the Criminal Code, Customs Law, etc.), regardless of who owns them, even a third party not an accused, when the necessity for their confiscation is recognized from the viewpoint of the state. Consequently, for me, the Customs Law, Article 118, which is in question, is obviously valid and I cannot accept the view which regards this article in itself unconstitutional, as the majority opinion holds.

3. However, even if the right to prosecute (right to make disposition) is found from the standpoint of substantive law to exercise such a right concretely, existence of this right to prosecute must, needless to say, be found concretely in accordance with the Criminal Procedure Code. The Constitution, Article 31 (providing that "no person shall be deprived of life or liberty nor shall any other criminal penalty be imposed, except according to procedure established by law"), clarifies this fundamental idea.

4. Under the Criminal Procedure Code, it is not appropriate for the direct effect of a decision against the accused to extend to third parties other than the accused. This principle not only applies to criminal procedure, but is one of the fundamental principles of established procedure law, including the Civil Procedure Code and the Bankruptcy Law [*Hasanho*]. Consequently, even though there is provision for recognizing confiscation of the property of a third party under substantive law, for the effectuation of such a provision, procedure is required that by some means (for instance, procedure for participation of the third party in a civil suit or the former procedure of incidental private action [*futai shiso*]) makes the third party a party to the lawsuit (at least the name of the third party must be stated in the decision itself [*hanketsusho*]). I cannot possibly approve an interpretation that although such procedural provisions are lacking, the effect of a declaration of confiscation as an additional penalty against an accused extends to third parties, by ignoring this fundamental theory of the law of procedure. This becomes more clear when considered from the standpoint of the third party. That is, without being called to court and while being unaware of the matter, his property might be confiscated; in other words, during such time of ignorance, by a decision made against another without his name even appearing (in the text of the decision), the right of ownership in a thing owned by him might be confiscated. What is worst, not being a litigant, he may not even make a *koso* appeal or *jokoku* appeal. Considering that even in the confiscation of an article owned by an accused, adjudication procedure [*saiban tetsuzuki*] is necessary, we cannot possibly permit imposition of the punishment of confiscation against a third party without going through any adjudication procedure, or allowing him to make any appeal. This is a contradiction arising from the fact that the majority opinion bases its argument on an interpretation contrary to the fundamental theory of procedure law, saying that the effect of a decision extends to persons other than the litigants.

5. Apparently one of the bases for the majority opinion flows from the past practice in the prosecutor's office to the effect that, when a so-called third-party indiscriminate confiscation decision [*daisansha musabetsu bosshu no hanketsu*] becomes final, its effect naturally extends to third parties, other than the accused

(of course their names are not stated in the decision), and a custom has arisen to effect execution [*shikko*] of confiscation against such third parties. But this is a practice from the era of the old Constitution, when there were no measures like administrative lawsuits by which to dispute and nullify administrative acts and dispositions made by administrative organs, and I consider that it is unacceptable, under the new Constitution, to ignore such basic procedure law theory and directly extend the effect of a decision against an accused to even a third party and by such decision deprive him of his rights.

6. Actually, the procurator's answer [*tobensho*] in this case says that "putting aside for the moment the basic problem whether it is permissible to challenge the propriety of this act concerning criminal proceedings by a *jokoku* appeal, we consider it should be interpreted permissible to bring a civil suit. This means that because of the legal principle of unjust enrichment [the person who has been unjustly enriched; in this case, the state] bears the duty to return such enrichment to the true owner, and the true owner may seek relief in court by a civil lawsuit." From the purport of this answer, we may see that the procurator will not handle a matter such that it will be regarded illegal (illegality is grounds for civil relief) so that the state will be liable for damages later; that is, regarding a judgment rendered against another as having effect against a third party, deprive him of his right of ownership in an article he owns by execution of the decision.

7. For the above reasons, I cannot accept the *jokoku* appeal in this case alleging unconstitutionality of the confiscation on the erroneous premise that the effect of the judgment below against the accused extends to a third party other than the accused and infringes on the third party's right of ownership.

8. In addition, since, under current law, confiscation is regarded as punishment by the express provision of the Criminal Code, Article 9, and as an additional penalty to be imposed along with the main punishment (there is no statutory authority for interpreting this as a disposition for the preservation of public order [*hoan shobun*]), and, moreover, so long as punishment is made against the accused himself, it is not consistent with such an idea of punishment to impose punishment (confiscation) on a third party. I understand confiscation to mean, under existing law, the deprivation of any legal benefits of property owned by the accused, and therefore that the effect of the declaration of confiscation against the accused deprives them of the right of ownership if they own the article, or deprives them of the right of possession if they merely have possession or use of the article. Therefore, confiscation from the accused still has meaning, even if the accused do not have the right of ownership of the article (the right of use or possession is sometimes more valuable than ownership; imposing punishment by not letting the accused keep or use the object confiscated is thus meaningful). Especially since, under the legal system in our country, an article is recognized only as the object of a right in any sense, and not as the possessor of a right, I feel that we should not deal with an article itself independently, or forfeit it to the national treasury by a decision without treating the owner or possessor as the object [of the decision].

9. For the above reasons, we should dismiss the *jokoku* appeal in this case.

Judge Yusuke Saito did not participate in the discussion of this case because of his retirement. Procurators Asaichi Murakami and Kinichi Hanakada were present at the hearing. (Chief Justice Kisaburo Yokota and Justices Hachiro

Fujita, Matasuke Kawamura, Toshio Irie, Katsu Ikeda, Katsumi Tarumi, Daisuke Kawamura, Masuo Shimoiizaka, Ken'ichi Okuno, Tsuneshichi Takagi, Shuichi Ishizaka, Sakunosuke Yamada, Kakiwa Gokijo, and Masatoshi Yokoto.)

Marbury v. Madison
(U.S.A., 1803)

At the December term 1801, William Marbury, Dennis Ramsay, Robert Townsend Hooe, and William Harper, by their counsel severally moved the court for a rule to James Madison, secretary of state of the United States, to show cause why a mandamus should not issue commanding him to cause to be delivered to them respectively their several commissions as justices of the peace in the district of Columbia. This motion was supported by affidavits of the following facts: that notice of this motion had been given to Mr. Madison; that Mr. Adams, the late president of the United States, nominated the applicants to the senate for their advice and consent to be appointed justices of the peace of the district of Columbia; that the senate advised and consented to the appointments; that commissions in due form were signed by the said president appointing them justices, &c. and that the seal of the United States was in due form affixed to the said commissions by the secretary of state; that the applicants have requested Mr. Madison to deliver them their said commissions, who has not complied with that request; and that their said commissions are withheld from them; that the applicants have made application to Mr. Madison as secretary of state of the United States at his office, for information whether the commissions were signed and sealed as aforesaid; that explicit and satisfactory information has not been given in answer to that inquiry, either by the secretary of state, or any officer in the department of state; that application has been made to the secretary of the senate for a certificate of the nomination of the applicants, and of the advice and consent of the senate, who has declined giving such a certificate; whereupon a rule was made to show cause on the fourth day of this term.

❊ ❊ ❊

Mr. Chief Justice MARSHALL delivered the opinion of the court.

At the last term, on the affidavits then read and filed with the clerk, a rule was granted in this case, requiring the secretary of state to show cause why a mandamus should not issue, directing him to deliver to William Marbury his commission as a justice of the peace for the county of Washington, in the district of Columbia.

No cause has been shown, and the present motion is for a mandamus. The peculiar delicacy of this case, the novelty of some of its circumstances, and the real difficulty attending the points which occur in it, require a complete exposition of the principles on which the opinion to be given by the court is founded.

These principles have been, on the side of the applicant, very ably argued at the bar. In rendering the opinion of the court, there will be some departure in form, though not in substance, from the points stated in that argument.

---

1 Cr. 137 (1803).

In the order in which the court has viewed this subject, the following questions have been considered and decided.

1. Has the applicant a right to the commission he demands?

2. If he has a right, and that right has been violated, do the laws of his country afford him a remedy?

3. If they do afford him a remedy, is it a mandamus issuing from this court? The first object of inquiry is,

1. Has the applicant a right to the commission he demands?

His right originates in an act of congress passed in February 1801, concerning the district of Columbia.

After dividing the district into two counties, the eleventh section of this law enacts, "that there shall be appointed in and for each of the said counties, such number of discreet persons to be justices of the peace as the president of the United States shall, from time to time, think expedient, to continue in office for five years."

It appears from the affidavits, that in compliance with this law, a commission for William Marbury as a justice of peace for the county of Washington was signed by John Adams, then president of the United States; after which the seal of the United States was affixed to it; but the commission has never reached the person for whom it was made out.

Mr. Marbury, then, since his commission was signed by the president and sealed by the secretary of state, was appointed; and as the law creating the office gave the officer a right to hold for five years independent of the executive, the appointment was not revocable; but vested in the officer legal rights which are protected by the laws of his country.

To withhold the commission, therefore, is an act deemed by the court not warranted by law, but violative of a vested legal right.

This brings us to the second inquiry; which is,

2. If he has a right, and that right has been violated, do the laws of his country afford him a remedy?

The very essence of civil liberty certainly consists in the right of every individual to claim the protection of the laws, whenever he receives an injury. One of the first duties of government is to afford that protection. In Great Britain, the king himself is sued in the respectful form of a petition, and he never fails to comply with the judgment of his court.

In the third volume of his Commentaries, page 23, Blackstone states two cases in which a remedy is afforded by mere operation of law.

"In all other cases," he says, "it is a general and indisputable rule, that where there is a legal right, there is also a legal remedy by suit or action at law whenever that right is invaded."

* * *

The government of the United States has been emphatically termed a government of laws, and not of men. It will certainly cease to deserve this high appellation, if the laws furnish no remedy for the violation of a vested legal right.

* * *

It is then the opinion of the court,

1. That by signing the commission of Mr. Marbury, the president of the United States appointed him a justice of peace for the county of Washington in the district of Columbia; and that the seal of the United States, affixed thereto by the secretary of state, is conclusive testimony of the verity of the signature,

and of the completion of the appointment; and that the appointment conferred on him a legal right to the office for the space of five years.

2. That, having this legal title to the office, he has a consequent right to the commission; a refusal to deliver which is a plain violation of that right, for which the laws of his country afford him a remedy.

It remains to be inquired whether,

3. He is entitled to the remedy for which he applies. This depends on,

1. The nature of the writ applied for. And,

2. The power of this court.

1. The nature of the writ.

Blackstone, in the third volume of his Commentaries, page 110, defines a mandamus to be, "a command issuing in the king's name from the court of king's bench, and directed to any person, corporation, or inferior court of judicature within the king's dominions, requiring them to do some particular thing therein specified which appertains to their office and duty, and which the court of king's bench has previously determined, or at least supposes, to be consonant to right and justice."

* * *

This writ, if awarded, would be directed to an officer of government, and its mandate to him would be, to use the words of Blackstone, "to do a particular thing therein specified, which appertains to his office and duty, and which the court has previously determined or at least supposes to be consonant to right and justice." . . . The applicant, in this case, has a right to execute an office of public concern, and is kept out of possession of that right.

These circumstances certainly concur in this case.

* * *

This, then, is a plain case of a mandamus, either to deliver the commission, or a copy of it from the record; and it only remains to be inquired,

Whether it can issue from this court.

The act to establish the judicial courts of the United States authorizes the supreme court "to issue writs of mandamus, in cases warranted by the principles and usages of law, to any courts appointed, or persons holding office, under the authority of the United States."

The secretary of state, being a person, holding an office under the authority of the United States, is precisely within the letter of the description; and if this court is not authorized to issue a writ of mandamus to such an officer, it must be because the law is unconstitutional, and therefore absolutely incapable of conferring the authority, and assigning the duties which its words purport to confer and assign.

The constitution vests the whole judicial power of the United States in one supreme court, and such inferior courts as congress shall, from time to time, ordain and establish. This power is expressly extended to all cases arising under the laws of the United States; and consequently, in some form, may be exercised over the present case; because the right claimed is given by a law of the United States.

In the distribution of this power it is declared that "the supreme court shall have original jurisdiction in all cases affecting ambassadors, other public ministers and consuls, and those in which a state shall be a party. In all other cases, the supreme court shall have appellate jurisdiction."

It has been insisted at the bar, that as the original grant of jurisdiction to the supreme and inferior courts is general, and the clause, assigning original jurisdiction to the supreme court, contains no negative or restrictive words; the power remains to the legislature to assign original jurisdiction to that court in other cases than those specified in the article which has been recited; provided those cases belong to the judicial power of the United States.

If it had been intended to leave it in the discretion of the legislature to apportion the judicial power between the supreme and inferior courts according to the will of that body, it would certainly have been useless to have proceeded further than to have defined the judicial power, and the tribunals in which it should be vested. The subsequent part of the section is mere surplusage, is entirely without meaning, if such is to be the construction. If congress remains at liberty to give this court appellate jurisdiction, where the constitution has declared their jurisdiction shall be original; and original jurisdiction where the constitution has declared it shall be appellate; the distribution of jurisdiction made in the constitution, is form without substance.

Affirmative words are often, in their operation, negative of other objects than those affirmed; and in this case, a negative or exclusive sense must be given to them or they have no operation at all.

It cannot be presumed that any clause in the constitution is intended to be without effect; and therefore such construction is inadmissible, unless the words require it.

If the solicitude of the convention, respecting our peace with foreign powers, induced a provision that the supreme court should take original jurisdiction in cases which might be supposed to affect them; yet the clause would have proceeded no further than to provide for such cases, if no further restriction on the powers of congress had been intended. That they should have appellate jurisdiction in all other cases, with such exceptions as congress might make, is no restriction; unless the words be deemed exclusive of original jurisdiction.

When an instrument organizing fundamentally a judicial system, divides it into one supreme, and so many inferior courts as the legislature may ordain and establish; then enumerates its powers, and proceeds so far to distribute them, as to define the jurisdiction of the supreme court by declaring the cases in which it shall take original jurisdiction, and that in others it shall take appellate jurisdiction, the plain import of the words seems to be, that in one class of cases its jurisdiction is original, and not appellate; in the other it is appellate, and not original. If any other construction would render the clause inoperative, that is an additional reason for rejecting such other construction, and for adhering to the obvious meaning.

To enable this court then to issue a mandamus, it must be shown to be an exercise of appellate jurisdiction, or to be necessary to enable them to exercise appellate jurisdiction.

It has been stated at the bar that the appellate jurisdiction may be exercised in a variety of forms, and that if it be the will of the legislature that a mandamus should be used for that purpose, that will must be obeyed. This is true; yet the jurisdiction must be appellate, not original.

It is the essential criterion of appellate jurisdiction, that it revises and corrects the proceedings in a case already instituted, and does not create that case. Although, therefore, a mandamus may be directed to courts, yet to issue such a writ to an officer for the delivery of a paper, is in effect the same as to sustain an original action for that paper, and therefore seems not to belong to appellate, but to original jurisdiction. Neither is it necessary in such a case as this, to enable the court to exercise its appellate jurisdiction.

The authority, therefore, given to the supreme court, by the act establishing the judicial courts of the United States, to issue writs of mandamus to public officers, appears not to be warranted by the constitution; and it becomes necessary to inquire whether a jurisdiction, so conferred, can be exercised.

The question, whether an act, repugnant to the constitution, can become the law of the land, is a question deeply interesting to the United States; but, happily, not of an intricacy proportioned to its interest. It seems only necessary to recognise certain principles, supposed to have been long and well established, to decide it.

That the people have an original right to establish, for their future government, such principles as, in their opinion, shall most conduce to their own happiness, is the basis on which the whole American fabric has been erected. The excise of this original right is a very great exertion; nor can it nor ought it to be frequently repeated. The principles, therefore, so established are deemed fundamental. And as the authority, from which they proceed, is supreme, and can seldom act, they are designed to be permanent.

This original and supreme will organizes the government, and assigns to different departments their respective powers. It may either stop here; or establish certain limits not to be transcended by those departments.

The government of the United States is of the latter description. The powers of the legislature are defined and limited; and that those limits may not be mistaken or forgotten, the constitution is written. To what purpose are powers limited, and to what purpose is that limitation committed to writing; if these limits may, at any time, be passed by those intended to be restrained? The distinction between a government with limited and unlimited powers is abolished, if those limits do not confine the persons on whom they are imposed, and if acts prohibited and acts allowed are of equal obligation. It is a proposition too plain to be contested, that the constitution controls any legislative act repugnant to it; or, that the legislature may alter the constitution by an ordinary act.

Between these alternatives there is no middle ground. The constitution is either a superior, paramount law, unchangeable by ordinary means, or it is on a level with ordinary legislative acts, and like other acts, is alterable when the legislature shall please to alter it.

If the former part of the alternative be true, then a legislative act contrary to the constitution is not law: if the latter part be true, then written constitutions are absurd attempts, on the part of the people, to limit a power in its own nature illimitable.

Certainly all those who have formed written constitutions contemplate them as forming the fundamental and paramount law of the nation, and consequently the theory of every such government must be, that an act of the legislature repugnant to the constitution is void.

This theory is essentially attached to a written constitution, and is consequently to be considered by this court as one of the fundamental principles of our society. It is not therefore to be lost sight of in the further consideration of this subject.

If an act of the legislature, repugnant to the constitution, is void, does it, notwithstanding its invalidity, bind the courts and oblige them to give it effect? Or, in other words, though it be not law, does it constitute a rule as operative as if it was a law? This would be to overthrow in fact what was established in theory; and would seem, at first view, an absurdity too gross to be insisted on. It shall, however, receive a more attentive consideration.

It is emphatically the province and duty of the judicial department to say what the law is. Those who apply the rule to particular cases, must of necessity expound and interpret that rule. If two laws conflict with each other, the courts must decide on the operation of each.

So if a law be in opposition to the constitution: if both the law and the constitution apply to a particular case, so that the court must either decide that case conformably to the law, disregarding the constitution; or conformably to the constitution, disregarding the law: the court must determine which of these conflicting rules governs the case. This is of the very essence of judicial duty.

If then the courts are to regard the constitution; and the constitution is superior to any ordinary act of the legislature; the constitution, and not such ordinary act, must govern the case to which they both apply.

Those then who controvert the principle that the constitution is to be considered, in court, as a paramount law, are reduced to the necessity of maintaining that courts must close their eyes on the constitution, and see only the law.

This doctrine would subvert the very foundation of all written constitutions. It would declare that an act, which, according to the principles and theory of our government, is entirely void, is yet, in practice, completely obligatory. It would declare, that if the legislature shall do what is expressly forbidden, such act, notwithstanding the express prohibition, is in reality effectual. It would be giving to the legislature a practical and real omnipotence with the same breath which professes to restrict their powers within narrow limits. It is prescribing limits, and declaring that those limits may be passed at pleasure.

That it thus reduces to nothing what we have deemed the greatest improvement on political institutions—a written constitution, would of itself be sufficient, in America where written constitutions have been viewed with so much reverence, for rejecting the construction. But the peculiar expressions of the constitution of the United States furnish additional arguments in favour of its rejection.

The judicial power of the United States is extended to all cases arising under the constitution.

Could it be the intention of those who gave this power, to say that, in using it, the constitution should not be looked into? That a case arising under the constitution should be decided without examining the instrument under which it arises?

This is too extravagant to be maintained.

In some cases then, the constitution must be looked into by the judges. And if they can open it at all, what part of it are they forbidden to read, or to obey?

There are many other parts of the constitution which serve to illustrate this subject.

It is declared that "no tax or duty shall be laid on articles exported from any state." Suppose a duty on the export of cotton, of tobacco, or of flour; and a suit instituted to recover it. Ought judgment to be rendered in such a case? ought the judges to close their eyes on the constitution, and only see the law?

The constitution declares that "no bill of attainder or ex post facto law shall be passed."

If, however, such a bill should be passed and a person should be prosecuted under it, must the court condemn to death those victims whom the constitution endeavours to preserve?

"No person," says the constitution, "shall be convicted of treason unless on the testimony of two witnesses to the same overt act, or on confession in open court."

Here the language of the constitution is addressed especially to the courts. It prescribes, directly for them, a rule of evidence not to be departed from. If the legislature should change that rule, and declare *one* witness, or a confession *out* of court, sufficient for conviction, must the constitutional principle yield to the legislative act?

From these and many other selections which might be made, it is apparent, that the framers of the constitution contemplated that instrument as a rule for the government of *courts,* as well as of the legislature.

Why otherwise does it direct the judges to take an oath to support it? This oath certainly applies, in an especial manner, to their conduct in their official character. How immoral to impose it on them, if they were to be used as the instruments, and the knowing instruments, for violating what they swear to support!

The oath of office, too, imposed by the legislature, is completely demonstrative of the legislative opinion on this subject. It is in these words: "I do solemnly swear that I will administer justice without respect to persons, and do equal right to the poor and to the rich; and that I will faithfully and impartially discharge all the duties incumbent on me as———, according to the best of my abilities and understanding, agreeably to the constitution and laws of the United States."

Why does a judge swear to discharge his duties agreeably to the constitution of the United States, if that constitution forms no rule for his government? if it is closed upon him and cannot be inspected by him.

If such be the real state of things, this is worse than solemn mockery. To prescribe, or to take this oath, becomes equally a crime.

It is also not entirely unworthy of observation, that in declaring what shall be the supreme law of the land, the constitution itself is first mentioned; and not the laws of the United States generally, but those only which shall be made in pursuance of the constitution, have that rank.

Thus, the particular phraseology of the constitution of the United States confirms and strengthens the principle, supposed to be essential to all written constitutions, that a law repugnant to the constitution is void, and that courts, as well as other departments, are bound by that instrument.

The rule must be discharged.

CHAPTER 6

VARIATIONS IN COURT STRUCTURE: LAY PARTICIPATION IN DECISION-MAKING

> My uncle used to say that the jury
> served the great purpose of ridding
> the neighborhood of its sons of
> bitches.
>
> —JUDGE CHARLES CURTIS

To THE AMERICAN MIND, the concept of lay participation in the court process almost inevitably conjures up visions of a jury trial. In all probability, most Americans think that this is the only way in which citizens without legal training could (or should) become involved in the decision-making aspects of the judicial process. Yet as late as 1947 a substantial portion of the highest court of the state of New Jersey (called the "Court of All Errors and No Appeals" by the bar at the time) was composed of lay judges. This combination of professional and amateur judges, as it were, is known as a mixed tribunal, and in many parts of the world the citizenry would consider it the only type of lay participation that is meaningful or appropriate or even democratic. Then there is the modern West German concept of the people's court, where certain criminal cases are heard by a panel of three judges and a jury of six laymen, all of whom vote together, with a majority vote necessary for a verdict, each man having one vote. This is very similar in structure to the Swedish *nämnd*, except that the professional judge in Sweden has a much weightier vote than any layman. Another variation on this general theme was the ancient Athenian court, where hundreds of common people sat simultaneously as judge and jury to weigh the fate of an accused. Socrates was tried before just such a jury court of 501 Athenians.

Legal and Political Propositions in the Literature

The institution of trial by a jury of one's peers has a relatively long and deep-rooted tradition in European, British, and American history. It is thought by some to be one of the bulwarks, indeed the crowning glory, of a democratic political system. However, even as some features of its form have been modified several times and its purpose has changed, its use has declined in many countries.[1] Nonetheless, it still seems to be highly valued by ordinary Americans, and it is frequently lauded in popular and professional media as one of the outstanding features of the American legal system and of the "democratic way of life." Mere hints of its elimination from the American legal scene stimulate the imaginations and type-writers of legions of defenders. One of the more novel apologies of late was to equate any demise of the American version of citizen-participation-as-a-juror with the ultimate victory of the faceless bureaucrat: "The jury is the last widely utilized institution of grass roots democracy; its disappearance would signal the victory of the specialist in government."[2]

Defenses of the jury system are usually more rousing, artful, or co-gent than this, for its defenders (if not idolators) have been around for quite some time. In fact, the ranks of sentinels and sentries for the jury system are staffed by many of the greats of jurisprudence. No less a philosopher than Blackstone himself applauded the jury as "the glory of English law," claiming that it is "the most transcendent privilege which any subject can enjoy or wish for, that he can not be affected either in his property, his liberty, or his person but by the unanimous consent of twelve of his neighbors and equals."[3] He further asserted that "the impartial administration of justice, which secures both our persons and our properties, is the great end of civil society,"[4] with the clear implication that trial by jury was not only instrumental to that end, but necessary to its attainment.

---

[1] Henry J. Abraham, *The Judicial Process: An Introductory Analysis of the Courts of the United States, England, and France*, 2nd ed. (New York: Oxford, 1968), p. 104. For a description of the differences between the English and American jury systems, see Delmar Karlen, *Anglo-American Criminal Justice* (Oxford: Clarendon Press, 1967). For some details on its decline and an argument for its abolition in civil cases in Scotland, see T. B. Smith, "Civil Jury Trial: A Scottish Assessment," *Virginia Law Review*, 50 (October, 1964), pp. 1076–95. It should be noted, however, that jury trials are increasing in criminal prosecution in England. This is due to the fact that juries are required when there is an indictment and a not-guilty plea, and that the use of indictment has increased substantially since World War II. See Arthur T. Vanderbilt, "Judges and Juries," *Boston University Law Review*, 36 (Winter, 1956), pp. 74–75.

[2] Beverly Blair Cook, *The Judicial Process in California* (Belmont, Calif.: Dickinson, 1967), p. 113.

[3] Sir William Blackstone, *Commentaries on the Laws of England*, vol. 3, adap. John L. Wendell (New York: Harper, 1854), quoted in Charles Joiner, *Civil Justice and the Jury* (Englewood Cliffs, N.J.: Prentice-Hall, 1962), p. 106.

[4] *Ibid.*

Blackstone concluded that "a competent number of sensible and upright jurymen, chosen by lot from among these of the middle rank, will be found the best investigators of truth, and the surest guardians of public justice."[5]

Two explicit legally oriented propositions may be formulated in connection with this part of Blackstone's thesis. (1) A properly chosen jury is the best available means for establishing truth, i.e., determining the facts in legal proceedings. (2) Juries are capable of deciding in an impartial, i.e., objective, manner. It is quite clear, however, from a thorough reading of Blackstone, that these pronouncements are not uttered on the grounds that he has proved these propositions to be true. These statements are based upon a *belief* that they are true, and on certain presuppositions that legislate (by means of certain normative statements) that if they are not true, they ought to be. Blackstone has used the language of factual statements to assimilate value premises into his argument. Further, even assuming his statements to be factual in character, he has by no means produced any empirical evidence by means of which one may assess the truth of these propositions.

The claims of Blackstone concerning the use of juries have been repeated in various forms by various writers since his time, and there have been numerous additions and clarifications. Alexis de Tocqueville, for one, drew a distinction between the legal and the political aspects of the institution, and directed his attention to the political ends served by its use.[6] Tocqueville asserts that the "greatest advantage" of the jury system is that it "contributes powerfully to form the judgment and to increase the natural intelligence of a people."[7] What might be called the values of political *education* and *participation* are explicated by Tocqueville's arguments, and he builds his case upon them. Clearly these uses of the jury are more political than legal. They are not at all related to accomplishment in the litigation process *per se*. These, then, are our propositions 3 and 4.

Tocqueville's argument, like Blackstone's, is probably based on value premises, though it too purports to be a statement of fact. Tocqueville tries to justify the existence of juries by resorting to some strange logic and exaggeration of fact. The defenders of the system have not been without resources. He writes of the jury as a judicial institution as follows:

A judicial institution which thus obtains the suffrages of a great people [the English] for so long a series of ages, which is zealously repro-

---

[5] *Ibid.*, p. 107.

[6] Alexis de Tocqueville, *Democracy in America,* vol. 1, 2nd ed., trans. Henry Reeve, ed. Francis Bowen (Cambridge: Sever & Francis, 1863), quoted in *ibid.*

[7] Tocqueville, *op. cit.*, vol. 1, trans. Henry Reeve, rev. Francis Bowen, corr. and ed. Phillips Bradley (New York: Knopf, 1945), p. 295.

duced at every stage of civilization, in all the climates of the earth, and under every form of human government, cannot be contrary to the spirit of justice.[8]

Even were all the clauses in the above excerpt true, still the conclusion, that the jury system "cannot be contrary to the spirit of justice," would not follow. I do not think I need labor the point. Moreover, the jury system was not nearly so widespread as Tocqueville imagined.

Yet it is to his credit that Tocqueville almost realized that a conflict may well exist between the theoretical legal and political ends served by the use of juries, for he observed, "I do not know whether the jury is useful to those who have lawsuits; but I am certain it is highly beneficial to those who judge them; and I look upon it as one of the most efficaceous means for the education of the people which society can employ."[9] Tocqueville, after all, was far more a political animal than a legal one.

In the *Federalist* papers, the value and utility of the jury trial are more or less taken for granted. There are no prolonged arguments or encomiums, so characteristic of these papers, on this subject, despite the fact that Hamilton in particular was quite concerned about many aspects of the construction and function of the judiciary. There was some talk, however, on limitations that should be placed on the jury. It appears that Hamilton was somewhat skeptical of the jury system. His primary concern was not to analyze the use of juries, but to show that they were not absolutely necessary to the dispensation of justice, especially in civil cases.

In *Federalist* no. 83, Hamilton praises the use of juries as "a valuable safeguard to liberty" and "the very palladium of free government."[10] On the other hand, he is of the opinion that such a mode of trial is not appropriate where complex legal issues are involved, where questions are "too complicated for a decision in that mode."[11] Not surprisingly, then, Hamilton (like Tocqueville) saw the importance of juries in their political, rather than legal, functionings.

Hamilton restricts the use of juries, in effect, by stating that juries are not qualified to rule on matters of law or to make public policy. In traditional language, he was careful to reserve the interpretation of law to the judicial branch of government. Moreover, in a subtle condemnation of the use of juries in civil cases he writes that "all are satisfied as to the utility of the institution, and of its friendly aspect to liberty. But I must

---

[8] *Ibid.*, p. 291.
[9] *Ibid.*, p. 296.
[10] *The Federalist*, ed. Benjamin F. Wright (Cambridge: Belknap Press of Harvard University Press, 1961), p. 521.
[11] *Ibid.*, p. 528.

acknowledge that I cannot readily discern the inseparable connection between the existence of liberty and the trial by jury in civil cases."[12] He sees its use only in certain criminal matters. Still, he is supporting another of our propositions: (5) The jury is a safeguard of the *liberties* of the population. It is, again, a political job of the jury variation in the judicial process.

There is one other major political proposition that is uttered by each observer who favors retaining the jury structure. I refer to the old saw that juries, because they are drawn from the population at large, are unencumbered by professionalism; have good old horse sense; dispense with adherence to the law when it would bring about hardship or be unfair under the circumstances, whatever they may be. In a word, juries are more flexible and just than judges are likely to be. There is, of course, another side to these arguments: juries are capricious and uncertain, and therefore unjust. The familiar response to this is: The justice of uncertainty is better than certain injustice. As Dale Broeder has stated in his own review of the literature, "For every charge leveled against the jury in this debate there is likewise to be found a vigorous defense."[13]

THE EMPIRICAL EVIDENCE ON THE LEGAL PROPOSITIONS

In these three aforementioned sources—one British, one European, one American—one can see the primary values that are believed to underlie the establishment, use, and advocacy of juries. These values are maintained by many later (even "modern") writers who recommend the continued use of juries. The factual considerations surrounding the issue are occasionally called into question, and when they are, dispute arises as to the desirability of the future employment of juries. I am appending to this chapter an edited version of the *Sheppard* case, wherein the Supreme Court in 1966 pointed to the difficulty of the jury's remaining impartial in the face of extreme local pressure and extraordinary publicity. It is included for a variety of reasons, the main one being that it illustrates methods by which the chances of (or degrees of) jury impartiality can be increased. The *Sheppard* case, far from providing a rationale for eliminating the jury from the American system, illustrates the strength of American belief in the ability of a jury to perform its legal functions properly, given ordinary structural support and usual conditions.

In witnessing the fierce argument among those who favor and disfavor juries, one may feel compelled to inquire whether there would be

---

12 *Ibid.*, p. 522.
13 Dale W. Broeder, "The University of Chicago Jury Project," *Nebraska Law Review*, 38 (May, 1959), p. 745.

any effect on the argument at all if it could be shown that there was little fact to bolster either view. In the many years since Blackstone, Tocqueville, and Hamilton, the assailants (as well as the defenders) of the jury system have sought and processed little evidence to support their contentions. It is only very recently that the evidence marshaled on one side or the other has gone beyond hunch, guess, and personal observation. Yet I think it will become clear that despite the growth in relevant knowledge, and though there have been some interesting and new applications of this knowledge to the legal and political theory concerning the jury, we are not much closer to confirming any aspect of this theory empirically than we ever were. At the very most, we are presented with more precise and involved tests. The contemporary writers who argue both for and against the use of juries, while they may be more precise, more cautious, and less inclined to generalize than writers of earlier years, still persist in drawing conclusions that are supported by, at best, meager evidence. Also, as will become clear, the major focus of this work is upon the strictly legal propositions and those that are only indirectly political.

Perhaps the most recent and far-reaching defense of the jury system based on contemporary social-scientific research is Charles Joiner's *Civil Justice and the Jury.*[14] Dean Joiner, well grounded in the canons of reason and causal inference, enters the tournament as a champion of the jury. Consider his following statements in support of the theoretical legal functioning of juries:

> The jury is a deliberative body. It does discuss, argue, and exchange ideas before it can report a decision. Therefore, it is not unfair to assume that the decision which it reaches may have fewer mistakes and fewer biases involved in it than would such a decision made by a single person.[15]

Joiner then produces a select list of psychological studies to document his contention that juries are better fact-finders than solitary problem-solvers:

> Most of these studies involved not juries, but other small groups with decision-making tasks. . . . The studies indicate that group decisions are fairer, more efficient, and more accurate in fact-finding than are the decisions of an individual. . . . It was found that the interaction during deliberation was the crucial difference that made group decisions more just than a pooling of individuals without the give-and-take of deliberation.[16]

The argument is surely a reasonable one, but it affords equally vigorous support to those who might advocate the merits of a panel of thirteen

---

[14] Charles Joiner, *Civil Justice and the Jury* (Englewood Cliffs, N.J.: Prentice-Hall, 1962).
[15] *Ibid.,* p. 26.
[16] *Ibid.,* pp. 26–27.

trial judges, a quintet of presidents, or a troika of chairmen. In addition it has some patent drawbacks. First, while portraying the jury as the supremely democratic small group, it downgrades the real possibility that there may be unique factors operating in jury deliberation. Second, it conveniently overlooks relevant facts and interpretations discussed in other social-scientific studies. Third, it was premature, as later work on juries has produced evidence capable of directly disconfirming Joiner's conclusions.

Juries may or may not be typical of small groups, since they operate in a unique context, are required (or are supposed) to follow special rules of law in reaching general verdicts, and so on. As an individual, each member is thrust into a novel environment, exposed to a strange tongue, and forced to assume a difficult professional role for which he is ill trained and to which he is introduced in haste and under pressure. The whole process is highly standardized from start to finish. It is hardly an ordinary small group, and one cannot help wondering to what extent, if any, the results of studies of other types of small groups can be applied to juries. I am not saying that such application is impossible. I am saying that the research on small groups and the research on the jury as a small group have not yet even approached a stage where we can have confidence in any such extrapolation. It must be viewed with more than a gram of suspicion.

Nevertheless, Joiner does employ the findings of such studies to justify the jury as an excellent fact-finder. This seems to be the grossest of oversimplifications. But what is worse is that the very same studies he cites, and a host of similar studies that he does not cite, can lead to precisely the opposite interpretation. Dean Joiner, for instance, is not unaware of some of the work done in social psychology that demonstrates the tendency of people in small groups to conform, contrary to their own opinion, to pressures exerted by the organization or by a strong leader. Moreover, there is evidence that when emotions are involved, the effectiveness of the group in problem-solving is impaired—and juries frequently have to face emotional situations.[17]

In interpreting the pertinent literature, Blau and Scott have stated the following:

> Not all studies, however, have found group performance to be superior to that of individuals. An examination of those tasks that groups do not perform as well as individuals will allow us to refine our analysis by specifying the conditions under which groups are generally su-

---

[17] Much of the literature relevant to this topic can be found in the following sources: A. Paul Hare, Edgar F. Borgatta, and Robert F. Bales, eds., *Small Groups* (New York: Knopf, 1965); Peter M. Blau and W. Richard Scott, *Formal Organizations* (San Francisco: Chandler, 1962); and Robert F. Golembiewski, "Small Groups and Large Organizations," in *Handbook of Organizations,* ed. James G. March (Chicago: Rand McNally, 1966).

perior. An experiment by Thorndike reports that groups were superior to individuals in *solving* crossword puzzles but that individuals were superior to groups in *constructing* them.[18]

Is a court case more like the solution of a factual situation or the construction of one? Can the tasks given to small groups in experimental situations be analogized to those given to a jury? Can studies that demonstrate that one person was less efficient in problem-solving than a group be valid in relationship to a situation where the one person is expert and the group is amateur? Joiner would also have difficulty with a finding by Taylor and Faust that "the fact that there were negligible differences between groups of two and of four either in number of questions or in elapsed time strongly suggests that *the optimum size group is not larger than four*."[19]

There is little question that the bulk of the research done on small groups does indicate that they have certain advantages over an individual in performing a variety of chores. Much of this work that was done before Joiner arrived at his conclusion and much of it that has been done since can be put together to make a good brief for continuing the jury system. Still, a good deal of it can be used to raise serious questions about the jury system as well. What is needed is a good deal of experimentation on juries or mock juries. There has been all too little of it, but what has been done can be used to contradict Joiner's views.

Fred Strodtbeck's Chicago data, for instance, indicated that several people emerged as the main contributors in each jury (and they were usually people of higher social status than the others). Not surprisingly, the highest degrees of satisfaction were reported by those who participated the most. Also, the few who were most active received the highest "helpfulness" scores from the jury as a whole. Given this picture of what goes on in the jury room, it might seem a bit odd that Strodtbeck has this to say about it: "The picture emerges that in the retrial in the jury room the jurors work like responsible citizens, with democratic recognition of competence where it is found."[20] It would appear that the elite theory of democracy is now finding its way into justification of the jury! Certainly the evidence can be interpreted to indicate as well that social conformity and clever manipulation by an oligarchic leadership brings a jury around.

Another recent report of empirical findings can be used to dent Joiner's optimism, despite the fact that its authors share Joiner's enthusiasm over

---

[18] Blau and Scott, *op. cit.*, pp. 118–19.

[19] Donald W. Taylor and William L. Faust, "Twenty Questions: Efficiency in Problem Solving as a Function of Size of Group," in *Small Groups*, ed. Hare *et al.*, p. 217 (emphasis mine).

[20] Fred Strodtbeck, "Social Process, the Law and the Jury," in *Law and Sociology*, ed. William Evan (New York: Free Press, 1962), p. 154.

the jury. The Ford Foundation granted a large sum of money to a group of scholars at the University of Chicago in the mid-fifties to study various aspects of the American jury system. Foremost among this group were Harry Kalven, Jr., Hans Zeisel, Fred Strodtbeck, Dale Broeder, and Rita James. Bit by bit, articles and books are accumulating on the results of their research. One of the most recent ones is *The American Jury,* by Kalven and Zeisel.[21]

The major theme of the Kalven-Zeisel volume is that there is a certain amount of difference between the outcomes of cases tried by judges and those tried by juries. For those who are jury fans, this finding will be read as a big difference; those who prefer judges will see the difference as small. This is due mainly to the interpretation by Zeisel and Kalven rather than to anything inherent in the data themselves. But more on that later. The point is that there were differences detected and that this information can be used to undermine Joiner's position (as well as to support it, of course).

The general method employed to discover the precise degree of disagreement (if any) and the conditions under which any disagreements might exist and vary was simple enough. A large sample of jury trials (3,576) was studied. For each trial, the judge was asked by questionnaire how he would have voted. If he disagreed with the jury, he was asked what he believed to be responsible for the divergence in opinion. Included were suggestions like "The composition of the jury?"; "Personalities in the case (defendant, witnesses, attorney)?" Many other questions were asked about the judge himself and about the case in its entirety. Also, there were two separate surveys taken, one in 1955 and one in 1959.

Two of their tables are particularly relevant for our purposes. Kalven and Zeisel interpret Table 6 as follows:

Reading the two shaded cells first, we obtain the percentage of cases in which judges and jury agree. They agree to acquit in 13.4 percent of all cases and to convict in 62.0 percent of all cases, thus yielding a total agreement rate of 75.4 percent.

---

[21] Boston: Little, Brown and Company [Inc.], 1966. This joint effort is extremely sophisticated and self-conscious in its methodology and rigorous in its collection and presentation of data. Though there are many serious questions about some of the authors' assumptions, which they discuss, they naturally resolve them all favorably to the continuance of their program of study. I do not intend to question them here; I shall assume that their data are reliable and valid and go on from there. Whatever its flaws, *The American Jury* will be hailed as a "classic" and a "landmark study" and "definitive." And there can be no question that it *is* an important step toward an eventual understanding of the judicial and jury decision-making processes. Yet, despite the fact that this book will increase the status of the social-scientific study of the jury process, it also threatens to abort, rather than stimulate, broader and independent research; not because of the massiveness of the project, but rather because of the overinterpretation of the data presented. It is fair to say that whatever the project has researched about the jury, it has left much unresearched, particularly on the political functions of the jury. The study is neither exhaustive nor definitive.

TABLE 6

Verdict of Jury and Judge
(In Percent of All 3,576 Trials)

| | | JURY | | | |
		Acquits	Convicts	Hangs	Total Judge
J U D G E	Acquits	13.4	2.2	1.1	16.7
	Convicts	16.9	62.0	4.4	83.3
	Total Jury	30.3	64.2	5.5	100.0%

◻ = Judge-jury agreement

SOURCE: Harry Kalven, Jr., and Hans Zeisel, *The American Jury* (Boston: Little, Brown and Company [Inc.], 1966), p. 56.

Looking next at the four unshaded cells, we see that the total disagreement, 24.6 percent of all cases, consists of $(16.9 + 2.2 =)$ 19.1 percent of cases in which judge and jury disagree on guilt, and $(1.1 + 4.4 =)$ 5.5 percent of cases in which the jury hangs.[22]

Kalven and Zeisel also point out that there is a 14.7 percent "net leniency" by the jury; that is, the jury acquits some 14.7 percent more often than the judge across the board. The phenomenon of greater leniency by the judge is termed a crossover.[23] Kalven and Zeisel then took the hung-jury figures and considered them to represent one-half for acquittal and one-half for conviction, and presto, we have Table 7. Here the net leniency is 16 percent.

Much of the Kalven-Zeisel study is devoted to determining the causes of this disagreement, both when the jury is more lenient than the judge and when the judge is more lenient than the jury. The nature of these factors is important to discuss, it is true, but they shall be relegated to footnote status in this book. For our purposes it is important to note only that Kalven and Zeisel believe that the evidence supports the view that the jury's leniency is due to its sense of equity, or its "modest war" with the law.[24] On the other hand, they note that there are other major factors, including trial evidence that is susceptible of various interpretations, and that by and

---

[22] *Ibid.*, pp. 56–57.
[23] *Ibid.*, p. 68n.
[24] *Ibid.*, p. 286.

TABLE 7

Verdict of Jury and Judge—Consolidated
(Percent of All 3,576 Trials)

| | | JURY | | |
		Acquits	Convicts	Total Judge
J U D G E	Acquits	14	3	17
	Convicts	19	64	83
	Total Jury	33	67	100%

⧄ = Judge-jury agreement

SOURCE: Harry Kalven, Jr., and Hans Zeisel, *The American Jury* (Boston: Little, Brown and Company [Inc.], 1966), p. 58.

large the jury process is so subtle as to prevent any interpretation of their data from being other than value-ridden itself.

This is just the point. I could apply these data to Joiner's statement and note that if the jury is such a good deliberating body, as opposed to a single decision-maker, how can he explain the fact that the lone judge arrives at similar conclusions some 83 percent of the time? How can we conclude that the 16–17 percent is the product of more, rather than less, rationality?

Other research findings published subsequent to Joiner's book are even more capable of nurturing doubt about the proposition that juries are fair and that group deliberation has significant impact on the final decision. In one experimental study, by Becker, Hildum, and Bateman, the original value positions of the jury seemed to be solely and directly determinative of the final verdict.[25] In this study of six simulated juries, if a jury was strongly prejudiced against mercy killing (the Catholic viewpoint) at the outset of the trial, it was harsh in its evaluation of the facts and interpreted the law quite literally and inflexibly. If, on the other hand, the jurors were likely to be sympathetic to a clear and tragic case of mercy killing (non-Catholic personnel), then they were lenient in their verdict and quite oblivious of the clear dictate of the law. The deliberation, if it accomplished anything, galvanized near unanimity into unanimity. These

---

[25] Theodore L. Becker, Donald C. Hildum, and Keith Bateman, "The Influence of Jurors' Values on Their Verdicts," *Southwestern Social Science Quarterly*, 46 (September, 1965), pp. 130–40.

findings were consistent with some earlier findings of the Chicago project. According to Dale Broeder:

> In virtually all of the cases a ballot was taken immediately. In thirty percent of the cases the first ballot was unanimous and that ended it. In seventy percent of the total cases, however, there was some division of opinion on the first ballot, and the striking fact about such cases is that the majority on the first ballot almost *always* won. The majority won in approximately ninety percent of such cases. . . . *The broad point suggested, of course, is that most criminal trials are decided during the trial and not during the deliberation.*[26]

In the Becker-Hildum-Bateman study, no jury held opposite to the majority position on the first ballot.

Joiner's confidence in the jury system resembles an act of faith more than it does an inductively derived theory. His reasoning and evidence do little to allay those fears so well summed up by a wag some seventy years ago who said, in scorning the scorners of the ancient practice of trial by ordeal:

> Let us not smile at the credulity of an age which could sanction such a device for the discovery of truth and the punishment of wrong. Our own boasted trial by jury, which affirms that all grades of capacity above driveling idiocy are alike fitted for the exalted office of sifting truth from error, may excite the derision of future times.[27]

Those who worship the jury system are not the only ones who torture the facts to suit their own preferences. Jerome Frank, for instance, offers perhaps the most articulate and persuasive antithesis to Joiner's position, and it is one of enduring notoriety. His attacks on the jury are frontal; he finds almost no redeeming benefits to it, either legally or politically. He sees no relationship between the ways it is supposed to function and the ways it actually does function. Most of his energies, since he was primarily a trial judge, are spent on attacking it from a legal perspective.

Frank's vendetta against juries is waged, by and large, in two works: *Law and the Modern Mind*[28] and *Courts on Trial*. His assault consists of two chief criticisms. First, he disputes the contention that the jury is intellectually capable or skilled enough to engage in the tedious and esoteric procedures of legal fact-finding and application of those facts to the law. Frank argues that the use of the general verdict clouds the issues and makes it impossible to determine upon what principles—law, logic, facts, evidence, etc.—the decision of the jury is grounded. There is no way to

---

[26] Broeder, *op. cit.*, p. 747 (emphasis mine).
[27] Quoted by Jerome Frank in his *Courts on Trial* (Princeton: Princeton University Press, 1949), pp. 138–39.
[28] Jerome Frank, *Law and the Modern Mind* (New York: Coward McCann, 1930).

decide whether it ignored the judge's instructions regarding the relevant law, compromised with them, or perhaps did not even understand them. "The truth is (as anyone can discover by questioning the average man who has served as a juror) that usually the jury are neither able to, nor do they attempt to, apply the instructions of the court."[29]

Frank's second major criticism concerns prejudice, capriciousness, and emotion.

> Many juries reaching their verdicts act on their emotional responses to the lawyers and witnesses; they like or dislike, not any legal rules, but they do like an artful lawyer for the plaintiff, the poor widow, the brunette with the soulful eyes, and they do dislike the big corporation, the Italian with the thick, foreign accent. We do not have uniform jury-nullification of harsh rules; we have juries avoiding— often in ignorance that they are doing so—excellent as well as bad rules, and in capricious fashion.[30]

Frank attempted to explode the myth that juries are impartial deliberative bodies acting in accordance with rules of law (including precedent given to them in a charge by the judge). The results, according to him, are that juries assume the roles of legislators and the effect is jury-made law.[31] In current terminology, Frank is saying that juries are almost completely situation-oriented. Unfortunately, Frank's criticisms are extreme and not cautiously made. While one can easily appreciate Frank's desire to play the role of the devil's advocate, as well as his challenging and refreshing prose, many of his statements cannot be taken seriously. His evidence, valuable though it may be, is limited to his own personal observations and does not support the absolutely damning nature of his generalizations.

This is not to say that there is any less truth to Frank's fears than there is to Joiner's optimism. All the data discussed in relationship to Joiner's generalizations can be used to undermine Frank's as well. Certainly it is true that the Becker-Hildum-Bateman study cited earlier suggests strongly that a man's life may depend on the initial attitude or value universe of those who comprise a jury. Yet Chapter 2 of this volume is replete with evidence that the values and attitudes of judges are salient factors in their decisions as well.

It is possible that both Joiner and Frank may be read to posit the proposition that juries *tend* to be either more or less objective, or better or worse at fact-finding. I doubt that Frank would be happy with the results of the Chicago study. After all, if jurors are as incompetent and emotional as he has said, then judges must be, too—at least a large percentage of them. The tone of the work of both Joiner and Frank and their staunchest

---

[29] Frank, *Courts on Trial,* p. 185.
[30] *Ibid.,* p. 130.
[31] *Ibid.,* chap. 9.

supporters would lead us to believe that they would expect a far larger difference than the Chicago results manifest.

An earlier study I conducted on judicial decision-making does not provide much ammunition for an extreme position, either.[32] This was a quasi experiment on law students (seniors) and undergraduates wherein they were to decide simulated cases. The precedent involved was varied; some cases had clear precedent and some had ambiguous precedent. The law-trained students did show a marked increase in precedent orientation over the students without legal training. Yet there was some indication that a lack of such training was not inconsistent with a desire to be objective and to follow precedent. The differences, though visible, were not, however, statistically significant along many of the relevant dimensions. This could be construed as lending support to those who have confidence in the layman's ability to comprehend the concept of judicial role and to follow it to a substantial degree. Again, it depends mostly upon one's point of view.

In sum, contemporary empirical studies tend to indicate that there is some degree of difference between the decision-making processes of the professionally trained judge or juror and those of one who has not been so trained. The conclusions they reach differ approximately 20 percent of the time. But there is absolutely no way for us to know whether this degree of difference is "too much" or "too little," or whether it is enough to support the arguments for retention or abolition of the present system of judge and jury as it is usually found in the United States. Some adore this degree of difference, some abhor it. All that scientific studies of it can accomplish is to provide explanations of the conditions of variance. We can draw no conclusions on the *legal*-function desirability or undesirability from these data alone. What we can do is: (*a*) estimate the result of a value judgment to be made by and implemented by the society; (*b*) speculate on what this judgment might mean in a *political*-functional sense; and (*c*) compare our findings with data obtained from foreign lands that employ other systems of lay participation. What political functions is our jury system supposed to have, and does it accomplish these better than other systems?

The Political Functions of the Jury System

I would like to reemphasize that the data and interpretations we have been discussing are at best only slightly related to any political-function hypothesis. Whether or not the jury and judge disagree, or whether one or

---

[32] Theodore L. Becker, *Political Behavioralism and Modern Jurisprudence* (Chicago: Rand McNally, 1965). See chap. 5.

the other is more or less objective and impartial, is relevant mainly to the legal system. It is only the degree to which this sort of finding is linked, explicitly or implicitly, to the concept of justice or the ultimate workings of the democratic process that it begins to touch on the political system.

I have noted before that justice is a value sought mainly through access to governmental institutions. When theorists speak of juries as being more flexible than judges (not relying heavily on precedent, i.e., being subjective), and therefore more just in their interpretation of the law, they are speaking of differences in decision-making behavior that have an influence on political rewards distributed by government. There is the opposite argument, equally political, that a judge's impartiality, i.e., willingness to be guided by precedent, is "evenhanded justice"; that is, a government of law and not of men. So what can we do about data on judge-jury differences in decision-making from this political perspective? We could say, in interpreting the Chicago data along these lines, that judges and juries were in the main equally just. Even so, some of the data on disagreement seem to indicate that juries occasionally act against a law. It is not a systematic rebellion, however. Kalven and Zeisel write, "We could not readily find any law against which the jury could be said to be in revolt, as it was a generation ago against Prohibition, and a century and a half ago against seditious libel."[33] Although Kalven and Zeisel call the jury "the law's most interesting critic,"[34] and note that "in an impressive number of cases we find that the explanation for this is that the jury's sense of justice leads it to policies which differ from official legal policies," they still conclude with the thought: "Despite the historical importance of this jury role, it is a commentary on the convergence of modern law and community sentiment that this list of unpopular laws is relatively short and the crimes on it are minor."[35]

This information, however, will simply be assimilated to fit the subjective beliefs of both the detractors and the supporters of the jury system. On the one hand, we will hear: "Well, there is that degree of justice, at any rate." From other quarters will come the view: "To that degree, the judge maintained a government of laws, not of men, and was therefore more just than the jurors." Sadly, as is so often the case, one man's justice is another man's tyranny.

> Where the prejudices of the community are shrouded in the verdict's mystery to carve out an exception from a rule whose normal operation would permit the defendant to go free, law-dispensing becomes

---

[33] Kalven and Zeisel, *op. cit.*, p. 286.
[34] *Ibid.*, p. 219.
[35] *Ibid.*

less palatable. The bona-fide white male conviction of a Negro for leering at a white girl at a distance of over sixty feet is a Southern exception to the ordinary assault rule.[36]

Pity the poor writers hoping to demonstrate in an objective, factual manner that justice must invariably lie in either role rigidity or situation flexbility when the hard, cold fact seems to be only that there exsts a certain degree of difference in the decision-making processes between professionals and laymen. Legal and political philosophers always run into trouble with possibilities, probabilities, and degrees. Their last resort is to protect their system by an overkill of eloquence, thereby hopelessly tranquilizing all would-be foes. Sir Patrick Devlin spoke of

> the English genius for arriving at a practical reconciliation of theoretical opposites. . . . Justice poses the problem of how to reconcile the rigidity of the law with the popular idea of what is fair and just. The English brought into being, as the basis of each solution, two institutions that have gained the admiration of the world—Parliament and the jury.[37]

Happily there are many other propositions of a political type in the literature dealing with the jury system that seem more amenable to empirical testing. These are not based on factual differences between judge and jury. Instead, they relate to the functions the jury has for the population of a society and for the government of that society. It is on proof of these, after all, that the jury must stand or fall, for as Tocqueville says, "The jury is pre-eminently a political institution."[38]

One of the most comprehensive political-functional statements is, once again, attributable to Dean Joiner:

> [The jury] is popular because it gives private citizens a broad participation in government. A significant job is performed without hiring new governmental employees or creating a new hierarchy. The jury provides for citizen participation in government unequalled elsewhere. If democracy is really to work . . . our citizens must not only be informed at election time but must know the meaning of making responsible decisions. Through the jury more private citizens participate in responsible decision-making than in all government put together. Certainly the decision of the juror is a responsible one, and he realizes it; and when he sees the difficulty in making it he cannot help but understand some of the problems that others, such as government officials, face when they have to make even more significant decisions than his.[39]

---

[36] Dale W. Broeder, "The Functions of the Jury," *University of Chicago Law Review,* 21 (Spring, 1954), p. 412.
[37] Sir Patrick Devlin, *Trial by Jury* (London: Stevens, 1956), p. 163.
[38] Tocqueville, *op. cit.* (Knopf ed.), p. 293.
[39] Joiner, *op. cit.,* p. 25.

Our first task, then, is to explicate and elaborate upon these functions. They fall into three main categories, under which a wide range of specific hypotheses is readily derivable.

Proposition 1 (Effect on the Citizen-Participant Himself)

Jury service, as a method of direct citizen participation in the governmental process, engenders a sense of efficacy among the citizenry.

    1.1.   Service on a jury allows some people to make important decisions (beyond their own personal lives) and thus engenders a sense of individual competence in all walks of life.

           (Note: the extrapolation of this might be: the greater the feelings of individual competency in the citizenry, the more open the society.)

    1.2.   Other forms of citizenship participation being relatively equal, a citizen who has participated on a jury will have greater feelings of efficacy in government than those who have not.

        (a)   Those who have participated in juries are more likely to participate more actively in other aspects of politics after their jury service.

    1.3.   The citizens of a democratic society that includes a jury system will have a greater sense of efficacy in their government than the citizens of a juryless "democratic" system.

        (a)   Those who have participated on a jury are more likely to feel that they can influence governmental policies than those who have not served on a jury.

Proposition 2 (Legitimacy Hypothesis)

Jury service engenders a greater understanding among citizens of the difficulties of governmental decision-making, and/or engenders greater loyalty to their government and its policies.

    2.1.   Those who have served on a jury are more sympathetic to (or have greater respect for) government officials, judges, and politicians.

    2.2.   When a case is controversial the citizenry is more likely to accept the verdict of a jury than that of a judge alone (the legitimacy hypothesis). This is more true of those citizens who have served on juries than those who have not.

    2.3.   Those who have participated in jury proceedings have greater loyalty to the government, in part or as a whole, than citizens who have not. They are also more likely to agree with government on its more controversial policies.

2.4. Citizens of a democratic society that provides jury trials have greater loyalty to their government than citizens of a government that does not provide them.

Proposition 3 (Fortress-of-Political-Liberty Hypothesis)

The existence of a jury system is a safeguard against the arbitrary use of the court system by government to prosecute its enemies for political purposes.

3.1. More political trials heard only by a judge end in conviction than political trials heard by jury.

3.2. There are fewer political trials in systems that provide juries than in systems that do not.

3.3. Political dissidents fear courts less in a system where trial by jury is available in political cases.

3.4. There are fewer convictions in political trials in systems where juries are available than in systems where they are not.

Generally speaking, there is some belief that the jury is one part of the American political system that stimulates positive affection toward itself as well as toward other parts of the government. This is supposed to occur (*a*) as a function of the ordinary citizen's desire to become directly exposed and involved in it, and (*b*) as a function of all citizens' equal chance to be called. Although there has been empirical study of feelings toward the jury itself on the part of former jurors and larger portions of the population, there is still no report of any empirical study explicitly designed to study the overflow of affect toward any other aspect of government or the political system as a whole. Still there is no paucity of inference along these lines. Herbert Jacob recently did an excellent job of collecting and citing most of these studies; his survey also affords an excellent illustration of the type of broad inference so frequently made.[40]

EFFECT ON THE CITIZEN PARTICIPANT HIMSELF (PROPOSITION 1)

The type of study and yield of information that seem to convince some people that jury duty influences political efficacy is the sort that demonstrates that the jury was satisfied, by and large, with the job it did,

---

[40] Herbert Jacob, *Justice in America* (Boston: Little, Brown and Company [Inc.], 1965). See also Charles P. Curtis, "The Trial Judge and the Jury," *Vanderbilt Law Review*, 5 (February, 1952), p. 157. This article is one of the best examples of a defense of the jury system based on anecdotes and negative reasoning. It is a statement of hallowed and hollow traditionalism.

or with the concept of the jury as the jurors came to understand it through their personal experiences. Joiner uses the small-group study to support his belief along these lines—but that study is as wobbly a foundation for this theory as it was for legal-systemic theory. On the other hand, Jacob notes that "ordinary Americans, in fact, value the opportunity that juries provide for popular participation in the judicial process."[41] This statement appears to mean more than that individual citizens feel they should discharge a duty. It would seem to indicate that they sense the extra possibility of personal accomplishment and political involvement through jury service. What data does he cite to support this inference?

> Those who have served on juries are on the whole pleased with their experience. In New York, 75 percent of those who served and were asked whether they would like to serve again unconditionally said Yes. In Wisconsin, most of those who served also liked their work. The Chicago Jury Project reported that among the general population that they sampled, only 36 percent would like to serve on a jury; but of those who had already served in recent years, 94 percent were willing to serve again.[42]

Certainly job satisfaction can be linked with feelings of efficacy, i.e., doing something through government, about government, and the like. On the other hand, it could be linked just as plausibly with a desire to break one's daily routine. One can be entertained by the workings of government and still not be affected appreciably in one's view of his own political capabilities. Such is one pitfall of inference when rival plausible hypotheses have not been disconfirmed. Furthermore, it is totally unacceptable to infer further relationship between this possible increase in political efficacy as a juror and an increase in a sense of efficacy in politics in general. Would a person who felt great frustration at his inability to influence government on the issue of the Vietnam war feel more politically effective after serving on a jury? I doubt it. Do Negroes who serve on urban juries feel less ineffective in their relationship to "the white power structure" than their brethren who have not served on juries? I doubt that too.

Ironically, though, one study quoted a Negro juror as stating that she felt great pride in being able to participate, and felt that the jury was a "wonderful way" of taking part in government.[43] Despite the fact that Negroes were found to be largely excluded from juries by the selection process and were largely ignored and somewhat disdained in jury-room deliberations, the few Negroes who served echoed this sentiment about

---

[41] Jacob, *op. cit.*, p. 120. See also W. J. Flynn, Jr., "Public Preference for the Jury," *New York State Bar Bulletin*, 32 (April, 1960), pp. 103–10.

[42] Jacob, *op. cit.*, p. 120.

[43] Dale W. Broeder, "The Negro in Court," *Duke Law Journal*, 1965 (Winter, 1965), p. 26.

jury functioning. How tragic that the best data to support Proposition 1 come from the mouths of people who are substantially barred from so much of ordinary American political life![44] Perhaps two subpropositions might be:

1. Jury service functions to make a small percentage of an alienated minority in a society feel political effectiveness.

2. Even the slim possibility of participation on a jury by members of a disadvantaged minority mitigates against feelings of total alienation on the part of a large percentage of that minority.

This might, if confirmed by study, become known as the "table scraps function." Some study of foreign legal systems produces evidence that a democratic society and a jury system are not very compatible at all. The jury system was introduced to Switzerland some 150 years ago, has been tried on and off federally and in several of the cantons, but is now said to be on its way to extinction in that land.[45] Indeed, if the existence of the jury system does function in fact as American writers believe, it is difficult to understand (*a*) why Swiss voters (who are notoriously eager to cast ballots) shun the election of jurors (a Swiss variation in juries), and (*b*) why, out of twenty-five cantons, fifteen do not even provide for jury trials in any kind of case. Moreover, as Francis O'Brien notes: "Surprisingly enough, this is true for the three cantons where 'pure' democracy still survives."[46] Some cynics would say that it is not surprising at all. Where democracy does truly exist there is no need for a form that pretends to the throne of democracy.

LEGITIMACY (PROPOSITION 2)

Another, perhaps more justifiable, inference is made from those studies that have sought a viewpoint from jurors (as well as from samples of a much larger population) on the desirability or undesirability of the jury trial. There is frequent allusion to a relationship between the jury system and the public's acceptance of legal decisions as fair, proper, just, and the like.[47] For instance, again according to Jacob:

> A Gallup Poll in 1957 reported that 58 percent of the respondents preferred a jury trial in automobile accident cases, and 51 percent in

---

[44] *Ibid.*; see the section "The Negro Juror: General Reactions," pp. 25–28.

[45] Francis William O'Brien, "The Jury in Switzerland," *Brooklyn Law Review*, 33 (Fall, 1966), pp. 58–69.

[46] *Ibid.*, p. 66.

[47] Some observers have speculated that the unanimity requirement, as opposed to a majority-vote variation, may be the factor that does most to instill confidence in jury verdicts among the population. See J. J. Cremona, "Jury System in Malta," *American Journal of Comparative Law*, 13 (Autumn, 1964), pp. 570–83.

serious criminal cases, whereas only 16 percent preferred trial by judge in the former cases and 35 percent in the latter. In Wisconsin a poll taken in 1963 indicated that 56 percent preferred trial by jury as against 16 percent who preferred trial by judge.[48]

Jacob himself may or may not be inferring legitimacy from such data. But there can be little doubt that these studies present the type of social-scientifically accumulated data only vaguely supportive of the plethora of literature proclaiming the legitimacy and fairness propositions to be clearly proved. Clearly, they are not. After all, it is equally possible that people may think that juries are a "softer touch," more easily fooled. This would hardly be the same as saying they were fairer. Thus the legitimacy function might really be the "put something over on the government" function. Or, to put it a bit more anomalously, it may be the "antilegitimacy" function.

FORTRESS OF POLITICAL LIBERTY (PROPOSITION 3)

As one might expect, there is similar breast-beating and stridency over Proposition 3 and its derivatives, but again sparse data and some internal inconsistency combine to undermine the argumentation. The tone of these utterances and their mode of presentation are frequently akin to those of a founding father offering a "self-evident truth." Indeed, many a leading political philosopher of yore has seen the jury as the leading symbol of individual political freedom within a society,[49] and this attitude continues to the present day. Botein states, for instance, that "it must be repeated that the jury system has always drawn nourishment as the defender of the individual against tyranny and oppression."[50] Jacob, after a thumbnail sketch of the history of the jury system, puts it like this: "In this way juries became instruments for limiting the arbitrary use of the courts against political opponents."[51] And Devlin affirms that trial by jury is "the lamp that shows that freedom lives."[52] No end of illustration could be provided, but to no good end.

The fact is simply that there is, once again, little systematically accumulated data relative to this area of political-judicial theory. On the other hand, there is also a fair amount of information that is convincing to the contrary.

---

[48] Jacob, *op. cit.*, pp. 119–20.
[49] See Montesquieu, *The Spirit of Laws*, trans. Thomas Nugent (New York: Hafner, 1949).
[50] Bernard Botein, *Trial Judge* (New York: Simon & Schuster, 1952), pp. 190–91.
[51] Jacob, *op. cit.*, p. 109.
[52] Devlin, *op. cit.*, p. 164.

In view of all the evidence of jury-railroading that American history has to offer, it is difficult to think of the jury as a citadel for the defense of individual eccentricity and nonconformity against an arbitrary, vengeful administration of justice. Particularly in the area of the political offense, there is very little reason to suspect that the jury would be more likely to acquit than a professionally trained judge (or less likely, for that matter), given the tremendous public pressures and hysteria often attending this kind of trial. There is some reason to believe that this is a systemic rather than an episodic flaw, for as government becomes more accessible and responsive to the popular mass, there is increased possibility that juries will go along with governmental acts of oppression, not oppose them. As one American judge stated after a lengthy administration of the Espionage Act during World War I:

> Most of the jurymen have sons in the war. They are all under the power of the passions which war engenders. For the first six months after June 15, 1917, I tried war cases before jurymen who were candid, sober, intelligent businessmen, whom I had known for thirty years, and who under ordinary circumstances would have had the highest respect for my declaration of law, but during that period they looked back into my eyes with the savagery of wild animals, saying by their manner, "Away with this twiddling, let us get at him." Men believed during that period that the only verdict in a war case, which could show loyalty, was a verdict of guilt.[53]

Furthermore, as Lewis Mayers observes:

> It is possible that local feeling favorable to the accused constitutes a graver weakness in trial by jury than does local hostility to him. The limited or totally absent provision in our law for a change of venue at the instance of the prosecutor has already been mentioned; nor is it of much value, even where available, if the popular feeling involved extends over a considerable region. Under these circumstances the jury, instead of being a shield to the innocent against official oppression, becomes a refuge for the guilty.[54]

The many southern prosecutors who have made valiant attempts to convict white racists for perpetrating physical attacks (sometimes fatal) on civil rights workers, white and black, can attest to the truth of this statement. This hardly works to the benefit of the liberty of disliked individuals or minorities. Do not the traditional odes to the jury become somewhat galling in the face of these widespread and repeated incidents?[55]

---

[53] Zechariah Chafee, *Free Speech in the United States* (Cambridge: Harvard University Press, 1948), p. 70.

[54] Lewis Mayers, *The American Legal System*, rev. ed. (New York: Harper & Row, 1964), pp. 117–18.

[55] The best collection of materials on the court practices in America's Southland to date is Leo Friedman, ed., *Southern Justice* (New York: Pantheon, 1966).

Also, in a historical vein, the use of juries as some sort of popular check on judiciaries (being a branch of government) is appropriate at least partially to the degree to which (*a*) the judiciary is not independent of the executive, and (*b*) the political system formally guarantees political liberties to individuals. The failure to recognize this has led to some legal practices that make little sense. For example, Mayers notes, in discussing jury waiver:

> In the remaining states constitutional provisions forbid such a waiver, and the defendant must be tried by a jury even though he might prefer to be tried by the judge alone. In some states and in the federal courts, the consent of the prosecution is required as well as the consent of the defendant, a rule which is difficult to justify in the light of the history of the right of trial by jury and its obvious purpose to protect the individual against a judge under the domination of the executive.[56]

My own examination of the data and interpretations has led me to this conclusion: We have much to learn but probably will continue to believe as we must. Extensive study of these topics could yield data more directly relevant to the theories and the controversy among them, but I do not foresee this occurring—particularly since the publication of the Kalven-Zeisel volume, with its thinly veiled reverence for juries. If I am correct, this would be unfortunate. Nor is the outlook very bright for the comparative studies necessary to test propositions like 1.3 and 2.4, or any of those derivable from Proposition 3. But it is possible that such studies may yet be done, since a comparative reorientation is taking place generally in political science. In the hope of some future systematic, comprehensive adventures in this area, I would like to turn now to the few foreign lay-participation studies that avoid being mainly legal in their perspective.[57]

Comparative Studies

The researchers of the Chicago jury project managed to collect the limited systematic comparative data and analyses available on juries as well as on the mixed tribunal. Their purpose was to compare them with their own data and conclusions. Though included as an aside (their Appendix

---

56 Mayers, *op. cit.*, p. 114.
57 For an example of the "mainly legal" variety, see Ruth Ginsburg, "The Jury and the Nämnd," *Cornell Law Quarterly*, 48 (Winter, 1963), pp. 253–73.

C), each of two studies is discussed briefly as to its design and its results. A third, an Austrian study, was still in progress at the time of publication of *The American Jury*. According to the Chicago group, these
studies represent the full (but lean) product of such research. The
authors of *The American Jury* find that these few works provide substantiation for the conclusions they draw from their study of the American
jury. However, since the comparative studies differ so radically in design
from the Chicago project, I think it best to examine their conclusions somewhat closely.

The first of these foreign studies is a careful, albeit impressionistic,
look at the work of English juries by Lord Chief Justice Parker of Wad-
dington. The lord chief justice was apparently impressed by the work of
the Chicago project, and following a visit by one or more of its members to
England he consulted the senior judges of the queen's bench on the question of judge-juror disagreement. Evidently Justice Parker asked the judges
of the queen's bench to respond to a question similar to one in the Chicago
questionnaire about the degree of accord and disagreement between judge
and jury in various cases. In reporting the findings, he noted duly that none
of the judges kept records of this, and that their replies were "largely a
matter of impression."[58] Justice Parker's data were sent to the authors of
The American Jury, and read as follows:

1. Cases of "ordinary crime" in which the Jury reaches a verdict which
   the Judge sitting alone would not have arrived at.
   (*a*) The cases in which the Judge would have acquitted where the
   Jury have convicted are very rare. Such cases as have been
   specifically referred to comprise sexual cases where the Jury
   have approached the matter in a common sense way whereas
   the Judge would have been more influenced by legal considerations such as the absence of corroboration.
   (*b*) Cases in which the Judge would have convicted where the
   Jury have acquitted range from 3% to 10%. These include
   cases when a Jury convicts of a minor offense rather than the
   grave offense, e.g., convicts of unlawful wounding and not
   wounding with intent to do grievous bodily harm.
2. Cases in which the Judge has been unable to say after consideration that the Jury may have been right, i.e., where the verdict is
   perverse, are very rare. The answers received describe them as
   "none," "negligible," "very rare," or "hardly ever."[59]

At this point, the authors of *The American Jury*, so very circumspect
in their methodological steps and assumptions, make a wide detour from
avenues of sound analysis. They attempt to "translate Lord Parker's letter

---

[58] Kalven and Zeisel, *op. cit.*, p. 514.
[59] *Ibid.*, pp. 514–15.

into the fourfold table used throughout [their] study [and] apply his data to trial statistics [for 1952] published for England and Wales." The tables that are the translations, so to speak, seem to me to be nothing more than a quasi-scientific façade. They inject infinitely more malaise than virtue into the analysis.

In the first place, why 1952 statistics on court cases were used is not explained. There is no indication that the judges of the queen's bench who were surveyed were thinking of that particular year, and 1952 is not even one of the years from which the American sample was drawn (1955 and 1959). Additionally, 1952 was a year of some political and social upheaval in England, the Attlee Labour government having tasted defeat only the previous year. Such a political reversal could be a conditioning agent for aberrant political behavior within the citizenry, and it is not implausible to suspect that ordinary citizens might have shown an unusual degree of deference to a particularly stable political institution, i.e., the courts, at that particular time. But this is the least of the intellectual horrors perpetrated in Appendix C of *The American Jury*.

Perhaps the worst is the assignment by the Chicago authors of specific numerical percentages to Justice Parker's verbal estimates ("very rare") on judge-jury disagreement, and their acceptance of his estimates of 3 percent and 10 percent as accurate measurements of the range of leniency of some unspecified number of judges. The assignment of particular percentages to these guesses was done to make the lord chief justice's information concretely comparable with the rigorously developed tables of American data. But it is clear that such a clumsy device is a pale imitation of scientifically oriented comparative analysis. Do Justice Parker's efforts indicate a comparable degree of dissent between English and American judges and juries? It is even impossible to know whether it would be more or less. Under no circumstances can these estimates support the Chicago statement that "there seems to be no doubt then that the English juries dissent less frequently from the judge than do their American counterparts."[60] Of course there is doubt, for "very rare" judge-acquitted/juror-convicted cases may well be somewhere between 5 and 10 percent. If we add this to an approximate 8 percent or 9 percent of judge-convicted/juror-acquitted cases, the total is about the same as the American percentage. Besides, estimates are not empirical proof. Furthermore, is a 3 to 10 percent range more or less than "very rare"? It is quite impossible to say; yet the Chicago authors blithely assume that it is more (in their Table 147). They arbitrarily assign the jury-convicted/judge-acquitted case percentage at a mere 1 percent and the jury-ac-

---

[60] *Ibid.*, p. 516.

quitted/judge-convicted case percentage at 7 percent. It is true that 1 percent is very rare, but in the minds of some, so is 5 percent. What does Justice Parker think? Even that would not be sufficient grounds for this type of gamesmanship with statistics.

The lone study that has collected information on the ratio of agreement to disagreement between professional and lay judges in a mixed tribunal is also described and commented upon in Appendix C. This study was conducted by F. Lucas, who was the presiding judge on a Danish appellate court that had three lay and three professional judges. Table 8 represents Table 149 of the Chicago study, which is extracted from the Danish study, first published in 1944.

It is significant to note, I think, that the authors of *The American Jury* feel compelled to notify the reader that "again, on the average, the lay judges were more favorable to the defendant."[61] This seems to be another illustration of a marked tendency in the Kalven-Zeisel work to interpret ambiguous data in favor of the jury. Though the authors caution readers early in their volume that many of their data are subject to diverse interpretations, their own consistent resolution of ambiguity in one direction makes their interpretation suspect.[62] For this reason, I feel inclined to treat

TABLE 8

Agreement and Dissent Between Three Lay and Three Learned Judges on the Issue of Guilt

		Percent
All six judges unanimous		85
Split vote		15
One lay judge for acquittal	4	
Two lay judges for acquittal	—	
Three lay judges for acquittal	2	
Three lay judges and one learned judge for acquittal	2	
One lay judge for lesser included offense	2	
Vote is split by details not indicated	5	
TOTAL		100%
Number of cases		123

SOURCE: Harry Kalven, Jr., and Hans Zeisel, *The American Jury* (Boston: Little, Brown and Company [Inc.], 1966), p. 517.

61 *Ibid.*, p. 519.

62 For a more fully explicated statement of the conservative nature of his bias, see Harry Kalven, Jr., "The Dignity of the Civil Jury," *Virginia Law Review*, 50 (October, 1964), pp. 1055–75. He admits, in his conclusion, that "I incline toward the view that old institutions should not be changed lightly." And he states his lately developed view that the institution of the jury system is, among other things, humane, sane, and responsible. It must be stated in Kalven's favor that he himself recognizes his own prejudice and the danger to interpretation that this implies.

the data presented throughout the text and the appendices with far more respect than the ancillary interpretations of it. One noteworthy datum, from a comparative point of view, is that the Danish percentage of split votes is extremely close to the American percentages as presented in the text of *The American Jury*. On the other hand, since these Danish data were first published in 1944, it seems likely that they were compiled on trials conducted during the Nazi occupation period. This may diminish their value as examples of Danish behavior or of the behavior of any citizenry under ordinary circumstances.

In addition to the presentation of data on judge-layman agreement, the Chicago group mentions, in embellishing these data and their own interpretation of them, that Judge Lucas himself was not impressed by the work of the laymen on his court. According to Kalven and Zeisel, "Judge Lucas's over-all conclusion is that in his experience the lay judges have made no significant contribution to his court."[63] Kalven and Zeisel chide Lucas for his comments about "questions that proved particularly difficult for the lay judges." At one point we find the Chicago people musing, "It must be difficult for the learned judge in a divided court to believe that the lay judges could be right."[64] Fortunately, the importance for comparative study of Mr. Lucas' observation does not lie in the Chicago group's analysis of it. In this instance, it lies in the literal translation and presentation of a statement on the Danish system by a Danish judge who, sufficiently convinced of the value of collecting data systematically and rigorously actually to do so, asserts his evaluation of this systemic variation. Lucas believed that some legal questions were particularly difficult for laymen, and that this accounted for "deviations from objective fact-finding." In other words, he apparently prefers mixed-tribunal duty to jury duty for laymen; for according to Kalven and Zeisel:

> In the jury trial the role of the learned judge is limited to presiding over the trial and he has no part in the deliberation. In the mixed tribunal, the learned judge is offered a chance for discussion, and, as Judge Lucas puts it, for a "clearing-up of misunderstandings."[65]

Lucas' evaluation presents a very interesting set of hypotheses to be tested on the legal efficiency of variations in the mixed-tribunal system. Unfortunately, like all of the others discussed in the body of the Chicago work itself and in Appendix C, this is of limited interest to students of comparative judicial politics from a substantive point of view. The subject matter is legal, not political. There is still no social-scientifically

---

[63] Kalven and Zeisel, *op. cit.*, p. 519.
[64] *Ibid.*
[65] *Ibid.*

oriented testing of any of the political propositions discussed earlier in this chapter. There are few empirical studies of any type on such phenomena. One of the rare exceptions is the political-journalistic effort by George Feifer mentioned earlier, *Justice in Moscow*.[66]

The main political questions to be answered in this area of judicial structural variation are: (1) Do any of the forms of citizen participation in the judiciary substantially add to feelings of individual political worth (efficacy), and, if so, (2) is the jury or the mixed tribunal more effective toward this end?

We have noted that American scholars who have studied the American jury system seem convinced that the jury system does make the average American feel more politically involved and effective, and it is assumed that this is the best method for achieving such feelings. Feifer spent a good deal of time observing and interviewing Muscovites who attended and participated in local judicial proceedings. He makes the following observation about the institution of the jury in the USSR: "It does not exist in Russia. A few liberal law professors suggested recently that it be re-established—fused to the court, like some of the juries of Western Europe —to decide questions of fact in the most serious cases. Their recommendations met overwhelming disapproval as 'bourgeois.' "[67] Who knows what manner of insult would be hurled at some American liberal law professor who suggested that a state adopt a lay-assessor system, even on an experimental basis? The word "communist" does come to mind.

Further examination into citizen participation at the lower judicial levels seems to confirm something that Feifer was told (and which he personally believes): that Russians think their system superior to a jury system. Moreover, they believe their system is truly and totally democratic. After all, not even the proudest American advocate of the jury system pretends that the jury has power equal to that of the professional judge. Feifer himself, as an observer, sees additional merit to the Russian argument.

Most of our viewpoint on the Soviet system of administration of justice in the courts has been formed through scholarly statutory interpretation, analysis of indigenous Soviet jurisprudence, observation of the highly visible but peculiar public purge trials, and discussions with Soviet jurisprudents at home and abroad. Feifer is one of the few to have regularly attended trials at the lowest levels of the Soviet court system. He is the first American to draft a report on the operations of the people's courts and comradely courts based on lengthy, firsthand, systematic observation

---

[66] George Feifer, *Justice in Moscow* (New York: Simon & Schuster, 1964).
[67] *Ibid.*, p. 80. Copyright © 1964 by George Feifer. Reprinted by permission of Simon & Schuster and Harold Matson Co., Inc.

and analysis. His descriptions leave us little choice but to reassess (*a*) our cherished view of the ultimate democratic value of the American jury system and (*b*) our belief in the authoritarian nature of the comradely courts.

In the first place, at the level of the people's courts, there are two lay assessors to each three-member tribunal; the third member is a professional judge. At the level of the comradely courts, the principle of *obshchestven-nost* (local community action) comes into play and no professional judge is to be found. The judges are common people who are elected and have no legal training. Feifer is quick to note that these elections are hotly contested and asserts that there is no party rigging or official influence on the outcome. Second, there are no trappings to set the rulers or officials apart from the public. No robes are worn. There is no raised dais to support any illusion that the questions or sentences emanate from on high. And no technical jargon is used. Third, and perhaps most important, in the comradely courts there is a good amount of interaction between the judge and the other people assembled in the courtroom. Rather than sitting back and passively listening, the spectators freely offer any "evidence" they wish.

> A Soviet trial is informal by any standard; there is nothing a layman cannot understand. The rules of the game (or compulsions of the ritual) are not treasured like intricate, ancient plumage. What the people in court have to say is more important than how they must say it. In the trials that I observed, when an interested observer had some relevant information to give, he gave it, even if it would have been inadmissible as evidence in a foreign court and even if he was not, at the moment, in the witness stand.[68]

Of course, sometimes this procedure becomes unwieldy. On the other hand, it is not necessarily what many American observers fear as mob justice or a kangaroo court. Despite the fact that open-and-shut cases are frequently put before the comradely courts (partially a function of exhaustive pretrial investigation), Feifer is convinced that there is no direction from above and that the courts operate under a sense of popular justice, according to accepted views of the general socialistic law and socialistic mercy. This is moving away from being a court, true, but its participatory function is obvious.[69] Feifer tells of the trial of five teen-age boys accused of hooliganism—harassment against a social worker:

> It was a classic case of "antisocial behavior," perfect raw material for a Comradely Court. It could put an end to an intolerable, though not criminal, human situation and preach the lessons of "socialistic mo-

---

[68] *Ibid.*, p. 50.
[69] Feifer agrees (*ibid.*, p. 113).

rality," "Communistic upbringing" and "comradely, communal living"
—all at the same time. . . .

It was a fiasco from the start: the auditorium lights went out for
ten-minute intervals, and the audience, restless in utter darkness,
shouted every kind of mocking comment. . . . When the lights worked,
the microphone did not, and the chairman, though bellowing at full
voice, could not be heard beyond the tenth row. No one seemed interested in hearing him anyway. The social worker was a sweet old
do-gooder. . . . But she was so obviously unsuited to working with
teen-age boys, so perfectly "square," that the audience mocked her
in spite of her woeful tales. "Put her in a kindergarten where she
belongs," "It's her own fault for babying the boys." . . . Paroxysms
of laughter followed these comments. . . . The audience became
noisier and noisier. The boys went on wisecracking marvelously.
The chairman kept trying to get someone to condemn the defendants' behavior. . . .

It lasted three hours, the audience had dwindled by half toward
the end, and that half booed wildly when the chairman shouted that it
would take at least a half hour to write the decision. He wrote it,
therefore, in five minutes; although the court found that the boys
had indeed behaved poorly, it "limited itself to a public examination
of the case," and it prescribed no punishment, since the boys "saw
the danger of their ways and promised to reform."[70]

Feifer's main point, a concise challenge to so many of our assumptions, is
expressed in the words of an old woman who came up to him and said,
"Do you understand how *obshchestvennost* works? The people decide.
That's democracy. It's the drawing of the people into the administration
of public affairs. It's truly people's justice."[71] Feifer adds: "And indeed,
everyone I knew who attended these meetings assured me that at this level
the rank and file *does* decide. It is not a rubber stamp."[72]

Conclusion

The Feifer study's cardinal novelty, again, is that his work is an extensive and intensive firsthand scholarly observation of a contrasting system of lay participation in the judicial process. It is comparative in intent
and in spirit. Its major value is less substantive than exemplary. Feifer's
study illustrates the vast potential for serious testing of the many political-
functional hypotheses that are comparative by their very nature. Up to
now, these hypotheses, when tested at all, were tested by inference from

[70] *Ibid.*, pp. 121–24.
[71] *Ibid.*, p. 126.
[72] *Ibid.*

data gathered only from American respondents and not intended to test such relationships directly. The bias of the respondents, compounded by the bias of the analysts, could result only in self-serving conclusions worded as confirmed propositions. We have still not come far from the goals and methods of Blackstone, Tocqueville, and Hamilton.

Comparative behavioral study explicitly designed to test such hypotheses would be simple to conceive and probably feasible to execute in many foreign countries. If we really want to know the varying effectiveness of different modes of citizen participation in the judicial process, the way is open. It is in comparative field research.

Another way to test these hypotheses would be through experimental work on small groups. It would be easy enough to set up models of the various forms of lay participation, structural types in contrast with control groups, and to put all of these hypotheses to thorough and objective test. The Chicago project people have attested to their strong belief in the validity of experimental study using mock juries. This view makes far more sense in the study of juries than in the simulated studies of nations in the field of international relations, where so many of such studies are conducted. Also, the small-group approach would eliminate the cultural variable in comparative study and show (we may hope) whether foreign variations would work in America.

We need to do more than play with science. We need to use it.

APPENDIX

Sheppard v. Maxwell

(U.S.A., 1966)

MR. JUSTICE CLARK delivered the opinion of the Court.

I.

Marilyn Sheppard, petitioner's pregnant wife, was bludgeoned to death in the upstairs bedroom of their lakeshore home in Bay Village, Ohio, a suburb of Cleveland. On the day of the tragedy, July 4, 1954, Sheppard pieced together for several local officials the following story: He and his wife had entertained neighborhood friends, the Aherns, on the previous evening at their home. After dinner they watched television in the living room. Sheppard became drowsy and dozed off to sleep on a couch. Later, Marilyn partially awoke him saying that she was going to bed. The next thing he remembered was hearing his wife cry out in the early morning hours. He hurried upstairs and in the dim light from the hall saw a "form" standing next to his wife's bed. As he struggled with the "form" he was struck on the back of the neck and rendered unconscious. On regaining his senses he found himself on the floor next to his wife's bed. He raised up, looked at her, took her pulse and "felt that she was gone." He then went to his son's room and found him unmolested. Hearing a noise, he hurried downstairs. He saw a "form" running out the door and pursued it to the lake shore. He grappled with it on the beach and again lost consciousness. Upon his recovery he was lying face down with the lower portion of his body in the water. He returned to his home, checked the pulse on his wife's neck, and "determined or thought that she was gone." He then went downstairs and called a neighbor, Mayor Houk of Bay Village. The Mayor and his wife came over at once, found Sheppard slumped in an easy chair downstairs and asked, "What happened?" Sheppard replied: "I don't know but somebody ought to try to do something for Marilyn." Mrs. Houk immediately went up to the bedroom. The Mayor told Sheppard, "Get hold of yourself. Can you tell me what happened?" Sheppard then related the above-outlined events. After Mrs. Houk discovered the body, the Mayor called the local police, Dr. Richard Sheppard, petitioner's brother, and Aherns. The local police were the first to arrive. They in turn notified the Coroner and Cleveland police.

* * *

From the outset officials focused suspicion on Sheppard. After a search of the house and premises on the morning of the tragedy, Dr. Gerber, the Coroner, is reported—and it is undenied—to have told his men, "Well, it is evident the doctor did this, so let's go get the confession out of him." He proceeded to interrogate and examine Sheppard while the latter was under sedation in his hospital room. On the same occasion, the Coroner was given the clothes Shep-

86 S. Ct. 1507 (1966). Footnotes have been renumbered. Citations have been omitted.

pard wore at the time of the tragedy together with the personal items in them. Later that afternoon Chief Eaton and two Cleveland police officers interrogated Sheppard at some length, confronting him with evidence and demanding explanations. Asked by Officer Shotke to take a lie detector test, Sheppard said he would if it were reliable. Shotke replied that it was "infallible" and "you might as well tell us all about it now." At the end of the interrogation Shotke told Sheppard: "I think you killed your wife." Still later in the same afternoon a physician sent by the Coroner was permitted to make a detailed examination of Sheppard. Until the Coroner's inquest on July 22, at which time he was subpoenaed, Sheppard made himself available for frequent and extended questioning without the presence of an attorney.

On July 7, the day of Marilyn Sheppard's funeral, a newspaper story appeared in which Assistant County Attorney Mahon—later the chief prosecutor of Sheppard—sharply criticized the refusal of the Sheppard family to permit his immediate questioning. From there on headline stories repeatedly stressed Sheppard's lack of cooperation with the police and other officials. Under the headline "Testify Now In Death, Bay Doctor Is Ordered," one story described a visit by Coroner Gerber and four police officers to the hospital on July 8. When Sheppard insisted that his lawyer be present, the Coroner wrote out a subpoena and served it on him. Sheppard then agreed to submit to questioning without counsel and the subpoena was torn up. The officers questioned him for several hours. On July 9, Sheppard, at the request of the Coroner, re-enacted the tragedy at his home before the Coroner, police officers, and a group of newsmen, who apparently were invited by the Coroner. The home was locked so that Sheppard was obliged to wait outside until the Coroner arrived. Sheppard's performance was reported in detail by the news media along with photographs. The newspapers also played up Sheppard's refusal to take a lie detector test and "the protective ring" thrown up by his family. Front-page newspaper headlines announced on the same day that "Doctor Balks at Lie Test; Retells Story." A column opposite that story contained an "exclusive" interview with Sheppard headlined: " 'Loved My Wife, She Loved Me,' Sheppard Tells News Reporters." The next day, another headline story disclosed that Sheppard had "again late yesterday refused to take a lie detector test" and quoted an Assistant County Attorney as saying that "at the end of a nine-hour questioning of Dr. Sheppard, I felt he was now ruling [a test] out completely." But subsequent newspaper articles reported that the Coroner was still pushing Sheppard for a lie detector test. More stories appeared when Sheppard would not allow authorities to inject him with "truth serum."

On the 20th, the "editorial artillery" opened fire with a front-page charge that somebody is "getting away with murder." The editorial attributed the ineptness of the investigation to "friendships, relationships, hired lawyers, a husband who ought to have been subjected instantly to the same third degree to which any person under similar circumstances is subjected. . . ." The following day, July 21, another page-one editorial was headed: "Why No Inquest? Do It Now, Dr. Gerber." The Coroner called an inquest the same day and subpoenaed Sheppard. It was staged the next day in a school gymnasium; the Coroner presided with the County Prosecutor as his advisor and two detectives as bailiffs. In the front of the room was a long table occupied by reporters, television and radio personnel, and broadcasting equipment. The hearing was broadcast with live microphones placed at the Coroner's seat and the witness stand. A swarm of reporters and photographers attended. Sheppard was brought into the room by police who searched him in full view of several hundred spectators. Sheppard's counsel were present during the three-day inquest but were not permitted to participate. When Sheppard's chief counsel attempted to place some documents in the record, he was forcibly ejected from the room by the Coroner, who received cheers, hugs, and kisses from ladies in the audience. Sheppard was questioned for five and one-half hours about his actions on the night of the murder, his married life, and a love affair with Susan Hayes. At the end of the hearing the Coroner announced that he "could" order Sheppard held for the grand jury, but did not do so.

Throughout this period the newspapers emphasized evidence that tended to incriminate Sheppard and pointed out discrepancies in his statements to authorities. At the same time, Sheppard made many public statements to the press and wrote feature articles asserting his innocence. During the inquest on July 26, a headline in large type stated: "Kerr [Captain of the Cleveland Police] Urges Sheppard's Arrest." In the story, Detective McArthur "disclosed that scientific tests at the Sheppard home have definitely established that the killer washed off a trail of blood from the murder bedroom to the downstairs section," a circumstance casting doubt on Sheppard's accounts of the murder. No such evidence was produced at trial. The newspapers also delved into Sheppard's personal life. Articles stressed his extra-marital love affairs as a motive for the crime. The newspapers portrayed Sheppard as a Lothario, fully explored his relationship with Susan Hayes, and named a number of other women who were allegedly involved with him. The testimony at trial never showed that Sheppard had any illicit relationships besides the one with Susan Hayes.

On July 28, an editorial entitled "Why Don't Police Quiz Top Suspect" demanded that Sheppard be taken to police headquarters. It described him in the following language: "Now proved under oath to be a liar, still free to go about his business, shielded by his family, protected by a smart lawyer who has made monkeys of the police and authorities, carrying a gun part of the time, left free to do whatever he pleases . . ." A front-page editorial on July 30 asked: "Why Isn't Sam Sheppard in Jail?" It was later titled "Quit Stalling—Bring Him In." After calling Sheppard "the most unusual murder suspect ever seen around these parts" the article said that "[e]xcept for some superficial questioning during Coroner Sam Gerber's inquest he has been scot-free of any official grilling. . . ." It asserted that he was "surrounded by an iron curtain of protection [and] concealment."

That night at 10 o'clock Sheppard was arrested at his father's home on a charge of murder. He was taken to the Bay Village City Hall where hundreds of people, newscasters, photographers and reporters were awaiting his arrival. He was immediately arraigned—having been denied a temporary delay to secure the presence of counsel—and bound over to the grand jury.

The publicity then grew in intensity until his indictment on August 17. Typical of the coverage during this period is a front-page interview entitled: "DR. SAM: 'I Wish There Was Something I Could Get Off My Chest—but There Isn't.' " Unfavorable publicity included items such as a cartoon of the body of a sphinx with Sheppard's head and the legend below: " 'I Will Do Everything In My Power to Help Solve This Terrible Murder.'—Dr. Sam Sheppard." Headlines announced, *inter alia*, that: "Doctor Evidence is Ready for Jury," "Corrigan Tactics Stall Quizzing," "Sheppard 'Gay Set' is Revealed by Houk," "Blood Is Found In Garage," "New Murder Evidence Is Found, Police Claim," "Dr. Sam Faces Quiz At Jail On Marilyn's Fear Of Him." On August 18, an article appeared under the headline "Dr. Sam Writes His Own Story." And reproduced across the entire front page was a portion of the typed statement signed by Sheppard: "I am not guilty of the murder of my wife, Marilyn. How could I, who have been trained to help people and devote my life to saving life, commit such a terrible and revolting crime?" We do not detail the coverage further. There are five volumes filled with similar clippings from each of the three Cleveland newspapers covering the period from the murder until Sheppard's conviction in December 1954. The record includes no excerpts from newscasts on radio and television but since space was reserved in the courtroom for these media we assume that their coverage was equally large.

II.

With this background the case came on for trial two weeks before the November general election at which the chief prosecutor was a candidate for municipal judge and the presiding judge, Judge Blythin, was a candidate to succeed himself. Twenty-five days before the case was set, a list of 75 veniremen were called as prospective jurors. This list, including the addresses of each venireman, was published in all three Cleveland newspapers. As a consequence, anonymous letters and telephone calls, as well as calls from friends, regarding the impending prosecution were received by all of the prospective jurors. The selection of the jury began on October 18, 1954.

The courtroom in which the trial was held measured 26 by 48 feet. A long temporary table was set up inside the bar, in back of the single counsel table. It ran the width of the courtroom, parallel to the bar railing, with one end less than three feet from the jury box. Approximately 20 representatives of newspapers and wire services were assigned seats at this table by the court. Behind the bar railing there were four rows of benches. These seats were likewise assigned by the court for the entire trial. The first row was occupied by representatives of television and radio stations, and the second and third rows by reporters from out-of-town newspapers and magazines. One side of the last row, which accommodated 14 people, was assigned to Sheppard's family and the other to Marilyn's. The public was permitted to fill vacancies in this row on special passes only. Representatives of the news media also used all the rooms on the courtroom floor, including the room where cases were ordinarily called and assigned for trial. Private telephone lines and telegraphic equipment were installed in these rooms so that reports from the trial could be speeded to the papers. Station WSRS was permitted to set up broadcasting facilities on the third floor of the courthouse next door to the jury room, where the jury rested during recesses in the trial and deliberated. Newscasts were made from this room throughout the trial, and while the jury reached its verdict.

On the sidewalk and steps in front of the courthouse, television and newsreel cameras were occasionally used to take motion pictures of the participants in the trial, including the jury and the judge. Indeed, one television broadcast carried a staged interview of the judge as he entered the courthouse. In the corridors outside the courtroom there was a host of photographers and television personnel with flash cameras, portable lights and motion picture cameras. This group photographed the prospective jurors during selection of the jury. After the trial opened, the witnesses, counsel, and jurors were photographed and televised whenever they entered or left the courtroom. Sheppard was brought to the courtroom about 10 minutes before each session began; he was surrounded by reporters and extensively photographed for the newspapers and television. A rule of court prohibited picture-taking in the courtroom during the actual sessions of the court, but no restraints were put on photographers during recesses, which were taken once each morning and afternoon, with a longer period for lunch.

All of these arrangements with the news media and their massive coverage of the trial continued during the entire nine weeks of the trial. The courtroom remained crowded to capacity with representatives of news media. Their movement in and out of the courtroom often caused so much confusion that, despite the loud speaker system installed in the courtroom, it was difficult for the witnesses and counsel to be heard. Furthermore, the reporters clustered within the bar of the small courtroom made confidential talk among Sheppard and his counsel almost impossible during the proceedings. They frequently had to leave the courtroom to obtain privacy. And many times when counsel wished to raise a point with the judge out of the hearing of the jury it was necessary to move to the judge's chambers. Even then, news media representatives so packed the judge's anteroom that counsel could hardly return from the chambers to the courtroom. The reporters vied with each other to find out what counsel and the judge had discussed, and often these matters later appeared in newspapers accessible to the jury.

The daily record of the proceedings was made available to the newspapers and the testimony of each witness was printed *verbatim* in the local editions, along with objections of counsel, and rulings by the judge. Pictures of Sheppard, the judge, counsel, pertinent witnesses, and the jury often accompanied the daily newspaper and television accounts. At times the newspapers published photographs of exhibits introduced at the trial, and the rooms of Sheppard's house were featured along with relevant testimony.

The jurors themselves were constantly exposed to the news media. Every juror, except one, testified at *voir dire* to reading about the case in the Cleveland papers or to having heard broadcasts about it. Seven of the 12 jurors who rendered the verdict had one or more Cleveland papers delivered in their homes; the remaining jurors were not interrogated on the point. Nor were there questions as to radios or television sets in the talesmen's homes, but we must assume that most of them owned such conveniences. As the selection of the jury progressed, individual pictures of prospective members appeared daily. During the trial, pictures of the jury appeared over 40 times in the Cleveland papers alone. The court permitted photographers to take pictures of the jury in the box, and individual pictures of the members in the jury room. One newspaper ran pictures of the jurors at the Sheppard home when they went there to view the scene of the murder. Another paper featured the home life of an alternate juror. The day before the verdict was rendered—while the jurors were at lunch and sequestered by two bailiffs—the jury was separated into two groups to pose for photographs which appeared in the newspapers.

III.

We now reach the conduct of the trial. While the intense publicity continued unabated, it is sufficient to relate only the more flagrant episodes:

1. On October 9, 1954, nine days before the case went to trial, an editorial in one of the newspapers criticized defense counsel's random poll of people on the streets as to their opinion of Sheppard's guilt or innocence in an effort to use

the resulting statistics to show the necessity for change of venue. The article said the survey "smacks of mass jury tampering," called on defense counsel to drop it, and stated that the bar association should do something about it. It characterized the poll as "non-judicial, non-legal, and nonsense." The article was called to the attention of the court but no action was taken.

2. On the second day of *voir dire* examination a debate was staged and broadcast live over WHK radio. The participants, newspaper reporters, accused Sheppard's counsel of throwing roadblocks in the way of the prosecution and asserted that Sheppard conceded his guilt by hiring a prominent criminal lawyer. Sheppard's counsel objected to this broadcast and requested a continuance, but the judge denied the motion. When counsel asked the court to give some protection from such events, the judge replied that "WHK doesn't have much coverage," and that "[a]fter all, we are not trying this case by radio or in newspapers or any other means. We confine ourselves seriously to it in this courtroom and do the very best we can."

* * *

5. On November 19, a Cleveland police officer gave testimony that tended to contradict details in the written statement Sheppard made to the Cleveland police. Two days later, in a broadcast heard over Station WHK in Cleveland, Robert Considine likened Sheppard to a perjurer and compared the episode to Alger Hiss' confrontation with Whittaker Chambers. Though defense counsel asked the judge to question the jury to ascertain how many heard the broadcast, the court refused to do so. The judge also overruled the motion for continuance based on the same ground, saying:

> Well, I don't know, we can't stop people, in any event, listening to it. It is a matter of free speech, and the court can't control everybody. . . . We are not going to harass the jury every morning. . . . It is getting to the point where if we do it every morning, we are suspecting the jury. I have confidence in this jury. . . .

6. On November 24, a story appeared under an eight-column headline: "Sam Called A 'Jekyll-Hyde' By Marilyn, Cousin To Testify." It related that Marilyn had recently told friends that Sheppard was a "Dr. Jekyll and Mr. Hyde" character. No such testimony was ever produced at the trial. The story went on to announce: "The prosecution has a 'bombshell witness' on tap who will testify to Dr. Sam's display of fiery temper—countering the defense claim that the defendant is a gentle physician with an even disposition." Defense counsel made motions for change of venue, continuance and mistrial, but they were denied. No action was taken by the court.

* * *

8. On December 9, while Sheppard was on the witness stand he testified that he had been mistreated by Cleveland detectives after his arrest. Although he was not at the trial, Captain Kerr of the Homicide Bureau issued a press statement denying Sheppard's allegations which appeared under the headline: " 'Bare-faced Liar,' Kerr Says of Sam." Captain Kerr never appeared as a witness at the trial.

* * *

IV.

[1] The principle that justice cannot survive behind walls of silence has long been reflected in the "Anglo-American distrust for secret trials." . . . A re-

sponsible press has always been regarded as the handmaiden of effective judicial administration, especially in the criminal field. Its function in this regard is documented by an impressive record of service over several centuries. The press does not simply publish information about trials but guards against the miscarriage of justice by subjecting the police, prosecutors, and judicial processes to extensive public scrutiny and criticism. . . . And where there was "no threat or menace to the integrity of the trial" . . . we have consistently required that the press have a free hand, even though we sometimes deplored its sensationalism.

[2,3] But the Court has also pointed out that "[l]egal trials are not like elections, to be won through the use of the meeting-hall, the radio, and the newspaper." . . .

* * *

[4] The undeviating rule of this Court was expressed by Mr. Justice Holmes over half a century ago in *Patterson* v. *State of Colorado ex rel. Attorney General*, 205 U.S. 454, 462, 27 S.Ct. 556, 558, 51 L.Ed. 879 (1907): "The theory of our system is that the conclusions to be reached in a case will be induced only by evidence and argument in open court, and not by any outside influence, whether of private talk or public print."

* * *

Only last Term in *Estes* v. *State of Texas*, 381 U.S. 532, 85 S.Ct. 1628, 14 L.Ed.2d 543 (1965), we set aside a conviction despite the absence of any showing of prejudice. We said there: "It is true that in most cases involving claims of due process deprivations we require a showing of identifiable prejudice to the accused. Nevertheless, at times a procedure employed by the State involves such a probability that prejudice will result that it is deemed inherently lacking in due process." . . .

* * *

V.

It is clear that the totality of circumstances in this case also warrant such an approach. Unlike Estes, Sheppard was not granted a change of venue to a locale away from where the publicity originated; nor was his jury sequestered. The Estes jury saw none of the television broadcasts from the courtroom. On the contrary, the Sheppard jurors were subjected to newspaper, radio and television coverage of the trial while not taking part in the proceedings. They were allowed to go their separate ways outside of the courtroom, without adequate directions not to read or listen to anything concerning the case. The judge's "admonitions" at the beginning of the trial are representative:

> I would suggest to you and caution you that you do not read any newspapers during the progress of this trial, that you do not listen to radio comments nor watch or listen to television comments, insofar as this case is concerned. You will feel very much better as the trial proceeds. . . .

* * *

At intervals during the trial, the judge simply repeated his "suggestions" and "requests" that the jury not expose themselves to comment upon the case. Moreover, the jurors were thrust into the role of celebrities by the judge's failure to insulate them from reporters and photographers. . . .

The press coverage of the Estes trial was not nearly as massive and pervasive as the attention given by the Cleveland newspapers and broadcasting stations to Sheppard's prosecution.[1] Sheppard stood indicted for the murder of his wife; the State was demanding the death penalty. For months the virulent publicity about Sheppard and the murder had made the case notorious. Charges and countercharges were aired in the news media besides those for which Sheppard was called to trial. In addition, only three months before trial, Sheppard was examined for more than five hours without counsel during a three-day inquest which ended in a public brawl. The inquest was televised live from a high school gymnasium seating hundreds of people. Furthermore, the trial began two weeks before a hotly contested election at which both Chief Prosecutor Mahon and Judge Blythin were candidates for judgeships.[2]

[5] While we cannot say that Sheppard was denied due process by the judge's refusal to take precautions against the influence of pretrial publicity alone, the court's later rulings must be considered against the setting in which the trial was held. In light of this background, we believe that the arrangements made by the judge with the news media caused Sheppard to be deprived of that "judicial serenity and calm to which [he] was entitled." . . . The fact is that bedlam reigned at the courthouse during the trial and newsmen took over practically the entire courtroom, hounding most of the participants in the trial, especially Sheppard. At a temporary table within a few feet of the jury box and counsel table sat some 20 reporters staring at Sheppard and taking notes. The erection of a press table for reporters inside the bar is unprecedented. The bar of the court is reserved for counsel, providing them a safe place in which to keep papers and exhibits, and to confer privately with client and co-counsel. It is designed to protect the witness and the jury from any distractions, intrusions or influences, and to permit bench discussions of the judge's rulings away from the hearing of the public and the jury. Having assigned almost all of the available seats in the courtroom to the news media, the judge lost his ability to supervise that environment. The movement of the reporters in and out of the courtroom caused frequent confusion and disruption of the trial. And the record reveals constant commotion within the bar. Moreover, the judge gave the throng of newsmen gathered in the corridors of the courthouse absolute free rein. Participants in the trial, including the jury, were forced to run a gantlet of reporters and photographers each time they entered or left the courtroom. The total lack of consideration for the privacy of the jury was demonstrated by the assignment to a broadcasting station of space next to the jury room on the floor above the court-

---

[1] Many more reporters and photographers attended the Sheppard trial. And it attracted several nationally famous commentators as well.

[2] At the commencement of trial, defense counsel made motions for continuance and change of venue. The judge postponed ruling on these motions until he determined whether an impartial jury could be impaneled. *Voir dire* examination showed that with one exception all members selected for jury service had read something about the case in the newspapers. Since, however, all of the jurors stated that they would not be influenced by what they had read or seen, the judge overruled both of the motions. *Without regard to whether the judge's actions in this respect reach dimensions that would justify issuance of the habeas writ, it should be noted that a short continuance would have alleviated any problem with regard to the judicial elections.* The court in *Delaney* v. *United States*, 199 F. 2d 107, 115 (C.A. 1st. Cir. 1952), recognized such a duty under similar circumstances, holding that "*if assurance of a fair trial would necessitate that the trial of the case be postponed until after the election, then we think the law required no less than that.*" [Italics added.]

room, as well as the fact that jurors were allowed to make telephone calls during their five-day deliberation.

VI.

There can be no question about the nature of the publicity which surrounded Sheppard's trial. We agree, as did the Court of Appeals, with the findings in Judge Bell's opinion for the Ohio Supreme Court:

> Murder and mystery, society, sex and suspense were combined in this case in such a manner as to intrigue and captivate the public fancy to a degree perhaps unparalleled in recent annals. Throughout the preindictment investigation, the subsequent legal skirmishes and the nine-week trial, circulation-conscious editors catered to the insatiable interest of the American public in the bizarre. . . . In this atmosphere of a "Roman holiday" for the news media, Sam Sheppard stood trial for his life. . . .

Indeed, every court that has considered this case, save the court that tried it, has deplored the manner in which the news media inflamed and prejudiced the public.

* * *

VII.

[6] The court's fundamental error is compounded by the holding that it lacked power to control the publicity about the trial. From the very inception of the proceedings the judge announced that neither he nor anyone else could restrict prejudicial news accounts. And he reiterated this view on numerous occasions. Since he viewed the news media as his target, the judge never considered other means that are often utilized to reduce the appearance of prejudicial material and to protect the jury from outside influence. We conclude that these procedures would have been sufficient to guarantee Sheppard a fair trial and so do not consider what sanctions might be available against a recalcitrant press nor the charges of bias now made against the state trial judge.[3]

* * *

[8–13] From the cases coming here we note that unfair and prejudicial news comment on pending trials has become increasingly prevalent. Due process requires that the accused receive a trial by an impartial jury free from outside influences. Given the pervasiveness of modern communications and the difficulty of effacing prejudicial publicity from the minds of the jurors, the trial courts must take strong measures to ensure that the balance is never weighed against the accused. And appellate tribunals have the duty to make an independent evaluation of the circumstances. Of course, there is nothing that proscribes the press from reporting events that transpire in the courtroom. But where there is a

---

[3] In an unsworn statement, which the parties agreed would have the status of a deposition, made 10 years after Sheppard's conviction and six years after Judge Blythin's death, Dorothy Kilgallen asserted that Judge Blythin had told her: "It's an open and shut case . . . he is guilty as hell." It is thus urged that Sheppard be released on the ground that the judge's bias infected the entire trial. But we need not reach this argument, since the judge's failure to insulate the proceedings from prejudicial publicity and disruptive influences deprived Sheppard of the chance to receive a fair hearing.

reasonable likelihood that prejudicial news prior to trial will prevent a fair trial, the judge should continue the case until the threat abates, or transfer it to another county not so permeated with publicity. In addition, sequestration of the jury was something the judge should have raised *sua sponte* with counsel. If publicity during the proceedings threatens the fairness of the trial, a new trial should be ordered. But we must remember that reversals are but palliatives; the cure lies in those remedial measures that will prevent the prejudice at its inception. The courts must take such steps by rule and regulation that will protect their processes from prejudicial outside interferences. Neither prosecutors, counsel for defense, the accused, witnesses, court staff nor enforcement officers coming under the jurisdiction of the court should be permitted to frustrate its function. Collaboration between counsel and the press as to information affecting the fairness of a criminal trial is not only subject to regulation, but is highly censurable and worthy of disciplinary measures.

[14] Since the state trial judge did not fulfill his duty to protect Sheppard from the inherently prejudicial publicity which saturated the community and to control disruptive influences in the courtroom, we must reverse the denial of the habeas petition. The case is remanded to the District Court with instructions to issue the writ and order that Sheppard be released from custody unless the State puts him to its charges again within a reasonable time.

It is so ordered.

MR. JUSTICE BLACK dissents.

CHAPTER 7

THE POLITICAL USE, ABUSE, AND MISUSE OF THE JUDICIAL STRUCTURE

> Were there arguments in his favor that had been overlooked? Of course there must be. Logic is doubtless unshakable, but it cannot withstand a man who wants to go on living. Where was the Judge, whom he had never seen? Where was the High Court, to which he had never penetrated? He raised his hands and spread out all his fingers.
> —FRANZ KAFKA
> *The Trial*

I NOTED IN CHAPTER 5 that the existence or nonexistence of judicial review is an important system variable. It is the most obvious illustration (to Americans) of the structural interplay between courts and other political structures of society. Yet it is not the sole such interaction; there are others, though they are ordinarily played down in American political science. This is due partly to past overemphasis on constitutional doctrine, partly to a confusion of ideology with theory, and party to pure oversight. Whatever the cause, the bald fact remains: little attention has been paid to the relative and direct uses and abuses of all courts in the grand game of politics.

Certain statements on the relative influence or significance of courts have never been thought through thoroughly, yet they pass as truisms. It is high time that the problem area was brought to the surface, as this is a variation in system that can perform crucial functions in society. It is important to recognize the many ways in which judicial structure is used as a method by which political power, in terms of *system control*, may be established, extended, and reinforced. Effective courts, properly run, are a political weapon of some magnitude. Courts have been a classic means of eliminating enemies of the state; that is, enemies of particular men in power. The almost total preoccupation of academic interest with the political functions of judicial review and the jury system may well be of far less importance than the level of significance of the courts in determining the *rules* and *outcomes* of the political game. Those who have judged that level by concentrating their attention on review, jury, and the like have been distracted from other, more critical, realities.

Level of Significance in Politics and on Policy

In considering relationships between the courts and other elements of the political structure, observers do comment upon their relative influence and degree of significance in the policy-making process. The judiciary is pictured as a lightweight, a ninety-seven-pound weakling. There seems to be nearly unanimous agreement that it is the "least dangerous branch."[1] It has been said that the courts are the weakest of the three branches of government,[2] and compliments are likely to be left-handed: "Judges are rulers, rulers in different and perhaps more limited ways than legislators or executive officials, but rulers nevertheless."[3] As Kirchheimer sees it, "Of the three [branches] the courts' share in the making of decisions is most limited."[4]

As we have observed, the first problem in any conceptualization process is to distinguish between the principal concept and those most closely related to it. In this case, I believe a clear boundary must be drawn between judicial influence and significance and judicial independence.

If I defined judicial independence and judicial significance in politics in a legalistic, formal sense, it would be a formidable undertaking to separate the two concepts. We would soon find ourselves talking about separa-ration of powers and checks and balances and coordinate branches; it would be civics revisited. The reader may recall that the definition of judicial independence used in Chapter 4 centered around attitudes of judges and other political actors, and such judicial behavior as actually opposed the conflicting desires of other political and social forces. This was to be discounted by retaliatory behavior, among other actions. Similarly, the degree of judicial influence, impact, and significance of the judiciary can

---

[1] Alexander Bickel, *The Least Dangerous Branch* (Indianapolis: Bobbs-Merrill, 1964).

[2] Henry J. Abraham, *The Judicial Process: An Introductory Analysis of the Courts of the United States, England, and France,* 2nd ed. (New York: Oxford University Press, 1968), pp. 340–41.

[3] Walter Murphy, *Elements of Judicial Strategy* (Chicago: University of Chicago Press, 1964), p. 1.

[4] Otto Kirchheimer, *Political Justice* (Princeton: Princeton University Press, 1961), p. 4.

be conceptualized along these lines. This is one way we can learn about the relative significance and functioning of various political structures with some exactitude.

The key concept, as I see it, is that of *significance*. It is a structural variable—as manifested in standardized attitudes, role expectations, and behavior patterns—that has weighty functions in a society. It is not a concept that has been explicated yet in judicial politics, and it needs to be. It is recklessly interchanged with the concepts of influence and power, much as I have done in the preceding paragraphs to illustrate the point. To my mind, a good way of separating them is to define *judicial level of significance* as the *sum of relative judicial influence (or power) plus relative judicial impact*.

INFLUENCE

For the purposes of my analysis of the courts in this volume I shall interchange the concepts of influence and power. Since the courts have no enforcement or sanctioning apparatus of their own, I shall collapse the concept of power under that of influence. Influence of the courts in the political system is defined as the judged utility of the courts by the various (or separate) sets of political actors.[5] The major operational dimensions of influence are two: First, there is the attitudinal judgment of various actors on the proper and feasible utilization of the courts. In other words, a researcher can examine the attitudes of various theoretically defined populations on whether, when, and how to use the courts.[6] Questions could be posed along the following lines: For problem X, would you first think of going to court in order to solve it? What are the various ways you can use courts to achieve your political goals? Or, if there were great controversy in your community on this issue, where might you go in order to get some resolution on the matter? Do you feel that people with a question about X should use the courts, the executive, or the legislature to get the issue settled? If more than one, which ones? In which sequence? Why?

There are other attitudes that comprise the factor of court influence as well; that is, there are the general attitudes about the law and the

---

[5] This includes the people at large, as they are thought to be a significant set of political actors at certain times and at certain points in the political system.

[6] Nathan Hakman did conduct a survey of officials of various organizations and found little appetite, on their part, for waging courtroom battles or getting involved in various aspects of litigation (*amicus curiae*, furnishing expert witnesses, helping finance the court costs, etc.). See Hakman, "The Supreme Court's Political Environment: The Processing of Non-Commercial Litigation," in *Frontiers of Judicial Research*, ed. Joel Grossman and Joseph Tanenhaus (New York: Wiley, 1969).

courts and judges that are held at the grass-roots level. An indirect measure of this dimension might be the prestige ranking of judges and lawyers. The reader may remember, in the discussion on the internal order function of the courts in Chapter 3, that the Japanese, as compared to Americans, rarely resort to litigation in order to resolve conflict. The Japanese lawyer has been held in relatively light regard since his debut in Japan in the mid-nineteenth century. Similarly, the Japanese judge has had low prestige ranking compared to many other occupations. Takaaki Hattori points out that today highly placed judges are beginning to score higher in prestige, but he believes that this is related to the fact that they were either high bureaucrats or law professors beforehand.[7] Another indicator of public attitudes toward the law and courts could be the number of lawyers and judges per unit of population. The data in Table 9 will further highlight the difference in court influence in the United States and Japan as late as 1960.[8]

There is still another set of attitudes that will relate to significance because it helps delineate a degree of influence of the judicial structure. These are, in a sense, pre-impact attitudes that condition the ultimate response of the citizenry (in official and nonofficial capacities) to court decisions. These would be much like the attitudes that were discussed in Chapter 5 on legitimacy. Prestige rankings of courts, judges, and the like could serve as indicators for this as well.

As I mentioned in the discussion of judicial independence, attitudinal indicators of factors are necessary but not sufficient in the analysis of these problems. This is as true in the scrutiny of court influence as it was of judicial independence. In like manner, then, the second and perhaps more

TABLE 9

Proportion of Lawyers and Judges, U.S.A. and Japan, 1960

Country	Population per Judge	Population per Lawyer
Japan	39,028	14,354
U.S.A.	3,740	728

---

[7] Takaaki Hattori (assisted by Richard W. Rabinowitz), "The Legal Profession in Japan: Its Historical Development and Present State," in *Law in Japan*, ed. Arthur von Mehren (Cambridge: Harvard University Press, 1963). See also David J. Danelski, "The People and the Court in Japan," in *Frontiers of Judicial Research*, ed. Grossman and Tanenhaus. Cf. Richard W. Rabinowitz, "The Japanese Lawyer—A Study in the Sociology of a Legal Profession" (unpublished Ph.D. dissertation, Harvard University, 1955).

[8] Hattori, *op. cit.*, p. 152.

significant operational judgment of utility is potential legal use coupled with the actual use of the courts by political actors. These may span a continuum from threats to go to court (very low) through preliminary proceedings (low) through diversionary and dilatory tactics (medium) through litigation to achieve a dispute-specific goal (high) to litigation to achieve a favorable policy statement in the form of a statutory interpretation or constitutional ruling (very high). Assessing weights of relative influence to various actions of the court is no easy task, but it seems worthy of some consideration.

In all political systems that have courts, the judge will exert some influence on inputs into and outcomes of the political process. The very existence of the judicial structure, by virtue of its interpretation of various laws, makes it a source of political force with which to contend. Still, court decisions are not as dramatic and finalizing as executive decisions on war, peace, and foreign policy. Furthermore, the original decision to formulate policy *appears* to have greater influence on the society than later decisions that interpret or even void some of these policies ("negative policy-making"). Moreover, reference is often made to the fact that since courts cannot choose what issues they are going to decide, and must relate their decisions to individual and specific cases, their ability to plan policy changes is unsubstantial.[9]

That the judicial structure engages in negative policy-making is quickly discounted as being a relatively minor power. But is this always true? Is a court decision to void a state statute allowing the creation of a state antisubversion committee really less significant than an executive decision to negotiate a treaty on wildlife? Is it less significant than a legislative decision to build two new community colleges in a certain county? Does the court really have less influence and impact on the distribution of major values? How many "major" decisions does the U.S. Congress make each session?

Much of the writing in this area embarks upon lengthy description of the "check and balance" system from historical and legal perspectives. Much is made of the legal power of the executive and legislature to appoint judges, impeach judges, limit court jurisdiction and size, alter laws in response to judicial decision, and evade or defy court decisions outright. Being at the mercy of Congress and at the sufferance of the President ("John Marshall has made his decision. Now let him enforce it.")[10] is the

---

[9] Vilhelm Aubert, "Courts and Conflict Resolution," *Journal of Conflict Resolution,* 11 (March, 1967), p. 43. I might add, though, that executives and legislatures also are constrained as to what issues they can decide—and by pressures that are less influential on courts.

[10] The case was *Worcester* v. *Georgia,* 6 Peters 515 (1832).

crucial factor, i.e., the factor that seems to convince many observers of the vulnerability, basic weakness, and lesser importance of the courts, for it is true that legal powers do bear some relationship to actual influence.

On the other hand, recognition is given to the various direct and indirect, formal and informal ways in which the court as an institution, or a judge personally, can exercise influence on the actors in other branches of government. Direct and formal ways, in addition to judicial review and statutory interpretation, might be advisory opinions and/or declaratory judgments. We are told that the judge has substantial power over administrators, and that "judicial review [of administrative action] tends to be more extensive . . . than in those [cases] involving governmental favors or services, or necessary functions of government. This difference is most apparent in the treatment of jurisdictive facts."[11] Direct and informal influence might result from the personal respect felt by some legislators or executives for a particular judge. His opinion would thus carry weight. These are the common run of instances cited as evidence of court influence. There are many others that are noticed only on rare occasions, but which demonstrate the wide influence of the courts in the American system.

Of no little interest and importance, for example, are the ways in which the very existence of a court system (even without a power of judicial review and with only a moderate measure of independence) may influence the bargaining process of the policy-formulators of a society. Murphy puts it this way:

> No less than in the broad wording of the Constitution, judges may find their own policy preferences in the vagaries of legislative language. As in constitutional interpretation, the task of applying the words of a statute to specific situations often demands rather than merely permits policy-making as well as policy application. Few important or controversial bills can run the legislative gauntlet without considerable compromise; *and vague, indefinite phrasing is a common means of obtaining general consensus. Certain points are agreed upon, and both sides tacitly consent to transfer to judges or administrators the authority to settle some of the issues on which agreement is impossible.*[12]

David Truman makes much the same point:

> In the American system the most significant discretionary judgments made by the courts are those interpreting statutes and particularly those deciding the constitutionality of acts of the national and state legislatures. The interpretation of statutes is as surely a source of judicial as of administrative discretion and for essentially the same reasons. Few statutes admit of only one interpretation. Although some

---

[11] J. Roland Pennock, *Administration and the Rule of Law* (New York: Rinehart, 1941), p. 182.
[12] Murphy, *op. cit.*, p. 14 (emphasis mine).

legislation is ambiguous, carelessness and sloppy draftsmanship—two already familiar sources of ambiguity—are probably of more importance. In the first place, when legislation delegates authority to the executive to deal flexibly with a changing and technical problem, the wording of the delegation is likely to be rather general, simply because the legislators cannot anticipate the detailed circumstances in which the law will be applied. The meaning of the statute in a particular situation is thus a matter of choice both for the administrator and the judge. In the second place, ambiguity in legislative language often represents an unresolved conflict among competing claims upon the lawmakers. Where the legislators feel a need to reconcile a set of fairly explicit and contradictory demands, the accepted formula is almost certain to be phrased broadly and in general terms. Just as such formulations shift to the administration the onus of developing specific and viable meanings in concrete cases, so they leave to the judiciary a broad freedom to interpret the statute in the light of detailed facts.[13]

These two illustrations make it quite clear that lawmakers have their uses for the judge and that these uses can be quite subtle. One is tempted to call this the "buck-passing function" of the courts, but it really indicates the influence of courts in the *positive* policy-making process. A proposition could be advanced that, in the bargaining type of policy-formulation process, which is highly sensitive to pressure, courts allow for compromise solutions as conflicts reach high levels. This being reasonably descriptive of the present system in West Germany, it is not surprising to find Karl Deutsch saying that "at times there has been a tendency in the Federal Republic to pass difficult political problems to the courts, and particularly to the Constitutional Court, so as to avoid the stresses and strains of handling them through the legislative and executive institutions."[14] It would be difficult to determine, however, whether a court system without judicial review would be considered by a legislature to be any different for this purpose than an administrative agency would be. While the reader is speculating about the relationship of such systemic differences to legislative motivations of this sort, it might occur to him that the courts might not serve the buck-passing function when the judiciary is part of the bureaucracy. Referring back to the Riggs hypothesis discussed in Chapter 4, one might guess that where the judiciary is less administrative and more professional-legal in its foundations, legislators are more likely to assign the resolution of disputes to it. In such systems, the legislator might feel he is shirking less of his legislative responsibility by "delegating" his decision-making to judges, as they are more immersed in the subtleties of the law

---

[13] David B. Truman, *The Governmental Process* (New York: Knopf, 1951), p. 480.
[14] Karl Deutsch (with the collaboration of Rupert Breitling), "The German Federal Republic," in *Modern Political Systems: Europe*, ed. Roy Macrides and Robert E. Ward (Englewood Cliffs, N.J.: Prentice-Hall, 1963), p. 358.

itself and less in administrative practicality. In this situation the judge's influence in the system is increased.

But how much? In what way should this influence be considered more or less than his sway over a particular president? Is it more or less than his power to void a law? Is it more or less than a legislator's power to introduce a bill? Furthermore, in judicial structures that do have the power of judicial review, how many "points of influence" do the courts get when they are the only decision-making body in the society that has the power to redefine the national system by itself? One need only consider *Marbury* v. *Madison, Baker* v. *Carr,* and the *Party Finance Case* to realize the tremendous and unparalleled influence of a court that can exercise judicial review.

Also, is it not true, from another perspective, that the Supreme Court exercises a unique and unparalleled influence of political leadership? Is it not a leadership exercisable when the so-called and widely reputed powerful agencies are powerless to act (and in particular to lead)? Schubert makes this point forcefully:

> On certain fundamental aspects of political equality, the Court began to produce consistently supporting majorities even during World War II. Among the policy components of this growing and increasingly dominant ideology of egalitarianism have been racial equality (through the elimination of the white primary and of restrictive covenants which precluded access to decent housing; and the assistance of Negroes to gain access first to higher education, next to public education generally, and then to a wide variety of other public facilities on an integrated basis); civic equality (for Americans residing abroad); voting equality (through insistence upon state legislative reapportionment); and equal justice for indigent persons accused of crimes (through assurance of the right to counsel, the right to be protected against conviction on the basis of testimonial compulsion, and the right to gain access to public records needed in order to appeal convictions). More recently the Court has given considerable emphasis to the right to privacy of persons living in an increasingly urbanized and mechanized society. The Court also has given some support to those citizens in local communities who have sought to resist the increasing efforts of various sectarians to use the public schools as an instrument for imposing their private faiths upon captive audiences of children. In every one of these policy areas, the Supreme Court not only has provided leadership: it has provided the *only* national political leadership in initiating and in encouraging political, economic, and social changes of fundamental significance for, and impact upon, American society.[15]

---

[15] Schubert, "Judges and Political Leadership," in *Political Leadership in Industrial Societies,* ed. Lewis Edinger (New York: Wiley, 1967), p. 257. M. J. C. Vile is equally impressed by the extent of judicial significance in Australia; see his "Judicial Review and Politics in Australia," *American Political Science Review,* 51 (June, 1957), pp. 386–91.

Schubert also observes that there are three functions of a high court: (1) to initiate, (2) to resist, and (3) to legitimate. One has to admit that each is a significant political influence in its own right, though the extent to which courts in various societies actually will use these, even where they formally may, varies tremendously.[16]

Kenneth Dolbeare dramatizes the tremendous range of judicial influence throughout the entire American judicial system by concentrating his attention on the local level of politics. Among other things, he takes into account the fact that much of what actually happens in the political system after a case leaves the Supreme Court as a decision depends on what the lower court judges (federal, state, and local) do with it—and they have enormous room to maneuver under numerous circumstances.[17] Additionally, Dolbeare observes that lower courts are adept at making important policy decisions either by a single case interpretation or through a connected series of decisions. Indeed, this power includes, as it does in type at the U.S. Supreme Court level, the capability of altering in significant fashion the structure of local politics and government.[18] Lastly, his analysis led him to the conclusion that the trial courts were most effectively used by individuals (in contrast to interest groups), and in particular by "politically isolated middle-class persons."[19]

The Dolbeare book is probably most useful, though, for its inclusion of the first assessment of the relative importance of the courts in a political system, defined concretely as the relative handling of the "important" political issues in that system. Dolbeare posits a scale of importance of various political disputes, as they are reported (degree of exposure) in the local press, and traces the use of the courts in resolving them. His study

---

[16] See Robert MacIver, *The Modern State* (London: Oxford University Press, 1926). According to MacIver, the rapid growth of the corporation and big business has "greatly extended" the power of the "executive and judicial functions of the state . . . in comparison with the legislative" (p. 311).

[17] Jack W. Peltason's *Fifty-Eight Lonely Men* (New York: Harcourt, Brace & World, 1961) is perhaps the classic statement of the ways in which lower court (federal district court and circuit court) judges' attitudes affect their interpretation of a vague Supreme Court edict, i.e., desegregate "with all deliberate speed." For other discussions of the leeways involved in lower court responses to higher court decisions, see Walter Murphy, "Lower Court Checks on Supreme Court Power," and Kenneth N. Vines, "Federal District Judges and Race Relations Cases in the South," both in *The Impact of the Supreme Court Decisions: Empirical Studies,* ed. Theodore L. Becker (New York: Oxford University Press, 1969).

[18] All of this is discussed in some detail in Kenneth M. Dolbeare, *Trial Courts in Urban Politics* (New York: Wiley, 1967), chap. 1. Dolbeare observes, too, that various factors make trial courts' impact more significant at the local than at the state level (p. 129). Also, he hypothesizes that the courts are particularly effective at the local level in urban areas: "The multiplicity of interests and the high level of potential conflict among them that characterize urban politics also suggest the probability of a substantial role for courts" (p. 9).

[19] *Ibid.,* p. 63.

provides some proof for those who would contend that courts are not utilized in much of the visible local political combat. In this strictly quantitative sense, they are not as important as other governmental structures.
Still, the study does suggest that certain genres of controversy are peculiarly suited for judicial amelioration alone, and that the courts' influence
contributes heavily to the shaping of the boundaries of governmental
power in the community.

An interesting comparative-historical example of tremendous influence by courts in politics is the Roman system. In that society, courts were
one of the major avenues to political power. Through prosecuting someone
successfully, one could gain the convicted person's official position, whatever it was.[20] This would seem to reflect a far more significant relationship
among the legal profession, the courts, and the political system than Eulau
and Sprague's concept of "professional convergence."[21] Skill as a lawyer
was not just a skill that could lead to political office because of the indirect
power inherent in the notoriety of the skill; it led to office directly and immediately. Lack of skill, I might note, was commensurately dangerous.

All of this seems to illustrate the type of thinking about interstructural
relationships and the relative influence of courts that has so far been largely
neglected. If we are ever to explicate even a working theory on this interrelationship, much more thought along these lines is required. Yet thought
is not enough by itself. We still would not be able to develop objective
criteria and test hypotheses by which to assess relative influence. We still
would not be able to work out a model that would allow us to discuss the
relevant causes and effects and sequences of events that are essential to a
comprehension of the mechanics of this phenomenon. With the exception
of Dolbeare's attempt to measure relative importance, the approaches that
are so commonly used to ponder and research these interrelationships seem
to me inadequate for the task. It is true that the historical, legalistic, and
anecdotal mélange can pinpoint isolated workings within the entire process, but these approaches (singly or in concert) cannot provide systematic,
comprehensive insight. This holds true even when historical and legal data
supplement a more social-scientifically based model of analysis. Even the
use of social-scientific theories, without sensitivity to potential operations
and rigorous research, can lead to erroneous conclusions on the research
potential of the behavioral movement to develop this area.

For instance, Murphy's *Elements of Judicial Strategy* is a rich lode of
reasoning and vignettes about the way men in the role of justice of the U.S.

---

[20] Lily Ross Taylor, *Party Politics in the Age of Caesar* (Los Angeles and Berkeley:
University of California Press, 1949), chap. 5.
[21] Heinz Eulau and John Sprague, *Lawyers in Politics: A Study in Professional
Convergence* (Indianapolis: Bobbs-Merrill, 1964).

Supreme Court can employ the judicial structure for political influence and policy purposes. Using Easton's model of political systems and subsystems, Murphy develops a novel categorization of interrelationships.[22] He avoids defining judicial system exclusively by formal legal structure, as he embellishes the model with a sprinkling of anecdotal materials, sociological and psychological in orientation. Two propositions that illustrate his sociological approach are:

> For their part the Justices have to remember that a prolonged conflict with lower court judges may strengthen rival agencies of government and weaken the whole court system. Furthermore, a large scale clash within the judicial system may encourage opposition to the Court's policy in other branches of government.[23]

> As in all organizations, there is a danger in the judicial process of conflict not only between the formal strata of authority but also between formal and informal hierarchies.[24]

A psychological, personal proposition is the following:

> Intellectual and emotional appeals can be aimed directly at legislators as well as at creating a general climate of opinion in the country as a whole. As in other tactical fields, these appeals can be contained in opinions, in speeches, in the Justice's own writings. . . .[25]

Murphy's conceptual perspective on systems and political strategies is sound and I believe it may prove highly heuristic for a multitude of case studies. Still, something is missing. It is precision, the lack of which is due to a methodological insensitivity so characteristic of this type of theoretical musing. Vagaries are no easier avenues toward comprehension when couched in systems-analysis jargon than they are in the lexicon of jurisprudence and civics. What is worse, though, is that this insensitivity to social-scientific methods can be misleading to policy-makers and to research-minded political scientists. For example:

> Thus the policy-oriented Justice in this model acts much like the rational man of economic theory. He has only a limited supply of such resources as time, energy, staff, prestige, reputation, and good will, and he must compute in terms of costs and revenues whether a particular choice is worth the price which is required to attain it. To be sure, neither in real life nor in this model can a Justice make precise mathematical calculations. He would be weighing intangibles and weighing them on a predictive basis. . . .[26]

---

[22] See David Easton, *Framework for Political Analysis* (Englewood Cliffs, N.J.: Prentice-Hall, 1965).

[23] Murphy, *op. cit.*, p. 111.

[24] *Ibid.*, p. 121.

[25] *Ibid.*, p. 162.

[26] *Ibid.*, pp. 35–36.

Murphy is wrong. If the reader examines this statement closely, he will see that most of the "intangibles" that Murphy believes make calculation so difficult are not so intangible after all. There is very good reason to expect that we can elevate such mystical concepts as good will, reputation, and prestige to tangibility; that is, make them operational, and even measurable, e.g., through interview schedules and questionnaires. The factors that Murphy feels are intangible are some of the very factors we must pin down in the study of judicial influence. The major reason for Murphy's failure to see this possibility, it seems to me, is that neither his conceptual scheme nor his approaches have been exploited in the search for data relevant to these inquiries.

In any event, I argue for the inclusion of both these operational dimensions (attitudes and actions) not only because they are consistent with the framework I have employed throughout this book, and because I judge this type of framework to be most useful in the study of comparative judicial politics, but for a third reason as well. The actual use of the courts tells what the actor is doing, e.g., he is or is not appearing in court. Attitudes tell how he feels about this appearance, or what his motivations might be. The combination of the two should allow us better to interpret the psychopolitical implications of his legal behavior. After all, the actor's use of the court system may be an indication that he sees the courts as a method to get what he wants, or it may be the legal equivalent of the Hopi rain dance—a ritual. Courts do have their latent functions. This could help us determine what, where, and when.

IMPACT

Murphy's skepticism about the possibilities of precision in the study of the influence of the judicial structure carries over into the other factor I have defined as being essential to the measurement of the relative judicial significance in a society: *impact*. For example, Murphy has this to say about predicting political reactions:

> Accurate prediction of a political reaction is hardly an easy task. It involves weighing of intangibles on a scale calibrated to the *unknown quantities of the future*. Yet this is the sort of problem which decision-makers in other government positions must regularly handle. Thus it is also the kind of problem which most Justices, considering their wide range of political experience before coming to the bench, have also frequently handled.[27]

What are these other intangibles, these immeasurable facts? According to Murphy, they are "newspaper reports," the facts from the *Congres-*

---

[27] *Ibid.,* p. 171 (emphasis mine).

sional Record, "committee reports," "presidential press conferences," and "statements by cabinet members." It does not seem too farfetched to expect that a good deal of precision will evolve soon from future refinements of the techniques of content analysis and factor analysis. They are readily available for time series studies of such documents and events, and thus can measure and possibly predict future political reaction.

Murphy also believes that estimates of the "chances of particular bills being passed" are forever to be the product of intuitive guesswork.[28] This is another of his "intangibles."

Yet in recent studies by Michael Shapiro and Cleo Cherryholmes, the outcomes of roll-call voting on House bills were simulated with striking accuracy.[29] Shapiro, for example, correctly simulated the outcome of twenty-one bills (out of twenty-one) in the 88th session of the House dealing with the expansion of the federal role. Basing his computer model on theories of predispositions and communicative behavior of the representatives, he even predicted correctly 84 percent of the individual roll-call votes on these twenty-one bills. Since when are we interested in solving only easy tasks?

Meanwhile, as I noted in Chapter 5, a flurry of studies on court impact in the last several years is greatly increasing our knowledge of the relative importance of the court system in the American political system and society. We have already seen, through this new work, that the court's significance in this society, whatever its degree, is not dependent on its ability to "legitimate." However, the Supreme Court's decisions do have some effect. How much? Under what conditions does the Court's impact vary? We would do well to take a fresh look at the impact studies from this perspective.

Judicial impact consists of attitudes and reactions attributable to the operation of the courts.[30] I shall use the concept to embrace a gaggle of similar ones scattered throughout the judicial politics literature—results,

---

28 *Ibid.,* p. 172.

29 Michael S. Shapiro, "The House and the Federal Role: A Computer Simulation of Roll Call Voting" (unpublished Ph.D. dissertation, Northwestern University, August, 1966); Cleo H. Cherryholmes, "The House and Foreign Affairs: A Computer Simulation of Roll Call Voting" (unpublished Ph.D. dissertation, Northwestern University, August, 1966). But see Cherryholmes and Shapiro, *Representatives and Roll Calls: A Computer Simulation of Voting in the Eighty-eighth Congress* (Indianapolis: Bobbs-Merrill, 1969).

30 Two recent calls for ever more judicial impact research have come from the halls of law schools. See Ernest M. Jones, "Impact Research and Sociology of Law: Some Tentative Proposals," *Wisconsin Law Review,* 1966 (Spring, 1966), pp. 331–39; Arthur S. Miller, "On the Need for Impact Analysis of Supreme Court Decisions," *Georgetown Law Journal,* 53 (Winter, 1965), pp. 365–401. Another recent call was also accompanied by specific suggestions for research designs. Its source was the discipline of sociology. See Richard Lempert, "Strategies of Research Design," *Law and Society Review,* 1 (November, 1966), pp. 111–32.

consequences, effects, and the like. Of course, the law is not interested in forming or reforming attitudes *qua* attitudes. Its interest is in directing behavior. It is concerned with affecting attitudes only as they may be responsible for certain patterns of action. Because of the close association between attitudes and behavior, most studies in this recent surge in the investigation of judicial impact by political scientists have treated both of these dimensions.

One area that has come under intense political science scrutiny lately is the impact of the recent Supreme Court decisions on Bible reading, schoolroom prayers, and the interrelationship of religion and education in general.[31] Another receiving its share of attention is the impact upon police of the court decisions concerning search and seizure and various station-house interrogation procedures.[32] Naturally, the ingenuity of various southern officials and northern private interests in avoiding the clear intent of the Supreme Court's wide assortment of decisions on desegregation has also captured the interest and energy of scholars.[33] The picture that is being unveiled is not a portraiture, but a collage. Compliance, resistance, evasion, delay, defiance—and all in various shades—do not show any clear-cut relationship with any single sociological or political factor, except perhaps the personal attitudes of the people in the society. Still, as I noted in Chapter 2, this is a multilevel and multidimensional concept that needs a great deal of explication and study in itself. For instance, Birkby, after failing to find a significant relationship between factors like degree of urbanization, extent of religious pluralism, and differences in the socioeconomic compositon of school boards and their compliance or noncompli-

---

[31] The pioneering political science work on judicial impact was in this area. See Gordon Patric, "The Impact of a Court Decision: Aftermath of the McCollum Case," *Journal of Public Law*, 6 (1957), pp. 455–64, and Frank J. Sorauf, "*Zorach v. Clauson:* The Impact of a Supreme Court Decision," *American Political Science Review*, 53 (September, 1959), pp. 777–91. Two of the most recent are Robert H. Birkby, "The Supreme Court and the Bible Belt: Tennessee Reaction to the 'Schempp' Decision," *Midwest Journal of Political Science*, 10 (August, 1966), pp. 304–19, and Richard Johnson, *The Dynamics of Compliance* (Evanston, Ill.: Northwestern University Press, 1967). Cf. William M. Beaney and Edward N. Beiser, "Prayer and Politics: The Impact of *Engel* and *Schempp* on the Political Process," *Journal of Public Law*, 13 (1965), pp. 475–503.

[32] Stuart S. Nagel, "Testing the Effects of Excluding Illegally Seized Evidence," *Wisconsin Law Review* (1965), pp. 283–310; Jerome Skolnik, *Justice without Trial* (New York: Wiley, 1966); Theodore Sourris, "Stop and Frisk or Arrest and Search—The Use and Misuse of Euphemisms," *Journal of Criminal Law, Criminology, and Police Science*, 57 (September, 1966), pp. 251–64; Michael Wald, Richard Ayers, David W. Hess, Mark Schantz, and Charles Whitebread II, "Interrogations in New Haven: The Impact of Miranda," *Yale Law Journal*, 76 (July, 1967), pp. 1519–1648.

[33] See Robert B. McKay, "'With All Deliberate Speed': A Study of School Desegregation," *New York University Law Review*, 31 (June, 1956), pp. 991–1090, and Albert Blaustein and Clarence Ferguson, *Desegregation and the Law* (New Brunswick, N.J.: Rutgers University Press, 1957).

ance with the court decision in *Schempp,* stated that "the Court-attitude [of people in the society] is only one of the variables affecting the impact of a judicial decision. The other major variable is the policy-maker's assessment of a commitment to the challenged program or activity."[34] Richard Johnson's study of the impact of the same decision on another community found essentially the same thing. His analysis gains depth by focusing exclusively on one locality that did comply with the Court's intent (in the face of extensive opposition):

> The Supreme Court's policy concerning religious practices in public schools ran counter to the prevailing values in the Eastville school district. Nevertheless, the central decision-maker for the school system, who found the policy congruent with his privately held notions, brought the system into a perceived state of compliance with the rulings. Rather than arousing a great deal of controversy, the action was generally supported or accepted in good grace. There are compelling factors that may offset private disagreement with the substance of the Court's policy. The legitimacy of the Court and its expertise are such offsetting factors. While an individual may feel that the ruling is an aid to groups he deplores, he may grudgingly acknowledge the duty to do what the Court has said because it is the appropriate body for making such a determination or because it possesses the necessary skills to discover what the Constitution "really means" in the "establishment" clause of the first amendment. On the other hand, those who stubbornly dispute a duty to comply with the Court's ruling may do so by countering the notion of a national legitimacy surrounding the Court with a notion of local legitimacy—the local system should dictate the solutions to such problems, not some far-off court. In Eastville, however, those acknowledging a duty to comply with the rulings are in the majority, particularly so in the case of the community "influentials." Consequently, the superintendent actually had a rather firm basis of support for the action he took; people who may have been antagonistic to this action were left without community leadership around which they could rally.[35]

The personal attitudes of those to be affected, once again, loom large in an explanatory picture. Yet the organizational context in which they exist can do much to mitigate their effect on behavior. An example is the courts' supervision of their own intent, as when they preclude the admission of evidence if it is found to be the fruit of a confession gained by unconstitutional procedures. In such a situation, despite very hostile attitudes, the impact on behavior is greater. Nevertheless, hostile attitudes on the part

---

[34] Reprinted from "The Supreme Court and the Bible Belt: Tennessee Reaction to the 'Schempp' Decision," *Midwest Journal of Political Science,* 10 (August, 1966), p. 315, by Robert H. Birkby, by permission of the Wayne State University Press. Copyright © by the Wayne State University Press.

[35] Richard Johnson, "Compliance and Supreme Court Decision-Making," *Wisconsin Law Review* (1967), p. 183.

of the police have been found to influence the style in which they adhere to the formal requirements of behavior demanded by the court—and this is not without some effect upon suspects being questioned, though it is nearly invisible to the judge who must determine whether the police have complied with the will of the court.[36] Thus, there may be formal compliance that does not eliminate the actual state of affairs deplored by the court. In any event, the literature on judicial impact is accumulating rapidly and promises to continue to do so.

By and large, however, the new surge in impact study in American political science circles is parochial. This is because it is confined, on the whole, merely to observing the impact of the United States Supreme Court on various political actors and the citizenry. At best, though, it will help us understand the mechanism of the impact of a single political structure on a single political system. True, this can have far-reaching policy-science ramifications. Political scientists can begin to populate the Supreme Court's research platoon and give advice about what kinds of decision will have what kinds of results under varying conditions. To spur and contribute to the development of a theory of politics, however, much more must be done. In the first place, we need to know the *relative impact* of courts as compared with the legislative organs and administrative-executive organs. For instance, do southerners obey Congress on civil rights any more than they obey the Court? Even more important, it seems to me, we must learn of the relative impact of courts cross-culturally. Both of these directions are vital to our understanding of the variable of significance of the courts; nothing has been done on this to date.

To assess the relative *significance* of the courts as contrasted to other political structures, we must consider, then, the influence and impact of these political structures in America. Impact and influence, like importance, are relative terms. Until we devise conceptual tools and research techniques by which we can at least approximate an understanding of what the differences might be, general statements about the relative significance of courts will continue to have no meaning. This is sad, since it is information about a structural variance, as I have stated before, that may well have important political functions in society.

It is clear that judicial independence can be high, yet the relative significance of the judiciary can vary. As the significance decreases, there could be a corresponding decline in any function that a particular judiciary served. Abel-Smith and Stevens, in their exhaustive study of the English court system, observed that the English courts, even as they have maintained their great impartiality and independence, have become increas-

---

[36] Particularly see Skolnik, *op. cit.*

ingly irrelevant to the operation of a modern, industrialized technocracy. As they have come to be used less and less (i.e., had less and less influence) and have thereby become less significant a force, the courts have come under fire as being "undemocratic," and their role in protecting civil liberties has come to be re-examined as well.[37]

This is what Danelski's essay on the prestige and visibility of the Japanese Supreme Court is all about—the significance of the courts. He recognized the fact that the Japanese Supreme Court had little influence and little impact on its own society. His theory was that the Japanese high court would gain in prestige as it began to exercise its legally supported independence, in addition to other factors (e.g., the appointment to the court of prestigeous men like Chief Justice Tanaka). Then the "requisite supportive political belief systems" could also take hold and prosper. What are these? They are popular and elite attitudes and values that would allow the court to exercise significant political power. Danelski is suggesting that if the Japanese Supreme Court is going to exercise the same political functions as that of its model (the U.S. Supreme Court), it needs to help create the prerequisite attitude distribution in sufficient strength to allow it to wield substantial political influence and cause significant impact by its decisions.

The relative significance of courts in a political system may well be as critical a variation in the expeditious performance of their peculiar functions as any other variation in judicial structure. If it has little importance, it may perform only paper functions, for example, in the resident texts and legal documentation. As the courts' significance increases, so do their manifest and latent functionings.

The Use of Court Systems to Gain and Consolidate Political Power

Going hand in glove with the type of theorizing discussed earlier in this book as to causes of courts (Chapter 3), there is a general acceptance, I think, of the proposition that courts (where they exist) are a reflection of a certain amount of political order and control. For instance, according to Edward Jencks, in his discussion of the gradual extension of medieval monarchy, "as the power of the State grew, the power of the local state

---

[37] Brian Abel-Smith and Robert B. Stevens, *Lawyers and the Courts: A Sociological Study of the English Legal System, 1750–1965* (Cambridge: Harvard University Press, 1967). M. J. C. Vile also remarks at length on the "decline of judicial power" in England (*Constitutionalism and the Separation of Powers* [New York: Oxford University Press, 1967]; see especially pp. 320–21).

courts grew likewise."[38] A corollary of this is that one interested in political power must first have a semblance of it before attempting to expand it, consolidate it, or maintain it through any use of courts. Sir Paul Vinogradoff, in agreeing with this position, believed that governmental power expanded as law or codes were accepted; only at that point could newer court procedures come into existence.[39] The court system is simply a mirror of a measure of political power already held. Still, further reading in medieval history and observation of some contemporary phenomena lead me to believe that, contrariwise, under certain conditions courts may well have been used to *aggrandize* general political power and may well be used for such purposes today and in the future. This is a potential function of its structure. Where it works in such a way, it becomes an added significance to the structure, as it will have demonstrated political influence and political impact.

Delving deep into the history of one modern developed nation and looking at it as one might observe a contemporary underdeveloped nation may help us to empathize with the dilemmas of these new nations and help us and them to understand their problems and suggest ways to solve them. Seymour Martin Lipset based one of his main studies partially upon this thesis. He stated:

> The United States was the first major colony successfully to revolt against colonial rule. In this sense, it was the first "new nation." For this reason, to see how, in the course of American history, its values took shape in institutions may help us to understand some of the problems faced by the new nations emerging today on the world scene. For the values which they must use to legitimate their political structure, and which thus become part of their political institutions, are also revolutionary. . . . The sociologist's analysis of value systems can contribute to the systematic study of the development of a nation's institutions.[40]

I would like to illustrate my point first by dipping into some English history. In feudal England there emerged, and then rapidly expanded, a network of royal courts, which had the effect of developing the power of

---

[38] Edward Jencks, *Law and Politics in the Middle Ages* (London: John Murray, 1919), p. 135.

[39] "The reign of St. Louis is as conspicuous for the progress of legal institutions as for its two crusades and its brilliant feats of chivalry. Trial by battle is relegated to the background in the Royal courts, and the production of evidence takes its place. . . . To this juridical revival two principal causes can be assigned—*the growth of royal authority* and a diligent study of Law" (Sir Paul Vinogradoff, *Roman Law in Medieval Europe*, 3rd ed. [New York: Oxford University Press, 1961], p. 78). Of course, this quotation and this theorizing can be used as further substantiation of the theory that formalized law is essential to the development of court systems.

[40] Seymour Martin Lipset, *The First New Nation* (New York: Basic Books, 1963), p. 2.

the crown relative to that of the local lords and barons. This expansion came in the form of an increase in the number of royal courts, their areas of jurisdiction, and the types of disputes handled by them. The royal court system was used as a political instrument by the king in a fluid and transitional age when two major factions, the royal household and the nobility, were vying for power. For its part, the crown was seeking both to gain and to centralize its power, while the barons wanted to retain the status quo. This meant that much power of the realm would remain diffused. It is a tenable hypothesis that the development of the royal court system played a significant part in determining the outcome of this struggle.

Until the crown got the urge to centralize its power, feudal society operated on a huge network of personal relationships and obligations, extending from the king down through the nobles to the serfs and back up again. Short of war or military action, no mechanism existed that was mutually acceptable to the monarchy and the nobility for the authoritative allocation of values at the societal level, partly because "no normal and constitutional way was provided by which a will opposed to the king's could act or even express itself. Feudal law did provide a way . . . but hardly one which we should call constitutional. It implied rebellion and civil war as its means of operation. . . ."[41] Peaceful ground rules for resolving political disputes were unknown. No institutions existed that were governmental in the sense of being a cut above the contending factions in politics. When a group faded away as a power or force in societal politics, its institutions were, for the most part, not taken over by the group that followed. Instead the new group created its own institutions. Thus in a society where military power counted for everything in political disputes, it behooved the several factions to acquire the means of allocating values at the subsocietal level, and the courts came to fit this need for the king.

Before feudalism was imported to England by the Normans, two independent court systems had developed. The first was the system of public courts, which originated at a time when most Englishmen were both part-time warriors and small farmers. Tribal living was the common pattern. In such a situation as this, "courts" consisted of several members within a tribe who heard and decided disputes brought before them by their fellows; that is, warrior-farmers. Disputes were usually decided by ordeal, and the judge was God. This procedure was a juridical form, but not a court.

Things began to change. Where once the crown and nobility were largely dependent on the volunteer services of the warrior-farmers in their armies, they became able to compel most of the English population

---

[41] George Burton Adams, *Constitutional History of England* (London: Jonathan Cape, 1960), p. 53.

to serve in their military exercises. This was due, as is so often the case in politics, to economic developments.

> One can imagine how easily in turbulent times such a community might be led to put itself under the protection of some powerful lord, and how easily also in the course of time the sums or service paid for such protection might begin to be regarded as resting upon the land and elements of the tenure by which it was held, so that land originally free became by degrees dependent or servile.[42]

Slowly the warrior-framer ceased to have an influential voice in local politics. With the loss of one's freedom, so goes power. At the same time a private system of courts was developing under the direction and control of the lords. The power to hold manorial and franchise courts, with jurisdictions that encroached upon the older public (tribal) "courts," was allowed to lords by various Anglo-Saxon kings. As yet the crown had not shown much interest in who controlled the courts, and only rarely did the royal household bother to adjudicate a dispute, except in certain offenses against the king.[43] These franchise and manorial courts came to be run much like the public courts of the earlier social structure. Though trial by ordeal was still commonplace, fines as a form of punishment increased, because the lords were entitled to all court profits. In addition to being a source of income, the court had a way of gaining deference from the mass of the population that fell under its jurisdiction. Moreover, the control of the courts guaranteed the safety of the lords with respect to the general population.

Eventually the crown seriously began to compete with the lords' courts and with the last remnants of the public courts. The crown had decided to try to extend its power to the society as a whole. "Monarchy and baronage stood over against one another as . . . the two most powerful forces of the time. . . ."[44] Naturally, the creation and subsequent expansion of the royal court system was only one aspect of a larger effort on the part of the crown to create a centralized system of government with itself as the center. "When England's need was for powerful and centralized government to combat the centrifugal forces that often accompanied feudalism, the kings gave their realm the centralized institutions and law that became common to all the kingdom."[45] In a sense, the royal household was

---

[42] *Ibid.*, p. 39.

[43] One reason for this was the fact that the king was forced to do much traveling in order to conduct his business. He had no fixed capital, and thus no place to keep records. Records and ministers followed him about the countryside. It was not till Henry II that even the Exchequer found its permanent home. See T. F. Tout, "The Emergence of a Bureaucracy," in *Reader in Bureaucracy*, ed. Robert K. Merton *et al.* (Glencoe, Ill.: Free Press, 1952).

[44] Adams, *op. cit.*, p. 75.

[45] Bryce Lyon, *Constitutional and Legal History of Medieval England* (New York: Harper & Row, 1960), p. 642.

starting from scratch, because "there was in England no tradition of well established and long continued strong central government . . . and . . . there was no definite institutional organization through which a strong government could be carried out."[46]

Somehow the crown had to circumvent or neutralize the diffused power of the lords. In the first stages of the conflict, since the crown was dependent to a great extent on the financial support of the lords, and since in a dispute between the king and the lords acting in concert the king would most likely come out second best, it behooved the royal household not to attack the lords directly. The crown aimed at a manifest, important, and vulnerable institution, the juridical type of court system of the lords. It established its own court system, and by doing so launched an indirect attack at the diffused power of the lords. Now if the emergence of the royal courts with their new jurisdictions did not represent an increase of the king's power, but was only a manifestation of power that he already had, why did he not abolish the private courts of the lords, or at least put them under his supervision? If the royal household was the mechanism by which authoritative allocation of values was made, why did the king allow a bastard to exist along with his legitimate system? The only authoritative way of deciding such a political question would have been by military means. Such a course of action could only have hurt the king's cause. The job had to be done another way.

By creating new sources of power and, for the time being, leaving that of the lords intact, the crown attempted to inch ahead of the lords. After all, political power is not a stable and static thing that is divided up among a number of people or groups until no more remains. The tactic seemed to be to grab up some of the expanding business and to leave the older, traditional business to the barons. The economy and the society were growing. A new middle class was beginning to emerge.[47]

---

[46] Adams, *op. cit.*, p. 52.

[47] As Vernon K. Dibble has pointed out:

Kings could not order feudal lords around. They could not replace feudal power with that of bureaucratic officials when a bureaucracy and the men to staff it did not exist. But kings could undercut feudal power by sharing power with a rural middle class that was independent of the great lords. That, in brief, was the story behind the expansion of the older conservator of the peace into the justice of the peace under Edward III (1327–1377). This was a period of lawlessness, of a weakened manorial system, and of the Black Death. The monarchy sought to subdue rebelliousness by the permanent establishment of justices of the peace in every county in England. Certain features of the office, as it developed during the first decades of its existence, remained ["The Organization of Traditional Authority: English County Government, 1558–1640," in *Handbook of Organizations*, ed. James March (Chicago: Rand McNally, 1965), chap. 21, p. 882. For further development of the theme during the sixteenth and seventeenth centuries, see the remainder of chap. 21].

Admittedly it is difficult to impute motives over this span of time, particularly when there is no direct evidence. Still, it is hard to believe that the crown was primarily interested in improving English courts or in ensuring justice for the peasantry. An explanation in terms of raw power politics seems more plausible. If the royal courts were to compete successfully with the lords' private courts, in some respect the royal courts had to be superior. The royal courts had to offer benefits their competitors did not and, even better, could not offer. For one thing, neither the manorial nor the public courts were administered from a common center, but the royal courts were. "To modern minds a single system of courts may appear logical, but to people in the twelfth century it was a novel development unsanctioned by custom. Courts 'belonged' to certain persons, who therefore had the rights to their revenues."[48]

Each manorial court differed from its neighbor, as the lords who presided over each court had varying notions of justice. The royal courts became popular among litigants for a number of reasons. (1) The ordeal was less commonly used as a means of determining guilt or innocence. (2) Fines were employed more often as a form of punishment. (3) The royal courts appeared less barbaric to contemporaries. (4) Officers of the court assumed the responsibility for carrying out its decisions, whereas before this duty often fell to the winner of a dispute. (5) There was a conscious attempt to develop precedents and principles by which to decide disputes. About this time, a royal justice wrote a book "which purports to give the law which the courts of the time applied, and apparently it does do so."[49] This contrasts sharply with the manorial courts, where the lords, more often than not, saw to it that disputes were decided according to their personal whim.

The crown continually reduced the business of the rival courts by making many types of disputes subject to decision solely in the royal courts. "By constantly placing more pleas under royal justice and by devising new writs that diverted causes into the royal courts, the Angevins [the Plantagenet kings] made sharp inroads into the jurisdiction of feudal courts and the profits of justice."[50] There was less reliance on God to indicate a man's innocence or guilt, and greater emphasis on the ability and right of representatives of the crown to decide this. The royal court system was triumphing over its opposition.

Only a few words need be said about the nonpublic courts—the feudal and the manorial. One word—decline—best characterizes their

---

[48] Colin Lovell, *English Constitutional and Legal History* (New York: Oxford University Press, 1962), p. 88.
[49] Adams, *op. cit.*, p. 83.
[50] Lyon, *op. cit.*, p. 314.

history. . . . Royal jurisdiction was extended to cover all disputes over possession of land as well as over right to land. All major criminal offenses were royal pleas. A lord lost jurisdiction over civil justice. . . .[51]

The same fate befell the remaining public courts.

How did the lords react to these events in which their power position had remained relatively stationary, but the king's had increased radically? One observer remarked: "The enormous extension of the judicial business of the royal courts upset the established balance of power between crown and barons. Hence a general readjustment was necessary."[52] Upon seeing a general decline in their relative power, the lords seized the only authoritative mechanism for the allocation of values: they revolted.

For a variety of causes, including the rise of the royal court system, civil war followed. The lords won a military victory over the crown, and in 1215 King John was forced to sign the Magna Charta, giving general guarantees that the process of centralization would be discontinued. Surprisingly enough, however, the royal courts were left almost intact. "This was not due to baronial ignorance of their ramifications. The barons knew them very well; many of them had used the royal courts for their own purposes. This was one reason why they showed such forbearance."[53]

The effect of the Magna Charta on societal politics was far-reaching. Previously the rules of the game were either nonexistent or unwritten. Now for the first time an agreement between the two chief groups in societal politics was reached and documented. Also for the first time, these same groups arrived at a consensus on the basic necessity of certain institutions to government. The functional administration and institutions started by the royal household were made acceptable to the lords so long as their control was shared to some extent by the nobility, and was not exclusively in the grasp of the crown. The royal court system fell into this category. This system, which originally arose as a tool of the crown to aid it in expanding its powers, was slowly coming to be administered not in the name or interest of a particular group, but rather in the name and interest of the state.

Two contemporary political scientists have noted this turnabout; namely, that the kings lost control of the developing common law court system, and concomitantly lost some degree of political control. Judiciaries, as we have noted, have a way of expanding and asserting their independence.

---

[51] *Ibid.*, p. 287.

[52] Sidney Painter, *Studies in the History of the English Feudal Barony* (Baltimore: Johns Hopkins Press, 1943), p. 195.

[53] Lovell, *op. cit.*, p. 116. Cf. George Burton Adams, *Council and Courts in Anglo-Norman England* (New York: Russell & Russell, 1965), especially chap. 9.

The common law judges, taking the view that the common law had precedence over statute law (and particularly over royal decrees that had not been sanctioned by parliament), might void a regulation from Westminster on the ground that it violated the ancient property right of English citizens. The monarch's attempts to develop mining as a crown monopoly were thwarted in this manner. . . .

Faced with the lax administration by the justices of the peace and the hostility of the common law courts, the king and the Privy Council were compelled to search for ways to reinforce the inadequate system of control.[54]

Subsequently, in the sixteenth century, the crown moved formally against the aristocracy in an attempt to put down a disrupting degree of local violence employed by the aristocracy against commoners and each other for many purposes, political and otherwise—mainly otherwise. Lawrence Stone believes that one avenue by which peace and order and a further centralization of power were reached was through the judiciary.[55] This was particularly effective after the fact; that is, the courts were then being used to *consolidate*, rather than gain, royal power by diverting the still strong aristocratic motivation toward violence into a more politically acceptable (to the crown) medium (because it was controlled by the crown). Stone states:

Once launched, the suit would with its complexity and prolixity consume their time, their energies, and their substance for years and years on end. The very deficiencies in the machinery of the law, its great cost, its appalling slowness, its obsession with irrelevant technical details, made it an admirable instrument for the sublimation of the bellicose instincts of a leisured class. Sixteenth century litigation combined the qualities of tedium, hardship, brutality, and injustice that tested character and endurance, with the element of pure chance that appealed to the gambler, the fear of defeat and ruin, and the hope of victory and the humiliation of the enemy. It had everything that war can offer save the delights of shedding blood. It gave shape and purpose to many otherwise empty lives.[56]

Professor Stone is not necessarily suggesting that the crown consciously used the courts for this purpose.[57] Indeed, it seems clear he con-

---

[54] Robert T. Holt and John E. Turner, *The Political Basis of Economic Development* (New York: Van Nostrand Reinhold, 1966), p. 125.

[55] Lawrence Stone, *The Crisis of the Aristocracy, 1558–1641* (Oxford: Clarendon Press, 1965).

[56] *Ibid.*, pp. 241–42. Reprinted by permission of the Clarendon Press, Oxford.

[57] Sir Patrick Devlin, however, does impute a certain royal consciousness in such a use for courts:

Henry II understood well the importance of extending the royal jurisdiction as a means of enlarging the royal power. . . . A jury which gave the King information for administrative purposes could also be used to give him information which would enable him to decide a dispute. The primitive nature

siders this employment of courts to be a latent function. As the crown muted violence, the courts became a sluice for the overflowing libidos of a morally bankrupt plutocracy.

A similar point, I think, has been made in Montesquieu's treatment of the development of a new form of trial (one far closer to our definition of court structure) as well as a code of laws promulgated by St. Louis in the thirteenth century. In many ways the conditions in France and England at that time, and the employment of the judicial structure to help centralize power, were amazingly similar. It was St. Louis, after all, who was the first to do away with the hideous device of trial by judicial combat (a public duel), which was in general use at the time in France, and to supplant it with a hearing and decision based on the testimony of witnesses. He did not force this upon the local lords, either. He simply allowed for the use of his method among various strata of the local populace and among the lords. This was done in conjunction with a new general code known as the Institutions. Some lords followed the new practices and some did not. And the new way prospered, and for a time the power of St. Louis did also. Montesquieu does not say that this was part of a conscious political strategy. He appears to believe it had to do instead with a sense of justice and humanity in the man. Be that as it may, the beginnings of centralization of political power again are traceable to a successful extension of courts.

> Thus this prince attained his end, though his regulations for the courts of the lords were not designed as a general law for the kingdom, but as a model which everyone might follow, and would even find his advantage in it. He removed the bad practice by showing them a better. When it appeared that his courts, and those of some lords, had chosen a form of proceeding more natural, more reasonable, more conformable to morality, to religion, to the public tranquility, and to the security of person and property, this form was soon adopted, and the other rejected.
>
> To allure when it is rash to constrain, to win by pleasing means when it is improper to exert authority, shows the man of abilities. Reason has a natural, and even a tyrannical sway; it meets with resistance, but this very resistance constitutes its triumph; for after a short struggle it commands an entire submission.[58]

---

of the older methods was in the second half of the twelfth century beginning to be recognized; the use of the jury was not only a superior procedure but was also one which could be used only in the King's Courts . . . [*Trial by Jury* (London: Stevens, 1956), p. 7].

[58] Baron de Montesquieu, *The Spirit of Laws*, trans. Thomas Nugent (New York: Hafner, 1949), vol. 2, pp. 144–45. The general run of material on St. Louis's changes can be found in sections 29ff. of vol. 2.

Finally, it should be noted that this may not be a gradual, simple development. It may be a multistage growth process with attendant disruptions.[59]

I do not mean to suggest that any direct parallel exists between medieval France, merrie England, and unhappy Vietnam of the mid-twentieth century. The epochal differences between a European country in the eleventh and twelfth and thirteen centuries and those Asian and African nations evolving in today's mad, mad world make one hesitant to venture a hypothesis on the basis of such data. Nonetheless, one might be struck by the possibilities in analogue, particularly upon coming across the likes of a reportorial observation on a strong resurgence of Huk strength in central Luzon in late 1966:

> The Huks are running their own courts and administering their own justice. "A case between landlord and tenant had been on the court lists for three years," said Mayor de Jesús. "Eventually they took their dispute to the Huks, who settled it in one day."
>
> Just as in Vietnam, the Huks, like the Viet Cong, use terror as a weapon but they also use it with discrimination. For the year ended July 31, they killed 46 people in Pampanga. These included good men like Mayor Gallardo who opposed them. But they also included cattle rustlers and others who preyed on the peasants. One known cattle rustler was .tried and beheaded. His headless body was left sticking upright in the mud of a paddyfield as a warning to others.[60]

Doesn't it make sense? Though the court (the judicial structure) may not dispense justice in an absolute or fair sense, if it is efficient enough to decide disputes for a population desperate for any order out of chaos, then that in itself can be an important function. In such an event, it can become an instrument of political power in itself. Moreover, the very trappings of the dispensation of justice, by symbolizing impartiality and objectivity through interpretation of rules, may satisfy a strong desire on the part of a deprived population for *some* justice in this life. Aside from this, it might even provide some satisfying distractions. Murray Edelman has written:

> The common element in the political settings mentioned . . . is their contrived character. They are unabashedly built up to emphasize a departure from men's daily routine, a special or heroic quality in the proceedings they are to frame. Massiveness, ornateness, and formality are the most common notes struck in the design of these scenes, and they are presented upon a scale which focuses constant attention upon

---

[59] See Marc Galanter, "The Modernization of Law," in *Modernization*, ed. Myron Weiner (New York: Basic Books, 1966), pp. 153–65. For a more detailed analysis of his several steps of development, particularly of the British experience in India, see his "Hindu Law and the Development of the Modern Legal System" (paper delivered at the annual meeting of the American Political Science Association, Chicago, 1964).

[60] Denis Warner, "Luzon: Another Viet Nam," *Honolulu Advertiser*, October 26, 1966.

the difference between everyday life and the special occasion when one appears in court. . . .[61]

There seems little doubt that the more overt policy-making branches of government can use the establishment of a court procedure and system to excellent advantage in fulfilling their desires for centralization or merely for amalgamation of local power. The court, with its *actual* practice of impartiality and objectivity, becomes a vital force toward political viability. I might suggest, however, this is true only when it is actually a court, and not merely a form. *Courts can induce political loyalty.* That is the hypothesis I think is suggested by the developments I have been surveying. Whether or not various trappings are necessary, or to what degree, is open to examination. Murphy has stated that the "judicial myth" (trappings of secrecy that shroud the objective elements of the process) has

> smoothed the path of acceptance for such decisions. People, it would seem, are more ready to accept unpleasant decisions which appear to be the ineluctable result of rigorously logical deductions from "the law" than they are of rulings which are frankly a medley of legal principle, personal preference, and educated guesses as to what is best for society.[62]

Whether this is so or not, in America or elsewhere, has yet to be subjected to any systematic and rigorous testing. The discussion in Chapter 3 would seem to cast some doubt on the proposition. A recent study has demonstrated that Soviet authorities tried court and law innovations in order to consolidate power in central Asia—and failed miserably![63] The cross-cultural study of Murphy and Tanenhaus, mentioned in Chapter 5, however, seems capable of furnishing at least some necessary preliminary data.

To think of the money that has been spent on researching other schemes—in the study of the "development" of underdeveloped political systems, for instance—and then to think of the directness and logic of this untested notion is to cause some dismay. Moreover, the tendency of some American policy and systems analysts to think of social change in terms of counterinsurgency is unfortunate. This puts too much emphasis on the police aspect of local systems of justice, which is quite the opposite of the

---

[61] Murray Edelman, *The Symbolic Uses of Politics* (Urbana: University of Illinois Press, 1964), p. 96.

[62] Murphy, *op. cit.*, p. 17.

[63] Gregory J. Massell, "Law as an Instrument of Revolutionary Change in a Traditional Milieu: The Case of Soviet Central Asia," *Law and Society Review*, 2 (February, 1968), pp. 179–228. But Massell, too, warns that "neither Soviet experience in Central Asia nor the lessons derived therefrom may be literally applicable to other milieus. They do not tell us . . . to what extent other methods of . . . judicial organization, applied under other political auspices, might have been more effective" (p. 228).

conception and phenomenon we have been discussing. The concomitant countereffect may be greater disloyalty.

The desire to promote indigenous and natural growth of judicial subsystems in an underdeveloped country is understandable and might even be laudable. Clearly, this would mean that some guessing and experimenting would have to be done to see what conditions and what form of central leadership could best succeed. The major pitfalls would lie in disturbing (by "foreign interference") the local conditions and thereby impeding and not allowing for failures in localized situations, if not *in toto*. In other words, effective and "just" courts might be neither a necessary nor a sufficient condition for the development of political loyalty in a particular area. If this should be so, it would be best to learn why, and let them fade away from disuse if they will. Practical-minded social scientists sometimes have too great a stake in their theories. When that happens, it is no longer social science, and no longer practical.

The Use of Court Procedures to Combat Political Enemies: The Political "Trial" and the Political Trial

Aside from simply assessing the relative significance of the judicial structure in policy-making, and from examining the potential value of courts in expanding and consolidating or centralizing political power, there is yet another important aspect of their political use to be studied. This involves the concepts of political trial and political "trial."

When one thinks of political trials, what enters his mind? The Dreyfus Case? The Rosenberg Case? The trial of Aaron Burr? The Russian purge trials? Probably all of these famous court proceedings are considered to fit within the genre of political trial. The underlying theme of each of these cases is treason or sedition, but trials for these activities are only the most obvious type of political trial. Governments and regimes have a far more splendid arsenal than mere enforcement of the proscription against sedition and treason.

There is no longer any doubt, for example, that the case against Sacco and Vanzetti was politically motivated, yet their trial was ostensibly for armed robbery and murder. Some men desired to rid the country of those considered to be enemies—and if a murder conviction was attainable, it was as effective a removal agent as a treason conviction.[64] If trespass

---

[64] Felix Frankfurter wrote:

But recently facts have been disclosed, and not denied by the prosecution, to show that the case against Sacco and Vanzetti for murder was part of a collusive effort between the District Attorney and agents of the Department of

and vagrancy statutes can be employed to sustain action against civil rights demonstrators in America's Southland, there is no less reason to call the court proceedings political trials. The incarceration of the leader or the intimidation of the followers is, for the period of time involved, an expurgation of the foe from the political arena. It is this, it seems to me, that is the essence of the usual notion of political trial. We may include as well libel suits, draft-evasion prosecutions (if not inducting "delinquents" into the army as punishment), and the like, when the obvious intent is to clear the political scene of threats to those trying to maintain the established political order. They are, in other words, attempting to employ the influence of the judicial structure—or a reasonable facsimile thereof—to help accomplish and/or justify their ends.

One caveat is in order before I proceed. The concept of the political trial is a limited one. Since this entire book is dedicated to the task of trying to illuminate the multitude of interactions between courts and politics, any trial could be considered political. To include all trials within the concept of political trial merely because courts are political agencies does not allow us to mark off this particular use of courts, i.e., direct purging of political enemies. I think we can utilize this particular symbolic shorthand since it has substantial grounding in the colloquial as well as in the traditional academic lexicon. In other words, I am simply interested, at this point, in the utilization of the judicial structure to engage political forces in combat by trial, and to dispose of opponents either permanently or temporarily. This, it need hardly be added, is *almost* the exclusive tactic of the party in power.[65] Sometimes the established judicial structure is

---

Justice to rid the country of these Italians because of their Red activities. In proof of this we have the affidavits of two former officers of the Government, one of whom served as post-office inspector for twenty-five years, and both of whom are in honorable civil employment. The names of Sacco and Vanzetti were on the files of the Department of Justice "as radicals to be watched"; the Department was eager for their deportation, but had not evidence enough to secure it, and inasmuch as the United States District Court for Massachusetts had checked abuses in deportation proceedings, the Department had become chary of resorting to deportation without adequate legal basis. The arrest of Sacco and Vanzetti, on the mistaken theory of Stewart, furnished the agents of the Department of Justice their opportunity. Although the opinion of the agents working on the case was that "the South Braintree crime was the work of professionals" and that Sacco and Vanzetti, "although anarchists and agitators, were not highway robbers, and had nothing to do with the South Braintree crime," yet they collaborated with the District Attorney in the prosecution of Sacco and Vanzetti for murder. For "it was the opinion of the Department agents here that a conviction of Sacco and Vanzetti for murder would be one way of disposing of these two men" [from *The Case of Sacco and Vanzetti* by Felix Frankfurter, by permission of Atlantic–Little, Brown and Co.; copyright 1927 by Felix Frankfurter].

[65] That this is not always true, and that frequently the "enemy" of the state provokes the inexorable activation of the trial, is the subject of my Introduction to *Political Trials* (Indianapolis: Bobbs-Merrill, forthcoming), as well as several of the essays therein.

activated, sometimes special or *ad hoc* courts are convened. A case brought before an *ad hoc* court might best be called a political "trial," for it is only a transparency and an illusion. It is the use of a judicial shadow, not of the judicial "essence."

In any event, American political science has spent very little of its time in studying these phenomena. It has developed almost no taxonomy. It has largely avoided any study of the causes of political trials or "trials," as well as their short-term and long-range effects. This neglect probably has much to do with American political science's preoccupation with American phenomena in general and the Supreme Court in particular. Nevertheless, the political trial and the political "trial" are important political phenomena, the provincialism of American political scientists notwithstanding.

Otto Kirchheimer is the one major "exception" to this rule.[66] Despite its relegation to relative obscurity, his work includes an excellent starter for classifying political trials, and it is loaded with interesting hypotheses. Political trials are placed in three major categories by Kirchheimer:

A. The trial involving a common crime committed for political purposes. . . .
B. The classic political trial: a regime's attempt to incriminate its foe's public behavior with a view to evicting him from the political scene.
C. The derivative political trial, where the weapons of defamation, perjury and contempt are manipulated in an effort to bring disrepute. . . .[67]

My concept of political "trial" seems close to his category of "derivative political trial." Three general areas of questions need to be answered in the future: (1) on strategy; (2) on the effect of the proceedings themselves upon the decision; and (3) on the consequences, both long term and short run, and particularly on the political system.

The goal is to eliminate an opponent, and there are many accessible routes. If the rulers want a permanent physical removal, there is the possibility of assassination, or exile, or execution after a closed administrative hearing. Why choose an open trial for treason or murder? The conditions that would account for one choice over another are far from clear. Surely the answer cannot be found simply in the existence of a constitutional form of government, though the presence of a constitution probably tends to force the rulers to resort to a court rather than to extraconstitutional means. This isn't too hazardous, as the judges are members of the ruling group— some measure of independence notwithstanding. The value systems of the judges tend to be similar to those of the rulers; they have a vested interest

---

[66] By birth and training, Kirchheimer was German.
[67] Kirchheimer, *op. cit.*, p. 46.

in the status quo, and certainly they have a deep concern for the maintenance of the form of government in which they are presiding officials.

On the other hand, judges may well (because of their role in a constitutionally defined system) have interests and values different from those of strong men, juntas, princes, premiers, presidents, councilmen, and the like. They may feel a greater compulsion to defer to the rule of law or freedom of expression or the open society (even where these are more dreams than even legal realities) than to what an executive or legislative body may deem a threat to the state at the moment. Judges may see a movement or a man as a threat only to a personal regime rather than to the survival of the society and its governmental form. What some might call the "judicial space" exists. It creates an area of uncertainty that a heavy-handed ruler would prefer to avoid. Still, that may be what gives it sex appeal to the top leadership. It may be for this very unpredictability that resort to the courts is chanced. If conviction ensues, it is thought to have that welcome stamp of legitimacy. It is at this point of juncture of the political and legal systems that this function *may* be performed most effectively. But let's take a closer look at this point too.

If consent of the masses is desired for an action against an enemy, it is widely believed that a successful court action is the best way to get it. We have seen earlier that this may be in error; not much attention is paid to the role of the courts. On the other hand, should attention be paid and should the people (or those from whom the rulers seek validation of their removal action) be basically sympathetic to the opponent or his position, a conviction by a court may well be viewed by them as being dictated by the rulers. I am suggesting that misreadings of even latent powerful interests may interdict the so-called legitimation effect, even if the regular court procedures are followed assiduously. Conversely, if the people are hostile to an opposing position or to the opponent personally, then I think the court proceeding is necessary only if it is essential to make the people feel self-righteous about a permanent removal. Because of the morality believed to inhere in the American legal system, for instance, its invocation is absolutely crucial for the disposal of even hated enemies. Otherwise, why didn't some government agent just shoot Sacco and Vanzetti with a pistol? Why all the time and expense? Why the legal maneuvering? In such a strong and old constitutional system as ours, even the police need the benediction a conviction in court bestows. It may not be so efficient as a Gestapo headquarters hearing, but then, German governmental structures did not embody any deep-seated notion of due process and did place great value on bureaucratic efficiency. Cultural variations in governmental structural values can furnish explanations for the fact that some societies will tolerate open political trials while others will not. They will determine whether rulers will deem it a necessity, a choice, or a convenience to go to trial.[68]

Aristede R. Zolberg provides us with an intriguing illustration and hypothesis.[69]

> Let us imagine, for example, that the government of country A, in an attempt to get some opponents out of the way, brings charges against them under existing laws, only to find that the judiciary has retained its own norms and refuses to recognize the validity of the charges. The government might therefore pass a law providing for the detention of these opponents without trial, then another law declaring certain of their past activities a crime, bring charges, and entrust the whole affair once again to the courts. If the judges come up with what is, from the point of view of the government, an undesirable verdict of acquittal, the executive replaces them with more sympathetic men, who finally declare the opponents guilty. All of this is reported in the local government-controlled press. From the point of view of observers accustomed to detecting authoritarian trends on the basis of violations of public liberties, such as an international commission of jurists, country A is guilty of having adopted an ex post facto law and a bill of attainder, of having violated the principle of independence of the judiciary and the right of habeas corpus. They travel to country B and are happy to find no bad laws on the books and judges whose tenure has not been disturbed since independence. In the conclusions of their report, country B is cited as an example which country A would do well to imitate. What they do not know, however, and what their procedure could not uncover, is that the government of country B has also eliminated its opponents, but has done so with more discretion. A group of party militiamen arrested them and kept them incarcerated in a private house; later, they were punished by a specially constituted party tribunal which was dissolved immediately afterwards. Little publicity was given to the whole process because country B is very conscious of its "image" abroad. Paradoxically, then, in reality country A has displayed a greater concern with the rule of law than country B! Thus, unless an attempt is made to compare broad patterns rather than collections of discrete events, misleading conclusions concerning differences between regimes might be drawn.

Why countries A and B chose different means to achieve approximately the same goal may stem in part from different legacies from the colonial era. Although the example above is somewhat exaggerated for the purpose of illustration, it does correspond to an important distinction between Ghana, on the one hand, and most of French-speaking Africa on the other. Although Apter was overly optimistic in viewing the Gold Coast as a successful case of institutional transfer of parliamentary democracy, he was correct in stressing that British norms generally had begun to take root in the Gold Coast. Hence the imple-

---

[68] *Ibid.*, pp. 419ff.
[69] Aristede R. Zolberg, *Creating Political Order: The Party-States of West Africa* (Chicago: Rand McNally, 1966), pp. 78–79.

mentation of the one-party ideology in Ghana has been a more complex process, reflecting obstacles stemming from the norms internalized by the leaders themselves as well as by significant groups in the society. . . . Finally . . . the opposition in Ghana had also come much closer to resembling the dominant movement than any other in the countries under consideration; more effort was required to eliminate it from the political scene. For all these reasons, to which we must add the fact of greater publicity, there is much more evidence of authoritarianism in Ghana than in any other West African country.

This, by the way, is an interesting example of the way we may sometimes have to go beyond legal forms *and* judicial behavior in order to get at degree of judicial significance.

The strategy behind the public political "trial" probably does not concern itself with galvanizing consent or perpetuating feelings of virtue. On the contrary, the political trial may be used to initiate or strengthen feelings of fear or subjugation in the populace, or to reinforce an ideological position in a population believed by the leadership to need such a lesson.

Once the government has decided to venture into the "judicial interstice" (as Kirchheimer calls it), there are various parts of the judicial structure that can impede the direct flow to the desired result. These parts are, of course, the various roles in the structure, but even more important, they are the process components of the peculiar interpretations of these roles by the individuals who are to perform them. These individual perceptions can vary drastically as a function of their personalities, values, ideology, attitudes, background and training, personal (idiosyncratic) responsiveness to various types of pressures, etc. We have discussed in earlier chapters the accumulated knowledge along these lines pertaining to judges, but there is reason to believe that some of these factors are even more important in relation to prosecutors, defense lawyers, witnesses, and jurors. There has been some work done on these factors as they pertain to American lawyers, jurors, and the like, but none of it focuses on comparing American political trials or "trials," and very little of it types them in any way; e.g., trials that take place in an atmosphere of public furor vs. trials conducted in a calm atmosphere. Very little comparative work has been done on the function of trial and "trial" in other cultures, and none that even makes any distinction of participant role variations in various types of trials.[70] There can be little doubt that this "space"—the uncertainties injected by the activity of the very unpredictable human animal—can be an uncomfortable one for rulers and their agents to enter. It would probably be correct to say that they will attempt to manipulate the *dramatis per-*

---

[70] Walter O. Weyrauch, *The Personality of Lawyers* (New Haven: Yale University Press, 1964).

sonae as much as they can without making their attempts (or successes) apparent.

As for judges, there is unquestionably tremendous variation in their outlooks on their position in the prosecution of an enemy of the state. In the inquisitorial type of system, the judge always appears as an interrogator, but the degree of his visible desire for conviction may vary greatly. This variation may well have impact on jurors or fellow judges in the degree to which the judge (in his role or personally) is respected. In "democratically centralized states," e.g., the Soviet Union, with its pervasive organization of the whole political system, there is little likelihood that a judge, professional or lay, will have very different values from those of other state officials. In accusatorial systems, the variations may be very great in the overt action of the judge and his interpretations, charges, and so forth. The judge may be cool and remote, or he may be an active antagonist, a near preacher—like Judge Thayer at the Sacco-Vanzetti trial, according to Felix Frankfurter:

> The first words of Judge Thayer's charge revived their memories of the war and sharpened their indignation against the two draft dodgers whose fate lay in their hands: "The Commonwealth of Massachusetts called upon you to render a most important service. Although you knew that such service would be arduous, painful and tiresome, yet you, like the true soldier, responded to that call in the spirit of supreme American loyalty. There is no better word in the English language than loyalty." It had been to the accompaniment of this same war motif that the jurors were first initiated into the case; by the license allowed to the prosecution it had been dinned into their ears; and now by the final and authoritative voice of the Court it was a soldier's loyalty which was made the measure of their duty.[71]

The lawyers, both for the state and for the defense, are also variables, though the prosecuting attorney is probably far more predictable as to his position, his zeal, and his belief in the cause. Although his competence or lack of it may have much to do with obtaining or losing a conviction, the competence of the trial lawyer seems more closely related to whether or not a political defendant will be found guilty as charged. Societies with sophisticated legal systems usually expect a lawyer to take the case of a political defendant and prepare and argue it with the same diligence he would use for any other client. Moreover, formally, at least, there is no assumption that the lawyer subscribes to the position of the defendant. Occasionally, however, counsel may plead too well and suffer official and/or unofficial penalties.

---

[71] From *The Case of Sacco and Vanzetti* by Felix Frankfurter, by permission of Atlantic–Little, Brown and Co. Copyright 1927 by Felix Frankfurter.

At any rate, what is really necessary is the development of a grand taxonomy and conceptual scheme that will assist in the original research to provide some systematically accumulated data upon which to build some theory in this area. What factors interact in what way to produce such errors in strategy as resulted in the acquittal of Aaron Burr and Adamafio, or in the compromise conviction of one such as Cailleaux in France in 1918 and Bonnard in Switzerland in 1954? Can we offer any explanation as to why the Rosenberg, Sacco-Vanzetti, and Daniel-Sinyavsky convictions were foregone conclusions?

If Adolf Eichmann had been acquitted, his trial could be explained (as an independent, individual anecdote) as simply having been staged to re-establish a feeling of history, purpose, and unity among Jewish Israelis. The trial would have been considered a device to reinvigorate the Jewish mission in Israel, and a conviction would have been unnecessary. When a "trial" results in the conviction and execution of a man who posed no threat to the regime, the motive of revenge and the release of tension must be considered important factors. But how could we have predicted the outcome? I, for one, was not as certain as most that the Israelis would lop off his head. I could see good policy arguments for suspending sentence and compromising. I could see certain motives served, certain functions carried out. Our task is to build theory that will allow us at least to guess and understand better the functional operation of the political "trial."

The judge in Genet's *The Balcony* makes it clear that various actors on the political stage depend on each other in carrying out their roles. To the convict who will be punished, to the citizen who will be deprived of some value or values, there is little to be gained in speculation upon the relative importance of the judge or executive or legislator or administrator in the process that decided his fate. For the political scientist, however, there is more than adequate reason to find out. There is compelling reason. The political scientist wants to see how the mechanism works for his own sake —and possibly to become a better policy or systems scientist.

Up to now, few steps have been taken along the path to these goals. In fact, if there is an importance in the role of courts in the political process, it has been greatly underestimated. Many of the ways in which courts might and do interact with the political process have been passed over lightly. Scientists cannot assess relative weights and measure interaction by ignoring phenomena. I hope I have suggested some taxonomic possibilities, a few theoretical link-ups, and demonstrated the existence of an exciting area of comparative study open to pioneering research of all styles and modes. We need to know much more about the political use, abuse, and misuse of the judicial structure.

CHAPTER 8

A FEW WORDS IN FAVOR OF FUNCTIONAL RESTRUCTURALISM

I was initially tempted to make the final section of this book another contribution to the "toward an empirical theory of" literature. Upon reflection, however, I felt that there were far too few data to support such a venture, and that such an enterprise was too limited in scope to embrace the substance of this book. If I have learned anything from applying structural-functional analysis to the subject of comparative judicial politics, it is that the analysis has at least proved its worth in subverting much of the established legal, philosophical, and political science writing (traditional and behavioral). Since vacuums are known to be inhospitable to growth, it seemed silly for me to pose as a Johnny Appleseed scattering theoretical ovules about. Thus, I have no positive conclusions about the subject matter and I have no general theory to offer.

Still, I hope the reader will agree that the tone of this book has been one of neither intellectual nihilism nor political despair. Frankly, I am buoyed by the results of this exercise. The mode of analysis utilized has played some havoc with much that has passed as knowledge and has raised some fundamental questions about a good deal of contemporary research. Concomitantly, it has been possible to see viable alternatives and to think creatively about future political system changes. In the Foreword, I stated that this book was going to be, at least partially, a redevelopment of a field of study. Redevelopment necessarily connotes a certain amount of destruction of existent edifices and the planning of future ones. This is valid whether we are talking about political science or political systems. There is good cause for dissatisfaction not only with the political science study of judicial politics, but also with the American system of judicial politics.

There is every reason to hope, however, that with a little bit of luck there'll be some changes made.

As for political science, there are certain bad habits that must be broken if the field of judicial politics is to flourish as an integrated body of knowledge and if it is ever to bear relevance to the society that sustains it. First, the perspective of political scientists who are interested in judicial politics desperately needs to be broadened. It should now be clear that numerous and important questions go begging for want of appropriate comparative research. The obsession with matters American, like most fetishes, defies ridicule, but it may ultimately be punctured by reason. To put it mildly: there are very few issues of significance, once you think long and hard about it, that can be resolved by studying the mechanics of a single system. Like a man with an old jalopy, early-twentieth-century vintage, we keep checking the engine and chassis, patching here and patching there while saying: "Well, it keeps going, doesn't it?" It does. But how well? What good is the ride if everyone is grumpy once the destination is reached? Improvements can be made on it that have become standard equipment on other models.

Once it is admitted that we are trying to build a science with some relevance for policy and system implementation, then comparative research becomes essential and must be given high priority. If this book does nothing else, it should make crystal clear how little work has been done in a comparative vein on judicial politics.

Another difficulty highlighted in the foregoing chapters is the effect that law or the legal system seems to have on researchers. It appears that "the law" has either a fatal attraction or a fatal repulsion for most scholars. Since we need a large quantity of comparative data about the courts' political role, it would be helpful if the comparative and general theorists would include the judicial aspect of government in their theories. They rarely do, and then their offerings are not up to par. We also need much comparative descriptive material, but we get precious little. On the other hand, those researchers to whom the legal system does have allure seldom see beyond judicial decisions, statute books, and constitutional provisions. To them, the study of judicial politics is tantamount to library research, whether they consider themselves traditional or behavioral researchers. Who could be more Austinian a positivist than he who finds truth in decisions of a court—whether it be legal or scientific truth? Naturally, there are exceptions in both camps. A few general comparativists have helped advance the cause of comparative judicial politics, and so have some refugees from the ranks of those who study the judicial processes in America. Still, the gulf remains wide; an entire field of data and theory necessary to the development of a middle level of political theory remains almost fallow.

Even where there is some gathering of pertinent information, a serious problem inheres in the basic attitudes of those who interpret it. A powerful inclination exists among American scholars in this area to justify and eulogize the American political system. It is almost impossible to find criticism of it from a comparative perspective. There may be some confession of problems, but there is unbridled optimism that they will be straightened out without extensive changes modeled on other systems. This conclusion is not too surprising, since the legal system is almost innately conservative, as perhaps are those who study it. However, if we are to see objectively the nature of various judicial-political systems, and assess any differences in consequence of those variations, we must be far more conscious of the bias that has preceded our past efforts. It will not do to encourage the kind of flag-waving that thrives in the American literature on judicial politics. I believe that the rather rigorous application of the structural-functional framework at least demonstrates that there is little support in reality for almost all the functional propositions in the literature. I'm quite certain this will bring a torrent of criticism down upon my head. That will be of little consequence if I am correct, and of even less consequence if I contribute to a bit more objectivity in analysis and interpretation in the study of judicial politics.

On a more substantive tack, the fact that so much that passes for judicial-politics theory is so hollow should jolt our complacency enough to open the way for considering potential alterations in our judicial system, alterations that might have desirable political results. For instance, there is the question of the degree of participation by the citizenry in the judicial process. Surely what has been observed about our jury system should muster some support for the adoption of the widespread European phenomenon of the lay assessor or mixed tribunal in the United States. In view of the great degree of agreement between judges and juries and the strong possibility that laymen might be sensitized to handling precedent in a short training course, the consequent participation seems infinitely more rewarding as an involvement. All trappings of subordination could be removed. All aspects of the decision could be in the hands of laymen. If they were elected, there would be even that much more democracy. Because laymen would be making the decisions, and in majority control of the proceedings, the populace might well view the judicial process as more representative of its interests. Moreover, we might just find some benefits accruing to the courts in terms of compliance. Most important, though, is the possibility that this could help to engage people in the governmental process, rather than alienate them from it. Political anomie and political cynicism are serious problems in our democratic United States. Since we seek methods to lessen them, I submit this proposal as a restructuring with great functional promise.

Another possibility of systemic adjustment is the adaptation of Moscow's technique of neighborhood courts to our larger cities. Considering the terrible problems that have developed in them, it is not surprising to find the residents of the inner cities calling for greater control of the instruments of government. After the Newark riot of 1967, the Governor's Select Commission on Civil Disorder recommended that the municipal courts in New Jersey be eliminated as such and merged into the state system of courts.[1] Although I think this suggestion might have some merit, it still does not go to the heart of the issue. There are all sorts of plans in circulation that wax eloquent over decentralizing the federal government. Some of these are plausible and seem feasible. However, none makes much sense in terms of court systems. In lieu of decentralizing federal or state courts, it does not appear too brash to suggest that neighborhood courts be established in various urban localities. This would allow the people there to feel, with some reason, that they had effective charge of a greater part of their own affairs, especially if lay assessors were incorporated into the system. There is little reason to suspect that there would be less order in those places with such a system. Each neighborhood could elect local people to sit with judges in certain low-level criminal actions, and in all local civil disruptions and civil causes of action. In this way, the values and perceptions of the residents of urban core areas, which differ so much from the "Establishment" judges (whether they be black or white), could enter the judicial process at precisely the spot where they would be most visible and thus do the most good for the immediate area of discontent. Once again, greater participation and a real voice could do wonders for individual egos, the morale of the locale, and the basic stability of the greater political system. This, too, is worth thinking about.

Another aspect of judicial politics that a structural functional analysis, in the context of some hard empirical data, calls into question is the relationship between actual functioning and real dysfunctioning that accompanies the exercise of judicial review. Without rehashing the arguments here, let me use them to grope a bit further. At the constitutional level, for example, the United States is very democratic. Yet at more concrete levels, with routine procedures and processes and informal traditions and customs, it is much less so. (Consider the filibuster, the seniority system for congressional committee chairmanships, the House Rules Committee, mal-

---

[1] Governor's Select Commission on Civil Disorder, State of New Jersey, *Report for Action* (February, 1968), pp. 165–66.

apportionment in state legislatures, jury selection processes, etc.) Thus, judicial review as an undemocratic (as distinguished from antidemocratic) political instrument is far more consistent with other substantial undemocratic and antidemocratic tendencies in our operating political system than most of its critics recognize in print. It functions latently as it must.

Judicial review in America has always been a vehicle for enabling an enlightened legal elite to juxtapose itself against basic democratic principles, all the while protecting democracy against putative forces that would destroy all semblance of it. The practice of judicial review in the United States today is not unlike that of a liberal parent who exhorts his prodigal son to be independent, supports his education, protects his interests diligently, and is surprised and disappointed when the son turns out to be wishy-washy, apathetic, and dependent. A healthy dose of judicial review can ward off antidemocratic bodies in a society, and in some circumstances, as in modern Japan, it can be said to help develop individual political responsibilities in the broad base of the people. We hear frequently enough that the Court educates the public in the meaning of the Constitution—as does its professional handmaiden, the bar. We hear of the wonderful job the Court has done in enlightening the public about its rights. Yet the facts show that these statements are at best arid aspirations and at worst pallid delusions. Our studies demonstrate that there is exceptionally little understanding of the content of the Constitution among our people. The modern American public is asleep on its rights, and the traditional practice of judicial review may very well be one of its sedatives.

Truly democratic institutions function in direct proportion to their visibility and prestige. One cannot exercise his rights if he does not know he has them. One cannot gain access to political channels if he is unaware that they exist. Furthermore, if an institution appears as a façade or as unimportant, it will not be used. Since the Court's real function has been by and large undemocratic, it did not need to be obtrusive (visible) in order to accomplish its major elite functions, and, as we have seen, the data of modern political science demonstrate how remarkably unostentatious a branch the Court has been. For the Court actually to educate the public in the values of democracy and actually to promote democratic processes, it must soar high. Paradoxically, however, it cannot do all this while retaining the power of judicial review. Only one solution seems possible. The way that the Court can promote and support democratic values and processes and become highly obtrusive as well is for it to overrule *Marbury v. Madison* as having outlived its proper function. The Court has indeed shielded democracy against some forces that would have destroyed it, but the conditions that yield the nourishment to invigorate democracy may well exist, and in abundance. The Court can generate understanding of this only by doing itself in.

Judicial review, as has been said frequently enough, is unnecessary in England because of the deeply embedded heritage of freedom there and the existence of a public consensus on the positive value of this tradition. It is high time that we seriously reconsider when we will have reached that point in America and be in a position to dispense with the institutional-structural check of judicial review, which has such clearly undemocratic tendencies. I submit that this time is approaching at jet speed. I have suggested that the Court seriously reflect on the desirability of overruling *Marbury* v. *Madison*. Constitutional review could then become a highly obtrusive practice and enter the ken of politics at the grass-roots level, where it belongs.

Today's public is more educated, wealthier, and far more worldly than was the American elite at the turn of the nineteenth century. Over some 150 years the Court has built a tremendous body of political theory—but by keeping it the province of lawyers, it has withheld it from the people. Legal theory, i.e., constitutional theory, can become and must become activated political theory. With our mass communications, we are able to leap continents in a single bound. Constitutional issues are fascinating and stirring issues; there is little reason to suspect that they will not be given much broadcast time for debate. Our modern technology has shrunk us to city-state size and has provided us with the economic and communicative conditions that can make democracy flourish.

The Australian practice of having referenda on constitutional issues that have been decided by the high court goes part of the way. In Australia the people are aware that they can directly overrule the court. But why have the court decide at all? It would be easy enough to stay enforcement on all statutes for six months until 500,000 voters could mount a petition (nationwide) to submit the issue for a vote on the most practicable election day. Is it quixotic to think that the nation would become heatedly involved in issues of constitutionality? I think not. The procedure might be expensive and cumbersome, and many institutions (including the educational establishment) would have to be overhauled to meet the challenge. Still, this is a small price to pay for the potentially substantial political involvement of the public at large.

It is not sufficient justification (or, indeed, any at all) to say that democracy in the United States is limited in many ways and therefore we ought not to tamper with judicial review. Discarding this one gadget might well stimulate thinking about the processes necessary to change others. James Reston recently noted that "thanks to television . . . the idea is getting

around that politics is too serious a business to be left to politicians."[2]
Thanks to television and our contemporary communications quantum
jump, perhaps we may soon realize that constitutionality is too serious a
business to be kept from the people.

Finally, we must also recognize that judicialness can be helpful in developing areas, as it was in the United States in a period of expanding
capital interests. Perhaps it can be overstressed in certain cultural milieus
and underplayed in others. As a method of administration, under certain
circumstances, it could well play an important role in amalgamating and/
or centralizing loyalties and thus power. Where conditions approach the
democratic threshhold, we might begin to ponder the wisdom of playing
down legal forms, upgrading political procedures, and removing some of
the insulation from administrative procedures. Where there are already
strong centralizing tendencies, the legal system may well tend to support
national oligarchies. In any event, it is time to reorient our thinking about
the significance of the courts in the development, maintenance, and distribution of power in emerging nations.

I sincerely hope no one has been led to believe that I claim my application of structural-functional analysis has demonstrated that the present
American legal system is a political failure and that my suggested alternatives are recommendations. To express dissatisfaction is not to charge
failure; to suggest is not to recommend. I have taken some pains to say that
I believe my analysis leaves much of what we accept almost axiomatically
and protect almost automatically open to grave reservation. I have also
tried to provide a rationale for grafting onto our system some alien innovations that seem capable of (*a*) lessening the dysfunctions that may well
flow from our existing system and (*b*) possibly producing consequences
more to our liking, more consistent with our ideology. These thoughts are
surmises based on an analysis of previous research and prior speculations.
They should be read as the reflections of one who has faith in the ideology
of America, who believes that we must constantly consider changes that
might make political realities closer to that ideology, and who believes that
a scientifically oriented study of judicial politics, based on comparative
research, can help reveal that the impossible dream is neither impossible
nor a dream.

---

[2] *New York Times*, March 27, 1968, p. 42M.

Name Index

387

Subject Index

Objectivity. *See* Impartiality.
Obshchestvennost, 118, 119, 332, 333
Occupational groups, represented in judiciary, 84, 85
Omachi et al. v. *Japan*, 283–94 *passim*
Opinions, judicial:
  analyzing, 34
  studied in judicial behavioral research, 28
Ownbey v. *Morgan*, 171

Pakistan:
  judicial independence in, 147–48, 152
  judicial review in, 206, 219, 220
  See also Snelson, Sir Edward, State v.
Pakistan, State of, v. *Mehraj-ud-Din*, 185
Pakistan through The Secretary, National Assembly v. *Khandker Ali*, 185
Party affiliation and judicial decision-making, 77–78, 81, 231n.
Party Finance Case, 209, 215, 247, 269–80, 352
Patterson v. *State of Colorado ex rel. Attorney General*, 341
Perkins v. *Elg*, 191
Personality:
  influence of, on judicial decision, 85, 86–89
  national, and legal-judicial system, 88–89
Personality-constraining role factors and decision-making process, 93–94
Philippines:
  Huk courts in, 370
  judicial independence in, 153, 158, 159–60
  judicial review in, 221
  judicial role in, 47, 48–50
  judiciary in:
    class origin of, 80
    and Hawaiian judiciary, 73
    prior experience and behavior of, 83
  legal code of, 161
  supreme court of, 159, 160
  See also Gonzales v. *Hechanova.*
Philosophy, legal, and judicial independence, 156–57, 161
Placation and judicial decision making, 111–12

Police:
  court invalidation of actions of, 152–53
  impact of court decisions on behavior of, 244–45, 358, 360
  as stage of development of legal system, 106
Policy making:
  as court function, 4
  positive, court influence in, 351
  significance of judiciary in, 346–61
Political change, courts as innovators of, 163
Political parties:
  and judicial decisions, 77–78, 81, 231n.
  Communist, public tolerance of, and supreme court decisions, 230
  in West Germany:
    institutionalization of, 215
    outlawed, 209, 227
Political science:
  relevance of, to judicial decision, 90–97
  and study of judicial politics, 380–81
  theoretical constructs involved in, 19–23
Political scientists:
  primary role of, 23
  and study of courts, 1–3, 23, 135–39
Political trials, 137
  concept of, 373–74
  derivative, 372–79 *passim*
  functions of, 374–79
  and jury system, 321, 325
  and value systems of societies, 375–77
Political units and public policy, 20
Politics:
  concept of, 16–19
  developmental, courts in, 136–39
  effect of, on judicial decisions, 83
  impact of judicial structure in, 356–61
  judicial, 18–19, 21, 380–81
  local, judicial influence in, 353
  relationship of courts to, 17–19, 136–39
  and social-class origin of judiciary, 84
  use of judicial structure in, 345–61
Positivism, Kelsenite, and judicial independence, 156

PRINTED IN U.S.A.